Contents

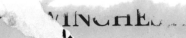

IBM SPSS STATISTICS 19

Made Simple

Colin D. Gray & Paul R. Kinnear

School of Psychology,
University of Aberdeen

Ψ **Psychology Press**
Taylor & Francis Group
HOVE AND NEW YORK

First published 2012 by Psychology Press
27 Church Road, Hove, East Sussex BN3 2FA

Simultaneously published in the USA and Canada
by Psychology Press, 711 Third Avenue, New York NY 10017

Psychology Press is an imprint of the Taylor & Francis Group, an informa business

Printed and bound in Great Britain by TJ International Ltd, Padstow, Cornwall,
from pdf files supplied by the authors.
Cover design by Hybert Design.

This publication has been produced with paper manufactured to strict environmental
standards and with pulp derived from sustainable forests.

British Library Cataloguing in Publication Data
A catalogue record for this book is available from the British Library.

Library of Congress Cataloging-in-Publication Data
Gray, Colin D.
  IBM SPSS statistics 19 made simple / Colin D. Gray and Paul R. Kinnear.
    p. cm.
    Includes bibliographical references and index.
  ISBN 978-1-84872-069-5 (soft cover)
  1. SPSS (Computer file) 2. Social sciences--Statistical methods--Computer programs. I. Kinnear, Paul
R. II. Title.
    HA32.G727 2012
    005.5'5--dc23
                                2011025014

ISBN: 978-1-84872-069-5 (pbk only)

CHAPTER 4   Describing and exploring your data *117*

CHAPTER 5   More on graphs and charts *161*

CHAPTER 15 Predicting category membership: logistic regression *564*

CHAPTER 16 The search for latent variables: factor analysis *601*

Preface

IBM SPSS Statistics 19 Made Simple is the latest in the *SPSS Made Simple* series. (In 2009, SPSS Inc. temporarily re-branded its software packages as *PASW* – Predictive Analytics SoftWare – but has reverted to *SPSS* once again.)

This new edition retains the practical and informal character of our previous books. No previous knowledge of SPSS is assumed. We have taught SPSS over a period of many years and the feedback and suggestions from our students have been invaluable in helping us to identify the principal causes of difficulty for the newcomer to statistical computing. Throughout the book, there is extensive use of annotated screen snapshots of dialog boxes and output in order to clarify the text. Where sequencing is important, the call-outs are numbered.

This is much more than a mere cookbook. In addition to clear practical instructions, the reader will find advice on the selection of appropriate statistical tests and an informal explanation of the rationale of each technique. The assumptions of the statistical model underlying each statistical test are described and, where necessary, there is advice on how to proceed should the data fail to meet the model's requirements. There is help with the interpretation of the output and there are suggestions for further reading.

The reporting of a statistical analysis requires care. As well as showing the reader how to use SPSS to run statistical analyses, we have also provided guidance on how the results of each test should be presented in scientific papers and reports, in line with the recommendations of the American Psychological Association (American Psychological Association, 2001).

In the present edition, as always, the coverage of SPSS has been updated to demonstrate the capabilities of the most up-to-date version of the software. SPSS graphical procedures, for example, have developed enormously, and charts and graphs are now much easier to edit. While there is advice on graphics throughout the book, Chapter 5 focuses upon some of the newest graphical techniques, chart editing and the use of chart templates to make an edited version of a chart available for future use.

Over the years, our coverage has been determined by several considerations. Many of our readers, with whom we have an extensive correspondence, are university lecturers and use the book for their courses. They often request new topics, as do researchers who have contacted us. The publishers regularly request appraisal from anonymous reviewers, who also make suggestions. In this edition, for example, in response to many requests, there is a new chapter on the analysis of covariance (ANCOVA).

There are powerful SPSS procedures, such as aggregation and file merging, which, although they have been available for many years, tend to get neglected. There is extensive coverage of such topics in this book. In recent editions, there has also been greater emphasis upon the use of Syntax, SPSS's control language, not only to save time when running the same analyis repeatedly on new data sets, but also for implementing such techniques as tests for simple effects, which cannot be accessed through the Windows dialogs.

We have always provided many practice examples, both for the benefit of the reader studying the subject on an individual basis and for use by the instructor. The examples are of two kinds. Some are designed to consolidate the material of a specific chapter and are clearly flagged as chapter-specific. Others, however, require the reader to analyse a data set without the cueing that a chapter context provides and are intended to help promote a sense of strategy in data analysis. The examples are available on our website at www.psypress.com/spss-made-simple. There, however, the reader will find not only examples of the two types just described, but also multiple-choice questions, PowerPoint presentations on various topics and notes on some of the statistical terms in the SPSS output that have proved to be stumbling-blocks over the years.

Throughout the preparation of this book, as with previous editions, we have benefited from the advice, encouragement and computing expertise of John Lemon, Student Liaison Officer at Aberdeen University's Directorate of Information Technology (DIT), who has also read parts of the manuscript and (as always) made helpful suggestions. We would also like to thank Philip Benson helping us with IT issues and for reading and commenting upon some of the material. John Crawford also gave us some useful IT advice. Jim Urquhart helped us to stay connected with the School and University networks. We shall always be grateful to Caroline Green, recently retired from her post of Senior Teaching Fellow in the School, for her helpful observations on the Exercises and her reports of students' progress with them in our SPSS practical classes over the years. We also very much appreciate the support that we have received from the Office staff in the School itself, from the DIT and from the Medical IT department at Foresterhill. We would like to thank Professor Peter McGeorge, Head of the School of Psychology in the College of Life Sciences and Medicine (now Vice-Principal, Learning and Teaching), for making the computing facilities of the University available to us. Finally, we would like to express our gratitude to all those who, though too numerous to mention individually, have helped us in some way to produce this book.

Colin Gray and Paul Kinnear

June, 2011

CHAPTER 1

Introduction

1.1   AIMS AND OBJECTIVES

This is not a comprehensive account of SPSS; nor is it a statistical text. The aim of this book is to help you to use SPSS to analyse your data. There are three main objectives: (1) to give you a useful working knowledge of SPSS; (2) to offer you some guidance in the choice of appropriate statistical techniques; (3) to help you to interpret SPSS output. In what follows, we have assumed that you are familiar, to at least some extent, with probability and statistics. This is very much a practical book and we have attempted no formal treatment of either topic.

The **Statistical Package for the Social Sciences** was designed to help researchers analyse data from disciplines in which the units of study are heterogeneous with respect to the properties that are being studied. In chemistry, there are books of physical **constants**, such as the temperature at which a substance melts or boils under specified conditions. In many other disciplines, in contrast, the characteristics of interest are **variables**. Properties such as blood pressure, resting heart rate, gender, nationality, height, weight and so on, vary between individuals; and some vary in the same individual from moment to moment. Research in such disciplines typically produces data in the form of numerical records of variables.

1.2   MEASUREMENTS AND DATA

Since this book is about the analysis of data, we shall begin with a survey of the kinds of data that result from research and introduce some key terms.

1.2.1   Variables: quantitative and qualitative

A **variable**, in the technical sense, is a characteristic or property of a person, an object or a situation, consisting of a set of different values or categories. Height is a variable, as are weight, blood type and gender. **Quantitative variables**, such as height, weight or age, are possessed in *degree* and can be measured on an independent scale with units. In contrast, **qualitative** or **categorical** variables, such as sex, blood group or nationality, are possessed only in *kind*: they cannot be expressed in units on a scale. With qualitative variables, we can only make counts of the cases falling into the various categories, as when the manager of a theatre might record that, on one evening, the audience consisted of 199 men and 201 women.

1.2.2   Levels of measurement: scale, ordinal and nominal data

A **data set** is a collection of numerical observations of variables. In this book, we shall use the term **measurement** rather generally to refer to the making of numerical records of *any* characteristic, whether quantitative or qualitative. The numbers in a data set can carry varying amounts of information about what is being recorded. Often, as with heights or weights, they are measurements on an independent scale with units; but sometimes, as with numerical records of category membership, they serve merely as labels. It is useful to identify three **levels of measurement**: (1) **scale** or **continuous**; (2) **ordinal**; (3) **nominal**.

Scale or continuous data

At the highest level, **scale** or **continuous** data are measurements on an independent scale with units. Heights and weights are obvious examples. So also are performance scores (such as the number of times a participant hits a target), IQs, responses to questionnaires and other psychometric data. In such a data set, each individual score (or **datum**) expresses the degree to which a property or characteristic is possessed on an independent scale, and so carries information independently of the other scores.

Ordinal data

At the next level of measurement, come data in the form of ranks. For example, if two judges rank 10 similar objects according to their perceived weight, assigning the rank 1 to the heaviest and 10 to the lightest, the data set will consist of 10 pairs of ranks, one pair for each object. Like scale data, ordinal data are also records of quantitative characteristics. Ranks, however, are not measures on an independent scale with units. Unlike a measurement such as a height or a weight, a rank has meaning only in relation to the other data in the set.

Nominal data

At the lowest level of measurement, **nominal** or **categorical** data relate to qualitative variables or attributes, such as gender or blood group, and are merely records of category membership, rather than true measurements. Nominal data, though numerical, are merely **labels**. They are numbers, but they do not express the degree to which any characteristic is possessed: they are arbitrary code numbers representing, say, different blood groups, genders or nationalities. Any other numbers (as long as they differentiated between categories) would have served the purpose just as well.

A grey area: ratings

Psychologists, market researchers and political pollsters frequently ask respondents to **rate** objects or people by assigning each to one of a set of ordered categories. There has been much debate about whether, from a statistical point of view, sets of ratings can be treated as scale data. Some argue that, unlike a rank, an individual rating carries information independently of the rest of the data. They do so on the grounds that, since raters are given reference or **anchor points** at the ends of the scale and are asked to express their judgements in relation to these, respondents are being measured on the same independent scale. Others, however, would say that if 100 participants in a research project are asked to rate, say, 30 objects by placing each object in one of seven ordered categories, where 1 is very good and 7 is very bad, the operation will result merely in 100 sets of **ranks with ties**: that is, ratings are merely ordinal data and should be treated as such in the statistical analysis. There would appear to be a fair consensus that the decision about how ratings should be treated depends upon several considerations, including the statistical properties of the data and the number of points on the rating scale.

1.2.3 Univariate, bivariate and multivariate data sets

It is useful to distinguish among data sets in terms of the number of measured variables they contain. In a **univariate** data set, all the data refer to just one variable. In a **bivariate** data set, there are data on two variables. In a **multivariate** data set, there are data on three or more variables.

With bivariate or multivariate data sets, there is the possibility of a statistical **association**, or **correlation**, between the variables that have been measured. Do people with higher incomes tend to score higher on psychometric tests? Is number of years of formal education an important factor in a person's income at the peak of his or her earning power? Is the amount of screen violence to which a child is exposed related to the child's own tendencies to actual violence?

With multivariate data sets, interest often centres on the extent to which certain variables can be accounted for or explained in terms of others in the data set. How well can we predict a person's final income from number of years of formal education, psychometric intelligence and parents' income? These are problems in **regression**.

1.3   DISTRIBUTIONS

The **frequency distribution** of a variable is a table or graph showing the profile of the frequencies (or relative frequencies) of values across the entire range of variation. A distribution tells you about the concentration, thickness-on-the ground or density of values in different regions of the entire range of the variable. If, for example, we have a set of heights or weights, we can depict their distribution by means of a type of graph called a **histogram**. In a histogram, the total range is divided into fixed **class intervals**, which are stepped out over the entire range, which is represented as a scale on the the horizontal axis. Upon each interval stands a rectangle whose height (or area) represents the frequency (or relative frequency) of observations falling within that interval.

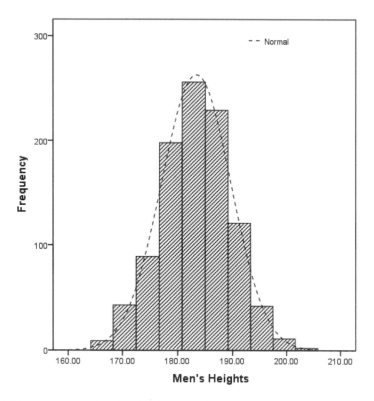

Output 1. A histogram showing the distribution of the heights of a thousand men

It is clear from the histogram in Output 1 that the distribution of men's heights is symmetrical and bell-shaped, with the greatest concentration of values in the centre of the range. Height is said to have an approximately **normal** distribution. The bell-shaped dotted line drawn through the tops of the rectangles of the histogram is a **normal curve**.

1.3.1 The three most important properties of a distribution

The three most important properties of a distribution (such as a set of heights, weights or scores on an attitude scale) are:

1. The typical value, **average** or **level** (as measured by the mean, the median, the mode or some other measure of **central tendency**).

2. The **spread** or **dispersion** of the scores around the average value, as measured by the standard deviation, the variance or a range measure.

3. The shape of the **distribution** (symmetric, normal, skewed and so on).

Output 2 from SPSS 19's Chart Builder shows four distributions with the same level, central tendency or average value (100), but with four different SDs.

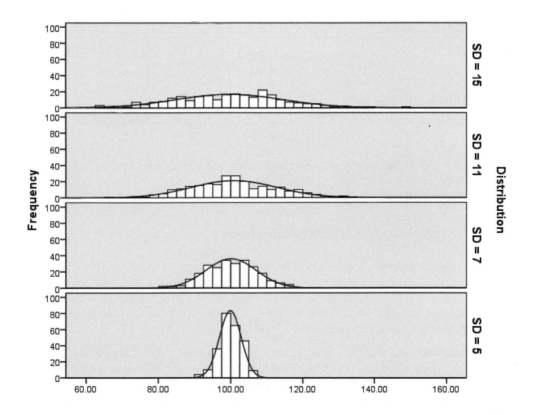

Output 2. Histograms of four distributions with the same central tendency or average, but with different spreads (SDs)

Output 3 shows four distributions with the same spread (SD = 15), but centred on four different mean values: 100, 110, 120 and 130.

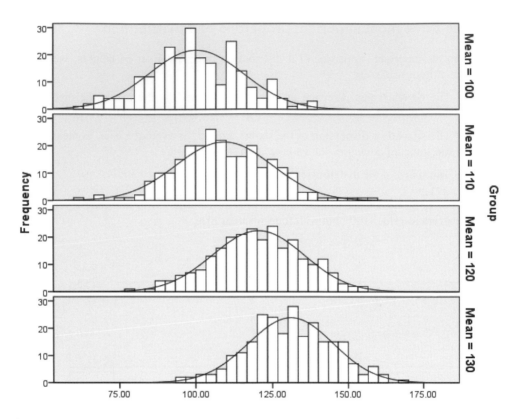

Output 3. Four distributions with the same spread (SD), but with different central tendencies or average values

1.3.2   Some common distribution shapes

Not all variables have normal (or even symmetrical) distributions. Output 4 shows a variety of distribution shapes, each of which is characteristic of some variable that has actually been measured. Heights and weights of people of either gender have (approximately) normal distributions; but reaction times and salaries are known to have **positively skewed** distributions with long tails to the right.

Positively skewed distributions are much more common than **negatively skewed distributions**, which have long tails to the left. Marks on an examination that is easy for most, but difficult for some, have a negatively skewed distribution; and so also does the result of an investment strategy which, while generally making a solid, steady (if unspectacular) profit, occasionally results in a heavy loss.

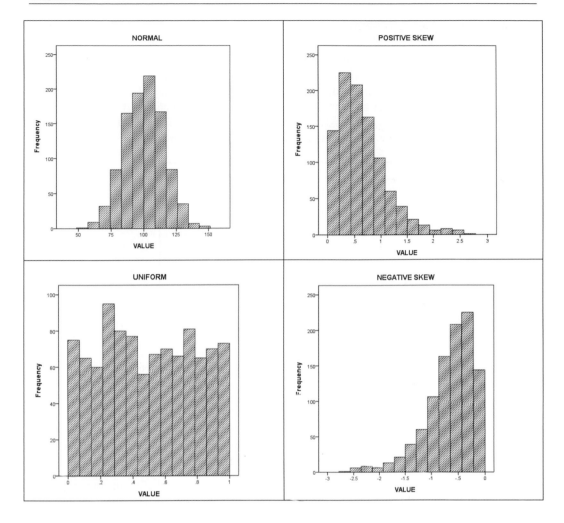

Output 4. Some common distribution shapes.

1.4   EXPERIMENTAL VERSUS CORRELATIONAL RESEARCH

We now come to a distinction which is of fundamental importance for an understanding of methodological issues and the correct choice of statistical techniques.   In some kinds of research, variables (blood pressure, leadership capabilities, reaction speed) are recorded as they occur in the individuals studied, with a view to identifying statistical associations among the variables. Such **correlational research** contrasts with experimental research, in which the researcher manipulates some variables known as **independent variables** to see whether they have a causal effect upon other variables, known as **dependent variables**.

1.4.1   A simple experiment

Sixty volunteers take part in an investigation designed to investigate the effects of caffeine upon skilled performance. Each volunteer is assigned, at random, to one of two groups. Thirty of the volunteers shoot at a target after ingesting a dose of caffeine. The remaining thirty volunteers also shoot at the target; but while the first group were receiving their caffeine, the second group were given a neutral saline solution as a **placebo**. Each volunteer receives a single accuracy score. Table 1 summarises the results of the experiment.

Table 1. Results of the caffeine experiment. Mean number of hits achieved by the Caffeine and Placebo groups		
	Placebo	Caffeine
Mean	10.06	12.45
SD	4.553	3.710

This study has all the characteristics of a true **experiment**. An **experiment** is the collection of *comparative* data under **controlled** conditions. One variable, known as the **independent variable (IV)** is manipulated by the investigator in order to determine whether it has a causal effect upon another variable, which is known as the **dependent variable (DV)**. Here the dependent variable is performance and the independent variable is the condition under which the participant performs. The Placebo condition serves as a comparison or **control**, with reference to which the performance of the actively treated group can be compared.

The IV is controlled by the investigator, and its values are determined before the experiment is carried out. This is achieved either by **random assignment** of the participants to the pre-set conditions or by testing each participant under all conditions, if that is feasible. The DV, on the other hand, is measured during the course of the investigation.

In the planning of an experiment, the researcher applies the **rule of one variable**: that is, the conditions under which participants in the different groups are tested must differ only with respect to the independent variable. In a poorly designed experiment, variables other than the independent variable may have a causal effect upon the dependent variable. In a well designed experiment, such **extraneous variables** are neutralised; that is, the experiment has adequate **controls**. The rule of one variable is one of the most important principles in experimental design. **Random assignment** to conditions is intended to ensure that any individual differences in ability between the experimental and **control groups** tend to cancel out, so that the groups are comparable in aggregate.

There are other methods of controlling extraneous variables, such as testing the same participants under all conditions, so that each participant serves as his or her own control. In fact, good experiments can be run with only a single participant. The strategy the researcher should adopt depends on many factors, including the nature of the research question, the ethical implications, the local situation and the resources available.

1.4.2   A more complex experiment

Suppose that in an investigation of the effects of four supposedly performance-enhancing drugs upon skilled performance, five groups of participants are tested:

1.   A control group, who have received a Placebo.

2.   A group who have received Drug A.

3.   A group who have received Drug B.

4.   A group who have received Drug C.

5.   A group who have received Drug D.

The results of the experiment are summarised in Table 2.

Table 2. Results of the drug experiment. Mean level of performance under four different drug conditions and a comparison, Placebo condition					
	Placebo	**Drug A**	**Drug B**	**Drug C**	**Drug D**
Mean	8.00	7.90	12.00	14.40	13.00
SD	1.83	2.13	2.49	4.50	3.74

Factors, levels and measures

In the terminology of experimental design, a **factor** is a set of related conditions or categories. The conditions or categories making up a factor are known as the **levels** of the factor, even though, as in the qualitative factors of gender or blood group, there is no sense in which one category can be said to be 'higher' or 'lower' than another. In the current drug experiment, there is one factor, Drug Condition, comprising five different conditions or levels: Placebo, Drug A, Drug B, Drug C and Drug D. In experimental design, the term **factor** has a meaning similar to the term **independent variable**, in the sense that the nature of the treatment is supposed to have a causal influence upon another variable, the **dependent variable (DV)**. In some experimental designs, however, (those having within subjects factors – see below), the dependent variable is known as a **measure**. In our current example, the dependent variable is the score that the participant achieved on the skilled task.

Between subjects and within subjects experiments

The 50 participants in the drug experiment were randomly assigned to the five conditions making up the treatment factor Drug Condition and each participant was tested only once. Such an experiment is said to be of **between subjects** design, in contrast to **within subjects** experiments, in which each participant is tested under all conditions.

1.4.3   A correlational study

A researcher believes that exposure to screen violence promotes actual violence in children. Ethical and practical considerations rule out an experiment in which the independent variable of amount of exposure to screen violence is manipulated to determine its effects upon the incidence of violent behaviour.   The investigator, therefore, decides upon a correlational strategy.   Twenty-seven children are measured on two variables: (1) their exposure to screen violence (Exposure); (2) their actual violence (Actual).

The researcher measures these variables in the expectation that they will show a positive association: there should be a tendency for those with high Exposure also to score highly on Actual violence; those low on Exposure should also be low on Actual violence; and those with average Exposure should fall within the normal range on Actual violence.   We may find that Actual violence is indeed correlated with Exposure to screened violence.   This correlational research, however, will not yield the strong evidence for causation that a true experiment would yield: all we can say is that the obtained correlation is at least consistent with the researcher's view that exposure to screen violence encourages actual violence in children.

The scatterplot

A correlational study of two variables will produce a **bivariate** data set, which can be depicted in a **scatterplot**.   The scatterplot of the children's actual violence against their exposure to screen violence is shown in Output 5.   In the scatterplot, each person is represented as a point, the coordinates of which are the person's scores on the Exposure and Actual scales, which are marked out on the horizontal and vertical axes, respectively.

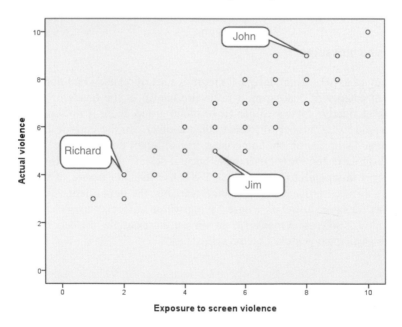

Output 5. Annotated SPSS scatterplot of Actual violence against Exposure to screen violence

In the violence study, as in the drugs project, the research was motivated by the hypothesis that one variable has a causal effect upon another: in the drug research, the hypothesis is that the ingestion of Drug X improves memory; in the second, it is that exposure to screen violence promotes actual violence.

From inspection of Output 5, it is quite clear that there is a marked tendency for those (e.g. John) who score highly on Exposure also to score highly on Actual violence. Those who score low on Exposure (e.g. Richard) tend to have low scores on Actual. And those in the middle of the Exposure range (e.g. Jim) tend to have intermediate scores on Actual. Our scatterplot, that is, gives strong evidence of an association, or **correlation**, between the two variables.

The Pearson correlation

When a scatterplot is elliptical, there is, to at least some degree, a linear relationship between the two variables. The narrower the ellipse, the stronger is the relationship. If the relationship is perfect, the points all lie along a straight line. A circular cloud of points indicates dissociation between the variables.

The **Pearson correlation** (*r*) is a statistic designed to measure the strength of a supposed linear association between two variables measured at the scale or continuous level. The Pearson correlation is so defined that it can have values only within the range from −1 to +1, inclusive. A value of zero indicates dissociation between the variables.

The sign of a correlation reflects the orientation of the elliptical cloud of points in the scatterplot: if the principal axis of the ellipse has a positive slope, the correlation has a positive sign; if the axis has a negative slope, the correlation is negative. The sign of a correlation does not reflect the strength of the association between the two variables: the values −0.6 and +0.6 indicate the same strength of association; but in the former case, one variable varies inversely with the other.

Output 6 shows two scatterplots: the first is the scatterplot of Actual violence upon Exposure to violence; the second is a scatterplot with the direction of the Exposure scale reversed (by multiplying the original Exposure scores by −1). In either case, the absolute value of the Pearson correlation is 0.90. A negative correlation of −0.90 represents the same (strong) degree of linear association as a positive correlation of +0.90.

A perfect linear association, with all the points in the scatterplot lying along the same straight line, would result in either a correlation of +1 or a correlation of −1: either value would represent perfect linearity.

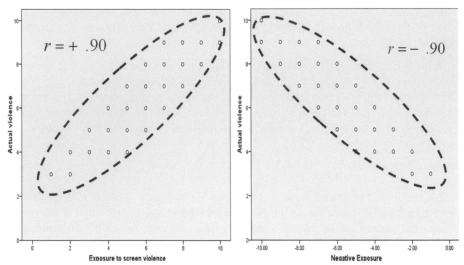

Output 6. Scatterplots of data sets showing the same degree of association, but with correlations of opposite sign

Correlation and causation

When interpreting the results of correlational research, we should bear in mind the dictum that *correlation does not imply causation*. The researcher may believe that Actual violence is, to at least some extent, a direct consequence of Exposure to violence. That, however, is only one of several possible interpretations of the correlation. Other variables may be involved. Do children with high levels of Exposure tend to live in violent households or, at any rate, in households where parents, if not actually physically violent, watch and obviously enjoy a rich diet of screen violence? In correlation research, the direction of causality itself may itself be in doubt: violent people may watch violent television and films; but has viewing screen violence over the years made the viewers violent or are such programmes merely the preferred entertainment of those with a violent disposition?

In an experiment, the IV, unlike gender, blood group, or nationality, is not an intrinsic property of the participants: the participants are assigned at random to the experimental and control groups. Such random assignment to different conditions confers upon the experiment a great advantage: should a difference be found between the groups in their performance, the researcher may reasonably draw the inference that the active experimental treatment has had a causal effect upon the dependent variable. If, on the other hand, all the variables in the study are measured as they occur in the individuals studied, it can be difficult or impossible to attribute causality to any of them.

1.4.4   Quasi-experiments

Does smoking shorten one's life? Researchers have conducted many studies comparing the longevity of smokers and non-smokers. In such research, those in the smoking and non-smoking groups are matched with respect to as many possible confounding variables as possible, such as socio-economic status, education, lifestyle and so on. In this way, it is hoped to achieve a comparison between two groups of people who differ only in their smoking category. A difference in longevity between smokers and non-smokers is taken as evidence for the hypothesis that smoking shortens life.

In such a **quasi-experiment**, as in a true experiment, the researcher attempts to control extraneous variables, so that the groups compared differ only with respect to the supposed causal variable. As in correlational research, however, the variables are properties of the participants: there is no random assignment to the smoking and non-smoking conditions. However careful the researchers have been to control the influence of extraneous variables, therefore, there remains the possibility that the groups may yet differ on some other crucial characteristic, such as personality or physical type. Arguably, the quasi-experiment is essentially a refinement of the correlational approach, where **statistical control** is used as an imperfect substitute for true experimental control.

1.5   CHOOSING A STATISTICAL TEST

It is common for authors of statistical texts to offer advice on choosing statistical tests in the form of a flow chart, decision tree or similar diagram. The numerous schemes that have been proposed vary considerably, and sometimes seem to contradict one another. Almost any system of classification tends to break down when the user encounters cases that straddle category boundaries. In this area, moreover, the correct choice of statistical technique for certain types of data has been hotly disputed.

On one matter at least, there is general agreement: there is no such thing as a decision tree that will automatically lead the investigator to the correct choice of a statistical test in all circumstances. Some of the later chapters contain illustrations of the penalties that an automated, scheme-reliant approach can incur. At best, a decision tree can serve only as a rough guideline. Ultimately, a safe decision requires careful reflection upon one's own research aims and a thorough preliminary exploration of the data. *Get to know your data before you proceed to make any formal statistical tests.*

1.5.1   Considerations in choosing a statistical test

The choice of a statistical test depends upon several considerations, including:

1.   Your research question.

2.   The plan, or **design**, of your research.

3.   The level of measurement of the data that you wish to analyse.

4.   The characteristics of your data, including their distribution.

In general, an important consideration in deciding upon a statistical analysis is whether the research is experimental or correlational. The experimenter is usually interested in making **comparisons** between the average performance level of participants tested under different conditions. Statistical methods such as *t* tests and analysis of variance (ANOVA) were designed for the purpose of making comparisons. The correlational researcher typically seeks statistical **associations** among the variables in the study, with a view to imputing causality to theoretically important variables. Correlation and regression are suitable techniques for that purpose.

1.5.2   Five common research situations

We shall identify five basic research situations in which formal statistical tests can be applied (Figure 1).

The questions are as follows:

1. Is a difference (between averages) significant? For example, is resting heart rate the same before and after a fitness course?

2. How strongly are variables associated? For example, do tall parents tend to have tall children?

3. Can scores on a target variable (or category membership, if the variable is qualitative) be predicted from data on other variables? For example, can university performance be predicted by scores on aptitude tests? Can final salary be predicted from number of years of formal education? Can we predict, from level of smoking, whether someone will develop a blood condition?

4. From a single sample of data, what can be said about the population? For example, a coin is tossed 100 times and comes up heads 80 times. Is the coin fair? A child, asked to select the correct object from a choice of two over a series of fifty trials, does so on 35 of the trials. Is this performance level better than chance? We test the speed at which 100 people in a driving-simulator can slam on their brakes in an emergency. How quickly do people in general react in this situation?

5. The user has a multivariate data set, perhaps people's scores on a battery of ability tests. Can these scores be accounted for (or classified) in terms of a smaller number of hypothetical latent variables or **factors**? For example, can performance in a variety of intellectual pursuits be accounted for in terms of general intelligence?

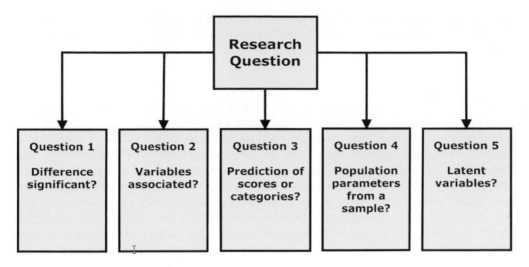

Figure 1. Five research questions

1.6 A SIGNIFICANT DIFFERENCE?

The question of whether two or more means are significantly different is one that arises naturally in the context of experimental or quasi-experimental research, where the performance of the participants under different conditions is being compared.

Suppose that in a drug experiment, performance under two different conditions (experimental and control) has been measured and that the means have somewhat different values. This may seem to support the experimenter's hypothesis; but would a similar difference be found if the experiment were to be repeated? Could the obtained difference merely be the result of sampling variability? Here the researcher wishes to test the statistical **significance** of the difference, that is, to establish that the difference is too large to have been merely a chance occurrence.

1.6.1 Independent or related samples?

Of crucial importance in the choice of an appropriate statistical test for comparing levels of performance is the question of whether the experiment would have resulted in **independent** or **related samples** of scores.

Independent samples

Suppose we select, say, 100 participants for an experiment and randomly assign half of them to an experimental condition and the rest to a control condition. With this procedure, the assignment of one person to a particular group has no effect upon the group to which another is assigned. The two **independent samples** of participants thus selected will produce two independent samples of scores, each consisting of 50 values. A useful criterion for deciding whether you have independent samples of data is that there must be no basis for **pairing** the scores in one sample with those in the other. An experiment in which independent samples of participants are tested under different conditions is known as a **between subjects** experiment.

Related samples

Suppose that each of fifty participants shoots ten times at a triangular target and ten times at a square target of the same area. For each target, each participant will have a score ranging from 0 (ten misses) to 10 (ten hits). As in the previous example, there will be two samples of 50 scores. This time, however, each score in either sample can be paired with the same participant's score with the other target. We have here two **related** or **paired** samples of scores. The scores in two related samples are likely to be substantially correlated, because participants who are better shots will tend to have higher scores with either target than those who are poorer shots. An experiment like this, in which each participant is tested under both (or all) conditions, is known as a **within subjects** experiment. Within subjects experiments are also said to have **repeated measures** on the treatment **factor** (the shape of the target).

There are other ways of obtaining **paired data**. Suppose that in the current example, the participants were pairs of identical or fraternal twins: each participant shoots at only one target and the twin shoots at the other. This experiment will also result in two related samples of scores, because, as in the repeated measures experiment, there is a basis for pairing the data. Different statistical tests are appropriate for use with independent and related samples of data.

1.6.2   Flow chart

Figure 2 outlines *some* of the considerations leading to a choice of a statistical test of the significance of differences between means (or frequencies, if one has nominal data). If there are more than two conditions or groups, an analysis of variance (ANOVA) may be applicable. In this section, we shall consider only the comparison between two groups or conditions, such as male versus female, or experimental group versus control group.

To use the chart, begin at the START box and consider how many conditions there are in the experiment. If there are two conditions, proceed down the chart to the next stage. The next questions are whether the samples are **independent** or **related** and whether the data are **scale** or **nominal** data. The appropriate test is shown in the bottom box.

See Chap. 6

The tests for making comparisons among scores obtained under three or more conditions will be discussed in Chapters 7-10, which are concerned with the **analysis of variance (ANOVA)**.

See Chaps
7-10

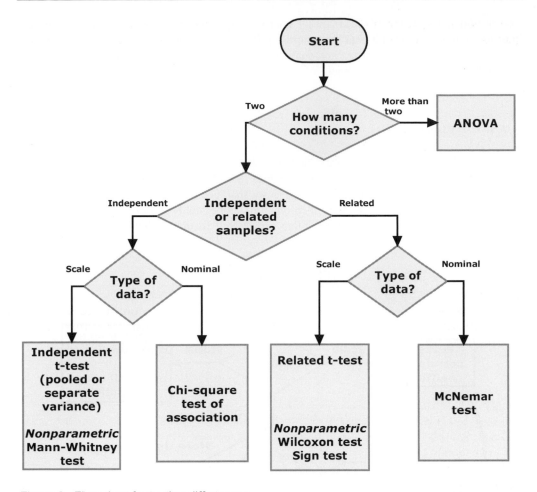

Figure 2. Flow chart for testing differences

In some schemes of this kind, there is a separate path for 'ordinal' data, along which the user is conducted to a choice of a **nonparametric test**, rather than a *t* test or analysis of variance. Ordinal data, however, are rare in experimental research, unless the researcher is working with ratings. Nonparametric tests can certainly be applied to scale data, but when this is done, the first step is the conversion of the original (scale) data to ranks, a process one might term 'ordinalisation' of the data. For this reason, in the scheme of Figure 2, the nonparametric tests appear at the end of the path for scale data.

1.7 ARE TWO VARIABLES ASSOCIATED?

Are those exposed to the most screen violence also the most violent in their actual behaviour? Do tall fathers tend to have tall sons, short fathers to have short sons and fathers of medium height to have sons of medium height? These questions concern a possible statistical

association between the two variables Father's Height and Son's Height. To answer the question, you would need a data set comprising the heights of a substantial sample of fathers and those of their (first) sons. For continuous or scale data such as these, the **Pearson correlation** measures the strength of association between the variables, provided the association is linear.

1.7.1   Flow chart

Begin at the START box in Figure 3 and consider whether the data are scale (continuous) or ordinal. If the two variables are continuous, a Pearson correlation should be considered. However, as we shall see in Chapter 11, there are circumstances in which the Pearson correlation can be highly misleading. It is essential to examine the data first before proceeding to obtain the Pearson correlation coefficient.

See Chap. 11

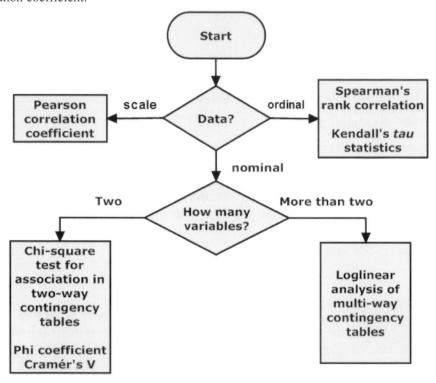

Figure 3. Flow chart showing measures of association

1.7.2   Measuring association in ordinal data

The collection of truly ordinal data is more likely to occur in the context of correlational, as opposed to experimental, research. Suppose we ask two judges to rank twenty paintings in order of preference. We shall have a data set consisting of twenty pairs of ranks. Do the judges agree?

Again, our question is one of a statistical association. However, since the data in their original form are ordinal, a **rank correlation** is an appropriate statistic to use. The two most common kinds of rank correlation are:

1. **Spearman's rank correlation**;

2. **Kendall tau** statistics.

Both measures are described in Chapter 11.

1.7.3   Measuring association in nominal data: Contingency tables

A medical researcher suspects that the incidence of an antibody may be higher in patients of tissue type X, compared with its incidence in patients of tissue types, A, B and C. Seventy-nine patients are tissue-typed and tested for the presence of the antibody. Such an exercise will result in a set of nominal data on two qualitative variables or attributes, Tissue Type (A, B, C, X) and Presence (Yes, No). Here the scientific hypothesis is that there is an association between the two variables. Table 3 is a **contingency table**, which shows the joint classification on the two variables of the seventy-nine patients in the study. (SPSS uses the term **crosstabulation** to denote a table of this type.) The expected association is indeed evident in the table: there is a much higher incidence of the antibody in type X patients.

Table 3.   A contingency table

Tissue type	Presence	
	No	Yes
A	14	8
B	11	7
C	5	7
X	6	21

The presence of an association can be confirmed by using a **chi-square** test (see Chapter 11). Since the value of the chi-square statistic depends partly upon the sample size, however, it is unsuitable as a measure of the *strength* of the association between two qualitative variables. Figure 3 identifies two statistics that measure strength of association between qualitative variables: **Cramér's V** and the **phi coefficient**. Both measures are discussed in Chapter 11.

1.7.4   Multi-way contingency tables

In recent years, there have been dramatic developments in the analysis of nominal data in the form of multi-way contingency tables. Previously, tables with three or more attributes were often 'collapsed' to produce two-way tables. The usual chi-square test could then be applied. Such 'collapsing', however, is fraught with risk, and the tests may give highly misleading results. The advent of modern **loglinear analysis** has made it possible to tease out the relationships among the attributes in a way that was not possible before (see Chapter 14).

See Chap. 14

1.8   MAKING PREDICTIONS

If there is an association between variables, it is natural to ask whether this can be exploited to predict scores on one variable from knowledge of those on another. For example, in some American universities, students take aptitude tests at matriculation and received an academic grade point average (GPA) at the end of their first year of study. Can students' GPAs be predicted from their earlier scores on the aptitude tests? Such prediction is indeed possible, and the methods by which this is achieved, which are known as **regression**, will be briefly reviewed in this section.

There are also circumstances in which one would wish to predict not scores on a target or criterion variable, but their category membership. For example, it is of medical and actuarial interest to be able to assign individuals to an 'at risk' category on the basis of their smoking and drinking habits. Statistical techniques have been specially devised for this purpose also.

The purpose of the methods reviewed here is to predict a target, or **criterion** variable (the term **dependent variable** is also used in this context) from scores on other variables, known variously (depending on the context) as **regressors**, **predictors**, **independent variables**, or **covariates**. The predictors need not always be quantitative variables: qualitative variables, such as gender and blood group, are often included among the predictor variables in research of this kind.

1.8.1   Flow chart

To use the flow chart (Figure 4) for selecting the appropriate prediction procedure, begin at the START box and consider whether the target variable is qualitative (e.g. a set of categories such as Pass and Fail) or quantitative (e.g. examination scores, which are scale data).

Begin at the START box and consider the purpose of the test. If it is to test for goodness-of-fit, move down the left-hand side of the chart. If it is to estimate the population mean or its probable range, move down the right-hand side. The next consideration is the nature of the data: different types of data require different tests. If the target variable is quantitative, a **regression** method should be considered. In **simple regression**, there is one predictor; in **multiple regression**, there are two or more (Chapter 12). If the criterion variable is qualitative, the techniques of **discriminant analysis** and **logistic regression** must be considered (Chapter 15).

See Chaps. 12 & 15

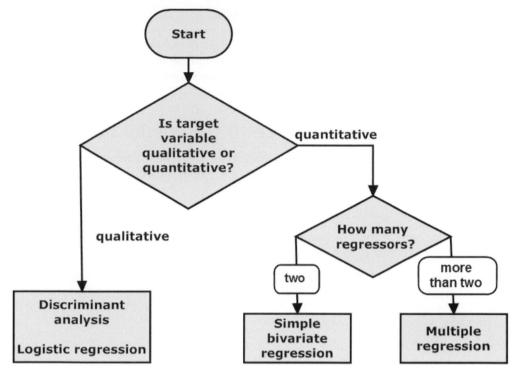

Figure 4. Flow chart showing procedures for prediction

1.8.2   Simple regression

In **simple regression**, a target or criterion variable is predicted from **one** predictor or regressor.

Suppose that, given a student's verbal aptitude score at matriculation, we want to predict the same student's grade point average a year later from the verbal aptitude score alone. Returning to our earlier example, can we predict a child's actual violence from the level of his exposure to screen violence? These are problems in simple regression, and the method is described in Chapter 12.

1.8.3   Multiple regression

A student's grade point average may be associated not only with verbal aptitude, but also with numerical ability. Can grade point average be predicted even more accurately when both verbal ability and numerical ability are taken into account? This is a problem in **multiple regression**. If grade point average is correlated with both verbal and numerical aptitude, multiple regression might produce (provided certain conditions are met) a more accurate prediction of a student's grade point average than would a simple regression upon either of the two regressors considered separately.

See
Chap.
12

1.8.4   Predicting category membership

Two statistical techniques designed to help the user make predictions of category membership are **discriminant analysis** and **logistic regression**.   (Logistic regression is described in Chapter 15). In recent years, logistic regression, being a somewhat more robust technique than discriminant analysis, has become the preferred method.

1.9   FROM A SINGLE SAMPLE TO THE POPULATION

Much psychological research involves the collection of two or more samples of data. This is by no means always true, however: sometimes the researcher draws a **single** sample of observations in order to study just **one** population.

The situations in which one might use a **one-sample test** are of two main kinds:

1.   One may wish to compare a sample distribution with a hypothetical distribution, such as the normal. This is a question of **goodness-of-fit**.

2.   One may wish to make inferences about the **parameters** of a single population from the statistics of a sample.

1.9.1   Flow chart

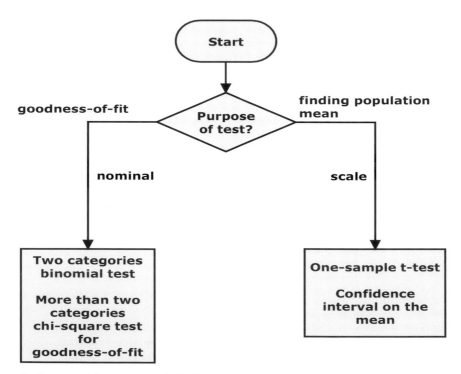

Figure 5. Flow chart for one-sample tests

Figure 5 summarises the circumstances in which a researcher might make various kinds of one-sample tests. The tests reviewed in this section are more fully considered in Chapters 6 and 11.

1.9.2   Goodness-of-fit: nominal data

Suppose a researcher wants to know whether 5-year-old children of a certain age show a preference for one of two types of toy (A or B). The choices of one hundred 5-year-olds are noted. Here the population comprises the choices (A or B) of 5-year-olds in general. Of the hundred children in the study, 60 choose toy A and 40 choose toy B. The null hypothesis states that the probability of choosing A (or B) is .5. More formally, as we shall see in Chapter 6, the null hypothesis states that we have sampled 100 times from a Bernoulli distribution with $p = 0.5$. Does this theoretical distribution fit our data? Figure 5 indicates that a **binomial test** can be used to test this hypothesis.

See Chap. 6

If, in the foregoing situation, there were three or more types of toys to choose from, the **chi-square** test of **goodness-of-fit** can be used to test the null hypothesis that the children have no preference for any particular toy.

1.9.3   Inferences about the mean of a single population

Suppose that a lecturer wishes to ascertain the typical reaction speed of first-year university students within a certain age group, say the 17 to 18 year-olds. The lecturer may have data on, say, two hundred first-year students; but the research question, being about the reaction speeds of first-year students in general, concerns the population of reaction times.

Figure 5 shows that a **one-sample *t* test** can be used to test the null hypothesis that a sample has been drawn from a population with a mean of a specified value. Often, however, as when the researcher is working with a non-standardised test, it may not be possible to specify any null hypothesis. The sample mean is a **point estimate** of the unknown population mean. The *t* distribution can also be used to build a **confidence interval** on the sample mean, so that the researcher has a range of values within which the true population mean can, with a specified degree of 'confidence', be assumed to lie.

See Chap. 6

The one-sample *t* test can also be used to test the difference between the means of two related samples of scores. If the difference between scores under the two conditions is found for each participant, we shall have a single sample of differences. If the null hypothesis is correct, the mean difference in the population is zero, which is equivalent to stating that, in the population, the mean scores under the two conditions have equal values. The related-samples *t* test and the one-sample *t* test, in fact, are exact equivalents and will produce exactly the same result.

1.10   THE SEARCH FOR LATENT VARIABLES

Suppose that 500 people are measured on twenty tests of ability and that the correlations between each test and every other test are arrayed in a square array known as a **correlation matrix (R-matrix)**. It is likely that, since those who are good at one thing tend also to be good at others, there will be substantial positive correlations among the tests in the battery.

Factor analysis (see Chapter 16) is a set of techniques which, on the basis of the correlations in an R-matrix, classify all the tests in a battery in terms of relatively few underlying (or **latent**) dimensions or **factors**. (The term factor has more than one meaning in statistics. In the **analysis of variance [ANOVA]**, a factor is an independent variable, that is, a set of related treatments or categories.) In **exploratory factor analysis**, the object is to find the minimum number of **factors** necessary to account for the correlations among the psychological tests. In **confirmatory factor analysis**, specified models are compared to see which of them gives the best account of the data.

See
Chap.
16

While factors are hypothetical underlying dimensions, they are estimated, essentially, by sums of participants' scores on all the tests in the battery. Thus, in addition to scores on the tests, each person also receives one or more **factor scores**, each of which represents that person's endowment with the latent variable in question.

1.11   MULTIVARIATE STATISTICS

Factor analysis and canonical correlation belong to a set of techniques collectively known as **multivariate statistics**. While these methods arise naturally in the context of correlational research, however, they are also applicable to certain kinds of experimental data.

In Section 1.4, where we considered experimental research, we spoke of the dependent variable (DV), which was measured during the course of the experiment and the independent variable (IV), which was manipulated by the experimenter with a view to showing that it had the power to affect the DV.

The DV in an experiment is often, in a sense, a representative or proxy variable. In a test of maze-learning proficiency, for instance, we may use the speed at which participants draw lines through the maze. Arguably, however, another aspect of performance, number of errors, also reflects maze-learning skill; indeed, in some situations there may be several reasonable potential dependent variables, any one of which could be taken as representative of proficiency.

Statistical methods designed for the analysis of data from experiments with a single DV are called **univariate statistics**. **Multivariate statistics** are methods designed for the analysis of data sets in which there are two or more DVs. In this context, however, the terms independent and dependent variable tend to be applied more generally to any research, whether experimental or correlational, in which some variables (the IVs) are thought to have a causal influence upon others (the DVs).

In experimental and quasi-experimental research, the *t* tests and ANOVA are generalised to **the multivariate analysis of variance (MANOVA)**. In correlational research, **factor analysis** explains associations among the observed variables (the DVs) in terms of latent 'causal' variables known as **factors** which, though they are sums of the observed variables, are taken to represent underlying psychological or health dimensions.

1.12   A FINAL WORD

In this chapter, we have offered some advice about using formal statistical tests to support the researcher's claim that what is true of a particular data set is likely to be true in the population.

At this point, however, a word of warning is appropriate. The making of a formal statistical test of significance always presupposes the applicability of a statistical **model**, that is, an interpretation (usually in the form of an equation) of the data set as having been generated in a specified manner. The model underlying the one-sample *t* test, for example, assumes that the data are from a normal population. To some extent, statistical tests have been shown to be robust to moderate violations of the assumptions of the models upon which they are based, that is, the actual error rates do not rise above acceptable levels. But there are limits to this robustness, and there are circumstances in which a result, declared by an incautious user to be significant beyond, say, the 0.05 level, may actually have been considerably more probable than that. There is no way of avoiding this pitfall other than by getting to know your data first (see Chapter 4) to ascertain their suitability for specified formal tests.

Recommended reading

Field, A., & Hole, G. (2003). *How to design and report experiments*. London: Sage.

Howell, D. C. (2007). *Statistical methods for psychology (6th ed.)*. Belmont, CA: Thomson/Wadsworth.

A useful dictionary of statistical terms

The following is a very useful reference book, with clear definitions.

Nelson, D. (2004). *The Penguin dictionary of statistics*. London: Penguin Books.

CHAPTER 2

Getting started with IBM SPSS Statistics 19

2.1   INTRODUCTION

There are three stages in the use of SPSS Statistics:

1.   Entry of the data into the **SPSS Statistics Data Editor**.

2.   The issue of commands.

3.   The examination and editing of the output in the **SPSS Statistics Viewer**.

Initially, the easiest way to issue commands is by making selections from drop-down menus at the top of the screen and completing **dialogs** in special windows called **dialog boxes**. Commands, however, can also be issued by writing them in a **control language** called **Syntax**. When the same procedure has to be used again and again, the completion of the same series of dialogs can become tedious and much time can be saved by recalling a stored Syntax command and re-running that. There are also procedures that can be accessed through Syntax only. For these reasons, Syntax is often the method of choice for the experienced SPSS user. We shall consider the use of Syntax in Section 2.5.

There are several ways of placing data in the **Data Editor**. The numbers (which SPSS terms **values**) can be typed in directly; or they can be read in from an SPSS data file that has already been created and stored. SPSS can also read data from files produced by other applications, such as EXCEL, R and STATISTICA. Sometimes such files must first be converted to text files; but recent versions of SPSS can read an EXCEL worksheet directly.

Once the data are in the **Data Editor**, a variety of editorial functions are available, enabling the user to reorganise the data in various ways and combine them with data from other files.

SPSS Statistics offers the user a formidable array of statistical techniques. In Chapter 1, we have tried to provide some general guidelines for the selection of appropriate descriptive statistics and formal tests. Before you make any formal statistical tests, first *get to know your data*. In addition to the standard descriptive statistics, SPSS offers a wide range of graphical methods for displaying a data set, most of which are described in Chapters 4 and 5. Graphs are particularly useful at the exploratory stage of a data analysis.

The results of the analysis appear in the **SPSS Statistics Viewer**. The Viewer itself offers powerful editing facilities, which can be used to improve the appearance and clarity of the output.

From the SPSS Statistics Viewer, material can readily be printed or transferred to other applications, such as Word.

In Chapter 1, we described an experiment in which the shooting accuracy of some volunteers who had ingested caffeine was compared with that of a control or placebo group. We shall use the caffeine experiment to illustrate the stages in a typical SPSS session. At this stage, we shall concentrate on the general procedure and run a simple descriptive analysis, leaving the making of formal statistical tests for later chapters. Table 1 shows the results of the experiment, the **raw data** from which the statistics in Table 1 of Chapter 1 were calculated.

The data shown in Table 1 are not in a form that the SPSS Statistics Data Editor will accept. In an SPSS data set, each row must contain data on just one **case**, **subject** or **participant**. The first row of entries in Table 1, however, contains data from ten different participants.

To make them suitable for analysis with SPSS, the data in Table 1 must be rearranged. In Table 2, the data in Table 1 have been re-tabulated, so that each row now contains data on only one case or participant.

In Table 2, the Condition or Group variable identifies the group to which each participant belongs by means of an arbitrary code number: 1 denotes the Placebo condition; 2 denotes the Caffeine condition. Unlike the numbers in the Score column, which express level of performance, the code numbers in the Condition or Group column serve merely as category labels: the Condition variable is a special kind of **categorical** variable (see Chapter 1) known as a **grouping variable**.

Table 1.   Results of the Caffeine experiment

Placebo Group					Caffeine Group				
13	21	3	3	16	14	17	15	8	8
4	8	12	10	13	14	8	12	21	15
6	4	5	10	12	10	18	11	13	15
10	6	13	7	10	10	10	16	12	9
11	15	11	6	8	8	7	7	13	16
9	18	16	15	7	17	10	11	19	12

Table 2. The data from Table 1, recast into a form suitable for entry into SPSS

Case or Participant	Condition or Group	Participant's Score
1	1	13
2	1	4
3	1	6
4	1	10
5	1	11
6	1	9
..	..	..
..	..	..
..	..	..
..	..	..
57	2	15
58	2	9
59	2	16
60	2	12

2.2 DESCRIBING THE DATA FROM THE THE CAFFEINE EXPERIMENT

In this section, we shall use SPSS to display the results of the caffeine experiment and summarise their characteristics with some statistics. We shall consider the making of formal statistical tests in Chapter 6.

The data set we shall be using is to be found in the file *Ch2 Caffeine experiment(60).sav*, which is available at http://www.psypress.com/spss-made-simple. We suggest, however, that you prepare the SPSS Statistics Data Editor as described below and type the data into Data View.

2.2.1 Opening SPSS

There are several ways of beginning a session with SPSS, depending upon whether you intend to build a new file or to access an old one. When SPSS is opened for the first time by clicking the SPSS icon, an opening **dialog box** will appear with the title SPSS Statistics 19. (See Figure 1.)

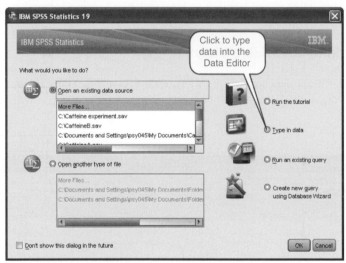

Figure 1. The **IBM SPSS Statistics 19** opening dialog box

Underneath the title is the question: 'What would you like to do?'. You have a choice of one of six small **radio buttons**. For the present, we shall assume that you wish to enter data manually into the Data Editor, in which case, click the button labelled **Type in data**. When you click **OK**, the **Data Editor** will appear on the screen.

Should you, at a later stage, wish to dispense with the introductory dialog, simply click the square in the bottom left corner labelled **Don't show this dialog in the future**.

2.2.2 The SPSS Statistics Data Editor

The **Data Editor** provides two alternative windows:

1. **Variable View** contains the names and details of the variables in the data set.

2. **Data View** is an array like a spreadsheet, into which the user can either type new data or enter data from a stored file.

Careful work in Variable View is time well spent. You should be able to return to the analysis of a data set at any time – perhaps after a considerable interval – and find everything clearly labelled and ready for immediate use. That would not be the case if, when the data were originally entered, the arbitrary values making up the grouping variables had not been assigned meaningful

> **Always assign value labels!**

value labels. Did the code values 0 and 1 indicate males and females, respectively; or was it the other way round? Were the right-handers and left-handers coded as 1 and 2, respectively – or was it vice versa? Such questions shouldn't arise when you return to a data set. Good work in Variable View can also make the output of your analysis much easier to understand, with any graphs clearly captioned and labelled and the variables bearing comprehensible names.

2.2.3 Working in Variable View

When the **Data Editor** appears, you may find that you are in **Data View**. If so, click the **Variable View** tab at the bottom left-hand side of the window and you will access **Variable View** (Figure 2).

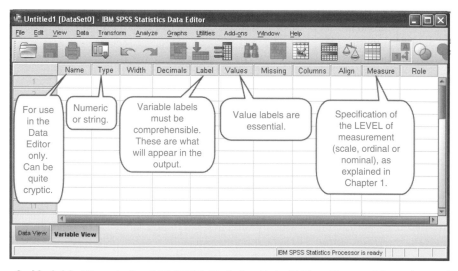

Figure 2. **Variable View** in the IBM SPSS Statistics Data Editor. (Some of the columns have been narrowed.)

When the **Data Editor** first appears, the caption in the title bar reads, '**Untitled1 [DataSet0]** – **IBM SPSS Statistics Data Editor**'. The word **Untitled** is a warning to the user that the contents of the Data Editor (as yet there are none) have yet to be saved to a file. The bracketed word **DataSet0** indicates that there are, as yet, no data in the Data Editor.

SPSS Statistics 19 allows more than one data set to be active during an SPSS session. (Only one data set, however, can be active at any moment.) Activation of the first data set is denoted by the appearance in the square brackets of 'DataSet1'; any additional data sets activated would be named 'DataSet2', 'DataSet 3' and so on. When you finish entering a set of data, you can supply your own name for the file by choosing the **Save As...** item from the **File** drop-down menu and entering a suitable name in the **File Name** box. After you have done this, the title bar in the Editor will display the new name for the file. (If you are typing a large data set into Data View, it is advisable to save frequently to the named file: this practice could save you hours of work should the system crash.)

> **Save your work frequently!**

The Name and Labels columns

Some of the column headings in **Variable View** (such as **Decimals**) are self-explanatory. SPSS calculates values to the same high level of precision, irrespective of the number of decimal places displayed in Data View. A good rule, therefore, is to display as few places of decimals as possible, to avoid clutter in Data View: e.g., **Decimals** should be set to zero for the values of a grouping variable.

The **Name** and **Labels** columns require some explanation. A **variable name** is an unbroken string of characters which will appear at the head of a column in **Data View**. *No spaces are allowed.* Digits can be included (var1, var2, var3), so long as the first character is a letter. A variable name is intended only as a convenient shorthand for use in the Data Editor. In contradistinction, a **variable label** is a full, meaningful caption of the type you would wish to see in a book or a journal article and the user is free to write the label as a meaningful phrase, complete with spaces between the words. You want the variable *label*, not the variable *name*, to appear in the output; but if you omit to supply a variable label, the variable name will appear in the output by default.

Here is a useful tip for entering variable names. Spaces in variable names aren't allowed, but you can simulate the spacing of words by using an underline thus: Time_of_Day. (To obtain an underline, press and hold down the shift key, then press the hyphen key.) Note that the phrasing has also been improved by using a mixture of lower and upper case. The name Time_of_Day will appear at the head of a column in Data View.

> **Tip**
> **Putting spaces in variable names**

Completing Variable View

To prepare the Data Editor for data in the form shown in Table 2, we shall have to enter three variables: Case; a grouping variable to indicate the group or condition to which a score belongs; and a third variable containing the participant's score.

- To name the variables Case, Group and Score, first check that the top leftmost cell has been highlighted in yellow. If necessary move the cursor there and click with the mouse.

- Type *Case* and make the entry by pressing the ↓ cursor key. Highlight the cell below by clicking the mouse there.

- Type *Group* into the second cell, press the ↓ cursor key to make the entry and click the next cell below to highlight that.

- Use the same procedure to enter the variable name Score in the leftmost cell of the third row from the top.

SPSS will accept eight different **types** of variable, two of the most important being **numeric** (numerals with a decimal point) and **string** (e.g. names of participants, cities or other non-numerical material). Initially, some of the format specifications of a variable are set by default, and the pre-set values will be seen as soon as the variable name has been typed and control transferred from the **Name** cell. Initially, it will be assumed that the variable is of the numeric type; and for most purposes, this is the correct type to use.

The number of places of decimals that will be displayed in **Data View** is pre-set at 2. Since the scores in Table 2 are all integers, however, it would be tedious to read entries such as 46.00, 34.00 and 54.00, as opposed to 46, 34 and 54. It is better to suppress the display of decimals in **Data View** as follows (Figure 3):

Figure 3. Changing the number of decimal places displayed for one variable only

Note that this countermanding of the default specification of two places of decimals will apply only to the variable concerned. Rather than over-riding the default specifications piecemeal in this way, you can reset the decimal display to zero for every numeric variable in the data set by choosing **Edit➔Options…➔Data** and resetting the number of decimal places to zero. See Chapter 3 for more details.

Variable labels are assigned by using the **Label** column. In order to make the output as clear as possible, it is important to devise meaningful labels for all the variables in the data set. The labels shown in Figure 4, Number of Hits and Treatment group, are more informative than the corresponding variable names Score

> **Assign variable labels!**

and Group, respectively which, though perfectly adequate for use by the researcher within the **Data Editor**, are too cryptic for a written report. No variable label need be assigned to the case numbers, since the variable Case will not appear in the most important tables and graphs in the output.

The **Values** column is for use with **grouping variables**, that is, sets of code numbers indicating category membership. By clicking on **Values**, the user can supply a key to the meanings of the code numbers making up the grouping variable. In this case, the grouping variable is Experimental Condition and we can arbitrarily decide that 1 = Placebo and 2 = Caffeine. Click the appropriate cell of the Values column and proceed as shown in Figure 5.

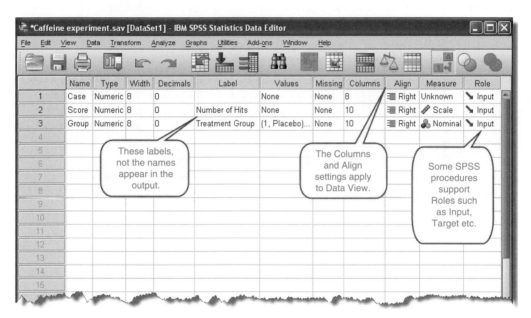

Figure 4. **Variable View** completed

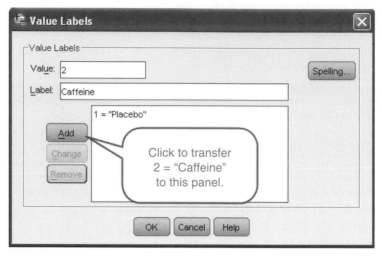

Figure 5. Assigning value labels

The Width column

If you are working with a string variable, the **Width** column controls the maximum length (in number of characters) of the string you will be allowed to enter when you are working in **Data View**. (Since you will normally be working with numeric variables, the width setting in Variable View will not usually be a concern. The Width setting, however, must be at least one more than the setting for the number of decimal places that will be displayed in Data View.)

The default setting for Width is 8, but this can be changed by choosing **Edit➔Options➔Data** and changing the **Width** setting there. For more details, see Chapter 3. If a string is too long for the set width, you will find that you will not see the extra letters when you go into **Data View**.

When you are working in either Variable View or Data View, you can easily widen the columns at any time by clicking and dragging on their boundary lines.

The Columns column

The cells of this column display, for all the variables in the data set, the actual widths of the columns that will appear in **Data View**. Initially, the cells in **Columns** will show the same setting as the **Width** column: 8. Were you to create a new numeric variable with a name whose length exceeded the preset width, only part of the name would be displayed in the **Name** column of **Variable View**. Moreover, in **Data View**, only part of the variable name would be visible at the head of the column for that variable.

To specify wider columns for a variable in **Data View** while working in **Variable View**, click the appropriate cell in **Columns** and adjust the setting there.

The Align column

This determines whether the data in Data View are **Left**, **Right** (the default) or **Center** aligned.

The Measure column

This enables the user to specify the **level of measurement** (Section 1.2.2) for each variable. You must declare whether the data are **Scale** (i.e. measurements on an independent scale with units), **Ordinal** or **Nominal.** The default specification is **Scale**. It is particularly important, however, to specify variables such as sex or blood group as **Nominal**, since this is a requirement for the use of some graphics procedures such as the **Chart Builder** and **Tables**. For our example, Case and Score would be entered in the Measure column as **Scale** and Group would be entered as **Nominal**.

The Role column

In some SPSS routines, variables must be assigned **roles** such as **input** or **output**, or made the basis of a partitioning of the data in some way. By default, all variables are **input**.

Copying settings

Values in the cells of **Variable View** can be copied and pasted to other cells in the usual way. For example, having adjusted the **Columns** setting to, say, 15 characters for one variable of the data set, the new setting can be applied to other variables by copying and pasting the contents of the cell with the entry 15 into the cells for the other variables.

Modified settings can also be copied to **Columns** from the **Width** Column. Having adjusted an entry in the **Width** column to, say, 16, the new setting can be copied and pasted into **Columns**. The effect will be to widen the columns in **Data View** for the variables to which the new **Columns** setting has been copied.

2.2.4   Working in Data View

Once you have entered the appropriate specifications in **Variable View**, click the **Data View** tab at the bottom of the **Variable View** window to enter **Data View**. At this stage, it is a good precaution to save the data to a named file – and to keep saving them at frequent intervals.

> **Keep saving your data!**

When **Data View** is accessed, the variable names Case, Group and Score will be the headings of the first three columns, as specified in **Variable View**. The default name *var*, which appears in the third, fourth and fifth columns, indicates that those columns have yet to be assigned to specified variables.

Running along the bottom of the **Data View** window is a horizontal band, in which various messages appear from time to time. When SPSS is accessed, the message reads: **SPSS Processor is ready**. This horizontal band is known as the **Status Bar**, because it reports not only whether SPSS is ready to begin, but also on the stage that a lengthy procedure has reached. If, for example, a large data set is being read from a file, progress is continually monitored, in blocks of cases, in the status bar. Occasionally, there will be a message indicating that the proceedings have been held up for some reason and the user will be need to take action.

Entering the data

Figure 6 shows a section of **Data View**, in which the data in Table 1 have been entered. The first variable, Case, contains the case numbers of the participants. Enter the number of each participant from 1 to 60. (Later, we shall see that there is a quick way of doing this.) The third variable, Group, identifies the condition under which each participant performed the task: 1 = Placebo; 2 = Drug. Enter thirty 1's into the first thirty rows of the Group variable, followed by thirty 2's. (There is a quick way of doing this as well.)

In the first ten cells of the Score column, enter the scores of the thirty participants who performed the task under the Placebo condition, followed by those of the thirty participants who performed under the Caffeine condition.

Notice that in Figure 6, location of control is indicated by the shaded cell in the 11th row of the second column. The value in this cell is 21, which is also displayed in a white area known as the **cell editor** just above the column headings. The value in the **cell editor** (and the cell itself) can be changed by clicking in the **cell editor**, selecting the present value, typing a new one and pressing ↵. The new value will appear in the grid.

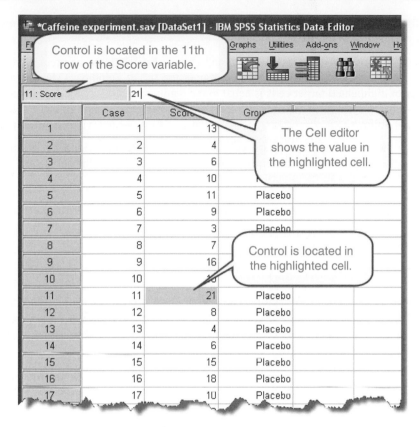

Figure 6. A fragment of **Data View** after the results in Table 1 have been entered

Blocking, copying and pasting

Initially, only one cell in **Data View** is highlighted. However, as we have seen, it is possible to highlight a whole **block** of cells, or even an entire row or column.

- To highlight a *whole row or column*, click the blue box containing the row number or the column heading. The highlighted row or column will turn yellow.

- To highlight a *block of cells* within a row or column, click on the first cell and (keeping the left button of the mouse pressed down) drag the pointer to the cell at the end of the block. The same result can be obtained by clicking the first cell in the block, pressing the **Shift** key and keeping it held down while using the appropriate cursor key (↑ or ↓) to move the highlighting along the entire block.

The blocking operation can be used to copy the values in one column into another or to place them elsewhere in the same column.

- Highlight a column of values that you wish to copy and then choose **Edit➔Copy** or use the key combination **Ctrl + C**.

- Highlight the cells of the target column and choose **Edit➔Paste** or press **Ctrl+V**. The values in the source column will now appear in the target column. (Make sure that the number of highlighted target cells is equal to the number of cells copied.) For example, the successions of 1's and 2's identifying the Placebo and Drug conditions could have been entered as follows.

  - Place the value 1 in the topmost cell of the Group column. Move the highlight away from the cell to complete the entry of the value 1 and highlight the cell again.

  - Choose **Edit➔Copy** or press **Ctrl + C** to store the value 1 in the clipboard.

  - Highlight cells 2 to 10 and choose **Edit➔Paste** or press **Ctrl + V** to place the value 1 in all the highlighted cells.

Deletion of values

Whether you are working in **Variable View** or in **Data View**, entries can be removed by selecting them in the manner described above and pressing the **Delete** key. Note that a period (.) indicates a missing value. Whole rows or columns can be deleted by selecting the whole row or column and clicking **Delete**.

Switching between Data View and Variable View

You can switch from one **Data Editor** display to the other at any point. While in **Data View**, for instance, you might want to return to **Variable View** to name further variables or add further details about existing ones. Just click the **Variable View** tab. When you have finished the new work in **Variable View**, click **Data View** to continue entering your data.

Creating more space for entries in Data View

While the widths of the columns in **Data View** can be controlled from **Variable View** in the manner described above, you can also control column width while working in **Data View**. To widen a column, click on the blue cell containing the variable name at the top of the column and click and drag the right-hand border to the right.

Displaying value labels in Data View

The values assigned to the numerical values of a grouping variable can be displayed in **Data View** (as in Figure 6) by clicking the **Value Labels** icon in the toolbar (right) or by choosing **View➔Value Labels**.

Should the Group column in **Data View** not be sufficiently wide to show the value labels completely, create more space by placing the cursor in the blue cell at the head of the column containing the label Group and click and drag the right-hand border of the cell to the right.

Using value labels when entering data

When you are typing data into **Data View**, you will find that, at first, it will accept only numerical values. (This is true even after you have assigned value labels in Variable View.) After you have typed in the value 1, however, you can display its value label in the usual way (**View➔Value Labels**). You will now see the label Placebo in the cell. You can now copy and paste this label to the other twenty-nine cases in the Placebo group in the usual way. When you come to the Drug group, however, you will need to type in 2 which, when you click another cell, will then appear as the label Caffeine. Data View will not accept the word Caffeine typed in directly; but you can copy and paste the second numerical label to the remaining cases in the Caffeine group. This procedure can be useful if, momentarily, as when your SPSS session has been interrupted, you have forgotten the number-label pairings you assigned in **Variable View**. Keeping the value labels in view also helps you to avoid transcription errors when transferring your data from response sheets.

Save your data frequently

Even modern computers can freeze up and if you haven't been saving as you go along, you can lose hours of work. Save your work by choosing **File➔Save As ...** , selecting an appropriate drive and/or folder and then entering a suitable name in the **File Name** box. After you have done this, the title bar of the Data Editor will display the name you assigned to the file. Note that if you do not save before ending the session, you will be prompted to supply a name for the data file at that point. If you are working in the Data Editor and save your work to a named file, you

> **Save your data frequently!**

can update the contents of the file easily by clicking the disk icon in the toolbar underneath the drop-down menus at the top of the window. In this way, you can continually update the file, thus keeping most of your work safe from mishaps.

2.2.5   Computing the group means

In this section, we shall use SPSS to summarise the results of the experiment by obtaining some descriptive statistics such as the mean and standard deviation of the scores for each treatment group (Placebo and Caffeine).

Several SPSS routines, including **Descriptives**, calculate means and standard deviations. In our example, however, the data contain a grouping variable and we want to compare the group means and other aspects of the group distributions. The **Means** procedure will do this for us. (**Descriptives** would be the wrong choice here, because it calculates the means of entire columns only.)

- From the drop-down **Analyze** menu, choose **Compare Means➔Means ...** (Figure 7).
- Click **Means...** to access the **Means** dialog box (Figure 8).

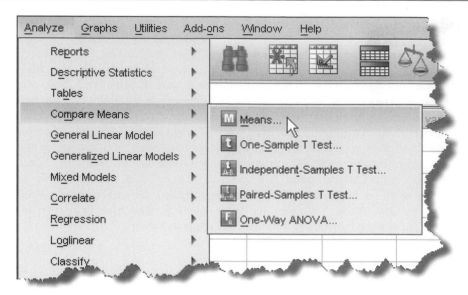

Figure 7. Finding the **Means** dialog box

- Click on Score to highlight it, then click the arrow pointing to the **Dependent List** box (Figure 8). The variable name and label will then be transferred to the **Dependent List** box. Alternatively, the variable names can be dragged and dropped into the appropriate box.

- In a similar manner, transfer the variable Treatment Group to the **Independent List** box (see Figure 8). (Were we to fail to do this, the Means procedure would simply calculate the means for the entire column of scores in Data View, which is what the Descriptives procedure would have done.)

- Click the **Options** button to access the **Means:Options** dialog box (Figure 9). Select some extra statistics (the median, the maximum and minimum scores and the range) and click **Continue** to return to the **Means** dialog (Figure 10).

- Click **OK** to run the analysis. The results will appear in a new window called the **SPSS Statistics Viewer**, a section of which is shown in Figure 11.

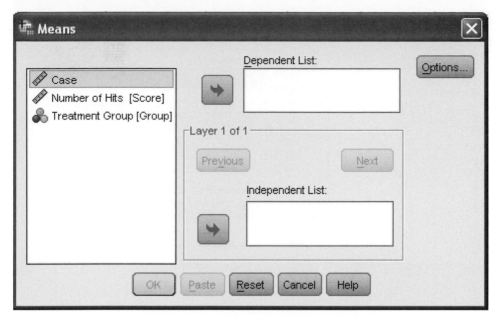

Figure 8. The **Means** dialog box

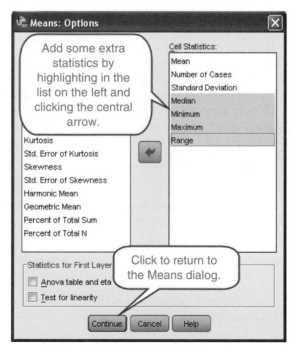

Figure 9. The **Means: Options** dialog box

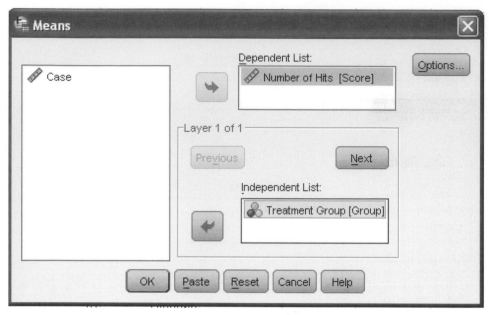

Figure 10. The completed **Means** dialog box

2.2.6 The SPSS Statistics Viewer

The **IBM SPSS Statistics Viewer** (Figure 11) consists of two panes, separated by a vertical common border. The relative widths of the panes can be adjusted by clicking on the border and dragging it to the left or to the right. The right-hand **contents pane** contains the output. The left hand **outline pane** contains labelled icons representing the items in the contents pane. The icons make up what is termed the **outline**. The icons can be manipulated in various ways to control the real items in the contents pane.

The labelled icons are of three types:

1. Icons representing individual items in the output. Initially, several of them appear with an open book icon, indicating that the actual item is visible in the contents pane.

2. Folder icons, in the form of ring-binders, which represent the output of named commands.

3. Log icons – one for each command – which contain the **control language**, or **Syntax** of the command concerned.

Hiding and revealing items in the Viewer

Double-clicking an item such as the Report in Figure 11 removes the open book icon and renders the item itself invisible in the contents pane. Another double-click on the icon, however, makes it visible once again.

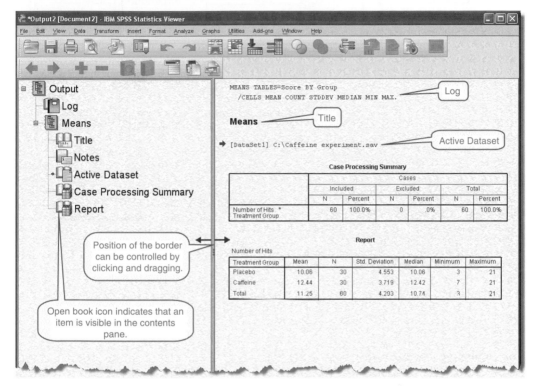

Figure 11. The **IBM SPSS Statistics Viewer** showing the output for the **Means** procedure

It is important to make a clear distinction between hiding an item and deleting it. You can easily remove an unwanted item by selecting it in either pane and pressing Delete. Once you have done this, however, the item has gone for good: you cannot restore it by clicking its icon. To recover a deleted item, you must re-run the procedure.

Figure 12 gives a closer view of the outline in the left-hand pane of the Viewer. Two of the icons, Output and Means, are yellow folders in the form of ring binders. On the left of each yellow folder is a blue square, which initially contains a minus sign. Clicking a square changes the sign to plus and hides the entire content of that particular folder, the pattern on the cover of which disappears (Figure 13a, 13b). When an icon disappears from the outline, the item itself can no longer be seen in the right-hand pane. The folders are arranged hierarchically, so that clicking on the leftmost square in the outline hides the entire contents of the Viewer (Figure 13b). Clicking the square to the left of the Means folder will hide the contents of that folder only, leaving the Log visible, both in the outline and in the right-hand pane. To restore the entire output of a procedure to view, simply click on the square beside the appropriate folder icon to see the minus sign once again. The icons of the items in the output will appear once again, as will the items themselves in the contents pane.

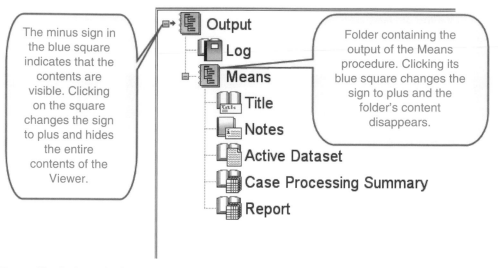

Figure 12. A closer look at the outline

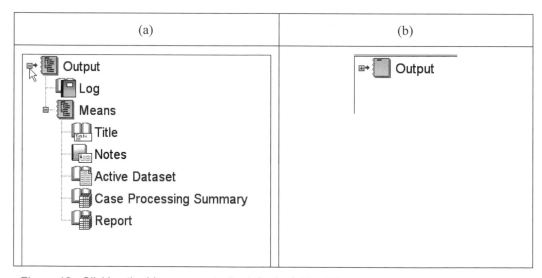

Figure 13. Clicking the blue square to the left of a folder hides its contents. (The sign changes to plus and the pattern on the folder's cover disappears.)

Selecting and deleting items in the Viewer

You can select any item in the Viewer by clicking on it or on its icon in the outline pane. You can make multiple selections by clicking on the first item, pressing and holding down the Control key, clicking on the second item and so on. Note that the items need not be adjacent in the Viewer.

> **Making multiple selections**

When an item has been selected, it can be deleted by pressing the Delete key. When multiple items have been selected, pressing the Delete key will remove all the items selected.

> **Making multiple deletions**

Copying and pasting items in the Viewer

An item in the contents pane can be copied by clicking on it to select it (a frame will appear around the item), pressing **Ctrl + C** and pasting it with **Ctrl + V**. There are situations in which it is useful to have a duplicate of an item in the Viewer, as when you want to compare an edited version with the original. A copying operation can also enable the different layers of a **pivot table** (see below) to be viewed side by side. Using exactly the same procedure, you can copy items of output to other applications, such as Word files.

Sometimes, when the output is extensive, you may want to re-arrange some of the items in the contents pane. Suppose that, in our current example, you want to relocate the Report above, rather than below, the Case Processing Summary. Simply click on the Report icon with the left mouse button and drag it upwards (Figure 14). As you drag the icon upwards, a red arrow appears in

> **Relocating an item in the Viewer**

the contents pane to the left of the item you have reached. Release the left mouse button when the red arrow is beside the icon below where you want the Report icon to be. In our present example, you would release the left mouse button when the red arrow is beside the Active Dataset icon (Figure 14, left pane).

You will find that the arrangement of the two items themselves in the right-hand pane has also changed to parallel the new arrangement of their icons in the outline pane.

You may sometimes find that the click-and-drag operation fails to move the target icon. If so, select the icon again and press **Ctrl + X** to remove it from the outline pane and place it in the buffer. Then select the item below which you want the target icon to be located and press **Ctrl + V** to paste the buffered icon in the desired position.

> **Trouble-shooting**

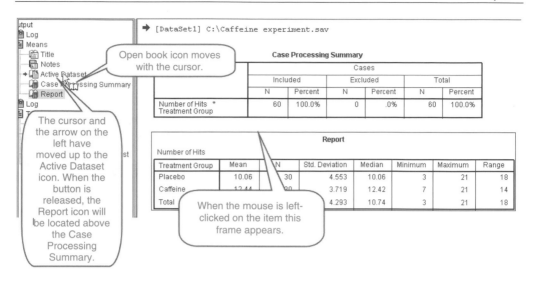

Figure 14. Moving the **Report** table to a new position above the **Case Processing Summary** by clicking and dragging with the left mouse button

2.2.7 The output from the Means procedure

The main item of interest is the **Report** (Output 1), which appears in the right pane. From the **Report**, it can be seen that the mean performance of those tested under the Caffeine condition was indeed higher than the mean of those tested under the Placebo condition.

Report

Number of Hits

Treatment Group	Mean	N	Std. Deviation	Median	Minimum	Maximum	Range
Placebo	10.06	30	4.553	10.06	3	21	18
Caffeine	12.44	30	3.719	12.42	7	21	14
Total	11.25	60	4.293	10.74	3	21	18

Output 1. The **Report** table showing the mean, median, standard deviation, and range statistics for each of the two groups

It would seem, therefore, that the results of the experiment support the scientific hypothesis. That, however, is insufficient: formal tests are necessary to confirm that the difference between the means is characteristic of the population and has not arisen from sampling error.

2.2.8 Histograms

Before making any formal statistical tests, you should first explore your data thoroughly. SPSS has an exploratory data analysis procedure, **Explore**, which offers a wide range of useful statistics. We shall consider **Explore** more fully in Chapter 4. For the moment, we note that, in Output 1 (from the Means procedure), the medians and means have very similar values, indicating that the distributions of scores under both conditions are symmetrical. On the other hand, the scores under the Placebo condition range rather more widely than do those under the Caffeine condition. The values of the standard deviations, however, indicate that the spread of scores is comparable in the two groups.

To supplement the descriptive statistics, we shall need to have a picture, or **graph** of our data. SPSS offers many different kinds of graph, but for the moment, a **histogram** will serve our purposes.

As we saw in Chapter 1, a **histogram** is a kind of graph in which the total range of values of a continuous or scale variable is stepped out in equal **class intervals** along the horizontal axis and upon each class interval is drawn a bar whose height (or area) is proportional to the frequency (or relative frequency) of values falling within the class interval.

- Choose **Graphs➔Chart Builder...** . A warning message will appear reminding you to specify the level of measurement of every variable in the data set and to assign value labels to the values of any grouping variables. Check the box marked **Don't show this dialog** again and click **OK** to enter the **Chart Builder** (Figure 15).

- Select the type of graph you want from the **Choose from** list. The appropriate array of choices will appear in the **Gallery**.

- Click on your choice from the array in the **Gallery** and drag the template into the **Chart Preview** area.

- From the **Variables** list, click and drag Score into the **Chart Preview** and position it in a box below the histogram.

- Click on **Element Properties**. Within the Element Properties dialog, click **Set Parameters** and choose the number of **bins** (class intervals) as shown in Figure 16. Click **Continue** to return to **Element Properties**.

- Back in **Element Properties**, check **Display normal curve** and click the **Apply** button to return to the **Chart Builder**. (See Figure 17.)

- In the **Chart Builder**, click the **Groups/Point ID** tab and check **Rows panel variable**. This choice produces a **rows panel** of figures (one figure for each group), one on top of the other. (A **columns panel** displays the figures side-by-side.) (See Figure 18.)

- You will see in the **Chart Preview** a box on the right marked **Panel?** Drag the grouping variable from the **Variables** list into the **Panel?** box in the **Chart Preview**. (See Figure 18.)

- Click **OK** to produce the histograms.

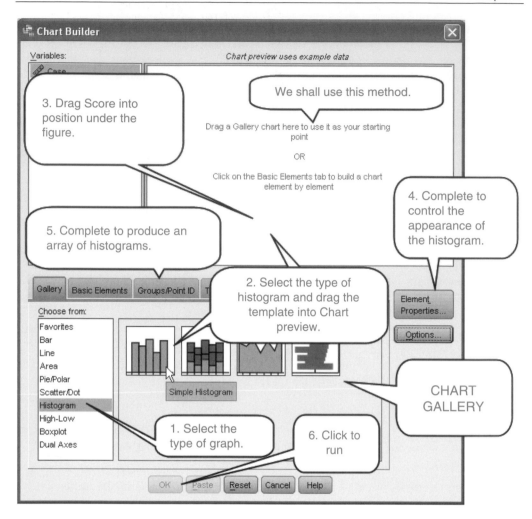

Figure 15. The **Chart Builder**, showing the six steps in the production of a simple histogram

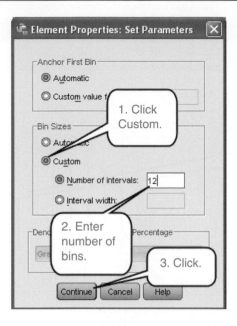

Figure 16. Controlling Bin Sizes in the **Element: Properties: Set Parameters** dialog box

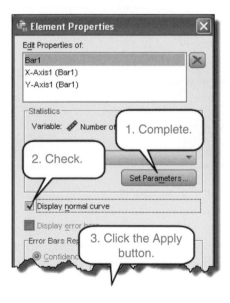

Figure 17. Ordering a normal curve in the **Element Properties** dialog box

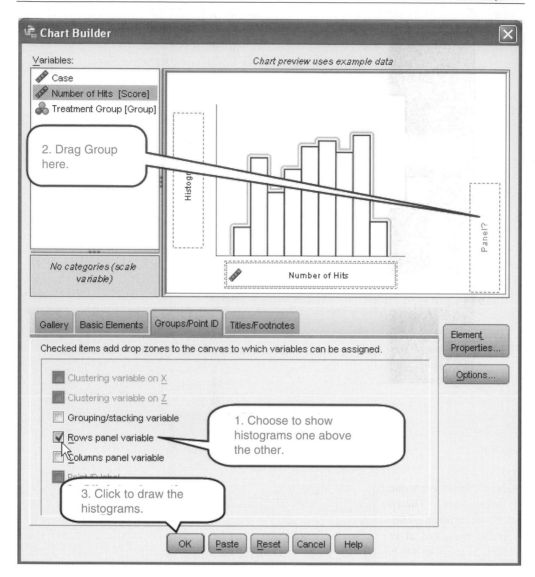

Figure 18. Ordering a rows panel of histograms

Output 2 shows histograms of the distributions of the scores in the Caffeine and Placebo groups. The initial histograms were edited in the **SPSS Statistics Viewer** by double-clicking on the figure to enter the **Chart Editor** and making some minor changes.

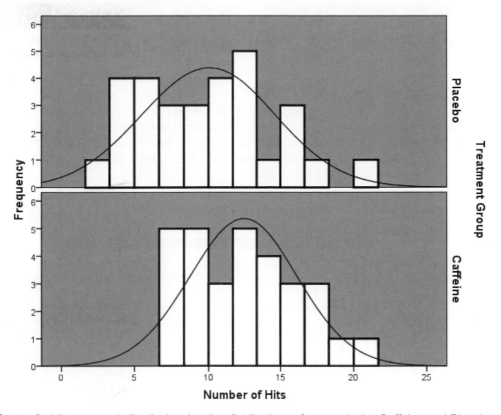

Output 2. Histograms (edited) showing the distributions of scores in the Caffeine and Placebo groups

Provided there are values within adjacent class intervals, there are no spaces between the bars of a histogram. (The space in the upper histogram in Output 2 reflects the absence of values within that range.) This is because a histogram is suitable for graphing the distribution of a variable measured at the **scale** or **continuous** level only.   The histogram must be sharply distinguished from the **bar chart**, in which the bars (which may also represent frequencies) are placed over the names of qualitatively different categories on the horizontal axis and therefore have spaces between them.

The two histograms in Output 2 show clearly that, although there is a tendency for the Caffeine group to score higher than the Placebo group, at least some participants in the Placebo group outperformed most of those in the Caffeine group; indeed the range statistics in Output 1 show that both distributions have the same maximum value.

The curves superimposed upon each of the histograms are normal curves with the same means and standard deviations as the scores in the two groups.   Many formal statistical tests make assumptions about the distributions from which the samples have been drawn. The t tests, for example (Chapter 6), assume normality of distribution and equality, in the population, of the variances in the two groups. (This is the **homogeneity of variance** assumption.) The statistics that we have examined in Output 1 and the appearance of the graphs in Output 2 give us no reason to question these assumptions.

2.2.9 Editing items in the Viewer

The **SPSS Statistics Viewer** offers powerful editing facilities, some of which can radically alter the appearance of a default table such as that shown in Output 1. Many of the tables in the output are **pivot tables**, that is, tables in which the columns and rows can be transposed and to which other radical alterations can be made.

Suppose, for example, that in the **Report** table shown in Output 1, you would prefer the experimental conditions Placebo and Drug to be column headings and the group means, medians, standard deviations, range statistics and N's to be below them. If you double-click the **Report**, a dotted border will appear around the table and the **Pivot** menu will appear (Figure 19). You have now entered the **Editor**.

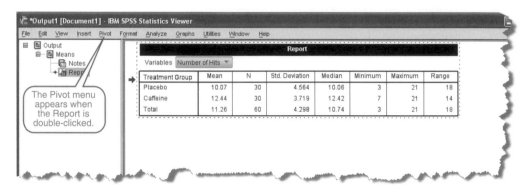

Figure 19. Accessing the **Pivot** menu

Choosing **Pivot➜Transpose Rows and Columns** will effect the transposition of the rows and columns of the table, as in Output 3.

Report

Number of Hits

	Treatment Group		
	Placebo	Caffeine	Total
Mean	10.06	12.44	11.25
N	30	30	60
Std. Deviation	4.553	3.719	4.293
Median	10.06	12.42	10.74
Minimum	3	7	3
Maximum	21	21	21
Range	18	14	18

Output 3. The transposed **Report** table

The descriptive statistics and experimental conditions now occupy the rows and columns, respectively, rather than vice versa as before.

The Pivot menu can be used to edit complex tables with three, four or more dimensions of classification. Such manipulation can be of great assistance in bringing out the most important features of your results. We shall return to the editing of pivot tables in Chapter 3.

2.2.10   Ending the session

SPSS is closed by choosing **Exit** from the **File** menu. If you have not yet saved the data or the output at any point, a default dialog box will appear with the question: **Save contents of data editor to untitled?** or **Save contents of output viewer to Output 1?** You must then click the **Yes**, **No** or **Cancel** button. If you choose **Yes**, you will be given a final opportunity to name the file that you wish to save.

At the risk of seeming repetitious, we suggest that by the closing stage of your session, you should already have been saving the data to a named file at frequent intervals. Output files, on the other hand, occupy considerable storage space, especially when they contain graphics. We therefore suggest that only selected items from the output should be saved.

2.2.11   Resuming work on a saved data set

There are several ways of resuming work on a saved data set. After opening SPSS and obtaining the introductory **SPSS Statistics 19** dialog box, you can click the radio button **Open an existing data source** (Figure 1). A list of saved files with the extension *.sav* will appear in the upper box. Select the appropriate file and click **OK**. (If you don't see the name of the file you are looking for, click on **More files …** .) When you click on the name of the target file, the data will appear in **Data View**. Other kinds of file, such as SPSS output files, can be retrieved from the lower box by clicking on the radio button labelled **Open another kind of file**. While you are in the **Data Editor**, it is always possible to access files by choosing **Open** from the **File** menu.

2.3   THE FOUR DRUGS EXPERIMENT

In Chapter 1, we described an experiment in which the performance of groups of participants who had ingested one of four different drugs (A, B, C and D) was compared with that of a comparison or control group, who had received a Placebo. The results of the experiment are shown in Table 3.

The file containing these data is *Placebo & four drugs.sav*, which is available on our website at http://www.psypress.com/spss-made-simple. As with the caffeine data, however, we suggest that, in order to familiarise yourself with SPSS, you should prepare the Data Editor as described below and type the scores in.

Table 3. The results of a one-factor, between subjects experiment

	Placebo	Drug A	Drug B	Drug C	Drug D	
	10	8	12	13	11	
	9	10	14	12	20	
	7	7	9	17	15	
	9	7	7	12	6	
	11	7	15	10	11	
	5	12	12	24	12	
	7	7	14	13	15	
	6	4	14	11	16	
	8	9	11	20	12	
	8	8	12	12	12	
Mean	8.00	7.90	12.00	14.40	13.00	M = 11.06
SD	1.83	2.13	2.49	4.50	3.74	grand mean

We should say at the outset that this is a miniature data set: the samples are nowhere near large enough for a proper experiment. We should need at least thirty participants in each group to produce results in which we could be reasonably confident. SPSS, of course, has no problems with large data sets. On the other hand, when you are finding your way around in SPSS, it's easier to see what is going on with small data sets than with large ones.

2.3.1   In Variable View

Earlier in the chapter, we described the entry of the results of the caffeine experiment into the SPSS Data Editor. We saw that the data shown in Table 1 are not in a form that the SPSS Statistics Data Editor will accept. In an SPSS data set, each row must contain data on just one participant; whereas the first row of entries in Table 1 contains data from ten different participants. The results shown in Table 3 must be similarly recast before they can be entered into the SPSS Data Editor.

As with the caffeine data, we shall need to define two variables:

1. A variable with a name such as Score, which contains all the scores in the data set. This is the dependent variable. It can also be given a more informative **variable label**, such as Performance Score.

2. A **grouping variable** with a simple variable name such as Group or Drug, which identifies the condition under which a score was achieved. (The grouping variable

should also be given a more informative variable label such as Drug Condition, because this is what will appear in the output.)

The grouping variable will consist of five values (one for the placebo condition and one for each of the four drugs). We shall arbitrarily assign value labels thus: 1 = Placebo; 2 = Drug A; 3 = Drug B; 4 = Drug C; 5 = Drug D. The captions attached to the numerical values are known as **value labels** and are assigned by making entries in the **Values** column in Variable View.

Proceed as follows:

- Open **Variable View** first and amend the settings so that when you enter **Data View**, your variables will already have been labelled and the scores will appear without unnecessary decimals: e.g. you certainly don't want any decimals for the arbitrary code numbers making up the grouping variable. Set **Decimals** to zero for both variables: we want to see integers only in Data View.

- Name the variables Score and Group.

- Assign a more self-explanatory **variable label** such as Drug Condition to the grouping variable.

- It is very important to assign **value labels**. Assign the value labels as shown in Figure 20.

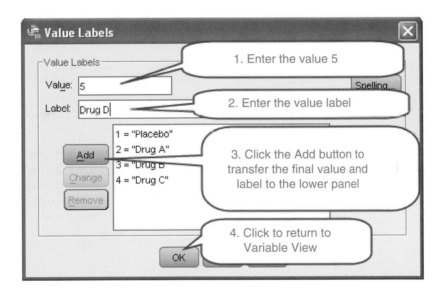

Figure 20. Assigning value labels to the code numbers making up the grouping variable. (The figure shows the value label 'Drug D' being given to the value 5.)

- In the **Measure** column of **Variable View**, specify the level of measurement of your grouping variable as **nominal** (Figure 21). (The numerical values that we have assigned to

the five treatment groups are quite arbitrary and serve merely as numerical labels for the
five different treatment conditions.)

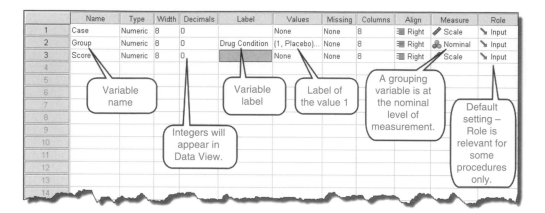

Figure 21. **Variable View** completed

Notice that in Figure 21, the variable label for the dependent variable has been omitted. As a
result, the variable name Score will appear in the output; whereas the grouping variable will
appear under its full variable label Drug Condition.

2.3.2   In Data View

When you enter Data View, you will find the columns labelled and the grid ready for entry of
the data. Many people find it helpful to have the value labels displayed, rather than the values
themselves.

Figure 22 shows two views of the same fragment of Data View. On the left, the
arbitrary code values making up the grouping variable are displayed; whereas on the
right, the value labels are displayed. To display the value lables, choose
View➜Value Labels or click on the **label icon** (shown at right) at the top of the
window.

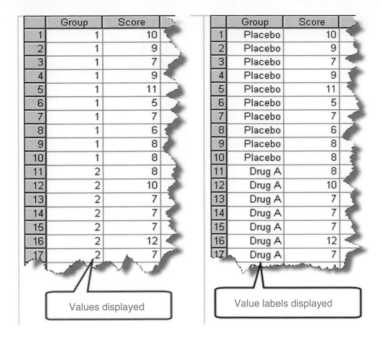

Figure 22. Two displays of the upper part of **Data View** after the data have been entered

2.3.3   Using the Means procedure

To obtain some statistics describing the five groups of scores, proceed as follows:

- Choose **Analyze➔Compare Means➔Means …**   to open the Means dialog box and proceed as shown in Figure 23. The results are shown in Output 4.

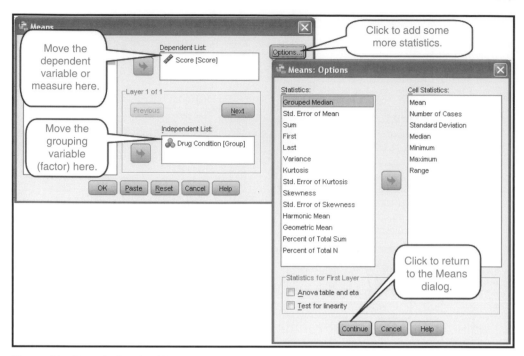

Figure 23. Completing the **Means** dialog

Report

Score

	Drug Condition					
	Placebo	Drug A	Drug B	Drug C	Drug D	Total
Mean	8.00	7.90	12.00	14.40	13.00	11.06
N	10	10	10	10	10	50
Std. Deviation	1.826	2.132	2.494	4.502	3.742	4.007
Median	8.00	7.50	12.00	12.50	12.00	11.00
Minimum	5	4	7	10	6	4
Maximum	11	12	15	24	20	24
Range	6	8	8	14	14	20

Output 4. Descriptive statistics of the scores in the five groups of the drug experiment

2.3.4   The histograms

To obtain histograms of the scores under the five treatment conditions, proceed almost exactly as described in Section 2.2.8 as follows:

- Choose **Graphs➔Chart Builder...** . A warning message will appear reminding you, in general, to specify the level of measurement of every variable in the data set and, in particular, to assign value labels to the values of any grouping variables. Check the box marked **Don't show this dialog** again and click **OK** to enter the **Chart Builder**.

- In the Gallery tab, select **Histogram** and click-and-drag the histogram template into the the **Chart Preview** box.

- Drag the DV (Score) to the drop zone under the horizontal axis of the histogram template in the Chart Preview.

- In the **Element Properties** dialog, check **Display normal curve** and click **Apply**.

- Click the **Groups/Point ID** tab and check the box labelled **Rows panel variable**.

- In the **Chart Preview** box, a new box will appear to the right of the histogram template. Click-and-drag the grouping variable to this box.

Click the **OK** button to run the procedure.

The histograms (Output 5) reveal considerable heterogeneity in the distributions of the scores in the different groups. The scores in the Drug C group, for example, appear to have a skewed distribution; whereas those in the Placebo group are more symmetrical.

The smooth curves superimposed upon the histograms are the normal distributions with the same means and standard deviations as the scores in the samples. Many formal statistical tests assume both normality of distribution and homogeneity of spread or variance from group to group. Clearly, in this case, there is considerable doubt about whether those requirements have been met; on the other hand, the samples are so small that there is insufficient evidence to decide either way.

Later, in Chapter 4, we shall use SPSS's **Explore** procedure to examine the data from the four drugs experiment more closely.

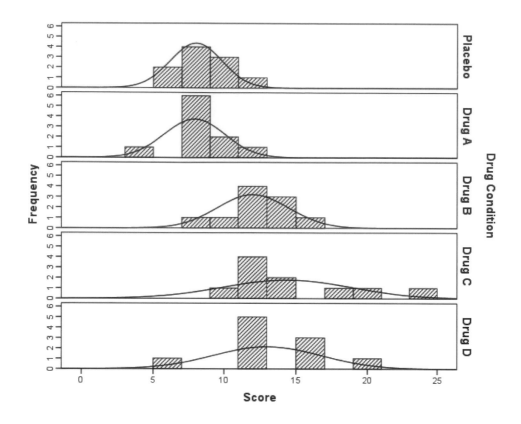

Output 5. Histograms of the scores from the five groups in the drug experiment

2.4   PRINTING FROM THE STATISTICS VIEWER

It is possible to make extensive use of SPSS without ever printing out the contents of the **Viewer**. Both the data in the Data Editor and the output can easily be backed up electronically by saving to disk; and important SPSS output is easily exported to the open Word document you actually want to print out. SPSS output can be extremely extensive and indiscriminate printing is wasteful. In the worst scenario, an inept printing operation could result in dozens of sheets of paper, with a single line of print on each sheet. There are, nevertheless, occasions on which it is both useful and necessary to print out selected items in the **Viewer**.

We strongly recommend that, before you print any output, you should make full use of the **Viewer**'s editing facilities to remove all irrelevant material. When using SPSS, one invariably requests output which, at the end of the day, proves to be superfluous. Moreover, as we have seen, radical changes in tables and other output can be made (with great economies in space) by using the **Viewer**'s powerful editing facilities. Since some of the output tables can be very wide, unnecessary columns can be removed.

For some kinds of material, it is better to use **landscape** orientation for the sheet, that is, have the shorter side vertical, rather than the more usual **portrait** orientation with the longer side vertical. It is easy to make such a specification while working in the Viewer before printing anything out. To clarify a batch of printed output, we also recommend that you add explanatory captions, such as Output for the Drugs Experiment. Otherwise, it is only too easy to accumulate pages of SPSS output, the purpose of which becomes increasingly unclear as time passes. All these things can easily be done while you are working in the Viewer. Often, however, even after you have severely pruned the Viewer's contents, you will be interested in printing out only a selection of the items.

We shall illustrate some aspects of printing from the **Viewer** with output from the Means and histograms produced either by the **Chart Builder** or the **Legacy Dialogs**.

Using Print Preview

- To view the content of the first page of the output that will be printed before any selection of items has been made, choose **File➜Print Preview...** (Figure 24).

- The contents of the other pages can be viewed by pressing the **PgDn** key as often as necessary. Alternatively, you can click on the **Next Page** button in the row of buttons at the top of the dialog box. You will see that, when no item has been selected, the output extends to several pages.

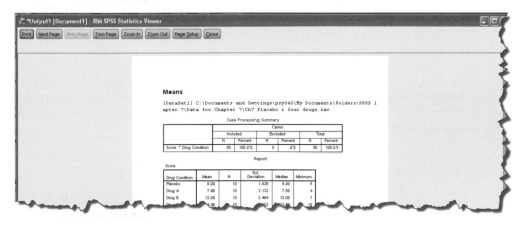

Figure 24. Part of the **Print Preview** dialog box (shrunk horizontally and vertically) for viewing the output before printing from the **SPSS Statistics Viewer**

Selecting items for printing

To select an item for printing, return to the Viewer and click the item. To select two or more items, click the first and, pressing the **Ctrl** key and keeping it held down, click the other items that you wish to select. (You will also need to hold down the **Ctrl** key if you are clicking icons in the left pane to achieve a multiple selection.) The items need not be adjacent. If you now choose **Print Preview**, you will see that it shows only the items you have selected, and it is

only those items that will actually be printed. There are
two ways of selecting items: you can click the item's icon
in the left pane of the **Viewer**; or you can click the item
itself in the right pane. Either way, a rectangle with a

single continuous border will appear around the item or items concerned. It is, perhaps, easier
to click on the items in the right pane directly to make it immediately clear what has been
selected.

Try selecting any item in the **Viewer** and choose **Print Preview**, to see the **SPSS Statistics
Viewer** window, which will display only the item you have selected. If you return to the **Print**
dialog box, you will see that the **Selection** radio button in the **Print range** panel has now been
activated. Were you to click **OK** at this point, only the selected item would be printed.

Inserting page breaks

You can also exert some control over the appearance of the output in the **Viewer** by creating a
page break between items that clearly belong to different categories. Back in the Viewer, …

- Click the item above which you want to create a page break.

- Choose **Insert→Page Break**. The break will be marked on the
  contents pane of the Viewer as shown at right. The Graph section
  will now appear on a new page of the printout.

  » **Graph**

- Click outside the selection rectangle to cancel the selection; otherwise only the selected
  item will appear in Print Preview.

If you now return to **Print Preview**, you will see that a page break has been created and the
item you selected is now at the top of a fresh page. Used in conjunction with re-ordering, page
breaks can help you to sort the items in the **Viewer**. Bear in mind, however, that creating page
breaks always increases the number of sheets of paper in the printed output.

Changing from portrait to landscape using Page Setup

For wide figures or tables, it may be better to have the base of the figure lying along the longer
side of the page (**landscape** orientation), rather than along the shorter side (**portrait**
orientation). To print with landscape orientation, proceed as follows:

- Choose **File→Page Setup...** to open the **Page Setup** dialog box (Figure 25). Check the radio button marked **Landscape**. The preview will change to landscape orientation.

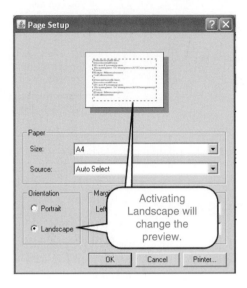

Figure 25. Using **Page Setup** to change the orientation to landscape

The SPSS Statistics Viewer's Print dialog box

- Access the SPSS Statistics Viewer's **Print** dialog box (Figure 26) by choosing **File→Print...**.

By default, the radio button labelled **All visible output** is active, which means that pressing **OK** will result in the *entire contents* of the **SPSS Statistics Viewer** being printed out indiscriminately. The default setting of copies is 1, but obviously increasing that value to 2 will double the volume of the printed output. If, however, you have selected one or more items in the Viewer, you will find the button labelled **Selected output** already checked, which is as it should be – one should be highly selective about printing output.

Make a selection!

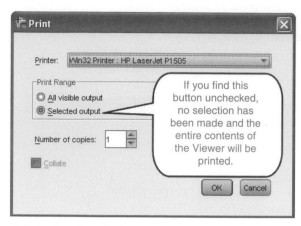

Figure 26. The **Print** dialog box for printing output from the **SPSS Statistics Viewer**

2.5   USING SPSS SYNTAX

So far throughout this book, the statistics provided by SPSS have been accessed by opening windows and completing dialog boxes. Although this is the easy way to learn SPSS, there is another way of using SPSS which, though it requires some practice, confers considerable additional benefits.

It is possible to run SPSS procedures and analyses by writing instructions in a **control language** known as **SPSS Syntax**. (In fact, until a few years ago, the only way of using any of the major mainframe statistical packages was by using control language.) It is still useful to learn how to use Syntax, however, if only because some SPSS routines are available through Syntax only. Moreover, the Syntax for a particular analysis (even one set up initially from dialog boxes) can be saved as a Syntax file and re-used later, with enormous savings in time.

The writing of Syntax, of course, is governed by rules which take a little time to learn. You can make good use of syntax, however, without actually writing any commands at all! If an analysis has been set up from dialog boxes, pressing **Paste** (instead of **OK**) in the main dialog box will paste the hitherto hidden syntax into the **Syntax Editor** from which it can be saved to a file in the usual way. Once an SPSS data file is active, the syntax file can be opened and the procedure can be run immediately: there is no need to complete any dialogs.

For a syntax file to run, the **Data Editor** must contain an active data set. This can be a data set that has already been saved to a file. You can open a saved file in the usual way from the SPSS Statistics opening window. In the Syntax Editor, you can write a **GET** command, which can activate a saved data set automatically. It is also possible to run syntax commands by entering a small data set **inline** into the **Syntax Editor** itself.

> **An active data set is essential!**

In no time at all, you will become practised in the use of Syntax and familiar with the general form of Syntax commands. We believe that the easiest way to learn SPSS Syntax is by pasting commands from the dialog boxes in this way, rather than ploughing through the available texts on the topic, which tend to be rather compendious and are better left until one has already acquired a good working knowledge of the language.

For the following exercise, open the file *Caffeine experiment(60).sav* , which is available on our website at http://www.psypress.com/spss-made-simple.

2.5.1   The Syntax Editor

The **SPSS Statistics Syntax Editor** window can be opened by choosing

File➔New➔Syntax (Figure 27).

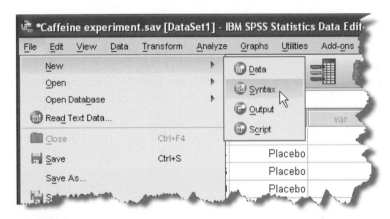

Figure 27. Accessing the **Syntax Editor** window

The window of the **IBM SPSS Statistics Syntax Editor** is shown in Figure 28. The commands are written in (or pasted into) the **editor pane** on the right. In the **navigation pane** on the left, commands that have been run are listed in outline. If the command is syntactically incorrect or refers to variables that do not exist, error messages will appear in an **error pane**, which opens below the editor pane. The editor and navigation panes are separated by an area called the **gutter**, which will eventually contain line numbers and other information about the commands written in the editor pane.

When a particular command in the window has been highlighted, it can be run by clicking the **Run Selection** icon (at right). The **Run** menu under the title bar, however, gives finer control over the selection and running of multiple commands in the syntax window: e.g., the commands in the **Syntax Editor** can be run step by step, either from the first command onwards or from a specified starting position.

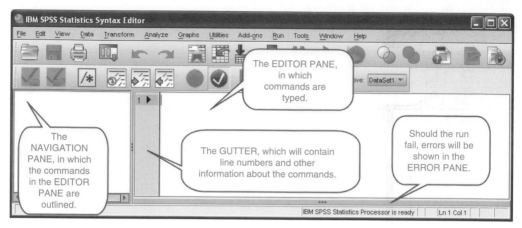

Figure 28. The **Syntax Editor** window

2.5.2   Running the Means procedure with Syntax

- Choose **Analyze➔Compare Means➔Means** and complete the **Means** dialog in the usual way, requesting, through **Options**, the median and the range statistics. Click the **Paste** button at the bottom of the dialog box (Figure 29) to paste the Syntax command into the **Syntax Editor** (Figure 30).

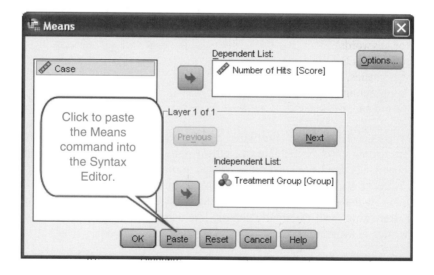

Figure 29. Pasting the **Means** command into the **Syntax Editor**

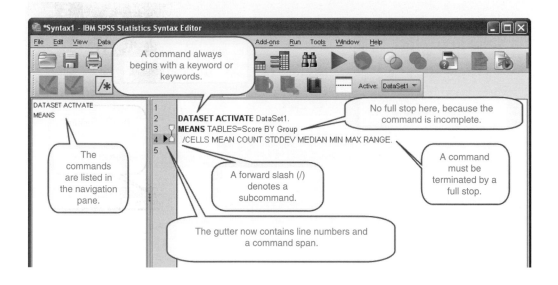

Figure 30. The **Means** command pasted into the **Syntax Editor**

In Figure 30, it will be noticed that the complete MEANS command has now been pasted into the editor pane of the Syntax Editor window. In fact, there are two commands in the editor pane: 1. the Means command itself; 2. The Dataset Activate command. (The Dataset Activate command isn't necessary if you type commands directly into the Syntax Editor, rather than pasting them in from a dialog box.) A command must begin with a recognised command **keyword** (or keywords) and end with a **terminator** in the form of a full stop. The forward slash (/) before CELLS indicates that CELLS is a **subcommand**. A command may contain several subcommands, in which case those subcommands that come in the middle of the command do not require terminators; in the present example the CELLS subcommand, being the only subcommand, is followed by the terminator of the MEANS command.

Notice that the CELLS subcommand includes the extra statistics that we ordered through **Options**: the median, the highest and lowest scores and the range. In Syntax commands, the keyword BY typically follows the name of the dependent variable and precedes the grouping variable or variables.

You will notice that when the terminating full stop has been added to the command, the keywords turn blue. Failure of the command keywords to turn blue indicates an error in the Syntax.

- Run the procedure by highlighting the entire MEANS command (which will then appear in inverse video) and clicking the **Run Selection** icon (at right), as shown in Figure 31.

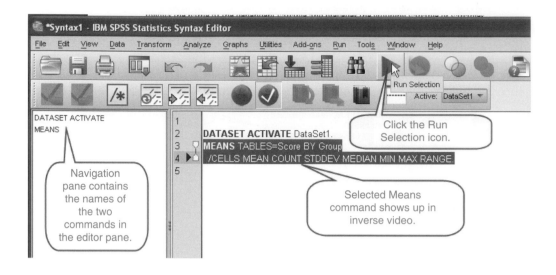

Figure 31. Running the **Means** command

The output is exactly the same as when we ran the Means command by completing the dialog and clicking the **OK** button.   Note also that the syntax appears as the Log in the Output Viewer window above the output for the Means procedure (Output 6):

```
GET
   FILE='C:\Caffeine experiment.sav'.
DATASET NAME DataSet1 WINDOW=FRONT.
MEANS TABLES=Score BY Group
   /CELLS MEAN COUNT STDDEV MEDIAN MIN MAX RANGE.
```

Output 6. Log containing the Syntax for the Means command from the Output Viewer

There will be, no doubt, occasions on which you will want to dispense with the appearance of the Log in the output every time you issue a command.   To hide the Log, proceed as follows:

• Choose **Edit➔Options➔Viewer (tab)**, deselect the **Log** by activating the radio button labelled **Hidden**, click the **Apply** button at the foot of the dialog and leave the dialog by clicking **OK**.

As a result of this move, the Log will no longer appear in the Viewer when a command is run.

2.5.3   Looping functions in Syntax

The scope and power of Syntax extend far beyond merely repeating routines without completing the same dialogs over and over again. Syntax can implement **looping functions**, that is, commands which, having performed an operation on a case or a variable, continually return control to the beginning of the operation and repeat it as often as required with fresh cases or variables. Looping functions can be invaluable in simulation and the investigation of sampling distributions. In an Appendix to this book, there is a short section on the use of four different looping structures.

2.6   A FINAL WORD

In this chapter, we have illustrated a typical SPSS session with the analysis of data from a simple experiment. In **Variable View**, the variables are named and labelled, values are assigned value labels, the level of measurement of each variable is specified, and the number of decimal places to which values will be displayed is set. Careful work in Data View, which includes clear naming and labelling of the variables and the assignment of value labels to the code numbers making up grouping variables, pays off handsomely when you come to work in Data View, where the availability of value labels can help you to avoid transcription errors when you are entering the data. Do save your work frequently, especially when entering a large data set by hand.

Since the data sets used in this chapter (the caffeine data and the drugs data) contain a grouping variable, the **Means** procedure was used to obtain descriptive statistics of the scores in the groups. The addition of the medians and range statistics to the means and standard deviations provided important additional information about the distributions of the scores in the different groups. The data in the groups were also examined by using the **Chart Builder** to draw histograms of the distributions.

The same analyses can be run by using **SPSS Syntax**, a control language. Syntax commands are written or pasted into the **Syntax Editor** and saved for future use with similar data sets. The scope of Syntax, however, extends far beyond the running of statistical tests and the production of graphs. An appendix describes the use of four different looped structures to draw samples from specified populations and investigate the sampling distribution of the mean.

SPSS Tutorials

For step-by-step tutorials on various SPSS topics, choose

Help➔Tutorial➔Using the Data Editor.

Exercises

Exercise 1 *Some simple operations with SPSS Statistics 19* and Exercise 2 *Questionnaire data* are available in www.psypress.com/spss-made-simple and click on Exercises.

CHAPTER 3

Editing data sets

3.1   MORE ON THE DATA EDITOR

In Chapter 2, we described the **Data Editor**, which has two windows: **Variable View** and **Data View**. In this section, we shall describe some further aspects of the use of each of these alternative (but coordinated) displays.

3.1.1   A preliminary check on the default settings

To ensure that the procedures we are about to describe work properly, you should first make a careful check on SPSS's default settings.

- Choose **Edit➔Options** to open the Options dialog box, the upper part of which is shown in Figure 1.   The call-outs indicate the changes that should be made.

At the base of each tab in Options is a button labelled **Apply**. If that button is live, click it to implement the change. If you are working on your own computer, rather than one on a network, the changes should survive a Shut Down.

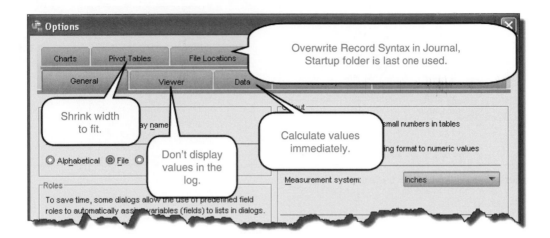

Figure 1. The upper part of the **Options** dialog box with the required settings

3.1.2   Inserting new variables

In the first of the following exercises, we shall be using the caffeine data, available in the file *Ch3 Caffeine experiment(60).sav*, at http://www.psypress.com/spss-made-simple.

An additional variable can be inserted in **Variable View** by highlighting any row (click the blue cell on the left to highlight the whole row, as in Figure 2a), and choosing **Edit➔Insert Variable** (Figure 2b).

In Variable View, the new variable, with the default name VAR00001, will appear *above* the row that was highlighted (Figure 3a). In Data View, it will appear to the *left* of the same variable (Figure 3b).

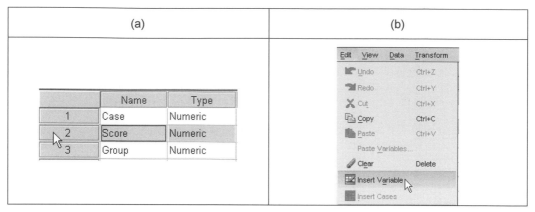

Figure 2. Inserting a new variable

	Name	Type
1	Case	Numeric
2	VAR00001	Numeric
3	Score	Numeric
4	Group	Numeric

Case	VAR00001	Score	Group
1	.	13	Placebo
2	.	4	Placebo
3	.	6	Placebo
4	.	10	Placebo
5	.	11	Placebo
6	.	9	Placebo

Figure 3. Positions of the new variable in **Variable View** and in **Data View**

3.1.3   Rearranging the order of variables in the Data Editor

The top-to-bottom ordering of the variables in Variable View determines their left-to-right order of appearance in Data View: if the former is Case, Score, then Group, the left-to-right order in Data View will also be Case, Score then Group.

Suppose, however, that you want to change the right-to-left order of the variables in **Data View**, so that the Score variable appears on the right of the Group variable, rather than on the left. In **Variable View**, click the blue box to the left of the Group variable to highlight the whole row (Figure 4a). (Click near the lower border of the highlighted leftmost box in the row to see a circle with a diagonal line across it. It is essential that you see the circle.) Holding the left mouse button down, drag the screen pointer upwards. A red line will appear above the Score row (Figure 4b). On release of the mouse button, the variable Group will now appear immediately above the Score variable (Figure 4c). In **Data View**, the variable Score will now appear to the right of the variable Group (Figure 4d).

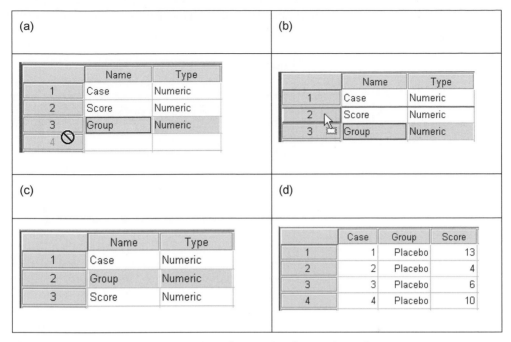

Figure 4. The arrangement of variables after moving Group above Score

3.1.4 Inserting case numbers

In the small data set we considered in Chapter 2, each row had a number which could be taken as representing one particular case or person. We didn't really need an additional Case variable. Suppose, however, that we had a much larger data set, perhaps the results of a study conducted over a considerable period of time, in which the same people were measured several times on the same variables. In such a study, some cases appearing early in the proceedings might not do so later on: indeed, such **subject attrition** can be expected in longitudinal research. From time to time, moreover, the researchers might change the order of the cases on the basis of the order of magnitude of one or more of the other variables in the data set. For many reasons, therefore, a particular row in the data set may not always contain data on the same person throughout the period of the investigation.

With any large data set, especially one that is continually changing, it is good practice to create, as the first variable, one with a name such as Case, which records each participant's original case number: 1, 2, ..., and so on. The advantage of doing this is that, even though a given person's data may occupy different rows at different points in the research, their data can always be identified and traced through the entire process of data entry and analysis.

In the following exercise, we shall use the data file *Ch3 Ungrouped Heights and Weights.sav*, at http://www.psypress.com/spss-made-simple.

Figure 5 shows Variable View and the first few lines of Data View in a data set consisting of the heights of 1000 men. As yet, however, that there are no case numbers in this data set. The object of this exercise is to insert a new variable, Case, containing the numbers from 1 to 1000, so that it appears as the leftmost variable in Data View (and the top variable in Variable View).

(a) Variable View	(b) Data View

	Name
1	MENS_HEIGHTS
2	MENS_WEIGHTS
3	
4	
5	

	MENS_HEIGHTS	MENS_WEIGHTS	va
1	176.99	81.36	
2	170.75	80.76	
3	181.77	80.43	
4	192.42	78.90	
5	172.94	95.81	
6	183.09	106.99	

Figure 5. Part of a data set consisting of the heights and weights of 1000 men

- Choose **Edit➜Options** and click the **Data** tab to see the settings for **Transformation and Merge Options**. The radio button marked **Calculate values immediately** should be checked (Figure 6).

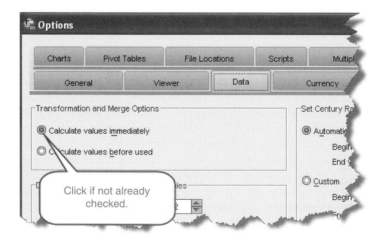

Figure 6. The correct setting for **Transformation and Merge Options**

- In Variable View, highlight the first variable, MENS_HEIGHTS by clicking on the blue rectangle on the left of the row, choose **Edit➜Insert Variable** and type *Case* as the name of the new variable. The effect of this move is to create, in the first column of Data View, a new column headed Case, which contains 1000 system-missing values (.).

- Copy the name Case with **Ctrl + C**. (Or choose **Edit➔Copy**.)

- Since the cases are whole numbers, set **Decimals** to zero.

- Choose **Transform➔Compute Variable…** to open the **Compute Variable** dialog box.

- Place the cursor in the **Target Variable** slot and paste the name Case into the **Target Variable** slot with **Ctrl +V** or **Edit➔Paste**. (If you have forgotten to copy the name you can type it in; but you won't be able to move it into the slot from the list below.)

- In the **Function group** panel on the right, click **All**, to reveal a list of functions in the **Special Functions and Variables** panel underneath, the first of which is $Casenum (Figure 7).

- Highlight $Casenum and click the arrow to transfer this name to the **Numeric Expression** panel (Figure 8).

- Click the **OK** button at the bottom of the dialog box to place the counting numbers from 1 to 1000 into the **Case** column in Data View (Figure 9).

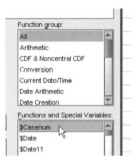

Figure 7. Finding the special variable $Casenum

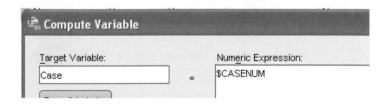

Figure 8. The special variable $Casenum has been transferred to the Numeric Expression panel

Case	MENS_HEIGHTS
1	176.99
2	170.75
3	181.77

Figure 9. The case numbers have now been inserted as the leftmost variable in Data View

3.1.5   Using Syntax to insert case numbers into a data set

Syntax can easily be used to insert case numbers into an existing data set. The procedure is described in the Appendix.

3.1.6   Inserting case numbers into an empty Data Editor

Suppose that before entering any data into the Data Editor, you want to create a Case variable containing the numbers from 1 to 1000. While this can be done mechanically, the process is laborious. The problem is that since an empty Data View grid will initially allow you to select only forty or so lines, you must take steps to make more lines available. If you intend to enter 1000 cases, you will have to repeat this releasing move several times.

Proceed as follows:

- Open a new SPSS file.

- In **Variable View**, choose **Edit➜Insert Variable** and type *Case* in the Name column of the new variable. Copy the name Case by selecting it and clicking Ctrl + C.

- Set **Decimals** to zero.

- In **Data View**, enter an arbitrary value (1 will do) into the top leftmost cell and click **Return**.

- Holding the left mouse down, drag downwards, highlighting the first allocation of forty or so rows. You will soon reach a point beyond which you can scroll down no further. Now, you must make the first releasing move.

- Click the first cell in row 40 and type in any number, say *1* (Figure 10a).

- When you press Enter, the **system-missing value** (.) will appear in all the cells up to the one in which you made the numerical entry (Figure 10b).

- Left-click and drag to scroll down again, until you reach the final row of your second allocation.

- Enter another arbitrary value (1 will do yet again) at the end of your second allocation of rows. When you have done this, you will see the system-missing value (.) appearing in all the preceding rows as before.

- Proceed in this manner, clicking and dragging to scroll down as far as possible then entering an arbitrary number and pressing Return, until each of the rows from 1 to 1000 contains either the system-missing value or a number.

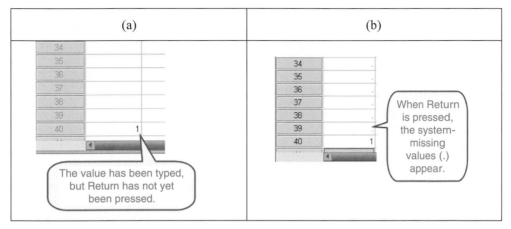

Figure 10. Increasing the size of the data set by entering arbitrary values and scrolling

- Choose **Transform➜Compute Variable**, paste the variable name Case into the **Target Variable** slot with Ctrl + V, and use the special $Casenum variable as before to insert the case numbers, which will replace the arbitrary numbers and system-missing values already in the Case variable.

3.1.7   Using Syntax to insert case numbers into an empty Data Editor

Syntax can be used to insert case numbers into a new, empty Data Editor. The procedure is described in the Appendix.

3.1.8   Changing the default settings for Width and Decimals

The default settings for variable width and number of places of decimals are 8 and 2, respectively. If you wish to enter several new variables and display them all as whole numbers (integers), choose **Edit➜Options➜Data**, click the **Data** tab and change the pre-set values.

The changes you have specified will apply only to any *new* numeric variables that you may create. You will find that, even after the default settings in Options have been amended, the appearance of numerical data already in Data View is unchanged.

If you are using a networked computer, the software and settings will be held on a central server. Any changes you may make by changing the entries in Options will apply only for the duration of your own session: when you log off, the system will restore the original default values.

3.1.9   String variables

In Variable View, there is a column headed **Type**. The Type column specifies the general form that an entry for a particular variable will take when it appears in the data set. By default, the variable type is assumed to be **numeric**; but seven other types of variable, including **string variables** can be specified in SPSS. In our experience, however, it is generally best to work with numeric variables and avoid using string variables wherever possible. There are also risks with storing potentially sensitive information about people in computer files. Many researchers code individuals numerically as case numbers and store the participants' names and case numbers in hard copy form only in a locked filing cabinet.

The code numbers making up a grouping variable are recognised by SPSS as numerical values, even though they are being used merely as labels for experimental conditions or group membership. In fact, such procedures as Descriptives can be used to calculate the mean and standard deviation of a grouping variable, even though these statistics don't mean anything.

A **string** is a sequence of characters, such as a person's name or a town or city, which is treated as a qualitative datum (not a number) by the system.   Suppose, for example, that we wanted to enter, in a variable called Town, the names of all the towns studied in a survey. Initially, the Data Editor will not accept non-numerical data of this kind.   To prepare the Data Editor for the input of a string variable, proceed as shown in Figures 11a and 11b.

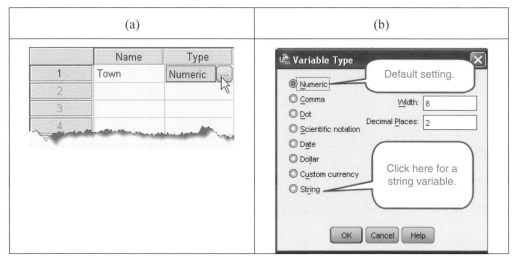

Figure 11. Preparing the Data Editor for input of a string variable

- Click the radio button marked **String** at the foot of the list (Figure 11b). The **Width** and **Decimal Places** boxes will immediately be replaced by a box labelled **Characters** (Figure 12).

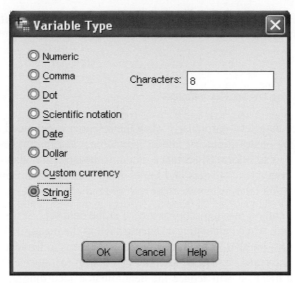

Figure 12. The Characters slot appears when the String radio button is activated

- In the **Characters** box, change the default value 8 to some larger number such as 20 to accommodate the longest likely town name. Do this by moving the cursor into the number box, highlighting the 8 and typing in 20.

- Click **OK**. In **Variable View**, the variable type String will now appear in the **Type** column and the cell for the Town variable in the **Width** column will now show 20 (Figure 13).

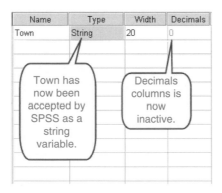

Figure 13. Acceptance of Town as a string variable by the system

- Copy the value 20 by highlighting it and choosing **Edit➜Copy** (or by using the key combination **Ctrl + C**).

- Click on the appropriate cell in **Columns**, highlight the value there and paste in the new **Width** specification (20), either by choosing **Edit➜Paste** or by using the key combination **Ctrl + V**. The effect of this move will be to make sufficient space available in **Data View** to see the longest town name in the data set. Alternatively, in **Data View**, the Name column can easily be widened by clicking the right hand column and dragging it to the right.

3.1.10   Specifying missing values

In research with large data sets, particularly when the research is extended over a considerable period of time, missing observations are almost inevitable. The researcher needs to be know, in the first instance, how to inform SPSS that a datum is missing; it is also important, however, to know how SPSS computes statistics and tables from data sets with missing values. (We shall address that question later, when we come to discuss the techniques concerned.)

It is a serious error to enter a missing score as a zero in the data set. SPSS will assume that the zero is a valid score and, when calculating a statistic such as the mean, will therefore divide the total score by too large a number. The correct procedure here is to leave a missing observation as a blank, then press Return. SPSS will supply a full stop to register the value as missing. When calculating the mean, it will reduce the denominator accordingly. In this context, the full stop is known as the **system-missing** value. Figure 14 shows part of a new data set in Data View (supposedly from another caffeine experiment), where the system-missing value (.) indicates a missing observation.

Case	Score	Group
1	13	Placebo
2	.	Placebo
3	6	Placebo
4	10	Placebo
5	.	Placebo
6	.	Placebo
7	3	Placebo
8	7	Placebo
9	16	Placebo
10	10	Placebo

Figure 14.   Part of Data View showing the system-missing value (.)

Now suppose, however, that the researcher has good reason to suspect that scores within the range from zero to two (of which there are several in this new data set) indicate that the participant failed to understand the instructions and therefore values in that range should be excluded from the analysis. The data also contain the value 20, which may have been a misreading of the handwritten entry of the value in the original recording sheet. The researcher wants to inform SPSS that this value too is to be treated as missing.

SPSS recognises two kinds of missing values:

1.   **system-missing** values, as described above;

2.   **user-missing values**, which the user flags as such by making an appropriate entry in the
      Missing column of Variable View.

- To define the range of values between 0 and 2, inclusive, and the point value 20 as user-
  missing, enter Variable View and click the blue rectangle (Figure 15a) to open the
  Missing Values Dialog box (Figure 15b).

- Make the entry shown and click the OK button to register these values as missing. Below
  the Dialog box in Figure 15b is a screen shot of the appropriate cell in the Missing
  Column in Variable View, showing that the user-missing value specifications have been
  entered into the system.

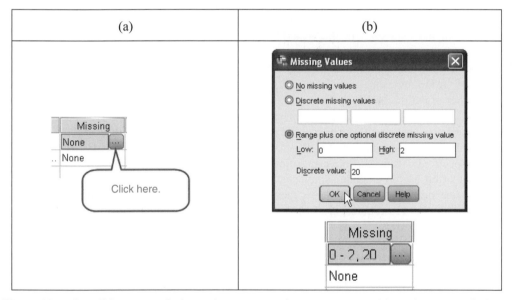

Figure 15.   Specifying user-missing values: a score between zero and 2; and a score of 20

In Output 1a, is the table in the output for **Descriptives** before the user-missing values have
been specified. There were forty participants; but since there are only 35 valid observations,
we know that there are 5 system-missing values in the data set.   In Output 1b, is the table in
the Descriptives output after the user-missing values have been defined, showing that, of the
forty observations, 15 have been treated as missing. You will notice that the removal of the
specified values from the analysis has made a considerable difference to the values of the
statistics.   When the data set is small, atypical scores can exert considerable influence or
leverage upon the values of traditional measures of spread such as the mean and SD.

(a)	(b)

Descriptive Statistics		
	Number of Hits	Valid N (listwise)
N	35	35
Range	20	
Minimum	0	
Maximum	20	
Mean	8.40	
Std. Deviation	5.441	

Descriptive Statistics		
	Number of Hits	Valid N (listwise)
N	25	25
Range	12	
Minimum	5	
Maximum	17	
Mean	10.64	
Std. Deviation	3.108	

Output 1.   The effect upon the **Descriptives** output of defining user-missing values

In Output 1, the term **listwise** appears under the column heading Valid N.   This means that, in order for a score to be accepted as a valid datum, the case must have valid values for all the variables in the data set.   In this example, we shall assume that all the entries for group membership had a numerical value of either 1 or 2 and are correct, in which case the valid N is the number of valid values of the variable Number of Hits.   Had a criterion been set for the values of Group and some cases had failed to meet it, the Valid N would have been less than the number of valid scores.

We should note that much of what can be achieved by informing SPSS of user-missing values as described in this section can also be achieved by the use of **Data➔Select Cases** to exclude data in specified categories from a statistical analysis. The present method would be preferred if the intention was to exclude some data from the analysis indefinitely; whereas the second, being easier to implement and reverse, enables data to be excluded and included in the analysis from occasion to occasion during a single session.

3.1.11   Changing the Alignment settings

In **Data View**, numbers are, by default, right-aligned and strings are left-aligned.   These settings can be changed in Variable View by clicking on the appropriate cell in the **Align** column and choosing **Left**, **Right** or **Center**.

3.1.12   Opening an SPSS file

Open a file from the SPSS opening window as follows:

• When the opening SPSS window appears, select **Open an existing data source**.

• Select the appropriate file. (To locate the target file, you may have to click **More files …** and locate, in that list, the file or the folder containing the file.)

- Click **OK** to open the file in **Data View**.

It is also possible to open a stored SPSS data file by proceeding at first as if you were going to type data into Data View directly:

- In the SPSS opening window, click the radio button labelled **Type in data** and then **OK** to bring **Data View** to the screen.

- In Data View, choose **File➜Open➜Data** to show the **Open File** dialog box. The target file can then be specified.

3.1.13   Entering data from other applications

Some researchers, having worked in another application such as Excel, have attempted to copy and paste blocks of data from the other application directly into Data View. With large data sets, this move can result in a chaotic display in Data View, because, as we saw in Section 3.1.6, Data View will initially make available only a limited number of lines. If you are going to attempt a pasting operation (which we would generally avoid), use the technique described in Section 3.1.6 to free up the necessary number of cases in Data View first.

It appears not to be generally realised that recent versions of SPSS Statistics, such as SPSS 18 and SPSS 19, can read an Excel worksheet directly, removing the necessity to do any pasting at all. Simply choose **File➜Open➜Data** and, from the **Files of type** menu, choose Excel (*.xls,*.xlsx,*.xlsm) as the file type. See Figure 16.

Should the application from which you wish to import data not have one of the many formats recognised by SPSS (Figure 16 shows only some of these), try saving the data to a **tab-delimited** file.   If you have an Excel file open, for example, the variable names will (or should) occupy the first line in the body of the spreadsheet. If you save the data as a tab-delimited file and open the file with SPSS 19, you will find that the variable names will appear in Variable View of the SPSS Data Editor and the values in Data View. The same applies if you wish to export data from SPSS to another application which does not read SPSS files: save the data to a tab-delimited file first.

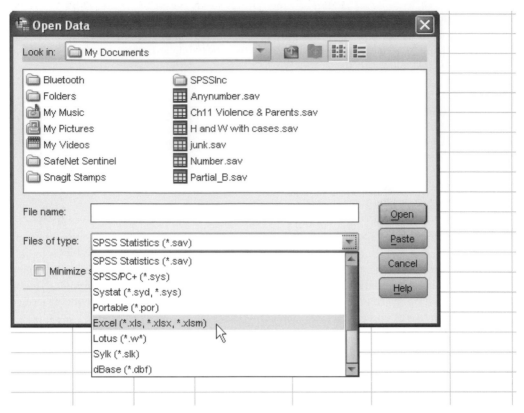

Figure 16.   Importing an Excel worksheet into SPSS

3.1.14   Creating new variables while in Data View

To add a new variable **to the right of those already in Data View**, you have only to type a value into a cell to the right of the present matrix of data. To add a new column **between two of those within the present data set**, proceed as follows:

- Highlight the variable **to the right of** the intended position of the new variable.

- Choose **Edit→Insert Variable** to create a new, empty, variable with a name such as VAR00001, to the left of the variable you have highlighted.

This procedure will also result in a new variable, VAR00001, appearing in Variable View above the name of the variable you highlighted in Data View. We do not recommend that you do this on a regular basis: it's much easier to keep track of your data by naming the variables in advance in Variable View before entering any data in Data View.

3.1.15 Adding new cases while in Data View

There are situations in which you simply must carry out manipulations in Data View directly. For example, you may have reached the end of your allocation of lines in Data View and want to add more cases to the variables already in the data set. We have seen that you can do this easily by pressing Return a few times, typing in an arbitrary number, pressing Return again a few times and so on. You can also choose **Edit➔Insert cases**, which will have the effect of adding new empty rows underneath the existing columns. If you need to insert a substantial number of new cases, however, proceed as described in Section 3.1.6 .

You may occasionally want to place rows for additional cases in the middle of the data set. Suppose that, in the caffeine experiment, you want to add data on an additional participant who has been tested under the Placebo condition. So you want to insert a new row of data at the foot of the scores of the participants in the Placebo group just above the scores of the Caffeine group. Proceed as follows.

- Click the blue cell on the left of the row of data *below* where you want to insert the new case. (This will be the row of data from the first participant who performed under the Caffeine condition.) The row will now be highlighted.

- Choose **Edit➔Insert Cases** to create a new empty row above the one you highlighted.

You can now type in the data from the additional Placebo participant. Actually, new cases can be added anywhere in the data set and re-ordered later by using **Data➔Sort Cases** (Section 3.6). If you sort according to the magnitude of the code numbers making up the grouping variable, the effect will be to bring all the scores from each condition or group together.

3.2   VALIDATION OF THE DATA

When entering data (especially a large data set) into a data file, it is only too easy to mistype a value, say 10, as 100; also, since successive case numbers may not be on successive lines, it is easy to enter the data on a particular case twice. In this subsection, we shall now describe two procedures for detecting rogue values and duplicate entries.

3.2.1   Validation of the data by defining rules

To illustrate the use of the Validation procedure, we shall use a data set like the results of the Caffeine experiment, but in which there have been some mistakes in transcription from the data sheets. There should be sixty cases, but there are actually 61, because the data for case 59 have been entered twice. A score should vary only within the range from 1 to 25, inclusive; but case 16's score of 18 has been wrongly entered as 81. Case 46 has been wrongly entered as Case 64. The code values making up the grouping variable should be 1 and 2 only; however, case 18 has been wrongly given the code number 0 instead of 1 as its group label.

The procedure for checking validity has two stages: the first stage consists of defining rules for acceptable entries; the second applies these rules to specified target variables. For example, suppose we wish to check that there are no duplicate case numbers and that no score is greater than 25 (the maximum possible score in the experiment). Proceed as follows:

- Choose **Data➔Validation➔Define Rules…** (Figure 17) to access the **Define Validation Rules** dialog box (Figure 18).

- In the **Define Validation Rules** window, type *Score Range* to replace the **Name** SingleVarRule1, and enter the values 1 and 25 into the **Minimum** and **Maximum** boxes respectively.

- Click **New** to hide the first rule and make way for you to specify your next rule.

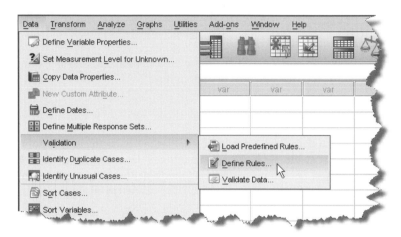

Figure 17. The **Validation** menu

- In the **Rule Definition** window, type *Value Range* to replace the **Name** SingleVarRule2, and enter the values 1 and 2 into the **Minimum** and **Maximum** boxes respectively.

- Add further rules as appropriate. For example, the third rule might specify the possible range of values of Case as 1 to 60.

- Click **OK** to register the rules. You are now ready to run the validation procedure.

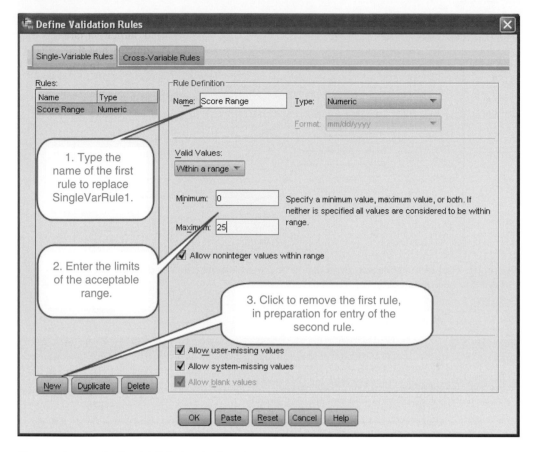

Figure 18. The **Define Validation Rules** dialog box showing the definition of the first rule.

Having defined the rules, the next step is to validate the target variables in the data set by applying the appropriate rules.

- Choose **Validation➔Validate Data...** to open the **Validate Data** dialog box (Figure 19).

- Select the variables Score and Group and click the arrow to transfer them to the **Analysis Variables** box. Transfer Case to the **Case Identifier Variables** panel below. Click the **Single-Variable Rules** tab to open the **Single-Variables Rules** dialog box (Figure 20).

- Click the variable names and the check boxes as shown in Figure 20 and then **OK** to run the validation procedure.

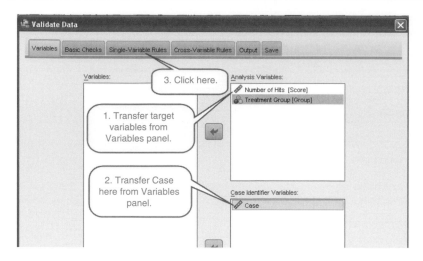

Figure 19. Part of the **Validate Data** dialog box showing the transfer of the names of the variables to be validated

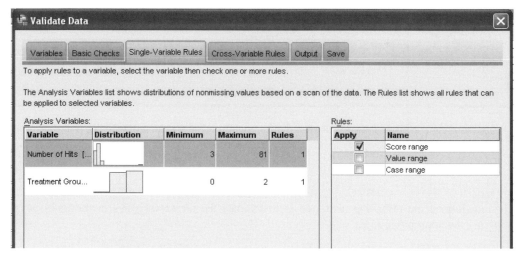

Figure 20. The **Validate Data** dialog box for associating variables with the appropriate rules

The output of the validation begins with warnings and variable checks, and a table of **Rule Descriptions** (not reproduced here). In Output 2, it can be seen that the validation procedure has detected the repetition of the entry for case 59.

Duplicate Identifiers

Duplicate Identifiers Group	Number of Duplicates	Cases with Duplicate Identifiers	Identifier Case
1	2	59, 60	59

Output 2. Table locating the duplication of the entry for case 59

Note that the idenfication of duplicate case numbers does not require prior formulation of any rules: it is sufficient merely to transfer the case identifier variable to the **Analysis Variables** panel in the **Validate Data** dialog.

Turning now to the validation of the data on the Score variable, we see from Output 2 that there has been one violation of our second rule: the data contain one score that lies outside the range from zero to 25. Case 16, as we know, was wrongly entered as scoring 81 instead of 18. The Case Report in Output 3 specifies case 16 as the source of the infringement.

Variable Summary

	Rule	Number of Violations
Number of Hits	Score range	1
	Total	1

Case Report

Case	Validation Rule Violations Single-Variable[a]	Identifier Case
16	Score range (1)	16

a. The number of variables that violated the rule follows each rule.

Output 3. Table showing the violation of the rule on the permissible range of scores

To investigate the grouping variable, we need only choose **Validation➔Validate Data…➔Single-Variable Rules (tab)** and pair the second rule with the grouping variable.

So far, the validation has not detected the wrong entry for case 46.   That is easily rectified by clicking the **Variables** tab, moving Case from the **Case Identifier Variables** box to the **Analysis Variables** box (by clicking on the central arrows), clicking the **Single-Variables Rules** tab, pairing the rule for **Case Range** with the Case variable and clicking **OK** to run the procedure.

Output 4 shows that there has been one violation of the Case Range rule requiring that the values of Case must be within the range from 1 to 60. The rogue case is shown to be case 46.

Variable Summary

	Rule	Number of Violations
Case	Case range	1
	Total	1

Case Report

	Validation Rule Violations
Case	Single-Variable[a]
46	Case range (1)

a. The number of variables that

violated the rule follows each rule.

Output 4.   Table showing a violation of the rule on the permissible range of Case

We have just seen how to use the **Validation** procedure to detect duplication of the same case number in the data set.   In the example above, we supposed that the researcher's mistake was to enter the data on the same case twice. The discovery of two records with identical case numbers and data, however, does not necessarily mean that the data from the same individual have been entered twice: the same case number could have been allocated to two individuals who got exactly the same score. This sort of ambiguity can only be resolved by going back to the original response sheets.

3.2.2   Handling multiple duplications in a large data set

Suppose that, at several points in the process of data entry, the researcher, when entering data on a new participant, assigned the case number of someone who was already in the data set. The mistake was repeated several times, so that there are several groups of records sharing a case number. **Identify Duplicate Cases** is a more specialised SPSS procedure, designed for this kind of problem.

- Choose **Analyze➜Identify Duplicate Cases …** to open the **Identify Duplicate Cases** dialog (Figure 21).

- Transfer Case to the **Define matching cases by** window.

- Assuming that later cases with the same case numbers have been incorrectly numbered, click the radio button **First case in each group is primary** to replace the default option **Last case in each group is primary**.

- Click **OK**.

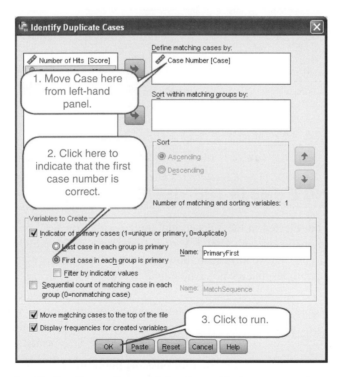

Figure 21. The **Identify Duplicate Cases** dialog box with the variable Case Number and the **First Case in each group is primary** option selected

After you click the **OK** button, you will find that the duplicated case numbers appear at the top of the data set (Figure 22). A new variable PrimaryFirst indicates the original entry with the value 1 and the duplicates with zeros. The **SPSS Statistics Viewer** also contains tables showing how many duplicated cases there are in the different groups.

	Case	Score	Group	PrimaryFirst
1	21	3	1	1
2	21	5	1	0
3	21	11	1	0
4	21	12	1	0

Figure 22. The first few cases of the data set with the new variable PrimaryFirst, which shows the original and the duplicated case numbers

In Variable View, it will be found that value labels have been added to the values 1 and 0. To display the labels in Data View, you have only to choose **View➜Value Labels** (Figure 23).

	Case	Score	Group	PrimaryFirst
1	21	3	Placebo	Primary Case
2	21	5	Placebo	Duplicate Case
3	21	11	Placebo	Duplicate Case
4	21	12	Placebo	Duplicate Case

Figure 23. Data View, showing value labels instead of values

3.3   EDITING ITEMS IN THE VIEWER

A table can easily be selected in the Viewer and copied with **Ctrl + C** or **Edit➜Copy** and pasted into a Word document with **Ctrl + V** or **Edit➜Paste.** The table can then be edited with Word's table tools. As we have seen, however, the Viewer has its own editor, which has several powerful capabilities that are not available in Word.

3.3.1   Changing the format of a table

If you are submitting an article to a journal for possible publication, you are likely to find that any tables in your paper must conform to certain formatting requirements, the most common being that the table must not have vertical lines separating the columns. SPSS offers a choice from a wide range of table formats. To convert the format of the Report table in Output 5 (which we worked on in Chapter 2) to one conforming to APA requirements, for example, double-click the table to get into the Viewer's editor and choose

Format➜TableLooks➜Academic (Figure 24).

Report

Number of Hits

Treatment Group	Mean	N	Std. Deviation	Median	Minimum	Maximum	Range
Placebo	10.06	30	4.553	10.06	3	21	18
Caffeine	12.44	30	3.719	12.42	7	21	14
Total	11.25	60	4.293	10.74	3	21	18

Output 5. The **Report** table in the output from the **Means** procedure

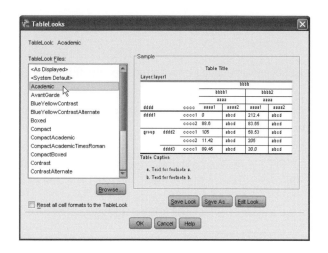

Figure 24. The **TableLooks** dialog box

The reformatted table is shown in Output 6.

Report

Number of Hits

Treatment Group	Mean	N	Std. Deviation	Median	Minimum	Maximum	Range
Placebo	10.06	30	4.553	10.06	3	21	18
Caffeine	12.44	30	3.719	12.42	7	21	14
Total	11.25	60	4.293	10.74	3	21	18

Output 6. The reformatted **Report** table

Should you wish to restore the Report table to its original format, you have only to choose **Format➜TableLooks➜Default** .

3.3.2   Widening, narrowing and hiding columns in a Report table

To edit a table such as Output 5, double-click it. The table will now be surrounded by a dotted box indicating that you are now in the **Viewer**'s editor and the title of the table will appear in inverse video (Output 7).

Report							
Variables Number of Hits ▼							

Treatment Group	Mean	N	Std. Deviation	Median	Minimum	Maximum	Range
Placebo	10.06	30	4.553	10.06	3	21	18
Caffeine	12.44	30	3.719	12.42	7	21	14
Total	11.25	60	4.293	10.74	3	21	18

Output 7.   Appearance of the **Report** table after double-clicking to enter the Editor

Once a selected item has been surrounded by a dotted box, the following changes can be made:

- To widen or narrow columns, move the cursor on to a vertical line in the table and click and drag the line to the left or the right.

- By clicking and dragging the rightmost margin to the left, the entire Range column can be made to disappear. Further clicking and dragging will hide more columns. In Figure 25, the Range column has been removed by clicking and dragging the rightmost margin of the table to the left. Further clicking and dragging will remove the Maximum column, the Minimum column, the Median column and others, if required.

In Output 8, only the means, sample sizes and standard deviations remain, after the rightmost margin has been clicked and dragged over the Range, Maximum, Minimum and Median columns.

Report						
Variables Number of Hits ▼						

Treatment Group	Mean	N	Std. Deviation	Median	Minimum	Maximum
Placebo	10.06	30	4.553	10.06	3	21
Caffeine	12.44	30	3.719	12.42	7	21
Total	11.25	60	4.293	10.74	3	21

Margin has been pulled to the left by left-clicking and dragging.

Figure 25.   Removal of columns and their contents by clicking and dragging the rightmost margin

Report

Number of Hits

Treatment Group	Mean	N	Std. Deviation
Placebo	10.06	30	4.553
Caffeine	12.44	30	3.719
Total	11.25	60	4.293

Output 8.   The **Report** table after the Range, Maximum, Minimum and Median columns have been removed by clicking and dragging the rightmost margin of the table

Note that the operation of hiding the columns is irreversible. Once columns have been hidden by clicking and dragging the right-hand margin as described, they cannot be revealed again by clicking and dragging the margin to the right again: that will serve only to widen the present rightmost column. When editing tables in the Viewer, it is often a good idea to copy the original table in case you should feel that your latest surgery has been too drastic.

> **When editing figures in the Viewer, keep a back-up copy of the original**

3.3.3   Deleting rows and columns from a Report table

Whole rows can be deleted by highlighting the values they contain and pressing the **Delete** key. For example, suppose that, in the **Report** table (Output 5), we want to dispense with the third row (Total) containing the statistics of all sixty scores in the data set, treated as if they were a single sample.   Proceed as follows:

- Click the first value (11.25) in the bottom (Total) row so that it is highlighted. (Don't click the row label itself.)

- Press the **Ctrl** button and, keeping it pressed, click the other cells in the Total row in succession so that they are all highlighted (Figure 26).

- Press the **Delete** key.   This move should cause the entire row, including the word Total in the first column, to disappear (Output 9).

- Should pressing the **Delete** key fail to remove the entire row, click the right-hand mouse button and select **Clear** from the drop-down menu.

> **Trouble-shooting**

- A column can be removed from the table in exactly the same way: double-click the table to get into the editor, click on the topmost *value* in the column (not the column heading) to highlight it, press **Ctrl** and keeping Ctrl pressed, successively highlight the remaining values in the column. Pressing the **Delete key** should remove the entire column, including the heading. Failing that, click the right-hand mouse button and select **Clear** from the drop-down menu.

Report

Variables Number of Hits ▼

Treatment Group	Mean	N	Std. Deviation	Median	Minimum	Maximum	Range
Placebo	10.06	30	4.553	10.06	3	21	18
Caffeine	12.44	30	3.719	12.42	7	21	14
Total	11.25	60	4.293	10.74	3	21	18

Figure 26. Deleting an entire row

Report

Number of Hits

Treatment Group	Mean	N	Std. Deviation	Minimum	Maximum	Range
Placebo	10.06	30	4.553	3	21	18
Caffeine	12.44	30	3.719	7	21	14

Output 9. The edited **Report** table after removing the Total row

3.3.4 Editing the captions in a table

Once you are in the Viewer's editor, it is often possible to edit the wording of a caption in a table by double-clicking it. If you can get a red cursor to show, you will be able to type in an amended version (Figure 27).

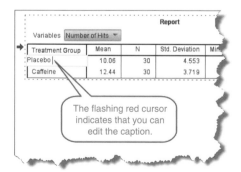

Figure 27. Editing text in a table

You can fine-tune the positioning of a row or column heading by double-clicking it, repositioning the red cursor behind the heading and either pressing the space bar to move the heading to the right or the back arrow to move it to the left.

3.3.5   Changing the number of decimal places displayed in a table

Should you find that a value in an output table does not show a sufficient number of places of decimals, highlight the value, press the *right* mouse button, select **Cell properties** from the drop-down menu, click the **Format Value** tab and change the specification of the number of decimal places displayed.

3.4   SELECTING CASES

Let us assume that, in **Data View**, we have the results of the caffeine experiment. In the original data set, there were two variables: Experimental Condition and Score. Suppose, however, that a grouping variable Sex has been added (where 1 = Male and 2 = Female), and that we want to examine the data from the female participants only.

The data for the following exercise are available in *Caffeine & Gender.sav*, at http://www.psypress.com/spss-made-simple.

- Choose **Data➜Select Cases...** to obtain the **Select Cases** dialog box (see Figure 28).

- Initially, the **All cases** radio button is marked. Click the **Select Cases: If** button and complete the **Select Cases: If** dialog box as shown in Figure 29. Click **Continue** to return to the **Select Cases** dialog box.

- Click **OK** to select only the female participants for analysis.

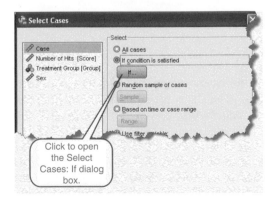

Figure 28. The **Select Cases** dialog box

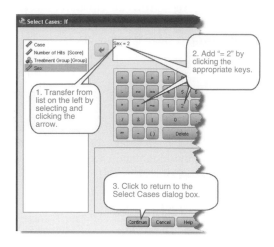

Figure 29. Part of the **Select Cases: If** dialog box with the expression for selecting only Gender = 2 (the female participants)

A section of **Data View** is shown in Figure 30. Another column, headed filter_$, has now appeared, containing the entries Not Selected and Selected.

	Case	Score	Group	Sex	filter_$	var	var
13	13	4	Placebo	Male	Not Selected		
14	14	6	Placebo	Male	Not Selected		
15	15	15	Placebo	Male	Not Selected		
16	16	18	Placebo	Female	Selected		
17	17	10	Placebo	Female	Selected		
18	18	6	Placebo	Female	Selected		
19	19	13	Placebo	Female	Selected		
20		8		F	S		

Figure 30. **Data View**, showing deselected cases

The row numbers of the unselected cases (the males) have been marked with an oblique bar. This is a useful indicator of **case selection status**. The status bar (if enabled at the foot of **Data View**) will carry the message **Filter On**. Any further analyses of the data set will exclude cases where Sex = 1.

Case selection can be **cancelled** as follows:

- From the **Data menu**, choose **Select Cases** and (in the **Select Cases** dialog box) click **All cases**.

- Click **OK**.

3.5   AGGREGATING DATA

In Chapter 1, we described an experiment in which the level of skilled performance (shooting accuracy) of people who had ingested one of four different drugs was compared with that of a Placebo group.   The results are summarised in Table 1.

Table 1. Results of the drug experiment.   Mean level of performance under four different drug conditions and a comparison, Placebo condition

	Placebo	Drug A	Drug B	Drug C	Drug D
Mean	8.00	7.90	12.00	14.40	13.00
SD	1.83	2.13	2.49	4.50	3.74

The Aggregate procedure will place, beside each score in Data View, a statistic or **Aggregate** such as the mean. In the **Aggregate** dialog, a grouping variable is termed a **break variable**. A break variable determines the groups of scores from which the means will be calculated. If no break variable is specified, the mean of all the scores in the data set will be placed beside each score.

- Choose   **Data➔Aggregate …**   to access the **Aggregate Data** dialog box (Figure 31) and proceed as shown in the figure.

Note the **Function** button which, if clicked, gives you the option of choosing another statistic (aggregate), such as the median or the size of the group.

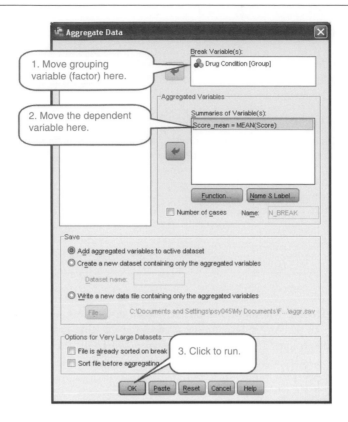

Figure 31.   The completed **Aggregate Data** dialog

Figure 32   is a section of Data View showing, beside each score, the mean of the group to which that participant was assigned in the experiment. The name of the new variable assigned by SPSS was Score_Mean; but, in Variable View, we amended the name to Group_Mean.

If no break variable is specified, the grand mean (not the group mean) will appear in Data View beside each score.

Case	Group	Score	Group_Mean	var	var
1	Placebo	10	8.00		
2	Placebo	9	8.00		
3	Placebo	7	8.00		
4	Placebo	9	8.00		
5	Placebo	11	8.00		
6	Placebo		8.00		
7	Placebo		8.00		
8	Placebo		8.00		
9	Placebo		8.00		
10	Placebo	8	8.00		
11	Drug A	8	7.90		
12	Drug A	10	7.90		
13	Drug A	7	7.90		
14	Drug A	7	7.90		
15	Drug A	7	7.90		
16	Drug A	12	7.90		
17	Drug A	7	7.90		
18	Drug A	4	7.90		

(callout: Group means)

Figure 32. **Data View** showing the new variable Group_Mean (originally named Score_Mean)

3.6   SORTING DATA

SPSS can sort case numbers according to the order of magnitude of the values of any variable in the data set. In the data set for the drugs experiment, the scores (and group mean) for the Drug A group are located below those for the Placebo group in Data View (Figure 32). This is simply because that is the way the data were entered into Data View in the first place: the five categories have no intrinsic "correct" order.   Suppose, however, that we wanted to sort the cases in order of the magnitude of the group means, so that the scores and mean for the Drug A group would come at the top of Data View.   This is easily done as follows:

- Choose: **Data➜Sort Cases …**   to open the **Sort Cases** dialog box (Figure 33).

- Complete the dialog as shown and click **OK** to rearrange the cases (Figure 34).

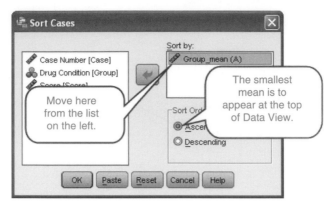

Figure 33.   The completed **Sort Cases** dialog

It can be seen from Figure 34 that, since every case within a group was paired with the group mean, the ordering of cases within groups has been preserved.   The Drug A group, however, now appears at the top of Data View, because the mean for that group is the smallest of the group means.   If, instead of the group mean, we had chosen Score as the sorting variable, the ordering of cases *within* groups would have been changed (Figure 35).

Case	Group	Score	Group_mean	var	var	va
11	Drug A	8	7.90			
12	Drug A	10	7.90			
13	Drug A	7	7.90			
14	Drug A	7	7.90			
15	Drug A	7	7.90			
16	Drug A	12	7.90			
17	Drug A	7	7.90			
18	Drug A	4	7.90			
19	Drug A	9	7.90			
20	Drug A	8	7.90			
1	Placebo	10	8.00			
2	Placebo	9	8.00			

Figure 34.   Cases sorted in ascending order of the magnitude of the group means

	Case	Group	Score	Group_Mean	var	va
1	18	Drug A	4	7.90		
2	6	Placebo	5	8.00		
3	8	Placebo	6	8.00		
4	44	Drug D	6	13.00		

Figure 35.   Cases rearranged in order of magnitude of the scores

3.7   FILE – MERGING: ADDING CASES

In the caffeine experiment, there were 60 cases: 30 in the Placebo group; 30 in the Caffeine group.   Now let us suppose that another researcher in the same team had also run this experiment and had transcribed the results into another SPSS data file, *Caffeine EXTRA.sav*, which is available on our website at http://www.psypress.com/spss-made-simple.   We shall begin at the point where we have opened the original data file with its 60 cases and want to import the data on the same variables from the other file.

A common reason for failure with file-merging operations is that the specifications in Variable View of the **active** (first) file are different from those of the **external** file.   In particular, it is essential that the entries in the Width column are the same in both files; but **Name**, **Width**, **Type** and **Values** should all be checked to make sure that they match.   It is also essential to ensure that the cases are **sorted** in **ascending order** in both files.

> **When merging files, make sure that the specifications of the variables match!**
>
> **Cases must be sorted in ascending order in both files**

Proceed as follows:

- Choose: **Data➔Merge Files➔Add Cases …**   to open the **Add Cases to** dialog box (Figure 36).

- When the **Browse** button is clicked, the **Add Cases: Read File** dialog appears.

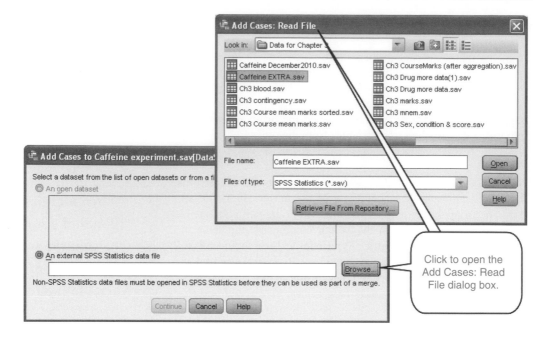

Figure 36.   Finding the target file with the **Add Cases: Read File** dialog

- When the path name of the target file (*Caffeine Extra.sav*) has been located and the **Open** button in the **Add Cases: Read File** dialog box is clicked, the path name will appear in the **Add Cases to ...** dialog box (Figure 37).

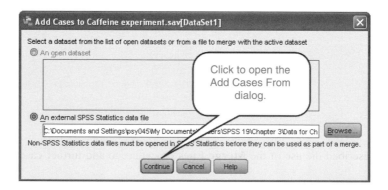

Figure 37.   The path name of the external file (Caffeine EXTRA.sav) appears in the **Add Cases to ...** dialog box

- Click the Continue button in the **Add Cases to ...** dialog to open the **Add Cases From** dialog box (Figure 38).

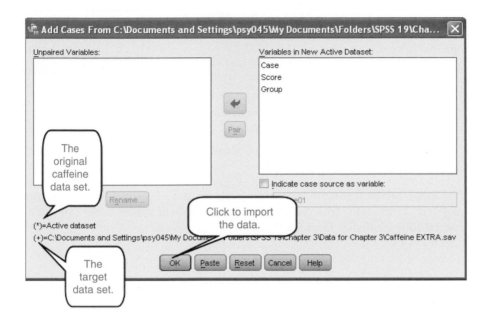

Figure 38.   Importing the data: the **Add Cases From** dialog box

- Click **OK** to import the data from the external file.

Data View will now contain 47 scores in the Caffeine group and 47 in the Placebo group.

3.8   FILE – MERGING: ADDING VARIABLES

We have just described the use of the **Merge Files** procedure to add further cases to a data set from a file containing more data on exactly the same variables. We can think of this operation as one of merging 'vertically', in the sense that the columns in the original data set become longer, but the number of columns (variables) in the data set remains the same. There was no change in the number of variables in the active data set.

We are now going to use the **Merge Files** procedure to import another variable, Gender, into the caffeine data set. Suppose there is available another file, containing only the case numbers of the active file and the gender of the participants. We want to use this second file as a **look-up file** and extract the gender information from it to add to the active file.   A requirement for this operation is that the active file and the look-up file must have a variable in common. In this example, the common variable is Case. The Case variable will be used as a **key** with which we can extract the gender information and add it to the active file.

In both the active file and the **look-up** (or **keyed**) **file**, the key variable must be sorted in ascending order. Check to make sure that this has been done.

> **Sort the key variable in ascending order in both files**

- Choose **Data→Merge Files→Add Variables…** to open the **Add Variables to** dialog box, click on the **Browse** button to open the **Add Variables: Read File** dialog box and find the target file (Figure 39).

- In the **Add Variables: Read File** dialog box, click **Open** to return to the **Add Variable to** dialog box, in which the path name of the look-up file will appear in the slot labelled **An External SPSS Statistics Data file** (Figure 41).

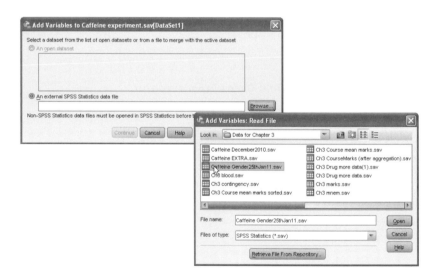

Figure 39. The **Add Variables to** and **Add Variables: Read File** dialog boxes

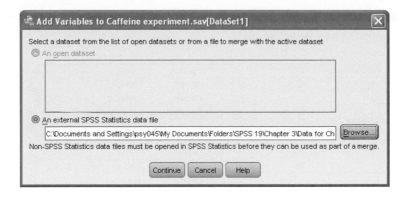

Figure 40. The external SPSS Statistics data file has now been located

- Click Continue to open the **Add Variables from** box (Figure 41).

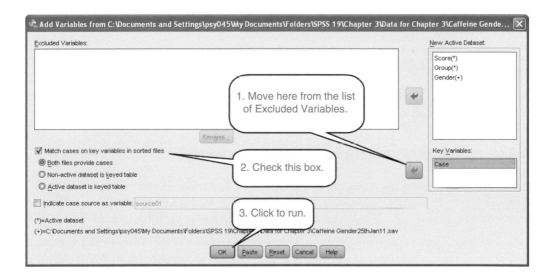

Figure 41. The **Add Variables from** box

- In the **Add Variables from** dialog box, click **OK** to run the procedure.   First, however, you will receive the following warning:

Figure 42 shows a fragment of Data View showing that the gender information has been successfully imported into the active file.

9	9	16	Placebo	Male	
10	10	10	Placebo	Male	
11	11	21	Placebo	Male	
12	12	8	Placebo	Male	
13	13	4	Placebo	Male	
14	14	6	Placebo	Male	
15	15	15	Placebo	Male	
16	16	18	Placebo	Female	
17	17	10	Placebo	Female	
18	18	6	Placebo	Female	
19	19	13	Placebo	Female	
20	20	8	Placebo	Female	
21	21	3	Placebo	Female	

Figure 42. A fragment of **Data View** showing the genders of some of the participants

3.9   THE COMPUTE VARIABLE COMMAND

We have already encountered the Compute Variable command on several occasions. We shall now look more closely at this powerful and versatile tool.

3.9.1   Calculating functions of several variables

Compute Variable (in the **Transform** menu) can be used to combine values of variables. Suppose you have a data set consisting of the marks of schoolchildren in their French, German and Spanish examinations. What is each child's mean score over the three examinations?

One way of doing this is to write your own numerical expression in the **Numerical Expression** box of the **Compute Variable** dialog box (e.g. name the target variable Mean_Mark and enter the expression (French + German + Spanish)/3. Should any child not have taken all three examinations, however, the mean would not be calculated and in Data View a system-missing mark (.) would appear in the Mean_Mark column.

Another way of obtaining the mean is to paste the **MEAN** function from the **Functions and Special Variables** list into the **Numerical Expression** box and transfer the variable names French, German and Spanish into the pasted function, taking care to have a comma between each variable name and to check that ? is no longer present [e.g. **MEAN**(French, German, Spanish)]. Should a child's mark be missing, the mean of the other two marks will be calculated. The function MEAN, therefore, calculates the mean from whatever valid values may be present. Only if a child has sat none of the three examinations, will a system-missing value for the mean be recorded.

Figure 43 is a section of **Data View** comparing the results of using the two methods of finding the mean. The variable Mean_by_Div (i.e. Mean by Division) contains the values of the mean from the first method and the variable MEAN contains the values of the mean calculated by the second method.

ChildsN	French	German	Spanish	MeanbyDiv	MEAN
Fred	67	78	23	56.00	56.00
Mary	50	50	.	.	50.00
John	.	.	.	.	.
Peter	0	50	50	33.33	33.33
Amy	0	.	.	.	.00
Jack	23	.	.	.	23.00

Figure 43. Two ways of computing the means of three variables

It can be seen from Figure 43 that the Mean by Division method works only when there are marks on all three examinations. It fails with Mary, John, Amy and Jack, because they didn't have three marks. The MEAN method fails to produce a result only with John, who did not sit any of the examinations. The MEAN function makes a clear distinction between zeros and missing values: Mary correctly receives the mean of the values 50 and 50; whereas Peter correctly receives the mean of 0, 50 and 50. Jack correctly receives a mean of 23, even though he sat only one examination.

3.9.2   Conditional transformations

A medical researcher has gathered some data on the drinking and substance intake of patients. Figure 44 shows a section from **Data View**. (The code values corresponding to the value labels displayed are: 0 = No Abuse and 1 = Abuse.)

	Patient	Alcohol	Substances
1	Sarah	No Abuse	No Abuse
2	Alan	Abuse	No Abuse
3	Jim	No Abuse	Abuse
4	Joe	Abuse	Abuse

Figure 44. A section of the data set for substance abuse in patients

The researcher wants to create a third variable, Addict (Addiction Level), with values as follows:

> 0 for patients with No Abuse on both variables
>
> 1 for patients with Abuse on Alcohol but No Abuse on Substances
>
> 2 for patients with No Abuse on Alcohol but Abuse on Substances
>
> 3 for patients with Abuse on both variables.

This problem can be solved in several ways. We could begin by using **Compute Variable** to create the variable Addict, where Addict = Alcohol + Substances + 1. We could then instruct the **Compute Variable** routine to proceed as follows. If either (Alcohol = Substances = 0) or (Alcohol = 1 and Substances = 0), subtract 1 from Addict. So a patient who neither smoked nor took subtances would receive a score of 0 on Addict: Addict = 0 + 0 + 1 – 1 = 0. A patient who took substances but not alcohol would receive an Addict score of 2 + 1 – 1 = 2. This will solve the problem, because the remaining combination fails to meet either condition and no subtraction takes place: for Joe, Addict = 1 + 1 + 1 = 3.

- Choose **Transform➜Compute Variable** to access the **Compute Variable** dialog box.

- Type *Addict* into the **Target Variable** box. Alternatively, name the variable Addict in Variable View, set Decimals to zero and copy the variable name so that you can paste it into the **Target Variable** slot in the **Compute Variable** dialog.

- Transfer the variable names Alcohol and Substances to the **Numeric Expression** box and create the expression: Alcohol + Substances + 1 (see Figure 45).

- Click **OK** to enter the values of Addict into the new column in Data View.

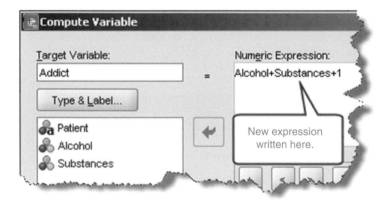

Figure 45. Part of the **Compute Variable** dialog box for computing values for the new variable Addict

The values of Addict will now appear in **Data View** as shown in Figure 46.

	Patient	Alcohol	Substances	Addict
1	Sarah	No Abuse	No Abuse	1
2	Alan	Abuse	No Abuse	2
3	Jim	No Abuse	Abuse	2
4	Joe	Abuse	Abuse	3

Figure 46. **Data View** showing the newly computed variable Addict

These values for Addict are correct except for Sarah and Alan, who should have the values 0 and 1 respectively. We must therefore modify the computation of these values of Addict by subtracting 1 from the total when both variables have 0, or if Alcohol = 1 and Substances = 0. This is done by constructing a conditional expression in the **Compute Variable: If Cases** dialog box.

- Return to the **Compute Variable** dialog and change the **Numeric Expression** entry to Addict – 1.

- Click the **If…** button to open the **Compute Variable: If Cases** dialog box.

- Click the radio button labelled **Include if Case satisfies condition:**

- In the box on the right enter the expression:

    (Alcohol = 0 & Substance = 0) | (Alcohol – 1 & Substances = 0).

    In this logical expression, the ampersand (**&**) denotes **AND** and the symbol | denotes **OR**. Care must be taken when inserting brackets in the conditional expression to ensure that the logical operators **AND** and **OR** operate appropriately.

- The top part of the completed dialog box will appear as in Figure 47.

- Click **Continue** to return to the **Compute Variable** dialog box.

- Click **OK** to compute the altered values of Addict.

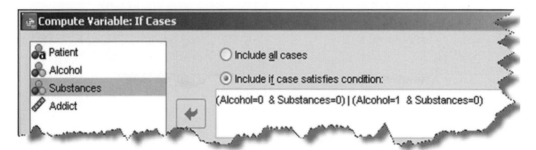

Figure 47. Top part of the **Compute Variables: If Cases** dialog box with the specially written conditional expression

The entries in **Data View** will now appear as shown in Figure 48.

	Patient	Alcohol	Substances	Addict
1	Sarah	No Abuse	No Abuse	0
2	Alan	Abuse	No Abuse	1
3	Jim	No Abuse	Abuse	2
4	Joe	Abuse	Abuse	3

Figure 48. The desired values for Addict after using a conditional expression in the **Compute Variable** dialog box

An alternative way of producing the Level of Addition variable (Addict) would be to compute Addict = Alcohol*10 + Substances and then use the **Recode** procedure (next Section) to recode the resulting set of values.

3.10   THE RECODE COMMAND

We have seen that the **Compute Variable** command operates upon one or more of the variables in the data set to produce a new variable that is a function of those already in the data set, so that the new variable has as many different values as the existing variables. In this section, we shall consider a command that assigns relatively few labels to ranges of values of a scale or continuous variable.

Suppose we have a set of 18 children's examination marks on a scale from 0 to 100 (Table 2). We want to **recode** the marks into three **bins** or intervals: 0-49 are Fails; 50-74 are Passes; 75-100 are Good. This can easily be done by using the **Recode** procedure on the **Transform** menu.

Table 2. Children's examination marks

Child	Mark	Child	Mark	Child	Mark
1	62	7	70	13	50
2	51	8	40	14	50
3	40	9	63	15	42
4	68	10	81	16	65
5	38	11	62	17	30
6	40	12	78	18	71

Enter the data into **Data View** in variables named Case and Marks and then:

- Choose **Transform➔Recode into Different Variables...** to open the **Recode into Different Variables** dialog box (Figure 49). Click Mark and the central arrow to transfer the name into the **Numeric Variable➔Output Variable** box, where you will see **Mark ➔**.

- Type *Grade* into the **Name** slot (Grade is the output variable) and click **Change** to insert the name into the **Numeric Variable➔Output Variable** box. In the **Numeric Variable➔Output Variable** box, you will now see **Mark➔ Grade**.

- Click the **Old and New Values** button to open the **Recode into Different Variables: Old and New Values** dialog box, a section of which is shown in Figure 50.

SPSS uses the term **through** to denote the higher or lower value of a specified interval: for example, the Fail interval is 'lowest through 49'; the middle interval (Pass) is '50 through 74'; the top interval (Good) is 'highest through 75'. So for the highest or lowest interval, you need specify only one value; but for intervening interval, you must specify two values (see Figure 50).

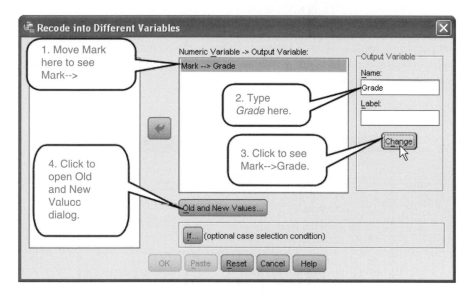

Figure 50. The **Recode into Different Variables** dialog box

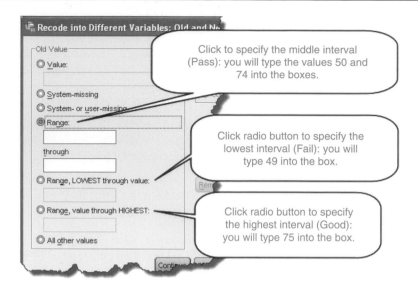

Figure 51. A section of the **Recode into Different Variables: Old and New values** dialog box

Figure 51 shows the steps in specifying the lowest interval. You need only enter one value: 49. Note that because you are creating a **string variable** as the output variable, you must check the box labelled **Output variables are strings**. (Otherwise, the dialog will expect you to enter numerical values in the **Values** box.)

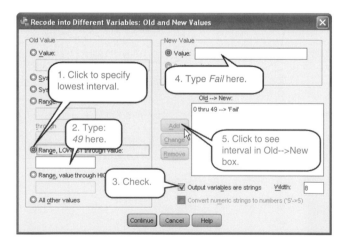

Figure 52. The **Recode into Different Variables**: **Old and New Values** dialog box showing the specification of the lowest Grade (Fail) as the interval between zero and 49, inclusive.

• Specify the middle and highest intervals by clicking the appropriate radio buttons and typing in the values specified in Figure 51.

Figure 52 shows the display in the **Old - - > New** box after all three intervals have been specified. After clicking **Continue** to return to the **Recode into Different Variables** dialog, click **Return**. A new string variable Grade containing the recoded labels Pass, Fail and Good will appear in **Data View** (Figure 54).

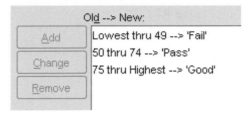

Figure 53. The appearance of the **Old - - > New** box after entering all the criteria

Child	Mark	Grade
1	62	Pass
2	51	Pass
3	40	Fail
4	68	Pass
5	38	Fail
6	40	Fail
7	70	Pass
8	40	Fail
9	63	Pass
10	81	Good
11	62	Pass
12	78	Good
13		Pass

Figure 54. Part of **Data View** showing the new string variable Grade with the labels Pass, Fail and Good

3.11   A FINAL WORD

In this chapter, we have considered, in some detail, various aspects of the editing systems of SPSS Statistics. Reading about these techniques is one thing; using them is quite another. Hands-on practice and experimentation on a daily basis are absolutely essential. SPSS itself now has some tutorials on various operations involving the Data Editor. Excellent though they are, however, merely clicking your way through the slides can engender a a false sense of security. There is no substitute for making up small data sets yourself and trying the various moves until they become second nature.

Exercises

Exercise 3 *Merging files – adding cases & variables* is available in www.psypress.com/spss-made-simple Click on Exercises.

Describing and exploring your data

4.1   INTRODUCTION

Description and exploration of your data are essential preliminaries to the making of any formal statistical tests. In this chapter, we shall consider the use of SPSS to describe various kinds of data.

We saw in Chapter 1 that the kinds of statistics the researcher uses to capture the most important features of a data set will depend very much on the nature of the data. For scale or continuous data, interest centres on the distribution of the data. What is the average value? To what extent are scores spread out around the average? What is the shape of the distribution? With categorical data, on the other hand, the questions change. How many participants fell into the different categories? Did a greater proportion of cases fall into Category A compared with Category B?

Different statistics are appropriate for data of different types: there is little point in finding the mean of a set of ranks, for example, because the resulting average would depend solely upon the number of people (or objects) in the sample. There would be little point in calculating the statistics of a grouping variable, because the numerical values of the code numbers are arbitrary and do not measure the extent to which any property is possessed by the unit of study.

Before embarking upon a descriptive analysis of a set of data, it is vital to check their integrity. In Chapter 3, we discussed the **validation** of a set of data, that is, the running of a set of checks to determine whether case numbers have been repeated, transcription errors have occurred or there are any impossible scores. There is more to exploring a set of data than validation, however.

A score may fall within the possible range of values for a variable and yet still create problems for statistical analysis. The presence of highly deviant scores can affect the values of statistics such as the mean and standard deviation so that they become poor measures of level and dispersion, respectively. Highly deviant scores, or **outliers**, exert undue leverage upon the values of statistics such as the mean and standard deviation, especially in small data sets. A similar problem occurs when the distribution of the data is highly skewed or asymmetrical in some other way. Fortunately, there are available measures of level and spread that are more resistant, or **robust**, to the influence of outliers.

In recent years, statisticians have devised a set of robust statistical methods specially designed for the purpose of examining small, unruly data sets. Together, they are known as **Exploratory Data Analysis (EDA)**. (For a readable account of EDA, see Howell, 2007, Chapter 2.) EDA statistics have now found their way into all good statistical computing packages, including SPSS. The EDA statistics are particularly good for capturing the most important characteristics of data sets with skewed distributions and highly deviant scores. As well as **robust** statistics, EDA includes a set of table-graph hybrids which EDA authors refer to as **displays**. We shall consider some EDA techniques and displays in this chapter.

In this chapter, we shall not attempt a comprehensive coverage of all that SPSS has to offer in the way of descriptive statistics, displays and graphs. Instead, we shall offer the reader some general guidelines for the selection of appropriate routines for specific research purposes.

To illustrate how SPSS can be used to describe and explore data, we shall first examine a large data set comprising two continuous variables, Weight and Height, and two categorical variables, Gender and Blood Group. (Later, we shall explore a small data set.)

The data are in *Correlated and grouped heights and weights.sav* , which is available on our website at http://www.psypress.com/spss-made-simple.

Figure 1 shows the first few lines of the large data set, which contains data on 2000 people. Some graphical procedures, such as the **Chart Builder** (Chapter 5), require that the level of measurement (scale, ordinal or nominal) must first be specified in **Variable View**. It is best, therefore, to specify the level of measurement of a variable as a matter of routine. In the **Measure** column of Variable View, the variables of Gender and Blood group must be set at the **Nominal** level. There is no need to make an entry for Weight or Height, because by default, all numerical variables are set at the **Scale** level of measurement.

Case	Height	Weight	Sex	Blood_group
541	172.31	54.48	Female	Group O
542	176.70	56.84	Female	Group O
543	164.05	50.08	Female	Group O
544	175.14	68.65	Male	Group A

Figure 1. The data on a few cases in a large data set

4.2   DESCRIBING NOMINAL DATA

Two of the variables in the data set, Gender and Blood Group, are categorical. In this section, we shall show how SPSS can be used to describe records of categorical variables, that is, **nominal** data.

Questions about nominal data are usually questions about **frequencies**: How many cases were there in each blood group? How many males and females were there in the two samples? Was the ratio of the number of males to the number of females the same in the different blood groups?

To answer the first two questions, we shall require tables showing the frequencies of observations in each category. Graphical displays, however, will also be helpful. A **bar chart**, for example, can be used to display the profile of frequencies of observations across groups. (A bar chart is a versatile type of graph, which can also be used to compare summaries of the distribution – means, medians – of a continuous or scale variable across categories. When used with nominal data, however, the bar chart becomes effectively a **bar graph**, which depicts a discrete frequency distribution.)

The third question is one of the possible **association** between two categorical variables or attributes, namely, Sex and Blood Group. To answer the question, we shall need a **contingency table** or **cross-tabulation** (Chapter 1), depicting the bivariate frequency distribution of the two attributes.

4.2.1   Describing nominal data on one attribute

Our first question about a data set containing a variable such as Gender or Blood group is: How many cases were there in each category? We can use the **Frequencies** procedure to answer this one. The Frequencies procedure can provide not only tables of frequencies, but also bar charts, which can often reveal the true nature of a distribution. Proceed as follows.

- Choose **Analyze➜Descriptive Statistics➜Frequencies...** to open the **Frequencies** dialog box (Figure 2)

- In the list in the left panel, highlight Blood Group and Gender and transfer them to the **Variable(s)** box by clicking the central arrow.

- Click **Charts** to obtain the **Frequencies: Charts** dialog box (Figure 2) and select the **Bar Chart(s)** radio button. There is also the choice of frequencies or percentages for the y-axis in the **Chart Values** box. Take the frequencies option.

- Click **Continue** to return to **Frequencies** and then **OK** to run the procedure.

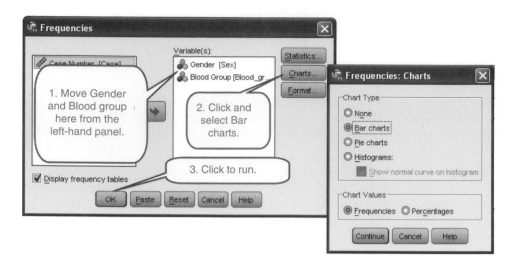

Figure 2. Completing the **Frequencies** dialog

The output consists of two tables (Output 1). The bar chart for Blood group (slightly edited) is shown in Output 2.

Gender

		Frequency	Percent	Valid Percent	Cumulative Percent
Valid	Male	1000	50.0	50.0	50.0
	Female	1000	50.0	50.0	100.0
	Total	2000	100.0	100.0	

Blood Group

		Frequency	Percent	Valid Percent	Cumulative Percent
Valid	Group O	880	44.0	44.0	44.0
	Group A	840	42.0	42.0	86.0
	Group B	200	10.0	10.0	96.0
	Group AB	80	4.0	4.0	100.0
	Total	2000	100.0	100.0	

Output 1. The Gender and Blood Group frequency tables

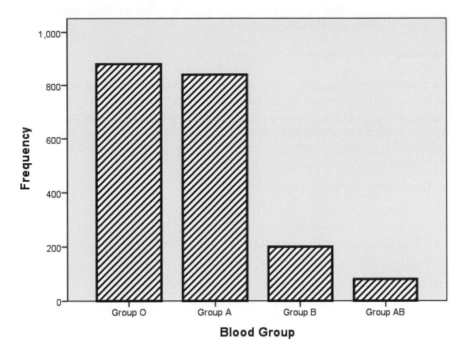

Output 2. Bar Chart for Blood Group

Note that the graph shown in Output 2 is usually referred to in statistical textboooks as a **bar graph**, that is, a depiction of a discrete frequency distribution. A clear distinction must be made between a bar chart or graph and a **histogram**, which is used to depict a *continuous* distribution. With continuous data, bar charts do not depict distributions: instead, they compare statistical summaries of the distributions of the same continuous variable across the categories of categorical variables.

4.2.2   Two attributes: contingency tables

When we have a data set comprising observations on two continuous or scale variables or attributes, interest centres on their **bivariate distribution**. Making a picture or graph of their bivariate distribution can tell the research whether the variables are associated. Where the variables are qualitative or categorical attributes, that is, the data are measurements at the **nominal** level, their bivariate distribution is best pictured by a **contingency table** or **crosstabulation**, as SPSS terms it. A contingency table is a two-way classification of the data, the cells of which contain the frequencies of occurrence of all combinations of the categories making up the attributes.

In this subsection, we shall describe the use of two procedures for obtaining contingency tables: (1) **Crosstabs**; (2) **Custom Tables**. **Crosstabs** is in the **Descriptive Statistics** menu and **Custom Tables** is in the **Tables** menu. We shall begin by using the **Crosstabs** procedure to obtain a contingency table for Blood Group and Gender.

Contingency tables with Crosstabs

Are the same proportions of men and women found in all blood groups?   In other words, is there a statistical association between the variables of Gender and Blood Group? A first step in answering this question is the construction of a   contingency table with the four blood groups as column headings and Male and Female as row headings.   As well as frequencies, it would be informative to have column percentages, that is, the percentages of males and females in each blood group sample. Proceed as follows:

- Choose **Analyze➔Descriptive Statistics➔Crosstabs…** to open the **Crosstabs** dialog box.

- Complete the dialog, as shown in Figure 3. (If one of the variables has four or more categories, it is better to have it in the **Rows** box, rather than in **Columns**, otherwise the output will be too wide for printing on a single page.)

- Click **OK** to obtain the contingency table.

The contingency table is shown in Output 3.   The differences in column frequencies are not at all surprising, since it is well known that some blood groups are more common than others. In all groups, however, the percentages of males and females have similar values, indicating that there is no evidence of an association between Gender and Blood Group in this data set.

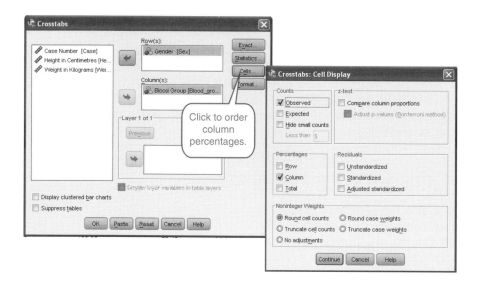

Figure 3. The **Crosstabs** dialog box,

Gender * Blood Group Crosstabulation

			Blood Group				Total
			Group O	Group A	Group B	Group AB	
Gender	Male	Count	448	413	101	38	1000
		% within Blood Group	50.9%	49.2%	50.5%	47.5%	50.0%
	Female	Count	432	427	99	42	1000
		% within Blood Group	49.1%	50.8%	49.5%	52.5%	50.0%
Total		Count	880	840	200	80	2000
		% within Blood Group	100.0%	100.0%	100.0%	100.0%	100.0%

Output 3. Contingency table from **Crosstabs** for Gender and Blood Group

More complex contingency tables: layering of pivot tables

Output 4 shows a three-way crosstabulation of the results of an experiment on helping behaviour. Male and female participants were each asked by either a male or a female interviewer whether they would or would not try to help someone in difficulties in a certain situation. The purpose of the investigation was to test the **opposite-sex dyadic hypothesis**, which holds that we are more likely to help someone of the opposite sex than someone of our own. The data are in *Ch4 Helping.sav* at http://www.psypress.com/spss-made-simple.

Count

			Sex of Participant		Total
Sex of Interviewer			Male	Female	
Male	Would you help?	Yes	4	16	20
		No	21	9	30
	Total		25	25	50
Female	Would you help?	Yes	11	11	22
		No	14	14	28
	Total		25	25	50
Total	Would you help?	Yes	15	27	42
		No	35	23	58
	Total		50	50	100

Output 4. A three-way cross-tabulation of the results of an experiment on helping behaviour

A three-way table like that shown in Output 4 can be made easier to read by a process known as **layering**, whereby a two-way contingency table involving the same two dimensions is shown at each level (or **layer**) of the third dimension, as in Figure 4. Any of the three variables can serve as the layer: the choice will depend upon your research question. In the present example, it would make sense to have Sex of Interviewer as the layer, so that we can compare the helpfulness of males and females with make and female interviewers.

Count Female		Sex of Participant		
		Male	Female	Total
Would you help?	Yes	11	11	22
	No	14	14	28
Total				

Count Male		Sex of Participant		
		Male	Female	Total
Would you help?	Yes	4	16	20
	No	21	9	30
Total		25	25	50

Figure 4. Layering of the cross-tabulation in Output 4. The layering variable is Sex of Interviewer

In Figure 4, the layers are the crosstabulations of Sex of Participant and Would you help? at each level of Sex of Interviewer, the layering variable.

To achieve the layering shown in Figure 4, proceed as follows:

- Double-click the three-way crosstabulation and choose **Pivot➜Pivoting Trays** to access the pivoting trays dialog box (Figure 5). In the dialog, the overlapping boxes will eventually represent the two layers of the table; but at this point, all three variables are at the same level, in the table on the right.

- Click and drag Sex of Interviewer from its position in the upper layer to the empty slot in the lower square labelled LAYER, as shown in Figure 5. The effect of this move is to produce the table shown in Output 5, which is the upper layer of the layered table.

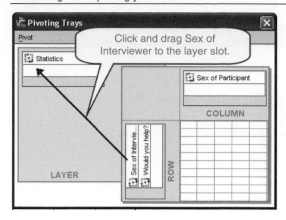

Figure 5. Making Sex of Interviewer the layering variable

Would you help? * Sex of Participant * Sex of Interviewer Crosstabulation

Count

Male

		Sex of Participant		Total
		Male	Female	
Would you help?	Yes	4	16	20
	No	21	9	30
Total		25	25	50

Output 5. The upper layer of the layered version of Output 4

Initially, the lower (Female) layer of the table is invisible. To see the lower layer, you must double-click the table and choose Female from the drop-down menu, as shown in Figure 6.

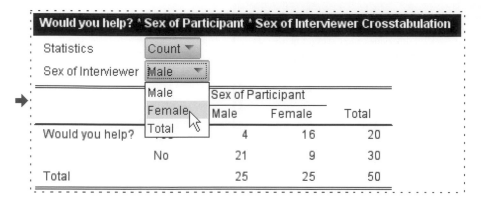

Figure 6. Seeing the lower, Female layer of the layered table

The effect of the move shown in Figure 6 is to produce the lower layer of the table (Output 6).

Would you help? * Sex of Participant * Sex of Interviewer Crosstabulation

Count

Female

		Sex of Participant		
		Male	Female	Total
Would you help?	Yes	11	11	22
	No	14	14	28
Total		25	25	50

Output 6. The previously hidden Female layer of the layered table

Should you wish to have both layers of the layered table available in the Viewer simultaneously, simply copy the original Male layer of the table, double-click on the lower version and make the choice shown in Figure 6 to obtain the Female layer shown in Output 6.

Contingency tables with the Custom Tables procedure

To illustrate the use of the **Custom Tables** procedure, we shall return to the large data set comprising the heights, weights, and blood groups of 1000 men and 1000 women and order the same Gender by Blood Group contingency table that we ordered before by using **Crosstabs**.

To obtain a table of frequencies with column percentages, proceed as follows:

- Choose **Analyze➔Tables➔Custom Tables…** to open the **Custom Tables** dialog box (Figure 7). If the warning box about labels appears, click **OK**. (You will, as a matter of routine, already have specified the level of measurement in Variable View.)

- The outline of the procedure is given in Figure 7. Note the sequencing.

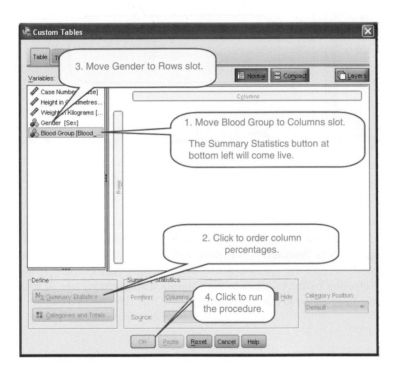

Figure 7. Outline of the procedure for obtaining a cross-tabulation with **Custom Tables**

- When moving Blood Group to the Columns slot, make sure the hand is visible and that the border of the Columns slot changes colour (Figure 8).

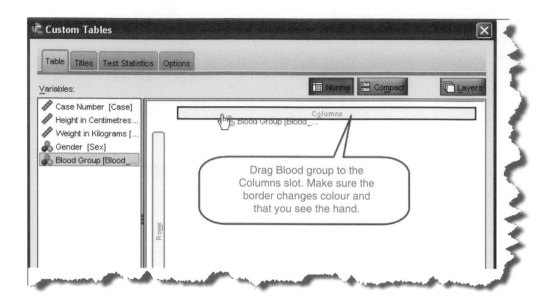

Figure 8. Correct procedure for moving Blood group to the Columns slot

Once Blood group has been transferred to the Columns slot, a sketch of a table will appear as shown in Figure 9. At the same time, the Button in the **Define** box at the bottom left of the dialog box labelled **N% Summary Statistics** will come live and the **Summary Statistics dialog** will appear (Figure 9). On completing the Summary Statistics dialog and pressing the **Apply to the Selection** button to return to the **Custom Tables** dialog box, it will be found that percentages have been added to the outline table.

- Drag Gender to the Rows slot. An outline of the complete crosstabulation will appear (Figure 10).

- Finally, click **OK** to obtain the crosstabulation, the transposed version of which is shown in Output 7. (The transposed version shown was obtained by double-clicking on the original table and choosing from the **Pivot** menu.)

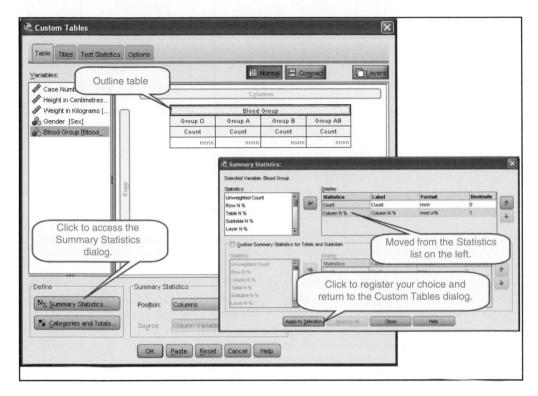

Figure 9. An outline table in **Custom Tables** and the **Summary Statistics** dialog

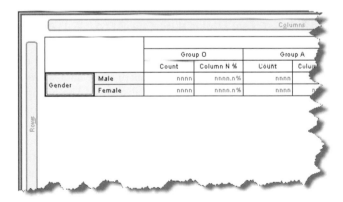

Figure 10. Outline of the crosstabulation

			Gender	
			Male	Female
Blood Group	Group O	Count	448	432
		Column N %	50.9%	49.1%
	Group A	Count	413	427
		Column N %	49.2%	50.8%
	Group B	Count	101	99
		Column N %	50.5%	49.5%
	Group AB	Count	38	42
		Column N %	47.5%	52.5%

Output 7. The crosstabulation. (The original table has been transposed by double-clicking and choosing from the **Pivot** menu.)

We have just used two different SPSS procedures to construct a contingency table: the **Crosstabs** procedure; and **Custom Tables**. Which procedure should we use? The older procedure, Crosstabs, is still a very useful tool; moreover, it produces rapid results. As you can see from this brief introduction, however, Custom Tables gives the user more control over the table during the construction process: the table previews serve as a very useful monitor. Crosstabs might be the method of choice at the exploratory stage of an analysis; whereas Custom Tables might prove more useful when putting the finishing touches to a table for a publication or seminar presentation.

4.3   DESCRIBING CONTINUOUS OR SCALE DATA

There are many procedures for describing and exploring data in the form of measurements on an independent scale with units. With such **continuous** or **scale** data, as with nominal data, we shall want to supplement the statistics with graphical displays. The histograms of the heights and weights of the males and the females can be expected to show approximate normality of distribution of either variable. (Other variables, however, such as salaries and reaction times, can be expected to have skewed distributions.)   Bar charts can be used to compare summaries of the distributions of the same variable in different categories: e.g. the statistics of the height and weight distributions of males and females can be compared by using bar charts.

Since long bones tend to weigh more than short ones, we can expect the variables of Height and Weight to be correlated; even though, of course, a short but stocky individual may weigh more than a considerably taller willowy one.

The present data contains records of the heights of 1000 men and 1000 women. While it would, of course, be possible to ignore the Gender variable and simply describe the data on all 2000 cases using either the **Descriptives** or the **Frequencies** procedures, the statistics of combined samples from different populations are often rather uninformative.

With bivariate and multivariate data sets, the question of possible **associations** among the variables arises. The **joint distributions** of continuous variables can be pictured by scatterplots. As with univariate graphs and statistics, however, scatterplots of data from combined samples can be misleading. As a preliminary to the investigation of the association between the two variables, therefore, we shall examine the scatterplots of weight against height for the Males and Females separately.

The file containing the data set we shall use for the following exercises is *Ch4 Correlated and grouped heights and weights.sav*, which is available on our website at http://www.psypress.com/spss-made-simple.

4.3.1   Histograms of height and weight for males and females

In Chapter 2, we described how to use the **Chart Builder** to produce **histograms** of the distributions of scores achieved under Placebo and Caffeine conditions. A histogram is an appropriate graph to use with continuous or scale data.

The basis of a histogram is a table called a **frequency distribution**, which divides the total range of values into arbitrary **class intervals** and gives the frequency of measurements that fall within each interval, that is, have values between the upper and lower **bounds** of the interval concerned. With data on height recorded in centimetres, for example, the total range would be divided into a sequence of class intervals such as 140–149, 150–159, 160–169, …, and so on, and the frequency distribution would give the frequencies of heights within each of these ranges. On top of the class intervals sit rectangles, the heights (and areas) of which represent the frequencies (or relative frequencies) of scores falling within the class intervals. Because the data are continuous, there are no spaces between neighbouring rectangles, provided there are scores in both of the adjacent class intervals.

In a **bar chart** (such as Output 2), the bars are separated because the horizontal axis contains names of unordered categories. The order of the bars in Output 2 is arbitrary: e.g. the Group AB bar could as well have followed the Group A bar, rather than vice versa, as in the figure. A histogram on the other hand, is appropriate for continuous or scale data.

To obtain histograms of the distributions of Height in the Males and the Females, proceed as follows:

- Choose **Data➜Select Cases** to select the data for the Males only. In the **Select Cases** dialog box, set Sex = 1, which is the code number for the Males in the data set.

> **See Section 2.2.8 for details of the Chart Builder**

- Choose **Graphs➜Chart Builder…** . A warning message will appear reminding you to specify the level of measurement of every variable in the data set and to assign value labels to the values of any grouping Select histogram from the **Choose from** list. The appropriate array of choices will appear in the **Gallery**.

- In the **Gallery** click **Simple histogram** and drag the template into the **Chart Preview** area.

- From the **Variables** list, click and drag Score into the **Chart Preview** and position it in a box below the histogram.

- Click on **Element Properties**. Within the Element Properties dialog, click **Set Parameters** and set the number of **bins** (class intervals) at 12. Click **Continue** to return to **Element Properties**.

- Back in **Element Properties**, check **Display normal curve** and click the **Apply** button to return to the **Chart Builder**.

- Click **OK** to produce the histograms.

By double-clicking on the initial histogram in the Viewer, you can use the Chart Editor to change the histograms in various ways. You can change the background colour to white. You can replace the colour of the rectangles by a pattern. Double-click on the Fill & Border tab, specify a white filler, choose a pattern for the bars. By double-clicking on the background outside the bars, you can change the background colour to white. Click **Apply** each time, to implement the chages.

The histogram is shown in Output 8.

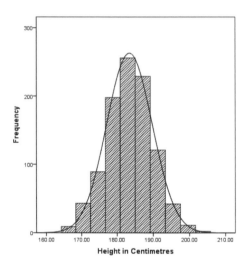

Output 8. Edited histogram of men's heights

The histogram of the distribution of Height in the Males shows an approximately normal distribution. The same is true of the histogram of Height in the Females. It will also be found that the distributions of Weight in the Males and Females are similarly bell-shaped.

4.3.2   Obtaining scatterplots of weight against height

To obtain the scatterplots of weight against height for the males and females separately, proceed as follows.

- Select the data for the females only by setting Gender = 2 in the **Select Cases** dialog.

- In the **Choose from** list, click **Scatter/Dot**. The appropriate array of choices will appear in the **Gallery**.

- In the **Gallery**, click on **Simple Scatter** and drag the template into the **Chart Preview** area.

- From the **Variables** list, click and drag Weight to the slot to the drop-off zone to the left of the vertical axis and Height to the drop-off zone below the horizontal axis.

- Click **OK** to produce the scatterplot (Output 9).

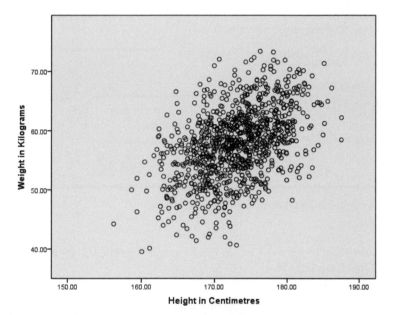

Output 9. Scatterplot of Weight against Height for the females

From Output 9, we can tell from inspection alone that there is a substantial correlation between the variables of Weight and Height in the region of $+0.4$ to $+0.6$ The topic of correlation, including the interpretation of a scatterplot, is discussed further in Chapter 11. An elliptical plot like that in Output 9 indicates that the Pearson correlation is a suitable statistic for use with this data set.

- Choose **Analyze➔Correlate➔Bivariate** to open the **Bivariate Correlations** dialog box (Figure 11).

- Complete the dialog as shown and click **OK** to run the procedure.

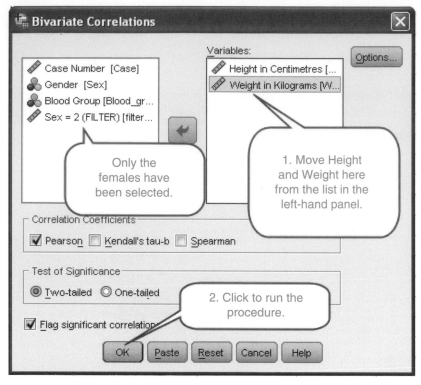

Figure 11. The completed **Bivariate Correlations** dialog

The correlation turns out to be + 0.456, as can be seen in Output 10. (We report: '$r(1000)$ = .456; $p < .01$' . See Chapter 11.)

Correlations

		Height in Centimetres	Weight in Kilograms
Height in Centimetres	Pearson Correlation	1	.456[**]
	Sig. (2-tailed)		.000
	N	1000	1000
Weight in Kilograms	Pearson Correlation	.456[**]	1
	Sig. (2-tailed)	.000	
	N	1000	1000

[**]. Correlation is significant at the 0.01 level (2-tailed).

Output 10. The Pearson correlation between Height and Weight in a thousand women

4.3.3   Statistics of height in males and females

This is a large data set, which the preliminary graphs have shown to be free of any obvious problems such as skewed distributions or outliers. A good procedure here for exploring the data further is **Frequencies**, which offers a selection of useful statistics, such as the mean, the median, quartiles and user-specified percentiles. The **Frequencies** procedure gives a much better selection of statistics than does **Descriptives**.

Proceed as follows:

*   Select the data on the males by choosing   **Data➔Select Cases** and, in the **Select Cases** dialog box, set Gender = 1, which will select the data on the Males only.

*   Choose **Analyze➔Descriptive Statistics➔Frequencies** to open the **Frequencies** dialog box (Figure 12).

*   In the **Frequencies** dialog, uncheck the **Display frequency tables** box.   If you omit to do this, the output will include a long list of scores.

*   Click the Statistics button to access the **Frequencies: Statistics** dialog box and complete that dialog as shown in Figure 13.

> **Uncheck Display frequency tables box**

*   Click **OK** to run the procedure.

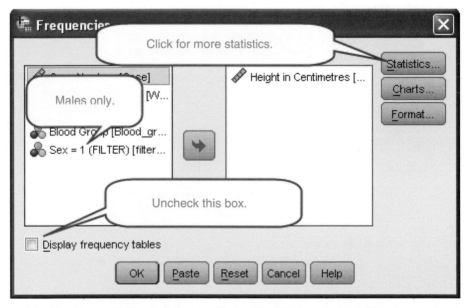

Figure 12.   The **Frequencies** dialog box with the **Display frequency tables** box unchecked

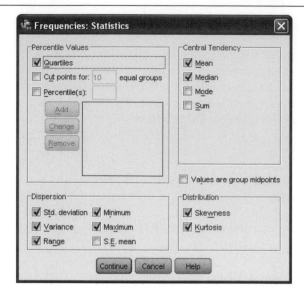

Figure 13. The completed **Frequencies: Statistics** dialog box

The requested statistics are shown in Output 11. Note that the mean and median have similar values, indicating that the distribution is symmetrical. The median is about half way between the upper and lower quartiles, which is another indication of symmetry.

Statistics

Height in Centimetres

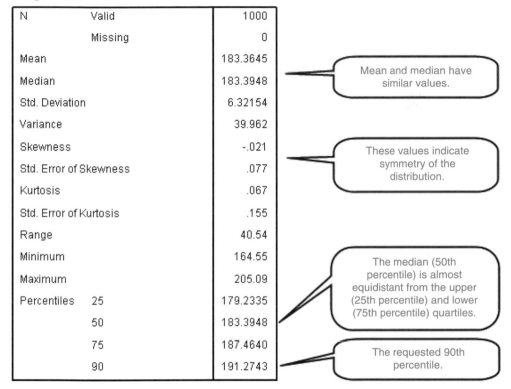

N	Valid	1000
	Missing	0
Mean		183.3645
Median		183.3948
Std. Deviation		6.32154
Variance		39.962
Skewness		-.021
Std. Error of Skewness		.077
Kurtosis		.067
Std. Error of Kurtosis		.155
Range		40.54
Minimum		164.55
Maximum		205.09
Percentiles	25	179.2335
	50	183.3948
	75	187.4640
	90	191.2743

Mean and median have similar values.

These values indicate symmetry of the distribution.

The median (50th percentile) is almost equidistant from the upper (25th percentile) and lower (75th percentile) quartiles.

The requested 90th percentile.

Output 11. The statistics from the **Frequencies** procedure

4.4   DESCRIBING SMALL DATA SETS

In the previous subsections, we explored a large data set using the **Frequencies** procedure, which is very useful for that purpose.   Often, however, our data are much less plentiful than we would wish and, should scarcity of data be combined with such features as skewness of distribution and the presence of markedly atypical scores in the samples, statistics such as the mean and standard deviation can present a misleading picture of the data. For small, unruly data sets, a set of special statistics has been devised, which are referred to collectively as **Exploratory Data Analysis (EDA)**. These special EDA statistics are much more resistant to the leverage exerted by outliers and asymmetry of distribution than are traditional statistics such as the mean and SD.

Another feature of EDA is a set of diagrams or **displays**, which might best be described as hybrids of tables and graphs. The EDA equivalent of the histogram, specially devised for use with small data sets, is the **stem-and-leaf display**. The counterpart of the bar chart is the **boxplot**, which summarises distributions of the same continuous variable such as height or weight in the different categories of a categorical attribute such as gender or blood group.

The **Explore** procedure (in the **Descriptive Statistics** menu) can be used with any size of data set. As well as traditional statistics and graphs, however, **Explore** also offers some EDA statistics and displays, which can be used to explore small data sets. The displays include the stem-and-leaf display and the boxplot, as well as the traditional histogram. (Boxplots are also available in the **Chart Builder**.)

4.4.1   The stem-and-leaf display and the boxplot

The data for the following exercise are contained in the file *Latencies.sav*, which is available on our website at http://www.psypress.com/spss-made-simple.

- Choose **Analyze➔Descriptive Statistics➔Explore…** to open the **Explore** dialog box.
- Follow the steps shown in Figure 14.

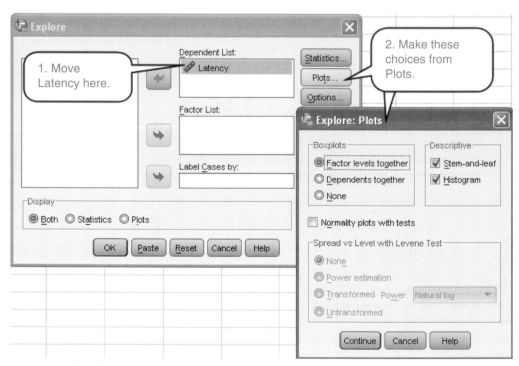

Figure 14. The **Explore** dialog box

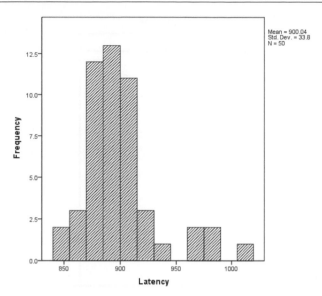

Output 12. Histogram of the latencies

The histogram in Output 12 is typical of reaction times: the distribution is **positively skewed**, that is, it has a long upper tail. This is because a set of reaction times invariably includes some unusually long latencies.

The statistics are shown in Output 13.   They are exactly as we should expect of a positively skewed data set.   The mean has been pulled upwards by the upper tail of long latencies; whereas the median has been more resistant to their influence. The skewness is given as 1.460, a value which is both positive and substantial: the standard error is 0.337.

The boxplot is shown in Output 14, which we have annotated with call-outs. Several outliers and one extreme score are identified.   The term **hinge** comes from Tukey (1977); but, essentially, the upper and lower hinges are the upper and lower quartiles, that is, the 75th and 25th percentiles, respectively, which encompass 50% of the distribution. The thick horizontal line across the interior of the box represents the median. The vertical lines outside the box, which are known as **whiskers**, run from the box to the largest and smallest values at either end of the distribution that are not sufficiently deviant to be marked as outliers or extreme cases: that is, the largest and smallest values in the data set that are less than 1.5 box lengths away from the upper and lower hinges of the box, respectively.   Should the data have contained no outliers, the whiskers would have run from the upper and lower hinges to the maximum and minimum score in the data set, respectively.   (This definition of whisker length is the one given by SPSS 19 in Help. There have been several different definitions of the length of a whisker, depending on the importance attached to normality of the distribution.   The percentiles 2%, 9%, 91% 98%, together with the hinges, make up the **seven-number summary** and, if the distribution is normal, are equally spaced. See McGill, Tukey & Larsen, 1978; Frigge, Hoaglin & Iglewicz, 1989.)

Descriptives

			Statistic	Std. Error
Latency	Mean		900.04	4.780
	95% Confidence Interval for Mean	Lower Bound	890.43	
		Upper Bound	909.65	
	5% Trimmed Mean		897.48	
	Median		896.50	
	Variance		1142.447	
	Std. Deviation		33.800	
	Minimum		849	
	Maximum		1013	
	Range		164	
	Interquartile Range		28	
	Skewness		1.460	.337
	Kurtosis		2.534	.662

Ouput 13. The Descriptives of the latencies

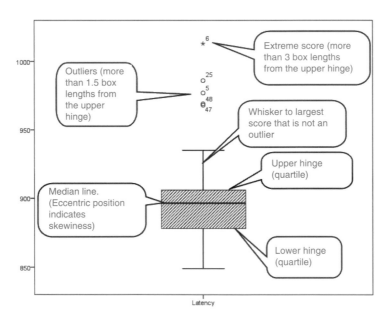

Ouput 14. Boxplot of the latencies

An **outlier** (marked as an o) is defined as a value more than 1.5 box-lengths away from the box; whereas an **extreme case** (*) is more than 3 box-lengths away from the box. The number(s) alongside o and * are the case numbers of the deviant observations concerned. The case numbers are either (by default, as in this example) the row numbers in **Data View** or the identifiers from the variable entered in the **Label Cases by** box.

Notice that the median line in the box is nearer to the upper hinge than to the lower, a strong indicator of positive skewness. The median, although more resistant than the mean to the influence of outliers, still gets dragged up to some extent as a result of the **leverage** exerted by the long upper tail of the distribution.

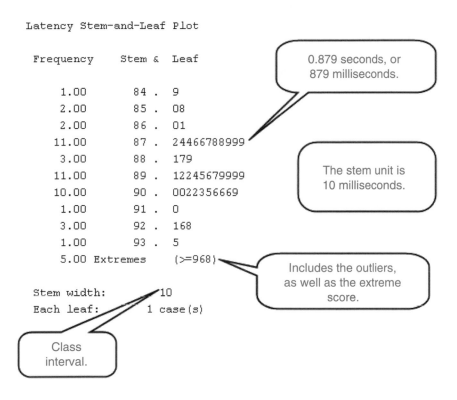

Ouput 15. Stem-and-leaf display of the latencies

Output 15 (annotated) shows a **stem-and-leaf display** of the latencies. In a **stem-and-leaf display**, the central column of numbers (84, 85, 86, ..., 93) is the **stem**, on which the class intervals are stepped out across the entire range. Each number on the stem is in units of 10 milliseconds: the first entry in the display is 849 ms. (The 'leaf' is 9.) In the stem-and-leaf display, the term **extreme** includes values that, in a boxplot, would be identified merely as outliers, not extreme scores.

4.4.2   Exploring a small data set

In this section, we shall use the **Explore** procedure to investigate a small data set consisting of data on 53 people (26 men and 27 women).   The data are available in the file *Small data set.sav*, which is available on our website at http://www.psypress.com/spss-made-simple. The first few lines of this data set are shown in Figure 15. The large case numbers reflect the fact that these data were drawn at random from the larger set that we examined earlier, by using the Sytax command:

SAMPLE .03.
LIST Cases.

Proportionate sample size.

	Case	Height	Weight	Sex	Blood_group	var
1	117	171.95	50.16	Male	Group A	
2	145	167.38	46.82	Female	Group A	
3	146	170.01	48.23	Female	Group O	
4	171	183.42	65.57	Male	Group A	
5	178	185.70	68.31	Male	Group A	
6	181	183.27	65.80	Male	Group O	
7	209	173.39	56.36	Male	Group A	
8	231	177.89	54.07	Female	Group O	
9	275	182.79	69.39	Male	Group A	
10	287	169.58	50.48	Female	Group O	
11	333	167.12	49.73	Female	Group A	
	336	176.92	55.0	Female	Group O	

Figure 15. The first few lines of the small data set

To run the **Explore** routine, proceed as follows:

- Choose **Analyze➔Descriptive Statistics➔Explore…** to open the **Explore** dialog box.

- Follow the steps shown in Figure 16.

- If there is a variable identifying the cases (e.g. Case), then click Case and transfer it with the arrow to the **Label Cases by** box. Outliers or extreme cases are identified in boxplots by their row numbers (the default output) or by the identifier in the variable entered in the **Label Cases by** box.

- Click **Plots** to open the **Explore: Plots** dialog box.   The default setting for the **Boxplots** is a side-by-side (**Factor levels together**) plot for each level of the factor (i.e. Female and Male) and **Stem-and-leaf** table. (Should you wish to have boxplots of two dependent variables side-by-side at each level of a classificatory variable, both dependent variables must be entered into the **Dependent List** box, and [in the **Boxplots** dialog box] the **Dependents together** radio button must be selected. In the present example, it would have made no sense to plot boxplots of Height and Weight side-by-side at each level of Gender, since height and weight measurements have different scales.)

- Click **Continue** and then **OK**.

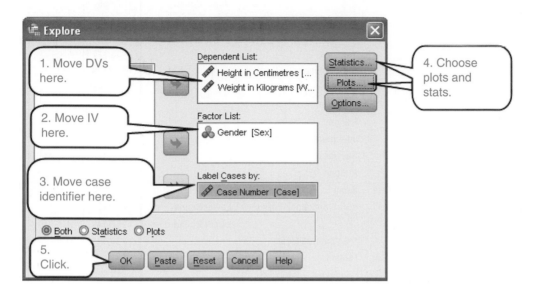

Figure 16.   The **Explore** dialog box for Height categorised by Gender

4.4.3   Some of the statistical output from Explore

The Descriptives for Height are shown in Output 16. These lists overlap considerably with those of similar tables in the output from the **Frequencies** routine. The **5% Trimmed Mean** (an EDA statistic) is the mean of the scores from which the extreme values at either end of the distribution have been removed. (A tenet of the philosophy of EDA is that it is better to describe 95% of the data well than 100% of them badly.) In both distributions, the trimmed mean, the traditional mean and the median all have similar values, suggesting that the distributions are symmetrical. In neither case, moreover, is the skewness as much as one standard error away from zero.

Descriptives

Gender				Statistic	Std. Error
Height in Centimetres	Male	Mean		184.7372	1.13206
		95% Confidence Interval for Mean	Lower Bound	182.4057	
			Upper Bound	187.0687	
		5% Trimmed Mean		184.6208	
		Median		184.7276	
		Variance		33.321	
		Std. Deviation		5.77239	
		Minimum		171.95	
		Maximum		201.31	
		Range		29.36	
		Interquartile Range		3.98	
		Skewness		.373	.456
		Kurtosis		2.474	.887
	Female	Mean		173.2002	1.12094
		95% Confidence Interval for Mean	Lower Bound	170.8961	
			Upper Bound	175.5043	
		5% Trimmed Mean		173.1645	
		Median		173.4456	
		Variance		33.926	
		Std. Deviation		5.82457	
		Minimum		163.01	
		Maximum		184.87	
		Range		21.86	
		Interquartile Range		9.94	
		Skewness		.041	.448
		Kurtosis		-1.001	.872

Output 16. The Descriptives for Height from the **Explore** output

Output 17 shows boxplots summarising the Height distributions in the Males and Females.   In either box, the central position of the median line indicates symmetry of the distribution.   In the distribution of male heights, however, there are more outliers and extreme scores.   There is, however, a reasonable balance between deviant scores at the upper and lower ends of the distribution; though the median has been moved upwards slightly from the central position.

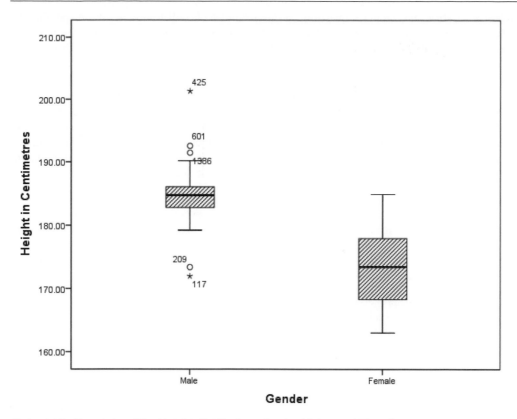

Output 17. Boxplots of the Height distributions for the Males and Females.

The stem-and-leaf plots of the distributions of height for males and females present a very similar picture to the boxplots and are not reproduced here. As before, the stem-and-leaf display for the male heights reports more 'extreme' scores than does the boxplot of the same data.

4.5 DESCRIBING DATA FROM MULTIPLE RESPONSE QUESTIONNAIRES

Some questionnaires contain items in the form of checklists from which the respondent can choose two or more items. For example, when asked which means of transport you use to get to work, you may be allowed to tick up to seven items from the following list: walking, cycling, taking the bus, driving a car on your own, using a motorbike, sharing a car and taking the train. On each working day, some commuters may use all seven methods to get to their work; whereas others may use just one. Most, however, will fall between these limits: Respondent A might drive his car to a station and then take a train; Respondent B might walk to a bus stop, take the bus to the railway station, take the train to a railway station near work and finally take another bus to complete her journey; and so on.

When a questionnaire includes questions in the form of a checklist allowing the respondent to tick one or more items, one cannot transcribe the responses to such a questionnaire into one variable of an SPSS data set, since we are allowed to enter only one value for each variable. Instead, we must create several elementary or **component** variables (e.g. Do you walk? Do you cycle?), one for each form of transport. There are two methods of coding responses. In the **multiple-dichotomy** method, which we shall follow in this section, the same code value (usually 1) is used for the positive response to every component question: e.g., if, for the question: 'Do you cycle?', the code value 1 indicates Yes, the same will be true for the question: 'Do you take the train?'. To capture a respondent's response to the checklist, we shall need as many variables as there are items in the list. The researcher can then enter a value of 1 for each of the items in the checklist that the respondent ticked.

The process of creating sets of component variables to capture a respondent's choices from a list is, of course, very laborious – particularly if there are several checklists in a questionnaire. Fortunately, special software is available for making the process less burdensome. In the example we shall use as an illustration in this section, we shall start with a data set containing a set of component variables for a single checklist that has been created by using the **SNAP** package of proprietary software.

We could, of course, proceed to analyse responses to the component variables separately by using SPSS procedures such as **Frequencies** and **Crosstabs**. Since the frequencies of positive responses to the items in the checklist are free to vary independently, there would certainly be something be gained from doing that. On the other hand, taken together, the questions form a meaningful set and it is therefore better to treat them as a coherent composite variable in the analysis. When comparing men and women in their use of various modes of transport, for example, there is interest not only in whether men use, say, cars more than women or vice versa, but also whether there is a difference in their selections of other modes of transport for parts of their journey to work. This is a question about *profiles* of transport mode, rather than simple comparison of the use of particular modes of transport in different groups of commuters.

The SPSS **Multiple Response** command integrates the component variables that carry responses to a checklist into a variable-like group known as a **multiple response set**. Up to 20 such sets can be defined. Were a questionnaire to present the respondent with 20 checklists, it would be reasonable to define 20 multiple response sets, each capturing the respondent's choices from one of the checklists. Should the researcher have a question about a subset of the listed items, however, a smaller multiple response set can easily be defined. For example, one might define a set containing only non-mechanised modes of transport (walk; cycle; run) and another containing mechanised modes of transport (bus; car; train). Like an ordinary variable, a multiple response set can be processed by some SPSS routines to display frequencies and optional percentages for its component items in univariate tables and bivariate and multivariate crosstabulations. Defined multiple response sets can be crosstabulated either with elementary variables or with other defined multiple response sets. The **Multiple Responses Crosstabs** procedure can produce cell, row, column and total counts and the corresponding percentages. The cell percentages can be based upon cases or upon responses. Such information can provide additional insights over and above an analysis with any single variable.

It should be noted that, although a multiple response set behaves like a categorical variable, it is supported by two SPSS routines only, namely, **Custom Tables** and the **Chart Builder**. A multiple response set is a special construct within a data file, which cannot be read by other

SPSS routines such as **Crosstabs** and **Frequencies**. Multiple response sets can be saved in data files, but they cannot be sent to or imported from other file formats.

4.5.1   Data for the Multiple Response procedure

We shall illustrate the **Multiple Response** procedure with a data set (in a file named *Multiple Responses*, which is available on our website at http://www.psypress.com/spss-made-simple) consisting of records of age, age group, sex and how the respondents travel to work. Our analysis begins at the stage where the details of how the respondents get to work have already been coded (by the software SNAP) into seven binary variables: Travel_walk, Travel_cycle, ..., Travel_train (Figure 17).

Travel_walk	Numeric	8	0	Do you walk?	{1, Yes}...
Travel_cycle	Numeric	8	0	Do you cycle?	{1, Yes}...
Travel_bus	Numeric	8	0	Do you take the bus?	{1, Yes}...
Travel_drivecar	Numeric	8	0	Do you drive a car?	{1, Yes}...
Travel_motorbike	Numeric	8	0	Do you drive a motorbike?	{1, Yes}...
Travel_sharecar	Numeric	8	0	Do you come by car with others	{1, Yes}...
Travel_train	Numeric	8	0	Do you come by train?	{1, Yes}...

Figure 17.   Part of **Variable View** showing the variables specifying seven modes of travel

Were you to click on the **Values** cell of any of the seven Travel variables listed in Figure 18, you would see the value 1 only: there is no zero (Figure 18). This is a peculiarity of the SNAP software, which has consequences for the appearance of **Data View**.

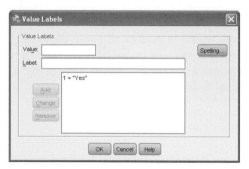

Figure 18. The **Value Labels** window for one of the component variables

Inspection of Data View, a section of which is shown in Figure 19 will show, in addition to case numbers and the grouping variables, seven columns, each headed with one of the variable names shown in Figure 19. In each column, the value 1 signifies that a respondent uses the mode of transport specified by the column heading. When a respondent does not use this mode of transport, however, a missing value will be recorded, rather than a zero. Had the researcher created the component variables without using the SNAP software, zeros for negative responses would have been entered in Data View, and the value label No would have been assigned to the code value 0 in the Values column of Variable View.

Travel_ walk	Travel_ cycle	Travel_ bus	Travel_driv ecar	Travel_m otorbike	Travel_s harecar	Travel_train
.	1	.	.	.	.	.
1	1	.	.	.	.	.
.	.	1	.	.	.	.
.	.	1	.	.	.	.
.	.	1	.	.	.	.
1	.	1	.	.	.	.

Figure 19.   A section of **Data View** in a file created by the SNAP software

The **Multiple Response** procedure has no problem at all with lots of system-missing values in Data View. We should note, however, that some of the routines in standard SPSS procedures such as **Compute Variable** cannot produce a result if there are missing values. Should we wish to run **Compute Variable**, for instance, we should have to replace the system-missing values in Data View with zeros. (This is easily done by using the **Recode** procedure.) The use of **Compute Variable** is necessary if the researcher has questions about the frequencies of specific combinations of different modes of travel. The **Multiple Response** procedure cannot answer questions of this type and we must turn to other methods.

Before we proceed to define a multiple response set, we should note that the **multiple-dichotomy** method of coding that we have chosen is the method of choice for recording responses to checklists, as in our current example. To understand the **Multiple Response Sets** dialog, however, we need to be aware that there is another method of coding, called **multiple-category** coding, by which you create a set of component variables, one for each mode of transport, but with a different value for the positive response for each component variable: thus, to the question, 'Do you walk?', a positive response could be coded as 1; to the question, 'Do you cycle?', a positive response could be coded as 2; and so on. Such **multiple category sets** are used when the maximum number of responses given by a respondent to a survey is significantly less than the total number of possible responses.

4.5.2   Creating a multiple response set

The first step in the **Multiple Response** procedure is to create a **Multiple Response Set** for the type of transport used to get to work. To do this, select **Analyze→Tables→Multiple Response Sets…** to access the **Define Multiple Response Sets** dialog box (Figure 20).

Complete the dialog box as shown in Figure 20 (assuming multiple dichotomy formatting, in which the value 1 always means Yes), remembering to enter the value 1 in the Counted Value slot. Click **OK** to run the procedure. Confirmation of the creation of a new Response Set named Travel_Mode with a label Ways of Travelling to Work will appear in the **SPSS Statistics Viewer** (Output 18).

(Had the variables been in multiple categories format [1 = Walk for the first variable, 2 = Cycle for the second variable, and so on], the radio button marked **Labels of counted value** in the left-hand **Category Labels Source** panel would have been clicked instead of the default **Variable labels** - see Figure 20.)

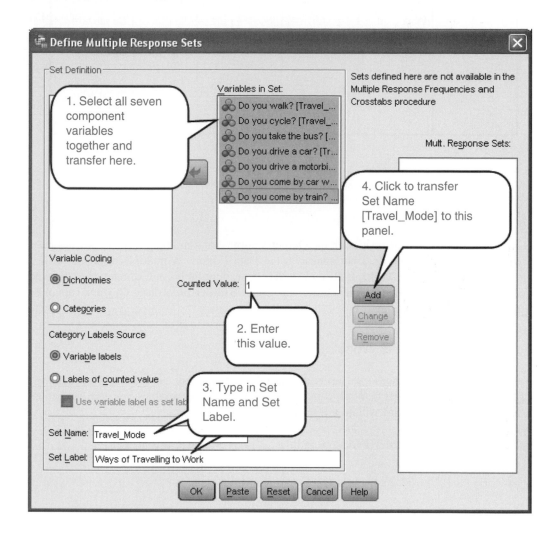

Figure 20. The **Define Multiple Response Sets** dialog box. Clicking **Add** will complete the dialog by transferring the Set Name to the right-hand panel

Multiple Response Sets

Name	Label	Coded As	Counted Value	Data Type	Elementary Variables
$Travel_Mode	Ways of Travelling to Work	Dichotomies	1	Numeric	Do you walk? Do you cycle? Do you take the bus? Do you drive a car? Do you drive a motorbike? Do you come by car with others? Do you come by train?

Output 18.   Confirmation that a multiple response set named Travel_Mode with the label 'Ways of Travelling to Work' has been created

Note that, despite the confirmation in the Output Viewer that a multiple response set has been created, this new variable does not appear in the Data Editor. A multiple response set is a special construct that the **Multiple Response Sets** procedure builds and stores within the data file. It is supported by the **Custom Tables** and **Chart Builder** procedures only and cannot be used by other SPSS procedures.

4.5.3   Obtaining the crosstabulations

Now that a Multiple Response Set has been created, the researcher can make a crosstabulation of the Response Set Travel to Work with the ordinary grouping variables Sex and AgeGroup. The **Custom Tables** routine will do this for us.

- Select **Analyze➜Tables➜Custom Tables…** to open the **Custom Tables** dialog box (Figure 21).

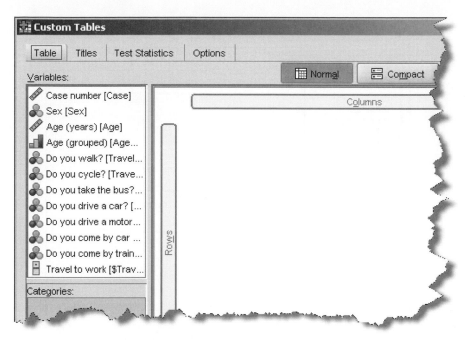

Figure 21.   Part of the **Custom Tables** dialog box

- Complete the dialog box as shown in Figure 22 and click **OK**.   As each variable name is dragged into either the **Columns** or the **Rows** panels, the display changes to show the constituent levels of the variables (Figure 23).

Other statistics such as percentages can be selected by highlighting sections of the table (e.g. Sex) in the dialog box (Figure 22), clicking **N% Summary Statistics** in the **Define** panel to open the **Summary Statistics** dialog box, selecting one (or more) of the options within the **Statistics** panel (e.g. **Row Valid N %**), clicking the arrow to transfer the chosen statistic to the next available row (or rows) in the **Display** panel, and clicking the **Apply to Selection** button. You will then be returned to the **Custom Tables** dialog box, where newly selected statistics are shown in the display. Finally click **OK** to obtain the contingency table. Care needs to be taken in selecting percentages: there are many options and the resulting table can easily become cluttered and difficult to read.

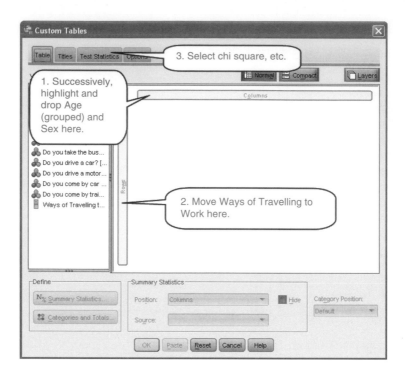

Figure 22.   Completing the **Custom Tables** dialog

			Sex							
			Female				Male			
			Age (grouped)				Age (grouped)			
			Female	21 - 30	31 - 40	41 - 50	Female	21 - 30	31 - 40	41 - 50
			Count	Count	Count	Count	Count	Count	Count	Count
	Ways of Travelling to Work	Do you take ...	nnnn	nnnn	nnnn	nnnn	nnnn	nnnn	nnnn	nnnn
		Do you cycle?	nnnn	nnnn	nnnn	nnnn	nnnn	nnnn	nnnn	nnnn
		Do you drive a ...	nnnn	nnnn	nnnn	nnnn	nnnn	nnnn	nnnn	nnnn
		Do you drive a ...	nnnn	nnnn	nnnn	nnnn	nnnn	nnnn	nnnn	nnnn
		Do you come .	nnnn	nnnn	nnnn	nnnn	nnnn	nnnn	nnnn	nnnn
		Do you come .	nnnn	nnnn	nnnn	nnnn	nnnn	nnnn	nnnn	nnnn
		Do you walk?	nnnn	nnnn	nnnn	nnnn	nnnn	nnnn	nnnn	nnnn

Figure 23.   Part of the completed **Custom Tables** dialog box for the contingency table of AgeGroup × Sex ×Travel to work

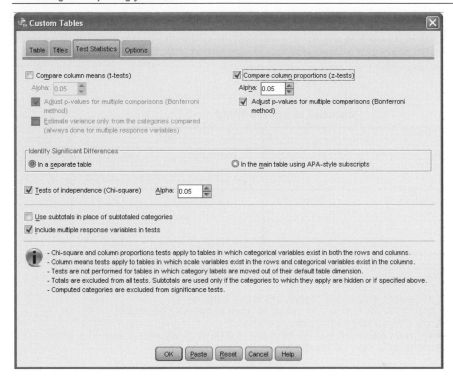

Figure 24 The **Test Statistics** tab

The contingency table is shown in Output 19.

		Sex							
		Female				Male			
		Age (grouped)				Age (grouped)			
		Female	21 - 30	31 - 40	41 - 50	Female	21 - 30	31 - 40	41 - 50
		Count	Count	Count	Count	Count	Count	Count	Count
Ways of Travelling to Work	Do you walk?	153	207	26	10	76	167	17	7
	Do you cycle?	5	22	7	5	13	33	8	5
	Do you take the bus?	69	72	14	8	39	41	6	2
	Do you drive a car?	46	67	44	41	28	57	34	16
	Do you drive a motorbike?	0	3	0	1	0	2	0	0
	Do you come by car with others?	8	8	2	3	5	4	1	1
	Do you come by train?	0	1	1	2	4	7	2	1

Output 19.   The contingency table of the various ways of getting to work categorised by Sex and AgeGroup

The chi-square test of independence (Output 20) shows that there are significant differences among the responses for How to get to work between the sexes in the two younger age groups but not in the two older ones. These differences are further teased out (Output 21) showing that cycling and taking the train are the critical responses for some of the age groups as shown by the letter A.

Pearson Chi-Square Tests

		Sex	
		Female	Male
		Age (grouped)	Age (grouped)
Ways of Travelling to Work	Chi-square	236.336	129.418
	df	21	21
	Sig.	.000[*,a,b]	.000[*,a,b]

Results are based on nonempty rows and columns in each innermost subtable.

*. The Chi-square statistic is significant at the 0.05 level.
a. More than 20% of cells in this subtable have expected cell counts less than 5. Chi-square results may be invalid.
b. The minimum expected cell count in this subtable is less than one. Chi-square results may be invalid.

Output 20. The chi-square tests showing sex differences for Travel to work for the Under 20 and 21-30 Age Groups only

It is clear from the cautions and caveats at the foot of the table in Output 21, that there are serious questions about the closeness of the distribution of the approximate chi-square variable to the true chi-square variable on the same degrees of freedom. In our view, it is better to regard the methods we have been describing as descriptive and exploratory, rather than confirmatory.

Comparisons of Column Proportions[b]

		Sex							
		Female				Male			
		Age (grouped)				Age (grouped)			
		Female	21 - 30	31 - 40	41 - 50	Female	21 - 30	31 - 40	41 - 50
		(A)	(B)	(C)	(D)	(A)	(B)	(C)	(D)
Ways of Travelling to Work	Do you walk?	C D	C D			C D	C D		
	Do you cycle?								
	Do you take the bus?	D				B C			
	Do you drive a car?			A B	A B			A B	A B
	Do you drive a motorbike?	,a		,a		,a		,a	,a
	Do you come by car with others?								
	Do you come by train?	,a			B				

Results are based on two-sided tests with significance level 0.05. For each significant pair, the key of the category with the smaller column proportion appears under the category with the larger column proportion.

a. This category is not used in comparisons because its column proportion is equal to zero or one.
b. Tests are adjusted for all pairwise comparisons within a row of each innermost subtable using the Bonferroni correction.

Output 21. The column proportions tests. The letter A shows which proportions are significantly different

The Response Set can also be used as one of the variables in a graph such as a clustered bar chart. This is illustrated in Output 22, which shows the Response Set plotted with Sex and AgeGroup.

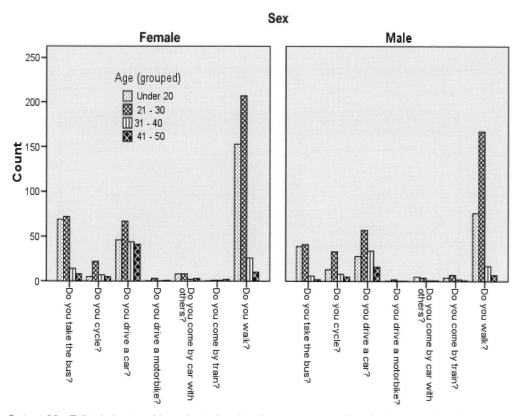

Output 22. Edited clustered bar chart showing the transport profiles for Sex and AgeGroup

4.5.4   Finding the frequencies of specific transport profiles

(Before reading the following subsection, we suggest the reader might first read the sections in Chapter 3 on the **Compute** and **Recode** commands.)

A respondent is quite likely to use more than one mode of transport to get to work. We might want to analyse the frequencies with which different *combinations* of modes of transport are used and compare these frequency profiles across groups: how many people cycle and take the bus? How many walk, cycle and drive? To determine the frequencies of the various combinations of modes of travel, we shall have to define a new composite variable with a name such as 'Combination', consisting of a set of new values, each value labelling one particular combination of modes of travel. After making a preliminary adjustment to the data set, we shall use the **Compute Variable** procedure to construct a new variable, Combination, which will code the various combinations of modes of travel.

The first step is to use the **Recode** procedure to convert the system-missing values in Data View into zeros. This is necessary because the **Compute Variable** procedure cannot run with system-missing values (represented as dots) in Data View. Proceed as follows.

- Choose **Transform➨Recode into the same variables** to open the **Recode into Same Variables** box and proceed as shown in Figure 25.

You will see that, in **Data View**, the system-missing value has been replaced with 0.

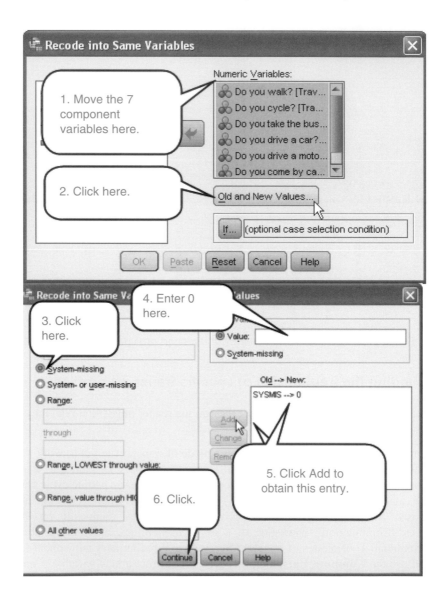

Figure 25.   Recoding the system-missing value (.) to zero

Constructing the new Combination variable

We want to identify each combination of possible modes of transport with a distinct code number. We can achieve this by creating a new variable named Combination, which is defined as a linear function of the seven modes of transport variables, in which each coefficient is a power of ten thus:

$$Combination = 10^0 * Travel\_walk + 10^1 * Travel\_cycle + 10^2 * Travel\_bus + ...$$
$$... + 10^3 * Travel\_drivecar + 10^4 * Travel\_motorbike + ...$$
$$... + 10^5 * Travel\_sharecar + 10^6 * Travel\_train$$

For a commuter who used all seven modes of transport, the value for the Combination variable would be:

$$Combination = 1 + 10 + 100 + ...$$
$$... + 1000 + 10,000 + ...$$
$$... + 100,000 + 1,000,000$$
$$= 1111111$$

The reason for the increasing powers of ten in the formula for the Combination variable is this: we do not want two respondents, both of whom chose, say, three modes of travel but selected different methods, to receive the same value for the Combination variable. Weighting the modes of travel with ascending powers of ten ensures that the sum will be different in the two cases.

We can now proceed with the **Compute Variable** procedure as shown in Figure 26. Simply build the formula for Combination into the Numeric Expression window, selecting the variable names on the left and clicking the arrow on the central pillar to transfer them to the appropriate places in the formula.

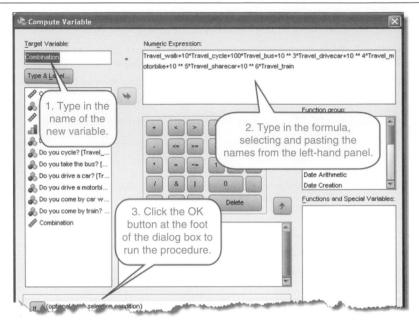

Figure 26. Using **Compute Variable** to calculate values of the new variable Combination

A fragment of the **Values** window in Variable View is shown in Figure 26.

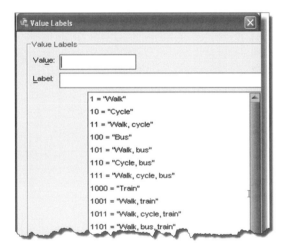

Figure 27. A fragment of the Value Labels window showing combinations with their value labels

The structure of the new variable named Combination enables the researcher to answer questions that cannot be answered by the **Multiple Response Sets** procedure. Suppose we want to compare the three age groups with respect to the number of respondents who travel to work by walking only. This question is different from any we have considered so far, because it is a question about a combination of responses. It is quite distinct from the question of how many respondents from each age group walked to get to work, because that might have been just one of several means of transport that they used. Proceed as follows:

- Choose **Data ➔ Select Cases** and, in the **Select Cases: If** window, set Combination = 1. (This is the code for walking only.)

- Choose **Analyze➔ Descriptive Statistics➔ Frequencies** and, to the **Variables** panel on the right-hand side of the dialog box, transfer the variables AgeGroup and Combination = 1. (This choice, rather than Combination, ensures that only those who said they made their entire journey to work by foot will be selected.) Click **OK** to run the procedure. The frequency distribution is shown in Output 23.

It would appear from Output 23 that most of those for whom the sole method of transport to work was walking were in their twenties.

Age (grouped)

		Frequency	Percent	Valid Percent	Cumulative Percent
Valid	Under 20	126	32.6	32.6	32.6
	21 - 30	232	60.1	60.1	92.7
	31 - 40	24	6.2	6.2	99.0
	41 - 50	4	1.0	1.0	100.0
	Total	386	100.0	100.0	

Output 23. The numbers of respondents in the different age groups for whom walking was their only means of transport

4.6   A FINAL WORD

In this chapter, we have described the use of SPSS Statistics 19 to describe various kinds of data in large and small data sets. Different statistics are appropriate for the description of data at the continuous (scale) and nominal levels of measurement.

Graphs and other displays can often reveal aspects of a distribution that a numerical statistical summary misses. For large sets of scale or continuous data, the histogram is a very useful graph for depicting the distributions; for small data sets, on the other hand, EDA displays such as the stem-and-leaf and the boxplot often present a truer picture of the distribution. The **Explore** procedure offers several EDA statistics and displays.

Association between categorical variables involves the construction of a contingency table. Contingency tables are readily available in **Crosstabs** and in **Tables**.

SPSS can be used to create **multiple response sets** and compare response profiles across such categorical variables as gender and age group.

Exercises

Exercise 4 *Correcting and preparing your data* and Exercise 5 *Preparing your data (continued)* are available in www.psypress.com/spss-made-simple and click on Exercises.

CHAPTER 5

More on graphs and charts

5.1   INTRODUCTION

SPSS offers a wide range of graphs and charts, some of which we have already made use of in Chapters 2, 3 and 4. In this chapter, we shall look more closely at some aspects of graph-drawing in SPSS.

For monochrome printing, the **Chart Editor** can be used once a graph or chart has appeared in the Viewer to remove the colours and replace them with patterns. It is better, however, to change the default settings beforehand as follows:

- Choose **Edit→Options...** and select the **Charts** tab in the **Options** dialog box.

- Within the **Style Cycle Preference** selection panel, select **Cycle through patterns only**.

- Click **Fills... .** Select the pattern you want for **Simple Charts** and delete the empty pattern box in **Grouped Charts** by clicking the radio button for **Grouped Charts**, selecting the empty box pattern and clicking **Remove**. Click **Continue**.

- Click **Apply**, then **OK**.

5.2   BAR CHARTS

This section describes the production of **simple bar charts**, **clustered bar charts**, and **panelled bar charts**.

5.2.1   Simple bar charts

A **simple bar chart** summaries the distributions of a scale or continuous variable at different levels of one categorical variable only, such as the experimental condition under which the participants in a study performed. We shall use the data from the caffeine experiment in *Ch5 Caffeine and Gender.sav* at http://www.psypress.com/spss-made-simple.

A simple bar chart for comparing the means scores of groups of participants such as those in the caffeine experiment (Chapter 2) can be obtained as follows:

- Choose **Graphs→Chart Builder…**

- A warning box will appear asking you to ensure that each variable has been defined in the **Measure** column of **Variable View** as **Scale**, **Ordinal** or **Nominal**, and that the values of categorical variables have been labelled. Should you have forgotten to do either of these things, you can enter the information at this point by completing the warning dialog. Otherwise, click **OK** to continue.

- In the **Choose From** list, highlight **Bar** to display, in the **Gallery**, pictures of the different kinds of bar chart. Click the first (top left) picture of simple bars to highlight it and then drag the template to the **Chart preview** in the panel above (Figure 1).

> **Chart Builder opening dialog in Section 2.2.8**

- In the **Element Properties** dialog box, check **Display error bars** and **Apply** to return to the Chart Builder and see the error bars included in the template.

- In the **Variables** list, click Score and drag it to the **Y-Axis** drop zone in the Chart preview. Move Experimental Condition to the **X-Axis** drop zone.

- To add a title, click **Titles/Footnotes** tab and then, in the list of check-boxes that will appear in place of the gallery of graphics choices, click **Title 1**. A panel will appear in the **Element Properties** dialog box, where a title such as 'Means and 95% Confidence Intervals' can be typed in. Click **Apply**, followed by **Close**. The marker **T1** will appear at the top of the preview if a title has been requested.

- Finally, back in the **Chart Builder**, click **OK** to create the chart (Output 1).

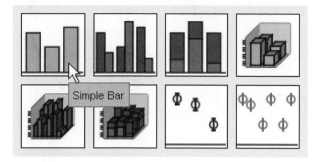

Figure 1. The bar chart gallery

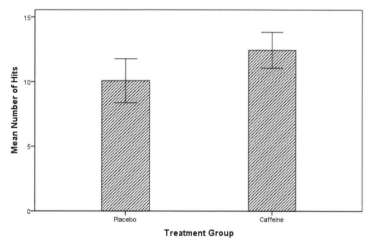

Output 1. A simple bar chart with error bars

5.2.2   Clustered bar charts

A **clustered bar chart** is a graph in which, instead of only a single bar over each of the categories on the horizontal axis, there is a **cluster** of bars, each bar in the cluster representing a category in a second categorical variable. Suppose that, in addition to the Experimental Condition variable, the data set also contained the Gender of the participants. A clustered bar chart could then be plotted with Experimental Condition as the first categorical variable and Gender as the clustering variable.

- Select Bar from the **Choose from** list. The appropriate array of choices will appear in the **Gallery** (Figure 2).

- Drag the **Clustered Bar** template into the **Chart Preview** area.

- From the **Variables** list, drag the three variables into their appropriate drop zones (Figure 3).

- In **Element Properties**, check **Display error bars** and click **Apply** to see the error bars added to the outline in the Chart preview (Figure 4).

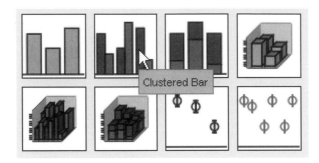

Figure 2. The **bar chart gallery**

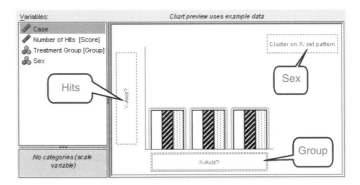

Figure 3. The three drop zones

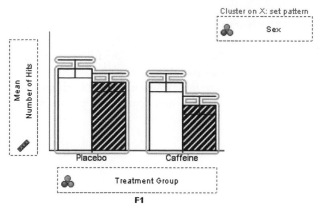

Figure 4.   Chart preview after specification of the cluster variable and error bars

• Click **OK** to produce the clustered bar chart (Output 2).

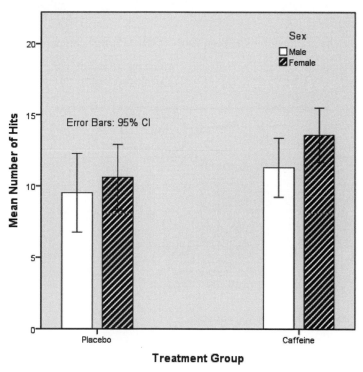

Output 2.   A clustered bar chart

5.2.3   Panelled bar charts

In Chapter 2, we showed how to display histograms for different groups either in rows or in columns. This operation is known as **panelling**. Bar charts can be panelled in exactly the same way as can histograms. Suppose that we want to display simple bar charts of the scores in the Caffeine experiment for the males and females in a side-by-side panelled display. Proceed as follows.

- Select **Bar** from the **Choose from** list. The appropriate array of choices will appear in the **Gallery**.

- Choose **Simple Bar** from the **Gallery** and drag the template into the **Chart Preview** area.

- From the **Variables** list, click and drag Score into Y-Axis drop zone in the **Chart Preview** and similarly transfer the grouping variable to the X-Axis drop zone.

- Click on **Element Properties**, order error bars and click **Apply** to return to the **Chart Builder** to see the error bars in the Chart preview.

- In the **Chart Builder**, click the **Groups/Point ID** tab and check **Columns panel variable**. (**Columns panelling** displays the figures in a row; **Rows panelling** displays them in a column.)

- Drag the grouping variable into the drop zone labelled **Panel?** (Figure 5)

- Click **OK** to produce the panelled bar charts, which are shown in Output 3.

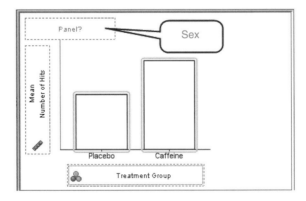

Figure 5.   Drop zone for the panelling variable

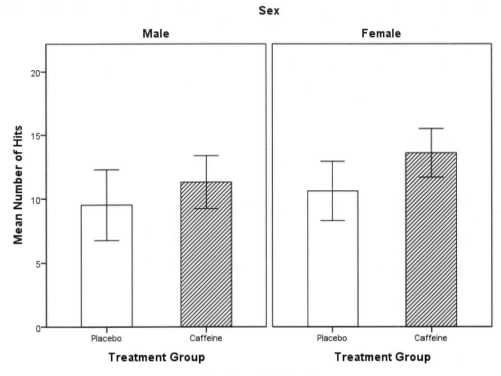

Output 3. Panelled bar charts

5.2.4   Editing a bar chart

The figure in Output 3 has been slightly edited: the thickness of the bars has been adjusted; and shading has been introduced to distinguish more sharply between the Caffeine and Placebo groups. The original version in the Viewer had thicker bars and no shading.

- Double-click the chart to open the **Chart Editor** (Figure 6). In the Editor, you will see the unedited figure that first appeared in the Viewer.

- Double-click on the bars to open the **Properties** dialog box. If necessary, click the **Fill & Border** tab.

- You will notice that all four bars are surrounded by a faint yellow border.   We want to change the fill of the Caffeine bars from a self-colour to a pattern. *Single*-click, say, the Caffeine bar in the Male part of the figure. You will see that this bar retains its yellow border; whereas the remaining bars lose theirs. This means that any editing requested will apply to that bar only.

TIP

Single-click one of the selected bars to select that bar alone

- In **Properties**, click the drop-down menu labelled **Pattern** and make a selection from the array (Figure 7). Click **Apply** to produce the pattern in the selected bar only.

- Single-click the other Caffeine bar to select that bar only and repeat the operation. Figure 7 shows the point where the selection has been made, but the **Apply** button has yet to be clicked and the target bar remains self-coloured.

- Click on the tab labelled **Bar Options** and adjust the width of the bars as shown in Figure 8.

- Click **Apply** to implement the change and **Close** to leave **Properties**.

- Back in the Chart Editor, choose **File➔Close** to leave the Chart Editor. The figure should now appear as in Output 3.

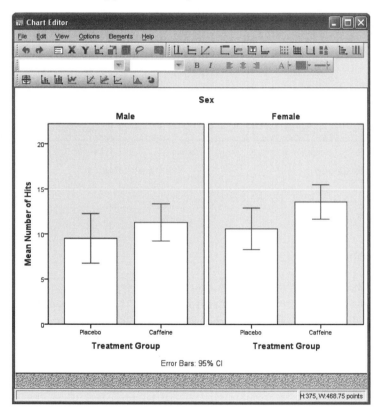

Figure 6. The **Chart Editor**

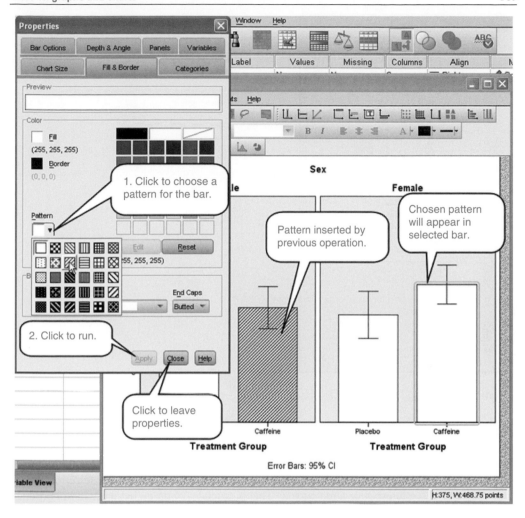

Figure 7. Selecting a filler pattern for the Caffeine bar in the Female column of the panel.

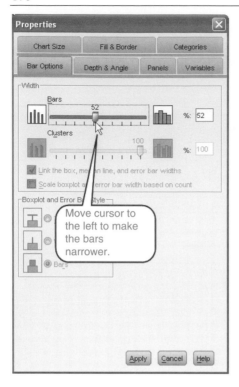

Figure 8. Adjusting the widths of the bars

Editing captions and titles on figures

When there is a figure in the Chart Editor, it is possible to edit titles, subtitles footnotes or captions by double-clicking on the area of the figure concerned to produce a selection frame, then *single*-clicking to produce a red cursor. This is crucial – *double*-clicking will not produce the cursor. See Figure 9.

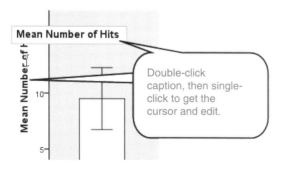

Figure 9. Editing captions in the **Chart Editor**

Changing the orientation of a label on the vertical axis of a graph

The initial orientation of the caption on the vertical axis of the figure was vertical: the text read in a bottom-up direction (Figure 9). To change the orientation of the caption, so that the text will read from right to left, proceed as shown in Figure 10.

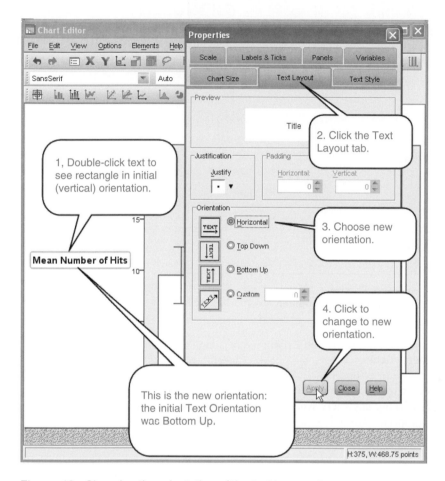

Figure 10. Changing the orientation of the text in a caption

5.3 ERROR BAR CHARTS

An alternative to a bar graph is an **Error Bar chart**, in which the mean of the scores in a particular category is represented by a single point. The spread is represented by a vertical line (T-bar or whiskers) passing through the point. The user can choose, as a measure of spread, the confidence interval on the mean, multiples of the standard deviation or multiples of the standard error of the mean. Output 4 is a clustered error bar chart summarising the results of the drug experiment.

The production of an error bar chart with the Chart Builder is analogous to the production of bar graphs and raises no new issues.

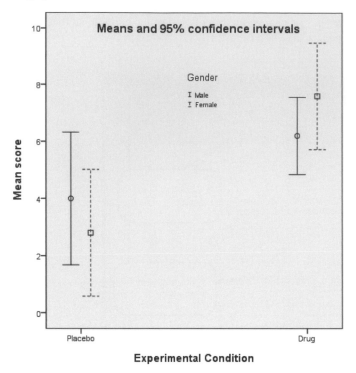

Output 4. A clustered error bar chart with Experimental Condition as the category variable and Gender as the cluster variable

The symbols used for the means and the form of the lines used for the error bars can be changed by double-clicking anywhere within the graphic to open the **Chart Editor**. Double-clicking on the appropriate symbol or line in the Gender key will open the corresponding **Properties** dialog box where changes can be made.

You will notice that in Output 4, there are no lines linking the error bars. This is entirely appropriate, since the bars represent qualitatively distinct categories. In other circumstances, however, as when the categories are ordered, it may be desirable to join up the points (when there are more than two) with interpolation lines. This is easily achieved in the **Chart Editor** by clicking the means to highlight them, selecting the **Elements** drop-down menu and clicking **Interpolation line** (or alternatively clicking the icon at right).

5.4 BOXPLOTS

Three types of boxplots are available in **Chart Builder**, the single boxplot (called **1-D Boxplot** in the gallery), the **simple boxplot** for plotting the boxplots across categories of a grouping variable and the **clustered boxplot** for plotting boxplots across categories of two grouping variables.

Output 5 shows the boxplots of Score for the Placebo and Caffeine groups, clustered by Sex. Notice in the output that there is one case identified as an outlier with 'o'. Any extreme case would have been identified with an asterisk (*).

The production of boxplots with the Chart Builder proceeds in a manner analogous to the drawing of histograms and bar charts and presents no new issues.

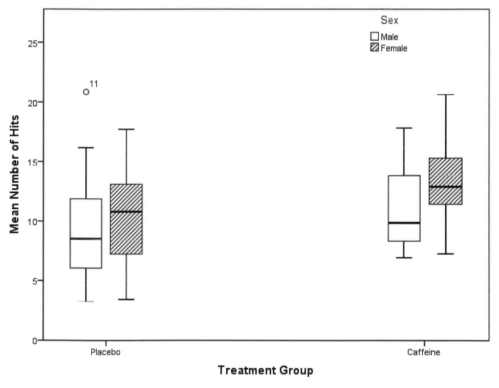

Output 5.   Boxplots of scores of the Placebo and Caffeine groups clustered by Sex

5.5 PIE CHARTS

The **pie chart** is an alternative to a bar graph, which provides a picturesque display of the frequency distribution of a qualitative variable. It is useful for displaying the relative frequencies of observations in the same set of categories over time or for bringing out the varying compositions of two things, such as conservative versus risky investment portfolios.

Pie charts can be panelled in a similar way to bar charts and histograms. Output 6 is a pie chart showing the percentages of the different blood groups in the sample we studied in Chapter 4. (The data are in *Ch4 Height, Weight, Sex & Blood group.sav* at http://www.psypress.com/spss-made-simple.)

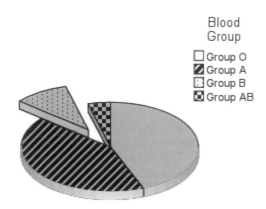

Blood
Group

☐ Group O
▨ Group A
⊞ Group B
▨ Group AB

Output 6. A 3-D **Pie Chart** showing the distribution of Blood Group with the Group B sector 'exploded' for greater salience

The pie chart in Output 6 has been edited in the Chart Editor to impart a three-dimensional appearance and 'explode' the Group B sector.

5.6   LINE GRAPHS

Like a scatterplot, a **line graph** depicts the relationship between two continuous or scale variables, such as weight and height. In a **line graph**, as in a histogram, the entire range of a one variable (say height) is stepped out in equal intervals along the horizontal axis. Above the midpoint of each interval, in the body of the graph, a point is placed with height on the y-axis proportional to the mean weight of all cases with heights falling within the interval on the horizontal axis. Finally, adjacent points are joined by straight lines.

Line graphs can be drawn with just one line or more than one line in the graph; and like bar charts and pie charts, they can also be panelled.

In this section, we shall use the **Chart Builder** to draw line graphs depicting the relationship between weight and height in the men and women in one of the data sets we explored in Chapter 4. To do this, we must first divide the total range of height into equal intervals, a task for which we need a special procedure known as **visual binning**.

5.6.1   The Visual Binning procedure

In order to draw the line graphs, we must first divide the entire range of the variable that is going to be on the horizontal axis of the graph (height) into equal intervals and specify a representative value for each interval.   This is done automatically in SPSS's **Histogram** procedure. In the histogram, the intervals are known as **class intervals**. Elsewhere, however, class intervals are known as **bins** and we shall need to use a special procedure known as **binning** to divide the total range of height into bins, with fixed **bin width**.

We shall use SPSS's **Visual Binning** procedure to divide the total range of the men's heights into intervals or bins, the largest and smallest of which are open-ended, so that all scores are included. Proceed as follows.

- Choose **Transform➜Visual Binning** to open the initial **Visual Binning** dialog box and transfer the variable Height to the **Variables to bin** box on the right. (See Figure 11.)

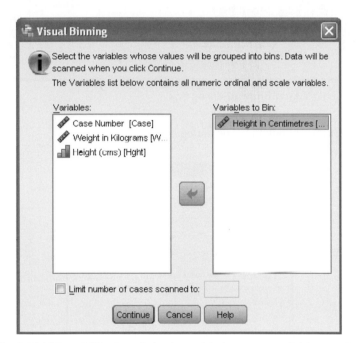

Figure 11.   The initial **Visual Binning** dialog box with the target variable transferred

Click the **Continue** button to enter the main **Visual Binning** dialog box, which shows a histogram of the distribution of Height, tells us that 2000 cases have been scanned and gives the minimum and maximum values of Height in our data set as 156.28cm and 205.09cm, respectively (See Figure 12).

We shall want about 12 class intervals or bins. The cutpoints will appear in the histogram when the bins are specified. We are going to enter, as Values in the Value column, the upper limits of the intervals. If we want 12 bins, we shall need to specify only 11 cutpoints.

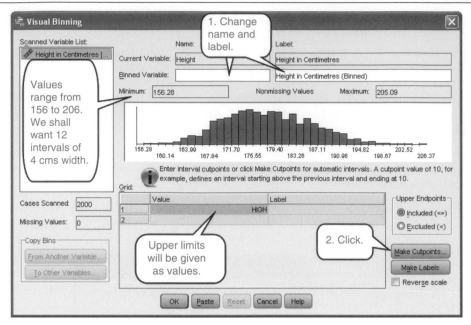

Figure 12.   The main **Visual Binning** dialog box

Click the **Make Cutpoints** button.   The dialog is shown in Figure 13.

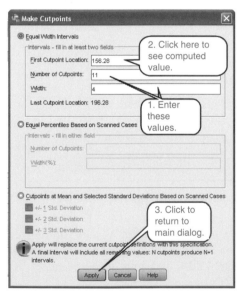

Figure 13. The Make Cutpoints dialog. The third slot must be clicked before the Apply button will become active.

On returning to the main Visual Binning dialog box, click the **Make Labels** Button. A column of labels now appears in the spaces under **Label**. Double-click on these to shorten them (Figure 18). Click the **OK** button to run the procedure.

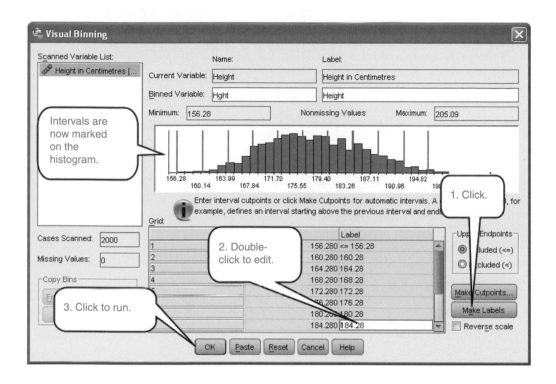

Figure 14. The main **Visual Binning** dialog box again, after clicking Make Labels and editing the labels

By choosing **View➔Value labels**, you can see, in Data View, the bin intervals shown in the Label column of the Visual Binning dialog. These intervals also appear in the Values column of Variable View for the variable Hght. With Value labels inactive, you would see only the ordinal numbers of the intervals. If, while in Variable View, you look in the Measure column, you will see that the binned version of Height has been automatically entered as an ordinal variable.

5.6.2 Plotting line graphs

We have used the Visual Binning procedure to divide the total range of heights of the participants into 11 bins. This binned version of the Height variable has been stored as the ordinal variable Hght. (Hght is fine for a variable name, provided the technical term **bin** does not appear in the variable label. You will need to edit the variable label in Variable View: a label such as 'Height in Centimeters (binned)' should be avoided.) We are going to plot line graphs of weight against height for the males and females and present them in a panelled display for comparison. Proceed as follows:

- Open the **Chart Builder**, select **Line** from the **Choose from** list, click the **Simple Line** picture in the gallery and drag it into the **Chart preview** box.

- Click the **Groups/Point ID** tab and choose **Columns panel variable**.

- Transfer the three variables to their correct drop zones, as shown in Figure 15.

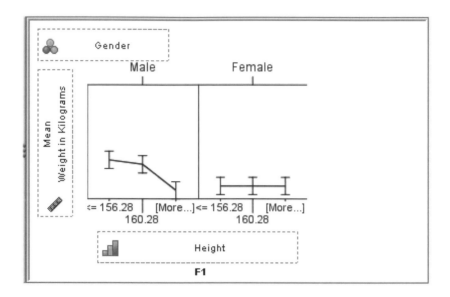

Figure 15.   Chart preview with the variables and error bars specified

- In **Element Properties**, specify that the statistic for the Y-axis is the mean. Order error bars as well.

- Click **OK** to run the procedure.

The panelled line graph is shown in Output 7. Output 7 has been edited by double-clicking to enter the Chart Editor and specify markers.

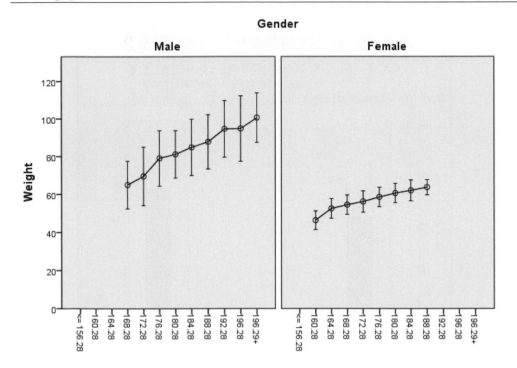

Output 7.   Panelled line graphs (edited) of Weight against Height for Males and Females

5.7   USING CHART TEMPLATES

Many or all of the attributes of an edited chart can be saved for future use, in what is known as a **chart template**. Should it be necessary to produce a similar chart on future occasions, time can be saved by opening the template, which will automatically incorporate the final attributes of the edited chart in the new chart that appears in the Viewer.   Such attributes include colour and shading and width and spacing of the bars, as well as headings, subheadings and footnotes.

Figure 16 shows the edited version of a chart in the Chart Editor.   (The right-hand margin has been dragged to the right to gain control of the position of the original footnote about the error bars.)   Realising that we may need to produce a similar chart in the future, we can store the edited version in a chart template as follows.

* Choose **File➔Save Chart Template...**   to open the **Save Chart Template** dialog box (Figure 17).

* Complete the **Save Chart Template** dialog as shown. On clicking **Continue**, you enter the **Save Template** dialog box.   Save the template somewhere in your own file space as shown in Figure 18.   Leave the Chart Editor.

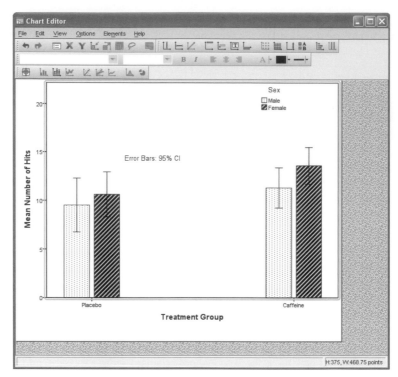

Figure 16.   An edited clustered bar chart in the **Chart Editor**

- Open the **Chart Builder** and order a clustered bar chart as before.

- Click the **Options** button to enter the **Options** dialog box, part of which is shown in Figure 19.

- Click the **Add** button, locate the folder in which you saved the file and open the file to see the file name appear in the **Template Files** box of the **Options** dialog box, below the **Add** button.

- Click **OK** to return to the **Chart Builder**. *At this stage you will see no change in the Chart preview.*

- In the **Chart Builder**, click **OK** to produce the chart (Output 8).

It is clear from Output 8, which appeared immediately in the Viewer, that the chart template has preserved all the features of the final edited version of the chart.

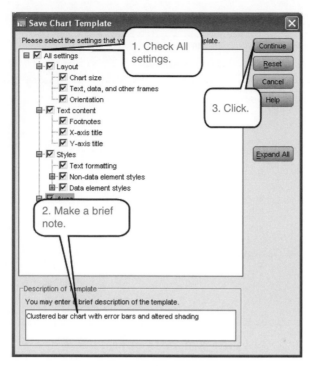

Figure 17. Completing the **Save Chart Template** dialog box

Figure 18. The **Save Template** dialog box

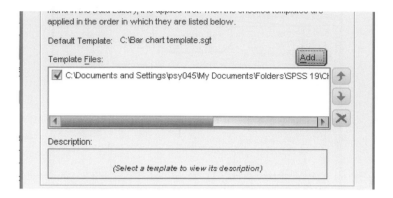

Figure 19.   Part of the **Options** dialog box in the **Chart Builder**

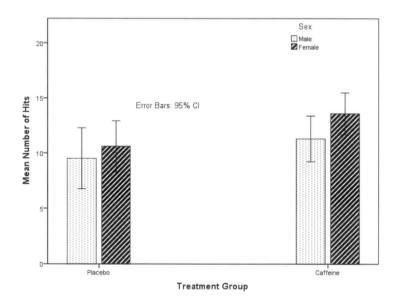

Output 8.   Replica of the edited clustered bar chart produced from a template

Chart templates are obviously very useful tools.   There are, however, some editorial changes that can be made in the Chart Editor, but which would not be preserved in a chart template.   In a simple bar chart, for example, you might want to use different shades or patterns for different bars.   Such a change would not be preserved in a template.   A similar problem would be encountered should you have used different patterns for selected categories of the x-axis variable separated by panel variable category. It can be done in the Chart Editor, but the change would not be preserved in the chart template. In this context, a clustered bar chart should be seen as two or more simple bar charts, one imposed upon the other: the bars in a cluster can be shaded differently, but are homogeneous within each of the simple component charts. Clustered bar charts, therefore, even when edited, are suitable for storage in a template. This requirement of pattern homogeneity within a simple chart unit, however, is not met when the categories of an X-variable have different patterns or colours across categories of a panel variable.

5.8   A FINAL WORD

In this chapter, we have tried to focus on some aspects of the editing of charts with which users often have difficulty. We have also looked more closely at the Chart Builder and drawn some new displays, such as line graphs.

When you are producing, say, a bar chart, you have the option of creating special effects, such as giving the graph a three-dimensional appearance. The fanciest graphs, however, do not necessarily present the clearest picture of the results of an investigation. Three-dimensional effects, for example, though aesthetically attractive to some, require careful handling; otherwise, they may actually obscure your presentation. The addition of error bars to such a figure creates the impression of tower blocks with a forest of radio masts on their roofs. It is sometimes difficult to discern, in such a cluttered display, the most important features of your results.

It is possible, having spent time editing a chart, to save many or all of its features in a chart template, which can be used to reproduce the final version instantly, whenever this is required.

Exercises

Exercise 6 *Charts and graphs,* and Exercise 7 *Recoding data; selecting cases, line graph* are available in www.psypress.com/spss-made-simple and click on Exercises.

CHAPTER 6

Comparing averages: Two-sample and one-sample tests

6.1   OVERVIEW

In Chapter 1, five research scenarios were described. In the first, the researcher has two or more samples of scores and wants to know whether the means are significantly different. As a guide to choosing an appropriate test in this kind of situation, we offered a flow chart with questions about the research question and the nature of the data. The first question asks for the number of groups or conditions. The main purpose of this chapter is to show you how to implement the tests recommended by the chart when there are two samples of scores.

In the fourth research scenario, the researcher has only a single sample of scores, on the basis of which an inference is to be about the mean of the population or a decision about whether the distribution of the sample is sufficiently well fitted by a theoretical distribution. One-sample tests, however, can sometimes be relevant to situations where there are two samples of scores. Where there are two related samples of scores in the form of continuous or scale data, for instance, the appropriate test for comparing the two means can be viewed as a one-sample test.

This is not a statistics textbook, and we must assume that you already have some knowledge of statistical terms. To understand SPSS output, you must be clear about the meaning of terms such as **probability**, **significance level**, *p*-**value** (which SPSS calls **Sig.**), **standard error**, **Type I and Type II errors**, **power**, **confidence interval** and so on. We have included some notes on some of the most common statistical terms on our website.

6.2   THE INDEPENDENT SAMPLES T TEST WITH SPSS

To illustrate the running of a *t* test on SPSS, we shall use the data from the caffeine experiment, which we explored in Chapter 2.   The data are available in the file *Caffeine experiment(60).sav*, at http://www.psypress.com/spss-made-simple.

We hope that, if you are a newcomer to SPSS, you will have already typed these data into the Data Editor and saved them to a file. Since we explored this data set in Chapter 2 and again in Chapter 4, we can omit most of the preliminaries at this point and cut to the chase.   Here, we shall start at the point where we have the data from the caffeine experiment in Data View, a fragment of which is shown in Figure 1.

	Case	Score	Group	var
1	1	13	Placebo	
2	2	4	Placebo	
3	3	6	Placebo	
4	4	10	Placebo	
5	5	11	Placebo	
6	6	9	Placebo	
7	7	3	Placebo	
8	8	7	Placebo	
9	9	16	Placebo	
10	10	10	Placebo	
11	11	21	Placebo	
12	12	8	Placebo	
13	13	4	Placebo	
14	14	6	Place	

Figure 1. A fragment of **Data View** showing some of the data from the caffeine experiment

6.2.1 Running the *t* test

- Choose **Analyze➔Compare Means➔Independent-Samples T Test ...** (Figure 2) to open the **Independent-Samples T Test** dialog box (Figure 3).

- Follow the steps in Figure 3 to open the **Define Groups** dialog (Figure 4). Follow the instructions in Figure 4 and click **Continue** to return to the **Independent Samples T Test dialog** box (Figure 5).

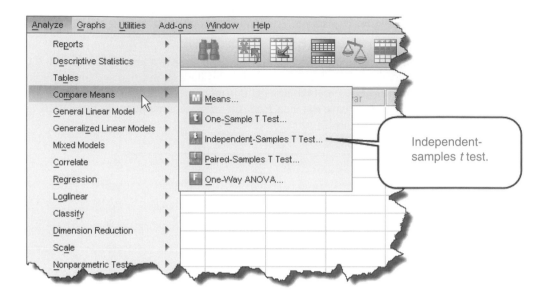

Figure 2. Opening the **Independent-Samples T Test** dialog box

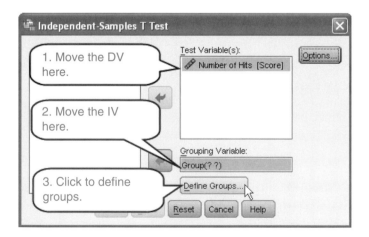

Figure 3. The **Independent-Samples T Test** dialog box

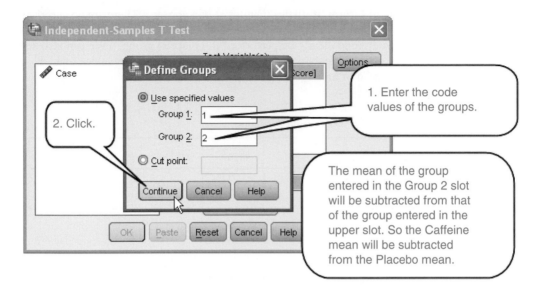

Figure 4.   Completing the **Define Groups** dialog box

The completed dialog box is shown in Figure 5. Click the **OK** button (which will have come live) to run the *t* test.

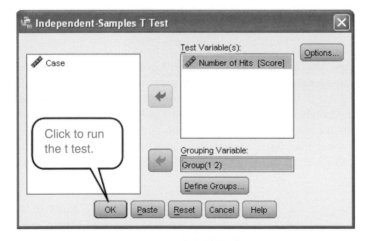

Figure 5. The completed **Independent-Samples T Test** dialog box

6.2.2 Interpreting the output

Early in the output, a table of **Group Statistics** (Output 1) will appear. There are no surprises here, since the values in the table are exactly those we obtained when we explored this data set in Chapter 2. The Caffeine group clearly outperformed the Placebo group. We can also see from Output 1 that the group standard deviations have rather similar values, which is compatible with the assumption of **homogeneity of variance**.

Group Statistics

	Treatment Group	N	Mean	Std. Deviation	Std. Error Mean
Number of Hits	Placebo	30	10.06	4.553	.831
	Caffeine	30	12.44	3.719	.679

Output 1. Summary table of the group statistics

The two means are certainly different but are they significantly different? Output 2 summarises the results of the t tests. (This table is actually the transpose of the original table in the SPSS output: the rows of the original table are now shown as columns in Output 2 and vice versa.) Notice that under the name of the dependent variable, Number of Hits, there are two columns, one headed **Equal variances assumed**, the other, on its right, headed **Equal variances not assumed**. The left column gives the result of the classical t test, which uses a pooled estimate of the supposedly constant population variance. The right column gives the result of the test with the **Behrens-Fisher statistic T**, in which the sample variance estimates are not pooled. Notice, too, that although the values of the two statistics are in close agreement, the degrees of freedom of T have been adjusted downwards slightly from 58 to 55.78. (The downward adjustment of the df was made with the **Welch-Satterthwaite formula**.)

Notice that the first two rows of Output 2 refer to **Levene's test**. Levene's test is a test of the assumption of **homogeneity of variance** and its purpose is to help us decide whether to accept the result of the t test in the **Equal variances assumed** column, or the **Equal variances not assumed** column. In Levene's test, the test statistic is F, not t. We shall discuss the F statistic in Chapter 7. For the moment, we need only look at the p-value of F, which is 0.295. Since this p-value is greater than 0.05, the variances can be assumed to be homogeneous and the **Equal Variances** column of values for the t test is the appropriate one to read for the results of the t test.

In this example, both the p-values and the values of t and T agree to several places of decimals. That would not have been the case with disparate sample variances: in some circumstances, the two tests can lead to different decisions about the null hypothesis.

The value of t is negative: -2.217. This is because, when we were completing the **Define Groups** dialog, we entered the code value 2 of the Caffeine group into the slot labelled **Group 2** and the code value 1 of the Placebo group into the slot labelled **Group 1**. As a result, when the difference between the Placebo and Caffeine means and the value of t were calculated, the

Caffeine mean was subtracted from the Placebo mean. Had we entered the value 2 into the **Group 1** slot and the value 1 into the **Group 2** slot, the value of *t* in Output 2 would have been positive, because the Placebo mean would have been subtracted from the Caffeine mean.

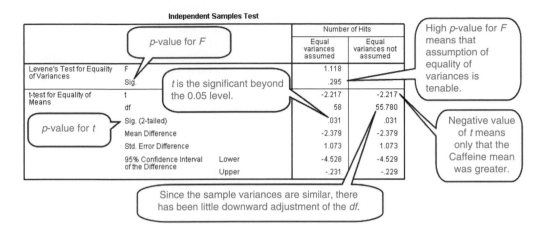

Output 2. T test output for **Independent Samples**

A **confidence interval** is a range of values built around the value of a sample statistic in such a way that in a specified percentage of samples, it would include the true value of the parameter (say the mean, or the difference between means) being estimated. The 95% confidence interval includes the value of the parameter on 95% of occasions; the 99% confidence interval includes the value of the parameter on 99% of occasions. A **confidence** is not a **probability**. A probability refers to a class of outcomes of a hypothetical future experiment of chance, such as tossing a coin, rolling dice or sampling from a population. Here the 'experiment' is over: the sample has been drawn. Think of a confidence interval as a ring that someone has been trying to throw over a fixed upright peg, but we don't know whether the hoop has fallen over the peg or not. The 'confidence' refers to the size of the hoop. We can be more confident that the 99% confidence interval has fallen over the peg than the 95% interval, which is narrower.

If the confidence interval on a statistic such as the mean or the difference between means fails to include the hypothetical value (zero in our example), the null hypothesis is rejected. This is equivalent to saying that the value of the test statistic (*t* or *T*) has fallen within the critical region and the test has shown significance.

The **95% confidence intervals** on the difference between means for the *t* and *T* tests are seen in Output 2 to be [–0.231, –4.528] and [–0.229, –4.529], respectively. The second interval, which does not assume homogeneity of variance, is only very slightly wider than the first. In neither case, does the value 0 (the *ex hypothesi* difference) fall within the confidence interval. (The null hypothesis states that, in the population, the two means are equal.) The *p*-value, however, although lower than 0.05, is greater than 0.01: the t test has shown significance beyond the 0.05 level, but not beyond the 0.01 level.

The 99% confidence intervals on the difference between the means both include zero. If you return to the **Independent-Samples T Test** dialog box and click the **Options** button (Figure

6), you will be able to re-specify the confidence as 99%, instead of the default value 95%. You will find that the 99% confidence intervals for the t and T tests are [–5.238, +0.479] and [–5.241, +0.483], respectively. These confidence intervals both include the value zero.

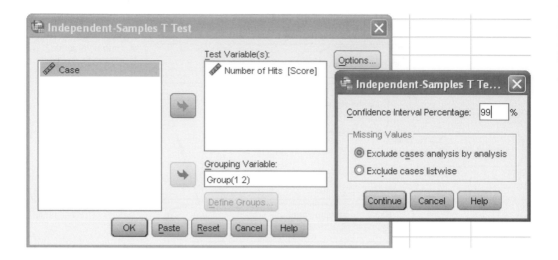

Figure 6. Ordering the 99% confidence interval

6.2.3 Two-tailed and one-tailed *p*-values

In Output 2, the *p*-value is given under the column headed **Sig. (2-tailed)**. In such a **two-tailed** test, the **critical region** for the test statistic is equally divided between the two tails of the distribution, so that the probability, under the null hypothesis, of a value in either tail is 0.025. In other words, we shall reject the null hypothesis if the value of t is either less than the 2.5th percentile or greater than the 97.5th percentile. This is entirely reasonable if the null hypothesis states simply that the two means are equal: a large difference in either direction casts doubt upon H_0 . That is why, although the value of t in Output 2 was negative, we were able to ignore the sign.

If we ignore the sign of t and thus always treat its value as positive, its *p*-value will always lie in the **upper tail** of the distribution of t. This is therefore known as a **one-tailed *p*-value**. But, since, under the null hypothesis, large *negative* values of t are just as likely as large positive values, an absolute value at least as great as the one we have obtained is actually twice as probable as the one-tailed *p*-value. SPSS calculates the **two-tailed *p*-value** by multiplying the one-tailed *p*-value by two.

Advocates of **one-tailed tests** will argue that the alternative hypothesis should coincide with the scientific hypothesis and therefore be directional. So if, as in our example, the researcher expects the Caffeine mean to be higher than, not simply different from, the Placebo mean, the critical region should be placed entirely in the *upper* tail of the distribution: that is, the critical value of t should be the 95th (rather than the 97.5th) percentile of the distribution. Clearly, therefore, the one-tailed t test has greater power to reject the null hypothesis, provided the difference between means is in the expected direction.

The down side of the one-tail approach is this: The one-tail tester must subtract the means in the direction dictated by the scientific hypothesis: the sign of t is now absolutely crucial. If the scientific or **alternative hypothesis H_1** is that μ_2 (the Caffeine mean) is *greater* than μ_1 (the Placebo mean), the null hypothesis H_0, being the negation of H_1, must state that μ_2 is *not* greater than μ_1, that is, H_0 must state that μ_2 is *less than or equal to* μ_1. When calculating the value of t, therefore, you must always subtract the Placebo mean from the Caffeine mean, even if the former has the greater value, in which case t would have a negative value. If t is negative, however large its absolute value, the one-tailed tester must still accept the null hypothesis. The one-tailed test cannot confirm an unexpected result.

6.2.4 Measuring effect size

The mean performance level of the Caffeine group was 2.38 units higher than that of the Placebo mean. We have seen that this is a significant difference; but is it also a *substantial* difference? Is it worth reporting as a contribution to scientific knowledge?

Cohen's d statistic

For the simple two-group between subjects experiment, Cohen (1988) suggested as a measure of effect size the statistic d, where

$$d = \frac{\mu_1 - \mu_2}{\sigma} \quad \text{- - - (1)} \quad \textbf{Cohen's effect size index}$$

Since Cohen's measure expresses the difference between the two population means in units of standard deviation, studies in which the same dependent variable has been measured in different units can be compared. Cohen's measure d is therefore used extensively in **meta-analysis**, the combination of statistics from several independent studies with a view to integrating all the evidence into a coherent body of knowledge. Cohen's index d was defined in terms of parameters, rather than statistics; but in practice, the parameters μ_1, μ_2 and σ are estimated from the means of the two samples and an estimate of the supposedly homogeneous population standard deviation.

As our estimate of σ, we can use the square root of the pooled variance estimate in the independent samples t test which, when the sample sizes are equal, is simply the mean of the two sample variances. Using the values given in Output 1, we have

$$s_{\text{pooled}} = \sqrt{\frac{s_1^2 + s_2^2}{2}} = \sqrt{\frac{4.553^2 + 3.719^2}{2}} = 4.157$$

Now, substituting the sample means in Output 1 and the pooled estimate of the standard deviation we have just calculated into formula (1), we have

$$d = \frac{M_1 - M_2}{s_{\text{pooled}}} = \frac{12.44 - 10.06}{4.157} = 0.57$$

We should note that if the sample sizes are unequal, the calculation of s_{pooled} is a little more complicated:

$$s_{\text{pooled}} = \sqrt{\frac{s_1^2(n_1-1) + s_2^2(n_2-1)}{n_1+n_2-2}} \quad \text{- - - (2)}$$

Making a pooled estimate of σ
when the sample sizes are unequal

You can see from formula (2) that in our estimate, we are weighting the contribution of each sample variance with its relative contribution to the total degrees of freedom of the t statistic. In this example, however, each sample variance will have a weighting of 0.5, so if you substitute the values in Output 1 into formula (2), you will get exactly the same value for the estimate of the pooled standard deviation as we did by simply taking the square root of the mean of the two sample variances.

If we already have the value of t, we can obtain that of Cohen's d very quickly from the following formula, in which n is the size of each sample:

$$d = t\sqrt{2/n} \quad \text{- - - (3)}$$

Obtaining the value of d from that of t

When we tested the difference between the means of the Caffeine and Placebo groups, we found that $t = 2.217$. From formula (1), found that $d = 0.57$. Applying formula (3) to this value of t, we have $d = t\sqrt{(2/n)} = 2.217\sqrt{(1/15)} = 0.57$, as before.

Interpreting values of *d*

On the basis of a study of a considerable body of published literature, Cohen (1962, 1988) has suggested a categorisation of effect size as shown in Table 1:

Table 1. Cohen's categories of effect size

Effect size (*d*)	Size of Effect	In words, …
$0.2 \leq d < 0.5$	Small	Less than 0.2 is Trivial
$0.5 \leq d < 0.8$	Medium	0.2 to 0.5 is Small
$d \geq 0.8$	Large	0.5 to 0.8 is Medium 0.8 or more is Large

Our value of d for the caffeine experiment is 0.57. Our experiment, therefore, has found caffeine to have a 'Medium' effect upon performance.

6.2.5   Reporting the results of a statistical test

Your research report may be read by someone who may not agree with your statistical analysis of the results. The general principle to follow is to try to provide the reader with sufficient information to understand exactly what you have done, so that they will be free to make up their own minds about the implications of the results of your study.

You may, for instance, have decided to make a one-tailed test. If so, your report must make it clear that your reported p-value is the *one-tailed* p-value, so that your reader, who may not accept your justification for a one-tailed test, is free to multiply the given value by two and evaluate your results accordingly.

Provide the descriptives

The reader should never be confronted with a bald statement of the results of a statistical test (or, worse, a list of test results) without also being given access, on the same page, to the corresponding descriptive statistics. Where possible, the descriptives should be given in the same paragraph as the test results; but failing that, they should appear in a table nearby, so that the reader can fully understand the meaning of the test result.

Provide a full report

It is insufficient merely to report that a t test has found a difference to be significant. Your report must include, not only the value of t, but also the p-value, the degrees of freedom and a statement of whether the result is significant and beyond which level. There should also be some measure of effect size. Confidence intervals can also be informative. When reporting the results of a t test, for example, include the value of Cohen's d or an equivalent index. This will allow the reader to appraise your results in relation to those reported by other researchers and evaluate them accordingly.

The p-value should be reported to two or three places of decimals, even for non-significant results. (The examples given in the APA Handbook imply that values should be given to two decimal places; but this is not explicitly stated and, arguably, three places of decimals is more appropriate.) A reported p-value of 0.951, for example, conveys the important information that the result of the test came nowhere near significance; whereas a value of 0.062, although statistically insignificant, casts some doubt upon the null hypothesis – especially if a scarcity of data indicates that the test was of low **power**.

Very small p-values should be reported as inequalities (<) thus: ' $p < .01$'; or, if the writer is reporting p-values to three places of decimals, '$p < .001$'. (The APA examples omit the leading zero from a decimal fraction such as 0.01. In our sample reports, therefore, we shall do likewise.)

A sample report

The t test that we have just carried out on the results of the caffeine experiment might be reported as follows:

'The mean score of the Caffeine group (M = 12.44; SD = 3.719) was significantly higher than that of the Placebo group (M = 10.06; SD = 4.553): $t(58) = 2.217$; $p = .031$ (two-tailed). Cohen's $d = .57$, a 'medium' effect. This result confirms the hypothesis that shooting accuracy is improved by the ingestion of caffeine.'

Some reviewers and journal editors like reports to contain confidence intervals (see Appendix) as well. Confidence intervals are included in the SPSS output. A confidence interval is equivalent to a test of significance, in the sense that if a difference is significant beyond, say, the 0.05 level, but not beyond the 0.01 level, the 95% confidence interval will not include zero, but the 99% interval will. A confidence interval, moreover, provides a whole range of possible values for the true population difference, any of which is compatible with the results of a particular study. Clearly, therefore, a confidence interval can be a useful addition to the report.

6.3   THE RELATED-SAMPLES (OR PAIRED-SAMPLES) T TEST

In an experiment on lateralisation of cortical functioning, a participant looks at a central spot on a computer screen and is told to press a key on recognition of a word that may appear on either side of the spot.

The experimental hypothesis is that words presented in the right visual field will be more quickly recognised than those in the left visual field, because the former are processed by the left cerebral hemisphere, which is thought to be better adapted to the processing of verbal information. For each participant, the median response time to forty words in both the right and the left visual fields is recorded, as indicated in Table 2. (The data are available in the file *Visual Field 5thApril2011.sav*, on our website at http://www.psypress.com/spss-made-simple.)

Also shown in Table 2 are the differences resulting from subtracting the right field scores from the left field scores. As the researcher had hoped, there is indeed a clear tendency for the differences to be positive, that is, the right field times are generally shorter.

Here, since each participant was tested with words in both visual hemifields, we have two **related** (or **paired**) samples of scores. A **related-samples *t* test** is therefore appropriate. (SPSS refers to this test as the **paired-samples t test**.)

Table 2. Median reaction times for words presented in the left and right visual fields

Case	Left Field	Right Field	Difference (d)
1	323	304	19
2	512	493	19
3	502	491	11
4	385	365	20
5	453	426	27
6	343	320	23
7	543	523	20
8	440	442	− 2
9	682	580	102
10	590	564	26

6.3.1 Preparing the data file

Proceed as follows:

- Open **Variable View** and type in the variable names *Case*, *Left_Field* and *Right_Field*. To improve the output, add less cryptic variable *labels*, such as Case Number, Left Visual Field and Right Visual Field.

- Now switch to **Data View** (which will now show the variable names) and enter the data.

Notice that, since in this example the same participants perform under both the Left Visual Field and the Right Visual Field conditions, there is no grouping variable. Notice too that there has been no opportunity either to name or to label the dependent variable, Median Reaction Time. You won't be able to do that until you complete the ANOVA dialog.

6.3.2 Exploring the data

Since each participant has p   consistency
in level of performance acrc   words in the

Left Visual Field should also be among the quickest with words in the Right Visual Field; those who are slowest in Left Visual Field recognition should also be among the slowest in Right Visual Field recognition. We can therefore expect a **positive correlation** between reaction times under Left Visual Field and Right Visual Field conditions. This positive correlation should be evident from the appearance of the scatterplot of Left_Field against Right-Field, or vice versa (Output 3).

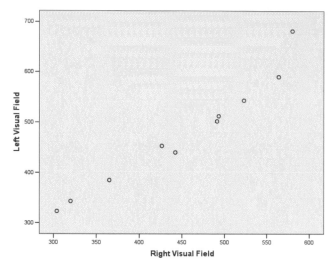

Output 3. The scatterplot of Left Visual Field against Right Visual Field

6.3.3 Running the *t* test

Proceed as follows:

- Choose **Analyze➜Compare Means➜Paired-Samples T Test ...** to open the **Paired-Samples T Test** dialog box, which is shown with dialog completed in Figure 7.

- Transfer the variable labels to the **Paired Variables** box on the right of the dialog as described in Figure 7. (They can be selected in pairs by using the Control button and transferred together to the **Paired Variables** panel.)

- Click **OK**.

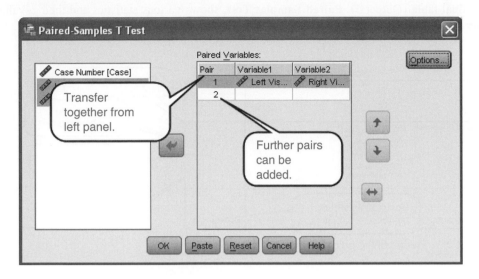

Figure 7. The **Paired-Samples T Test** dialog box

6.3.4 Interpreting the output

Since it is possible to run *t* tests on several pairs of variables at the same time, the output specifies the pair under consideration in each sub-table. In this example, there is only one pair. The upper part of Output 4, **Paired Samples Statistics**, tabulates the statistics for each variable in the pair. The second output table (lower part of Output 4), **Paired Samples Correlations,** gives the value of the correlation coefficient, which is 0.97.

Paired Samples Statistics

		Mean	N	Std. Deviation	Std. Error Mean
Pair 1	Left Visual Field	477.30	10	112.09	35.45
	Right Visual Field	450.80	10	97.09	30.70

Paired Samples Correlations

		N	Correlation	Sig.
Pair 1	Left Visual Field & Right Visual Field	10	.97	.00

Output 4. Paired samples statistics and correlations

The final table (Output 5), **Paired Samples Test,** shows various statistics and their *p*-values. (The table is the transpose of the original in the SPSS output.)

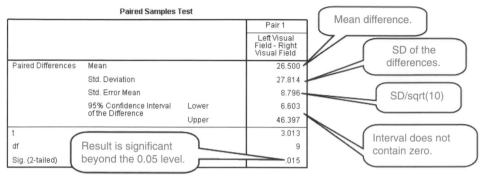

Output 5.   Result of the paired samples T test

The 95% confidence interval on the difference between the means excludes zero. Were you, however, to specify the 99% confidence interval (by clicking the **Options** button and changing the default setting),   you would find that the interval included zero: the test has shown significance beyond the 0.05 level, but not the 0.01 level.

6.3.5 Measuring effect size

As with the independent samples *t* test, effect size can be measured with the Cohen's *d* statistic, where *d* is estimated with

$$d = \frac{M_1 - M_2}{s_{pooled}}$$

From the upper table in Output 4, we have

$$s_{pooled} = \sqrt{\frac{s_1^2 + s_2^2}{2}} = \sqrt{\frac{112.09^2 + 97.09^2}{2}} = 104.86$$

Substituting the values in Output 4 and our estimate of the population standard deviation into formula (1), we have

$$d = \frac{M_1 - M_2}{s_{pooled}} = \frac{477.30 - 450.80}{104.86} = 0.25$$

From Table 1, we see that this is a 'small' effect – only a quarter of a standard deviation.

6.3.6 Reporting the results of the test

We can report the results of the test as follows.

> 'The mean response latency for the Left Visual Field (M = 477.30, SD = 112.09) was greater than the mean for the Right Visual Field (M = 450.80, SD = 97.09). A related-samples *t* test showed significance beyond the .05 level: t(9) = 3.01; p = .02 (two-tailed). The 95% confidence interval on the difference was [6.60, 46.40], which does not include the value of zero specified by the null hypothesis. Cohen's *d* = .25, which is a small effect.'

6.3.7 A one-sample test

The related-samples *t* test is actually a **one-sample test**. The null hypothesis of equality of the two treatment means is restated as the proposition that we have a single sample from a population of differences *d* with a mean of zero. All the statements in Output 5, therefore, refer to the set of *differences d*, rather than the raw scores *X*.

Notice the entry labelled 'Std. Error Mean'. Its value, 8.80, was obtained as follows:

$$s_{M_d} = \frac{s_d}{\sqrt{n}} = \frac{27.81}{\sqrt{10}} = 8.80$$

We see that the value of *t* (on 9 degrees of freedom) is 3.01, and that the *p*-value, 'Sig. (2-tailed)', is 0.015. The result of the *t* test is significant beyond the 0.05 level.

6.4   NONPARAMETRIC TESTS

The *t* test is an example of a **parametric test**: that is, it is assumed that the data are samples from two normally distributed populations with the same variance. Other tests, known as **nonparametric tests**, are based upon models of the data that make fewer assumptions about the population distributions. (Nonparametric models do not assume normality of distribution; nor do they assume homogeneity of variance. They do, however, assume homogeneity of distribution shape.) A nonparametric alternative to the independent-samples *t* test is the **Mann-Whitney U test**. (An equivalent test is the **Wilcoxon Rank Sum Test**.) Two nonparametric alternatives to the related-samples *t* test are the **Wilcoxon Signed-Ranks test** and the **Sign test**.

Planned experiments usually produce scale or continuous data; although data in the form of ratings are not uncommon in areas such as experimental aesthetics. With data in the form of ratings, many journal editors would insist that you use a nonparametric test, rather than a *t* test.

Occasionally, one might run an experiment in which each participant attempts a task and either a pass or a fail is recorded. If so, a two-group experiment will yield two independent samples of **nominal data**. Here the research question is still one of the significance of a difference, albeit the difference between two relative frequencies, rather than the difference between two means. With independent samples, a **chi-square test for association** will answer the question of whether the success rates in the two groups are significantly different (see Chapter 11).

Most nonparametric methods are more resistant to the influence of outliers and skewness than are their parametric counterparts. The disadvantage is a loss in the power of the test to reject the null hypothesis should that be false. This is likely to be a real issue with the sorts of small, badly behaved data sets upon which the researcher is most likely to consider running nonparametric tests rather than a *t* test.

With large samples, several of the most common nonparametric test statistics have sampling distributions approximating to known continuous distributions and the approximation is close enough to provide serviceable estimates of *p*-values. (The term **asymptotic** means that the approximation to the theoretical distribution becomes ever closer as the sample size grows larger.) With small samples, however, the approximation can be very poor and the incautious user runs a heightened risk of making a false inference.

Fortunately, as well as providing approximate, **asymptotic** *p*-values, SPSS can also compute **exact** *p*-values. We recommend that, when the data are scarce, you should report the exact *p*-values for nonparametric tests, rather than the asymptotic *p*-values.

6.4.1   Nonparametric tests in SPSS

SPSS offers a wide selection of nonparametric tests, which can be accessed through the **Nonparametric Tests** menu (Figure 8).

Figure 8.   The **Nonparametric Tests** menu

The choices **One Sample...**, **Independent Samples...** and **Related Samples...** were introduced in SPSS 18. They offer a considerably wider range of tests and options than do the older **Legacy Dialogs**. (The Legacy Dialogs, however, are still very convenient and useful; in fact, they sometimes contain information that is missing from the more recent output.)

6.4.2   Independent samples: the Mann-Whitney U test

Once again, we shall use the caffeine data, which are available in the file *Caffeine experiment(60).sav*, at http://www.psypress.com/spss-made-simple.   (We would not normally consider running a nonparametric test with such a substantial and well-behaved data set, but the comparison between the outcomes of the two tests is informative.)

- Choose **Analyze➜Nonparametric Tests➜Independent Samples...** to open the **Nonparametric Tests: Two or More Independent Samples** dialog box (Figure 9). You will find that you are in the dialog under the **Objective** tab. The default settings there can be left as they are.

- Click the **Fields** tab to specify the IV and the DV (Figure 10). This step is *essential*.

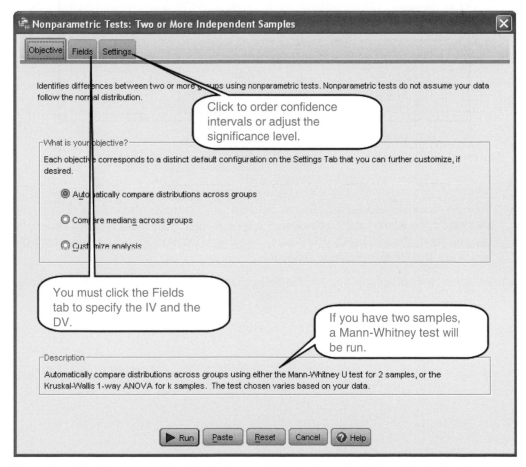

Figure 9.   The **Nonparametric Tests: Two or More Independent Samples** dialog box

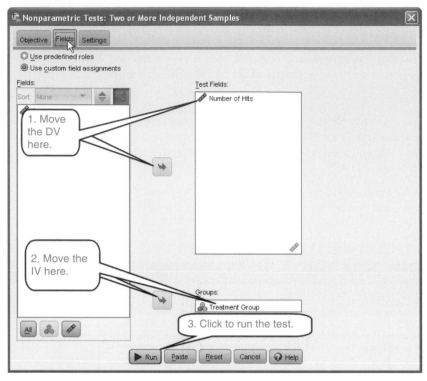

Figure 10.   Specifying the **Test Fields** and **Groups** variables

- To order a confidence interval, click the **Settings** tab.   In the **Settings** dialog (Figure 11), check the radio button labelled **Customize tests** and check the **Mann-Whitney** option. In the panel at the bottom labelled **Estimate Confidence Interval across Groups**, check the button labelled **Hodges-Lehman estimate**.

- Click the **Run** button at the foot of the dialog to run the Mann-Whitney test and obtain the confidence interval.

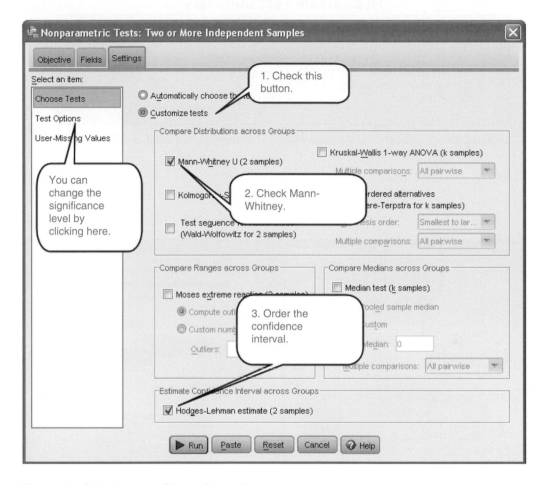

Figure 11. Ordering a confidence interval

6.4.3 Output from the Mann-Whitney U test

The initial output is shown in Output 6. The initial display gives the asymptotic p-value as 0.035, which is only slightly greater than the p-value from the t test. To obtain more details about the results of the test, double-click the table in Output 6 to see the **Model Viewer** (Output 7).

Hypothesis Test Summary

	Null Hypothesis	Test	Sig.	Decision
1	The distribution of Number of Hits is the same across categories of Treatment Group.	Independent-Samples Mann-Whitney U Test	.035	Reject the null hypothesis.

Asymptotic significances are displayed. The significance level is .05.

Output 6.   The initial output of the **Mann-Whitney U test**

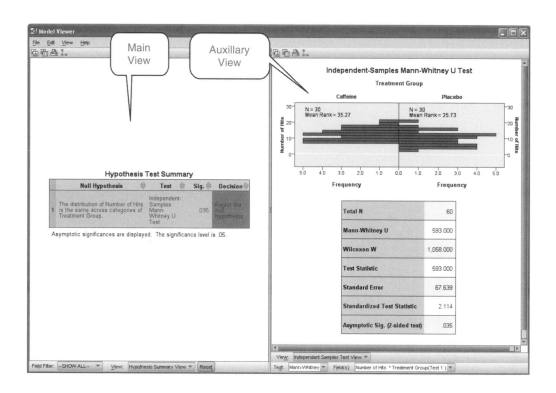

Output 7.   The **Model Viewer**

The **Model Viewer**, like the **SPSS Statistics Viewer**, is divided into two panes separated by a vertical border. The left-hand pane, which is known as the **main view**, contains the table that appeared in the Output Viewer. The right-hand pane, known as the **auxiliary view**, contains the details of the results of the test: the value of the U statistic, the standardised test statistic and so on. In addition, there is a **population pyramid**, consisting of back-to-back histograms of the distributions of the scores in the Caffeine and Placebo groups.

At the foot of the main view is a drop-down menu, which is set initially at **Hypothesis Summary View**. Click on the arrow to obtain the **Confidence Interval Summary View**, as shown in Figure 12.

Figure 12. Bringing the confidence interval to Main View

Confidence Interval Summary

Confidence Interval Type	Parameter	Estimate	95% Confidence Interval	
			Lower	Upper
Independent-Samples Hodges-Lehman Median Difference	Difference between medians of Number of Hits across categories of Treatment Group.	-2.495	-4.728	-.187

Output 8. The Hodges-Lehman confidence interval

The confidence interval is shown in Output 8. The interval is [–4.728, –0.187], which does not include zero. This is consistent with the finding that the *p*-value from the Mann-Whitney test is less than 0.05. Were you to click **Test Options** and reset the confidence interval to 99%, however, you would obtain the interval [–5.488, 0.539], which does include the value 0. This is exactly what we should expect, given that the test has shown significance beyond the 0.05 level, but not the 0.01 level.

6.4.4 Exact tests

The small data set in the lower part of Figure 13 was obtained by running the Syntax in the upper part of the table.

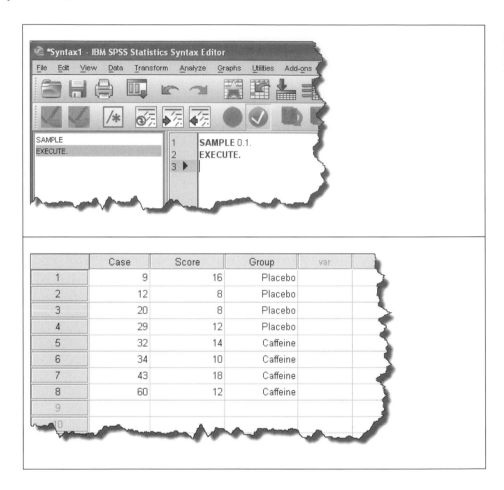

Figure 13.   A small data set obtained from the caffeine data by running Syntax

If you run the Mann-Whitney test on these data, Auxiliary View (Output 9) will show, in addition to the asymptotic p-value, the **exact p-value**.

Total N	8
Mann-Whitney U	11.000
Wilcoxon W	21.000
Test Statistic	11.000
Standard Error	3.464
Standardized Test Statistic	.866
Asymptotic Sig. (2-sided test)	.386
Exact Sig. (2-sided test)	.486

Output 9.   The exact p-value for the **Mann-Whitney U test** is included when the samples are small

6.4.5 Effect size

At this point, we should perhaps say that we would normally consider running a nonparametric test on a small unruly data set only, especially one consisting of ratings. With ratings data, the variance estimates are highly constrained and depend very much upon how near the group means are to the ends of the rating scale. With such data, measures such as Cohen's d may be inappropriate.

Several indices of effect size for use with the Mann-Whitney U test have been proposed. Let M_1 and M_2 be the mean ranks for Group 1 and Group 2, respectively. As a measure of effect size, King and Minium (2003) advocate the **Glass rank biserial correlation coefficient r_g**, where

$$r_g = \frac{2(M_1 - M_2)}{n_1 + n_2} \quad \text{- - - (4)}$$

The Glass rank biserial correlation coefficient

Note that in formula (4), M_1 and M_2 are the mean **ranks** of the scores in the two groups, not the means of the original scores. In the denominator, n_1 and n_2 are the sizes of the two samples.

The mean ranks are not included in the output from the new **Independent Samples** procedure (they are included in the output from the Legacy dialog); but they can easily be obtained by converting all the scores to ranks, and then using the Means procedure.   In our current example,

$$r_g = \frac{2(M_1 - M_2)}{n_1 + n_2} = \frac{2(35.27 - 25.73)}{60} = +0.318$$

Cohen (1988) offers guidelines for interpreting the value of a correlation. Table 3 below is an interpretation of Cohen's guidelines. It is clear from the table that the obtained difference in mean ranks is an effect of 'medium' size.

In Chapter 11, it is explained that, although the value of a correlation is in itself a perfectly good measure of effect strength, the square of the correlation, which is termed the **coefficient of determination** is also useful, because it measures the proportion of the total variance of either variable that is shared between the two variables. (In Chapter 12, we shall also see that the coefficient of determination is the proportion of the variance of one variable that is accounted for or explained by **regression** upon another variable.)

6.4.6 The report

The report of the result of the significance test should include not only the details of the test statistic and the p-value, but also a measure of effect size, such as Glass's rank correlation coefficient.

Your report of the results of the **Mann-Whitney U test** might read as follows:

'The median number of hits for the Placebo group (Median = 10.06, Range = 18.00) was less than the median number of hits for the Caffeine group (Median = 12.42, Range = 14.00). A Mann-Whitney U test showed this difference to be significant: U = 593; $p < .035$ (two-tailed). The Glass rank biserial correlation = +.318, a medium effect in Cohen's (1988) classification.'

Table 3. Guidelines (from Cohen, 1988) for classifying association strength, as measured by a correlation coefficient

Absolute value of r	r squared	Size of effect
$0.1 \leq r < 0.30$	$0.01 \leq r^2 < 0.09$	**Small**
$0.30 \leq r < 0.50$	$0.09 \leq r^2 < 0.25$	**Medium**
$r \geq 0.50$	$r^2 \geq 0.25$	**Large**

A correlation less than 0.1 is TRIVIAL.

A correlation between 0.1 and 0.3 is SMALL. Between 1% and 8% of the variance is shared.

A correlation between 0.3 and 0.5 is MEDIUM. Between 9% and 25% of the variance is shared.

A correlation of 0.5 or greater is LARGE. At least 25% of the variance is shared.

6.5   THE WILCOXON MATCHED-PAIRS TEST

We shall turn now to the comparison of performance levels when the data are from an experiment of **within subjects** design, that is each participant is tested under both conditions. (The data are available at http://www.psypress.com/spss-made-simple. in the file *Visual Field 5thApril2011.sav*.)

The **Wilcoxon Matched-Pairs Test** is applicable to data of this kind and carries fewer assumptions about the distribution of the data than does the related-samples (or paired samples) *t* test.

6.5.1 The Wilcoxon matched-pairs test in SPSS

With the lateralisation data in **Data View**,

- Choose **Analyze➜Nonparametric Tests➜Related Samples...** to obtain the **Nonparametric Tests: Two or More Related Samples** dialog box (which is similar to the one for independent samples).

- Click the **Fields** tab to open the next dialog box (Figure 15). Transfer both Left Visual Field and Right Visual Field to the Test Fields box. (There is no grouping variable.)

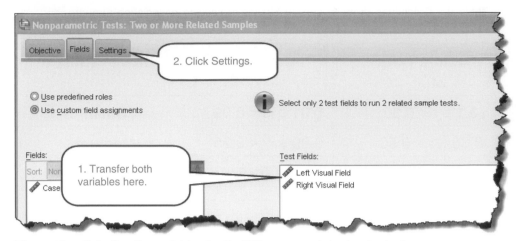

Figure 15.   Selecting the variables for the **Wilcoxon matched-pairs** test

- Click the **Settings** Tab to specify the tests and order a confidence interval (Figure 16).

- Click **Run**.

6.5.2 The output

The initial output (Output 10) summarises the result of the test. Notice that the null hypothesis is about the medians (not the means) of the populations. The null hypothesis must be rejected: the *p*-value is 0.007.

Hypothesis Test Summary

	Null Hypothesis	Test	Sig.	Decision
1	The median of differences between Left Visual Field and Right Visual Field equals 0.	Related-Samples Wilcoxon Signed Ranks Test	.007	Reject the null hypothesis.

Asymptotic significances are displayed. The significance level is .05.

Output 10. The initial output of the **Two Related Samples** test

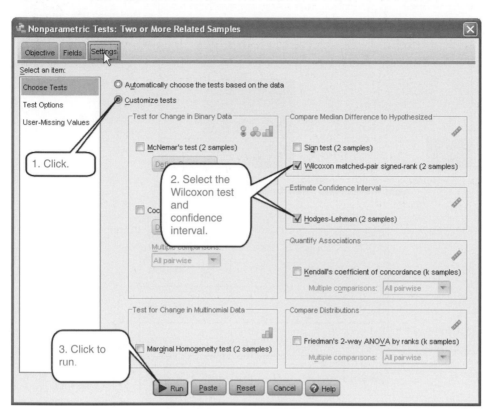

Figure 16. Selecting the variables for the **Wilcoxon matched-pairs** test

The auxiliary view (right-hand pane) of the **Model Viewer** (Output 11) is obtained by double-clicking on Output 10.

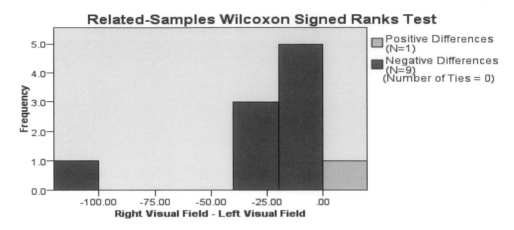

Output 11. The auxiliary view of the Model Viewer for the **Wilcoxon test**

In the **Wilcoxon test**, each participant's score under the Right Visual Field condition is paired with the same person's score under the Left Visual Field condition. A set of difference scores is obtained by consistently subtracting the Left Visual Field score in each pair from the Right Visual Field score. The histogram in Output 11 shows that in 9 out of 10 cases, the Left Visual Field score was greater than that for the Right Visual Field. The differences are then ranked in order of their *absolute* values: that is, they are ranked in order of magnitude, regardless of sign. The signs are then restored and the sums of the positive and negative ranks calculated. The test statistic W is the smaller of the two sums of ranks of the same sign: in this case, $W = 1$.

The asymptotic *p*-value (**Asymptotic Sig.**) specifies the two-tailed *p*-value for the test statistic. Clearly the test has shown significance beyond the 0.01 level.

In the main view (left-hand pane) of the Model Viewer, click **Confidence Interval Summary View** at the foot of the Viewer to obtain the **Hodges-Lehman confidence interval** (Output 12).

Confidence Interval Summary

Confidence Interval Type	Parameter	Estimate	95% Confidence Interval	
			Lower	Upper
Related-Samples Hodges-Lehman Median Difference	Median of the difference between Left Visual Field and Right Visual Field.	-21.000	-56.500	-12.000

Output 12. The Hodges-Lehman 95% confidence interval

The 95% confidence interval is [–56.5, –12.00], which does not include the value zero. Try changing the settings and running the test again, with the significance level set at 0.01 and the confidence interval at 99%. The 99% confidence interval is shown in Output 13.

Confidence Interval Summary

Confidence Interval Type	Parameter	Estimate	99% Confidence Interval	
			Lower	Upper
Related-Samples Hodges-Lehman Median Difference	Median of the difference between Left Visual Field and Right Visual Field.	-21.000	-64.000	-8.500

Output 13. The Hodges-Lehman 99% confidence interval

The 99% confidence interval is [–64.00, –8.50]. This interval, although considerably wider than the 95% interval, still excludes zero, which is consistent with the very low *p*-value of 0.007.

6.5.3 Effect size

As a measure of effect size following the Wilcoxon Matched-Pairs test, King and Minium (2003; p.457) prescribe the **matched-pairs rank biserial correlation**. If the sums of the positive and negative ranks are R_+ and R_-, respectively, T is the smaller of these two values, and N is the number of pairs of scores, the formula for the correlation r is:

$$r = \frac{4\left|T - \left(\frac{R_+ + R_-}{2}\right)\right|}{N(N+1)} \quad \text{- - - (5)}$$

The matched-pairs rank biserial correlation

In formula (5), the vertical lines denote the absolute value of the expression inside: that is, even if the difference is negative, the value is treated as if it were positive.

The output from the **Related Samples** procedure does not include the sums of the positive and negative ranks; though they can, of course, be obtained by a series of **Compute Variable** commands. Easier by far is to choose **Analyze➜Nonparametric Tests➜Legacy Dialogs➜2 Related Samples…** and run the Wilcoxon Test, obtaining the table shown in Output 14.

Ranks

		N	Mean Rank	Sum of Ranks
Right Visual Field - Left Visual Field	Negative Ranks	9[a]	6.00	54.00
	Positive Ranks	1[b]	1.00	1.00
	Ties	0[c]		
	Total	10		

a. Right Visual Field < Left Visual Field
b. Right Visual Field > Left Visual Field
c. Right Visual Field = Left Visual Field

Output 14. The Ranks table from Output of the **2 Related Samples** procedure from the **Legacy Dialogs**

Substituting the values given in Output 14 into formula (5), we have

$$r = \frac{4\left|T - \left(\frac{R_+ + R_-}{2}\right)\right|}{N(N+1)} = \frac{4\left|1 - \left(\frac{1+54}{2}\right)\right|}{10(11)} = 0.96$$

Since this index of effect size measure is a correlation, we don't need any table to see immediately that this is very strong effect indeed.

6.5.4 The report

In Output 11, the Standardized Test Statistic is the basis of the asymptotic p-value. (Should you want the exact p-value, you would have to use the **2 Related Samples** procedure in the **Legacy Dialogs**, in which an exact test is an option.) Your report of the results of this test might read as follows:

'A Wilcoxon matched-pairs, signed ranks test showed that the difference between the median response time for words presented in the left visual field (Md = 477.50 ms, Range = 359ms, Min, max = 323, 682) and the right visual field (Md = 466.50 ms; Range = 276 ms, Min, max = 304, 580) was significant beyond the .01 level: exact $p < .01$ (two-tailed). The sums of ranks were 54 and 1 for the negative and positive ranks, respectively, therefore $W = 1$. The matched-pairs rank biserial correlation is .96, which (in Cohen' classification) is a 'large' effect.'

6.6   THE SIGN AND BINOMIAL TESTS

While the Wilcoxon matched pairs test assumes neither normality of distribution nor homogeneity of variance, it does assume that, in the population, the positive and negative differences have identical distributions. Like the Mann-Whitney test, the Wilcoxon test is vulnerable to the influence of extreme scores or outliers. In this subsection, we shall describe a test which makes no assumptions whatever about the original distributions.

The **sign test** is yet another alternative to the related- or paired-samples t test, and is applicable to a data set such as the hemifield data. (This test is actually an application of the **binomial test**, which we shall describe later in this section.) When used with scale or continuous data, the sign test jettisons even more information from the raw data than does the Wilcoxon Matched-pairs test, with an even greater reduction in power.

Recall that in the related-samples t test, the basis of the analysis is a column of difference scores, obtained by consistently subtracting Left Visual Field scores from the Right Visual Field scores (or vice-versa). In the Wilcoxon Matched-Pairs Test, those differences were transformed to ranks and the test statistic was the smaller of the sums of the negative and positive ranks. In the sign test, the only information used is the *signs* of the ranks, so that the starting point for the test is a string of pluses and minuses (Table 4).

Table 4. The table of differences

Difference (d)	Sign
−19	−
−19	−
−11	−
−20	−
−27	−
−23	−
−20	−
+ 2	+
−102	−
−26	−

If the null hypothesis is true and the populations of response times for the right and left visual fields are identical, there should, in the long run, be as many positive signs as there are negative signs: that is, the proportion of either sign in the population of signs should be 0.5. Even in this small data set, this null hypothesis seems false, but a formal test is necessary to confirm the pattern of predominance of positive signs.

6.6.1 The sign test in SPSS

With the hemifield data in **Data View**,

- Choose **Analyze➔Nonparametric Tests➔Related Samples...** to obtain the **Nonparametric Tests: Two or More Related Samples** dialog box (not shown).

- Click the **Fields** tab and transfer the variables in the usual way.

- Click the **Settings** tab to open the dialog box for selecting a test, check the **Customize tests** radio button and select **Sign Test**.

- Click **Run** to run the Sign test.

Output for the sign test

The result of the sign test is shown in Outputs 15 and 16. The exact p-value is 0.021, so there is evidence against the null hypothesis; the asymptotic p-value (0.027) also shows significance well beyond the 0.05 level.

Hypothesis Test Summary

	Null Hypothesis	Test	Sig.	Decision
1	The median of differences between Right Visual Field and Left Visual Field equals 0.	Related-Samples Sign Test	.021[1]	Reject the null hypothesis.

Asymptotic significances are displayed. The significance level is .05.

[1]Exact significance is displayed for this test.

Output 15. The initial output in the **SPSS Statistics Viewer** for the sign test

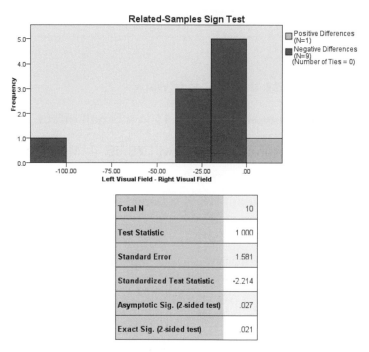

Total N	10
Test Statistic	1.000
Standard Error	1.581
Standardized Test Statistic	-2.214
Asymptotic Sig. (2-sided test)	.027
Exact Sig. (2-sided test)	.021

1. The exact p-value is computed based on the binomial distribution because there are 25 or fewer cases.

Output 16. The auxiliary view of the **Model Viewer**

Effect size

As an index of effect size following the binomial and sign tests, Cohen (1988; pp.147–151) suggests the statistic g, which is the difference between P, the proportion of outcomes in the target category and p, the probability of the outcome under the null hypothesis:

$$g = |P - p| \quad \text{- - - (6)}$$

Cohen's Effect size index (two-sided) for binomial test

To evaluate a value of g, Cohen suggests that we can regard the values 0.05, 0.15 and 0.25 as Small, Medium and Large effects, respectively. This advice can be interpreted as shown in Table 5.

Table 5. Guidelines (from Cohen, 1988) for interpreting the effect size index g

Value of g	Size of effect
$0.05 \leq g < 0.15$	Small
$0.15 \leq g < 0.25$	Medium
$g \geq 0.25$	Large

In words …

A value less than .05 is trivial.

A value between .05 and .15 is a Small effect.

A value between .15 and .25 is a Medium effect.

A value of at least .25 is a Large effect.

Output 16 shows that 90% of participants showed negative difference scores; whereas the proportion under the null hypothesis is 0.5. Substituting in formula (6), we have

$$g = |P - p| = 0.9 - 0.5 = 0.4$$

which, according to Table 5 is a 'Large' effect.

Our report of the results of the sign test might read as follows:

> 'The Median response time was higher for words presented in the left visual field (Md = 477.50 ms, Range = 359ms, Min, max = 323, 682) than it was for words in the right visual field (Md = 466.50 ms; Range = 276 ms, Min, max = 304, 580). When the response times for the left visual field were consistently subtracted from those for the right visual field, there were nine negative differences and one positive difference. A sign test showed an exact p-value of .02. Cohen's g = .4, a large effect.'

6.6.2   Bernoulli trials: the binomial test

If a coin is tossed, say, 20 times, and the outcome (H or T) is noted each time, we may end up with a sequence such as H, H, T, T, T, T, H, T, T, T, H, H, T, H, H, T, T, T, H, H.

This set of trials has the following properties:

1.   There is a *fixed number* of identical experiments or trials.

2.   The outcomes of every trial can be divided into the same two *dichotomous categories*, one of which can be regarded as a 'success', the other as a 'failure'. ('Heads you win, tails you lose.')

3.   The outcomes of the trials are *independent*.

4.   The probability of a 'success' is *the same on all trials*. If the coin is fair, that fixed probability is 0.5.

Such a series is known as a set of **Bernoulli trials**. Note that property (2) does not imply that there are only two possible outcomes, only that we can divide the outcomes into two mutually exclusive categories.   Suppose that a candidate sitting a 50-question multiple-choice examination with six alternatives per question were (having no knowledge of the topic) to choose the answer by rolling a die each time. In that case, although there are six outcomes per question, they can be classified dichotomously into Pass (with a probability of 1/6) and Fail (with a probability of 5/6). Here too, we have a set of Bernoulli trials.

The **binomial probability model** enables us to assign probabilities to specified numbers of heads or tails over n Bernoulli trials. Is a coin biased? Suppose we were to obtain 16 heads in 20 tosses. The binomial model can give us the probability, given that $p = 0.5$, of obtaining more than 15 heads or fewer than five heads in 20 tosses. If that probability is less than 0.05, we have evidence against the claim that the coin is fair.

Returning to the hemifield example and supposing that the null hypothesis is true, we can think of the random selection of ten participants for the experiment as ten Bernoulli trials, because on each trial we can classify the outcome in the same way as + or − . If there is indeed no tendency in the population for response times to be different for the right and left visual fields, the probability of a + (or a –) on each trial is 0.5. In our experiment, we obtained nine – signs and one + sign. The binomial model shows that the two-tailed probability of such a bias under the null hypothesis is less than 0.05. (The 'two-tailed *p*-value' is obtained by multiplying the probability of at least nine minus signs by two. We shall want to report a marked difference between the hemifield scores, regardless of direction.)

As a second example, suppose that a researcher wants to know whether 5-year-old children of a certain age show a preference for one of two toys (A or B). The choices of one hundred 5-year-olds are noted, of whom 60 choose toy A and 40 toy B. Can we confirm the apparent preference for toy A by means of a formal statistical test?

If the null hypothesis is true so that, in the population, there is no tendency for children to prefer toy A, we can regard the selection of the children and the noting of the preference (A or B) of each child as a set of 100 Bernoulli trials. Under the null hypothesis, the probability of any child preferring toy A is ½ . The binomial probability model can give us the probability that at least 60 children (or less than 40 children) would say that they preferred toy A.

We should note that, in the sign test, the application of the binomial probability model tests only the null hypothesis that $p = 0.5$. In the **binomial test** procedure, which we shall now describe, the value of p can be set to any value between 0 and 1.

The binomial test in SPSS

To illustrate the binomial test, we shall use our first example of the children's choices between two toys. Of the 100 five-year-olds studied, 60 chose toy A and 40 chose toy B. Proceed as follows:

- Assign code numbers to the two choices, say 1 to toy A and 2 to toy B.

- In **Variable View**, name a variable Toy, give the values 1 to Toy A and 2 to Toy B and assign variable labels to the values. Change **Scale** to **Nominal** in the **Measure** column.

- Name a second variable Frequency for the number of choices.

- Enter the data in **Data View**.

- In order to ensure that, in the statistical analysis, the two choices will be weighted by their frequencies of occurrence, select **Weight Cases…** in the **Data** menu to obtain the **Weight Cases** dialog box, select the **Weight Cases by** radio button, transfer Frequency to the **Frequency Variable** box, and click **OK**. Note that if each child's choice were to be entered individually into the data set (a more realistic scenario), there would be no need to use the **Weight Cases** procedure.

With the data in **Data View**,

- Choose **Analyze➔Nonparametric Tests➔One Sample...** to obtain the **One-Sample Nonparametric Tests** dialog box (not shown).

- Click the **Fields** tab to open the variable selection dialog box and transfer the variable name Toy to the **Test Fields** panel.

- Click the **Settings** tab to open the dialog box for selecting a test. Click the radio button marked **Customize tests** and check the box describing the binomial test.

- Click the **Options** box and the **Binomial Options** dialog box will appear (Figure 16).

With a null hypothesis of two equally likely options, the default probability level of 0.5 applies. This is appropriate for the present test, because if the experiment was conducted properly and the children had no preference, the probability of each choice is 0.5. In other situations, however, that would not be the case, as when a candidate is guessing the correct answers to the questions in a multiple-choice examination, in which case, if there were four choices, the **Test Proportion** would be 0.25.

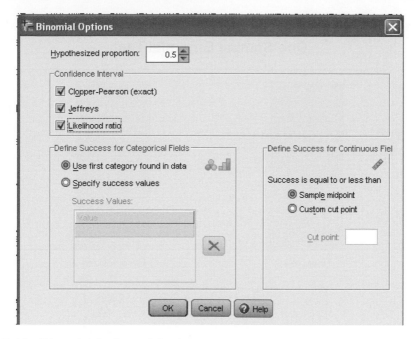

Figure 17. The **Binomial Options** dialog box

The output

The results of the binomial test are shown in Outputs 17, 18 and 19.

Hypothesis Test Summary

	Null Hypothesis	Test	Sig.	Decision
1	The categories defined by Toy = Toy A and Toy D occur with probabilities 0.5 and 0.5.	One-Sample Binomial Test	.057	Retain the null hypothesis.

Asymptotic significances are displayed. The significance level is .05.

Output 17. The initial output for the **Binomial test**

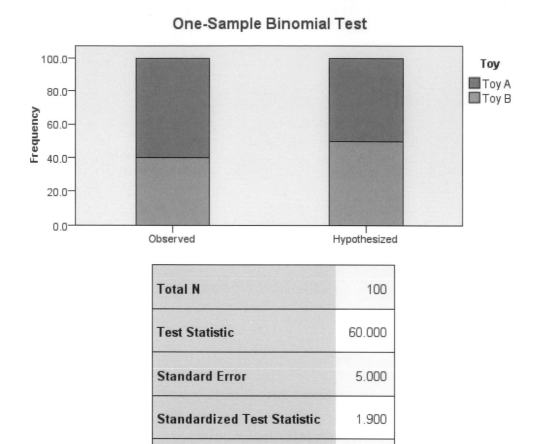

Output 18. The **Model Viewer** for the **Binomial Test**

Notice that the symptotic *p*-value is given in Output 18. With large samples, as in our example with *n* = 100, the exact and asymptotic *p*-values agree to many places of decimals; with a small sample, however, the two *p*-values can be far from identical and could lead to different conclusions about the null hypothesis. In such cases, both *p*-values would be included in the output. In our example, since the *p*-value is approximately 0.057, the null hypothesis cannot be rejected.

On double-clicking the initial output, the **Model Viewer** will appear giving further statistics and a stacked bar chart showing the observed frequencies of choices of Toy A and Toy B with the expected frequencies under the null hypothesis for comparison. From the left-hand bar in the bar chart in Output 18, we see that the value of Cohen's statistic *g* is $0.6 - 0.5 = 0.1$. This is a 'small' effect.

At the base of the left-hand pane of the Model Viewer is a drop-down menu initially set at **Hypothesis Summary View**. Reset this to **Confidence Interval Summary View** to see the requested confidence intervals on the proportion of 'successes' in the sample. The three requested confidence intervals are shown in Output 19. It can be seen that all three intervals agree broadly that the 95% confidence interval is [0.5 to 0.7], inclusive. In other words, a range of values up to 0.7 are compatible with the data; but so also is the *ex hypothesi* value 0.5. We have here no compelling evidence against the null hypothesis.

Confidence Interval Summary

Confidence Interval Type	Parameter	Estimate	95% Confidence Interval	
			Lower	Upper
One-Sample Binomial Success Rate (Clopper-Pearson)	Probability (Toy=Toy A).	.600	.497	.697
One-Sample Binomial Success Rate (Jeffreys)	Probability (Toy=Toy A).	.600	.502	.692
One-Sample Binomial Success Rate (Likelihood)	Probability (Toy=Toy A).	.600	.502	.693

Output 19. The confidence intervals

The result of the binomial test could be reported as follows:

> 'Although more children (60%) chose toy A than toy B (40%), a binomial test failed to reject the hypothesis that there is no preference: Exact p = .06 (two-tailed). Cohen's g = .1, which is a 'small' effect.'

6.7   EFFECT SIZE, POWER AND THE NUMBER OF PARTICIPANTS

The power P of a statistical test is the probability that the null hypothesis will be rejected if it is false. When planning an experiment, the researcher must decide upon the numbers of participants necessary to ensure that statistical tests have sufficient power. There is a fair consensus that tests should have a power level of at least 0.75.

Since the power of a test depends upon the difference, in the population, between the means under the null and alternative hypotheses, the researcher must decide upon the smallest difference that is worth confirming by tests and reporting as a contribution to knowledge.

How many participants shall I need for my experiment?

Suppose that you plan to carry out an experiment comparing the performance of a group of participants who have taken a supposedly performance-enhancing drug with that of a placebo group. You wish to make a *t* test that will reveal an effect of medium size (i.e. Cohen's *d* is at least 0.5) and achieve a power of 0.75. How many participants will you need? It is quite possible to answer questions like this by using the cumulative distribution functions in the SPSS Compute menu, but one needs a clear grasp of the underlying statistical theory and the conventions for specifying these functions. An easier approach is to use a dedicated software package such as **G*Power 3**, which is freely available on the Internet and can be downloaded on to your computer (Erdfelder *et al.*, 1996; Faul *et al.*, 2007).

G*Power asks the user to enter values for several of the effect size indices suggested by Cohen (1988). To obtain the answer to the present question, we must type the value 0.5 in the *d* slot. The output is shown in the lower right part of Figure 17.

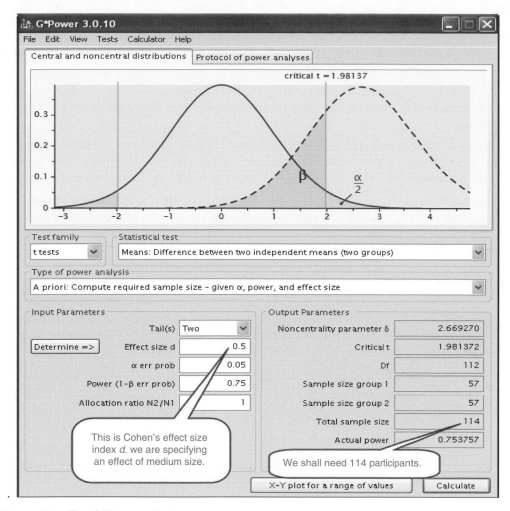

Figure 18.   The **G*Power** window

6.8   A FINAL WORD

In this chapter, we described some tests for comparing the performance levels of participants in experiments with two groups or treatment conditions.   We also considered some useful tests that could be made on the statistics of a single sample of scores. We first considered the **parametric *t* tests**.   A difference between the means in a between subjects experiment can be tested with an **independent-samples *t* test**.   A difference between the means in a within subjects experiment can be tested with a **related- or paired-samples *t* test**.

The parametric *t* tests carry several assumptions (such as homogeneity of variance and normality of distribution), which are often not true of data sets.   There are, therefore, those who advocate **nonparametric** alternatives to the *t* tests, which carry fewer assumptions about the data.   The **Mann-Whitney U test** is a nonparametric alternative to the independent-samples *t* test and the **Wilcoxon Matched-Pairs test** is a nonparametric alternative to the related- or paired-samples *t* test. In both nonparametric tests, the original scores are converted to ranks, a process which reduces the power of the test to reject the null hypothesis, if that is false.

The **Sign test** is another alternative to the related-samples *t* test, in which even more information from the original data is shed: only the signs of the differences are retained for the analysis.

Advocates of nonparametric tests emphasise their greater robustness to the influence of skewness, outliers and extreme scores. They are not, however, totally immune to the leverage exerted by outliers; moreover their use always incurs an immediate penalty of a loss in power.

There has been much controversy about the use of nonparametric tests instead of t tests with some kinds of data, especially ratings. Many journal editors would insist that ratings, with which the values of group means constrain the variances, should always be analysed by nonparametric tests in preference to the t tests.

Exercises

Exercise 8 *Comparing the averages of two independent samples of data,* Exercise 9 *Comparing the averages of two related samples of data* and Exercise 10 *One-sample tests* are available in www.psypress.com/spss-made-simple. Click on Exercises.

CHAPTER 7

The one-way ANOVA

7.1   INTRODUCTION

In Chapter 6, we discussed the use of the t test and other techniques for comparing mean performance levels under two different conditions. In this chapter, we shall be describing one of a set of techniques for comparing means in more complex experiments with three or more conditions or groups. These methods are known collectively as the **analysis of variance (ANOVA)**.

The term **factor** was introduced in Chapter 1. In the context of experimental design, a factor is a set of related conditions thought to affect performance on some **measure**, or **dependent variable** (DV), recorded during the course of the experiment. In a **completely randomised** (between subjects) experiment, there is just one **between subjects** factor, that is, each participant is tested under a single condition. Participants or subjects are randomly assigned to the conditions. The **one-way ANOVA** was designed for use with data from this type of experiment.

In Chapter 1, we described an experiment in which each of five groups of participants performed under a different drug-related condition: a comparison, placebo condition and four different drug conditions: A, B, C and D. In Table 1 below, in addition to the groups means and standard deviations, the raw data are also given. Does any of the four drugs affect level of performance? The **scientific hypothesis** is that at least one of them does. The statistical **null hypothesis** (H_0), however (and the one directly tested in the ANOVA), is the negation of this assertion: in the *population* (the reference set of all possible scores that might be obtained under these conditions) the mean performance score is the same under all five conditions. If H_0 is correct, any differences among the group means are attributable to **sampling error**.

By analogy with the two-group experiment, we write:

$$H_0: \mu_1 = \mu_2 = \mu_3 = \mu_4 = \mu_5 \quad \text{- - -} (1)$$

The null hypothesis

Table 1. The results of a one-factor, between subjects experiment

	Placebo	Drug A	Drug B	Drug C	Drug D	
	10	8	12	13	11	
	9	10	14	12	20	
	7	7	9	17	15	
	9	7	7	12	6	
	11	7	15	10	11	
	5	12	12	24	12	
	7	7	14	13	15	
	6	4	14	11	16	
	8	9	11	20	12	
	8	8	12	12	12	
Mean	8.00	7.90	12.00	14.40	13.00	$M^* = 11.06$
SD	1.83	2.13	2.49	4.50	3.74	
						* Grand Mean

Between groups and within groups variance estimates

In Table 1, the treatment means show considerable variability, or variance. On the other hand, the group means could not be expected to have exactly the same value from group to group: Sample means from the same population are subject to **sampling error**. According to the null hypothesis, the differences among the group means that we see in Table 1 merely reflect sampling error, not differences among the population means.   In other words, according to the null hypothesis, the marked differences we see among the means in Table 1 merely reflect data noise.

We can measure error variance or data noise by forgetting about the group means and looking at the variances of the scores within the five treatment groups. Table 1 shows the standard deviations, but if we square those values, we have variance estimates.   In the ANOVA, these within groups variance estimates are averaged to produce a **within groups variance estimate**.

In the ANOVA, a variance estimate is known as a **mean square (*MS*)**. The numerator of the mean square is known as a **sum of squares (*SS*)**, and the denominator as the *degrees of freedom (df)*, so that

$$MS = \frac{SS}{df} \quad \text{- - - (2)}$$

ANOVA notation for a variance estimate

The within groups variance estimate or **within groups mean square**, is denoted by the term MS_{within}. We can calculate its value by taking the mean of the squares of the five standard deviations in Table 1 thus:

$$MS_{within} = \frac{\left(1.83^2 + 2.13^2 + 2.49^2 + 4.50^2 + 3.74^2\right)}{5} = 9.67$$

Suppose we were to add or subtract a constant to or from the scores in some groups, so that all five group means had exactly the same value. That operation would have no effect at all on the values of the SDs in Table 1. The value of the within groups mean square would remain exactly the same: 9.67.

The within groups mean square has been calculated by averaging five variance estimates. Since each variance estimate was based upon 10 scores, it has 9 degrees of freedom, because one parameter (the group mean) was estimated and deviations about the mean sum to zero. Since there are five variance estimates, the degrees of freedom of the within groups estimate is $5 \times 9 = 45$.

In the one-way ANOVA, a second variance estimate is calculated, which does reflect the sizes of differences between the group means; in fact it is calculated from the values of the group means (and grand mean) only. This second estimate is called the **between groups variance estimate** (or the **between groups mean square**) and is termed $MS_{between}$. To obtain the between groups sum of squares, we take the sum of squares of the deviations of the group means from the grand mean and multiply this by the number of observations in each group (10) thus:

$$SS_{between} = 10\left[(8.00 - 11.06)^2 + (7.90 - 11.06)^2 + ... + (13.00 - 11.03)^2\right]$$
$$= 351.520$$

This sum of squares was calculated from the deviations of the 5 group means from the grand mean. Since deviations about the mean sum to zero and one parameter has been estimated, the between groups sum of squares has $(5 - 1) = 4$ degrees of freedom. Therefore $MS_{between} = 351.520/4 = 87.880$.

We have calculated two variance estimates, the between groups mean square and the within groups mean square. We have also seen that they both reflect sampling error. The between groups estimate, however, will also reflect any real differences there may be among the population means. If, however, there are actually no differences among the five population means, the values of the between and within mean squares both reflect error variance only.

The F statistic

The one-way ANOVA works by comparing the between groups variance with the within groups variance. The comparison is made by means of a statistic F, where

$$F = \frac{MS_{between}}{MS_{within}} \quad \text{- - - (3)} \; \textbf{The } \textit{F} \textbf{ statistic}$$

$$F = \frac{MS_{between}}{MS_{within}} = \frac{87.880}{9.673} = 9.09$$

The denominator of the F statistic is known as the **error term**. If the null hypothesis is true, both mean squares reflect within groups or error variance only and the value of F should be close to 1. If the null hypothesis is false, the numerator of F will be inflated by differences among the population means and F may be very large. If so, there is evidence against the null hypothesis (Figure 1).

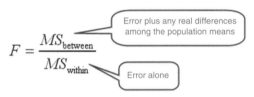

Figure 1. What F is measuring

The one-way ANOVA can be represented schematically as shown in Figure 2.

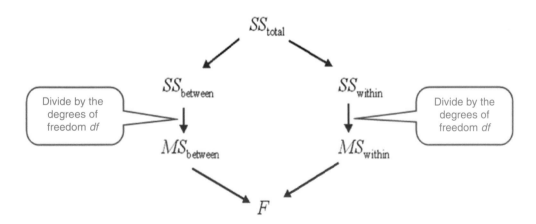

Figure 2. Schematic picture of the one-way ANOVA

Testing *F* for significance

If the null hypothesis is true, both the within groups and within groups mean squares are measuring error variance. If so, the value of *F* should, more often than not, be close to 1. The value of *F* that we have calculated from the data (9.09), however, is nine times the expected value of *F* under the null hypothesis. But is this value of *F* large enough for us to be able to reject H_0?

Suppose that the null hypothesis is true and that our drug experiment were to be repeated many times. Through sampling error, we can expect large values of *F* to occur occasionally. The distribution of *F* is known as its **sampling distribution**. To make a test of significance, we must locate our obtained value within the sampling distribution of *F* so that we can determine its ***p*-value**, that is, the probability, under the null hypothesis, of obtaining a value at least as extreme as the one we obtained.

Parameters of the *F* distribution

To specify a particular *F* distribution, we must assign values to its **parameters**.

The *F* distribution has *two* parameters:

1. The degrees of freedom of the between groups mean square $df_{between}$;
2. The degrees of freedom of the within groups mean square df_{within} .

We want to refer our value of F (9.09) to the distribution of F on 4 and 45 degrees of freedom, that is, F(4, 45). This distribution is shown in Figure 3.

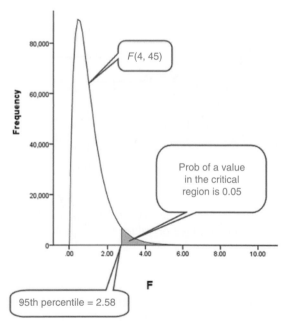

Figure 3. Distribution of *F* on 4 and 45 degrees of freedom. The critical value 2.58 is the 95th percentile of this distribution

The critical region and the critical value of F

We need now to consider the range of possible values of F. Since a variance, which is the sum of squared deviations, cannot have a negative value, the value of F cannot be less than zero. On the other hand, F has no upper limit. Since only large values of F cast doubt upon the null hypothesis, therefore, we shall locate the critical region entirely in the upper tail of the distribution. It can be seen from Figure 3 that, under the null hypothesis, only 5% of values in the distribution of $F(4, 45)$ are as great as 2.58. The critical region, therefore, comprises values of 2.58 and greater.

The p-value of the obtained value of a test statistic is the probability (under the null hypothesis) of a value at least as extreme as that value. In this case, the p-value of the obtained value of F is 1 minus its cumulative probability. The p-value is the probability of a value of F at least as far into the upper tail of the sampling distribution as the one obtained. (See Figure 4.) (Actually our obtained value of F is much higher than that shown in Figure 4, which was intended only to illustrate the meaning of a p-value.)

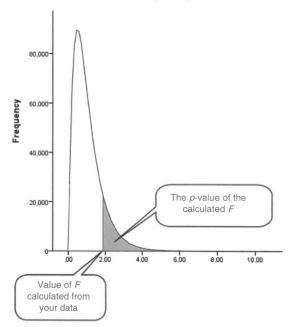

Figure 4. The p-value of an obtained value of F in the sampling distribution F(4, 45)

It is important to make a clear distinction between, on the one hand, the probability of a value falling within the critical region, a range of values with a probability equal to the pre-fixed **significance level** (0.05), and the p-value, which can only be determined after the data have been gathered.

If the p-value is less than the pre-set significance level, the obtained value of F will fall within the critical region. If so, the result of the test is deemed to be statistically **significant** and will be taken as evidence against the null hypothesis. Our obtained value of F (9.09) exceeds the critical value and is therefore significant beyond the 0.05 level.

The p-value conveys additional information over and above the question of the significance of the result of the test: a very small p-value indicates that the value of the test statistic falls well within the critical region; whereas a large p-value such as 0.8 or 0.9 indicates that the value lies well within the range one would expect if the null hypothesis is true. The p-value of our obtained value of F is 0.000018, which is very small indeed. The null hypothesis of equality, in the population, of the treatment means is therefore rejected.

The ANOVA summary table

It is useful for the researcher to have what is known as the ANOVA **summary table**, which includes, not only the value of F, but also the between groups and within groups sums of squares and mean squares, with their respective degrees of freedom. The ANOVA summary table is not always included in the body of a research paper; but it is, nevertheless, a valuable source of information about the results of the analysis.

Table 2 is the ANOVA summary table for our present example.

Table 2.   The ANOVA Summary Table

	Sum of squares	df	Mean square	F	p-value*
Between groups	351.520	4	87.880	9.085	< 0.01
Within groups	435.30	45	9.673		
Total	786.820	49			
*SPSS terms the p-value 'Sig.'					

7.2   ENTERING THE DATA

The data in Table 1 are not in a form suitable for entry into the SPSS Data Editor. Each line in Data View must contain information on one participant or case only; whereas in Table 1, each row of the table contains data on five different participants. The correct format is achieved by carrying the information about participants' scores and their group membership in separate variables (columns) in Data View.

In **Variable View**, as with the independent samples t test, you will need to define two variables:

1. A variable with a name such as Score, which contains all the scores in the data set. This is the dependent variable. It can be given a more informative variable label, such as Performance Score.

2. A grouping variable with a simple variable name such as Group or Drug, which identifies the condition under which a score was achieved. (The grouping variable should also be given a more specific variable label such as Drug Condition, because it is the variable label that will appear in the output.)

The grouping variable will consist of five values (one for the placebo condition and one for each of the four drugs). We shall arbitrarily assign value labels thus: 1 = Placebo; 2 = Drug A; 3 = Drug B; 4 = Drug C; 5 = Drug D. The captions attached to the numerical values are known as **value labels** and are assigned by making entries in the **Values** column in Variable View.

* Open **Variable View** first, to name the variables and amend the settings so that when you enter **Data View**, the columns will already have meaningful headings and the scores will appear without unnecessary decimals.

* In the **Values** column, assign clear value labels to the code numbers you have chosen for grouping variables (Figure 5). When you are typing data into **Data View**, having the value labels displayed there can help you to avoid transcription errors. It also ensures that some graphs have labels, rather than code numbers, on their axes.

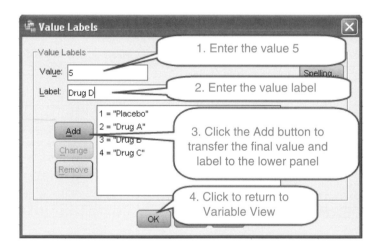

Figure 5.   Assigning value labels to the code numbers making up the grouping variable. The figure shows the last label being assigned to the value 5

* Set **Decimals** to zero for both variables: we want to see integers only in Data View.

* In the **Measure** column of **Variable View**, specify the level of measurement of the grouping variable (the treatment factor), which is at the **nominal** level of measurement (Figure 6).

Figure 6.   The completed **Variable View** window, specifying the nominal level of measurement for the grouping variable Drug Condition

Notice that in Figure 6, the variable label for the dependent variable has been omitted. As a consequence, in the SPSS output, the variable *name* Score will appear; whereas the grouping variable will appear under its full variable *label* Drug Condition. (You might want to type in a more informative variable label for Score, such as *Number of Hits*.)

	Group	Score			Group	Score
1	1	10		1	Placebo	10
2	1	9		2	Placebo	9
3	1	7		3	Placebo	7
4	1	9		4	Placebo	9
5	1	11		5	Placebo	11
6	1	5		6	Placebo	5
7	1	7		7	Placebo	7
8	1	6		8	Placebo	6
9	1	8		9	Placebo	8
10	1	8		10	Placebo	8
11	2	8		11	Drug A	8
12	2	10		12	Drug A	10
13	2	7		13	Drug A	7
14	2	7		14	Drug A	7
15	2	7		15	Drug A	7
16	2	12		16	Drug A	12
17	2	7		17	Drug A	7

Values displayed

Value labels displayed

Figure 7. Two displays of the same part of **Data View** after the data have been entered: on the left, in the Group column, the values are shown; on the right, in the same column, the value labels are shown

Having prepared the ground in this way while in **Variable View**, you will find that when you enter **Data View**, the names of the variables appear at the heads of the first two columns. When you type in the values of the grouping variable, you can view their labels by checking the **Value Labels** option in the **View** menu or by clicking the **Value Labels** icon (shown right). Figure 7 shows the same part of **Data View** after the data have been entered, with and without value labels.

7.3   RUNNING THE ONE-WAY ANOVA ON GLM

There are several ways of running a one-way ANOVA on SPSS. Here we shall use the **Univariate** procedure in the **GLM (General Linear Model)** menu. First, we may need to introduce some new terms.

In all the experiments we have considered so far, there has been a single DV. In the current example, the DV is the score a participant achieves on a task. The one-way ANOVA and the *t* test are **univariate tests**, because they were designed for the analysis of data from experiments with a single DV. If, however, we had also recorded the time the participant took to complete the task, we should have had two DVs. **Multivariate tests** are techniques designed for the analysis of data from experiments with two or more DVs. An example of a multivariate technique is **Multivariate Analysis of Variance (MANOVA)**, which is a generalisation of the univariate ANOVA to the analysis of data from experiments with several DVs. This technique is briefly described and illustrated in Chapter 10.

7.3.1   Finding the GLM menu

- Choose **Analyze➔General Linear Model➔Univariate...** . (The menu is shown in Figure 8.)

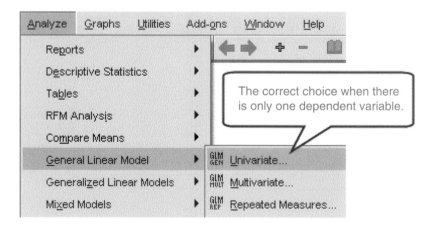

Figure 8. The **General Linear Model (GLM)** menu

The **Univariate** dialog box is shown in Figure 9.   Some of the terms in the dialog may be unfamiliar.

Factors with fixed and random effects

The selection of experimental conditions for an experiment is usually driven either by theory or by the need to resolve some practical issue. A factor consisting of a set of theoretically-determined conditions is said to have **fixed effects**. Most factors in experimental research are fixed effects factors.

There are occasions, however, on which the conditions making up a factor can be viewed as a random sample from a large (perhaps infinitely large) pool of possible conditions. In research on reading skills, for example, an investigator studying the effects of sentence length upon passage readability may select or prepare some passages which vary systematically in sentence length. With such a procedure, however, reading performance may reflect passage properties other than sentence length; moreover, these additional properties cannot be expected to remain the same from passage to passage. The effects of using different passages should, arguably, be included as a factor in the analysis, even though the experimenter is not primarily interested in this nuisance variable. Since passage characteristics other than average sentence length can be viewed as a random sample from a pool of possible conditions, the passage factor is said to have **random effects**. Factors with random effects arise more commonly in applied, correlational research and their presence has important implications for the analysis.

Covariates: the analysis of covariance (ANCOVA)

A **covariate** is a variable which, because it can be expected to correlate (i.e. 'co-vary') with the DV, is likely to add to the variability (or 'noisiness') of the data and inflate the error term, resulting in a reduction of the power of the statistical test to reject the null hypothesis. An obvious example of a covariate is IQ, which can be expected to correlate substantially with almost any measure of cognitive or skilled performance and add considerably to the 'noisiness' of the data.

The **analysis of covariance** (**ANCOVA**) is a technique whereby the effects of a covariate upon the DV are removed from the data, thus reducing error and increasing the power of the F test. The manner in which this is achieved is described in statistical texts such as Winer, Brown & Michels (1991) and Keppel & Wickens (2004). The analysis of covariance is described at a practical level in Chapter 13.

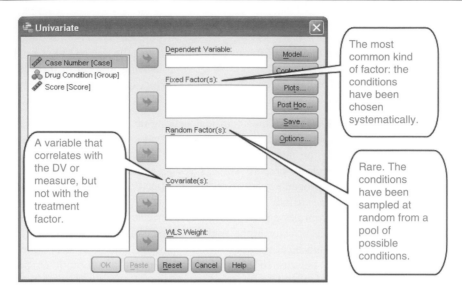

Figure 9. The **Univariate** dialog box, with explanations of some of the terms

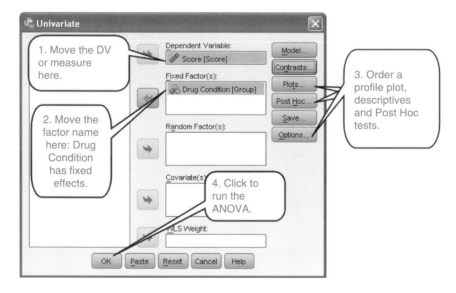

Figure 10. Running the one-way ANOVA

- Complete the **Univariate** dialog as shown in Figure 10.

- Order Descriptive statistics by clicking the **Options** button and following the instructions in Figure 11.

- Click the **Plots...** button to open the **Profile Plots** dialog box and follow the procedure shown in Figure 12.

- Click the **Post Hoc...** button to open the **Post Hoc** dialog box (Figure 13). Follow the directions in Figure 13 in order to run the **Bonferroni**, **Sidak**, **Tukey** and **Dunnett** tests. For the **Dunnett** test, which compares active experimental conditions with a control condition, specify which group is the control or comparison group. By default, SPSS will assume that the last group is the comparison group, so check the radio button marked First.

- Back in the **Univariate** dialog, click the **Run button**.

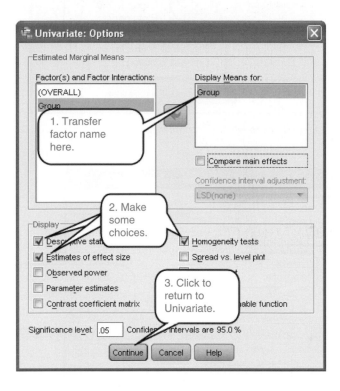

Figure 11. Ordering descriptive statistics

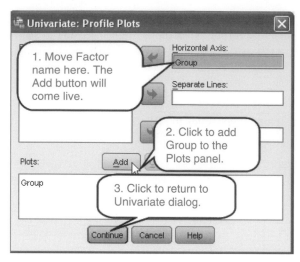

Figure 12. Requesting a **Profile Plot** of the means

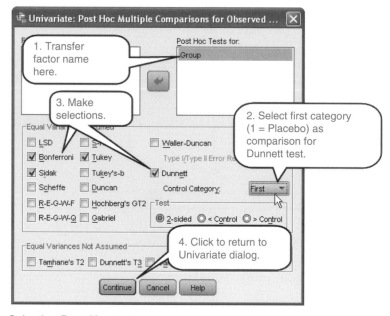

Figure 13. Selecting **Post Hoc** tests

7.3.2 Descriptives and the ANOVA summary table

Output 1 is a table of **Descriptive Statistics**.

Descriptive Statistics

Dependent Variable:Score

Drug Condition	Mean	Std. Deviation	N
Placebo	8.00	1.826	10
Drug A	7.90	2.132	10
Drug B	12.00	2.494	10
Drug C	14.40	4.502	10
Drug D	13.00	3.742	10
Total	11.06	4.007	50

Output 1. The **Descriptive Statistics** table

The model for the one-way ANOVA assumes **homogeneity of variance**: in the population, the error variance is constant across treatment conditions. In the one-way ANOVA, the sample variances are pooled to give an estimate of this supposedly constant error variance. Should the assumption of homogeneity of variance be false, there is the danger that the ANOVA may produce too many (or two few) significant results. Output 2 shows the result of Levene's test for homogeneity of variance.

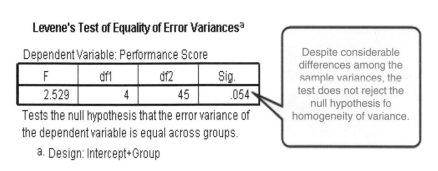

Levene's Test of Equality of Error Variances[a]

Dependent Variable: Performance Score

F	df1	df2	Sig.
2.529	4	45	.054

Tests the null hypothesis that the error variance of the dependent variable is equal across groups.

a. Design: Intercept+Group

> Despite considerable differences among the sample variances, the test does not reject the null hypothesis fo homogeneity of variance.

Output 2. **Levene's Test** for homogeneity of variance

The non-significance of the Levene F Statistic for the test of equality of error variances (homogeneity of variances) indicates that the assumption of homogeneity of variance is tenable; however, considerable differences among the variances are apparent from inspection. The one-way ANOVA is to some extent robust to violations of the assumption of homogeneity of variance, especially when, as in the present example, there are equal numbers of observations in the different groups. When there are marked differences in sample size from group to group, however, this robustness tends to break down and the true Type I or Type II error rates may increase to unacceptable levels.

Now we come to the ANOVA summary table itself. Output 3 shows the **Tests of Between-Subjects Effects** table, with Table 2 below it for comparison. The two tables contain a common core of results. In the GLM summary table, the rows labelled **Group**, **Error** and **Corrected Total** contain exactly the same information as we shall find in the **Between Groups**, **Within Groups** and **Total** rows of the One-Way ANOVA table reproduced underneath it for comparison. The values of F are also exactly the same in both tables. The GLM table, however, contains some additional terms, including **Intercept** and **R Squared**. These are terms from another statistical technique called **regression**, which is discussed in Chapter 12. It is quite possible to recast the one-way ANOVA (or, indeed, *any* ANOVA) as a problem in regression and make exactly the same test of the null hypothesis. If that is done (as in the GLM procedure), the mean squares, their degrees of freedom, the value of F and the *p*-value will all be exactly the same as those produced by the ANOVA procedure.

Tests of Between-Subjects Effects

Dependent Variable:Score

Source	Type III Sum of Squares	df	Mean Square	F	Sig.	Partial Eta Squared
Corrected Model	351.520[a]	4	87.880	9.085	.000	.447
Intercept	6116.180	1	6116.180	632.272	.000	.934
Group	351.520	4	87.880	9.085	.000	.447
Error	435.300	45	9.673			
Total	6903.000	50				
Corrected Total	786.820	49				

a. R Squared = .447 (Adjusted R Squared = .398)

Table 2. The ANOVA Summary Table

	Sum of squares	df	Mean square	F	p-value*
Between groups	351.520	4	87.880	9.085	< 0.01
Within groups	435.30	45	9.673		
Total	786.820	49			
*SPSS calls the *p*-value 'Sig.'					

Output 3. The **Tests of Between-Subjects Effects** table, with Table 2 copied below it for comparison

7.3.3   The profile plot

The requested profile plot of the means is shown in Output 4. Observe that the zero point of the vertical scale does not appear on the axis. This is something that still happens in default profile plots in SPSS. Always be suspicious of such a graph, because it can give the appearance of a strong effect when actually there is very little happening. The difficulty can easily be remedied by double-clicking on the graph to bring it into the **Chart Editor**, double-clicking on the vertical axis and specifying zero as the minimum point on the vertical scale.

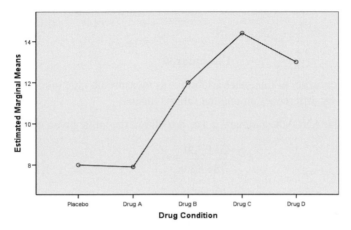

Output 4. The default profile plot in the SPSS Statistics Viewer

The result is shown in Output 5. The effect of including the zero point on the vertical scale, can sometimes be quite dramatic: with some data sets, an exciting-looking range of peaks suddenly becomes a featureless plain. In this case, however, it is clear that even when the zero point is shown on the vertical axis, something really is happening in this data set.

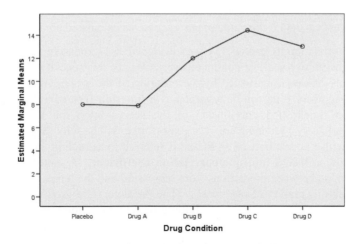

Output 5. The plot of the means with the vertical scale now including zero

7.3.4   Measuring effect size

Several measures of effect size for use with the ANOVA have been proposed, the earliest of which was a statistic known as **eta squared** (η^2), where eta is known as the **correlation ratio**.

Eta and eta squared

The eta squared statistic is the between groups sum of squares divided by the total sum of squares:

$$\eta^2 = \frac{SS_{between}}{SS_{total}} = \frac{SS_{between}}{SS_{between} + SS_{within}} \quad \text{- - - (4)}$$

Eta squared

Eta squared is the proportion of the total variability (as measured by the total sum of squares) that is accounted for by differences among the sample means.

Using the values in the ANOVA summary table, we obtain the value given in Output 3:

$$\eta^2 = \frac{351.520}{786.820} = 0.447$$

The value of eta (the correlation ratio itself) is:

$$\eta = \sqrt{\frac{SS_{between}}{SS_{between} + SS_{within}}} = \sqrt{.447} = 0.67$$

The term **correlation ratio** is not particularly transparent. Eta, however, is indeed, as we have just seen, a ratio. Moreover, it is also a correlation. If each of the fifty scores in our data set is paired with its group mean, the correlation between the scores and the group means has the value of eta. You can confirm this easily and quickly by using the **Aggregate** command in the **Data** menu to place, opposite each score in Data View, its group mean. (In the Aggregate dialog, use the grouping variable as the **break variable**.) You will find that the **Pearson correlation** between the column of scores and the column of means is 0.66840, the square of which is 0.447, the value of eta squared, as calculated above.

The Pearson correlation (Chapter 11) was designed as a measure of a supposed linear relationship between two scale or continuous variables. In this special situation, however, the value of the correlation is unaffected by the ordering of the groups, which are identified by arbitrary code numbers. Eta can be regarded as a **function-free correlation** expressing the total regression (linear and curvilinear) of the scores upon the treatments, which are represented as arbitrary code numbers. For reasons that will be fully explained in Chapter 12, eta squared can also be symbolised as R^2 and is referred to as such in the SPSS output. This is because eta is, in fact, a **multiple correlation coefficient**. A multiple correlation is the Pearson correlation between predictions from regression and the target variable. In this case, the target variable is the set of raw scores. The predictors are grouping variables carrying information about group membership. Multiple regression of the scores upon the grouping variables will predict, as the estimate of each score, its group mean. Thus the multiple correlation coefficient (eta) is the correlation between the scores and their group means, which explains why eta cannot have a negative value.

Cohen's f statistic

Cohen (1988) suggested another measure of effect size which he called f. While eta squared is the variance of the population treatment means as a proportion of the total variance, that is, the variance of the population means plus error, Cohen's f is the ratio of the standard deviation of the population treatment means to the error standard deviation. Since both statistics are defined in terms of exactly the same parameters, one can readily be transformed to the other and vice versa:

$$f = \sqrt{\frac{\eta^2}{1-\eta^2}}$$

$$\eta = \sqrt{\frac{f^2}{1+f^2}} \qquad \text{---(5)}$$

Relation between Cohen's f and eta

We have found that for the results of the drug experiment, the value of eta squared is 0.447. Substituting in formula (5), we obtain

$$f = \sqrt{\frac{0.447}{1-0.447}} = 0.90$$

Interpreting values of Cohen's f

Cohen (1988) has offered guidelines for the interpretation of values of his own statistic f and equivalent values of eta squared (both defined in terms of population parameters). His guidelines are interpreted in Table 3 below.

Table 3. Guidelines for assessing values of eta squared (or bias-corrected measures such as omega squared) and the equivalent values of Cohen's f.

Size of Effect	Eta squared	Cohen's f
Small	$0.01 \leq \eta^2 < 0.06$	$0.10 \leq f < 0.25$
Medium	$0.06 \leq \eta^2 < 0.14$	$0.25 \leq f < 0.40$
Large	$\eta^2 \geq 0.14$	$f \geq 0.40$

Since our obtained value for eta squared is 0.45, the treatment factor of Drug Condition can be said to have had a 'large' effect. Since several treatments were involved, however, this fact conveys a limited amount of information. Did all four drugs have an effect or just some of them? How large were the effects of the different drugs considered individually? We shall return to the question of effect size when we consider the making of comparisons among the individual treatment means.

Other estimates of effect size: omega squared

As measures of effect size, the statistics eta and eta squared are purely descriptive of the data set in hand. As estimates of effect size in the population, however, they are positively biased. For some ANOVA designs, the statistic known as **omega squared** can be calculated. While omega squared incorporates a correction for positive bias, however, there are ANOVA designs for which its calculation is difficult or impossible. The omega squared statistic is not an option in SPSS.

In terms of the one-way ANOVA, the value of omega squared can be calculated directly from the value of F by means of the following formula:

$$\hat{\omega}^2 = \frac{(k-1)(F-1)}{(k-1)(F-1)+kn} \quad \text{- - - (6)} \quad \textbf{Omega squared}$$

In formula (6), k is the number of treatment groups, and n is the number of participants in each group. In the present example, $k = 5$, $F = 9.085$ and $n = 10$. Substituting in formula (6), we have

$$\hat{\omega}^2 = \frac{(5-1)(9.085-1)}{(5-1)(9.085-1)+50} = 0.39$$

The square root of the omega squared statistic can be viewed as an estimate of the correlation ratio in the population and, as such, is an improvement upon the sample value of eta. The value of omega squared can be interpreted by using the ranges of values for eta squared given in Table 3.

7.3.5   Report of the analysis

In Chapter 6, the reader was advised never to present the results of a statistical test without also giving the descriptives, either in the same paragraph or in a nearby table on the same page. A bald statement of the results of a one-way ANOVA is even less informative than a value of t, because a significant value of F gives no indication of where the difference or differences among an array of means might lie.

Even if F is significant and it seems clear from the descriptives that only a few of the differences are large enough to account for the significant value of F, further follow-up tests are necessary to confirm these impressions. We shall discuss such tests later in the chapter. For now, we suggest that a report of the results of the one-way ANOVA might begin as follows:

> 'The mean performance level for the placebo was M = 8.00 (SD = 1.83) and for the four drug conditions A, B, C and D, the means were M = 7.90 (SD = 2.13); M = 12.00 (SD = 2.49); M = 14.40 (SD = 4.50); M = 13.00 (SD = 3.74), respectively. The one-way ANOVA showed F to be significant beyond the .01 level: $F(4, 45) = 9.08$; p <.01. Eta is .67 which, according to Cohen's (1988) classification, is a large effect.'

7.4   MAKING COMPARISONS AMONG THE TREATMENT MEANS

We have found evidence against the null hypothesis; but what can we conclude from this? If H_0 states that all the means are equal, the alternative hypothesis is simply that they are not all equal. The falsity of H_0, however, does not imply that the difference between any and every pair of group means is significant. If the ANOVA F test is significant, there should be at least one difference *somewhere* among the means; but we cannot claim that the mean for any particular group is significantly different from the mean of any other group. Further analysis is necessary to confirm whatever differences there may appear to be among the individual treatment means. In this section, we shall describe some methods for testing comparisons among the group means.

7.4.1   Planned and unplanned comparisons

Before running an experiment such as the one in our current example, the experimenter may have some very specific questions in mind. It might be expected, for example (perhaps on theoretical grounds), that the mean score of every group who have ingested one of the drugs will be greater than the mean score of the Placebo group. This expectation would be tested by comparing each drug group with the Placebo group. Perhaps, on the other hand, the experimenter has theoretical reasons to suspect that Drugs A and B should enhance performance, but Drugs C and D should not. That hypothesis could be tested by comparing the Placebo mean with the average score for groups A and B combined and with the average score for groups B and C combined. These are examples of **planned comparisons**.

Often, however, the experimenter, perhaps because the field has been little explored, has only a sketchy idea of how the results will turn out. There may be good reason to expect that *some* of the drugs will enhance performance; but it may not be possible, a priori, to be more specific. Unplanned, or **post hoc**, comparisons are part of the 'data-snooping' that inevitably follows the initial analysis of variance.

The per comparison and familywise Type I error rates

When we use the t test to compare two means, the significance level α is the probability of a Type I error, that is, the rejection of the null hypothesis when it is actually true. When, however, we intend to make several comparisons among a group of means, we must distinguish between the individual comparison and the whole set, or **family**, of comparisons that we intend to make. It can be shown that if we make a set of comparisons, the probability, under the null hypothesis, of *at least one* of them being significant may be considerably greater than α. We must, therefore, distinguish between the Type I error rate **per comparison** (α) and the **familywise** Type I error rate (α_{family}).

If we plan to make c comparisons, the **familywise** Type I error rate can be shown to be approximately $c\alpha$.

$$\alpha_{family} \approx c\alpha \quad \text{- - - (7)}$$

The familywise Type I error rate

It is clear from formula (7) that, when the researcher is making many comparisons among the treatment means of data from complex experiments, the probability of at least one test showing significance can be very high: with a large array of treatment means, the probability of obtaining at least one significant difference might be 0.8, 0.9 or greater, even when there are no differences in the population at all! It is therefore essential to control the familywise Type I error rate by making data-snooping tests more conservative. Several procedures for doing this have been proposed.

The Bonferroni correction and other conservative tests

Formula (7) is the basis of the **Bonferroni method** of controlling the familywise Type I error rate. If c is the number of comparisons in the family, the p-value for each test is multiplied by c. Alternatively, we can fix the alpha-rate per comparison at α/c. This procedure obviously makes the test of a comparison more conservative. For example, suppose that, having decided to make 4 comparisons, we were to make an ordinary t test of one comparison and find that the p-value is 0.04. In the Bonferroni procedure, we must now multiply this p-value by 4, obtaining 0.16, a value well above the desired familywise error rate of 0.05. We must, therefore, accept the null hypothesis. Alternatively, rather than set the per comparison significance level at 0.05, we could set it at $0.05/4 = 0.01$, approximately. Either approach leads to the same decision about the null hypothesis.

It is common practice, following the running of an experiment with several different conditions, to make unplanned or **post hoc** multiple pairwise comparisons among the treatment means: that is, the difference between every possible pair of means is tested for significance. Here, the Bonferroni method can result in extremely conservative tests, because in this situation c (the size of the comparison family) is arguably the number of different pairs that can be drawn from the array of k treatment means. (This is also true of the **Sidak correction**, which is slightly less conservative than the Bonferroni.) The Bonferroni and Sidak tests can be conservative to the point that they may have very little power to reject the null hypothesis.

The **Tukey** tests and the **Newman-Keuls** test are less conservative, the **Tukey HSD test** (or a variant known as **Tukey-b**) being generally preferred for post hoc tests of pairwise differences following the one-way ANOVA. For more complex comparisons, such as the comparison of one mean with the mean of several others, the **Scheffé test** is highly regarded; but it is thought to be over-conservative when used for pairwise comparisons.

The situation may arise in which the researcher wishes to compare performance under each of several active conditions with that of a baseline control group. The **Dunnett test**, described in Howell (2007; p.374), is regarded as the most powerful test available for this purpose.

These tests (and many others) are available in SPSS. While several of them are also available in the One-Way procedure, we shall confine ourselves to GLM, which offers a better selection of options.

Unplanned or post hoc multiple comparisons with SPSS

Output 6 is only part of an extensive table of the results of multiple pairwise comparisons with the **Tukey**, **Bonferroni, Sidak** and **Dunnett** tests. The most conservative test of the three, the Bonferroni, has the widest confidence intervals and the largest p-values. The Sidak test has somewhat tighter confidence limits and smaller p-values, but is still very conservative; the Dunnett test, has the narrowest confidence intervals and the smallest p-values.

	(I) Drug Condition	(J) Drug Condition	95% Confidence Interval	
			Lower Bound	Upper Bound
Tukey HSD	Placebo	Drug A	-3.85	4.05
		Drug B	-7.95	-.05
		Drug C	-10.35	-2.45
		Drug D	-8.95	-1.05
Bonferroni	Placebo	Drug A	-4.01	4.21
		Drug B	-8.11	.11
		Drug C	-10.51	-2.29
		Drug D	-9.11	-.89
Sidak	Placebo	Drug A	-3.99	4.19
		Drug B	-8.09	.09
		Drug C	-10.49	-2.31
		Drug D	-9.09	-.91
Dunnett t (2-sided)[a]	Drug A	Placebo	-3.62	3.42
	Drug B	Placebo	.48	7.52
	Drug C	Placebo	2.00	9.92
	Drug D	Placebo	1.48	8.52

Output 6. Comparison of the outputs for the **Tukey**, **Bonferroni, Sidak** and **Dunnett** tests

Output 7 shows a second part of the output for the **Tukey** test. The output shows that there are two subgroups of tests. Within each subgroup there are no significant pairwise differences; on the other hand, any member of either subgroup is significantly different from any member of the other subgroup. For example, there are no differences among Drugs B, C and D; but each of those is significantly different from both the Placebo and Drug A. In fact, of the four drugs tested, the only one not to produce an improvement over the Placebo was Drug A.

Homogeneous Subsets

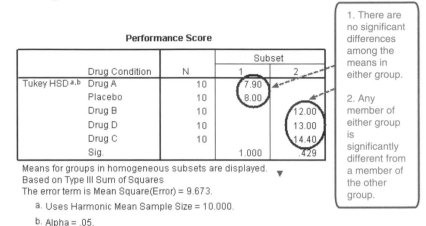

Performance Score

	Drug Condition	N	Subset 1	Subset 2
Tukey HSD [a,b]	Drug A	10	7.90	
	Placebo	10	8.00	
	Drug B	10		12.00
	Drug D	10		13.00
	Drug C	10		14.40
	Sig.		1.000	.429

Means for groups in homogeneous subsets are displayed.
Based on Type III Sum of Squares
The error term is Mean Square(Error) = 9.673.
  a. Uses Harmonic Mean Sample Size = 10.000.
  b. Alpha = .05.

1. There are no significant differences among the means in either group.

2. Any member of either group is significantly different from a member of the other group.

Output 7. The two subgroups of treatment means identified by the **Tukey** multiple comparisons test

Reporting the results of the Tukey test

We suggest your report of the results of the Tukey test might read as follows:

'The Tukey HSD test was used to make pairwise comparisons among the individual treatment means, with the familywise significance level set at .05. The test confirmed the differences between the Placebo mean and those for Drugs B, C and D; but the difference between the Placebo and Drug A means is insignificant. The conservative p-values for the differences between the Plabeco mean and those for Drugs A, B, C and D are, respectively, 1.00, .046, < .001 and .007. The differences between the Placebo mean and those for Drugs B, C and D are 4.0, 6.4 and 5.0, respectively. If the population standard deviation is estimated as the square root of the within groups mean square (3.11), the values of Cohen's d statistic for the three differences are 1.29, 2.06 and 1.61, respectively. All these differences are large in Cohen's classification.'

Cohen's guidelines for d are repeated in Table 4 for your convenience.

Table 4. Cohen's categories of effect size

Value of Cohen's d	Size of Effect	In words, ...
$0.2 \leq d < 0.5$	Small	Less than 0.2 is Trivial 0.2 to 0.5 is Small
$0.5 \leq d < 0.8$	Medium	0.5 to 0.8 is Medium 0.8 or greater is Large
$d \geq 0.8$	Large	

7.4.2   Linear contrasts

We have data from a one-factor between subject experiment with five treatment groups. Let M_1, M_2, M_3, M_4 and M_5 be the mean performance levels for the Placebo, Drug A, Drug B, Drug C and Drug D conditions, respectively.

A comparison between two of an array of k treatment means (or combinations of the means) can be expressed as a **linear contrast**, that is, a linear sum of the five treatment means, with the constraint that the coefficients (weights) add up to zero. Suppose we want to compare M_1 with M_2. The difference $M_1 - M_2$ can be expressed as the **linear contrast C**, where

$$C = (1)M_1 + (-1)M_2 + (0)M_3 + (0)M_4 + (0)M_5 \quad \text{- - - (8)}$$

A linear contrast

Since we are interested in comparing only two of the five means, the inclusion of all five means in formula (8) may seem highly artificial; but we need to develop a notation for a whole *set* of contrasts that might be made among a given set of treatment means. We must have the same number of terms in all contrasts, even if we have to have coefficients of zero for the irrelevant terms. In a situation such as our current example, in which there are five treatment means, one of which is a control or comparison, the researcher may wish to compare the control mean with each of the others. Such pairwise contrasts are known as **simple contrasts**. As in formula (8), the formulation of each of a set of simple contrasts must include all the treatments means, the irrelevant means having coefficients of zero:

$$M_2 - M_1 = (-1)M_1 + (+1)M_2 + (0)M_3 + (0)M_4 + (0)M_5$$
$$M_3 - M_1 = (-1)M_1 + (0)M_2 + (+1)M_3 + (0)M_4 + (0)M_5$$
$$M_4 - M_1 = (-1)M_1 + (0)M_2 + (0)M_3 + (+1)M_4 + (0)M_5$$
$$M_5 - M_1 = (-1)M_1 + (0)M_2 + (0)M_3 + (0)M_4 + (+1)M_5$$

This set of four simple contrasts can be represented more compactly by the four rows of coefficients alone:

$$\begin{pmatrix} -1 & +1 & 0 & 0 & 0 \\ -1 & 0 & +1 & 0 & 0 \\ -1 & 0 & 0 & +1 & 0 \\ -1 & 0 & 0 & 0 & +1 \end{pmatrix}$$

The same notation extends easily to more **complex contrasts**, that is, contrasts involving three or more treatment means. If we wish to compare M_3 with the mean of M_1 and M_2, the difference can be expressed as the complex linear contrast D, where

$$D = (-0.5)M_1 + (-0.5)M_2 + (1)M_3 + (0)M_4 + (0)M_5 \ \text{---} \ (9)$$

A complex linear contrast

It is worth bearing in mind that although in (9) three of the five treament means have non-zero coefficients, the contrast is between only *two* means: (1) M_3 and (2) a composite mean derived from M_1 and M_2. This has the important implication that *a contrast sum of squares must always have one degree of freedom*, however complex the contrast and however many means may be involved.

7.4.3 Helmert contrasts

Suppose, as in our present example, we have an array of five treatment means. We construct a set of **Helmert contrasts** as follows:

1. We compare the first mean with the average of the other four means.

2. We drop the first mean and compare the second mean with the average of means three, four and five.

3. We drop the second mean and compare the third with the average of means four and five.

4. Finally, we compare the fourth mean with the fifth.

This set of contrasts can be represented by four rows of coefficients as follows:

$$\begin{pmatrix} +1 & -1/4 & -1/4 & -1/4 & -1/4 \\ 0 & +1 & -1/3 & -1/3 & -1/3 \\ 0 & 0 & +1 & -1/2 & -1/2 \\ 0 & 0 & 0 & +1 & -1 \end{pmatrix}$$

We can remove the fractions by multiplying each of the coefficients in the first row by 4, those of the second by 3, and those of the third by two thus:

$$\begin{pmatrix} +4 & -1 & -1 & -1 & -1 \\ 0 & +3 & -1 & -1 & -1 \\ 0 & 0 & +2 & -1 & -1 \\ 0 & 0 & 0 & +1 & -1 \end{pmatrix}$$

Helmert contrasts have, as we shall see, a very important property.

Orthogonal contrast sets

In a set of Helmert contrasts, each contrast is independent of the others: that is, its value is neither constrained by, nor does it constrain, those of any of the other contrasts in the set. The first contrast does not affect the value of the second, because the first mean is not involved in the second contrast. Similarly, the values of neither of the first two contrasts affect the value of the third, because the latter involves neither of the first two means. Finally, the fourth contrast is independent of the first three, because the first three means have now been dropped. Taken together, these Helmert contrasts are said to make up a set of **orthogonal contrasts**.

In either version of the set of Helmert contrasts (the matrix containing the fractions or the matrix with the whole numbers), the sum of the products of the corresponding coefficients in any two rows is zero. For contrasts 1 and 2, for instance, if we let c_1 and c_2 be the coefficients in row 1 and row 2, respectively, $\Sigma c_1 c_2 = 0$. This is the criterion for the orthogonality (independence) of a set of contrasts. You might wish to confirm, for example, that the sum of products of the corresponding coefficients in the first two rows of either matrix is zero; moreover, you can easily check that the sum of products is zero for *any* two rows.

In our current example, with five treatment means, we were able to construct a set of four orthogonal contrasts. In general, with k treatment means, sets of only $(k - 1)$ orthogonal contrasts are possible; though it may be possible to construct more than one orthogonal set. The limit to the size of any one set of orthogonal contrasts is, of course, the degrees of freedom of the between groups sum of squares.

Running contrasts in the GLM procedure

Table 5 shows the different types of contrasts that can be requested from the GLM dialog box. We shall illustrate the procedure by requesting a set of simple contrasts.

- In the **Univariate** dialog box, Click the **Contrasts...** button to open the **Contrasts** dialog box. Follow the directions in Figure 14. It is essential to click the **Change** button.

- Check that the settings are now as in Figure 15. Click **Continue** to return to the Univariate dialog box.

Table 5. The types of contrast sets available on GLM

Type	Description
Simple	A pre-specified reference or control mean is compared with each of the other means.
Helmert	Starting from the leftmost mean in the array, each mean is compared with the mean of the remaining means.
Difference (Reverse Helmert)	Starting from the leftmost mean in the array, each mean is compared with the mean of the means that preceded it.
Repeated	First with second, second with third, third with fourth, …
Deviation	Each mean is compared with the grand mean.

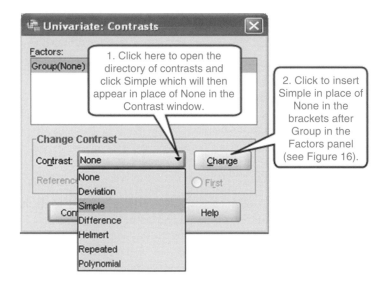

Figure 14. Ordering simple contrasts: the first step

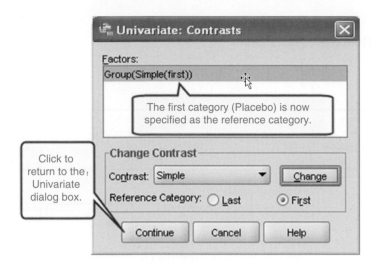

Figure 15. Appearance of the **Contrasts** dialog box after specifying simple contrasts with the first category as the comparison

Output 8 shows part of the table of results of the set of simple contrasts. No t-values are given; but if the 95% confidence interval fails to include zero, the contrast is significant. To obtain the value of t, we need only divide the 'Contrast Estimate' by the 'Std. Error':

$$t = \frac{-0.10}{1.391} = -0.07$$

Custom Hypothesis Tests

Contrast Results (K Matrix)

Drug Condition Simple Contrast[a]			Dependent Variable Performance Score
Level 2 vs. Level 1	Contrast Estimate		-.100
	Hypothesized Value		0
	Difference (Estimate - Hypothesized)		-.100
	Std. Error	Not significant since p-value >.05	1.391
	Sig.		.943
	95% Confidence Interval for Difference	Lower Bound	-2.901
		Upper Bound	2.701
Level 3 vs. Level 1	Contrast Estimate		4.000
	Hypothesized Value		0
	Difference (Estimate - Hypothesized)		4.000
	Std. Error	Significant since p-value <.05	1.391
	Sig.		.006
	95% Confidence Interval for Difference	Lower Bound	1.199
		Upper Bound	6.801
Level 4 vs. Level 1	Contrast Estimate		6.400

Output 8.   Part of the **Simple Contrasts** output with *Placebo* as the reference category

Measuring the effect size of a contrast

We have seen that, when the F test from the one-way ANOVA has shown significance, we can obtain some idea of overall effect size by calculating a measure such as Cohen's f, eta squared or an equivalent statistic such as adjusted R^2 or estimated omega squared. Such overall measures, however, are of limited value, because while they may confirm that *something* is going on, they do not tell us exactly *what* it is.

Planned contrasts confirm that, in our drug experiment, some drugs resulted in a very substantial improvement in performance, whereas others did not. The addition of a measure of effect size to a significant contrast arguably makes a greater contribution to knowledge than any overall measure of effect size.

Since any contrast, however complex, is basically a comparison between two means, Cohen's d statistic affords a useful measure of effect size here also. In Chapter 6, we saw that Cohen's d statistic was defined as the difference between the two means divided by the supposedly constant population standard deviation. The formula for d is reproduced below.

$$d = \frac{\mu_1 - \mu_2}{\sigma} \quad \text{- - -}\ (10)$$

Cohen's effect size index

In practice, we would estimate the within groups standard deviation with the square root of the average of the sample variances, incorporating, where necessary, a weighting for sample size. In the context of the ANOVA, the pooled variance estimate in the usual t test formula can be replaced by the ANOVA within groups mean square MS_{within}.

If we already have the value of t, we can obtain that of Cohen's d very quickly from the following formula, in which n is the size of each sample:

$$d = t\sqrt{2/n} \quad \text{- - -}\ (11)$$

Obtaining the value of d from that of t

In Chapter 6, we found that, when we tested the difference between the means of the Caffeine and Placebo groups, $t = 2.217$. We also found (from formula 10) that $d = 0.57$. Applying formula (11) to this value of t, we have

$$d = t\sqrt{2/n} = 2.217\sqrt{1/15} = 0.57$$

This value is in agreement with that obtained from the defining formula.

Turning now to contrasts, in the equal-n case, we must replace the factor $\sqrt{(2/n)}$ in formula (11) with

$$\sqrt{\sum_j^k c_j^2 / n},$$

where c_j is the contrast coefficient for group j and k is the number of groups. The formula for obtaining the value of d from that of t now becomes:

$$d = t\sqrt{\sum_j^k c_j^2 / n} \quad \text{- - -}\ (12)$$

Cohen's d for a contrast

For the second simple contrast in Output 8, $t = 4/1.391 = 2.876$. The coefficients are $-1, 0, +1, 0, 0$, therefore $\Sigma c_j^2 = 2$.

$$d = t\sqrt{\sum_j^k c_j^2 / n} = 2.876\sqrt{\frac{2}{10}} = 1.29$$

In Cohen's classification, this is a (very) large effect.

7.5   POWER AND EFFECT SIZE IN THE ONE-WAY ANOVA

When planning research, it is now standard practice to calculate the numbers of observations that will enable tests of sufficient power to be made. (The power of a statistical test is the probability that the test will show significance if the null hypothesis is false.)   One determinant of the power of a test is the size of the effect that is being studied: a given test has greater power to obtain significance when there is a large effect than when there is a small one.   In order to plan a test with a specified power, a decision must be made about the minimum size that effects must reach before they are sufficiently substantial to be worth reporting.

There are several other determinants of the power of a statistical test. The factor most under the control of the researcher, however, is usually the size of the sample: the more data you have, the greater the power of your statistical tests.

Statistical textbooks show that the sample sizes necessary to achieve an acceptable level of power (at least 0.75) for small, medium and large effects vary considerably: to be sufficiently powerful to reject the null hypothesis when there is a small effect, a sample must be several times as large as one necessary to reject the null hypothesis when there is a large effect. The higher the level of power you require, the greater the differential in sample sizes needed for the three different minimum effect sizes (Keppel & Wickens, 2004; p.169, Figure 8.1).

Using G*Power 3

The easiest way to answer questions about power and sample size is to use a dedicated statistical package such as   **G*Power 3** (Erdfelder, Faul & Buchner, 1996; Faul, Erdfelder, Lang & Buchner, 2007). The answers G*Power gives to questions about power and sample size agree with those that you would obtain if you were to consult standard tables or use a statistical computing package such as SPSS.

Questions about power and sample size cannot be answered without specifying the minimum effect size for which a test at a specified level of power is to be made.   As a measure of minimum effect size, G*Power requires the user to specify a value of Cohen's f statistic.

G*Power also requires the user to input a value for the **noncentrality parameter**, which we shall now consider.

The central F distribution

When the null hypothesis is true, the expected value of F is *about* 1. (More precisely, the expected value of F is $df_{error}/(df_{error} - 2)$, which approaches unity as the error degrees of freedom become large.)   The expected value of F under the null hypothesis is the mean of the **central F distribution,** that is, the sampling distribution of F that is 'centred' around the expected value under the null hypothesis.

The noncentral F distribution

If the null hypothesis is false, the distribution of F is centred on a value greater than $df_{error}/(df_{error} - 2)$ and is said to be distributed as **noncentral F**. The noncentral F distribution has three parameters: $df_{between}$, df_{within} and the **noncentrality parameter (lambda λ)**, which is related to Cohen's f according to:

$$\lambda = f^2 \times N \quad \text{- - -} \ (13)$$

The noncentrality parameter

In formula (13), N is the *total* sample size.

The noncentrality parameter locates the centre of the noncentral F distribution on the real number line somewhere to the right of that of the central F distribution. The larger the value of f, the less overlap there will be between the two distributions, the lower will be the Type II error rate and the greater will be the power of the F test to reject the null hypothesis if that is false.

Open G*Power 3, and select **Tests→Means→Many groups: ANOVA: One-way (one independent variable)** to open the dialog box (Figure 16). Then follow the steps shown in Figure 16. Figure 16 shows the output from G*Power 3, with the central and noncentral F distributions at the top and, in the right-hand lower panel, the total sample size necessary to achieve a power level of 0.75 to detect an effect of 'medium' size, that is a Cohen's f of at least 0.25. (These specifications are entered in the appropriate slots of the left-hand lower panel labelled **Input Parameters**.) In the **Output Parameters** panel at bottom right, we see that 180 participants will be required, that is, 36 participants in each of the five groups.

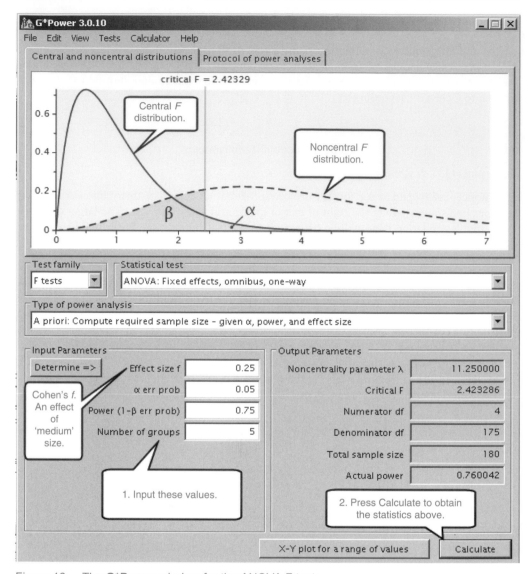

Figure 16.   The **G*Power** window for the ANOVA F test

7.6   ALTERNATIVES TO THE ONE-WAY ANOVA

Monte Carlo studies have shown that the one-way ANOVA is, to some extent, robust to small to moderate violations of the assumptions of the model and will tolerate some heterogeneity of variance and skewness of distribution.   The general import of these studies is that, if the sample sizes are similar in the various groups, and the distributions of the populations are, if not normal, at least similar from group to group, variances can differ by a factor of four without the Type I or Type II error rates rising unacceptably (see Howell, 2007; p.316).

The risk of error, however, increases considerably in data sets with unequal sample sizes in the groups. Occasionally, a data set, even when 'cleaned up' to the greatest possible extent by the removal of obviously aberrant extreme scores, may still show contraindications against the use of the usual one-way ANOVA.

The techniques described by Welch (1951) and Brown and Forsythe (1974) were specially designed for use with data sets showing marked heterogeneity of variance. They are thought to keep the error rates within acceptable limits in most circumstances. Both are available within SPSS and we feel that these (rather than nonparametric tests) should generally be one's first port of call when there are strong contraindications against the usual ANOVA procedure.

When the data are in the form of ratings, however, some journal editors and reviewers would object to the use of any kind of parametric method (even a robust test, such as those of Welch or Brown and Forsythe).

The **Kruskal-Wallis** test is a nonparametric alternative to the one-way ANOVA. It assumes neither normality of distribution nor homogeneity of variance; though it does assume that the populations have distributions of the same shape. The Kruskal-Wallis test, though less vulnerable to the presence of extreme scores and outliers than the one-way ANOVA, is by no means immune to their influence.

The Kruskal-Wallis method tests the null hypothesis of equality of medians in the population.

Some recommend that nonparametric tests should be used with many kinds of data. The first step in the running of a test such as the Kruskal-Wallis, however, is the conversion of the original scale data to ranks, a process which might be termed 'ordinalisation'. Such ordinalisation incurs the immediate penalty of a loss in power, which is a consideration when the data are scarcer than the researcher would have liked. To illustrate the test, however, we shall use the same data that we used for the one-way ANOVA.

Running the Kruskal-Wallis k-sample test

Proceed as follows:

- Choose **Analyze**➔**Nonparametric Tests**➔**Independent Samples...** to open the **Nonparametric Tests: Two or More Independent Samples** dialog box.

- Click the **Fields** tab to enter the **Fields** dialog. Transfer Score (the DV) to the **Test Fields** box and Drug Condition to the **Groups** slot.

- Click the **Settings** tab and, in the Settings dialog, click the **Customize Tests** radio button and check the **Kruskal-Wallis 1-way ANOVA (k samples)** box (Figure 17).

- Click the **Run** button at the foot of the dialog.

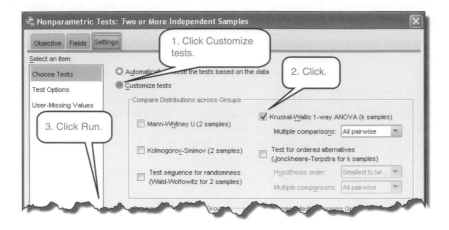

Figure 17.   Choosing the Kruskal-Wallis test

The output

The first item to appear (in the SPSS Statistics Viewer) is the **Hypothesis Test Summary** (Output 9).   Unsurprisingly, the Kruskal-Wallis test decides against the null hypothesis.

Hypothesis Test Summary

	Null Hypothesis	Test	Sig.	Decision
1	The distribution of Score is the same across categories of Drug Condition.	Independent-Samples Kruskal-Wallis Test	.000	Reject the null hypothesis.

Asymptotic significances are displayed. The significance level is .05.

Output 9.   The Hypothesis Test Summary

- Double-click on the Hypothesis Test Summary to enter the **Model Viewer**.

Output 10 shows the contents of **Auxiliary View**. The results of the pairwise comparisons can be obtained by clicking on the drop-down menu under Auxiliary View labelled Test and choosing **Pairwise Comparisons**.

You may have difficulty in seeing the entire contents of Auxiliary View, which now contains a large table. If so, proceed as follows:

- In the Model Viewer, Choose **Edit➔Copy Auxiliary View** and, in the SPSS Statistics Viewer, choose **Edit➔Paste After**.

You will now see the entire contents of Auxiliary View in the SPSS Statistics Output Viewer.

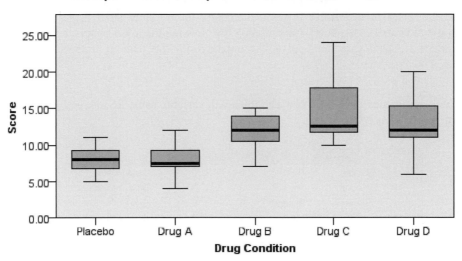

Total N	50
Test Statistic	25.376
Degrees of Freedom	4
Asymptotic Sig. (2-sided test)	.000

1. The test statistic is adjusted for ties.

Output 10. Auxiliary View in the Model Viewer

Effect size

As an overall measure of effect size following a significant Kruskal-Wallis test result, King and Minium (2003, p. 459) offer a statistic known as **epsilon-squared** (E^2).

Epsilon is the exact analogue, for ranks, of eta squared, where eta is the correlation ratio. If all the raw scores are ranked, irrespective of their groups, and each score's overall rank is paired with the mean of the ranks in its group, the correlation between the overall ranks and the group mean ranks is the square root of epsilon.

To calculate epsilon, proceed as follows:

- Choose **Transform➔Rank Cases** and transfer the variable label Score to the upper right-hand panel of the **Rank Cases** dialog box, leaving the lower panel empty. This will produce a column containing the rank of every score in the data set, irrespective of which group it came from.

SPSS will automatically create a new variable, with variable name RScore and variable label Rank of Score (Figure 18).

	Name	Type	Width	Decimals	Label
1	Case	Numeric	8	0	Case Number
2	Group	Numeric	8	0	Drug Condition
3	Score	Numeric	8	0	Score
4	RScore	Numeric	9	3	Rank of Score

Figure 18.   **Variable View**, showing that a new variable has been named and labelled

- Select **Data➔Aggregate** to enter the **Aggregate Data** dialog box (Figure 19). Move the variable label Rank of Score to the Summaries of Variable(s) panel on the right and Drug Condition to the Break Variable(s) panel. Click the OK button. This will have the effect of creating another new variable, named RScore_mean (Figure 20).

- Select **Analyze➔Correlate➔Bivariate** to access the **Bivariate Correlations** dialog box. Transfer the two new variables, RScore and RScore_mean, to the **Variables** panel on the right of the dialog and run the correlation.

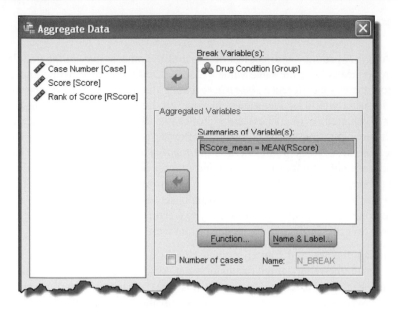

Figure 19.   The **Aggregate Data** dialog box

	Name	Type	Width	Decimals	Label
1	Case	Numeric	8	0	Case Number
2	Group	Numeric	8	0	Drug Condition
3	Score	Numeric	8	0	Score
4	RScore	Numeric	9	3	Rank of Score
5	RScore_mean	Numeric	8	2	

Figure 20. The mean ranks have been calculated

The output will show that the correlation between the overall ranks of the scores and their group mean ranks is 0.72, the square of which is 0.52. This, within rounding error, is the value of epsilon squared.

One potential problem with some of the statistics in the output for a nonparametric test is that neither ranks nor mean ranks have any meaning beyond the data from which they have been calculated. It is therefore best, in the tables and graphs in the body of the paper, to report the usual statistics such as the means and standard deviations of the original scores, rather than the rank statistics. The report of the test itself might read as follows:

'The Kruskal-Wallis chi-square test is significant beyond the .01 level: χ^2 (4) = 25.38; $p < .01$. Epsilon squared is .52 which, in Cohen's classification, is a large effect.'

7.7   A FINAL WORD

The one-way ANOVA provides a direct test of the null hypothesis that, in the population, all treatment or group means have the same value. A significant value of F, while implying that, in the population, there is a difference *somewhere* among the treatment means, does not locate the difference for us: it would be illegitimate to infer, on the basis of a significant F, that any two means (or combinations of means) are significantly different. On the other hand, the process of data-snooping, that is, the making of follow-up statistical tests, runs a heightened risk of a **Type I error**. A key notion here is the *familywise* Type I error rate. This is the probability, under the null hypothesis, of obtaining *at least one* significant result when several tests are made subsequently. The familywise Type I error rate may be very much higher than the *per comparison* Type I error rate, which is usually set at 0.05. It is essential to distinguish the Type I error rate per comparison with the Type I error rate familywise. Several ways of achieving control over the familywise Type I error rate were discussed.

Since statistical significance and a small *p*-value do not necessarily mean that a substantial effect has been found, the report of the results of a statistical test is now expected to include a measure of effect size, such as eta squared or (if possible) a bias-corrected measure such as omega squared. Where specific contrasts are of central interest, measures of effect size for those are often of more interest than an overall measure. The measure known as Cohen's *d* can easily be adapted as a measure of effect size for use with specific contrasts by taking into consideration the values of the contrast coefficients.

The researcher should try to ensure that sufficient numbers of participants are tested to allow statistical tests of adequate power to be made.

When there are strong contraindications against the use of the normal one-way ANOVA, as when the sample variances and sizes vary markedly, the researcher must consider more robust methods, some of which are available as alternatives to the ANOVA in the same SPSS program. These robust variants of ANOVA should be the first alternatives to be considered; also available, however, are nonparametric counterparts of the one-way ANOVA which, since they involve an initial process of converting scores on the original scale to ranks, incur an automatic loss in power. The case for their use, arguably, is strongest for data in the form of ratings.

When the conditions making up the treatment factor vary along a continuous dimension, as when different groups of participants perform a skilled tasks after ingestion of varying doses of the same drug, the technique of trend analysis can be used to investigate the polynomial components of the functional relationship between the independent and dependent variables. In trend analysis, the components of trend are captured in contrasts whose coefficients are values of polynomials of specified order. These contrasts (and the trends they capture) can be tested for significance in the usual way.

Recommended reading

Howell, D. C. (2007). *Statistical methods for psychology (6th ed.)*. Belmont, CA: Thomson/Wadsworth.

Keppel, G., & Wickens, T. D. (2004). *Design and Analysis: A researcher's handbook (4th ed.)*. Upper Saddle River, NJ: Pearson/Prentice Hall.

Exercise

Exercise 11   *The one-factor between subjects ANOVA* is available at
http://www.psypress.com/spss-made-simple.

CHAPTER 8

Between subjects factorial experiments

8.1   INTRODUCTION

Experiments with two or more factors are known as **factorial** experiments. In the simplest case, there is a different sample of participants for each possible combination of conditions. This arrangement is known as a **between subjects** (or **completely randomised**) **factorial** experiment. In this chapter, we shall discuss between subjects factorial experiments with two and three factors. For the analysis of data from such experiments, the **two-way** and the **three-way ANOVA** are appropriate techniques.

8.1.1   An experiment with two treatment factors

Suppose that a researcher has been commissioned to investigate the effects upon simulated driving performance of two new anti-hay fever drugs, A and B. It is suspected that at least one of the drugs may have different effects upon fresh and tired drivers, and the firm developing the drugs needs to ensure that neither drug has an adverse effect upon driving performance.

The researcher decides to carry out a two-factor factorial experiment, in which the factors are:

1.   Drug Treatment, with levels Placebo, Drug A and Drug B;

2.   Alertness, with levels Fresh and Tired.

All participants are asked to take a flavoured drink containing either (in the Drug A and Drug B conditions) a small quantity of the drug or (in the control or Placebo condition) no drug. Half the participants are tested immediately on rising; the others are tested after doing without sleep for twenty-four hours. A different sample of ten participants is tested under each of the six treatment combinations: (Fresh, Placebo); (Fresh, Drug A); (Fresh, Drug B); (Tired, Placebo); (Tired, Drug A); (Tired, Drug B).

In this experiment, each level of either factor is to be found in combination with every level of the other; the two factors, that is, are said to **cross**. There are experimental designs in which the factors do not cross (not all combinations of conditions or groups are present), but such designs will not be considered in this book. The two-factor between subjects factorial experiment can be represented as a table in which each row or column represents a particular level of one of the treatment factors, and a **cell** of the table (i.e. a single rectangle in the grid) represents one particular treatment combination (Table 1). In Table 1, the cell on the bottom right represents the combination (Tired, Drug B). The participants in Group 6 were tested under that particular treatment combination.

Table 1. A completely randomised, two-factor factorial experiment on the effects of two factors upon simulated driving performance

Alertness	Drug Treatment		
	Placebo	Drug A	Drug B
Fresh	Group 1	Group 2	Group 3
Tired	Group 4	Group 5	Group 6

The mean scores of the participants are shown in Table 2. The row and column means are known as **marginal means**. They are the means of all the scores at each level of either factor, ignoring the other factor in the classification. Inspection of the column means shows that the mean score of all those who ingested Drug B, irrespective of whether they were fresh or tired, is 19.0, a higher level of performance than that of the Placebo or Drug A groups. Inspection of the row means shows that the mean score of the Fresh participants, ignoring the drug group to which they had been assigned, is greater than that of the Tired participants.

Table 2. Mean scores achieved by the participants in the drugs experiment

	Placebo	Drug A	Drug B	Mean
Fresh	21.0	12.0	22.0	18.3
Tired	10.0	18.0	16.0	14.7
Mean	15.5	15.0	19.0	16.5

To say that the mean for the fresh participants is greater than that for the tired participants does not, of course, imply that this superiority is necessarily true of the scores at any particular level of the Drug Treatment factor. In fact, when we move from consideration of the marginal means to the cell means in the body of the table, we see that with the scores achieved under the Drug A condition, the opposite is the case: the Tired participants outperformed the Fresh participants!

The most interesting features of the data from factorial experiments often emerge from consideration of the cell means in the body of the table, rather than the marginal means. This is because the cell means show how the factors in a factorial experiment interplay or **interact**, often in complex ways. The interaction of the factors is a source of variance over and above any main effect and the possibility of such an interaction is often the principal motivation for a factorial experiment.

8.1.2   Main effects and interactions

The introduction of a second factor into the experimental design extends the range of questions that can be investigated. In this two-way factorial experiment, there are two kinds of effects, both of which can be tested with an appropriate F statistic:

1.   **main effects**;

2.   the **interaction**.

Main effects may be evident from inspection of the marginal means. Should at least one of the differences among the column means for the three levels of the Drug factor be sufficiently great as to indicate a difference in the population and should this pattern be confirmed by statistical testing, the Drug Treatment factor is said to have a **main effect**. Similarly, a large difference between the two row means would indicate that the Alertness factor also has a main effect. Since Table 2 shows that there are indeed marked differences among both row and column marginal means, it looks as if both factors have main effects. Not surprisingly, the fresh participants, on average, outperformed the tired participants. In the participants as a whole, Drug A did not produce a higher overall level of performance in comparison with the mean score of those participants who received a placebo. Drug B, on the other hand, did produce a higher overall level of performance.

Simple main effects

The effect of one treatment factor (such as Alertness) at one particular level of another factor (e.g. on the Drug A participants only) is known as a **simple main effect**. From inspection of Table 2, it would appear that the Alertness factor has different simple main effects at different levels of the Drug factor: its effect is diminished with Drug B and actually reversed with Drug A: the ingestion of the drug actually *impairs* performance compared with the Placebo group.

Interactions

When the simple main effects of one treatment factor are not homogeneous at all levels of another, the two factors are said to **interact**. An interaction between two factors, such as Drug Treatment and Alertness, is indicated by a multiplication sign thus: Drug Treatment × Alertness. (In computer output, multiplication is indicated by an asterisk: Drug Treatment*Alertness.) The results of the drug experiment, therefore, suggest the presence of a Drug Treatment × Alertness interaction.

8.1.3   Profile plots

The interaction pattern that we have just described can be depicted graphically, as plots of the cell means for the Fresh and the Tired participants against Drug Treatment (see Output 1). Such graphs are called **profile plots**.   In the present example, the Fresh participants' performance profile is V-shaped, plunging under the Drug A condition.   The Tired participants' profile, on the other hand, rises to higher levels under both the Drug A and Drug B conditions. The presence of an interaction is indicated by **profile heterogeneity** from level to level of one of the factors, that is, by *non-parallel* profiles. This is certainly the case with the profiles of the Fresh and Tired participants in the present example across the three Drug Treatment conditions.

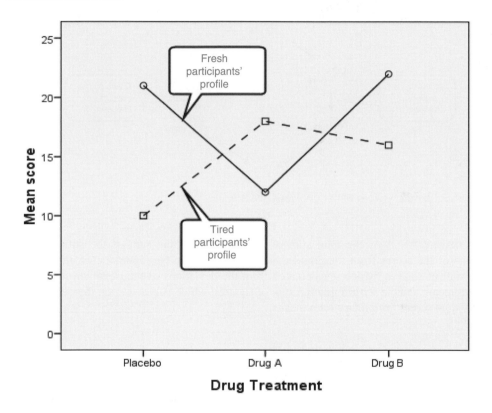

Output 1 (Annotated). A pattern of cell means suggestive of an interaction

It is important to be clear that an interaction effect is a source of variance over and above the effect of either factor considered alone or, indeed, the main effects of both factors combined. Main effects and interactions are independent: it is quite possible to obtain significant main effects without any significant interaction between the factors; it is also possible to have significant interactions without any significant main effects. As well as showing an interaction pattern, however, the appearance of the profiles in Output 1 is affected partly by the presence of main effects.   Had there been an even greater difference in overall performance level between the Fresh and Tired participants, for example, the Fresh and Tired profiles might have become completely separated at all three levels of the Drug Treatment factor. It is the *convergence* or *divergence* of the profiles, rather than their separation or slope, that indicates the presence of an interaction: there is no need for the profiles to cross one another. When the profiles are parallel, there is no interaction – even if they both slope sharply upwards or downwards or are widely separated on the vertical axis of the graph. Either of those tendencies indicates a main effect, not an interaction.

8.2 HOW THE TWO-WAY ANOVA WORKS

In Figure 1, we reproduce the graphical summary of the one-way ANOVA from Chapter 7.

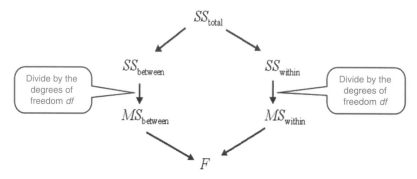

Figure 1.   Schematic picture of the one-way ANOVA

In the one-way ANOVA, the total sum of squares, that is, the sum of the squares of the deviations of the scores from the grand mean, is divided into two components: the **between groups** sum of squares, which is calculated from the deviations of the treatment means from the grand mean; and the **within groups** sum of squares, which is based upon the deviations of the individual scores from their group means.

8.2.1   The two-way ANOVA

As in the one-way ANOVA, a within subjects (error) sum of squares can be calculated by averaging the variances of the scores in the individual cells, i.e., their dispersion about their group means.

In the two-way ANOVA, the counterpart of the between groups sum of squares is the sum of squares of the deviations of the *cell means* from the grand mean. This between groups sum of squares, however, can itself be further divided into three components:

1. a **main effect** sum of squares for the Drug Treatment factor;

2. a **main effect** sum of squares for the Alertness factor;

3. an **interaction** sum of squares.

The two main effect sum of squares and the interaction sum of squares are now divided by their respective degrees of freedom to obtain mean squares, that is, variance estimates for the main effects and the interaction. As in the one-way ANOVA, the within groups sum of squares can be divided by its degrees of freedom to obtain an estimate of the error (within cell) variance. Finally, the two main effects and the interaction are tested with three F statistics, each of which has the same within groups mean square as its error term or denominator:

$$F_{\text{Alertness}} = \frac{MS_{\text{Alertness}}}{MS_{\text{within}}}$$

$$F_{\text{Drug}} = \frac{MS_{\text{Drug}}}{MS_{\text{within}}} \qquad \text{- - - (1)}$$

$$F_{\text{Alertness} \times \text{Drug}} = \frac{MS_{\text{Alertness} \times \text{Drug}}}{MS_{\text{within}}}$$

The three F tests in the two-way ANOVA

Figure 2 summarises the two-way ANOVA. (In the Figure, the specific labels Drug, Alertness and Alertness × Drug have been replaced by the more compact symbols A, B and A × B.)

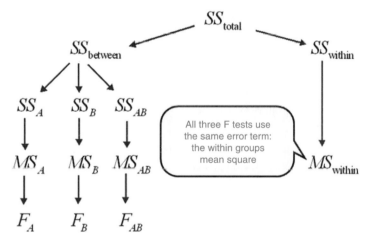

Figure 2.   Diagram summarising the two-way ANOVA

8.2.2   Degrees of freedom

In more complex designs, it is particularly important to be clear about the degrees of freedom of the various sources; otherwise it can be difficult to follow the reports of tests in the output.

Degrees of freedom of the main effects

In the one-way ANOVA of data from an experiment with k treatment groups, the degrees of freedom df of the between groups mean square is the number of treatment groups minus one: $df = k - 1$. In a similar way, in a two-way ANOVA, the degrees of freedom of each of the source mean squares for main effects is the number of levels making up the source, minus one: thus for the Alertness factor (Fresh, Tired), $df = (2 - 1) = 1$; for the Drug Treatment factor (Placebo, Drug A, Drug B), $df = (3 - 1) = 2$.

Degrees of freedom of the interaction

Turning now to the degrees of freedom of the interaction, the rule is as follows: the degrees of freedom of an interaction mean square is the product of the degrees of freedom of the factors involved. Since $df_{Alertness} = 1$ and $df_{Drug} = 2$, $df_{interaction} = 1 \times 2 = 2$.

Degrees of freedom of the error term

In the two-way ANOVA, the within groups mean square is the average of all the cell variances. In the present example, there are 6 cells, each cell representing a different combination of the factors of Alertness (2 levels) and Drug Treatment (3 levels). Each of the six cells yields a variance estimate which, since it is based upon 10 observations, has 9 degrees of freedom. The pooled within cells variance estimate, therefore, has $6 \times 9 = 54$ degrees of freedom.

In the two-way ANOVA, the within cell pooled variance estimate MS_{within} is the error term in all three F tests.

8.2.3   The two-way ANOVA summary table

Table 3 shows the ANOVA summary table for the data summarised in Table 2. Notice that there are three F statistics: one for each of the two factors considered separately; the third for the interaction. Consistent with our inspection of Table 2, the two-way ANOVA has shown that all three tests show significance beyond the 0.05 level; and the Alertness factor and the interaction are significant beyond the 0.01 level.

The precise manner in which the quantities in Table 3 are calculated is lucidly described in many excellent textbooks, such as Howell (2007) and Keppel & Wickens (2004).

Table 3. The two-way ANOVA summary table

Source	df	SS	MS	F	p	Partial eta squared
Main effects						
Alertness (A)	1	201.67	201.67	8.71	< 0.01	0.14
Drug (D)	2	190.00	95.00	4.10	0.02	0.13
Interaction						
Interaction (A × D)	2	763.33	381.67	16.49	< 0.01	0.38
Error						
Within groups (Error)	54	1250.00	23.15			
Total	59	2405.0				

The two-way ANOVA has confirmed the most interesting feature of the data, namely, the presence of an interaction between the Drug Treatment and Alertness factors: while the drug improved the performance of the tired participants, it impeded the performance of the fresh participants. It is this ability to confirm the existence of an interaction that accounts for the fact that the factorial ANOVA is one of the most widely used statistical techniques in some fields of research, such as experimental psychology; indeed, the main effects of factors considered separately are often of little interest in themselves. It is not surprising, for example, to learn that fresh participants outperform tired participants; but it is of considerable interest to learn that while a drug improves the performance of tired participants, this effect is reversed with fresh participants.

The entries under the heading **Partial eta squared** (an option in SPSS) are included in Table 3 at this point for the sake of completeness. Partial eta squared is a measure of effect size. We shall return to the measurement of effect size in a later section.

8.3   THE TWO-WAY ANOVA WITH SPSS

Table 4 shows the raw data from the two-factor factorial Drug × Alertness experiment.

Table 4. Results of the Drug Treatment × Alertness factorial experiment

| Alertness | Drug Treatment | | |
	Placebo	A	B
Fresh	24 25 13 22 16	18 8 9 14 16	27 14 19 29 27
	23 18 19 24 26	15 6 9 8 17	23 19 17 20 25
Tired	13 12 14 16 17	21 24 22 23 20	21 11 14 22 19
	13 4 3 2 6	13 11 17 13 16	9 14 11 21 18

8.3.1   Entering the data

Since there are two factors, two **grouping variables**, Alertness and Drug Treatment, will be required to specify the treatment combination under which each score was achieved. The dependent variable or measure is Driving Performance. In the **SPSS Statistics Data Editor**, we shall need a column for case numbers, two for the grouping variables, and a fourth column for Driving Performance.

- In **Variable View**, use the **Name** column to assign names to the variables, as described in Chapter 2. Here, the variables Case Number, Drug Treatment and Driving Performance must be given more compact variable names such as Participant, Drug and DrivingPerf, respectively, comforming to the requirement that a variable name must be a single string with no spaces. (The shift and hyphen keys, however, can be used to achieve partial separation among the characters, as in Driving_Perf.)

- In the **Decimals** column, change the values to 0 to display whole numbers.

- In the **Label** column, type the full variable labels: *Participant Number, Alertness, Drug Treatment,* and *Driving Performance*. This is essential for the quality of the output.

- In the **Values** column, enter the values and labels for the grouping variables, such as 1 and 2 (with labels Fresh and Tired, respectively) for the Alertness factor and 1, 2, and 3 (with labels Placebo, Drug A, and Drug B, respectively) for Drug Treatment.

- In the **Measure** column, specify that Participant and DrivingPerf are Scale variables, and that Drug and Alertness are Nominal variables.

- Enter **Data View**. To display the labels for the values entered for the grouping variables, check the View menu to make sure that **Value Labels** is ticked.

Some of the data in **Data View** are shown in Figure 3. Note that the values for the grouping variables Alertness and Drug have been replaced by their corresponding labels. For example, in case 28, the value 1 has been replaced by Fresh and 2 has been replaced by Drug B. Likewise, in case 31, the value 2 has been replaced by Tired and 1 by Placebo.

	Participant	Alertness	Drug	DrivingPerf	va
27	27	Fresh	Drug B	19	
28	28	Fresh	Drug B	17	
29	29	Fresh	Drug B	20	
30	30	Fresh	Drug B	25	
31	31	Tired	Placebo	13	
32	32	Tired	Placebo	12	
33	33	Tired	Placebo	14	
34	34	Tired	Placebo	16	
35	35	Tired	Placebo	17	
	26	Tired		3	

Figure 3. Part of **Data View** showing some of the data from Table 4

8.3.2 Exploring the data: boxplots

Before running the ANOVA, it is important to explore the data to check for any problems with the distributions. Clustered boxplots, for example, can be used to obtain summaries of the distributions of scores under the six combinations of the two treatment factors.

8.3.3 Choosing a factorial ANOVA

In SPSS, a factorial ANOVA is run by choosing from the **General Linear Model (GLM)** menu (see Figure 8 in Chapter 7).

For a between subjects factorial ANOVA, we must choose **Univariate**, bearing in mind that, although there are two independent variables (factors), namely, Drug Treatment and Alertness, this is still essentially a **univariate data** set, because there is only one dependent variable, Driving Performance.

Completing the Univariate dialog box

The **Univariate** dialog box has already been discussed in Chapter 7, and the meanings of terms such as **fixed factor** and **covariate** were explained in Section 7.3. For the two-way ANOVA, the names of both factors, Alertness and Drug Treatment, are transferred to the **Fixed Factor(s)** panel on the right of the dialog. The procedure and completed dialog are shown in Figure 4.

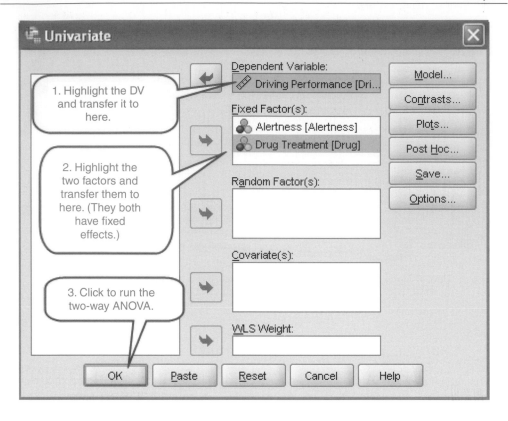

Figure 4. The completed **Univariate** dialog

Ordering profile plots

To obtain a profile plot of the means, click **Plots…** in the **Univariate** dialog box to open the **Univariate: Profile Plots** dialog box and follow the steps in Figure 5.

Note that by completing the dialog as we have in Figure 5, we have requested the profile plot shown in Output 1, with the three drug conditions on the horizontal axis and the profiles of the fresh and tired participants across the three conditions. For some purposes, however, we might want to profile the three drug conditions over the two states of alertness, in which case we should have transferred Alertness to the slot labelled **Horizontal Axis** and Drug Treatment to the **Separate Lines** slot. We shall do that later in the chapter.

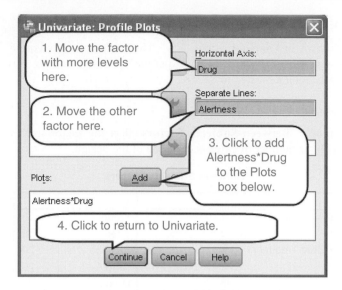

Figure 5. The **Profile Plots** dialog box for plotting the two Alertness profiles against Drug Treatment, the three levels of which will appear on the horizontal axis

Ordering descriptives and other useful measures

Click the **Options** button and order descriptive statistics and other useful measures, as shown in Figure 6.

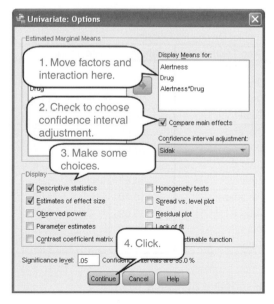

Figure 6. Ordering descriptives and other useful measures and tests from Options

8.3.4   Output for a factorial ANOVA

The results are shown in Output Listings 2-5. The earliest items require close attention, because they show whether the nature of the experimental design and the variables in the data set have been clearly communicated to SPSS.

Design specifications

The table in Output 2, **Between-Subjects Factors**, lists the factor names and their value labels, together with the number of cases in each cell of the design.

Between-Subjects Factors

		Value Label	N
Alertness	1	Fresh	30
	2	Tired	30
Drug Treatment	1	Placebo	20
	2	Drug A	20
	3	Drug B	20

Output 2. The table of **Between-Subjects Factors**

Descriptive statistics

Output 3 is the table of descriptive statistics requested from **Options…**

Descriptive Statistics

Dependent Variable: Driving Performance

Alertness	Drug Treatment	Mean	Std. Deviation	N
Fresh	Placebo	21.00	4.29	10
	Drug A	12.00	4.42	10
	Drug B	22.00	4.94	10
	Total	18.33	6.35	30
Tired	Placebo	10.00	5.66	10
	Drug A	18.00	4.64	10
	Drug B	16.00	4.78	10
	Total	14.67	5.97	30
Total	Placebo	15.50	7.47	20
	Drug A	15.00	5.38	20
	Drug B	19.00	5.65	20
	Total	16.50	6.38	60

Output 3. The table of **Descriptive Statistics**

The ANOVA summary table

The table in Output 4, **Tests of Between-Subjects Effects**, is the ANOVA summary table, which tabulates the sources of variation, their **Sums of Squares**, degrees of freedom (*df*), mean squares, *F* ratios and *p*-values (**Sig.**). Note that, in the between subjects factorial ANOVA, each *F* ratio is the Mean Square for the source divided by the Error Mean Square (23.15). The final column **Partial Eta Squared** contains estimates of effect size.

The table in Output 4 was edited in **SPSS Viewer** to reduce the display of values from three decimal places to two decimal places. This was done by double-clicking the whole table so that it showed a hashed border, highlighting the five columns of numbers so that they appeared in inverse video, clicking the right-hand mouse button to show a menu, selecting the item **Cell Properties...**, selecting in the **Format** box the item **#.#**, changing the number of decimals shown in the **Decimals** box to 2, and finally clicking **OK**.

The terms **Corrected Model** and **Intercept** refer to the regression method used to carry out the ANOVA and can be ignored. The three rows **Alertness, Drug** and **Alertness*Drug** are of most interest, since these report tests for the two main effects and the interaction. Note the **Sig.** (i.e. *p*-value, or tail probability) for each *F* ratio. There are significant main effects for both the Alertness and Drug Treatment factors: the former is significant beyond the 0.01 level, the latter beyond the 0.05 level, but not beyond the 0.01 level. In addition to main effects of both treatment factors, there is a significant interaction. The *p*-value is given as .000, which means that it is less than 0.0005. Write '$p < .01$', not '$p = .000$'. Clearly, the Drug Treatment factor has different effects upon Fresh and Tired participants. To ascertain the nature of these effects, however, we shall need to examine the pattern of the treatment means more closely.

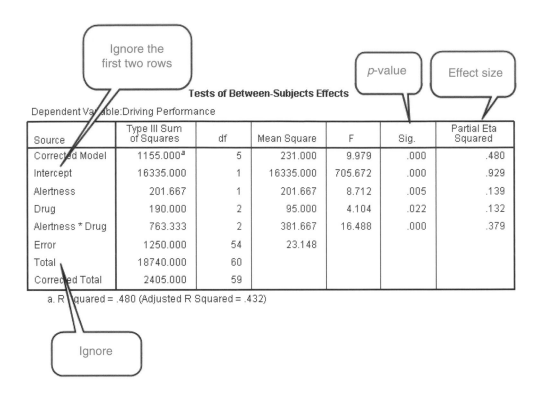

Output 4. The **ANOVA** summary table

8.3.5   Measuring effect size in the two-way ANOVA

In Chapter 7, we introduced the measure of effect size known as **eta squared (η^2)**, which is an estimate of the proportion of variance in the dependent variable accounted for by differences in the levels of the independent variable. In the case of the one-way ANOVA, eta squared is defined as follows:

$$\eta^2 = \frac{SS_{\text{treatment}}}{SS_{\text{total}}} = \frac{SS_{\text{between}}}{SS_{\text{total}}} \quad \text{- - - (2)}$$

Eta squared in the one-way ANOVA

Complete eta squared

Let Factor A and Factor B be the factors in a two-way ANOVA. We have seen that in the two-way ANOVA, there are three between groups sources of variance: the two main effect sources and the interaction. For Factor A, the measure of effect size known as **complete eta squared (η^2)** is defined as follows:

$$\eta^2 = \frac{SS_A}{SS_{total}} = \frac{SS_A}{SS_A + SS_B + SS_{AB} + SS_{within}} \quad \text{---(3)}$$

Complete eta squared

Applying formula (5) to the information in Table 3, we find that, for the Alertness factor,

$$\eta^2 = \frac{SS_{Alertness}}{SS_{total}}$$

$$= \frac{SS_{Alertness}}{SS_{Alertness} + SS_{Drug} + SS_{Alertness \times Drug} + SS_{within}}$$

$$= \frac{201.67}{2405.00} = 0.08$$

Partial eta squared

There are two major problems with complete eta squared. One is that its value is affected by the variance arising from the presence of the other factors in the experiment, which would make it difficult to compare the effect size of the same factor in two experiments with different numbers of factors. Some authors therefore advocate an alternative form of η^2, called **partial η^2** or η_p^2 in which the variance of the sums of squares for a particular effect is expressed as a proportion, not of the *total* sum of squares, but of the sum of squares of *that effect alone* plus the error sum of squares:

$$\eta_p^2 = \frac{SS_A}{SS_A + SS_{within}} \quad \text{---(4)} \quad \textbf{Partial eta squared}$$

Applying formula (4) to the information in Table 3, we find that, for the Alertness factor, the value of partial eta squared is

$$\eta_p^2 = \frac{201.667}{201.667 + 1250} = 0.139$$

which is the value given in Table 3 and Output 4. The value of partial eta squared is, of course, appreciably larger than that of complete eta squared for the same effect. SPSS includes partial eta squared as an option (**Estimates of effect size**) in the **Options...** dialog box. The choice between the **complete η^2** and **partial η^2** statistics depends upon the design of the experiment and purpose of the investigation (see Keppel & Wickens, 2004; p.235). As we shall see, however, better measures of effect size are available for some designs.

Complete and partial omega squared

The other major problem with eta squared (and this applies to both the complete and partial versions) is that it is a purely descriptive measure and overestimates the strength of the effect in the population. The estimated omega squared statistics correct this positive bias and allow for shrinkage with re-sampling.

The estimated omega squared statistics corresponding to eta squared and partial eta squared are, respectively, **complete omega squared** and **partial omega squared** – see Keppel & Wickens, 2004; pp.232–233.

The formula for the estimate of complete omega squared is

$$\hat{\omega}^2_{source} = \frac{df_{source}\left(F_{source}-1\right)}{\displaystyle\sum_{\substack{all\ treatment \\ sources}} df_{source}\left(F_{source}-1\right)+abn} \quad \text{- - - (5) \textbf{Complete omega squared}}$$

Applying Formula (7) to the information in Table 3, we see that, for the Alertness factor, the value of the estimate of complete omega squared is

$$\hat{\omega}^2_{Alertness} = \frac{df_{Alertness}\left(F_{Alertness}-1\right)}{\displaystyle\sum_{\substack{all\ treatment \\ sources}} \left(df_{source}-1\right)+abn}$$

$$= \frac{1(7.712)}{1(7.712)+2(3.10)+2(15.49)+60} = 0.07$$

The formula for partial omega squared is as follows:

$$\hat{\omega}^2_{source} = \frac{df_{source}\left(F_{source}-1\right)}{df_{source}\left(F_{source}-1\right)+abn} \quad \text{- - - (6) \textbf{Partial omega squared}}$$

where a, b and n are the number of levels of Factor A, the number of levels of Factor B and the number of observations per cell, respectively.

Returning to Table 3, we see that, for the Alertness factor, partial eta squared is given as .14. Applying Formula (6), we find that the estimate of partial omega squared for the same source is

$$\hat{\omega}^2_p = \frac{df_{Alertness}\left(F_{Alertness}-1\right)}{df_{Alertness}\left(F_{Alertness}-1\right)+\left(2\times3\times10\right)}$$

$$= \frac{1\times7.712}{1\times7.712+60} = 0.114$$

As we should expect, this value is somewhat less than the value of partial eta squared for the same source (0.139), because the estimate of omega squared incorporates a correction for positive bias.

Since the estimate of complete omega squared has the full denominator and incorporates the correction for bias, we can expect it to be the smallest of the four estimates that we have calculated.

Interpreting values of eta squared and omega squared: equivalent ranges of Cohen's *f*

In Chapter 7, in addition to eta squared and omega squared, we introduced a third measure of effect size, **Cohen's *f***. We did so because values of *f* are required as input for **G*Power 3**, a package which computes the sample sizes necessary to achieve specified levels of power to reject the null hypothesis in the presence of effects of specified minimum size.

Here (Table 5) we reproduce the table from Chapter 7 comparing the size ranges for Cohen's measure of effect size *f* with those for eta squared and omega squared. In terms of population parameters, eta squared and omega squared are identical; the estimate of partial omega squared, however, corrects for the positive bias in partial eta squared.

Table 5. A scheme for assessing values of partial eta squared/omega squared and Cohen's *f*

Size of Effect	Partial eta squared (or partial omega squared)	Cohen's *f*
Small	$0.01 \leq \eta^2 < 0.06$	$0.10 \leq f < 0.25$
Medium	$0.06 \leq \eta^2 < 0.14$	$0.25 \leq f < 0.40$
Large	$\eta^2 \geq 0.14$	$f \geq 0.40$

8.3.6 Reporting the results of the two-way ANOVA

The results of the three F tests shown in Table 3 should be reported by specifying the name of the factor, followed by the value of the *F* ratio (with the *df* of the numerator and denominator separated by a comma in brackets), the *p*-value and a measure of effect size as follows:

For the Alertness factor: $F(1, 54) = 8.71$; $p < .01$; partial eta squared = .14.
For the Drug factor: $F(2, 54) = 4.10$; $p = .02$; partial eta squared = .13.
For the interaction: $F(2, 54) = 16.49$; $p < .01$; partial eta squared = .38.

A reader, however, should never be confronted with the result of a statistical test (or, worse, a list of results like this) without also being given instant access to the descriptive statistics, either in the body of the text or in a table or figure nearby. The following report embodies these requirements; though a table would have made it less cluttered. The main thing is, the descriptives must be available as well as the test results. Note that *p*-values are given to two places of decimals only; with probabilities less than 0.01, the inequality sign < is used thus: *p* < .01. Probabilities *greater* than 0.05 should also be given (to two places of decimals). Insignificant results are also of interest. The report might read as follows:

'The mean Driving Performance scores for the Fresh (M = 18.33, SD = 6.35) and Tired (M = 14.67, SD = 5.97) conditions of the Alertness factor differed significantly beyond the .01 level: $F(1, 54) = 8.71$; $p < .01$. Partial eta squared = .14, a 'large' effect. The means and standard deviations of the three conditions making up the Drug Treatment factor were: Placebo (M = 15.5, SD = 7.47); Drug A (M = 15.0, SD = 5.38); Drug B (M = 19.00, SD = 5.65). The Drug Treatment factor had a significant main effect: $F(2, 54) = 4.10$; $p = .02$. Partial eta squared = .13, a 'medium' effect. There was also a significant Alertness × Drug interaction: $F(2, 54) = 16.49$; $p < .01$. Partial eta squared = .38, a 'large' effect.'

8.4   FURTHER ANALYSIS

In Chapter 7, we observed that the ANOVA itself is just the first stage in the analysis of a set of data from a complex experiment: inevitably, further analysis will be required to clarify the result of the initial ANOVA F test. This is true, *a fortiori*, of the factorial ANOVA. In the first place, the researcher will wish to establish (using measures such as those discussed above) the strengths of the effects that the experiment has demonstrated. It will also be necessary to pinpoint and confirm differences among the group means. Should a significant interaction be obtained, it may be necessary to 'unpack' it by making comparisons among the individual cell means.

8.4.1   A problem with multiple comparisons

A data set from a complex experiment with two or more treatment factors may well show some interesting patterns: the more complex the experiment, in fact, the more likely you are to find something interesting in the results. Unfortunately, this 'discovery' might be the result of sampling variability! You will therefore want to follow up the original ANOVA with additional analysis and make several (perhaps many) additional tests of significance. The problem with that procedure, however, is that the more significance tests you make, the more significant results you will obtain – even if the null hypothesis is true!

By making many tests of significance without taking certain precautions, the researcher is 'capitalising upon chance'. In order to avoid that mistake, the researcher must make conservative tests in order to control the **familywise** Type I error rate, that is, the probability, under the null hypothesis, that at least one test will show significance. There has been much dispute about which of several possible strategies one should follow and none has emerged as a clear winner. Here, we outline just one approach.

8.4.2   Unpacking significant main effects: post hoc tests

If the two-way ANOVA has shown a factor with three or more levels to have a significant main effect, the researcher may wish to make further comparisons among the individual marginal means. Unplanned or post hoc pairwise (or more complex) comparisons can be run by clicking the **Post Hoc** button in the **Univariate** dialog box.

The optional **Tukey** Post Hoc test results for the Drug Treatment factor are shown in Output 5. It can be seen that the means for Drug A and Drug B differ significantly from one another, but neither differs significantly from the Placebo mean.

Multiple Comparisons

Dependent Variable: Driving Performance

Tukey HSD

(I) Drug Treatment	(J) Drug Treatment	Mean Difference (I-J)	Std. Error	Sig.
Placebo	Drug A	.50	1.52	.942
	Drug B	-3.50	1.52	.064
Drug A	Placebo	-.50	1.52	.942
	Drug B	-4.00*	1.52	.029
Drug B	Placebo	3.50	1.52	.064
	Drug A	4.00*	1.52	.029

Based on observed means.

*. The mean difference is significant at the .05 level.

> The only difference with a p-value <.05 is *Drug A* and *Drug B*.
> Note these rows are highlighted with *

Output 5. Results of the Tukey multiple comparisons

8.4.3   The analysis of interactions

When the two-way ANOVA has confirmed a significant interaction between the two factors, it is often necessary to 'unpack' the interaction to determine which differences among the individual treatment or group means are significant.

An alternative profile plot

In Output 6, we have re-plotted the means from the drug experiment, so that the profiles are now the three different Drug Treatment conditions across the levels of the Alertness factor. Having the factor with the greater number of levels on the horizontal axis, as in Output 1, is more aesthetically pleasing. We have re-plotted the means with the scales reversed, however, because ultimately we shall want to make comparisons among the means for the three drug conditions and the new arrangement helps to highlight the key comparisons.

From the graph it is clear that, in the Fresh participants, performance is considerably better under the Placebo and Drug B conditions than it was under Drug A; whereas in the Tired participants, performance with both drugs seems superior to performance under the Placebo condition. Are these differences significant: that is, would these patterns survive a replication of the experiment?

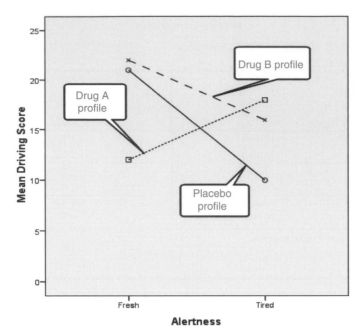

Output 6. Profile plots of the three drug treatments against levels of Alertness

One approach to the problem of making conservative multiple comparisons among the individual means is to pretend that this is really a one-factor experiment with six groups and request a **Tukey** test. (That would entail adding a new grouping variable with six values to the data set.) The problem with that approach is that, even with an array of six means, the number of possible pairwise comparisons is quite large (15) and this is reflected in a large critical value for the **studentized range statistic (q)**. The **Bonferroni and Sidak corrections** impose even tougher critera for significance. In the next subsection, we shall describe another strategy, which provides a justification for defining a smaller comparison 'family', thus enabling the user to make tests of greater power.

Testing for simple main effects

The ANOVA summary table has confirmed the interaction pattern that was strikingly evident in Ouput 1 (and in Output 6). Further analysis, however, is necessary in order to confirm the differences among the cell means. We have seen that in a factorial experiment, a **simple main effect** is the effect of a factor at one particular level of another. It would appear from Ouput 6 that there is a simple main effect of the Drug Treatment factor at each of the two levels of the Alertness factor. If we could demonstrate that each of these effects is robust, we should have a justification for defining the comparison families on the basis of three means, rather than six, and so run more powerful **Tukey** (or perhaps **Sidak-corrected**) pairwise multiple comparisons tests.

8.5   TESTING FOR SIMPLE MAIN EFFECTS WITH SYNTAX

Tests for simple main effects cannot be run simply by completing dialogs in the windowed ANOVA procedure. To test for a simple main effect of the Drug Treatment factor with the Fresh participants only, one could select the data for the fresh participants only and run a one-way ANOVA on those data alone. Subdividing the data in this way, however, entails a loss in power. The use of SPSS control language, or syntax, to test for the presence of simple main effects is the preferred approach.

8.5.1   Using the MANOVA command to run the univariate ANOVA

In the ANOVA, there is just one dependent variable or measure, no matter how many independent variables or factors there may be. The ANOVA, therefore, is a **univariate** statistical technique – even though there may be several factors in the design. In **multivariate statistics**, there are two or more dependent variables. The **multivariate analysis of variance (MANOVA)** is a generalisation of the ANOVA to data sets in which there are two or more dependent variables or measures. We shall have more to say about MANOVA in later chapters. For present purposes, it is only necessary to bear in mind that, for some purposes, the ANOVA can be viewed as a special case of MANOVA and can be run with the MANOVA command. Simple effects analysis for the ANOVA, in fact, can only be accessed by taking the MANOVA route: tests for simple effects are not an option in the ANOVA command itself.

Running a two-way ANOVA on the MANOVA command

Figure 7 shows a syntax command which will run a two-way ANOVA on the same drug and alertness data that we have already analysed, but under the aegis of the MANOVA command. Note the following points. The first word of the syntax must be the command keyword MANOVA and the command must end with a full stop or period. In the middle of the command is the keyword BY, on the left of which is the measure or dependent variable and on the right is the list of between subjects factors. The numbers in brackets after each factor name are the lowest and highest code numbers assigned to the groups or conditions.

The ANOVA summary table

The ANOVA summary table is shown in Output 7. The values of the sums of squares, the mean squares, the degrees of freedom and F are exactly as they were in Output 4. The term UNIQUE indicates that a univariate ANOVA has been run by using the MANOVA command. This is a special application of MANOVA: the MANOVA output normally looks very different from this.

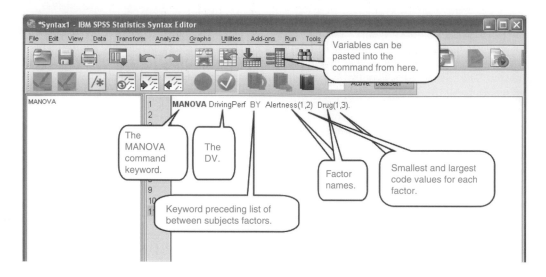

Figure 7.   Syntax for running ANOVA with the MANOVA command

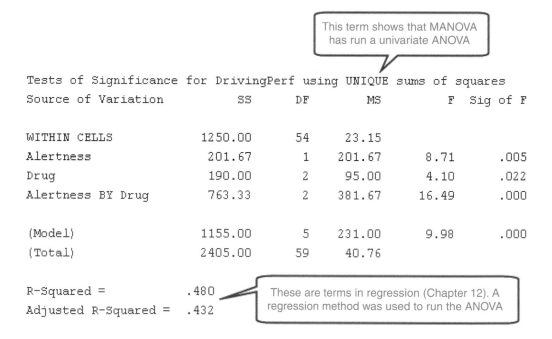

Output 7. The **ANOVA summary table** obtained from running the MANOVA command

8.5.2   Including simple effects in a MANOVA subcommand

There is more than one way of writing the syntax for simple main effects. The easiest way is shown in Figure 8.

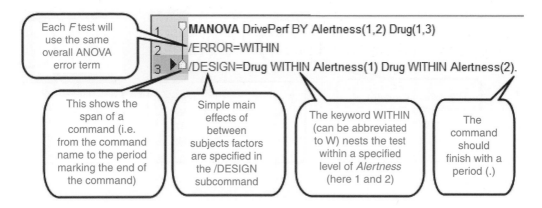

Figure 8. Syntax for testing for simple main effects of the Drug Treatment at each level of Alertness

The subcommand /DESIGN is used for tests of simple main effects. The commands for all the simple main effects of one factor at the different levels of another can be included within the same /DESIGN subcommand.

Note carefully the subcommand /ERROR. If this subcommand is not included, MANOVA will use a composite error term that includes an extra RESIDUAL component. The inclusion of the /ERROR subcommand is not the only way of avoiding this problem: as we shall see, it is possible to absorb the residual component of the error term into the effect sums of squares by amending the /DESIGN subcommand.

Output for the simple main effects analysis

Part of the output from the simple effects analysis is shown in Output 8. The analysis has confirmed the presence of simple effects of the Drug Treatment factor at both levels of Alertness: both p-values are very small. The correct error term has been used, as requested in the /ERROR subcommand. (Compare with the values of SS and DF in the full two-way ANOVA summary table in Output 7.)

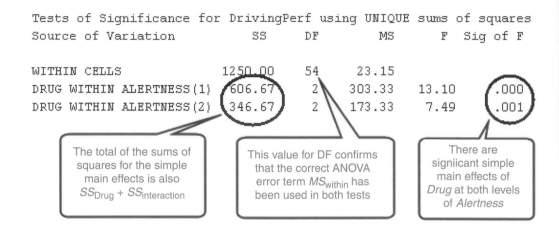

Output 8. Results of tests for simple main effects of the Drug Treatment factor at each level of Alertness

The comparison of the values in Output 8 with the ANOVA summary table in Output 7 also confirms another interesting identity. Earlier, we observed that the appearance of profile plots reflects, in part, the presence of the main effect of the factor whose simple main effects we are testing, as well as the interaction. In Output 8, you can see that

$$SS_{\text{Drug at Alertness(1)}} + SS_{\text{Drug at Alertness(2)}} = 606.666 + 346.666$$
$$= 953.33$$

This is the total of the sums of squares for the Drug Treatment factor and the interaction in the ANOVA summary table (Output 7):

$$SS_{\text{Drug}} + SS_{\text{Alertness} \times \text{Drug}} = 190.00 + 763.33$$
$$= 953.33$$

The above comparison illustrates the general point that, in a factorial experiment of A × B design, the sums of squares of the simple main effects of A at B_1, A at B_2, …, across all levels of B, add up to the sum of squares for the main effect of A plus the sum of squares for the interaction. Effectively, the simple main effects terms in Output 8 have replaced the main effect and interaction terms in the full ANOVA shown in Output 7.

An alternative syntax for testing simple main effects

The manner in which the ANOVA run by the MANOVA procedure has re-divided (or, to use the technical term, **re-partitioned**) the sums of squares becomes explicit when another wording of the MANOVA syntax command is used to test for the same simple main effects.

We have seen that the full ANOVA can be run from the MANOVA command with a single line of syntax, namely,

MANOVA DrivingPerf BY Alertness(1,2) Drug(1,3).

By adding a /DESIGN subcommand as in Figure 9, however, it is possible to repartition the between groups sum of squares into a main effect of Alertness, plus the simple effects of the Drug factor at each level of Alertness. This will have the effect of reallocating the sums of squares that would usually be attributed to the main effects of the Drug factor and the Drug by Alertness interaction to the simple effects, so that in the output, no Drug or interaction source will appear explicitly.

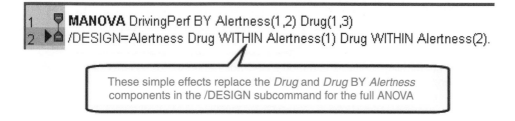

Figure 9. Specifying tests for simple main effects without also specifying the error term

Output 9 shows the result of the analysis. The source labelled WITHIN + RESIDUAL is actually the WITHIN error term in the full ANOVA, as you can see from the degrees of freedom (54) and the agreement between the sum of squares value (1250) and that given as WITHIN CELLS in Output 8. The sums of squares for ALERTNESS and (Total) have exactly the same values as those given in the full ANOVA summary table (Output 7). The sums of squares for the simple effects of the Drug Treatment factor at the different levels of Alertness sum to the total of the Drug and Drug × Alertness sums of squares in the full ANOVA.

```
Tests of Significance for DrivingPerf using UNIQUE sums of squares
Source of Variation          SS        DF      MS        F   Sig of F

WITHIN+RESIDUAL            1250.00     54     23.15
ALERTNESS                  201.67      1     201.67     8.71    .005
DRUG WITHIN ALERTNESS(1)   606.67      2     303.33    13.10    .000
DRUG WITHIN ALERTNESS(2)   346.67      2     173.33     7.49    .001

(Model)                   1155.00      5     231.00     9.98    .000
(Total)                   2405.00     59     40.76
```

R-Squared =   .480
Adjusted R-Squared =   .432

> These sources replace the main effect of Drug and the Drug*Alertness interaction in the full ANOVA summary table

Output 9. Tests for simple effects in a model re-dividing the sum of squares of the main effect of the Drug factor plus that of the Drug × Alertness interaction

Multiple comparisons following tests of simple main effects

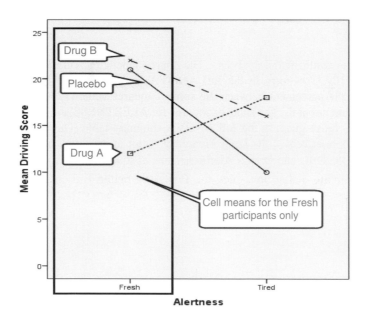

Output 10. Profile plots of the three drug conditions over the two levels of Alertness

Output 10 (annotated) is an alternative set of profile plots of the two-way table of means for the Drug and Alertness experiment, with the profiles for the three different drug conditions plotted against the two levels of the Alertness factor on the horizontal axis. From the graph, it would appear that, with the Fresh participants, Drug A lowered the performance level in comparison with the Drug B and Placebo conditions, which produced similar levels of performance.

Now that we have established that there is a significant simple main effect of the Drug Treatment factor with the Fresh participants, some would proceed with post hoc pairwise comparisons on the basis that the comparison 'family' is the number of possible pairs in the three cell means for the Fresh participants. From Output 10, we can expect that the mean for Drug A will turn out to be significantly less than the means for the Placebo and Drug B groups; whereas it seems likely that there is no significant difference between Drug B and the Placebo.

To select Fresh participants only, choose **Data➔Select Cases...** and click the **If condition satisfied** radio button to open the **Select Cases: If** dialog box (Figure 10). Complete the dialog as in Figure 10 and then click **OK** in the **Select Cases** dialog box.

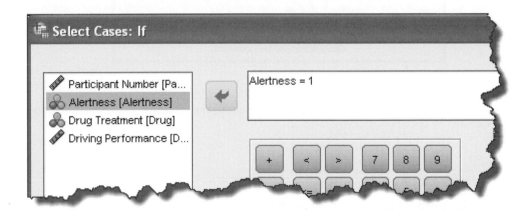

Figure 10. Selecting the data on the fresh participants only

Back in the **Univariate** dialog box, click the **Post Hoc** button and choose the **Tukey** test, specifying the factor as Drug Treatment (Figure 11). (It is instructive to choose some other methods, such as the Sidak and Bonferroni, for comparison.)

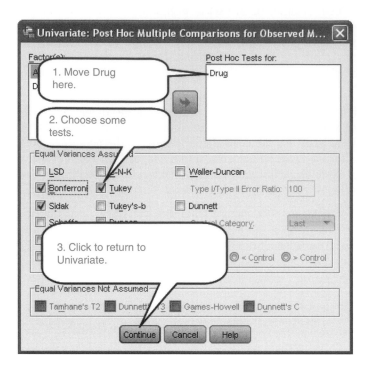

Figure 11. Choosing **Tukey** post hoc tests (and Bonferroni and Sidak for comparison) for the Drug Treatment factor

Output for the Tukey test

Output 11 shows that the **Tukey** test has identified two subgroups:

1.   The mean for Drug A;

2.   The means for the Placebo and Drug B groups.

Should you require further details for your report, the SPSS output includes another table showing the p-values and confidence intervals for these tests. We do not show this table here, but the Bonferroni and Sidak tests agree with the Tukey about which differences are significant.

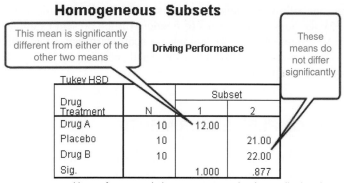

Homogeneous Subsets

Driving Performance

This mean is significantly different from either of the other two means

These means do not differ significantly

Tukey HSD

Drug Treatment	N	Subset 1	Subset 2
Drug A	10	12.00	
Placebo	10		21.00
Drug B	10		22.00
Sig.		1.000	.877

Means for groups in homogeneous subsets are displayed.
Based on observed means.
The error term is Mean Square(Error) = 20.815.

Output 11. Tukey homogeneous subsets table. (The means within each group do not differ signficantly from one another; but those in any group differ significantly from all members of the other groups.)

The **Tukey** test has clearly confirmed that, in the data from the Fresh participants only, the mean for the Drug A group is significantly lower than the means for either the Drug B group or the Placebo group, which do not differ significantly from one another.

Since the Drug Treatment factor also has a significant main effect upon the Tired participants, a similar Tukey test can be run on those data as well to confirm the pattern of differences that appears in Output 10.

8.6   HOW MANY PARTICIPANTS SHALL I NEED?

Suppose that we plan to run a two-factor between subjects factorial experiment of the same design as the one in our current example. How many people would we need to test in order to achieve, say, a power of 0.75 for an effect of medium size, that is, Cohen's $f = 0.25$?

When deciding upon the numbers of participants necessary to achieve a specified level of power for, say, an effect of 'medium' size ($f = 0.25$) the user should bear in mind that in factorial experiments, the tests of the various effects do not always have the same power to reject the null hypothesis: e.g. if both factors have three or more levels, the test for an interaction will have less power than a test for a main effect. You may have sufficient participants to achieve a power of at least 0.75 for your tests of main effects; but your test for an interaction may have lower power. Since the interaction is often the main focus in a factorial experiment, the researcher should give this effect source special attention.

As with the earlier versions, **G*Power 3** will answer questions about the power of an experimental design with specified numbers of participants and about the numbers of participants that will be needed to achieve tests at a minimum specified level of power. Open G*Power 3 and select **Tests→Means→Many groups: ANOVA: Main effects and interactions (two or more independent variables)**. Returning to our original question, we shall need to enter the following items: the effect size (0.25); the alpha-level (0.05); the desired power level (0.75); the numerator degrees of freedom (in the present example, $df_{\text{interaction}} = 2$; the total number of groups (6). In the output, we shall learn that a total sample size of 141 will be required. In practical terms, this means we shall actually require 24 participants in each group, i.e. 144 participants in all.

8.7   MORE COMPLEX EXPERIMENTS

SPSS can readily be used to analyse data from more complex factorial experiments, with three or more treatment factors. In Section 8.2, we described the two-way ANOVA, which we illustrated with data from an imaginary investigation of the effects of two new anti-hay fever drugs, A and B, upon simulated driving performance. It was suspected that at least one of the drugs might have different effects upon fresh and tired drivers, and the firm developing the drugs needed to ensure that neither had an adverse effect upon driving performance. It was found that Drug A did indeed have different effects upon fresh and tired participants: it improved the performance of tired drivers; but it impaired the performance of fresh drivers. The two-factor drugs-and-driving experiment demonstrated the presence of an interaction between the two treatment factors of Alertness (Fresh, Tired) and Drug Treatment (Placebo, Drug A, Drug B).

Our hypothetical researcher was aware that much of the previous research on the hay fever drugs had used male participants. Recent pilot work, however, had suggested that the striking interaction between Alertness and Drug Treatment might not occur in female drivers. It was therefore decided to include females in a new investigation and run a **three-factor between subjects factorial experiment**, in which the factors were:

1.   Drug Treatment, with levels Placebo, Drug A and Drug B.

2.   Alertness, with levels Fresh and Tired.

3.   Sex, with levels Female and Male.

An experiment with three factors allows the investigation of more complex hypotheses than does a two-factor experiment: in particular, the addition of the third factor brings the possibility of a complex interplay among all three factors known as a **three-way interaction**.

8.7.1   Three-way interactions

In a factorial experiment with three factors, the interaction between two factors at one particular level of the third factor is known as a **simple interaction**. For example, the interaction between the Drug Treatment and Alertness factors in the female participants only is a simple interaction, as is the interaction between the same two factors in the male participants.

What is a three-way interaction?

A **three-way interaction** is said to occur when the simple interactions between two factors are not the same at all levels of a third factor. This is exactly what is implied by the investigator's hypothesis: we can expect a three-way interaction among the factors of Alertness, Drug

Treatment and Sex because we have reason to suspect that the simple interaction between Drug Treatment and Alertness may not be the same in the two sexes.

It is quite clear from the graphs in Output 12 that the two-way interaction between the Alertness and Drug Treatment factors is different in the female and male participants: while the simple interaction is strikingly evident in the males, it is not apparent in the data from the females. Here we have what appears to be a three-way interaction among the factors Alertness, Drug Treatment and Sex. We can hope that the three-way ANOVA will confirm this complex interaction.

In the males, Drug A had a dampening effect on the performance of the fresh participants; whereas the same drug improved the performance of the tired participants. In the female participants, there is little sign of an interaction; though the Drug A profile is shallower than those of the Drug B or Placebo groups. There is here no evidence that either drug boosted the performance of tired female drivers.

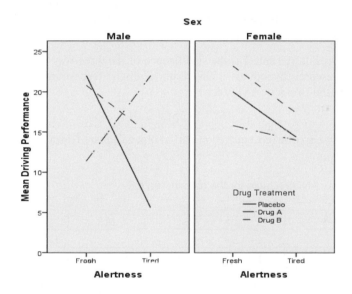

Output 12. The two-way graphs for the female and male participants, illustrating a three-way interaction among the factors of Alertness, Drug Treatment and Sex

8.7.2   The three-way ANOVA

The results of the experiment are shown in Table 6. The data are available in *Alert Sex Drug Drive (Mk II).sav* at http://www.psypress.com/spss-made-simple.

Table 6. Results of a three-way factorial experiment

Levels of the **Alertness** factor:	Levels of the **Sex** factor:	Drug Treatment		
		Placebo	A	B
Fresh	Male	23 18 19 24 26	11 16 11 8 11	23 19 17 20 25
	Female	24 25 13 22 16	14 18 15 18 14	27 14 19 29 27
Tired	Male	13 4 3 2 6	21 19 25 21 24	9 14 11 21 18
	Female	13 12 14 16 17	13 16 14 15 12	21 11 14 22 19

The three-way ANOVA summary table is shown in Table 7. It is worth examining Table 7 carefully and comparing it with the two-way table. There are now tests for three main effects: Drug Treatment, Alertness and Sex. There are also tests for each of the three possible two-way interactions: Alertness × Drug Treatment, Alertness × Sex and Drug Treatment × Sex. Finally, there is a test for a three-way interaction.

The most interesting result in Table 7 is the significance of the three-way interaction, which is consistent with the research hypothesis. The result of this F test would be reported in the manner described for the two-way ANOVA:

$$‘F(2, 48) = 11.15; p < .01’$$

A measure of effect size (partial eta squared or partial omega squared) would also be included.

Table 7. Three-way ANOVA table for the data in Table 6

Source	df	SS	MS	F	p
Main effects					
Alertness (A)	1	264.60	264.60	17.49	<0.01
Drug (D)	2	150.53	75.27	4.97	0.01
Sex (S)	1	29.40	29.40	1.94	0.17
Two-way interactions					
A × D	2	617.20	308.60	20.39	<0.01
A × S	1	0.60	0.60	0.04	0.84
D × S	2	78.40	39.20	2.59	0.09
Three-way interaction					
A × D × S	2	337.60	168.80	11.15	<0.01
Error term					
Within groups (Error)	48	726.40	15.13		
Total	59	2204.73			

In this context, it is worth observing that a list of ANOVA test results means very little without a clear demonstration of the patterns of differences responsible for each result. The mere fact that the three-way interaction is significant does not necessarily mean that the cell means show the patterns of those in Output 12. Rather than presenting the reader with a long list of results of the seven F tests, you should 'talk the reader through' the patterns of means in a graph such as Output 12 or a table, explaining the relevant significant (and insignificant) results with reference to the descriptive statistics.

8.7.3   How the three-way ANOVA works

The rationale of the three-way ANOVA is a simple extension of that of the two-way ANOVA.

In the three-way ANOVA, the between groups sums of squares is partitioned into three main effects sums of squares, three two-way interaction sums of squares and the three-way interaction sum of squares. As with the one-way and two-way ANOVA, the mean squares are obtained by dividing the sums of squares by their degrees of freedom. The general form of the F statistic for any between subjects factorial design is as follows:

$$F\left(df_{source}, df_{within}\right) = \frac{MS_{source}}{MS_{within}} \quad \text{- - - (7)}$$

General form of the F statistic in the between subjects factorial ANOVA

Degrees of freedom of the mean squares

It is important, with complex experimental designs especially, to be clear about the degrees of freedom of the various sources in the ANOVA. This knowledge is very helpful when you are interpreting the SPSS output, or when you want to use a package such as **G*Power 3** to determine the number of participants that will be needed in a study you plan to run.

The degrees of freedom are obtained in a manner analogous with the one-way and two-way ANOVA. For main effects, df is the number of conditions or groups minus 1. In our current example,

$$df_{Drug} = (3-1) = 2; \quad df_{Alertness} = (2-1) = 1; \quad df_{Sex} = (2-1) = 1$$

For two-way interactions, the df is the product of the degrees of freedom of the main effects of the sources involved in the interaction. In our current example,

$$df_{Alertness \times Drug} = (2-1)(3-1) = 2;$$
$$df_{Alertness \times Sex} = (2-1)(2-1) = 1;$$
$$df_{Drug \times Sex} = (3-1)(2-1) = 2$$

The degrees of freedom of the three-way interaction is the product of the degrees of freedom of the three component sources. In our current example, if A, B and C are the Alertness, Drug Treatment and Sex factors, respectively, then

$$df_{A \times B \times C} = (2-1)(3-1)(2-1) = 2$$

The error term for the three-way ANOVA

As in the two-way ANOVA, all the F tests in the three-way ANOVA have the same denominator, namely, MS_{within}. As in the one-way and two-way ANOVA, the within groups mean square is the average of the variance estimates calculated from each sample of participants.

The number of samples is the number of cells in the three-way design and therefore the product of the numbers of levels making up the different treatment factors. In our current example, the number of samples = $2 \times 3 \times 2 = 12$. If there are 5 scores in each sample, each variance estimate has 4 degrees of freedom. The pooled error term, therefore, has $12 \times 4 = 48$ degrees of freedom. This is the value given in Table 7.

8.7.4 The three-way ANOVA with SPSS

For the three-way ANOVA, the data set in **Data View** will now include three grouping variables (Alertness, Sex, and Drug), as well as a column for the dependent variable DrivingPerf. (It is good practice also to include a column of case or participant numbers as well.) Figure 12 shows a section of **Data View**, showing the third grouping variable Sex, representing the third factor in the experimental design.

	Participant	Alertness	Drug	Sex	DrivingPerf
1	1	Fresh	Placebo	Female	24
2	2	Fresh	Placebo	Female	25
3	3	Fresh	Placebo	Female	13
4	4	Fresh	Placebo	Female	22
5	5	Fresh	Placebo	Female	16
6	6	Fresh	Placebo	Male	23
7	7	Fresh	Placebo	Male	18
8	8	Fresh	Placebo	Male	19
9	9	Fresh	Placebo	Male	24

Figure 12.   Part of **Data View** showing some of the data in Table 6

- Open the **Univariate** dialog box and complete the dialog by moving Driving Performance to the **Dependent Variable** box and the three grouping factors Alertness, Drug Treatment and Sex to the **Fixed Factors** box.

- Click the **Options** button and select **Descriptive statistics** and **Estimates of effect size**. Click **Continue** to return to the **Univariate** dialog, and **Post Hoc** to order **Tukey** tests. (Try some of the others as well, such as Bonferroni and Sidak.)

- To obtain the profile plots of the means that we have shown in Output 12, click **Plots...** to open the **Univariate: Profile Plots** dialog box. Select Alertness for the **Horizontal Axis** box, Drug Treatment for the **Separate Lines** box and Sex for the **Separate Plots** box. Click **Add** to add the plot to the **Plots** list and then **Continue** to return to the **Univariate** dialog box. (Note that, should you want to have the Drug Treatment factor on the horizontal axis of the graphs and show the profiles of the two Alertness conditions, you would transfer Drug Treatment to the Horizontal Axis box, Alertness to the **Separate Lines** box and Sex to the **Separate Plots** box as before.)

- Click **OK**.

The first table in the output lists the factors in the experiment, their value labels and the number of cases in each cell (Output 13). Check this information carefully to ensure that there have been no transcription errors and that the design specifications have been correctly communicated to SPSS.

Between-Subjects Factors

		Value Label	N
Alertness	1	Fresh	30
	2	Tired	30
Drug Treatment	1	Placebo	20
	2	Drug A	20
	3	Drug B	20
Sex	1	Male	30
	2	Female	30

Output 13. The table of **Between-Subjects Factors**

The next table in the output (not reproduced here) shows the descriptive statistics you should always request in the **Options...** dialog box.

The ANOVA summary table (Output 14) shows that of the three main effects, Alertness and Drug are significant but Sex is insignificant. Of the three two-way interactions, Alertness × Drug is significant, but neither Alertness × Sex nor Drug × Sex is significant. There is a significant three-way interaction, in line with the experimental hypothesis.

The full SPSS ANOVA summary table is a useful source of information for the researcher who is analysing data with a view to publishing a research paper. Such a table, on the other hand, would rarely appear in the body of the text of a paper; moreover, little would be achieved by including, in the body of the text, a comprehensive list of all the test results in the ANOVA summary table. Instead, the reader should be guided through only those results that are relevant to the principal research hypotheses, each result being explained with reference to the appropriate descriptive statistics. Whether a table or a graph is the more suitable vehicle for the descriptive statistics is a matter of opinion and journal editors can differ on this issue. With a complex experiment such as the present one, we think it makes life easier for the reader to be (at least initially) referred to a graph such as Output 12, rather than a complex table.

Tests of Between-Subjects Effects

Dependent Variable:Driving Performance

Source	Type III Sum of Squares	df	Mean Square	F	Sig.	Partial Eta Squared
Alertness	264.600	1	264.600	17.485	.000	.267
Drug	150.533	2	75.267	4.974	.011	.172
Sex	29.400	1	29.400	1.943	.170	.039
Alertness * Drug	617.200	2	308.600	20.392	.000	.459
Alertness * Sex	.600	1	.600	.040	.843	.001
Drug * Sex	78.400	2	39.200	2.590	.085	.097
Alertness * Drug * Sex	337.600	2	168.800	11.154	.000	.317
Error	726.400	48	15.133			
Corrected Total	2204.733	59				

Output 14. The three-way factorial **ANOVA** summary table (edited)

8.7.5   Follow-up analysis following a significant three-way interaction

Having obtained a three-way interaction, you will certainly want to follow this up with further analysis. In an experiment of this degree of complexity, however, the perils of data-snooping are even greater than they are in a two-factor experiment. As far as we can see from our study of the literature, there seems to be no generally acceptable way of avoiding inflation of the **Familywise Type I error** rate to at least some extent. The following suggestions, though defended by some, would certainly not be accepted by everyone.

It might be argued that the risk of capitalising upon chance is reduced by following a multistage decision process, in which tests at any stage are only made if the previous stage has shown a significant result. For example, only if the three-way interaction has proved significant, would one proceed to test for simple interactions between Drug Treatment and Alertness at each level of Sex. Should you obtain a significant simple interaction only with the males, this would provide additional confirmation of the research hypothesis. As with testing for simple main effects in the two-factor experiment, the **Bonferroni or Sidak correction** could be used to make a more conservative test for simple two-way interactions in the three-factor experiment. Since there are two possible simple interactions, one for the males, the other for the females, you would require that each test should show significance beyond the 0.025 level, rather than merely beyond the 0.05 level.

Should a simple interaction prove to be significant, you will naturally wish to make unplanned comparisons among the individual cell means. In the two-factor experiment, there was the difficulty that if one bases the size of the comparison family upon the set of means involved in the entire interaction, the criterion for significance is very stringent. Arguably, a significant test for a simple main effect might justify basing the size of the comparison family upon those means at one level only of the other factor. The same problem arises in the analysis following a significant three-way interaction. In order to justify limiting the size of the comparison 'family', you could proceed to test for a main effect of the Drug Treatment factor at specific combinations of the factors of Alertness and Sex. Should you find, for example, that there is a significant main effect of the Drug Treatment factor in those participants who were both Fresh and Male, you could then proceed to run a **Tukey** test on the three cell means involved, basing the size of the comparison family upon those means alone, rather than upon all those involved in the interaction. A test for a main effect of one factor at a specific combination of two other factors is known as a **simple, simple main effect**. A significant simple, simple main effect would arguably justify reducing the size of the comparison family when making unplanned multiple comparison among the cell means. Once again, the test for a significant simple, simple main effect should be protected by the **Bonferroni** procedure: in the present example, the test would have to show significance beyond the 0.025 level, rather than the 0.05 level.

In the next section, we shall describe the use of SPSS syntax to test for simple interactions and simple, simple main effects.

8.7.6   Testing for simple interactions and simple, simple main effects

Tests for simple effects of various kinds in completely randomised factorial experiments are accessed by the use of the DESIGN subcommand within the MANOVA command. Here we shall consider the syntax for simple interactions and simple, simple main effects separately. In practice, of course, both types of subcommand could be included in the same MANOVA command.

The full three-way ANOVA with syntax

The full ANOVA can be run with a one-line MANOVA command very similar to the one we used for the two-factor ANOVA (Figure 13):

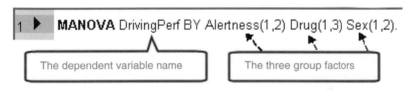

Figure 13. The three-way ANOVA with Syntax

The ANOVA summary table is shown in Output 15. The values given, of course, agree exactly with the corresponding values in the GLM output (Output 14).

```
Tests of Significance for DrivingPerf using UNIQUE sums of squares
Source of Variation            SS        DF        MS         F  Sig of F

WITHIN CELLS                726.40      48     15.13
Alertness                   264.60       1    264.60      17.48    .000
Drug                        150.53       2     75.27       4.97    .011
Sex                          29.40       1     29.40       1.94    .170
Alertness BY Drug           617.20       2    308.60      20.39    .000
Alertness BY Sex              .60        1      .60         .04    .843
Drug BY Sex                  78.40       2     39.20       2.59    .085
Alertness BY Drug BY        337.60       2    168.80      11.15    .000
 Sex

(Model)                    1478.33      11    134.39       8.88    .000
(Total)                    2204.73      59     37.37


R-Squared =           .671
Adjusted R-Squared =  .595
```

Output 15.   The three-way ANOVA summary table from Syntax

Testing for simple interactions

Figure 14 shows the syntax for tests of simple interactions at each level of the Sex factor.   In the /DESIGN subcommand, the keyword BY is used to specify an interaction.

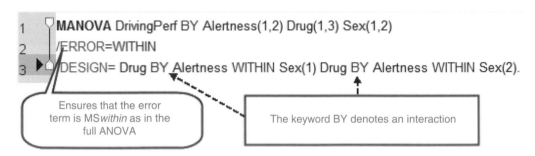

Figure 14.   Testing for simple interactions with Syntax

The results of the tests for simple interactions are shown in Output 16.

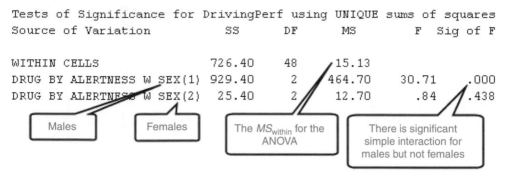

Output 16. Tests for a simple interaction between Drug Treatment and Alertness at each level of Sex

There is a significant simple Drug Treatment × Alertness interaction in the Males, but not in the Females. This result is consistent with the experimenter's hypothesis that the interaction may not occur in Female drivers.

Notice that if we add the sums of squares for the two simple interactions, we obtain the sum of the sums of squares for the Drug × Alertness interaction and the Drug × Alertness × Sex interaction from the full ANOVA summary table. Simple effects confound the target interaction with certain lower-order effects: simple main effects confound the two-way interaction with the main effect; simple interactions confound the three-way interaction with the two-way interaction. Simple effects, then, are a blend of effects at different levels, and it is for that reason that some are opposed to their use.

Testing for a simple, simple main effect of the Drug Treatment factor at each level of Sex

Figure 15 shows the syntax for testing for simple, simple main effects. A specific combination of Alertness and Sex is specified by a second use of the keyword WITHIN.

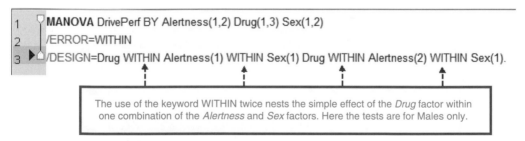

Figure 15. Testing for simple, simple main effects of the Drug Treatment factor at different combinations of Alertness and Sex

The results of the tests for simple, simple main effects are shown in Output 17.

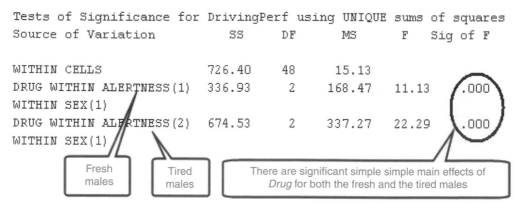

```
Tests of Significance for DrivingPerf using UNIQUE sums of squares
Source of Variation              SS       DF       MS       F    Sig of F

WITHIN CELLS                   726.40     48     15.13
DRUG WITHIN ALERTNESS(1)       336.93      2    168.47    11.13    .000
WITHIN SEX(1)
DRUG WITHIN ALERTNESS(2)       674.53      2    337.27    22.29    .000
WITHIN SEX(1)
```

| Fresh males | Tired males | There are significant simple simple main effects of *Drug* for both the fresh and the tired males |

Output 17. Tests (edited) for simple, simple main effects of the Drug Treatment factor at each level of Alertness in the Male participants only

Since both tests show significance beyond the 0.01 level, there is, some would argue, justification for making unplanned multiple comparisons among the three cell means at either level of Alertness.

8.7.7   Unplanned multiple comparisons

We have seen that the appearance of the cell means in Output 12 has been confirmed by the finding that there is a significant simple interaction between the factors of Drug Treatment and Alertness among the male participants. We have also found that there is a significant simple, simple main effect of the Drug Treatment factor in the data from the Fresh Males. We now want to unpack the interaction more completely by making unplanned multiple comparisons among the Placebo, Drug A and Drug B cell means from the data on the Fresh Males only. The first step is to filter out all the data except the scores obtained by the Fresh Male participants. Figure 16 shows the appropriate **Select Cases: If** command.

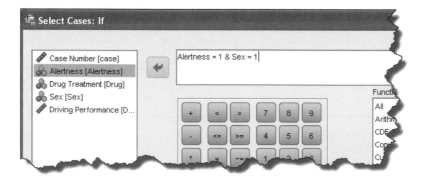

Figure 16. Selecting the data for Fresh Males only

Figure 17 shows the appearance of part of Data View with the filter in operation. It will be seen that only the data from the Fresh Males have been selected for the Tukey analysis.

	Case	Alertness	Drug	Sex	DrivingPerf	filter_$
8	8	Fresh	Placebo	Male	19	Selected
9	9	Fresh	Placebo	Male	24	Selected
10	10	Fresh	Placebo	Male	26	Selected
11	11	Fresh	Drug A	Female	14	Not Selected
12	12	Fresh	Drug A	Female	18	Not Selected
13	13	Fresh	Drug A	Female	15	Not Selected
14	14	Fresh	Drug A	Female	18	Not Selected
15	15	Fresh	Drug A	Female	14	Not Selected
16	16	Fresh	Drug A	Male	11	Selected
17	17	Fresh	Drug A	Male	16	Selected

Figure 17. Data View, showing that only the data from the Fresh Males will be subjected to further analysis

Since the testing of various multiple comparisons raises no new issues, we shall not describe the procedure here.

8.8   A FINAL WORD

In this chapter, we have tried to convey something of the power of factorial experiments to answer complex scientific questions. The interpretation of the results of complex experiments, however, particularly unplanned tests made during the data-snooping phase following the ANOVA proper, is fraught with risk and there is a heightened risk of capitalising upon chance.

We strongly recommend that you should try to avoid factorial designs with more than three factors. While we agree that participants' scores are likely to depend on many variables, it is usually possible to arrange that theoretically unimportant potential sources of variance, such as positional and sequential contingencies, can be neutralised by careful experimental design and need not emerge explicitly as factors in the analysis.

There are several good reasons for avoiding complex factorial designs with four or more factors. Four-way interactions are exceedingly difficult to interpret. Moreover, although the follow-up methods we have described can, in principle, be extended to the analysis of more complex experiments, there remains the potential problem of over-analysis and hence capitalising upon chance. The more factors there are, the greater the risk that the analysis will turn up an unexpected and striking effect that would not be confirmed by a re-run of the experiment. If a comparison is of such vital theoretical importance, there is much to be said for designing a new, simpler experiment to confirm that it has nor arisen merely through sampling error.

Some would certainly disapprove of the use of simple effects analysis to reduce the size of the comparison 'family' when one is unpacking a significant interaction; and the testing of simple, simple main effects for the purpose of reducing the size of the comparison family when unpacking a significant three-way interaction is even more questionable. Others, however, would agree that if such analyses are untaken only after an interaction (or simple interaction) has proved to be significant, the risk of capitalising upon chance has at least been reduced. In our view, an experiment of complex factorial design is perhaps most appropriate when the hypotheses driving the research are still somewhat tentative. At a later stage, when the focal hypothesis has crystallised, the researcher should test it with an experiment of simpler design.

Recommended Reading

In this chapter, we could do no more than touch upon the analysis of data from complex factorial experiments. Howell (2007; Chapter 13) gives a lucid treatment of the analysis of interactions.

Howell, D. C. (2007). *Statistical methods for psychology (6th ed.)*. Belmont, CA: Thomson/Wadsworth.

Exercise

Exercise 12 *Between subjects factorial ANOVA (two-way ANOVA)* is available in www.psypress.com/spss-made-simple. Click on Exercises.

CHAPTER 9

Within subjects experiments

9.1   INTRODUCTION

In this chapter, we turn to experiments in which each participant (or subject) is tested under all the different conditions in the experimental design. Such repeated testing obviously makes fullest use of the participant's presence. As we shall see, however, the taking of **repeated measures** on the same participants also has disadvantages.

9.1.1   Rationale of a within subjects experiment

A potential problem with between subjects experiments (Chapters 7 & 8) is that if there are large individual differences in performance, searching for a meaningful pattern in the data can be like trying to listen to an old-fashioned radio against a loud background crackle of interference. For example, in a Drug experiment such as the one described in Chapter 7, some of the scores obtained by participants in the Placebo condition may well be higher than those of participants tested under any of the drug conditions. There are some people who can bring a natural dexterity and flair to almost any test of skill; in others, on the other hand, those qualities are consistently less evident. Since, in a between subjects experiment, a different sample of participants performs under each condition, variation in natural aptitude is likely to introduce considerable **noise** into the data and inflate the error terms of the F statistics.

Another drawback with the between subjects experiment is that it is wasteful of participants: if the experimental procedure is a short one, a participant may spend more time travelling to and from the place of testing than actually performing the experimental task. We shall now consider another experimental strategy which not only allows the researcher to make fuller use of the participant's time, but also results in more powerful statistical tests.

A researcher wishes to investigate the effects upon shooting accuracy of the shape of a target. Participants are asked to shoot twenty times at each of four differently-shaped targets. Since each participant is tested under all the conditions making up the factor of target shape, this experiment is said to be of **within subjects** design, or to have **repeated measures** on the factor of target shape. Table 1 compares the design of this one-factor, within subjects experiment with that of a one-factor between subjects experiment similar to the drug experiment in Chapter 7.

Table 1. Between subjects and within subjects experiments in which there is one treatment factor with four levels

(a)	A one-factor between subjects experiment		
	Levels of the Drug factor		
	Control	Drug A	Drug B	Drug C
Participants	Group 1	Group 2	Group 3	Group 4
(b)	A one-factor within subjects experiment		
	Levels of the Shape factor		
	Circle	Square	Triangle	Diamond
Participants	The same participants perform with all four shapes. The order of presentation of the four conditions is varied, or **counterbalanced**, so that each condition occurs with equal frequency in each of the four ordinal positions across all the participants in the study.		

The variance in the scores from our experiment on target shape and shooting accuracy will certainly reflect individual differences every bit as marked as they are likely to be in the drug experiment. There is, however, an important difference between the two experiments. In being tested under every condition, each participant is effectively serving as his or her own control. That person's average performance over all conditions can serve as a baseline against which their performance under the different conditions can be evaluated.

While the within subjects experiment has obvious advantages over the between subjects experiment, it should also be said that this data-gathering strategy raises problems that are not encountered with the between subjects experiment. All these difficulties stem ultimately from the fact that within subjects experiments yield correlated data. The manner in which the data are correlated has important implications, both for the making of the statistical tests in the ANOVA itself and for such considerations as the measure of power and effect size.

9.1.2   How the within subjects ANOVA works

In Figure 1, we reproduce from Chapter 7 a diagram of the one-way between subjects ANOVA. In the one-way ANOVA, two estimates of variance are made: the between groups mean square $MS_{between}$, which is calculated from the values of the group means only; and the within groups means square MS_{within}, which is the average of the variances of the individual scores within the groups. The null hypothesis of equality, in the population, of the treatment means was tested with the statistic F, where $F = MS_{between} / MS_{within}$.

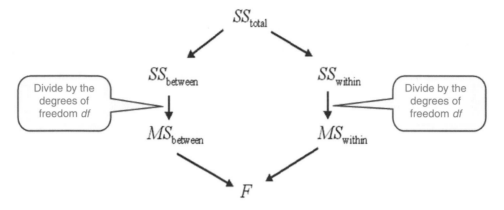

Figure 1. Summary of the one-way (between groups) ANOVA

In the one-factor within subjects ANOVA, the participants are not grouped, so there is no between groups sum of squares. The participants are tested under all conditions, however, which makes it possible to calculate a mean score for each participant. Since each participant is tested at all levels of the treatment factor, we could regard Subjects as a second factor which **crosses** with Treatments, that is, every combination of Subjects and Treatments is present in the design of the experiment. In fact, we can think of the within subjects experiment as a two-factor experiment with one observation per cell, which is why some textbooks use the term **Subjects × Treatments** to refer to this type of experiment.

The Subjects × Treatments designation makes explicit the possibility of an interaction between the Subjects 'factor' and the true treatments factor. If there are n participants, the Subjects factor has n levels. If the treatment factor has k levels, the interaction between the Subjects and Treatments factors has $(n-1)(k-1)$ degrees of freedom.

It is this interaction between Subjects and Treatments that serves as the error term for the F test in the one-factor, within subjects ANOVA. The corresponding variance estimate is known as the **residual** mean square, because it represents what remains of the total variance when the contributions of the treatment factor and the Subjects factor have both been removed.

$$MS_{residual} = MS_{Subjects \times Treatments} = \frac{SS_{residual}}{df_{residual}} = \frac{SS_{residual}}{(n-1)(k-1)} \quad \text{--- (1)}$$

**The error term in the
one-factor within subjects experiment**

Figure 2 summarises the one-factor within subjects ANOVA:

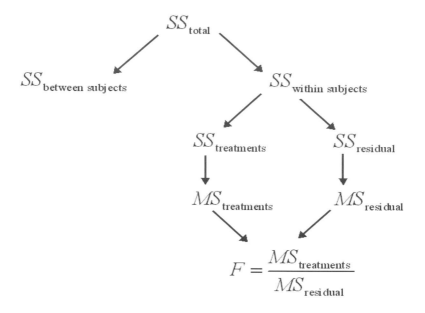

Figure 2. Summary of the one-factor within subjects ANOVA

It can be seen from Figure 2 that in the one-factor within subjects ANOVA, no estimate of the between subjects variance is actually made. However, the between subjects sum of squares is removed from the total sum of squares and the mean squares for the treatment factor and the error term are both calculated from the within subjects sum of squares.

If Subjects is a 'factor', it is one with **random effects**: that is, the participants in the experiment are assumed to be a random sample from a large pool of possible participants. This is why the residual (Subjects × Treatments) mean square is suitable as the error term for the F test. (Howell, 2007, gives a lucid discussion of the rationales of the F tests in the ANOVA, including the within subjects ANOVA.)

When we compare Figure 2 with Figure 1 (the diagram of the one-way ANOVA), it is clear that the within subjects design allows the extraction of a considerable amount of the variance from the data and results in an error term that does not reflect the main effect of the Subjects factor. (The residual error term, however, does reflect the interaction between Treatments and Subjects.)

In our within subject experiment, the treatment factor has four levels.   If there are ten participants or subjects, the experiment will result in forty scores. The equivalent one-factor between subjects experiment would have forty participants, one group of ten for each of the four treatment conditions. In the within subjects ANOVA, the residual sum of squares has only $(10 - 1)(4 - 1) = 27$ degrees of freedom; whereas in the one-way (between subjects) ANOVA, the within groups mean square MS_{within} has $4(9) = 36$ degrees of freedom.

Since the degrees of freedom of the residual sum of squares are less than the df of MS_{within}, the critical value for F is larger. In practice, however, the partialling out of a major part of the variance arising from individual differences results in an increase in the power of the F test, so that the power efficiency (that is, power in relation to the number of participants) of the within subjects experiment is greater than that of the between subjects experiment.

In summary, therefore, the within subjects experiment has two advantages over the between subjects experiment:

1. It makes more efficient use of time and resources, requiring fewer participants and making more use of those participants.

2. It cuts down data noise, resulting in a test of greater power in relation to the number of participants in the experiment.

The within subjects experiment, however, also has disadvantages, which in some circumstances can outweigh considerations of convenience and the maximisation of the signal-to-noise ratio. We shall consider some of those problems presently.

9.1.3   A within subjects experiment on the effect of target shape on shooting accuracy

Table 2 shows the results of an experiment on the effects of target shape on shooting accuracy. (In this experiment, there were three target shapes only.) The order of presentation of the three targets was counterbalanced across participants in an attempt to neutralise any order effects.

Table 2. Results of a one-factor within subjects experiment

	Target		
Participant (Subject)	Circle	Square	Triangle
1	10	12	14
2	18	10	16
3	20	15	16
4	12	10	12
5	19	20	21
6	25	22	20
7	18	16	17
8	22	18	18
9	17	14	12
10	23	20	18

The ANOVA summary table is shown in Table 3.

Table 3. The ANOVA summary table

Source	df	SS	MS	F	p
Shape	2	39.267	19.633	4.86	0.02
Subjects	9	370.170	40.608		
Residual (Shape × Subjects)	18	72.730	4.04		
Total	29	482.167			

We can report the result of the F test as follows:

‘The factor of Target Shape had a significant main effect: $F(2, 18) = 4.86$; $p = .02$.’

In a scientific report, this result would be accompanied by the descriptive statistics (preferably in a table or graph) and some measure of effect size such as partial eta squared or partial omega squared.

9.1.4   Order effects: counterbalancing

A potential problem with repeated measures is that a participant's performance on one task may be affected by the experience of having performed another task, particularly when the two tasks are attempted in close succession. Such an effect upon performance is an example of a **carry-over** (or **order**) **effect**. Sometimes, of course, carry-over effects are of focal interest, as in memory research, where the researcher might wish to demonstrate the proactive interference of learning one list of words with the recall of the words in another list learned subsequently. Usually, however, carry-over effects in within subjects experiments are potential **confounds**, the influence of which can be difficult to disentangle from that of the treatment factor itself.

If participants are tested on a succession of tasks, their performance on the later tasks may improve through a **practice effect**. Practice effects, however, are only one type of carry-over effect. Not all carry-over effects are positive: proactive and retroactive interference in memory are negative carry-over effects. In within subjects experiments, carry-over effects are potential **extraneous variables**, whose effects may be confounded with those of the treatment factor.

The possibility of carry-over effects confounding the effects of the treatment factor is reduced by the procedure known as **counterbalancing**, in which the order of the conditions making up a within subjects factor is varied from participant to participant, in the hope that carry-over effects will balance out across conditions. Counterbalancing is not always effective, however, because order effects can be very asymmetrical. There are also situations in which a within subjects strategy would be quite inappropriate: the drug experiment in Chapter 7 is a good example.

9.1.5 Assumptions underlying the within subjects ANOVA: homogeneity of covariance

We shall not describe the model underlying the within subjects ANOVA explicitly here. Recall, however, that in the model for the one-way ANOVA, certain assumptions are made about the random error component of each score, such as normality of distribution and homogeneity of variance.

Another important assumption in the one-way ANOVA is the independence of the error components of different scores. The within subjects ANOVA, however, is based upon a model of a situation in which the same participant is tested under all experimental conditions. Here, the assumption of independence of the error components is untenable. The within subjects model, while acknowledging that the data are correlated, makes an additional assumption about the scores, namely, that they have the property of **homogeneity of covariance**, or **sphericity**.

The covariance

Since the same participants shoot at all three targets, we can expect a positive correlation between the scores that the participants achieved under any two of the conditions: high scores with one target are likely to be paired with high scores on the other; and low scores on one target are likely to be accompanied by low scores on the other. The actual correlations among the scores for the three targets confirm this expectation: the correlation between the scores on the Circle and Square targets is 0.802; the correlation between Circle and Triangle is 0.729; and the correlation between Square and Triangle is 0.826.

The **covariance** is a measure of strength of association which, unlike the correlation coefficient (actually a special case of the covariance), has no upper or lower limits. For a bivariate data set comprising n (X, Y) pairs, the covariance between X and Y, $COV(X, Y)$ is:

$$COV(X,Y) = \frac{\sum (X - M_X)(Y - M_Y)}{n-1} \quad \text{--- (2)} \quad \textbf{The covariance}$$

Formula (2) resembles the formula for the sample variance, except that the sum of the squared deviations from the mean has been replaced by the sum of the products of the deviations of X and Y from their respective means. In fact, the variance is the covariance of a variable with itself!

The variance-covariance matrix

In Table 4, are shown the covariances of each of the three conditions in the experiment with the other two conditions.

In the cells on the **principal diagonal** of this array or matrix, that is, the diagonal that runs from top left to bottom right, are the variances of the scores for each condition: each diagonal cell, that is, contains the covariance of the scores achieved under one particular condition with themselves. The off-diagonal elements contain the covariances between heterogeneous pairs of conditions. In summary, the values in bold along the diagonal (21.60; 18.23; 9.38) are the variances; the off-diagonal elements are the covariances.

Table 4. Variance-covariance matrix for the scores in Table 2. (The grey cells along the principal diagonal contain variances; the off-diagonal cells contain covariances.)

	Circle	Square	Triangle
Circle	21.60	15.91	10.38
Square	15.91	18.23	10.80
Triangle	10.38	10.80	9.38

Notice the symmetry of the variance-covariance matrix: the covariance of X with Y is identical with the covariance of Y with X, so the entries in the cells below the principal diagonal duplicate those in the cells above it.

The values in the variance-covariance matrix must show a uniformity or consistency known as **homogeneity of covariance** or **sphericity**: that is, there should be comparable levels of association among the scores at different levels of the treatments factor. If this assumption is violated, the **Type I error rate** (i.e. the probability of rejecting H_0 when it is true) may be inflated. Tests for homogeneity of covariance are made on the variance-covariance matrix. For this purpose, SPSS uses the **Mauchly Sphericity Test**. Should the data fail the sphericity test (i.e. p-value < 0.05), the ANOVA F test must be modified to make it more **conservative** (less likely to reject the null hypothesis). SPSS offers three such conservative tests, varying in their degree of conservativeness: the **Greenhouse-Geisser**, the **Huynh-Feldt**, and the **Lower-bound**. All three tests reduce the degrees of freedom of the numerator and the denominator of the F ratio (by multiplying them by a factor termed **epsilon**), thus increasing the value of F required for significance.

9.2 A ONE-FACTOR WITHIN SUBJECTS ANOVA WITH SPSS

The one-factor within subjects ANOVA is accessed through **Repeated Measures...** in the **General Linear Model** menu. As always, we strongly recommend that you begin your analysis by getting to know your data first, before embarking on any formal statistical tests. Here, however, we shall assume that you have already done this and we can proceed with the ANOVA directly. The data can be found in *Ch9 Shooting accuracy.sav* at http://www.psypress.com/spss-made-simple.

9.2.1   Entering the data

Since the participants have not been divided into groups, no grouping variable is required for entry of these data into the **SPSS Statistics Data Editor**. In **Variable View**, using the procedures described in Chapter 2, enter the variables Case (or Participant), Circle, Square and Triangle. Using the **Label** column, expand the variable names to Case Number, Circle Target, Square Target and Triangle Target. To avoid clutter in Data View, set the number of decimal places displayed to zero. In **Data View**, enter the case numbers and the data from Table 2 into the first four (pre-labelled) columns.

9.2.2   Running the one-factor within subjects ANOVA

So far, we have merely created a data set in Data View consisting of three variables: Circle, Square and Triangle. Hitherto, SPSS will have assumed that the values in the Circle, Square and Triangle variables are related to three quite different properties or characteristics. There is no mention of the treatment factor Shape anywhere in this data set, in contrast to the appearance of Data View before a one-way ANOVA, in which the treatment factor is one of the named variables. SPSS must now be informed that these data are all Accuracy scores and are the results of a within subjects experiment with one treatment factor (Shape), consisting of three levels. When we do this, SPSS will present a frame into which we can insert the names Circle, Square and Triangle as the names of the three levels of the treatment factor Shape.

- Select **Analyze→General Linear Model→Repeated Measures…** to open the **Repeated Measures Define Factors** dialog box (Figure 3).

- Follow the steps described in Figure 3 and click **Define** to view the **Repeated Measures** dialog box (Figure 4), which will show, above the **Within-Subjects Variables box**, the name (Shape) of the within subjects factor that has just been defined. In the box itself, is a frame for the variable names making up the levels of the newly-defined within subjects factor.

- Transfer the three variables en masse to the frame by selecting them while keeping the **Ctrl** key pressed and clicking the central arrow. The question marks on the frame will be replaced by the variable names (Figure 5).

- Order a profile plot of the levels of the within subjects factor by clicking **Plots…** and following the steps shown in Figure 6. Click **Continue** to return to the original dialog box.

- A table of **Descriptive statistics**, **Estimates of effect size** and a table of **Sidak-adjusted pairwise comparisons** among the levels of the within subjects factor are requested by clicking **Options…** in the **Repeated Measures** dialog box and following the steps shown in Figure 7. Click **Continue** to return to the original dialog box.

- Click **OK** to run the procedure.

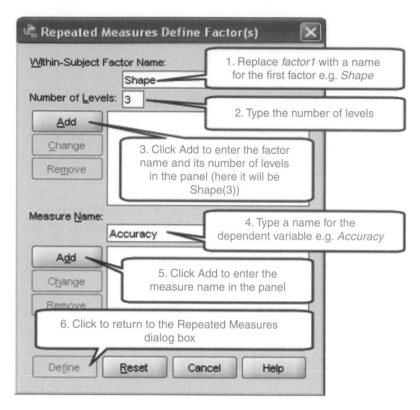

Figure 3. The **Repeated Measures Define Factor(s)** dialog box

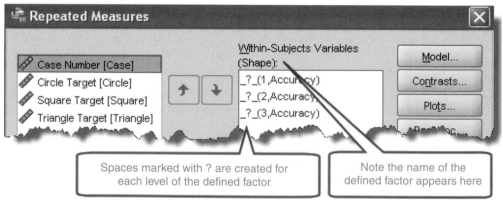

Figure 4. The upper half of the **Repeated Measures** dialog box after defining the **Within-Subjects Variables** factor as Shape with three levels and naming the measure as Accuracy

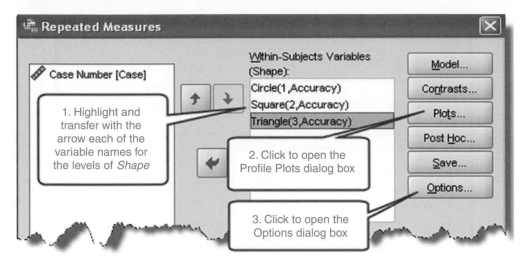

Figure 5. The completed **Repeated Measures** dialog box

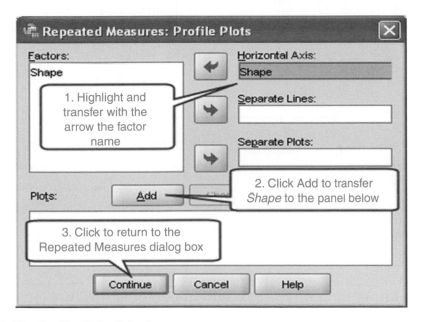

Figure 6. The **Profile Plots** dialog box

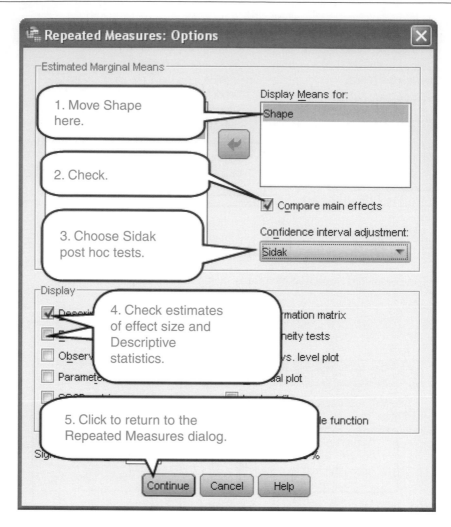

Figure 7. The completed **Options** dialog box requesting **Descriptive statistics**, **Estimates of effect size** and **Sidak** comparisons

9.2.3   Output for a one-factor within subjects ANOVA

The output is extensive, but not all of it is required for a within subjects ANOVA. Eventually, you may find it convenient to remove some of the items by highlighting their icons in the outline pane in the SPSS Statistics Viewer and pressing Delete. Meantime, we shall consider the items of principal interest.

Details of the experimental design and descriptive statistics

Output 1 shows the **Title**, the **Within-Subjects Factors** list for the measure Accuracy and the specially requested **Descriptive Statistics** table.

Within-Subjects Factors

Measure: Accuracy

Shape	Dependent Variable
1	Circle
2	Square
3	Triangle

Descriptive Statistics

	Mean	Std. Deviation	N
Circle Target	18.40	4.648	10
Square Target	15.70	4.270	10
Triangle Target	16.40	3.062	10

Output 1. The **Within-Subjects Factors** list and **Descriptive Statistics** table

The Mauchly Test of Sphericity

Output 2 reports the result of the **Mauchly's Test of Sphericity**, a test for homogeneity of covariance (see Section 9.1.5). There are two possible results. If the p-value (**Sig.**) is greater than 0.05, the null hypothesis of homogeneity of covariance (sphericity) is accepted. If the p-value is less than 0.05, the null hypothesis of homogeneity of covariance is rejected.

> The chi-square value is 0.76 and its associated p-value (Sig.) is 0.68 (i.e. not significant)

Mauchly's Test of Sphericity[b]

Measure: Accuracy

Within Subjects Effect	Mauchly's W	Approx. Chi-Square	df	Sig.	Epsilon[a] Greenhouse-Geisser	Huynh Feldt	Lower-bound
Shape	.909	.760	2	.684	.917	1.000	.500

Tests the null hypothesis that the error covariance matrix of the orthonormalized transformed dependent variables is proportional to an identity matrix.

a. May be used to adjust the degrees of freedom for the averaged tests of significance. Corrected tests are displayed in the Tests of Within-Subjects Effects table.

b.
Design: Intercept
Within Subjects Design: Shape

Output 2. **Mauchly's Test of Sphericity** and values of epsilon for conservative **ANOVA** F tests

The result of Mauchly's Test indicates how we should read the final ANOVA summary table. If the result is insignificant, we can concentrate on those rows of the ANOVA summary table that are marked as assuming sphericity, or homogeneity of covariance; but if the test has shown significance, we should report the results of, say, the Greenhouse-Geisser conservative F test.

The ANOVA summary table

The ANOVA summary table (Output 3) shows the results of four F tests of the null hypothesis that, in the population, shooting accuracy for all three shapes is the same.

The results of the tests are given in separated rows, labelled **Sphericity Assumed**, **Greenhouse-Geisser**, **Huynh-Feldt** and **Lower-Bound**. In the lower part of the table, the same row labels are used for the error terms of the four F statistics reported in the top half of the table. Each F ratio was obtained by dividing the treatment mean square in its row by the error mean square in the row of the same name in the lower half of the table. If Mauchly's Test does not show significance, we need only read, in the ANOVA summary table, the rows labelled **Sphericity Assumed**. If Mauchly's Test does show significance, we suggest that, in the ANOVA summary table, you read only the rows labelled **Greenhouse-Geisser**.

The conservative test only makes a difference when:

1.   There is heterogeneity of covariance (i.e. Mauchly's Test is significant).

2.   The F with unadjusted degrees of freedom (i.e. the values shown in the **Sphericity Assumed** rows) is barely significant beyond the 0.05 level.

Should F have a low tail probability (say $p < 0.01$), the null hypothesis can be safely rejected without making a conservative test. In the present case, Mauchly's Test gives a p-value of 0.68, so there is no evidence of heterogeneity of covariance. The usual ANOVA F test can therefore be made.

Tests of Within-Subjects Effects

Measure:Accuracy

Source		Type III Sum of Squares	df	Mean Square	F	Sig.	Partial Eta Squared
Shape	Sphericity Assumed	39.27	2	19.63	4.86	.021	.351
	Greenhouse-Geisser	39.27	1.83	21.41	4.86	.024	.351
	Huynh-Feldt	39.27	2.00	19.63	4.86	.021	.351
	Lower-bound	39.27	1.00	39.27	4.86	.055	.351
Error(Shape)	Sphericity Assumed	72.73	18	4.041			
	Greenhouse-Geisser	72.73	16.50	4.41			
	Huynh-Feldt	72.73	18.00	4.04			
	Lower-bound	72.73	9.00	8.08			

Since the Mauchly result was not significant, the Sphericity Assumed rows apply. The other rows could be deleted	For *F*=4.86 with a p-value of 0.02, the factor *Shape* is significant	The value of partial eta squared is 35% (i.e. a large effect size)

Output 3. The **ANOVA** summary table for the **Within-Subjects Effects**

The main result in Output 3 is the value of *F* and its associated *p*-value (**Sig.**) for the within subjects factor Shape. The table has been edited by narrowing some columns and reducing the number of decimal places displayed.

In the row labelled **Error (Shape) Sphericity Assumed**, the *df* for the error term is given as 18; but in the other rows, smaller values for the *df* are given for the conservative tests. In the present case, there was no need to make a conservative *F* test because Mauchly's Test is not significant. It is apparent from the **Sig.** column that, *in this particular example*, most of the conservative tests make no difference to the result of the ANOVA *F* test.

In the case of the factor Shape, note that the *p*-value for *F* in the **Sphericity Assumed** row is 0.021: that is, the obtained value of *F* is significant beyond the five per cent (0.05) level, but not beyond the 0.01 level. We can therefore conclude that Shape does affect shooting accuracy. We can write this result as follows:

> 'The mean scores for the three shapes of target differed significantly at the 5% level: $F(2, 18) = 4.86$; $p = .02$ Partial eta squared = .35, which is a large effect.'

...ied multiple comparisons

...e is evidence to suggest that, following significant main effects of within subjects factors, ... **Tukey test** affords insufficient protection against inflation of the per family type I error ...ate. The **Bonferroni** adjustment is a more conservative test. The **Sidak** adjustment is slightly less conservative than the Bonferroni. Output 4 shows the results of Sidak-corrected tests of pairwise comparisons. The results of the Bonferroni tests are shown below the Sidak table for comparison.

Pairwise Comparisons

Measure:Accuracy

(I) Shape	(J) Shape	Mean Difference (I-J)	Std. Error	Sig.ª	95% Confidence Interval for Differenceª	
					Lower Bound	Upper Bound
1	2	2.700*	.895	.043	.084	5.316
	3	2.000	1.011	.220	-.955	4.955
2	1	-2.700*	.895	.043	-5.316	-.084
	3	-.700	.775	.773	-2.966	1.566
3	1	-2.000	1.011	.220	-4.955	.955
	2	.700	.775	.773	-1.566	2.966

Based on estimated marginal means

*. The mean difference is significant at the .05 level.
a. Adjustment for multiple comparisons: Sidak.

Pairwise Comparisons

Measure: Accuracy

(I) Shape	(J) Shape	Mean Difference (I-J)	Std. Error	Sig.ª	95% Confidence Interval for Differenceª	
					Lower Bound	Upper Bound
1	2	2.70*	.90	.044	.075	5.325
	3	2.00	1.01	.238	-.966	4.966
2	1	-2.70*	.90	.044	-5.325	-.075
	3	-.70	.78	1.000	-2.974	1.574
3	1	-2.00	1.01	.238	-4.966	.966
	2	.70	.78	1.000	-1.574	2.974

Based on estimated marginal means

*. The mean difference is significant at the .05 level.
a. Adjustment for multiple comparisons: Bonferroni.

Only one comparison has a p-value (Sig.) <.05

Output 4. The Sidak- and Bonferroni-adjusted **Pairwise Comparisons** among the levels of the within subjects factor Shape for the measure Accuracy

It can be seen from Output 4 that, on both the Bonferroni and Sidak post hoc tests of the three possible pairwise comparisons among the three treatment means, only the difference between the means for the Circle and Square conditions is significant. The other two comparisons fall well short of significance.

The profile plot

The requested profile plot is shown in Output 5, which is an edited version of the default plot, adjusted to include zero on the vertical scale. The default plot, with only a small section of the scale on the vertical axis, makes the differences among the means look enormous.

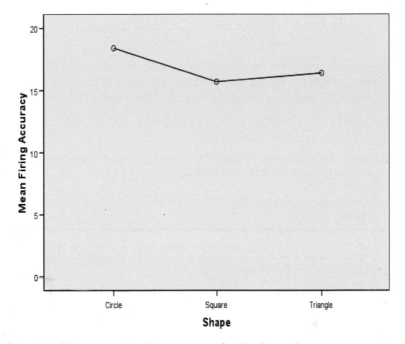

Output 5. The plot of the mean shooting accuracy for the three shapes

9.2.4 Effect size in the within subjects ANOVA

We have seen that the one-factor within subjects ANOVA can be viewed as a Subjects × Treatments factorial experiment with one observation per cell. We need to take that view in order to understand the measures of effect size that have been proposed. Even when there is only one treatment factor, the presence of the Subjects factor in the design means that the question of a partial (rather than a complete) measure of effect size arises. For the one-factor within subjects experiment, partial measures express the variance attributable to the treatment factor as a proportion, not of the total variance, but of the source variance plus the residual variance.

Partial eta sqared

As with the between subjects ANOVA, SPSS provides, as a measure of the size of the effect of a treatment source (a factor or an interaction), the statistic known as **partial eta squared** η_p^2, where

$$\eta_p^2 = \frac{SS_{treatment}}{SS_{treatment} + SS_{residual}} \text{ --- (3) \textbf{Partial eta squared}}$$

From Table 3 (the ANOVA summary table), we find that $SS_{Shape} = 39.267$ and $SS_{residual} = 72.730$. Substituting these values into formula (3), we have

$$\eta_p^2 = \frac{SS_{treatment}}{SS_{treatment} + SS_{residual}} = \frac{39.267}{39.267 + 72.730} = 0.35$$

This value agrees with that given in the ANOVA summary table. Below, in Table 5, we reproduce Cohen's guidelines for the interpretation of values of eta squared (or partial eta squared) and Cohen's f. In Cohen's classification, the Shape factor has a 'large' effect.

Table 5.   Guidelines for assessing values of eta squared (or bias-corrected measures such as omega squared) and the equivalent values of Cohen's f

Size of Effect	Eta squared	Cohen's f
Small	$0.01 \leq \eta^2 < 0.06$	$0.10 \leq f < 0.25$
Medium	$0.06 \leq \eta^2 < 0.14$	$0.25 \leq f < 0.40$
Large	$\eta^2 \geq 0.14$	$f \geq 0.40$

We should note that, although the eta squared measures can readily be extended to within subjects designs with two or more factors, the use of bias-corrected measures such as omega squared is often problematic. (See, for example, Keppel & Wickens, 2004; p.427.) For a detailed discussion of these issues, see Dodd & Schultz (1973).

9.3   HOW MANY PARTICIPANTS SHALL I NEED?

The correlated nature of the data from within subjects experiments has implications for the determination of power and effect size. To determine the power of the F test in a within subjects experiment, we shall need to be able to locate the critical value for F in the noncentral F distribution, where its cumulative probability is β, the Type II error rate, and $(1 - \beta)$ is the power of the test. In Chapter 7, we saw that for the kind to data to which the one-way ANOVA is applicable, the noncentrality parameter lambda is simply the square of Cohen's f statistic multiplied by N, the total sample size. In the one-factor within subjects experiment, which will yield correlated data, matters are by no means as simple. The noncentrality parameter is affected by several factors, including the average correlation among the scores at the different levels of the treatment factor. It is also affected by epsilon, the multiplier for the degrees of freedom that is obtained from the variance-covariance matrix. The import of these considerations is that, in order to determine, a priori, the power of a within subjects experiment that you are planning to run, you will require information that may not readily be available unless you have already run some pilot studies of the measures you intend to use in your experiment.

The **G*Power 3** package, which is available freely on the Internet (Erdfelder, Faul & Buchner, 1996; Faul, Erdfelder, Lang & Buchner, 2007), can also answer questions about power and effect size in within subjects experiments. For within subjects experiments, however, the G*Power interface will require information that the user is unlikely to have, such as the average inter-correlation between scores at different levels of the within subjects factor. Some pilot work with the planned measures would enable the researcher to supply the necessary information. Failing that, you could specify the design of the experiment as between subjects and arrive at conservative recommendations that would certainly ensure that your tests had sufficient power.

9.4   NONPARAMETRIC EQUIVALENTS OF THE WITHIN SUBJECTS ANOVA

As with the one-factor completely randomised experiment, nonparametric methods are available for the analysis of ordinal and nominal data. Once again, we suggest that if your measurements are at the scale or continuous level, the first possibility to consider is the running of the within subjects ANOVA on a cleaned-up data set, rather than 'ordinalising' the data by converting them to ranks, which is effectively what happens when one runs a nonparametric test. The decision to opt for a nonparametric test in this situation incurs the immediate penalty of a loss of power. In the next example, however, the raw data are ranks in the first place and the researcher has no option but to use a nonparametric test.

9.4.1   The Friedman test for ordinal data

Suppose that six people rank five objects in order of 'pleasingness', assigning the rank of 1 to the most pleasing object and 5 to the least pleasing. Their decisions might appear as in Table 6. (The data are available in *Ch9 Friedman.sav* at http://www.psypress.com/spss-made-simple.)

Table 6. Six people's ranks of five objects in order of 'pleasingness'

	Object 1	Object 2	Object 3	Object 4	Object 5
Person 1	2	1	5	4	3
Person 2	1	2	5	4	3
Person 3	1	3	4	2	5
Person 4	2	1	3	5	4
Person 5	2	1	5	4	3
Person 6	1	2	5	3	4

From Table 6, it would appear that Object 1 is more pleasing to most of the raters than, say, Object 3. Since, however, the numbers in Table 6 are not independent measurements but ranks, the one-factor within subjects ANOVA cannot be used here to confirm differences among the average ratings assigned to the objects. With data in the form of ranks, the Friedman test is the nonparametric equivalent of the one-factor within subjects ANOVA. The null hypothesis tested, however, is that the five samples of ranks are from populations with identical distributions, which is often taken as the statement that the medians are equal.

Running the Friedman test

In **Variable View**, name the variables Object1, Object2, ... Object5. In **Data View**, enter the data in the usual way.

To run the Friedman test:

- Check that, in Variable View, the level of measurement is set at the scale level. This is very important – the procedure will not run otherwise.

- Choose **Analyze➔Nonparametric Tests➔Two or More Related Samples...** to enter the **Nonparametric Tests: Two or More Related Samples** dialog.

- Click the **Fields** tab and, in the **Fields** dialog, transfer the five variables to the **Test Fields** box on the right.

- Click the **Settings** tab and, in the **Settings** dialog, check the **Customize** radio button and the box labelled **Friedman's 2-way ANOVA by ranks (k samples)**. The completed dialog is shown in Figure 8.

- Click the **Run** button at the foot of the dialog to run the test.

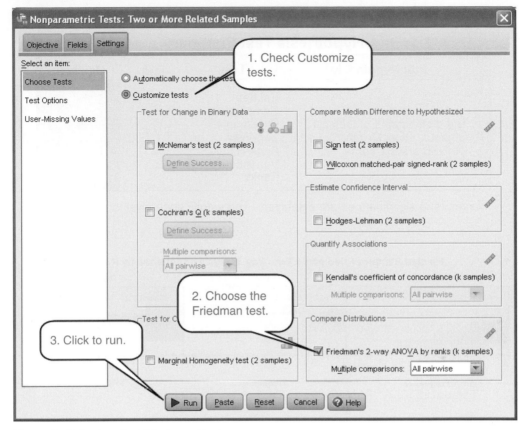

Figure 8. Selecting the **Friedman** Test

Output from the Friedman test

The **Friedman Test** results are shown in Output 6. Underneath the Test Summary in the SPSS Statistics Viewer, is the content of the auxiliary pane of the Model Viewer. (To see the whole pane, it may be necessary to copy it and paste it into the SPSS Statistics Viewer.) Clearly the rankings differ significantly across the objects since the *p*-value is less than 0.01. In this test, the test statistic is an approximate chi-square on degrees of freedom one less than the number of objects. We can write this result as:

$$`\chi^2 (4) = 17.2; p < .01.`$$

The Friedman procedure also produces a neat table of multiple comparisons, which can be viewed by clicking on the drop-down menu at the foot of the auxiliary pane of the Model Viewer.

It is worth noting that, had we run the Friedman test on the data set upon the Shape data, the chi-square test would have failed to show significance: $\chi^2(4) = 5.421; p = 0.065$. That result, however, is a consequence of the loss in power resulting from the conversion to ranks of data that were originally at the continuous or scale level of measurement. We certainly would not recommend such a transformation.

Hypothesis Test Summary

	Null Hypothesis	Test	Sig.	Decision
1	The distributions of Object1, Object2, Object3, Object4 and Object5 are the same.	Related-Samples Friedman's Two-Way Analysis of Variance by Ranks	.002	Reject the null hypothesis.

Asymptotic significances are displayed. The significance level is .05.

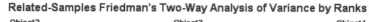

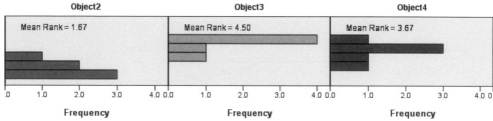

Total N	6
Test Statistic	17.200
Degrees of Freedom	4
Asymptotic Sig. (2-sided test)	.002

Output 6. **Friedman** test results

Measuring effect size with the coefficient of concordance

As a follow-up measure of effect size following a significant Friedman test result, King & Minium (2003; p.462) recommend the **coefficient of concordance (*W*)**. If N is the total number of data points, k is the number of conditions and χ^2 is the Friedman test statistic, the formula for W is

$$W = \frac{\chi^2}{N(k-1)} \quad \text{--- (4)}$$

The coefficient of concordance

Substituting the values in Output 8 for χ^2, N and k in formula (4), we have

$$W = \frac{\chi^2}{N(k-1)} = \frac{17.2}{6(4)} = 0.72$$

The coefficient of concordance can take values in the range from zero to 1, inclusive. To interpret a value of W, therefore, we can use the usual Cohen benchmarks (Chapter 6, Table 5) for classifying the size of a correlation and, since W is greater than 0.5, conclude that a value of 0.72 represents a 'large' effect.

Unplanned multiple comparisons following a significant Friedman test result

Following a significant result of the Friedman test, pairwise multiple comparisons can be made among the different conditions by using the Wilcoxon signed–ranks test, applying the Bonferroni correction to protect against inflation of the familywise Type I error rate. For example, if Object 1 is regarded as a comparison object, we could compare the level of ranking for Object 1 with those for Objects 2, 3, 4 and 5, setting our per comparison Type 1 error rate at $0.05/4 = 0.01$.

9.4.2   Cochran's Q test for nominal data

Suppose that six children were asked to imagine they were in five different situations and had to choose between Course of Action A (coded 0) and B (coded 1). The results might appear as in Table 7. Inspection of Table 7, shows that B (i.e. cells containing 1) was chosen more often in some scenarios than in others. A suitable confirmatory test of this trend is **Cochran's Q** test, which was designed for use with related samples of dichotomous nominal data.

Table 7. Courses of action chosen by six children in five scenarios

	Scene 1	Scene 2	Scene 3	Scene 4	Scene 5
Child 1	0	0	1	1	1
Child 2	0	1	0	1	1
Child 3	1	1	1	1	1
Child 4	0	0	0	1	0
Child 5	0	0	0	0	0
Child 6	0	0	0	1	1

The data are available in *Ch9 Cochran.sav* at http://www.psypress.com/spss-made-simple.

Running Cochran's Q test

To run Cochran's Q test:

- Check that, in Variable View, the level of measurement for the five variables is set at the nominal level.

- Choose **Analyze➔Nonparametric Tests➔Two or More Related Samples…** to enter the **Nonparametric Tests: Two or More Related Samples** dialog.

- Click the **Fields** tab and, in the **Fields** dialog, transfer the five variables to the **Test Fields** box on the right.

- Click the **Settings** tab and, in the **Settings** dialog, check the **Customize** radio button and the box labelled **Cochran's Q (k samples)**.

- Click the **Run** button at the foot of the dialog to run the test.

The results are shown in Output 7, from which it is clear that the same course of action is not taken in equally often in all five scenarios. Your report might read:

'Cochran $Q = 9.82$; $df = 4$; $p = .04$.'

By clicking on the drop-down menu at the foot of Auxiliary View, you can see a table of the results of tests of multiple comparisons.

Hypothesis Test Summary

	Null Hypothesis	Test	Sig.	Decision
1	The distributions of Scenario 1, Scenario 2, Scenario 3, Scenario 4 and Scenario 5 are the same.	Related-Samples Cochran's Q Test	.044	Reject the null hypothesis.

Asymptotic significances are displayed. The significance level is .05.

Related-Samples Cochran's Q Test

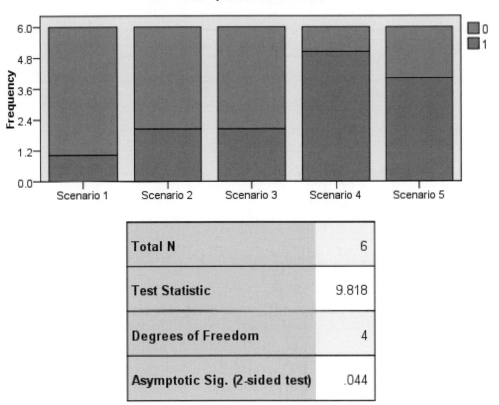

Total N	6
Test Statistic	9.818
Degrees of Freedom	4
Asymptotic Sig. (2-sided test)	.044

Output 7. **Cochran Test** results

9.5 THE TWO-FACTOR WITHIN SUBJECTS ANOVA

An experiment was designed to investigate the effects of the shape and solidity of patterns shown on a screen upon the ease with which they are detected. The dependent variable (DV) was the Number of Errors made in responding to a pattern. There were two treatment factors: Shape (Circle, Square, or Triangle) and Solidity (Outline or Solid). Each participant was tested under all six combinations of the two treatment factors: that is, both factors were within subjects. The results and the ANOVA summary table are shown in Table 8 and Table 9. The data are available in *Ch9 Shape Solidity 2ndMay2011.sav* at http://www.psypress.com/spss-made-simple.)

Table 8. Results of a two-factor within subjects experiment

SHAPE:-	Circle		Square		Triangle	
SOLIDITY:-	Solid	Outline	Solid	Outline	Solid	Outline
Participant						
1	8	2	3	8	5	7
2	7	6	3	6	6	11
3	6	10	3	5	3	5
4	5	8	6	5	2	11
5	8	6	5	5	3	12
6	7	6	5	6	7	14
7	11	12	3	6	2	10
8	10	10	10	5	0	12
9	8	5	8	6	6	14
10	6	12	13	8	8	14

Table 9 is the summary table for the ANOVA of the data in Table 8.

There are three treatment sources of variance in this ANOVA: the two main effect sources, Shape and Solidity; and the Shape × Solidity interaction. The *F* test for each of these sources has its own error term. The error term is always the interaction between the source (i.e. Shape, Solidity or Shape × Solidity) and Subjects. So the error term for Shape is the Shape × Subjects interaction, with 2 × 9 = 18 degrees of freedom; the error term for Solidity is the Solidity × Subjects interaction, with 1 × 9 = 9 degrees of freedom; the error term for Shape × Solidity is Shape × Solidity × Subjects, with 2 × 1 × 9 = 18 degrees of freedom.

A full explanation of this rule for finding the correct error term lies beyond the scope of this book. Basically, the Subjects source can be regarded as a factor with random effects, so that the various combinations of Subjects and treatments do not cancel out across the experiment as a whole. The interaction, therefore, adds to the expected value of the treatments sum of squares. (For more on this, see a statistical textbook such as Howell, 2007 or Keppel & Wickens, 2004.)

Table 9. Summary table for the ANOVA of the data in Table 8

Source	Degrees of freedom	Sum of squares	Mean square	F	p
Subjects	9				
Shape	2	37.433	18.717	2.662	0.097
Error (Shape)	18	126.567	7.031		
Solidity	1	81.667	81.667	46.915	<0.01
Error (Solidity)	9	15.667	1.741		
Shape × Solidity	2	149.633	74.817	9.828	<0.01
Error (Shape × Solidity)	18	137.033	7.613		

9.5.1 Preparing the data set

The first four rows of data in **Data View** appear as in Figure 9.

Case	CircleSolid	CircleOutline	SquareSolid	SquareOutline	TriangleSolid	TriangleOutline
1	8	2	3	8	5	7
2	7	6	3	6	6	11
3	6	10	3	5	3	5
4	5	8	6	5	2	11
5	8	6	5	5	3	

Figure 9. Part of **Data View** for the two-factor within subjects ANOVA

Extra care is needed when entering data from experiments with two or more within subjects factors. It is essential to ensure that SPSS understands which data were obtained under which combination of factors. In the present example, there are six scores for each participant, each score having being achieved under one combination of the Shape and Solidity factors. We can name the data variables in the data set CircleSolid, CircleOutline, SquareSolid, SquareOutline, TriangleSolid and TriangleOutline, representing all possible combinations of the shape and solidity factors. Such systematic, left-to-right naming not only helps to avoid transcription errors at the data entry stage, but also prevents incorrect responses when you are in the **Repeated-Measures Define Variable(s)** dialog box and are naming the within subjects factors.

Note that the left-to-right ordering of the variable names in Data View (Figure 9) is exactly the order in which they appeared in the original table of results (Table 8).

9.5.2 Running the two-factor within subjects ANOVA

- Select **Analyze➔General Linear Model➔Repeated Measures...** and complete the various dialog boxes by analogy with the one-factor example, defining a second within subjects (repeated measures) factor and naming the dependent measure as Errors.

- The completed **Repeated Measures Define Factor(s)** dialog box, with the two within subjects factor names Shape and Solidity, is shown in Figure 10, together with the measure name Errors.

- After **Define** has been clicked, the **Repeated Measures** dialog box appears with the six variables listed in alphabetical order on the left. (The top half is reproduced in Figure 11).

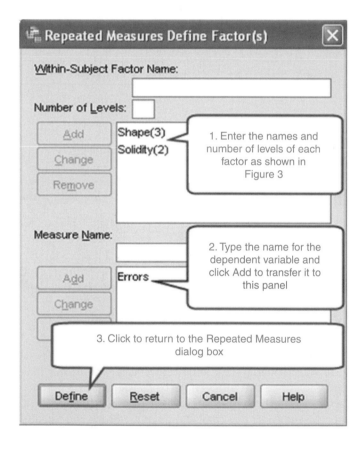

Figure 10. The **Repeated Measures Define Factor(s)** dialog box with two factors and their numbers of levels defined as well as a name for the dependent variable

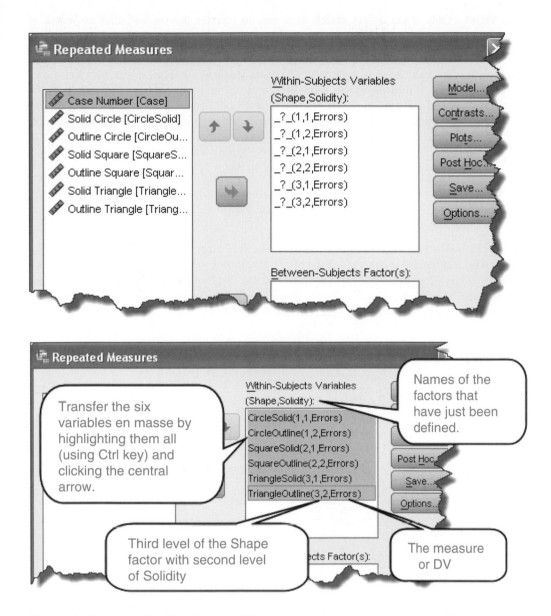

Figure 11. The top half of the **Repeated Measures** dialog box for two factors Shape and Solidity before and after transferring the variable names

Over the box on the right labelled **Within-Subjects Variables** (just underneath the label), appears the expression (Shape, Solidity), telling us the names of the two within subjects factors that have just been defined and the order in which they were defined (Figure 11). In the box itself, appears a list of the various combinations of the code numbers representing the levels of each of the two treatment factors. It will be noticed that, as one reads down the list, the first number in each pair changes more slowly than the second. Check that the downward order of the variable names in the left-hand panel matches the order of the names in **Variable View** (or

Data View). Only if the orders match, is it safe to transfer the six variables en masse as instructed in Figure 11; otherwise, the variables much be transferred singly to the appropriate slots.

Should your experiment be more complex, with more levels in the factors, it is safer to transfer the variables to the **Within-Subjects Variables** slots one at a time, noting the numbers in the square brackets and referring to the names of the newly defined within subjects factors (in this case Shape and Solidity) inside the square brackets in the caption above the **Within-Subjects Variables** box.

- There are some useful options associated with a repeated measures ANOVA. Request a profile plot of the levels of one of the factors across the levels of the other factor by clicking **Plots...** and following the steps shown in Figure 12. Click **Continue** to return to the original dialog box.

- A table of **descriptive statistics**, **estimates of effect sizes** and a table of post hoc **Sidak pairwise comparisons** among the levels of within subjects factors with more than two levels (Shape has three levels) are requested by clicking the **Options...** button in the **Repeated Measures** dialog box and following the steps shown earlier. Click **Continue** to return to the original dialog box and then **OK** to run the analysis.

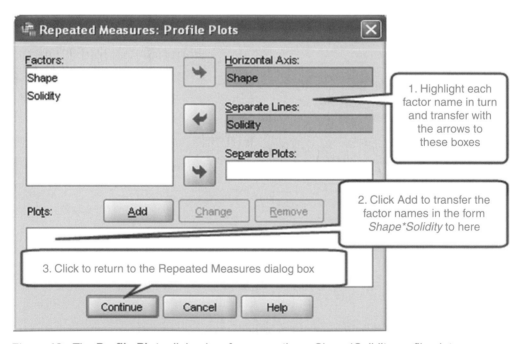

Figure 12. The **Profile Plots** dialog box for requesting a Shape*Solidity profile plot

9.5.3   Output for a two-factor within subjects ANOVA

As in the case of the one-factor within subjects ANOVA, the output is extensive, and not all of it is required. You can make life easier by pruning some items and removing others altogether. It is easiest to highlight an item's icon in the outline in the left pane and click the Delete button to remove the item altogether.

Experimental design and descriptive statistics

Output 8 shows the **Within-Subjects Factors** list and the specially requested **Descriptive Statistics** table.

Within-Subjects Factors

Measure:Errors

Shape	Solidity	Dependent Variable
1	1	CircleSolid
	2	CircleOutline
2	1	SquareSolid
	2	SquareOutline
3	1	TriangleSolid
	2	TriangleOutline

Descriptive Statistics

	Mean	Std. Deviation	N
Solid Circle	7.60	1.838	10
Outline Circle	7.70	3.268	10
Solid Square	5.90	3.446	10
Outline Square	6.00	1.155	10
Solid Triangle	4.20	2.573	10
Outline Triangle	11.00	3.018	10

Output 8. The **Within-Subjects Factors** list and **Descriptive Statistics** table

Results of the Mauchly test

The next table (Output 9) reports the result of the **Mauchly's Test of Sphericity** for homogeneity of covariance (see Section 9.2).

The table is more extensive than that in Output 3, because there are two factors. Notice that the test is not applied when a factor has only two levels (as in the case of Solidity) because, when there is only a single covariance, the question of homogeneity of covariance does not arise. The test does not show significance (i.e. there is no evidence of heterogeneity of covariance), either for Shape or for the interaction between Shape and Solidity, so the significance levels in the rows labelled **Sphericity Assumed** can be accepted. You should now remove from the ANOVA table the rows giving the results of the various conservative *F* tests.

Mauchly's Test of Sphericity[b]

Measure:Errors

		Within Subjects Effect		
		Shape	Solidity	Shape * Solidity
Mauchly's W		.635	1.000	.906
Approx. Chi-Square		3.635	.000	.789
df		2	0	2
Sig.		.162	.	.674
Epsilon[a]	Greenhouse-Geisser	.733	1.000	.914
	Huynh-Feldt	.839	1.000	1.000
	Lower-bound	.500	1.000	.500

Tests the null hypothesis that the error covariance matrix of the orthonormalized transformed dependent variables is proportional to an identity matrix.

a. May be used to adjust the degrees of freedom for the averaged tests of significance. Corrected tests are displayed in the Tests of Within-Subjects Effects table.
b. Design: Intercept
Within Subjects Design: Shape + Solidity + Shape * Solidity

Output 9. **Mauchly's Test of Sphericity** and more conservative statistics for Shape and for the interaction between Shape and Solidity

The ANOVA summary table

The edited ANOVA summary table (minus the rows with the conservative tests and the words Sphericity Assumed) for the within subjects factors Shape and Solidity, and their interaction is shown in Output 10. Notice that, in contrast with a two-factor between subjects ANOVA, there are three error terms, one for each main effect and one for the interaction.

Tests of Within-Subjects Effects

Measure:Errors

Source	Type III Sum of Squares	df	Mean Square	F	Sig.	Partial Eta Squared
Shape	37.433	2	18.717	2.662	.097	.228
Error(Shape)	126.567	18	7.031			
Solidity	81.667	1	81.667	46.915	.000	.839
Error(Solidity)	15.667	9	1.741			
Shape * Solidity	149.633	2	74.817	9.828	.001	.522
Error(Shape*Solidity)	137.033	18	7.613			

Output 10.   The edited **ANOVA** summary table for the **Within-Subjects Effects**

Output 10 shows that the factor Shape has no significant main effect, since the p-value for F in the column headed **Sig.** is greater than 0.05. We can write this result as follows:

'There was no significant effect of the Shape factor: $F(2, 18) = 2.67$; $p = .097$.'

The factor Solidity is significant, since its p-value is less than 0.01 (the output value '.000' means that the p-value is less than 0.0005). We can write this result as:

'The Solidity factor had a main effect that was significant beyond the 1% level: $F(1, 9) - 54.6$; $p < .01$. Partial eta squared = .86. This is a large effect.'

Finally, there is a significant Shape $\times$ Solidity interaction: $F(2, 18) = 9.828$; $p < 0.01$.

Since there is no significant effect of Shape, the output of the multiple comparisons tests is ignored.

Profile plots

The edited profile plot is shown in Output 11. An interaction is indicated when the profiles cross one another, diverge or converge. The plot shows that the significant interaction has been driven entirely by the greater error rate of the participants when they were shooting at the outline target.

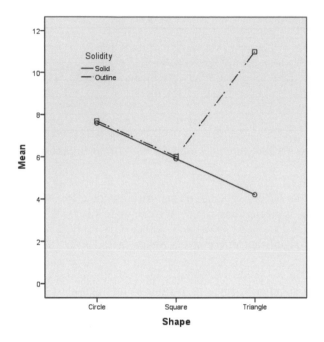

Output 11. The profile plots of the two levels of Solidity across the three shapes

9.5.4   Unpacking a significant interaction with multiple comparisons

The appearance of the profiles in Output 11 suggest that if we test for simple main effects of Solidity at each of the three levels of the Shape factor, we can expect to confirm the existence of an effect with the triangle only. The SPSS syntax for testing for simple main effects of Solidity at the Circle, Triangle and Square levels of Shape is shown in Figure 13.

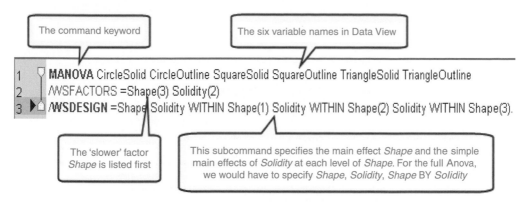

Figure 13. Syntax for testing simple main effects of Solidity at the Circle, Triangle and Square levels of Shape. Note that for within subjects factors, the subcommand /WSDESIGN replaces /DESIGN

The results of the tests for simple main effects are shown in Output 12. They are entirely consistent with the pattern that is so evident in the graph: there is a significant simple main effect of Solidity at the Triangle level of Shape, but none at the Square or Circle levels. From the point of view of making unplanned multiple comparisons, the confirmation of a simple main effect of one factor at one particular level of another might be regarded as a justification for calculating the size of the comparison family from the cell means at that level only. The **Bonferroni** or **Sidak** corrections might be made on that basis.

```
Tests involving 'SOLIDITY W SHAPE(1)' Within-Subject Effect.

Tests of Significance for T4 using UNIQUE sums of squares
Source of Variation            SS        DF        MS        F   Sig of F

WITHIN+RESIDUAL               56.45       9        6.27
SOLIDITY W SHAPE(1)             .05       1         .05      .01     .931
```

> No simple main effect of *Solidity* at Shape(1)

```
Tests involving 'SOLIDITY W SHAPE(2)' Within-Subject Effect.

Tests of Significance for T5 using UNIQUE sums of squares
Source of Variation            SS        DF        MS        F   Sig of F

WITHIN+RESIDUAL               51.45       9        5.72
SOLIDITY W SHAPE(2)             .05       1         .05      .01     .928
```

> No simple main effect of *Solidity* at Shape(2)

```
Tests involving 'SOLIDITY W SHAPE(3)' Within-Subject Effect.

Tests of Significance for T6 using UNIQUE sums of squares
Source of Variation            SS        DF        MS        F   Sig of F

WITHIN+RESIDUAL               44.80       9        4.98
SOLIDITY W SHAPE(3)          231.20       1      231.20    46.45     .000
```

> A significant simple main effect of *Solidity* at Shape(3)

Output 12. The results of tests (edited) for simple main effects of the Solidity factor at the three levels of Shape

9.6   A FINAL WORD

In this chapter, we have considered the analysis of variance of data from within subject experiments, in which the participant performs at every level of each of the treatment factors. Despite the practical efficiency of this research strategy and the increase in power that results from using participants as their own controls, the within subjects ANOVA raises issues that do not arise with between subjects experiments.

Within subjects experiments produce correlated data; and therein lies the heart of the difficulty. The within subjects ANOVA model carries the additional assumption of homogeneity of covariance or sphericity. Violation of this requirement can have serious consequences for the ANOVA, arising from the failure of the F statistics to have the distributions specified by the degrees of freedom, with consequent inflation of the error rates. There are available tests for homogeneity of covariance and adjustments that can be made to the F tests as a result of violation of this assumption. Heterogeneity of covariance, however, has ramifications that extend beyond the ANOVA itself which, as we have pointed out, is usually merely the first stage in the analysis of a set of data. The measurement of power and the making of specific contrasts, for example, are problematic: even if the data meet the requirement of sphericity, the researcher requires information that may be difficult or impossible to obtain.

There is, however, another approach to the analysis of the data from within subjects experiments. Rather than viewing the participant's performance under the k different conditions making up a treatment factor as values of one dependent variable measured under different conditions, the same data could be viewed as measures on k different dependent variables. The **Multivariate Analysis of Variance** (or **MANOVA** for short) is a generalisation of ANOVA which is applicable to correlated experimental data and yet does not require homogeneity of covariance. In the next chapter, we shall take a closer look at the MANOVA and its application to within subjects experiments.

Recommended reading

There are available several readable textbooks with clear yet comprehensive accounts of within subjects ANOVA. The treatments of ANOVA in the following books are particularly accessible.

Field, A. (2009). *Discovering statistics using SPSS (3rd ed.)*. London: Sage.

Howell, D. C. (2007). *Statistical methods for psychology (6th ed.)*. Belmont, CA: Thomson/Wadsworth.

Keppel, G., & Wickens, T. D. (2004). *Design and analysis: A researcher's handbook (4th ed.)*. Upper Saddle River, NJ: Pearson Prentice Hall.

Tabachnick, B.G., & Fidell, L.S. (2007). *Using multivariate Statistics (5th ed.)*. Boston: Allyn & Bacon (Pearson International Edition).

Two useful additional references

Dodd, D. H., & Schultz, R. F. (1973). Computational procedures for estimating magnitude of effect for some analysis of variance designs. *Psychological Bulletin, 79*, 391-395.

Faul, F., Erdfelder, E., Lang, A-G., and Buchner, A. (2007). G*Power 3: A flexible statistical power analysis program for the social, behavioral and biomedical sciences. *Behavior Research Methods, 39*, 175 – 191.

Exercises

Exercise 13 *One-factor within subjects (repeated measures) ANOVA* and Exercise 14 *Two-factor within subjects ANOVA* are available in www.psypress.com/spss-made-simple. Click on Exercises.

Mixed factorial experiments

10.1   INTRODUCTION

In the factorial designs we have considered so far, all the factors have been either between subjects or within subjects: in the **between subjects** factorial experiment, all factors are between subjects; in the **within subjects** factorial experiment they are within subjects. In this chapter, we shall consider **mixed factorial** experiments, in which there are both between subjects and within subjects factors. (An older term for this type of experimental design is **split-plot**, reflecting its original agronomic context.)

10.1.1   A mixed factorial experiment

A researcher designs an experiment to explore the hypothesis that engineering students, because of their training in two-dimensional representation of three-dimensional structures, have a more strongly developed sense of shape discrimination than do psychology students, whose training places a greater emphasis upon verbal and numerical skills. This, he reasons, should enable the engineers to make more accurate drawings of projections in the fronto-parallel plane of the gable-ends of buildings photographed from varying angles.   The investigator creates a set of solid building-like structures with triangular, square and rectangular 'gable-ends' and the participant is required to judge which of a set of comparison shapes presented on a screen is the correct projection, in the fronto-parallel plane, of the gable-end of the object. A scoring system is devised which assigns the highest marks for selections that are closest to the correct projection of the gable end of the real structure. The dependent variable (or measure) is the participant's score. The results of the experiment are shown in Table 1.

It can be seen from Table 1 that there were two factors in this experiment:

    1.   Student Category, with levels Psychology and Engineering.

    2.   Shape, with levels Triangle, Square and Rectangle.

Student Category is, of course, a between subjects factor; but since each participant was tested with all three shapes, Shape is a within subjects factor.

Table 1. Results of a two-factor mixed factorial experiment with one within subjects factor and one between subjects factor

Group	Case	Shape		
		Triangle	Square	Rectangle
	1	2	12	7
	2	8	10	9
Psychology	3	4	15	3
	4	6	9	7
	5	9	13	8
	6	7	14	8
	7	13	3	35
	8	21	4	30
Engineering	9	26	10	35
	10	22	8	30
	11	20	9	28
	12	19	8	27

10.1.2   Classifying mixed factorial designs

In this chapter, we shall follow a common convention for labelling different kinds of mixed factorial designs, in which the between subjects factors are represented by letters without brackets and the within subjects factors are bracketed. The present experiment, for example, is of design A × (B), where Factor A is Category of Student, Factor B is Shape and the brackets around B indicate that there are repeated measures on Shape.

Later in the chapter, we shall consider more complex mixed factorial experiments with three factors:

1. Design A × (B × C), which has one between subjects factor and two within subjects factors;

2. Design A × B × (C), which has two between subjects factors and one within subjects factor.

In the same notation, the completely randomised one-factor experiment is of type A, the two-factor between subjects factorial experiment is of type A × B and the two-factor within subjects factorial experiment is S × A × B. (Subjects crosses with the treatment factors.)

In Table 2, are shown three experimental designs with two factors, A and B. The two-factor mixed factorial experiment of which our current experiment is an example, is depicted schematically in Table 2c. This design is clearly a hybrid of the completely randomised and within subjects designs. It is like a between subjects one-factor between subjects experiment, except that each participant, instead of being tested just once, undergoes a within subjects S × B (Subjects by Treatments) experiment and is tested three times, once at each level of factor B.

10.1.3   Rationale of the mixed ANOVA

The ANOVA of the data in Table 1 is a hybrid of the ANOVA for the between subjects and within subjects experiments. If we were to ignore the Shape factor, calculate the mean performance of each participant across shapes and treat that mean as a single score, we should have data suitable for a one-way ANOVA, the results of which are shown in Output 1.

Table 2. Completely randomised, within subjects and mixed factorial experimental designs

(a) Completely randomised two-factor factorial experiment (design A × B)

Factor A	Factor B		
	B1	B2	B3
A1	Group 1	Group 2	Group 3
A2	Group 4	Group 5	Group 6

(b) Two-factor, within subjects factorial experiment (design S × A × B)

A1			A2		
B1	B2	B3	B1	B2	B3

Each participant is tested under all combinations of the two treatment factors. The ordering of the treatment combinations is counterbalanced, so that, across all the participants, each combination occurs equally often in each serial position (1st, 2nd,..., 6th).

(c) Two-factor, mixed factorial experiment [design A × (B)]

Factor A (group)	Factor B		
	B1	B2	B3
A1	Each participant is tested at all three levels of factor B		
A2	Each participant is tested at all three levels of factor B		

ANOVA

Mean

	Sum of Squares	df	Mean Square	F	Sig.
Between Groups	359.343	1	359.343	98.952	.000
Within Groups	36.315	10	3.631		
Total	395.657	11			

Output 1. The ANOVA summary table for the one-way ANOVA of the mean scores of participants in the two groups, averaged across the three shapes

In Chapter 9, we saw that in the two-factor within subjects S × A × B experiment, the Subjects 'factor' crosses with the two treatment factors, so that the correct error term for the F-test of the interaction A × B is the three way interaction A × B × S, remembering that the Subjects factor (S) has random effects. In the present case, however, it is clear that the Subjects 'factor' (S) does not cross with the Group factor, so that there can be no A × B × S interaction; there is, however, a B × S (i.e. Shape × Subjects) interaction nested within levels of the group factor A. These nested interactions are pooled to give the error term for the F tests for the within subjects sources. (It can be shown that, because the Subjects 'factor' has random effects, the expected value of this pooled error term includes not only an A × B component, but also a three-way A × B × S component. This pooled mean square is therefore also the appropriate error term for the test for the presence of a two-factor interaction. For a full explanation, see a statistics textbook such as Howell, 2007, or Keppel & Wickens, 2004.)

The ANOVA summary table is shown in Table 3. There are both between subjects and within subjects sources. We have already seen that the between groups sources are Group and the Within Groups error term. Within each professional group, are the results of a Subjects × Treatments (one-factor within subjects) experiment, with Shape as the single factor. In the experiment as a whole, however, the Group and Shape factor cross, so that we can include the Group × Shape interaction as another within subjects source of variance in the analysis of variance.

In this mixed two-factor ANOVA, there are three F tests:

1. A test for a main effect of the group factor, Category of Student;

2. a test for a main effect of the Shape factor;

3. a test for an interaction between Shape and Category of Student.

In the first F test, the error term is the usual one-way ANOVA within groups mean square (Output 1). In the second and third tests, the error term is the pooled Shape by Subjects interaction, which is termed **Error (Shape)** in the SPSS output.

We said earlier that the term **Error (Shape)** is a pooled variance estimate constructed from the Shape × Subjects interactions in the two groups. You can see this from the degrees of freedom: since there are six participants (subjects) within each group, the degrees of freedom of the error term for either one-factor within subjects experiment is $(6 - 1)(3 - 1) = 10$. Pooling across both groups doubles this value, producing the tabled *df* value of 20 for the within subjects error term **Error (Shape)**.

Table 3. ANOVA summary table for the data in Table 1

Source	df	SS	MS	F	p
Between subjects					
Group	1	1078.03	1078.83	98.95	<.01
Error: Within Groups	10	108.94	10.89		
Within subjects					
Shape	2	533.56	266.78	32.62	<.01
Shape × Group	2	1308.22	654.11	79.99	<.01
Error (Shape): Pooled Shape × Subjects	20	163.56	8.18		

10.2   THE TWO-FACTOR MIXED FACTORIAL ANOVA WITH SPSS

In Chapter 9, we saw that the within subjects ANOVA is available in the **General Linear Model** menu, under **Repeated Measures**. The mixed ANOVA is also run with the **Repeated Measures** procedure.

The data are available at http://www.psypress.com/spss-made-simple in the file *Shapes for Psychs & Engineers.sav*.

10.2.1   Preparing the SPSS data set

In Table 1, we represented the experimental design with the levels of the within subjects factor arrayed horizontally (as column headings) and those of the between subjects factor stacked vertically (as row labels), with Engineering under Psychology. We did so because this arrangement corresponds to the way in which the results will be arranged in **Data View**.

As always, the first column of **Data View** will contain the case numbers. The second column will contain a single grouping variable Category representing the Psychologists (code value: 1) and the Engineers (code value: 2). The third, fourth and fifth columns will contain the scores at the three levels of the Shape factor (Triangle, Square, and Rectangle).

- Enter **Variable View** and name five variables: Case, Category (the grouping variable), Triangle, Square, and Rectangle. Use the **Label** column to assign more meaningful variable names (Case Number, Category of Student) and the **Values** column to assign full labels to the numerical values of the grouping variable Category (such as 1 = 'Psychology Student', 2 = 'Engineering Student'). Set the **Decimals** column to zero for each variable to avoid needless clutter in **Data View**.

Click the **Data View** tab and enter the data into **Data View** (Figure 1). If values rather than labels appear in the variable Category, enter the **View** menu and click **Value Labels**.

Case	Category	Triangle	Square	Rectangle
1	Psychology Student	2	12	7
2	Psychology Student	8	10	9
3	Psychology Student	4	15	3
4	Psychology Student	6	9	7
5	Psychology Student	9	13	8
6	Psychology Student	7	14	8
7	Engineering Student	13	3	35
8	Engineering Student	21	4	30
9	Engineering Student	26	10	35
10	Engineering Student	22	8	30
11	Engineering Student	20	9	28
12	Engineering Student	19	8	27

Figure 1. The data from Table 1 in **Data View**

10.2.2 Running the ANOVA

As we observed in Chapter 9, the analysis of a within subjects experiment begins with three variables in Data View, each of which consists of a column of scores. There is no grouping variable coding the levels of a between subjects treatment factor. At a later stage, SPSS is informed that there is, in fact, a single dependent variable (the measure), which has been taken at the different levels making up a within subjects treatment factor. In the current example, Data View contains the name of the between subjects (group) factor; but the within subjects factor (Shape) has yet to be defined (Figure 1).

- Select **Analyze➜General Linear Model➜Repeated Measures...** to open the **Repeated Measures Define Factor(s)** dialog box. (The partially completed dialog is shown in Figure 2.)

- In the **Within-Subject Factor Name** box, delete the entry 'factor1' and type a generic name (such as Shape) for the repeated measures factor. This variable name must not be that of any of the three levels making up the factor. It must also conform to the rules governing the assignment of variable names: e.g. no spaces are allowed. (Spaces can be approximated, however, by use of the shift and hyphen keys.) In the **Number of Levels** box, type the number of levels (3) making up the repeated measures factor. Click **Add** and, in the middle box in Figure 2, the entry Shape(3) will appear. As the **Measure Name** (the name of the dependent variable in the experiment), type *Score*. Clicking on the **Add** button will cause the name Score to appear in the bottom panel.

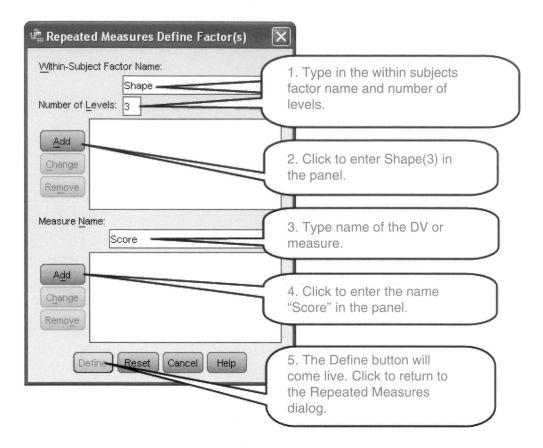

Figure 2. The **Repeated Measures Define Factor(s)** for three levels of Shape

- Click **Define** to open the **Repeated Measures ANOVA** dialog box.

- Transfer the variable names Triangle, Rectangle and Square to the **Within-Subjects Variables** box as shown in Figure 3.

- Transfer the factor name Category of Student to the **Between-Subjects Factor(s)** box.

- There are some useful additional options. A profile plot of the levels of the within subjects factor Shape for each level of the between subjects factor Category is requested by clicking **Plots...** . Move Shape to the **Horizontal Axis** slot and Category to the **Separate Lines** slot. Click **Continue** to return to the **Repeated Measures** dialog box.

- A table of **descriptive statistics**, **estimates of effect size** and a table of **Bonferroni** or **Sidak adjusted pairwise comparisons** among the levels of the within subjects factor Shape can be requested by clicking **Options…** and following the steps described in Chapter 9. Click **Continue** to return to the **Repeated Measures** dialog box.

- Had there been more than two levels in the between subjects variable Category, a Tukey post-hoc test could have been requested by clicking **Post Hoc…**, transferring the variable name Category to the **Post Hoc Tests for** box, and clicking the **Tukey** check box. Click **Continue** to return to the original dialog box.

- Click **OK** to run the ANOVA.

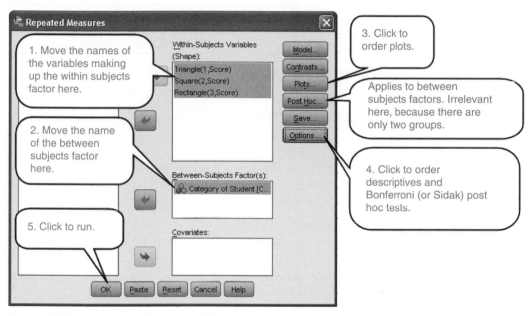

Figure 3. The completed **Repeated Measures** dialog

10.2.3   Output for the two-factor mixed ANOVA

The output from a mixed ANOVA is extensive, particularly for more complex experiments with three or more factors. The first step is to do some editing and remove some of the items. You will find the table of contents in the **SPSS Statistics Viewer** particularly helpful for navigating the extensive output.   Two items, **Multivariate Tests** and **Tests of Within-Subjects Contrasts**, can be deleted immediately by highlighting each in turn and pressing the **Delete** key on the keyboard. In the **Estimated Marginal Means** section, the **Multivariate Tests** table can also be deleted.

Design specifications

It is important to check that the nature of the design has been correctly communicated to SPSS. Output 2 shows the two SPSS tables identifying the levels of the **Within-Subjects Factors** and the levels of the **Between-Subjects Factors**.

Within-Subjects Factors

Measure: Score

Shape	Dependent Variable
1	Triangle
2	Square
3	Rectangle

Between-Subjects Factors

		Value Label	N
Category of Student	1	Psychology Student	6
	2	Engineering Student	6

Output 2. The **Within-Subjects Factors** list of levels and the **Between-Subjects Factors** list of levels

Check that the levels of each of the factors have been correctly labelled. Check that the value labels for the between subjects factor have been correctly assigned. Make sure also that the levels of the within subjects factor are listed in the order that they appear from left to right in Data View.

Note that, although Shape is the dependent variable in this study, Triangle, Square and Rectangle are described as DVs in the Within-Subjects Factors table. This is because SPSS runs the repeated measures ANOVA as a multivariate analysis, in which the levels of the within subjects factor are treated as separate dependent variables.

The descriptive statistics

Output 3 shows the table of descriptive statistics requested in **Options**. Inspection of the means shows different profiles across the factor Shape for the two student categories, suggesting the presence of an interaction between the two factors.

Descriptive Statistics

	Category of Student	Mean	Std. Deviation	N
Triangle	Psychology Student	6.00	2.61	6
	Engineering Student	20.17	4.26	6
	Total	13.08	8.13	12
Square	Psychology Student	12.17	2.32	6
	Engineering Student	7.00	2.83	6
	Total	9.58	3.65	12
Rectangle	Psychology Student	7.00	2.10	6
	Engineering Student	30.83	3.43	6
	Total	18.92	12.74	12

Output 3. The optional table of **Descriptive Statistics**

The Mauchly test

The next table, in Output 4, reports the result of the **Mauchly's Test of Sphericity**, or homogeneity of covariance.   (Actually, for reasons of space, we show the transpose of the original table.)

Mauchly's Test of Sphericity[b]

Measure:Score

	Within ...
	Shape
Mauchly's W	.903
Approx. Chi-Square	.921
df	2
Sig.	.631
Epsilon[a] Greenhouse-Geisser	.911
Huynh-Feldt	1.000
Lower-bound	.500

Tests the null hypothesis that the error
covariance matrix of the orthonormalized
transformed dependent variables is
proportional to an identity matrix.

a. May be used to adjust the degrees of
freedom for the averaged tests of
significance. Corrected tests are displayed
in the Tests of Within-Subjects Effects table.
b. Design: Intercept + Category
Within Subjects Design: Shape

Output 4. **Mauchly's Test of Sphericity** and values of **Epsilon** for more conservative tests.
(They aren't necessary in this example, because W is not significant.)

In the present case, the **Mauchly** statistic has a p-value of 0.63, so there is no evidence of heterogeneity of covariance. The usual (**Sphericity Assumed**) F test can therefore be used. You should therefore simplify the ANOVA table by removing the rows containing information about the conservative F tests.

Tests for within subjects effects

The edited table is shown in Output 5. Note that the factor Shape is significant beyond the 1 per cent level: the p-value (**Sig.**) '.000' is computerese for 'less than 0.0005'. Write '$p < .01$' (or '$p <.001$'), not '.000'. This result would be reported as follows:

'The Shape factor is significant beyond the .01 level: $F(2, 20) = 32.62$; $p < .01$. Partial eta squared = .765, a large effect (Cohen, 1988).'

The Category × Shape interaction is also significant beyond the 1% level: the *p*-value is less than 0.0005. This result would be reported as follows:

> 'There was a significant interaction between Category and Shape: $F(2, 20) = 79.99$; $p < .01$. Partial eta squared = .889, a large effect (Cohen, 1988).'

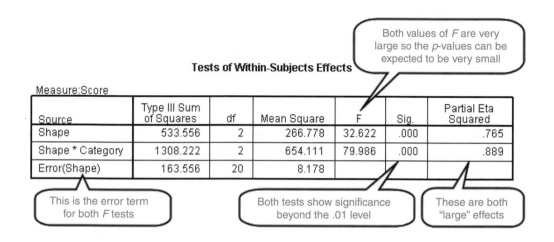

Both values of *F* are very large so the *p*-values can be expected to be very small

Tests of Within-Subjects Effects

Measure:Score

Source	Type III Sum of Squares	df	Mean Square	F	Sig.	Partial Eta Squared
Shape	533.556	2	266.778	32.622	.000	.765
Shape * Category	1308.222	2	654.111	79.986	.000	.889
Error(Shape)	163.556	20	8.178			

This is the error term for both *F* tests

Both tests show significance beyond the .01 level

These are both "large" effects

Output 5. The edited **ANOVA summary table** for the within-subjects factor Shape and its interaction with the between-subjects factor Category

Tests for between subjects effects

Output 6 shows the ANOVA summary table for the between subjects factor Category.

Ignore the terms **Intercept** and **Type III**: these refer to the regression method that was used to perform the analysis. With a *p*-value (**Sig.**) of less than 0.0005, there is clearly a significant difference in performance between the two groups of students. This result would be reported as follows:

> 'The mean scores for the categories of student differed significantly at the 1% level: $F(1,10) = 98.95$; $p < .01$. Partial eta squared = .91, a large effect (Cohen, 1988).'

The ANOVA strongly confirms the patterns discernible in Table 3: the Shape and Category factors both have significant main effects; and the interaction between the factors is also significant. You will notice, however, that although the value given for *F* is exactly the same as in the one-way ANOVA of the mean scores of the participants over all three shapes, the mean squares for the Category and Error sources have three times the values in the one-way table shown in Output 1. For each of the six means for each group, there were three times that number of raw scores, increasing the multiplier of the sum of the squares of the deviations by a factor of three.

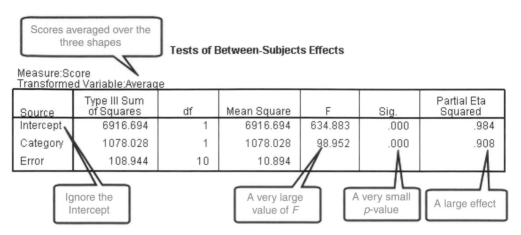

Output 6. The ANOVA summary table for the between-subjects factor Category

Bonferroni Pairwise Comparisons for the within subjects factor

Output 7 shows the pairwise comparisons requested in **Options**.   The upper table shows the results of the Sidak-corrected comparisons.   For comparison, the results of the Bonferroni-corrected comparisons are shown in the lower table.   The results are very similar; but you can see that The Sidak confidence intervals are somewhat tighter, indicating a slightly less conservative test.

Pairwise Comparisons

Measure:Score

(I) Shape	(J) Shape	Mean Difference (I-J)	Std. Error	Sig.[a]	95% Confidence Interval for Difference[a]	
					Lower Bound	Upper Bound
1	2	3.500[*]	.973	.015	.716	6.284
	3	-5.833[*]	1.222	.002	-9.330	-2.337
2	1	-3.500[*]	.973	.015	-6.284	-.716
	3	-9.333[*]	1.283	.000	-13.004	-5.662
3	1	5.833[*]	1.222	.002	2.337	9.330
	2	9.333[*]	1.283	.000	5.662	13.004

Based on estimated marginal means

*. The mean difference is significant at the .05 level.
a. Adjustment for multiple comparisons: Sidak.

Pairwise Comparisons

Measure:Score

(I) Shape	(J) Shape	Mean Difference (I-J)	Std. Error	Sig.[a]	95% Confidence Interval for Difference[a]	
					Lower Bound	Upper Bound
1	2	3.500[*]	.973	.015	.707	6.293
	3	-5.833[*]	1.222	.002	-9.342	-2.325
2	1	-3.500[*]	.973	.015	-6.293	-.707
	3	-9.333[*]	1.283	.000	-13.017	-5.650
3	1	5.833[*]	1.222	.002	2.325	9.342
	2	9.333[*]	1.283	.000	5.650	13.017

Based on estimated marginal means

*. The mean difference is significant at the .05 level.
a. Adjustment for multiple comparisons: Bonferroni.

Output 7. The Sidak- and Bonferroni-corrected pairwise comparisons for the factor Shape

The profile plots

The requested profile plot is shown (edited) in Output 8. With squares, the Psychology students improved, while the Engineering students' scores tended to slump in that condition.

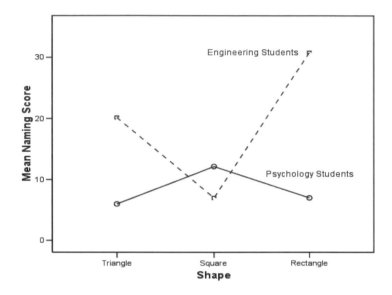

Output 8. The performance profiles over the three levels of Shape for each student category

10.2.4 Simple effects analysis with syntax

Given that the Group × Shape interaction has proved significant, the researcher might wish to 'unpack' this interaction by making tests for the simple effects of Group at each of the three levels of the Shape factor.

The syntax for testing for simple main effects of a factor in a mixed design at specific levels of a factor of the opposite type (i.e. a between factor at one level of a within factor and vice versa) is tricky, because the /DESIGN subcommand permits the explicit mention of between subjects factors only; whereas the /WSDESIGN subcommand permits reference to within subjects factors only. In other words, for an experiment of mixed factorial A × (B) design, a phrase such as A WITHIN B(1) will not be permitted in either the /DESIGN or the /WSDESIGN subcommand.

Simple main effects of the between subjects factor

The trick here is that, when (in the two-factor mixed factorial A × (B) experiment) we want to specify the simple main effect of the between subjects factor A at each level of B, we use the keyword MWITHIN to refer to the effects of A. This reference, however, is in the /WSDESIGN subcommand which, hitherto, we have used exclusively for within subjects sources (Figure 4).

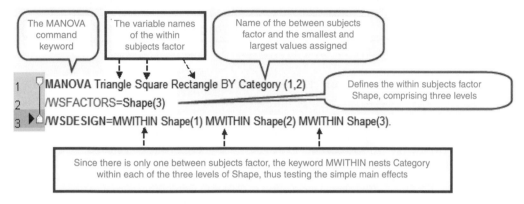

Figure 4. Syntax for simple main effects of the between factor at each level of the within factor

In this particular example, where there is only one between subjects factor, there will be an automatic link between that factor and the MWITHIN statements. In more complex mixed designs, where there are two or more between subjects factors, we shall need to write an additional /DESIGN subcommand to resolve the ambiguity and make the link between the specific between subjects effect that we want to test and the MWITHIN phrase in the /WSDESIGN subcommand.

The results of the tests for simple main effects of the Group factor at the three levels of the Shape factor are shown in Output 9 (edited). The desired simple main effects are labelled as if they were interactions: that is, the keyword BY which, hitherto has always indicated an interaction, appears before MWITHIN. The simple main effect of Group at the first level of Shape is labelled as 'Category BY MWITHIN SHAPE(1); the simple main effect of Group at the second level of Shape is 'Category BY MWITHIN SHAPE(2)'. These are NOT interactions: they are simple effects. The sources labelled 'MWITHIN SHAPE(1)' and 'MWITHIN SHAPE(2)' test the null hypothesis that the average score across the groups is zero within each level of Shape. Unless we are dealing with difference scores, this test is not usually of interest, because the null hypothesis will always be false.

We can see from Output 9 that formal testing has confirmed the existence of simple main effects of Group at all three levels of Shape. Since there were only two groups, we can infer that the difference between the two group means is significant at all three levels of the Shape factor.

```
Tests involving 'MWITHIN SHAPE(1)' Within-Subject Effect.

 Tests of Significance for T1 using UNIQUE sums of squares
 Source of Variation                    SS   DF        MS         F  Sig of F

 WITHIN+RESIDUAL          ( Ignore )   124.83   10     12.48
 MWITHIN SHAPE(1)                      2054.08    1   2054.08    164.55    .000
 Category BY MWITHIN SHAPE(1)  602.08    1    602.08     48.23    .000
```

The simple main effect of Category at the first level of Shape

```
Tests involving 'MWITHIN SHAPE(2)' Within-Subject Effect.

 Tests of Significance for T2 using UNIQUE sums of squares
 Source of Variation                    SS   DF        MS         F  Sig of F

 WITHIN+RESIDUAL          ( Ignore )    66.83   10      6.68
 MWITHIN SHAPE(2)                      1102.08    1   1102.08    164.90    .000
 Category BY MWITHIN SHAPE(2)   80.08    1     80.08     11.98    .006
```

The simple main effect of Category at the second level of Shape

```
Tests involving 'MWITHIN SHAPE(3)' Within-Subject Effect.

 Tests of Significance for T3 using UNIQUE sums of squares
 Source of Variation                    SS   DF        MS         F  Sig of F

 WITHIN+RESIDUAL          ( Ignore )    80.83   10      8.08
 MWITHIN SHAPE(3)                      4294.08    1   4294.08    531.23    .000
 Category BY MWITHIN SHAPE(3) 1704.08    1   1704.08    210.81    .000
```

The simple main effect of Category at the third level of Shape

Output 9. Results of the tests for simple main effects of Category at each level of Shape

Simple main effects of the within factor at each level of the between factor

The syntax for testing for simple main effects of Shape at each level of the Group factor is shown in Figure 5.

Note once again that, although we are testing for simple main effects of the within subjects factor, we use the /DESIGN subcommand, not /WSDESIGN. This is because only the /DESIGN subcommand allows you to name a between subjects factor. Since there are only two factors, the link between MWITHIN and the within subjects factor is unambiguous.

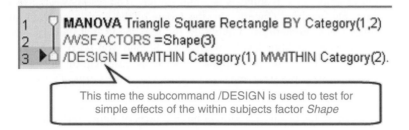

Figure 5. Syntax for testing for simple main effects of the within subjects factor (Shape) at each level of the between groups factor

The results of the simple effects analysis are shown in Output 10.

```
Tests of Between-Subjects Effects.   [ These are not generally of interest. Ignore! ]

Tests of Significance for T1 using UNIQUE sums of squares
Source of Variation          SS       DF      MS        F   Sig of F

WITHIN+RESIDUAL            108.94      10    10.89
MWITHIN CATEGORY(1)       1266.72       1  1266.72    116.27     .000
MWITHIN CATEGORY(2)       6728.00       1  6728.00    617.56     .000


                                          [ Tests for simple main effects of
Tests involving 'SHAPE' Within-Subject Effect.    Shape at each level of Group. ]

AVERAGED Tests of Significance for MEAS.1 using UNIQUE sums of squares
Source of Variation          SS       DF      MS        F   Sig of F

WITHIN+RESIDUAL            163.56      20     8.18
MWITHIN CATEGORY(1)       131.44       2    65.72      8.04     .003
BY SHAPE
MWITHIN CATEGORY(2)      1710.33       2   855.17    104.57     .000
BY SHAPE
```

[Despite the keyword BY, these are simple *main* effects.]

Output 10. Tests for simple main effects of the within subjects factor Shape at each level of the between groups factor

The arrangement of this output is somewhat different from the output for the simple main effects of Group at each level of Shape: the output is divided explicitly into between subjects and within subjects effects. The same points about the output, however, apply here too. In the between subjects output, the sources MWITHIN GROUP(1) and MWITHIN GROUP(2) test the hypothesis that, within each group, the mean score averaged across the three shapes is zero.

In the context of our example, this hypothesis is a non-starter. The results we are looking for are in the within subjects section. Once again, the labels of the simple effects contain the keyword BY as if they were interactions. Output 10 (edited) shows that there are significant simple main effects of Shape at both levels of Group. Should you wish to make multiple comparisons among the cell means, this might be seen as justification for defining the comparison family in relation to the three means at each level of the Group factor, rather than the six means in the entire experiment.

Figure 6 presents the syntax for testing for simple main effects of either factor in the A × (B) design in more abstract notation, representing the scores obtained under the conditions of the within subjects factor B as B1 and B2. In the current example, B1, B2, B3 and A are Triangle, Square, Rectangle and Student Category, respectively.

Including /DESIGN and /WSDESIGN subcommands in the same MANOVA command

In Figure 6, the /DESIGN and /WSDESIGN subcommands are presented as alternatives, the choice between them depending upon which set of simple main effects are required. Both subcommands, however, can be run on a single MANOVA command. Have a separate subcommand for each set of simple main effects: the two sets of simple effects are alternative partitions of the same interaction and main effect terms in the model.

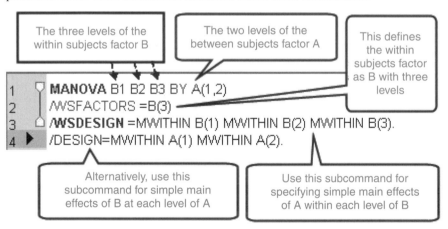

Figure 6. Using the MWITHIN keyword to test for simple main effects in the A × (B) mixed design. (The period at the end of line 3 can be dispensed with, in which case both subcommands will be run.)

Including comments with SPSS syntax

As an *aide-memoire*, it can be useful, in syntax files, to include reminders of the purpose of various subcommands and phrases. If added in the proper format, such comments are ignored by the computer and the syntax will run in the usual way. The rules for comments are as follows.

- If a comment requires several lines, write it before or after a command.

- If a comment occurs in the middle of a command, it must not spill over into a second line.

- All comments begin with an asterisk * and end with a period or full stop.

- When a comment occurs before or after a command, the asterisk and full stop, respectively, are all that is necessary.

- A comment in the middle of a line of syntax must begin with the /* and end with a full stop, followed by the two characters */ . (There is no additional full stop after the forward slash /.)

- When a comment comes in the middle of a command, but at the end of a line, the right-hand sequence of characters */ after the period is unnecessary.

The format for comments in various positions is illustrated in Figure 7.

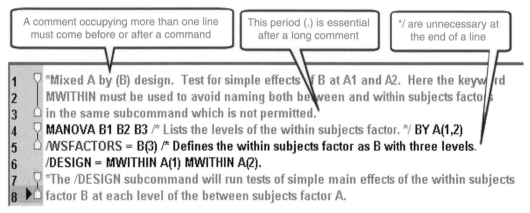

Figure 7. Illustration of the formatting for comments inserted in syntax

10.3   THE THREE-FACTOR MIXED ANOVA

The procedures described in Section 10.2 can readily be extended to the analysis of data from mixed factorial experiments with three treatment factors. To make the correct ANOVA choice, however, the user must be clear about the different possible experimental designs, for each of which there is a particular model and ANOVA procedure.

10.3.1   The two three-factor mixed designs

In Table 4 below are shown the most common mixed ANOVA designs, all of which can be seen as elaborations of between subjects experiments, the simplest of which we shall term the 'Type A' design. In Table 4, the within subject factors are bracketed.

There are two possible three-factor mixed factorial experiments:
1. Two within subjects factors and one between subjects factor: $A \times (B \times C)$
2. One within subjects factor and two between subjects factors: $A \times B \times (C)$.

Table 4. The 'mixed' or 'split-plot' experimental designs, as elaborations of the simple, two-group between subjects experiment (Type A)

(a)	Women		Men		
Type A design	Group 1		Group 2		

(b)	**Gender**	**Task:**	Task 1	Task 2	Task3
Type A × (B)	Women			Group 1	
design	Men			Group 2	

(c)		**Task:**	Task 1		Task 2		Task3	
Type A × (B×C)	**Gender**	**Hand:**	L	R	L	R	L	R
design	Women				Group 1			
	Men				Group 2			

(d)	**Gender**	**Hand**	**Task:**	Task 1	Task 2	Task 3
Type A × B × (C)	F	R			Group 1	
design		L			Group 2	
	M	R			Group 3	
		L			Group 4	

10.3.2   Two within subjects factors

Suppose that to the experiment described in Section 10.2, we were to add an additional within subjects factor, such as Solidity (of the shape), with two levels, Solid or Outline.   The participants (either Psychology or Engineering students) now have to try to recognise both Solid and Outline Triangles, Squares, and Rectangles. The data are contained in the file *Ch10 Shape, Solidity, Category.sav* at http://www.psypress.com/spss-made-simple.

Entering the data

Since there are six combinations of the Shape and Solidity factors, we shall need to have six variables in **Data View** to contain all the scores. Prepare the named columns systematically in **Variable View** by taking the first level of one factor (say, Shape) and combining it successively with each of the levels of the second factor (Solidity), and then doing the same with the second and third levels of the first factor. The top part of **Data View** might appear as in Figure 8, which shows the headings of the columns and the data for the first few participants. As we read from left to right across the variable labels for the various combinations of Shape and Solidity, we see that, whereas the second column is still a triangle (we are still at the first level of the Shape factor, i.e., Triangle), the level of the Solidity factor has changed to Outline. In this sense, the levels of the Shape factor can be said to 'change more slowly' than those of the Solidity factor as we scan the variable names from left to right.

The data are contained in the file *Ch11 Tissue type (large sample).sav*, which is available at http://www.psypress.com/spss-made-simple.

Case	Category	Rectangle Solid	Rectangle Outline	Square Solid	Square Outline	Triangle Solid	Triangle Outline	
1	Psychology	2	12	3	1	4	5	
2	Psychology	13	22	5	9	6	8	
3	Psychology	14	20	8	7	5	7	
4	Engineering	12	1	3	9	6	10	
5	Engineering	11	2	8	10	5	9	
6	Engineering	12	7	2	4	4	10	

Figure 8. The variable names for a three-factor mixed factorial experiment with two within subjects factors

Running the analysis

As usual, we must define our within subjects factors to create a framework into which the variables in Data View can be slotted. If the data are arranged as in Figure 8, the within subjects factors will be defined in the order: Shape (3), Solidity (2). (See Figure 9.) The 'slower' factor in the sense described above is defined first. Once the factors have been defined, a grid will appear in the **Within-Subject Variables** panel, waiting for the appropriate variable names to be inserted in the slots.

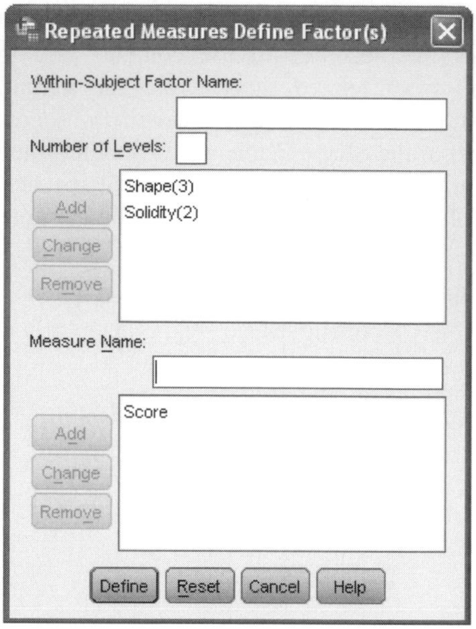

Figure 9. Defining the within subjects factors

When you are working in the **Repeated Measures** dialog box, take care when transferring variable names from the list in the panel on the left to the slots in **Within-Subjects Variables** panel on the right. If, in **Data View**, you have arranged the variables systematically as we have described, you will be able to transfer the variables *en bloc* to the Within-Subjects Variables panel, where each will occupy the correct slot. The numerical contents of the slots in the panel are determined by the order in which the factors were defined and the numbers of levels that were given for each factor. In this case, since the Shape factor (with 3 levels) was defined first, the contents of the brackets should read as follows: (1, 1), (1, 2), (2, 1), (2, 2), (3, 1), (3, 2). Should the order of the variables in the left-hand panel fail to correspond with the numbering in the right-hand panel, something has gone wrong. You may, for instance, have defined the factors in the wrong order. Had you defined the factors in the order Solidity(2), Shape(3), the numbering in the slots would have been wrong for some of the variables: the third slot would still contain the data for the variable SquareSolid, but the programme would treat this variable as the scores for the solid triangle; and the slot that should contain data for the solid triangle would be treated as an outline square.

The completed dialog box is shown in Figure 10.

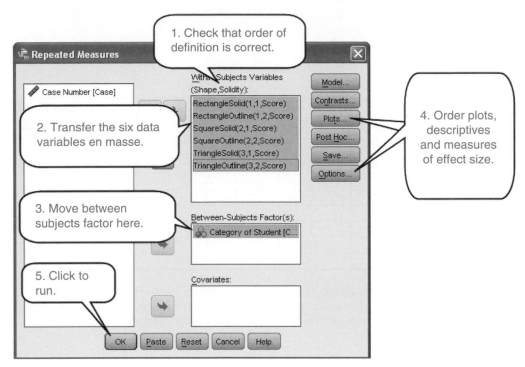

Figure 10. The upper part of the **Repeated Measures** dialog box for a three-factor mixed factorial experiment, with two within subjects factors and one between subjects factor

The ANOVA summary tables

The output includes Output 11, which shows the tests for the main effects of the within subjects factors and their various interactions with each other and with the between subjects factor. Output 12 shows the test for the between subjects factor.

In the ANOVA, having equal sample sizes ensures that the sums of squares for the various effects can vary independently. Nevertheless, a significant higher order effect is often of more interest than a lower order effect and supersedes the former as the focus of attention and further analysis. In Output 11, for example, we see that the Shape × Solidity interaction is not significant. The finding that there is a significant three-way Shape × Solidity × Category interaction, however, shows that a more fine-grained analysis of the two-way interaction within the data from each group of participants is indicated. One obvious possibility is that the Shape × Solidity interaction may occur in one participant category but not in the other; on the other hand, there may be simple interactions in both groups of participants, but the patterns they show may be different.

Tests of Within-Subjects Effects

Measure:**Score**

Source	Type III Sum of Squares	df	Mean Square	F	Sig.	Partial Eta Squared
Shape	166.17	2	83.08	7.11	.017	.640
Shape * Category	109.06	2	54.53	4.67	.045	.539
Error(Shape)	93.44	8	11.68			
Solidity	25.00	1	25.00	11.25	.028	.738
Solidity * Category	28.44	1	28.44	12.80	.023	.762
Error(Solidity)	8.89	4	2.22			
Shape * Solidity	15.17	2	7.58	2.74	.124	.407
Shape * Solidity * Category	193.39	2	96.69	34.98	.000	.897
Error(Shape*Solidity)	22.11	8	2.76			

Output 11. The edited **Within-Subjects Effects** table showing the **F ratio** and **Partial Eta Squared** for the within subjects factors Shape and Solidity and their various double and triple interactions with each other and with the between subjects factor Category

Tests of Between-Subjects Effects

Measure:Score
Transformed Variable:Average

Source	Type III Sum of Squares	df	Mean Square	F	Sig.	Partial Eta Squared
Category	18.78	1	18.78	.538	.504	.119
Error	139.56	4	34.89			

Output 12. The edited **Between-Subjects Effects** table showing the **F ratio** and **Partial Eta Squared** for the between subjects factor Category

The profile plots

The profile plots of Shape against Solidity for the two student groups are shown in Output 13. Comparison of the profile plots in the two groups strongly suggests heterogeneity of the simple interactions: the Engineers show a striking cross-over pattern; whereas the psychologists' profiles converge. The patterns shown by the two sets of profiles are quite consistent with the finding from the ANOVA that the three-way interaction is significant.

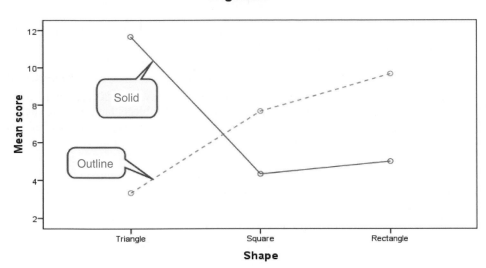

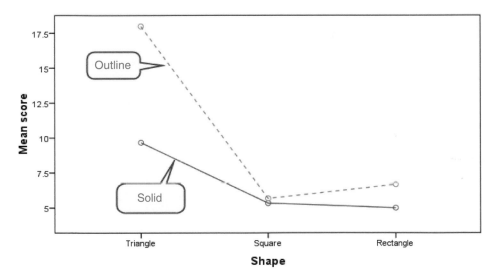

Output 13. Profile plots of Solidity against Shape for the two groups of participants

10.3.3   Using syntax to test for simple effects

Since the three-way interaction has proved to be significant, the researcher might wish to 'unpack' it by making further tests. Should at least one of the simple interactions turn out be significant, one might consider further analysis of simple, simple main effects of Solidity at different levels of the Category factor (i.e. in the psychologists and the engineers considered separately).

As we observed in our discussion of the syntax for simple effects in the two-factor A × (B) mixed factorial experiment, in order to avoid naming both a between subjects factor and a within subjects factor in the same subcommand (whether that is /DESIGN or /WSDESIGN), we shall need to use the keyword MWITHIN. If the experimental design is of the type A × (B × C), for instance, a statement such as B BY C at A(1), for instance, is unacceptable in either subcommand, because it names both within subjects and between subjects factors. Once again, the MWITHIN keyword is included in the subcommand we would normally use for effects of the other type: that is, if we want simple effects of within subjects factors (or their simple interactions), the MWITHIN keyword is included in the /DESIGN command, not the /WSDESIGN subcommand, as might be expected. The same is true of simple effects and (in designs with more than one between subjects factor) interactions among between subjects sources: in such cases, the MWITHIN keyword occurs in the /WSDESIGN, not the /DESIGN, subcommand.

For a mixed factorial design of type A × (B × C), that is, one in which factor A is between subjects and B and C are within subjects as in the current example, the following syntax (Figure 11) will run the full ANOVA:

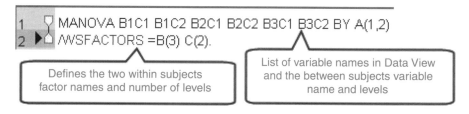

Figure 11. Syntax for a mixed factorial design of type A × (B × C)

In terms of the factors and the names of the variables in Data View in our current example, the syntax for the mixed ANOVA will appear as in Figure 12.

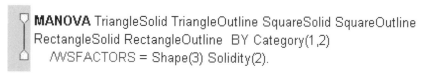

Figure 12. Syntax for the current example with Shape and Solidity as within subjects factors and Category as the between subjects factor

We shall be testing the simple interactions between Shape and Solidity at each level of the Category factor. As a check on the output, we shall want to satisfy ourselves that the sum of the sums of squares for the simple interactions is equal to the sum of squares for the three-way interaction plus the sums of squares for the two-way interaction between Shape and Solidity.

We expect this because, in general,

$$\sum_{j} SS_{BC \; at \; A_j} = SS_{BC} + SS_{ABC} \quad - - - (1)$$

Alternative partitioning of interaction sums of squares

We shall not show the MANOVA output for the full ANOVA again, since the values given are identical with those shown in Outputs 11 and 12. We note from Output 11 that

$$SS_{Shape \times Solidity} + SS_{Shape \times Solidity \times Category} = 15.17 + 193.39 = 208.56$$

We shall make use of this value when we examine the output for the tests for simple interactions.

The syntax for testing for simple interactions between two within subjects factors at specified levels of a between subjects factor is shown in Figure 13.

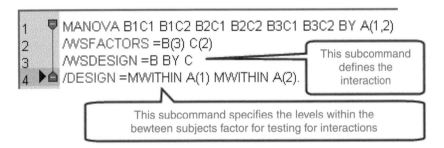

Figure 13. Syntax for testing simple interactions between two within subjects factors

Notice that, since there are three factors in the current experiment, we shall need both /DESIGN and /WSDESIGN subcommands to link the simple interactions to the MWITHIN statements. In terms of the variable names in the current example, the syntax for testing for simple interactions between Shape and Solidity at each level of the Category factor is as shown in Figure 14.

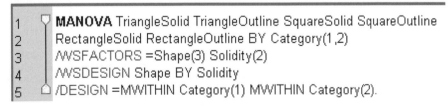

Figure 14. Syntax for testing the simple interactions between Shape and Solidity in each of the two groups

The results of the tests for simple interactions are shown in Output 14, which forms the final part of an extensive list of test results, the rest of which has been omitted. Notice that, once again, the second occurrence of the keyword BY in connexion with the keyword MWITHIN suggests a three-factor interaction; but these are simple two-factor interactions of Shape with Solidity at each level of the Category factor.

When we add together the sums of squares for the sources labelled as MWITHIN CATEGORY(1) BY SHAPE BY SOLIDITY and MWITHIN CATEGORY(2) BY SHAPE BY SOLIDITY, we obtain the value 208.56, which, as we have seen (1), is the sum of the sums of squares for the Shape × Solidity interaction and the Shape × Solidity × Category interaction.

```
Tests involving 'SHAPE BY SOLIDITY' Within-Subject Effect.

AVERAGED Tests of Significance for MEAS.1 using UNIQUE sums of squares
Source of Variation              SS        DF        MS        F  Sig of F

WITHIN+RESIDUAL                22.11        8       2.76
MWITHIN CATEGORY(1)            55.11        2      27.56      9.97      .007
BY SHAPE BY SOLIDITY

MWITHIN CATEGORY(2)           153.44        2      76.72     27.76      .000
BY SHAPE BY SOLIDITY
```

Output 14. Tests for simple interactions Shape and Solidity at both levels of the Category factor

Our formal tests have confirmed the existence of simple interactions between Shape and Solidity in both groups of participants. Arguably, therefore, we can proceed to test for simple, simple main effects of solidity in order to cast further light on the profile patterns in Output 13. The syntax for these tests is as shown in Figure 15.

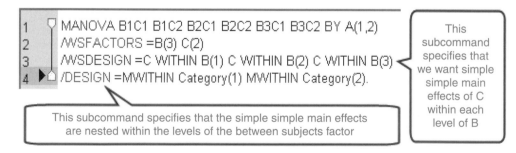

```
1    MANOVA B1C1 B1C2 B2C1 B2C2 B3C1 B3C2 BY A(1,2)
2    /WSFACTORS =B(3) C(2)
3    /WSDESIGN =C WITHIN B(1) C WITHIN B(2) C WITHIN B(3)
4    /DESIGN =MWITHIN Category(1) MWITHIN Category(2).
```

This subcommand specifies that we want simple simple main effects of C within each level of B

This subcommand specifies that the simple simple main effects are nested within the levels of the between subjects factor

Figure 15. Syntax for simple simple main effects for an A × (B × C) design

In terms of the variable names and other design specifications of the current example, the syntax reads as in Figure 16.

```
1    MANOVA TriangleSolid TriangleOutline SquareSolid SquareOutline
2    RectangleSolid RectangleOutline BY Category(1,2)
3    /WSFACTORS = Shape(3) Solidity(2)
4    /WSDESIGN = Solidity WITHIN Shape(1) Solidity WITHIN Shape(2) Solidity WITHIN Shape(3)
5    /DESIGN =MWITHIN Category(1) MWITHIN Category(2).
```

Figure 16. Syntax for testing simple simple main effects

Since the MWITHIN keywords in the /DESIGN subcommand nest the three simple main effects within each level of the between subjects factor Category, the analysis will run tests of six simple, simple main effects: Solidity at Shape(1), Shape(2) and Shape(3) at Category(1); and Solidity at Shape(1), Shape(2) and Shape(3) at Category(2).

Output 15 shows the results of the six tests for simple simple main effects of Solidity at the six combinations of the Shape and Solidity factors.

Source of Variation	SS	DF	MS	F	Sig of F
WITHIN+RESIDUAL	13.67	4	3.42		
MWITHIN CATEGORY(1) BY SOLIDITY W SHAPE(1)	104.17	1	104.17	30.49	.005
MWITHIN CATEGORY(2) BY SOLIDITY W SHAPE(1)	104.17	1	104.17	30.49	.005
WITHIN+RESIDUAL	15.67	4	3.92		
MWITHIN CATEGORY(1) BY SOLIDITY W SHAPE(2)	.17	1	.17	.04	.847
MWITHIN CATEGORY(2) BY SOLIDITY W SHAPE(2)	16.67	1	16.67	4.26	.108
WITHIN+RESIDUAL	1.67	4	.42		
MWITHIN CATEGORY(1) BY SOLIDITY W SHAPE(3)	4.17	1	4.17	10.00	.034
MWITHIN CATEGORY(2) BY SOLIDITY W SHAPE(3)	32.67	1	32.67	78.40	.001

C at B(1)A(1)
C at B(1)A(2)
C at B(2)A(1)
C at B(2)A(2)
C at B(3)A(1)
C at B(3)A(2)

Output 15. Tests for simple, simple main effects of Solidity at each of the six combinations of Shape and Category

Since the factor of Solidity has only two levels, a significant simple, simple main effect implies that the difference between the means for the Solid and Outline conditions is also significant.

Had we tested for simple, simple main effects of Shape at each of the four combinations of the Solidity and Category factors, further testing of pairwise comparisons would have been required.   The presence of a significant simple, simple main effect might be seen as justification for defining the size of the comparison family on the basis of three means only.

10.3.4   One within subjects factor and two between subjects factors: the A × B × (C) mixed factorial design

Suppose the experiment described in Section 10.3.2 were to have an additional between subjects factor, such as Sex (Male, Female) but just one within subjects factor Shape. Our mixed factorial design is now of type A × B × (C). The participants (Psychology and Engineering Students, Male and Female) are asked to try to recognise targets of three different shapes (Triangles, Squares and Rectangles).

Preparing the data set

The data for this final example of a mixed factorial ANOVA are in the file *Ch11 One factor within, two factors between.sav* at www.psypress.com/spss-made-simple.

In **Variable View**, it will now be necessary to add a second grouping variable, Sex. Figure 17 shows the first row of values in Data View. The names of the two grouping variables, Category and Sex, can also be seen.

Case	Category	Sex	Triangle	Square	Rectangle
1	Psychology Student	Male	2	12	7

Figure 17. The variable names for a three-factor mixed factorial experiment with one within subjects and two between subjects factors

Running the ANOVA

The completed **Repeated Measures ANOVA** dialog box is shown in Figure 18. Notice that the Between-Subjects Factor(s) box now contains the labels of two grouping variables, Category of Student and Sex.

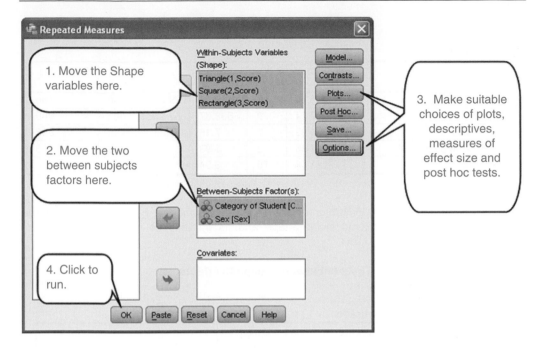

Figure 18. The upper part of the **Repeated Measures** dialog box for a three-factor mixed factorial experiment with one within subjects factor and two between subjects factors

The output

The output, as usual, is extensive, so we shall draw your attention to the key tables only. Output 16 shows the tests of the within subjects factor Shape and its various interactions with the two between subjects factors. Output 17 shows the tests of the between subjects factors Category and Sex. The results in Output 17 show that Shape and the interaction between Shape and Category are significant beyond the 1% level; but neither the interaction between Shape and Sex nor the triple interaction is significant. The results in Output 17 show that the factor Category is significant at the 1% level but neither the factor Sex nor the interaction between Sex and Category is significant.

Tests of Within-Subjects Effects

Measure: Score

Source	Type III Sum of Squares	df	Mean Square	F	Sig.	Partial Eta Squared
Shape	519.62	2	259.81	29.39	.000	.786
Shape * Category	1277.74	2	638.87	72.27	.000	.900
Shape * Sex	14.92	2	7.46	.84	.448	.095
Shape * Category * Sex	7.86	2	3.93	.44	.649	.053
Error(Shape)	141.44	16	8.84			

Output 16. The edited **Within-Subjects Effects** table showing the **F ratio** and **Partial Eta Squared** for the within subjects factor Shape and its interactions with the two between subjects factors Category and Sex

Tests of Between-Subjects Effects

Measure: Score

Transformed Variable: Average

Source	Type III Sum of Squares	df	Mean Square	F	Sig.	Partial Eta Squared
Category	1093.34	1	1093.34	107.69	.000	.931
Sex	22.75	1	22.75	2.24	.173	.219
Category * Sex	6.28	1	6.28	.62	.454	.072
Error	81.22	8	10.15			

Output 17. The edited **Between-Subjects Effects** table showing the **F ratio** and **Partial Eta Squared** for the two between subjects factors Category and Sex together with their interaction

The profile plot

Output 18 shows that the significant interaction between Shape and Category arises because the profiles of the psychologists and engineers show a cross-over pattern.

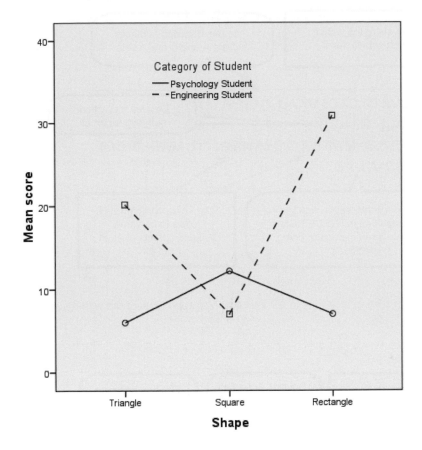

Output 18. The profile plot showing the significant interaction of Shape with Category

Testing for simple main effects and interactions

In the event of a significant two-factor interaction, the researcher might well proceed to test for simple main effects. Since the procedure presents no new issues, we shall not describe the syntax for the tests for simple main effects here.

Since, in the current example, the three-factor interaction is statistically insignificant, we would not go on to test for simple interactions. Had the interaction proved to be significant, however, we would certainly have considered testing the simple interactions for significance.

In general notation, the syntax for testing for a simple interaction between factors A and B at each of the three levels of factor C is shown in Figure 19. The syntax for our current example is shown in Figure 20.

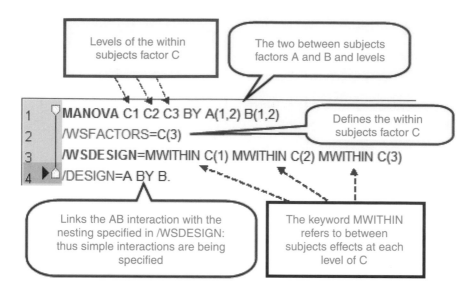

Figure 19.   Syntax for testing for a simple AB interaction at each level of the within subjects factor C

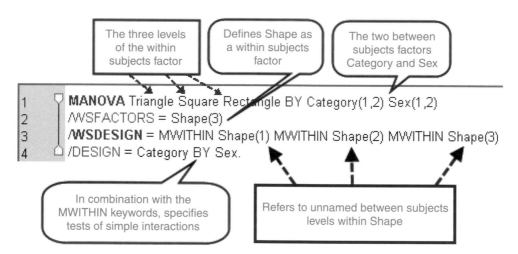

Figure 20.   Syntax for testing for a simple Category by Sex interaction at each level of the within subjects factor Shape

Output 19 shows the output for the test for a simple interaction between Category and Sex at one level only of the Shape factor: Triangle.

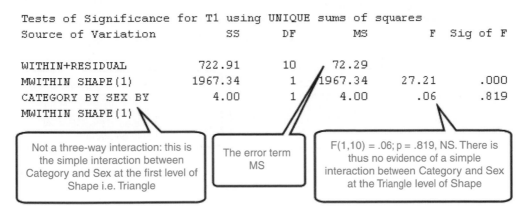

```
Tests involving 'MWITHIN SHAPE(1)' Within-Subject Effect.

Tests of Significance for T1 using UNIQUE sums of squares
Source of Variation              SS       DF       MS          F  Sig of F

WITHIN+RESIDUAL               722.91      10      72.29
MWITHIN SHAPE(1)             1967.34       1    1967.34      27.21      .000
CATEGORY BY SEX BY              4.00       1       4.00        .06      .819
MWITHIN SHAPE(1)
```

Not a three-way interaction: this is the simple interaction between Category and Sex at the first level of Shape i.e. Triangle

The error term MS

F(1,10) = .06; p = .819, NS. There is thus no evidence of a simple interaction between Category and Sex at the Triangle level of Shape

Output 19. Some of the output, showing that there is no significant simple interaction between Category and Sex in the data from the Triangles condition

Testing for simple, simple main effects following a significant three-factor interaction

Since, in the current example, there was no three-factor interaction, the question of unpacking the interaction by testing for simple, simple main effects does not arise. Should a test for a simple interaction show significance, you might wish to proceed to make tests of simple, simple main effects. The syntax is shown in Figure 21.

Here, we are asking for tests of simple, simple main effects of factor A at combinations of factors B and C: B(1)C(1), B(2)C(1), B(3)C(1) and so on. In the output (not shown here), these simple, simple main effects will look like interactions, because their labels contain the keyword BY with MWITHIN.

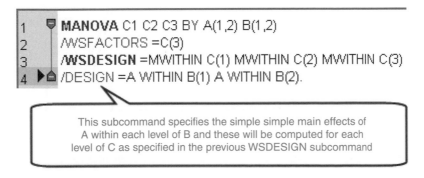

```
1    MANOVA C1 C2 C3 BY A(1,2) B(1,2)
2    /WSFACTORS =C(3)
3    /WSDESIGN =MWITHIN C(1) MWITHIN C(2) MWITHIN C(3)
4    /DESIGN =A WITHIN B(1) A WITHIN B(2).
```

This subcommand specifies the simple simple main effects of A within each level of B and these will be computed for each level of C as specified in the previous WSDESIGN subcommand

Figure 21. Syntax for testing simple simple main effects in an A × B × (C) design

In the current example, the syntax for testing simple, simple main effects appears as in Figure 22.

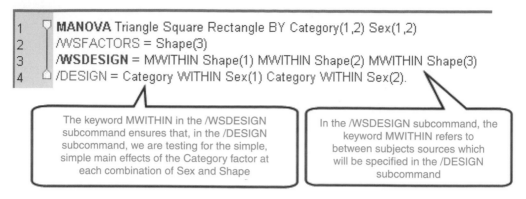

```
1    MANOVA Triangle Square Rectangle BY Category(1,2) Sex(1,2)
2    /WSFACTORS = Shape(3)
3    /WSDESIGN = MWITHIN Shape(1) MWITHIN Shape(2) MWITHIN Shape(3)
4    /DESIGN = Category WITHIN Sex(1) Category WITHIN Sex(2).
```

The keyword MWITHIN in the /WSDESIGN subcommand ensures that, in the /DESIGN subcommand, we are testing for the simple, simple main effects of the Category factor at each combination of Sex and Shape

In the /WSDESIGN subcommand, the keyword MWITHIN refers to between subjects sources which will be specified in the /DESIGN subcommand

Figure 21. Syntax for testing for simple simple main effects of Category at each combination of Shape and Sex

Notice that, once again, although we can use the keyword MWITHIN in the /WSDESIGN subcommand to refer to between subjects sources, we need an additional /DESIGN subcommand to specify that we want an interaction.

Output 20 shows a fragment of the output: the test for simple simple effects of Category at the combinations of Triangle Shape with Male and Female Participants.

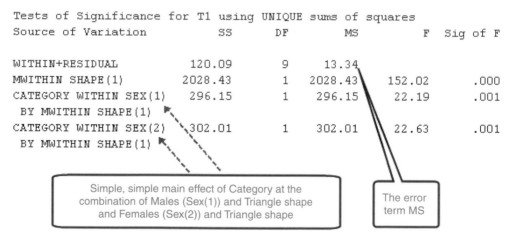

```
Tests involving 'MWITHIN SHAPE(1)' Within-Subject Effect.

 Tests of Significance for T1 using UNIQUE sums of squares
 Source of Variation            SS        DF        MS          F  Sig of F

 WITHIN+RESIDUAL             120.09        9      13.34
 MWITHIN SHAPE(1)           2028.43        1    2028.43     152.02     .000
 CATEGORY WITHIN SEX(1)      296.15        1     296.15      22.19     .001
   BY MWITHIN SHAPE(1)
 CATEGORY WITHIN SEX(2)      302.01        1     302.01      22.63     .001
   BY MWITHIN SHAPE(1)
```

Simple, simple main effect of Category at the combination of Males (Sex(1)) and Triangle shape and Females (Sex(2)) and Triangle shape

The error term MS

Output 20. Tests for simple simple main effects of Category at the combinations of Triangle Shape with Male and Female participants

Finally, we should perhaps say that the foregoing testing of simple, simple main effects is included for the sake of completeness: although both of the tests for simple, simple main effects reported in Output 20 show significance beyond the 0.01 level, we should not normally proceed with such further testing were the test for the three-factor interaction to prove insignificant, which is the case in our present example.

10.4 THE MULTIVARIATE ANALYSIS OF VARIANCE (MANOVA)

In the analysis of variance (ANOVA), there is just ONE dependent variable. There may, as we have seen, be several factors (that is, independent variables) and, as a consequence, **Data View** will contain several variables. Such a data set, however, is still regarded as **univariate**, because it contains only one measured variable, namely the DV, that is of central interest and is recorded during the investigation. This is still essentially true if the researcher has further data on the participants in the form of measurements on a **covariate**, that is, a variable which correlates (or covaries) with the DV and may inflate the error term in the F tests. We shall have two measured variables; but interest still focuses on the DV and the purpose of the technique known as **analysis of covariance (ANCOVA)** is to 'purify' the data by removing the effects of the covariate, thereby reducing data 'noise' and enabling the researcher to make a more powerful ANOVA F test. (The ANCOVA is described in Chapter 13.)

A researcher, however, will often wish to study the effects of experimental or group factors upon *two or more* DVs. For example, in an experiment on the influence of drugs upon skilled performance, the researcher might wish to take measures of speed and errors, as well as the participant's performance score. Such an experiment will result in a **bivariate** or **multivariate** data set, that is, one in which two or more of the variables are measured during the course of the investigation with a view to investigating how they are affected by the factors in the experimental design. Such additional DVs are quite different from covariates, in that, far from being merely potential contributors to data noise, they are of central interest in their own right.

A researcher with a multivariate data set of this kind might consider running a univariate ANOVA on each of the DVs in the study. This, indeed, has been (and still is) a very common approach to the analysis of multivariate data. A major problem, however, is that the DVs are highly likely to be correlated, because the same people are being measured on the different DVs and the DVs are likely to be similarly affected by the treatment factors. As a result, the outcomes of the various univariate ANOVAs are not independent. This can have serious consequences for the interpretation of the p-values from the F tests: the type I error rate, for example, may increase to an unacceptably high level.

The **multivariate analysis of variance (MANOVA)** is a set of techniques designed specially for the purpose of analysing simultaneously the results of experiments with several DVs.

10.4.1 What the MANOVA does

The MANOVA is an extension or generalisation of the univariate ANOVA to multivariate data sets. We have seen that the one-way ANOVA tests the null hypothesis that any differences there may be among the group means on a single DV have arisen merely through sampling error. In MANOVA, the object of the exercise is, firstly, to find a linear function of the DVs with respect to which the groups are spread as widely as possible. This linear function of the DVs is known as a **discriminant function**; in fact, the one-way MANOVA was originally termed **discriminant analysis**. The next step is to determine whether differences among the group means with respect to participants' scores on the discriminant function (these means are known as **centroids**) could have arisen merely through sampling error, the null hypothesis being that, in the population, the mean discriminant score or centroid is the same for all groups.

A discriminant function

A discriminant function has the following general form. If we suppose that there are p dependent variables in the experiment, $DV_1, DV_2, ..., DV_p$, the formula for the discriminant function is

$$D = b_0 + b_1DV_1 + b_2DV_2 + ... + b_pDV_p \quad \text{- - - (2)}$$

A discriminant function

Each of the participants in the experiment will receive, in addition to scores on the DVs, an additional score on the discriminant function D. The values of the constants $b_0, b_1, ...b_p$ are chosen so that the distributions of D among the groups (i.e., the group means or centroids) are spread out across the range of variation of D to the greatest possible extent: that is, the variability of D between groups is maximised. In this sense, the function D can be said to 'discriminate' among the groups.

If there are more than two groups, more than one discriminant function can be extracted. If there are k groups, $k - 1$ uncorrelated (or **orthogonal**) discriminant functions can be extracted. During the MANOVA, the extraction of the first discriminant function D_1 is followed by the extraction of the second discriminant function D_2, which is uncorrelated with (or **orthogonal to**) D_1. The process continues until all $k - 1$ discriminant functions have been extracted. Each participant will now have, in addition to a score on each DV, $(k - 1)$ extra scores, one on each of the discriminant functions.

MANOVA or discriminant analysis?

We have already said that the one-way MANOVA is identical with the technique known as discriminant analysis (DA). Both the MANOVA and DA, however, are options in SPSS. The choice between them depends upon the research situation. The MANOVA is applicable in experimental (or quasi-experimental research), where the researcher is primarily interested in comparing groups or conditions. DA, on the other hand, is applicable in correlational research, in which the researcher is more interested in the possible associations among a set of measured variables and wants to predict category membership from other measures in the data set. The researcher, for instance, might use a DA to predict patients' diagnostic categories from their scores on a battery of clinical scales. The use of discriminant functions to categorise people in this way is known as **classification**. The output from SPSS's discriminant analysis procedure (see Chapter 15) reflects the difference in orientation between the MANOVA and DA. Although the DA and MANOVA outputs contain the same core statistics, the DA output also includes additional statistics of particular interest to the researcher who is trying to predict group membership.

While the discriminant functions from the MANOVA could each be analysed with a univariate, one-way ANOVA to compare the group centroids or means, additional techniques are available for measuring the relative contribution of each discriminant function to the between groups variance and of the DVs to the variance accounted for by each discriminant function.

10.4.2 How the MANOVA works

The presence of several DVs makes the mathematics of the MANOVA more complicated than that of the ANOVA. In the one-way ANOVA, the total variability, as measured by the total sum of squares, is partitioned into between groups and within groups components and (after adjustments for their different degrees of freedom), the two variance estimates are compared by means of an F ratio to test the null hypothesis of equality, in the population, of the group means. Each of the two variance estimates has a single (or **point**) value.

Something basically similar happens in the MANOVA as well; but the analogues of point values such as the between and within sums of squares in the univariate ANOVA are rectangular arrays of numbers known as **matrices**. Conceptually, though, the parallels are close.

We have already encountered the **variance-covariance** matrix in Chapter 9, where we discussed the within subjects ANOVA. The values running along the principal diagonal of the variance-covariance matrix (the line of cells running from the top left of the matrix to the bottom right) are variances and the off-diagonal values are covariances between pairs of the repeated measures. The safe use of the within subjects ANOVA requires that the variance-covariance matrix must have the property of **sphericity**, that is, the values of the covariances must be (within sampling error) uniform. One of the great advantages of the MANOVA over the within subjects ANOVA is that sphericity is not a requirement. This is especially relevant when the MANOVA is used as an alternative to the ANOVA for the analysis of data from within subjects experiments (see below).

Variance-covariance matrices in MANOVA

In the MANOVA, the point values embodying the total variability, the between groups variability and the within groups variability that are used in the ANOVA, namely, SS_{total}, $SS_{between}$ and SS_{within}, and, respectively, are replaced by equivalent values calculated from variance-covariance matrices. In Chapter 9, we saw that the building block from which a covariance is calculated is the **cross-product** $(X - M_X)(Y - M_Y)$. The numerator of the covariance is the sum of cross-products SP, where $SP = \Sigma(X - M_X)(Y - M_Y)$. If we take deviations of the scores on the DVs from their respective grand means, ignoring the group means, we have a variance-covariance matrix T, which is the analogue of the total sum of squares in the ANOVA. If we take the deviations of the group means from the grand means, we have a matrix B corresponding to the between groups sum of squares in ANOVA. If we take the deviations of the scores from their group means, we have a matrix W corresponding to the within groups sum of squares in the ANOVA. Rather than merely measuring variance or variability, however, as in the ANOVA, these matrices also measure covariance, or shared variability.

Partition of the total variance-covariance matrix

Matrices, such as T, B and W, that all have the same number of rows r and columns c (that is, they have the same **dimensions**), can be added to produce another matrix with r rows and c columns, whose elements are the sums of the corresponding elements in the component matrices. For example,

$$\begin{pmatrix} 2 & 1 & 3 & 1 \\ 5 & 0 & 1 & 2 \end{pmatrix} + \begin{pmatrix} 6 & 0 & 9 & 1 \\ 3 & 3 & 4 & 6 \end{pmatrix} = \begin{pmatrix} 8 & 1 & 12 & 2 \\ 8 & 3 & 5 & 8 \end{pmatrix}$$

$$\qquad M_1 \qquad\qquad M_2 \qquad\qquad M_3 = M_1 + M_2 \quad \text{- - - (3)}$$

$$\qquad (2\times 4) \qquad\quad (2\times 4) \qquad\qquad\quad (2\times 4)$$

Matrix addition

In the MANOVA, the between groups and within groups variance-covariance matrices of cross-products have the same dimensions (same numbers of rows and columns) and can therefore be added together. It can be shown that when this is done, we have the total variance-covariance matrix. So, in MANOVA, we have a partition of the total variance-covariance matrix into between groups and within groups components thus:

$$T = B + W \quad \text{- - - (4)}$$

Partition of the total variance-covariance matrix in the MANOVA

A multivariate analogue of the variance: the determinant and Wilks' lambda

We have stressed that T, B and W are *matrices*, that is, rectangular arrays of values, not point values. From such a matrix, however, a point analogue of the variance can be calculated, namely, the **determinant** of the variance-covariance matrix. The determinant can be thought of as measuring variance plus covariance. A determinant is denoted by the use of two vertical lines: | |. The determinants of the between groups and within groups matrices are |B| and |W|, respectively.

In the one-way ANOVA, the F statistic is used to test the null hypothesis of equality of the group means. In MANOVA, several statistics have been proposed for testing the null hypothesis of equality of the group centroids. These statistics include **Wilks's lambda**, **Pillai's criterion**, **Hotelling's trace** and **Roy's principal root**. Wilks' lambda divides the determinant of the within groups matrix by the sum of the determinants of the within groups and between groups matrices:

$$\Lambda = \frac{|W|}{|W| + |B|} \quad \text{- - - (5)} \quad \textbf{Wilks' lambda}$$

We can think of Wilks' lambda as expressing the error variance as a proportion of the total variance. From Wilks' lambda, an approximate F statistic can be calculated. (An approximate chi-square statistic can also be used.) The degrees of freedom of F are given by complex formulae with which we shall not concern ourselves here (see Tabachnick & Fidell, 2007, p.259). The values of the degrees of freedom are included in the SPSS output.

Wilks' lambda and eta squared

Recall that in univariate one-way ANOVA, a measure of effect size is **eta squared (η^2)**, where

$$\eta^2 = \frac{SS_{between}}{SS_{total}} \quad \text{- - - (6) \ Eta squared}$$

Eta squared is the proportion of the total variability in the scores that is accounted for by variability among the group means.

For simplicity, **Wilks's lambda (Λ)**, can be thought of as the proportion of the total variance that is *within* groups, rather than *between* groups, as in eta squared: in fact, in the context of the one-way ANOVA (where there is just one DV), lambda is simply 1 minus eta squared:

$$\Lambda = 1 - \eta^2 \quad \text{- - - (7)}$$

**Wilks' lambda and eta squared in
the special case of one DV**

This comparison extends to the situation where, rather than one DV, we have a discriminant function of several DVs. The value of Λ, like that of η^2, can range in value from 0 to 1. Since, however, lambda is measuring *within* groups rather than *between* groups variability, a value of Λ close to zero indicates a *large* separation among the means; whereas a value close to unity indicates a *small* separation.

How discriminant functions are constructed: eigenvectors and eigenvalues

A **vector** is a row or column of values, as opposed to a **scalar**, which is a single value. In a matrix, any row or column is a vector. From some matrices, it is possible to calculate a special vector known as an **eigenvector**. In the MANOVA, the values in an eigenvector are the coefficients of a discriminant function: there is an eigenvector for each discriminant function extracted by the MANOVA. Associated with each eigenvector and discriminant function is an **eigenvalue (λ)** (or **characteristic root**). The eigenvalue measures the proportion of the variance accounted for by that function. An eigenvalue has a maximum value of 1, which would mean that its discriminant function accounts for 100% of the variance.

Eigenvectors and eigenvalues are ubiquitous in multivariate statistics: 'Most of the multivariate procedures rely on eigenvalues and their corresponding eigenvectors (also called characteristic roots and vectors) in one way or another because they consolidate the variance in a matrix (the *eigenvalue*) while providing the linear combination of variables (the *eigenvector*) to do it' (Tabachnick & Fidell, 2007; p.931).

Eigenvalues and Wilks' lambda

We have already looked at Wilks's lambda in the context of the comparison between within groups and between groups variance-covariance matrices. Lambda can also be expressed in terms of eigenvalues:

$$\Lambda = \prod_{i}^{d} \frac{1}{1+\lambda_{i}} \quad \text{- - - (8)}$$

Wilks's lambda expressed in terms of eigenvalues

In formula (8), d is the number of discriminant functions extracted by the MANOVA. The symbol $\prod$ (pi) stands for 'product': it is an operator, like Σ, but this time the d terms $1/(1 + \lambda_i)$ are multiplied together, not added. The greater the eigenvalues, the smaller the value of Wilks's lambda, bearing in mind that lambda is the *error* variance-covariance expressed as a proportion: the *smaller* the value of lambda, the *greater* the power of the discriminant function to discriminate among the groups.

The other principal statistics that appear in the SPSS MANOVA output, namely, the **Pillai-Bartlett trace**, **Hotellings T^2 (Hotelling-Lawley trace)** and **Roy's largest root**, are all functions of the eigenvalues λ. The simplest of these measures, Roy's largest root, is simply the largest value of λ. Since the first eigenvector (and discriminant function) to be extracted has the largest eigenvalue, Roy's statistic is the ratio of the between groups to the within groups variance/covariance for the first discriminant function.

10.4.3   Assumptions of the MANOVA

In univariate ANOVA, the data should be normally distributed. In MANOVA, the distributions of the DVs should be **multivariate normal**: if there are k DVs, then for any set of fixed values of $k - 1$ of them, the distribution of the remaining variable is also normal. The assumption of multivariate normality is the counterpart, in multivariate statistics, of the assumption of normality of distribution in the univariate ANOVA.

In the univariate ANOVA, the data should meet the requirement of homogeneity of variance. In MANOVA, the counterpart of this assumption is **homogeneity of variance-covariance matrices**: that is, it is assumed that the variance-covariance matrices in the different groups have all been sampled from the same population and so can be combined to give a pooled estimate of error, just as in the ANOVA, the cell variances are combined in the within groups mean square. The assumption of homogeneity of variance-covariance matrices (which is tested by **Box's test**) is quite a separate property from **sphericity**, that is, the homogeneity of the covariances among the repeated measures in the within subjects ANOVA, which is tested with the Mauchly test: variance-covariance matrices can be homogeneous across groups, but the individual matrices may not have the property of sphericity. The great advantage of MANOVA is that homogeneity of covariance is not a requirement and for this reason, some prefer to use MANOVA for the analysis of data from within subjects experiments.

To some extent, MANOVA is robust to violation of the assumptions of multivariate normality and homogeneity of variance-covariance matrices. As in the case of between subjects ANOVA, when sample sizes are large and equal among groups, all is likely to be well as far as Type I and Type II error rates are concerned. In the ANOVA, the greatest threat to the accuracy of the p-values of the F tests is a combination of unequal sample sizes and heterogeneity of variance. In the MANOVA, the parallel of these contraindications is a combination of unequal sample sizes and disparities among the variance-covariance matrices in different groups: if the larger samples have larger variances and covariances, the p-values are likely to be too large; whereas if the smaller samples have larger variances and covariances, the *p*-values are likely to be too small (Tabachnick & Fidell, 2007; p252). This consideration has implications for the choice between the various test statistics that are available.

The presence of strong associations among the variables is known as **multicollinearity**. In the extreme case of a perfect correlation between two of the DVs, the variance-covariance matrix is **singular**, that is, the determinant does not exist and the key statistics cannot be calculated. If the data show multicollinearity, one or more of the dependent variables must be removed before the MANOVA can run successfully.

10.4.4 Application of the MANOVA to the shape recognition experiment

In Section 10.2, we described the analysis of data from an experiment of design A × (B), specifically, Category × Shape, using the mixed or split-plot ANOVA. This technique is available through the **Repeated Measures** procedure in the **GLM** menu. Included in the SPSS output is a table of **Multivariate Tests**, which we omitted from that section, but which is shown in Output 21 below. This table summarises the results of the MANOVA of the same data set.

Multivariate Tests[b]

Effect		Value	F	Hypothesis df	Error df	Sig.	Partial Eta Squared
Shape	Pillai's Trace	.841	23.884[a]	2.000	9.000	.000	.841
	Wilks' Lambda	.159	23.884[a]	2.000	9.000	.000	.841
	Hotelling's Trace	5.308	23.884[a]	2.000	9.000	.000	.841
	Roy's Largest Root	5.308	23.884[a]	2.000	9.000	.000	.841
Shape * Category	Pillai's Trace	.941	71.159[a]	2.000	9.000	.000	.941
	Wilks' Lambda	.059	71.159[a]	2.000	9.000	.000	.941
	Hotelling's Trace	15.813	71.159[a]	2.000	9.000	.000	.941
	Roy's Largest Root	15.813	71.159[a]	2.000	9.000	.000	.941

a. Exact statistic

b. Design: Intercept + Category
Within Subjects Design: Shape

Output 21. Table of results of multivariate tests for the data in Table 1

The results of the tests made by the MANOVA are clearly in agreement with those of the ANOVA: there is a significant main effect of the Shape factor and also a significant Shape by Category interaction. (We should note, however, that the ANOVA and the MANOVA don't always produce the same results.) You will notice that the values of partial eta squared for the Shape factor and Shape by Category interaction are somewhat larger than those given for the same sources of variance in the Repeated Measures ANOVA output. The values given in Output 21 are 1 minus the value of Wilks' lambda for each source of variance.

The results of the approximate F test can be reported in the usual way, including information about the degrees of freedom, the p-values and measures of effect size, as when reporting the results of a univariate ANOVA F test.

Testing within subjects sources for significance

The MANOVA procedure is obtainable by choosing the **Multivariate** option in the **GLM** menu. If, in the MANOVA dialog box, you were to enter Category of Student as the Fixed Factor and Triangle, Square and Rectangle as the dependent variables and run the MANOVA procedure, you would obtain a test of the Category of Student factor. The procedure would find a discriminant function of Triangle, Square and Rectangle that maximises the separation of the group means or centroids and tests the null hypothesis that, in the population, the two group centroids are equal. The output would also include comparisons of the two groups on each of the three dependent variables considered separately. The output, however, would contain neither a test of the within subjects Shape factor nor of its interaction with the grouping factor Category of Student.

Essentially, the Repeated Measures procedure uses MANOVA to test within subjects sources of variance by creating, from the variables in the data set, certain additional variables and entering those (rather than Triangle, Square and Rectangle) into the MANOVA. The output will then include the desired tests of within subjects sources.

How the Repeated Measures procedure uses MANOVA to test within subjects sources

You might wish to choose the Multivariate option and use MANOVA yourself to see how the Repeated Measures procedure makes tests of within subjects factors and their interactions.

In Figure 23, is shown the original data set, including participants' scores under the Triangle, Square and Rectangle conditions, plus two new variables, SquareMinusTriangle and RectangleMinusSquare. These were produced by using the **Compute** command in the **Transform** menu to produce two columns of **difference scores**: the first was obtained by subtracting each Triangle score from the same participant's Square score; the second was obtained by subtracting the Square score from the corresponding Rectangle score (Figure 24).

	Case	Category	Triangle	Square	Rectangle	SquareMinus Triangle	RectangleMinus Square
1	1	1	2	12	7	10	-5
2	2	1	8	10	9	2	-1
3	3	1	4	15	3	11	-12
4	4	1	6	9	7	3	-2
5	5	1	9	13	8	4	-5
6	6	1	7	14	8	7	-6
7	7	2	13	3	35	-10	32
8	8	2	21	4	30	-17	26
9	9	2	26	10	35	-16	25
10	10	2	22	8	30	-14	22
11	11	2	20	9	28	-11	19
12	12	2	19	8	27	-11	19

Figure 23. **Data View**, showing the addition to the data set of two difference variables

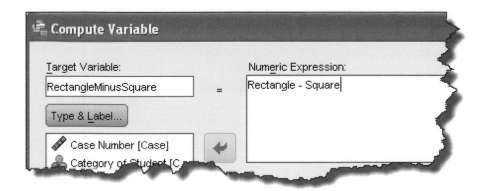

Figure 24. Compute Rectangle – Square with the **Compute Variable** command

Considering first the within subjects factor Shape, the null hypothesis holds that, in the population, the mean scores for the three shapes, Triangle, Square and Rectangle, are equal. If this is true, the values, in the population, of the means of the difference scores SquareMinusTriangle and RectangleMinusSquare are both zero. If the two difference variables are input as DVs into the MANOVA, the procedure will test this hypothesis and we shall have a test for a main effect of Shape.

If, in addition to the two difference variables, we input the grouping variable Category, the MANOVA procedure will compute a discriminant function of the two difference scores, which maximises the difference between the group means or centroids. Think of that discriminant function as a simple contrast between the two difference scores. If there is no interaction present, the value of that contrast will be similar in the two groups and the discriminant function will not be able to discriminate reliably between them. If an interaction is present, the mean values of the function (the centroids) will be further apart and the discriminant function will be able to discriminate reliably between the two groups.

Running the MANOVA

To run the MANOVA

- Select **Analyze→General Linear Model→Multivariate...** to open the **Multivariate** dialog box (Figure 25).

- Transfer the DVs, that is, the two difference variables, to the **Dependent Variables** box.

- Click **Options** and select **Descriptive statistics**, **Estimates of effect size**, and **Homogeneity tests** for checking the assumption of homogeneity of the variance-covariance matrix. Click **Continue** to return to the **MANOVA** dialog box.

- Click **OK** to run the MANOVA.

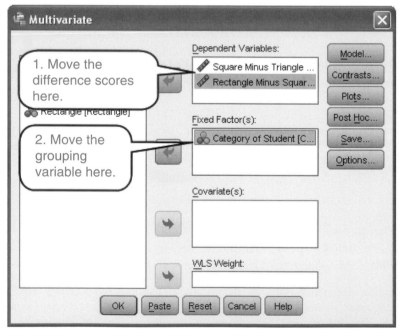

Figure 25. The **Multivariate** dialog box with the two difference scores transferred to the **Dependent Variables** box and the IV to the **Fixed Factor(s)** box

The MANOVA output

The results of the MANOVA are summarised in Output 22.

The multivariate equivalent of the main effect of Shape

Multivariate Tests[b]

Effect		Value	F	Hypothesis df	Error df	Sig.
Intercept	Pillai's Trace	.841	23.884[a]	2.000	9.000	.000
	Wilks' Lambda	.159	23.884[a]	2.000	9.000	.000
	Hotelling's Trace	5.308	23.884[a]	2.000	9.000	.000
	Roy's Largest Root	5.308	23.884[a]	2.000	9.000	.000
Category	Pillai's Trace	.941	71.159[a]	2.000	9.000	.000
	Wilks' Lambda	.059	71.159[a]	2.000	9.000	.000
	Hotelling's Trace	15.813	71.159[a]	2.000	9.000	.000
	Roy's Largest Root	15.813	71.159[a]	2.000	9.000	.000

a. Exact statistic

b. Design: Intercept + Category

The multivariate equivalent of the Shape*Category interaction

Output 22. Results of the MANOVA of the difference variables SquareMinusTriangle and RectangleMinusSquare

Although the upper and lower part of the table are labelled 'Intercept' and 'Category', respectively, we have the same results of the tests for a main effect of the Shape factor and the Shape × Category interaction as were presented in Output 21 from the **Repeated Measures** procedure. The use of difference variables rather than raw scores as input for the MANOVA has captured both the main effect of Shape and the Shape × Category interaction. The Repeated Measures procedure creates difference variables in a similar way and inputs them to the MANOVA, but outputs a table in which the name of the within subjects factor and the interaction are correctly labelled.

There are several ways of proceeding when a MANOVA main effect or an interaction is significant, but the details of these lie beyond the scope of this book. SPSS provides a step-by-step tutorial: click the **Help** button in the **MANOVA** dialog box and then click **Show me** at the foot of the resulting text box. Statistical textbooks, such as Tabachnick & Fidell (2007) and Field (2005, 2009), suggest further procedures such as Roy-Bargmann Stepdown Analysis and Discriminant Analysis.

10.5   A FINAL WORD

In this chapter, we have described the analysis of data from experiments of mixed factorial (or split-plot) design, in which some (but not all) factors have repeated measures. Experiments of this type are very widespread in research.

On the positive side, the presence of within subjects factors affords both convenience and improved power for the statistical tests. On the negative side, the difficulties with within subjects designs that we discussed in Chapter 9, together with their implications for the determination of power and effect size and their consequences for error rates, all apply to the designs we have described in this chapter. The main problem is that having repeated measures on some factors produces correlated data; and the patterns of those correlations can have consequences for the statistical tests. Should the variance-covariance matrices lack the property of homogeneity of covariance or sphericity, the ANOVA F tests will produce too many significant results. Conservative tests are available to attempt to control the **Type I error rate**; but there has been considerable debate about how effective they really are.

An alternative approach to the analysis of data from experiments of mixed factorial design is the multivariate analysis of variance (MANOVA). The MANOVA does not assume sphericity; however, the variance-covariance matrices in the various groups should be homogeneous.

We have taken only a very brief look at MANOVA using a simple example. MANOVA designs can have two or more factors and DVs as well as covariates, and can include contrast analyses. To learn more about these techniques, you should consult textbooks such as those already cited before embarking on a MANOVA.

Recommended reading

There are many readable textbooks on ANOVA, which provide extensive coverage of within subjects ANOVA. These include:

Dugard, P., Todman, J., & Staines, H. (2010). *Approaching multivariate analysis: A practical introduction (2nd ed.)*. London & New York: Routledge.

Field, A. (2009). *Discovering Statistics Using SPSS (3nd ed.)*. London: Sage.

Howell, D. C. (2007). *Statistical methods for psychology (6th ed.)*. Belmont, CA: Thomson/Wadsworth.

Keppel, G., & Wickens, T. D. (2004). *Design and analysis: A researcher's handbook (4th ed.)*. Upper Saddle River, NJ: Pearson Prentice Hall.

There are several excellent textbooks on multivariate statistics, including the MANOVA. These include:

Tabachnick, B. G., & Fidell, L. S. (2007). *Using multivariate statistics (5th ed.)*. Boston: Allyn & Bacon (Pearson International Edition).

Exercises

Exercise 15 *Mixed ANOVA: two-factor experiment* and Exercise 16 *Mixed ANOVA: three-factor experiment* are available in www.psypress.com/spss-made-simple Click on Exercises.

CHAPTER 11

Measuring statistical association

11.1   INTRODUCTION

So far, this book has been concerned with comparing the averages of different samples with respect to one variable, measured at the continuous or scale level: for example, on a measure of skilled performance, a drug group might be compared with a placebo group; right-handed people might be compared with left-handed people; the trained might be compared with the untrained; males might be compared with females. In such data sets, there is only one measured variable, the dependent variable: the other variables are grouping variables specifying the conditions under which the participants were tested or the natural groups to which they belonged; or the research might focus upon the performance of the same participants under the different conditions making up a within subjects factor. In this chapter, we move to correlational as opposed to experimental reseach and consider situations in which participants, rather than being assigned to different conditions created by the experimenter, are simply measured on two or more characteristics without any manipulation of conditions by the experimenter. Here interest centres on the question of whether there exists an association between the measured variables and, if so, the strength of that association.

In the early part of the chapter, we shall be concerned with data at the continuous or scale level of measurement only. Later, however, we shall turn to the analysis of nominal and ordinal data.

In the final part of the chapter, we shall be concerned with some issues that arise in correlational research and some of the ways in which they can be resolved.

11.1.1 A correlational study

In Chapter 1, we described a correlational study designed to investigate the extent to which children's Actual violence is related to their level of Exposure to screen violence.

The researcher has measured these variables in the expectation that they will show a positive association: there should be a tendency for those with high Exposure to score highly on Actual violence also; those low on Exposure should also be low on Actual violence; and those with average Exposure should fall within the normal range on Actual violence. This research strategy will not yield the strong evidence for causation that a true experiment would yield; however, an association would at least be consistent with the researcher's hypothesis that exposure to screened violence encourages actual violence in children.

Correlational research like this results in a **bivariate** data set, which can be pictured in a **scatterplot**. The scatterplot of the children's actual violence against their exposure to screen violence is shown in Output 1. In the scatterplot, each person is represented as a point, the coordinates of which are the person's scores on the Exposure and Actual scales, which are marked out on the horizontal and vertical axes, respectively.

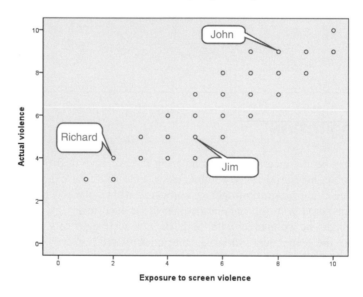

Ouput 1. Scatterplot of Actual Violence against Exposure to Screen Violence

It is evident from the scatterplot that there is indeed an association between the variables of Exposure to and Actual violence: John was highest on Exposure and he was also the most violent of the three children identified in the figure; Richard, with least Exposure, was also the least violent; Jim had intermediate scores on both variables. On the other hand, the association is imperfect: four children, including Jim, scored 5 on Exposure; but their Actual violence scores ranged from 4 to 7.

11.1.2   Linear relationships

One variable is said to be a **linear function** of another if the graph of the first upon the second is a straight line. Temperature in degrees Fahrenheit is a linear function of temperature in degrees Celsius, as shown in Output 2.

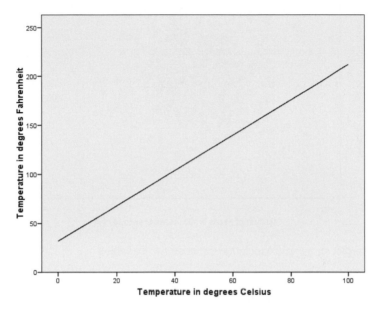

Output 2. A linear (straight line) relationship

The elliptical shape of the points in Output 1 arises because, although the relationship between the variables is *basically* linear, each score has a random, error component. It should be this error alone that "fattens up" the plot. The elliptical shape of the scatterplot, however, indicates that no other systematic trend (such as a quadratic or cubic relationship) is present.

If two variables are **dissociated** or independent, their scatterplot will be a circular cloud of points. Suppose two coins are each tossed 100 times and the number of heads recorded for each. The experiment is repeated 1000 times. There are two variables here: Number of Heads on the First coin and Number of Heads on the Second coin. Each repetition of the experiment will produce another pair of scores, one on each variable, so that at the end of the exercise we shall have 1000 pairs of scores. Here, however, the pairing is arbitrary: the outcomes should be independent and we should not expect any association between the two variables. The scatterplot will appear as in Output 3.

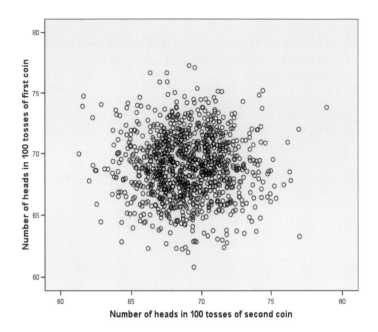

Output 3. Scatterplot showing dissociation between two variables

11.2   THE PEARSON CORRELATION

We made the acquaintance of the Pearson correlation in Chapter 1. The Pearson correlation is a measure of a supposed linear relationship between two variables, both measured at the continuous or scale level. The word 'supposed' is important here. Should the variables be in a nonlinear relationship (i.e., the graph of one against the other is curved in some way), the Pearson correlation can be highly misleading as a measure of strength of association. The true nature of the relationship between two continuous variables will be evident from the appearance of their scatterplot and the plot should always be viewed when that is possible.

11.2.1 Formula for the Pearson correlation

There are several different formulae for the Pearson correlation, one of the most common of which is as follows:

$$r_{XY} = \frac{\Sigma(X - M_X)(Y - M_Y)}{\sqrt{\Sigma(X - M_X)^2\ \Sigma(Y - M_Y)^2}} = \frac{SP}{\sqrt{SS_X\, SS_Y}} \quad ---(1)$$

The Pearson correlation

In the SS/SP version of this formula, *SS* stands for 'Sum of Squares' (i.e. the squared **deviations** from the mean summed over all the participants in the study) and SP stands for 'Sum of Products' (the product of the **deviations** of X and Y from M_X and M_Y, respectively, summed over all participants).

11.2.2   The range of values of the Pearson correlation

It can be shown that the value of r can vary only within the range from -1 to $+1$, inclusive.

$$-1 \leq r \leq +1 \quad \text{---(2)}$$

Range of possible values of r

This property confers upon the Pearson correlation a great advantage over another measure of association known as the **covariance**, which was described in Chapter 9. The covariance has no upper or lower limit; moreover, its value depends upon the scale on which each of the two variables is measured: if a data set contains the heights and weights of 100 people, measured in feet and stones, respectively, and these measurements are transformed to inches and pounds, the value of the covariance will also change. The *absolute* value of the correlation coefficient, on the other hand (its value with the sign ignored), remains unchanged by any linear transformation of the units of measurement. (If the slope of the transformation is negative, however, the correlation changes in sign.) A correlation between the heights and weights of fifty people measured in centimetres and grams respectively has the same value as the correlation between their heights and weights measured in inches and pounds. The correlation thus has the great advantage of being 'unit-free', and can be used to compare the degrees of association between pairs of variables measured in different units.

The Pearson correlation is actually the covariance between two sets of scores X and Y after they have been transformed to standard (z) scores z_X and z_Y by subtracting their respective means and dividing these deviation scores by their respective standard deviations. The formula for the Pearson correlation, therefore, may also be written as follows:

$$r_{XY} = \frac{\sum z_X z_Y}{n-1} \quad \text{---(3)}$$

**Standard score formula for
the Pearson correlation**

Comparison of formula (3) with formula (2) in Chapter 9 shows that the Pearson correlation is the covariance between two standardised variables.

11.2.3   The sign of a correlation

The sign of a correlation sometimes reflects the intrinsic natures of the variables being measured: one would not expect height to correlate negatively with weight. Often, however, the sign of a correlation is merely a matter of definition and scaling and therefore arbitrary. If we label an obsessive-compulsive scale as Decisiveness, the zero point will represent extreme *indecisiveness* and the highest value extreme decisiveness; but if we label the same scale Indecisiveness, the zero point will represent extreme *decisiveness*. Since the purpose of a correlation coefficient is primarily to measure the strength of a statistical association, the researcher's attention usually focuses upon the *absolute* value of r, that is, its numerical value with the sign ignored. Figure 1 shows two scatterplots: the first is the scatterplot of Actual violence upon Exposure to violence; the second is a scatterplot with the direction of the Exposure scale reversed by multiplying the original Exposure scores by -1. (The reversal would make psychological sense if the variable name Exposure were to be changed to Degree of Censorship.) In either case, the absolute value of the Pearson correlation is 0.90. A negative correlation of -0.90 represents the same (very strong) degree of linear association as a positive correlation of $+0.90$.

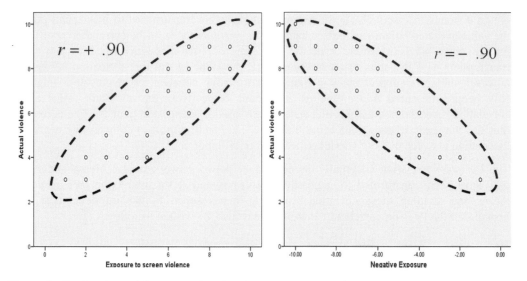

Figure 1. Scatterplots of data sets showing the same degree of association, but with correlations of opposite sign

A perfect linear association, with all the points in the scatterplot lying along the same straight line, would be reflected either in a correlation of $+1$ or a correlation of -1: either value would represent a perfect linear relationship.

11.2.4   Testing an obtained value of *r* for significance

The test for the significance of a correlation coefficient presupposes that the data have the property of **bivariate normality**, that is, at any particular value of either variable, the other variable has a normal distribution.   An elliptical cloud of points in the scatterplot indicates that the assumption of bivariate normality has been met and that it is safe to proceed with the formal test.

The test of the null hypothesis that, in the bivariate normal population, the correlation is zero is made with the statistic *t*, where

$$t(n-2) = \frac{r\sqrt{(n-2)}}{\sqrt{(1-r^2)}} \quad \text{---(4)}$$

Testing *r* for significance

In formula (4), *n* is the number of pairs of scores.   If the assumption of bivariate normality holds, this test statistic is distributed as *t* on $n-2$ degrees of freedom.

11.2.5   A word of warning about the correlation coefficient

It is quite possible, from inspection of a scatterplot, to do two useful things:

1. Establish that there is indeed a linear relationship between the variables, in which case the Pearson correlation would be a meaningful statistic to use;

2. Guess fairly accurately what the value of the Pearson correlation would be if it were to be calculated.

In other words, from inspection of the scatterplot alone, one can discern the most important features of the true relationship (if any) between two variables.   So if we reason from the scatterplot to the statistics, we shall never go seriously wrong.

The converse, however, is not true: given only the value of a Pearson correlation, one can say nothing whatsoever about the nature of the relationship between two variables.   Many years ago, in a famous paper, Anscombe (1973) presented some bivariate data sets which illustrate how misleading the value of the Pearson correlation can be. In one set, for instance, the correlation is high, yet the scatterplot shows no association whatsoever; in another, the correlation is zero, but the scatterplot shows a perfect, but nonlinear, association. The moral of this cautionary tale is clear: when studying the association between two variables, always construct a scatterplot, and interpret (or disregard) the Pearson correlation accordingly.

In the same paper, Anscombe gave us a useful rule for deciding whether there really is a robust linear relationship between two variables: should the shape of the scatterplot be unaltered by the removal of a few observations at random, the plot is an accurate depiction of the true relationship between the variables.   In one of the sets Anscombe devised, a substantial correlation is driven by a single outlier and disappears when the outlier is removed.

To sum up, the Pearson correlation is a measure of a *supposed* linear relationship between two variables; but the supposition of linearity must always be confirmed by inspection of the scatterplot.

11.2.6   Effect size

Unlike t, F or chi-square, the value of a correlation is, in itself, a measure of "effect size", bearing in mind, of course, that correlation does not imply causation. For the purposes of comparison with other measures of effect size, however, the **square** of the correlation r^2, which is known as the **coefficient of determination**, is often used instead. The reason for this will be explained more fully in Chapter 12, where we shall see that the square of the Pearson correlation is an estimate of the proportion of the variance of the scores on the target or criterion variable that is accounted for by regression upon another variable. In the data set depicted in Output 1, the Pearson correlation between the Actual and Exposure scores is +0.89. The value of the coefficient of determination (CD) is therefore $0.89^2 = 0.80$. In other words, 80% of the variance of the Actual scores is accounted for by regression upon Exposure.

The coefficient of determination is the proportion of the variance of either variable that is shared with the other variable. This sharing of variance can be depicted by two overlapping circles, the area of each representing 100% of the variance of either variable and the overlapping area representing the proportion of the variance that is shared (Figure 2).

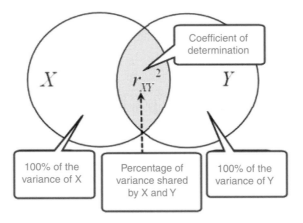

Figure 2. The coefficient of determination as the percentage of the variance of either variable that is shared with the other

In the coefficient of determination (r^2), we have a measure of effect size which can be interpreted along guidelines suggested by Cohen (1988). Cohen's guidelines are shown in Table 1. A correlation of less than 0.1 is trivial. A correlation between 0.1 and 0.3 is "small". A correlation between 0.3 and 0.5 is "medium". A correlation of 0.5 or greater is "large". Also given in Table 1 are the equivalent ranges for the coefficient of determination.

Table 1. Guidelines (from Cohen, 1988) for classifying association strength, as measured by a correlation coefficient

Absolute value of r	r squared	Size of effect
$0.1 \leq |r| < 0.30$	$0.01 \leq r^2 < 0.09$	Small
$0.30 \leq |r| < 0.50$	$0.09 \leq r^2 < 0.25$	Medium
$|r| \geq 0.50$	$r^2 \geq 0.25$	Large

A correlation less than 0.1 is trivial.

If a correlation is **between 0.1 and 0.3** (ignoring the sign), the association is **SMALL**. Between 1% and 8% of the variance is shared.

If a correlation is **between 0.3 and 0.5**, the association is **MEDIUM**. Between 9% and 25% of the variance is shared.

If a correlation is **0.5 or greater**, the association is **LARGE**. At least 25% of the variance is shared.

11.3   CORRELATION WITH SPSS

Table 2 shows the raw data that were pictured in the scatterplot in Figure 1.   These data are available in the file *Ch11 Violence and Parents.sav* at www.psypress.com/spss-made-simple . To the newcomer to SPSS, however, we suggest that, since this is a very small data set, it would be a useful exercise to enter the data by hand into the Data Editor, rather than simply downloading the file from the website.

11.3.1 Preparing the SPSS data set

As usual, begin in **Variable View**. Name the variables Actual and Exposure and assign full **variable labels**, such as Actual Violence and Exposure to Screen Violence. (The variable *labels*, not the variable *names*, will appear in the output.) Set the **Decimals** specification to zero in order to avoid unnecessary clutter in **Data View**. Switch to **Data View** and enter the data. Save the data set.

Table 2. The raw data from the violence study

Case	Exposure	Actual
1	1	3
2	2	3
3	2	4
4	3	4
5	4	4
6	5	4
7	3	5
8	4	5
9	5	5
10	6	5
11	4	6
12	5	6
13	6	6
14	7	6

Case	Exposure	Actual
15	5	7
16	6	7
17	7	7
18	8	7
19	6	8
20	7	8
21	8	8
22	9	8
23	7	9
24	8	9
25	9	9
26	10	9
27	10	10

11.3.2   Obtaining the scatterplot

We have already described the use of the Chart Builder to draw a scatterplot.

See
Chapter 5

11.3.3   Obtaining the Pearson correlation

We described how to obtain the Pearson correlation between two variables in Chapter 4. Confirm, using the **Bivariate Correlations** procedure, that the correlation between Exposure and Actual is +0.892.

See
Chapter 4

11.3.4   Output for the Pearson correlation

Output 4 is the **Correlations** table produced by the **Bivariate Correlations** procedure. The table contains the Pearson correlation, its p-value and the number of paired data points. The value for r is 0.892, which is significant beyond the 0.01 level. This is written as:

"$r(27) = .892$; p $< .01$. Effect size $r^2 = .80$, a Large effect."

Since 80% of the variance is shared, the association is obviously a strong one.

Correlations

		Exposure to Screen Violence	Actual Violence
Exposure to Screen Violence	Pearson Correlation	1	.892**
	Sig. (2-tailed)		.000
	N	27	27
Actual Violence	Pearson Correlation	.892**	1
	Sig. (2-tailed)	.000	
	N	27	27

r = 0.892 and is significant at .01 level

There are 27 pairs of values

**. Correlation is significant at the 0.01 level (2-tailed).

Since the correlation of Exposure with Actual is the same as the correlation of Actual with Exposure, the second row is a repeat of the first row

Output 4. The Pearson **Correlations** table

Notice that in Output 4, the information we need in the upper right cell of the table (the value of *r*, the number of pairs of data and the *p*-value) is duplicated in the lower left cell of the table, because the correlation of A with B is the same as the correlation of B with A.

Had there been more than two variables, the results would have appeared in the form of a square matrix with entries above the **principal diagonal** (which runs from the top left of the matrix to the bottom right) being duplicated in the cells below it. When there are more than two variables, SPSS can be commanded to construct this **correlation matrix (or R-matrix)** simply by entering as many variable names as required into the **Variables** box of the **Correlations** dialog.

11.4   OTHER MEASURES OF ASSOCIATION

The Pearson correlation is suitable for continuous or scale data only. With ordinal or nominal data, other statistics must be used.

11.4.1   Spearman's rank correlation

The term **ordinal data** includes both ranks and assignments to ordered categories. When the same objects are ranked independently by two judges, the question arises as to the extent to which the judges agree. This is a question about the strength of association between two variables which, although quantitative, are measured at the ordinal level. Suppose that the ranks assigned to ten paintings by two judges are as in Table 3.

Table 3. Ranks assigned by two judges to each of ten paintings

Painting	A	B	C	D	E	F	G	H	I	J
First Judge	1	2	3	4	5	6	7	8	9	10
Second Judge	1	3	2	4	6	5	8	7	10	9

It is obvious that the judges generally agree closely in their rankings: at most, their assignments differ by a single rank. One way of measuring the level of agreement between the two judges is by calculating the Pearson correlation between the two sets of ranks. This correlation is known as the **Spearman rank correlation** (r_S) or **Spearman's rho** (ρ). Like eta squared, Spearman's rho is a *statistic*, not a parameter, and is thus another exception to the general rule about reserving Greek and Roman letters for parameters and statistics, respectively. While the defining formula for the Spearman rank correlation looks very different from that for the Pearson correlation, the two formulae are exactly equivalent, provided that no ties are allowed.

The use of the Spearman rank correlation is not confined to ordinal data. Suppose the scatterplot of the bivariate distribution of two continuous variables shows that they are in a **monotonic** relationship (when one increases or decreases, so does the other), but the relationship is non-linear, so that the Pearson correlation is an unsuitable measure of degree of association. The scores on both variables can be converted to ranks and the Spearman rank correlation calculated instead. Arguably, in this situation, the value of the rank correlation is a truer reflection of the degree of association between the two variables than is the value of the Pearson correlation.

11.4.2   Kendall's tau statistics

The **Kendall's tau** (τ) statistics offer an alternative to the Spearman rank correlation as measures of agreement between rankings, or assignments to ordered categories. The basic idea is that one set of ranks can be converted into another by a succession of reversals of pairs of ranks in one set: the fewer the reversals needed to achieve the conversion (in relation to the total number of possible reversals), the larger the value of tau. The numerator of Kendall's tau is the difference between the number of pairs of objects whose ranks are concordant (i.e. they go in the same direction) and the number of discordant pairs. If the former predominate, the sign of tau is positive; if the latter predominate, tau is negative.

There are three different versions of Kendall's tau: **tau-a**, **tau-b** and **tau-c**. All three measures have the same numerator, the difference between the numbers of concordant and discordant pairs. In their denominators, however, they differ in the way they handle tied observations.

The denominator of the correlation **tau-a** is simply the total number of pairs. The problem with tau-a is that when there are ties, its range quickly becomes restricted, to the point where it becomes difficult to interpret.

The correlation **tau-b** has terms in the denominator that consider, in either variable, pairs that are tied on one variable but not on the other. (When there are no ties, the values of tau-a and tau-b are identical.)

The correlation **tau-c** was designed for situations where one wishes to measure agreement between assignments to unequal-sized sets of ordered categories. Provided the data meet certain requirements, the appropriate tau correlation can vary throughout the complete range from −1 to +1.

Note that the calculation of Kendall's statistics with ordinal data, in the form of assignments of target objects to ordered categories, is best handled by the **Crosstabs** procedure (see next section); indeed, **tau-c** can be obtained only by using **Crosstabs**.

11.4.3   Rank correlations with SPSS

In **Variable View**, name two variables, *Judge1* and *Judge2*. Click the **Data View** tab to switch to **Data View** and, from Table 3, enter the ranks assigned by the first judge into the Judge1 column and those assigned by the second judge into the Judge2 column.

- Choose **Analyze➔Correlate➔Bivariate…** to obtain the **Bivariate Correlations** dialog box (Figure 3). By default, the **Pearson** check box will be marked. Click off the **Pearson** check box and click the **Kendall's tau-b** and the **Spearman** check boxes.

- Transfer the variable names Judge1 and Judge2 to the **Variables:** box.

- Click **OK** to obtain the correlations shown in Output 5.

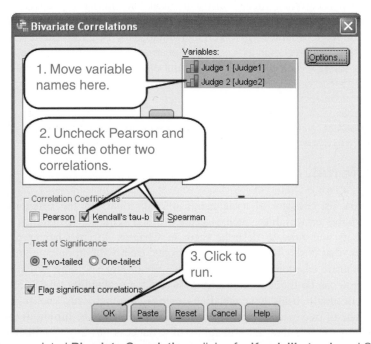

Figure 3. The completed **Bivariate Correlations** dialog for **Kendall's tau-b** and Spearman's rho

Correlations

			Judge 1	Judge 2
Kendall's tau_b	Judge 1	Correlation Coefficient	1.000	.822**
		Sig. (2-tailed)	.	.001
		N	10	10
	Judge 2	Correlation Coefficient	.822**	1.000
		Sig. (2-tailed)	.001	.
		N	10	10
Spearman's rho	Judge 1	Correlation Coefficient	1.000	.952**
		Sig. (2-tailed)	.	.000
		N	10	10
	Judge 2	Correlation Coefficient	.952**	1.000
		Sig. (2-tailed)	.000	.
		N	10	10

Tau-b correlation is .822 with an associated p-value <.01

Spearman's correlation is .952 with an associated p-value <.01

**. Correlation is significant at the 0.01 level (2-tailed).

Output 5. **Kendall** and **Spearman**'s rank correlations

Output 5 shows that the **Kendall correlation** is +0.82 and the **Spearman correlation** is +0.95. These values differ, but there is nothing untoward in this. The two statistics are based on quite different theoretical foundations and often take noticeably different values when calculated from the same data set. In tests for significance, each statistic is referred to its own sampling distribution to obtain its p-value. Incidentally, the Pearson option would have given the same value for the correlation as would the Spearman (+0.95), because the latter procedure first transforms the raw data to ranks. The results of the Spearman test would be written as follows:

"rho $(10) = .95$; $p = < .01$.

rho^2 $= .91$, a large effect".

11.5   NOMINAL DATA

A **nominal** data set consists of assignments of individuals to the categories making up qualitative attributes or variables, such as gender, blood group or nationality. We discussed nominal data sets and how to describe them in Chapter 4. In Chapter 6, we discussed **Bernoulli trials**, that is sets of identical experiments, each with an outcome that can fall into one of two qualitative categories (Heads or Tails, Six or Not Six, Pass or Fail, Toy A or Toy B). One outcome can be thought of as a Success and the probability of a Success is the same on all trials. Bernoulli trials generate **dichotomous** nominal data: each observation is an assignment to one of two categories. In Chapter 6, we saw that the **binomial test** can be used to test the null hypothesis that the probability of a Success has any specified value between zero and 1.

In Chapter 6, the binomial test was illustrated with an example in which each of 100 children selected one of two toys. Sixty children selected Toy A and forty selected Toy B. Here the null hypothesis was that, in the population, there is no tendency for children to prefer one toy over the other. In that example, the **observed** frequencies (60 and 40) were insufficiently different from the **expected** frequencies under the null hypothesis (50 and 50) to reject the null hypothesis and provide evidence for a preference.

In the example of the two toys, the binomial test was being used as a test of the **goodness-of-fit** of the distribution of expected frequencies (50, 50) to the observed distribution (60, 40). In statistics, the **expectation** of a statistic is its long run mean value were the same experiment to be run an unthinkably large number of times. In the example of the two toys, the distribution of expected frequencies is a sufficiently good fit to the observed distribution for the null hypothesis to be accepted.

11.5.1   The one-sample approximate chi-square goodness-of-fit test with three or more categories

To extend the example of toy preferences, suppose that there are three or more toys to choose from. In that situation, in which there is a single property or **attribute** consisting of three or more categories, the **chi-square approximate goodness-of-fit test** can be used to test the null hypothesis that, in the population, all the toys are equally attractive to children.

Suppose that there were three toys, A, B and C and that ninety children were asked which of the toys they most preferred. Of 90 children tested, the numbers choosing the three toys were 20, 41 and 29, respectively (see Table 4). This is the distribution of **observed frequencies** (*O*). If there is no preference in the population (the null hypothesis), we should expect that 30 children would choose each of the three toys. This is the distribution of **expected frequencies** (*E*). The null hypothesis of no preference in the population implies that the preferences among the three categories have a **discrete uniform distribution**. In testing the null hypothesis of no preference among the three toys, we are asking whether the theoretical (uniform) distribution is a good fit to the observed distribution of frequencies. The test of **goodness-of-fit** is made by running an **approximate chi-square (χ^2) test**.

Table 1. A nominal data set showing the observed and expected frequencies (O and E, respectively)

	A	B	C
O	20	41	29
E	30	30	30

The test is 'approximate' because the true chi-square variable is defined in the context of a normally distributed variable and is therefore continuous. The statistic we are about to describe is only approximately distributed as χ^2. The chi-square statistic is defined as follows:

$$\chi^2 = \sum \frac{(O-E)^2}{E} \quad \text{- - - (5)}$$

Approximate chi-square statistic

(In formula 5, the symbol Σ means 'Sum': the formula instructs us to add up, over all three toys, the values of $\dfrac{(O-E)^2}{E}$.)

A chi-square distribution has one parameter, the **degrees of freedom (*df*)**. In the context of nominal data in a one-way classification, the value of the degrees of freedom (*df*) is one less than the number of categories in the one-way classification. In this example, $df = 3 - 1 = 2$. A chi-square variate has a lower limit of zero, but no upper limit. The distribution is positively skewed, with a long tail to the right. The critical region lies above the 95th percentile of the distribution of chi-square on 2 degrees of freedom, which is 6.0 . (You can confirm this by using the INVCDF function in the Compute Variable command to calculate the 95th percentile of the chi square distribution on 2 degrees of freedom.)

How well does the theoretical **uniform distribution** fit the observed distribution? It is clear from the formula that the greater the differences between the observed and expected frequencies, the greater will be the magnitude of the χ^2 statistic. The value of chi-square is:

$$\chi^2 = \frac{(-10)^2}{30} + \frac{(11)^2}{30} + \frac{(-1)^2}{30} = \frac{222}{30} = 7.4$$

The null hypothesis that the distribution is uniform is rejected: $\chi^2(2) = 7.4;\ p = 0.03$.

11.5.2   Running a chi-square goodness-of-fit test on SPSS

The results of the three toys experiment can either be entered into the data editor on an individual basis (in which case there would be 90 rows in **Data View**) or as frequencies (in which case there would only be three rows). We shall assume that the researcher has already computed the frequency distribution and that **Data View** appears as in Figure 4.

	Preference	Frequency
1	Toy A	20
2	Toy B	41
3	Toy C	29
4		

Figure 4. Data View showing data in the form of a frequency distribution

If the data are entered in the form of a frequency distribution as in Figure 4, it is essential to make this clear to SPSS by following the **Weight Cases** procedure (in the **Data** menu). In this case, the values of the variable Preference must be weighted with those in the Frequency variable. The procedure is shown in Figure 5:

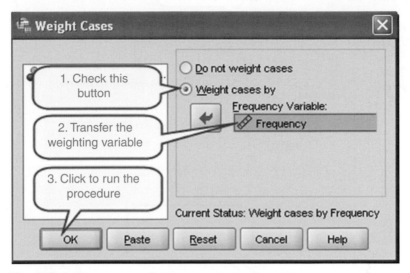

Figure 5.   The **Weight Cases** procedure

The **Chi-square goodness-of-fit test** is run as follows:

- In **Variable View** name the variables Preference and Frequency. The Preference variable comprises 3 categories, to which are assigned the values 1, 2 and 3, with value labels Toy A, Toy B and Toy C, respectively.   For the Preference variable, change the **Scale** setting to **Nominal**.

- Enter the data in **Data View**.

- Use **Weight Cases...** to weight the values in Frequency as described in Figure 5.

- Choose **Analyze➔Nonparametric Tests➔One Sample...** to open the **One-Sample Nonparametric Tests** dialog box. The opening dialog will have the tab **Objective** at the top.   Click the Fields tab and transfer Preference to the **Test Fields** box. (Leave the Frequency variable behind: SPSS has already been informed that Frequency will be used to weight the cases.)

- Click the **Settings** tab and complete the dialog as shown in Figure 6.

- Click The **Run** button.

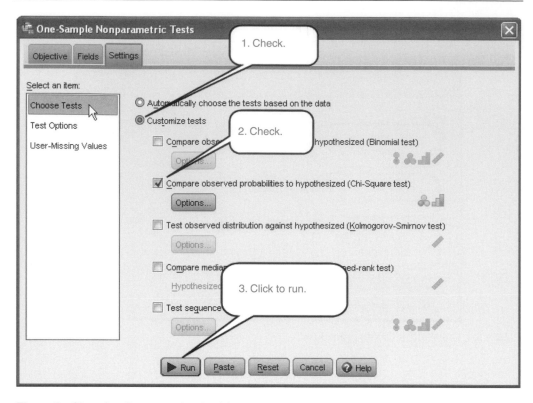

Figure 6. Choosing the approximate chi-square test

Output 6 is the first item to appear in the Output Viewer. Double-click on the table to see the Auxiliary View of the Model Viewer (Output 7).

Hypothesis Test Summary

	Null Hypothesis	Test	Sig.	Decision
1	The categories of Preference occur with equal probabilities.	One-Sample Chi-Square Test	.025	Reject the null hypothesis.

Asymptotic significances are displayed. The significance level is .05.

Output 6. The summary table in the Output Viewer

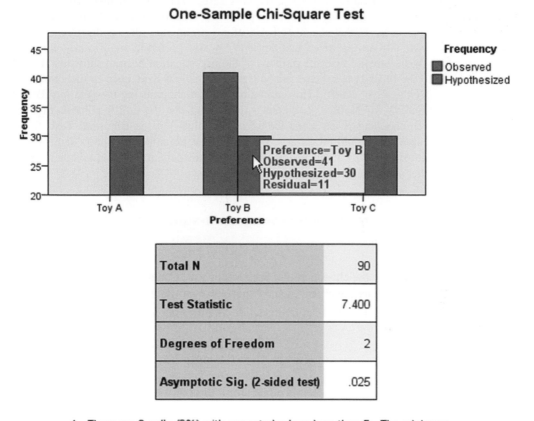

Output 7. The auxiliary pane of the Model Viewer showing details of the approximate chi-square test of goodness-of-fit

Notice that, in Output 7, the Test Statistic has exactly the value that we calculated for the approximate chi-square statistic. When the cursor is placed on a bar on the bar chart, the values of the observed and expected frequencies and the residual $[O, E \text{ and } (O - E)]$ will appear.

The results of the test might be reported as follows:

"Inspection of the frequency distribution shows that twice as many children (41) chose Toy B as chose Toy A (20). Approximately the expected number (29) preferred Toy C. A an approximate chi-square test of the null hypothesis that the three toys were equally attractive to the children showed significance beyond the .05 level: $\chi^2 (2) = 7.4$; $p = .025$ ".

The interpretation of the results of this test requires care. The experimenter may have had theoretical reason to expect that Toy B would be preferred to the other toys. All the chi-square test has shown, however, is that the hypothesis of no preference among the three toys is untenable. We have not demonstrated that any one toy was preferred significantly more (or less) than either of the others. Had the purpose of the investigation been to show that Toy B was preferable to the other two, a better analytic strategy would have been to dichotomise a child's choice as either B or NotB. This can be done by dichotomising the data into B and NotB: 49 for *B* and 41 for NotB. A binomial test would test the null hypothesis that the number of children choosing B exceeded the expected value. In the **Binomial Test** dialog box, the **Test Proportion** would be set at $1/3 = 0.33$. The binomial test shows significance beyond the 0.05 level: $p = 0.01$. This result does support the scientific hypothesis that Toy B is preferred to either of the other two toys.

11.5.3   Measuring effect size following a chi-square test of goodness-of-fit

As an effect size index for the chi-square goodness-of-fit test, Cohen (1988) has proposed the statistic *w*. If P_O and P_E are the observed and expected proportions, obtained from the values of *O* and *E* by dividing them by the total frequency *N*, the formula for *w* is

$$w = \sqrt{\sum \frac{\left(P_o - P_E\right)^2}{P_E}} \quad \text{- - - (5)}$$

Cohen's effect size index

The value of *w* can be calculated very easily from that of chi-square. In our current example, N = 90 and $\chi^2 = 7.4$. The value of *w*, therefore, is:

$$w = \sqrt{\sum \frac{\left(P_O - P_E\right)^2}{P_E}} = \sqrt{\frac{\chi^2}{N}} = \sqrt{\frac{7.4}{30}} = 0.50$$

Cohen suggests the values 0.1, 0.3 and 0.5 as Small, Medium and Large effects respectively. We have interpreted these guidelines in Table 5. Our obtained value 0.50, therefore, is a Large effect.

Table 5.   Guidelines (from Cohen, 1988) for
interpreting his effect size index

Value of w	Size of effect
$0.1 \leq w < 0.3$	Small
$0.3 \leq w < 0.5$	Medium
$w \geq 0.5$	Large

A value less than 0.1 is trivial.

A value between 0.1 and 0.3 is a Small effect.

A value between 0.3 and 0.5 is a Medium effect.

A value at least 0.5 is a Large effect.

To sum up, we have just discussed the use of the approximate **chi-square statistic** χ^2 to test the **goodness-of-fit** of a theoretical distribution of expected frequencies E to the distribution of the observed frequencies O over a set of categories making up a single qualitative variable or attribute.

In the general case, if the attribute has k categories, the value of chi-square ($df = k - 1$) for the goodness-of-fit test is given by

$$\chi^2 = \sum_{\text{all categories}} \frac{(O-E)^2}{E} \quad \text{- - - (6)}$$

Chi-square goodness-of-fit test

11.5.4   Testing for association between two qualitative variables in a contingency table

In Chapter 1, we saw that when people's membership of two sets of mutually exclusive and exhaustive categories is recorded, the bivariate distribution of the two attributes can be examined by constructing a **crosstabulation**, or **contingency table**. The crosstabulation of nominal data is the equivalent of the use of the scatterplot to examine the bivariate distribution of variables measured at the scale or continuous level. Like the scatterplot, the contingency table provides an excellent means of inspecting a discrete bivariate distribution in order to ascertain the presence of an association between the variables concerned.

Suppose that a researcher has reason to believe that there should be a higher incidence of a potentially harmful antibody in patients whose tissue is of a certain 'critical' type. In a study of 79 patients, the incidence of the antibody in patients of four different tissue types, including the 'critical' category, are recorded. The results are presented in Table 6.

Table 6. Contingency table with a pattern of observed frequencies suggesting an association between Tissue Type and Presence of an antibody

Tissue type	Presence		Total
	No	Yes	
Critical	6	21	27
A	5	7	12
B	11	7	18
C	14	8	22
Total	36	43	79

The chi-square statistic

The pattern of the frequencies appears to confirm the research hypothesis: there is a noticeably higher incidence of the antibody in the Critical group.

The researcher's hypothesis is that there is an association between the variables of Group (the type of tissue) and the Presence (Yes or No) of the antibody. The null hypothesis H_0 is the negation of this: there is no association between the two attributes. While it would appear from Table 6 that the null hypothesis is false, a formal statistical test is required to confirm this.

The null hypothesis that there is no association between the Group and Presence variables can be tested with the **chi-square test for association**. For each cell of the contingency table, the expected frequency E is calculated on the assumption that the attributes of Group and

Presence are independent, and the values of E are compared with the corresponding observed frequencies O by means of the statistic χ^2, where

$$\chi^2(3) = \sum_{\text{all cells}} \frac{(O-E)^2}{E} \quad \text{---}(7)$$

Chi-square test for association

In general, if variables A and B consist of a and b categories, respectively, the value of the degrees of freedom of this chi-square statistic is given by

$$df = (a-1)(b-1) \quad \text{---}(8)$$

General formula for the degrees of freedom
in two-way contingency tables

In the present example, $df = (4-1)(2-1) = 3$. In a 4×2 table with fixed marginal totals, the assignment of frequencies to only three cells completely determines the values of the frequencies in the remaining five cells.

The expected frequencies are calculated using estimates of probability derived from the marginal totals and the total frequency N in the following way. If R and C are the marginal totals of the row and the column that locate the cell in the contingency table, the expected frequency E_{RC} is given by

$$E_{RC} = \frac{R \times C}{N} \quad \text{---}(9) \text{ **Expected frequency**}$$

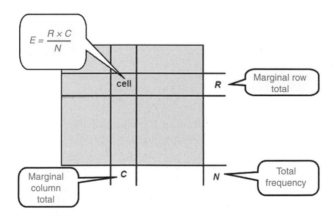

Figure 7. Calculation of the expected cell frequencies (E) in a contingency table

For example, for the top left cell in the contingency table, $E = (27 \times 36)/79 = 12.30$. The expected frequencies (referred to by SPSS as **Expected Counts**) in all eight cells of the table are shown in Output 8.

Tissue Type * Presence Crosstabulation

			Presence No	Presence Yes	Total
Tissue Type	Critical	Count	6	21	27
		Expected Count	12.3	14.7	27.0
	Type C	Count	5	7	12
		Expected Count	5.5	6.5	12.0
	Type B	Count	11	7	18
		Expected Count	8.2	9.8	18.0
	Type A	Count	14	8	22
		Expected Count	10.0	12.0	22.0
Total		Count	36	43	79
		Expected Count	36.0	43.0	79.0

Output 8. The observed and expected frequencies of observations in the cells of the contingency table in Table 6

The value of chi-square is

$$\chi^2 = \sum_{\text{all cells}} \frac{(O-E)^2}{E} = \frac{(6-12.3)^2}{12.3} + \frac{(21-14.7)^2}{14.7} + \ldots + \frac{(14-10.0)^2}{10.0} + \frac{(8-12.0)^2}{12.0} = 10.66$$

The p-value of the chi-square value 10.66 on $df = 3$ is < 0.05. The null hypothesis is therefore rejected and we report this result as follows:

$$\text{"}\chi^2(3) = 10.66; \ p < .05\text{"}$$

Formula (10) is a straightforward application of the multiplication rule for independent events in elementary probability. Events are independent if the probability of their joint occurrence is the product of their separate probabilities: for example, if a coin is tossed and a die is rolled, the joint probability of a head and a six is $1/2 \times 1/6 = 1/12$. If, in a two-way contingency table, the row and columns represent attributes A and B, respectively, and R and C are the marginal totals of the row and column intersecting in a cell of the table, the probabilities of those particular levels of A and B are R/N and C/N, respectively. According to the null hypothesis, the occurrence of this level of A with that level of B are independent events, so the probability of their joint occurrence $p = (R/N)(C/N)$. We can regard the total frequency N as the number of times an experiment of chance is replicated, so the expected cell frequency E is given by $E = (R/N)(C/N)N = RC/N$.

Measuring effect size in contingency tables

The rejection of the null hypothesis establishes the presence of an association between the two attributes. The chi-square statistic itself, however, is not a satisfactory measure of association strength, because its magnitude is affected by the total frequency of observations in the contingency table. From the chi-square statistic, however, several measures of strength of association have been devised.

An ideal measure of association should mimic the correlation coefficient by having a maximum absolute value of 1 for a perfect association, and a value of 0 for dissociation or independence. The choice of the appropriate statistic depends on whether the contingency table is 2×2 (each variable has two categories) or larger. Some statistics, such as the **phi coefficient**, cannot achieve the full range of variation from 0 to 1 when the number of columns is not equal to the number of rows.

A useful measure of effect size for use with two-way contingency tables is what SPSS calls **Cramer's V**, the formula for which is as follows:

$$V = \sqrt{\frac{\chi^2}{N(a-1)}} \quad \text{- - - (10) Cramer's } V$$

Formula (10) is applicable to an $a \times b$ contingency table, in which a is no greater than b.

In our current example, $V = 0.367$.

For the purposes of evaluating Cramer's V, we can transform Cramer's V into the equivalent value of Cohen's index of effect size w by applying the following formula:

$$w = V\sqrt{(a-1)} \quad \text{- - - (11) Obtaining Cohen's } w \text{ from } V$$

Applying formula (11) to the current example, we have

$$w = V\sqrt{(a-1)} = .367\sqrt{(2-1)} = 0.367$$

We can now consult Cohen's table and interpret the effect size (Table 5). The value 0.367 is of Medium size.

Some measures of association, such as **Goodman & Kruskal's lambda**, measure the proportional reduction in error achieved when membership of a category on one attribute is used to predict category membership on the other.

More information on the various measures of association can be found by clicking the SPSS **Help** box in the **Crosstabs: Statistics** dialog box.

Likelihood ratio (or Maximum Likelihood) chi-square

So far, both in testing for goodness-of-fit and association, we have used the traditional **Pearson chi-square** statistic. Both types of tests, however, can also be made with another approximate chi-square statistic known variously as the **likelihood ratio**, **maximum likelihood** or **log-likelihood** chi-square. Like the Pearson chi-square, the likelihood ratio chi-square is distributed approximately as a true chi-square variable on the same number of degrees of freedom; although for small samples, the Pearson chi-square is perhaps the better approximation (Agresti, 1990).

For a test of goodness-of-fit with a single qualitative variable comprising g categories, the formula for the likelihood-ratio chi-square is

$$\chi^2 = 2 \sum_{\text{all categories}} O \ln\left(\frac{O}{E}\right) \quad \text{- - - (12)}$$

LR goodness-of-fit chi-square

where the function ln is the natural log (to the base e) of the ratio of the observed to the expected frequency. For a test of association, the formula is

$$\chi^2 (r-1)(c-1) = 2 \sum_{\text{all cells}} O \ln\left(\frac{O}{E}\right) \quad \text{- - - (13)}$$

LR association chi-square

where r and c are the numbers of rows and columns, respectively, in the contingency table. The likelihood ratio chi-square is distributed approximately as chi-square on $(r-1)(c-1)$ degrees of freedom.

For the data in Table 6, the value of the likelihood ratio chi-square is

$$\chi^2 (3) = 2 \sum_{\text{all groups}} O \left[\ln\left(\frac{O}{E}\right) \right]$$

$$= 2 \left[6 \ln\left(\frac{6}{12.3}\right) + 21 \ln\left(\frac{21}{14.7}\right) + \dots + 14 \ln\left(\frac{14}{10.0}\right) + 8 \ln\left(\frac{8}{12.0}\right) \right]$$

$$= 11.09$$

which is close to 10.66, the value of the value of the Pearson chi-square.

The likelihood ratio chi-square is ubiquitous in log-linear analysis (Chapter 13) because, unlike the Pearson chi-square, the values of chi-square associated with the various components in a model add up to the total chi-square value: the likelihood chi-square is thus said to have the **additive property**.

Two by two contingency tables: the odds and odds ratio

Table 7 is a contingency table in which both attributes (Presence of the antibody and tissue Group) are dichotomous, i.e., they consist of only two categories. (Table 7 was constructed from Table 6 by 'collapsing' across the three non-critical tissue types to produce a single category named 'Other'.)

Table 7. A 2 × 2 contingency table

Tissue type	Presence		Total
	No	Yes	
Critical	6	21	27
Other	30	22	52
Total	36	43	79

The **Odds** is a measure of likelihood which, like probability, arises in the context of an experiment of chance, that is, a procedure with an uncertain outcome, such as tossing a coin or rolling a die. The odds in favour of an outcome is the number of ways in which the outcome could occur divided by the number of ways in which it could fail to occur.

$$\text{Odds} = \frac{\begin{bmatrix}\text{number of ways in which} \\ \text{an outcome can occur}\end{bmatrix}}{\begin{bmatrix}\text{number of ways in} \\ \text{which it can fail to occur}\end{bmatrix}} \quad \text{- - - (14) \textbf{The Odds}}$$

When a die is rolled, for example, the odds in favour of a six are 1 to 5 or, to express this as a fraction, 1/5.

We can compare the incidence of an outcome in two groups of participants simply by dividing the odds in favour of the outcome in one category by the odds in favour of the same outcome in the other category, the resulting statistic being known as the **odds ratio (OR)**:

$$\text{OR} = \frac{[\text{odds in favour in first group}]}{[\text{odds in favour in second group}]} \quad \text{- - - (15) \textbf{The Odds Ratio}}$$

In Table 7, we see that for the Critical category, the value of the odds in favour of the presence of the antibody is 21/6 = 3.5 and for the category Other, Odds = 22/30 = 0 .7333. The odds ratio is calculated simply by dividing the odds for the Critical group by the odds for the Other group: OR = 3.5/0.7333 = 4.77. The odds ratio tells us that when we move from the category Other to the Critical category, the odds in favour of the occurrence of the antibody increase nearly fivefold.

The odds ratio is useful for exploring any contingency table where at least two of the attributes are dichotomous. We shall make use of this statistic later, when we consider multi-way frequency tables in Chapter 13.

11.5.5   Analysis of contingency tables with SPSS

To illustrate the computerisation of the analysis, we shall return to the contingency table shown in Table 6. The data are contained in the file Ch11 Tissue type (large sample).sav, which is available at http://www.psypress.com/spss-made-simple.

We shall enter the data in the form of a frequency distribution, rather than case by case. When the data have already been grouped in this way, the data set for a contingency table must include two grouping variables to identify the various cell counts, one representing the rows (Group), and the other the columns (Presence) of the contingency table in Table 6. In this example, since the data are counts, not individual records of presence or absence, a third variable (Count) is needed for the cell frequencies.

- In **Variable View**, name the variables Group, Presence, and Count.

- In the Measure column, set the levels of measurement at **Nominal** for Group and Presence.

- In the **Values** column, assign the value labels Type A, Type B, Type C and Critical to the numerical values 1, 2, 3 and 4, respectively. For the Presence variable, assign the value labels No and Yes to the numerical values 1 and 2, respectively.

- When you have finished working in Variable View, Click the **Data View** tab to switch to **Data View** and enter the data into the three columns, as shown in Figure 8. (It is easier to enter the data when the value labels are displayed, rather than the values themselves.)

	Group	Presence	Count
1	Type A	No	14
2	Type A	Yes	8
3	Type B	No	11
4	Type B	Yes	7
5	Type C	No	5
6	Type C	Yes	7
7	Critical	No	6
8	Critical	Yes	21

Figure 8. **Data View** showing the two grouping variables and the counts of presence or absence of the antibody

When you have grouped data as in this example, the next step is essential. Since the data in the Count column represent cell frequencies of a variable (not values), SPSS must be informed of this by means of the **Weight Cases** procedure in the **Data** menu, which we described in section 11.5.2. Had the data been recorded case by case in the data file (i.e. not collated), there would have been no need to use the **Weight Cases** procedure because the **Crosstabs** procedure would have counted up the cases automatically.

- Choose **Analyze➜Descriptives➜Crosstabs...** to enter the Crosstabs dialog (Figure 9). Proceed as shown in the figure.

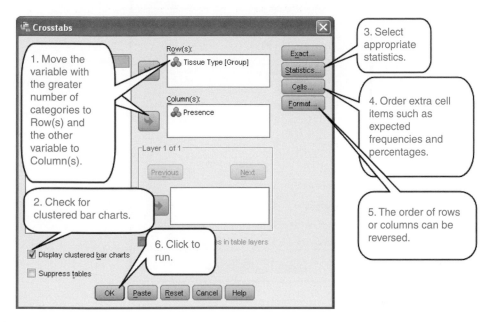

Figure 9. Completing the Crosstabs dialog

- Complete the **Statistics...**, and **Cells...**, dialog boxes as shown in Figures 10 and 11.

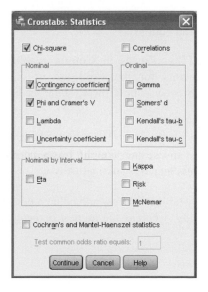

Figure 10. The Crosstabs: Statistics dialog box

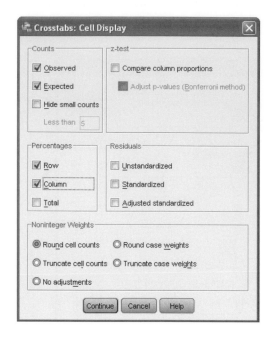

Figure 11. The Crosstabs: Cell Display dialog box

The **Format…** dialog controls the order in which rows for the values of the grouping variable appear in the contingency table. The default setting is **Ascending**, meaning that the top row of entries in the table will be the data for the value 1 and the bottom row will be the data for the value 4 (the Critical group). By changing the setting to **Descending**, this order will be reversed: the row with the value 4 (the Critical group) will now appear at the top and the row with the value 1 will appear at the bottom.

The option of **Expected** cell frequencies in **Counts** enables the user to check that the prescribed minimum requirements for the valid use of chi-square have been fulfilled. Although there has been much debate about these, some leading authorities have proscribed the use of chi-square when:

     1.   In 2 × 2 tables, any of the expected frequencies is less than 5;

     2.   In larger tables, any of the expected frequencies is less than 1 or more than 20% are less than 5.

Output 9 shows the contingency table, with row and column percentages. In the Critical group, 77.8% of cases had the antibody; whereas the highest percentage in any of the other groups was 58.3%.

Tissue Type * Presence Crosstabulation

			Presence		Total
			No	Yes	
Tissue Type	Type A	Count	14	8	22
		Expected Count	10.0	12.0	22.0
		% within Tissue Type	63.6%	36.4%	100.0%
		% within Presence	38.9%	18.6%	27.8%
	Type B	Count	11	7	18
		Expected Count	8.2	9.8	18.0
		% within Tissue Type	61.1%	38.9%	100.0%
		% within Presence	30.6%	16.3%	22.8%
	Type C	Count	5	7	12
		Expected Count	5.5	6.5	12.0
		% within Tissue Type	41.7%	58.3%	100.0%
		% within Presence	13.9%	16.3%	15.2%
	Critical	Count	6	21	27
		Expected Count	12.3	14.7	27.0
		% within Tissue Type	22.2%	77.8%	100.0%
		% within Presence	16.7%	48.8%	34.2%
Total		Count	36	43	79
		Expected Count	36.0	43.0	79.0
		% within Tissue Type	45.6%	54.4%	100.0%
		% within Presence	100.0%	100.0%	100.0%

Output 9. The contingency table, to which have been added the row and column percentages

Output 10 shows the (edited) clustered bar chart, in which the colours in the original chart have been replaced by black and white patterns. The chart provides a striking demonstration of the predominance of the antibody in the Critical tissue group.

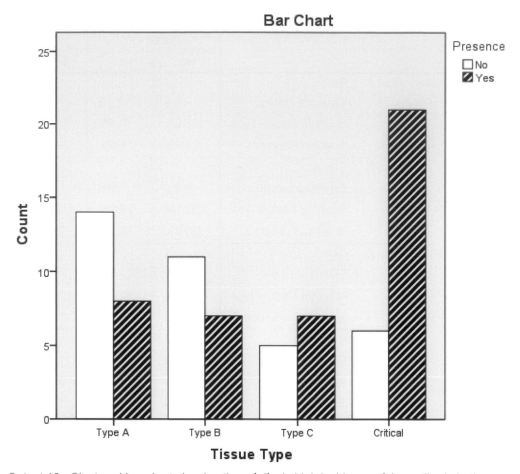

Output 10. Clustered bar chart showing the relatively high incidence of the antibody in the Critical tissue group

Output 11 shows the results of the chi-square test. The chi-square value 10.66 is significant beyond the 0.05 level:

$$\chi^2(3) = 10.66; \quad p < 0.05$$

Note the remark under the table in Output 11 about expected cell frequencies, which assures the user that the data are sufficiently plentiful to permit the usual chi-square test.

Output 12 gives the values of the tests of strength of association. In this particular example, where one of the attributes is a dichotomy, the values of phi and Cramer's V are the same. That would not necessarily be so in more complex tables.

Chi-Square Tests

	Value	df	Asymp. Sig. (2-sided)
Pearson Chi-Square	10.655[a]	3	.014
Likelihood Ratio	11.093	3	.011
Linear-by-Linear Association	9.850	1	.002
N of Valid Cases	79		

a. 0 cells (.0%) have expected count less than 5. The minimum expected count is 5.47.

Output 11. Results of the chi-square tests

Symmetric Measures

		Value	Approx. Sig.
Nominal by Nominal	Phi	.367	.014
	Cramer's V	.367	.014
	Contingency Coefficient	.345	.014
N of Valid Cases		79	

Output 12. Statistics measuring the strength of the association between Tissue Type and presence of the antibody

11.5.6   Getting help with the output

Should any item in the SPSS output be unfamiliar, you can find an explanation by double-clicking on the item to highlight it and right-clicking with the mouse (Figure 12).

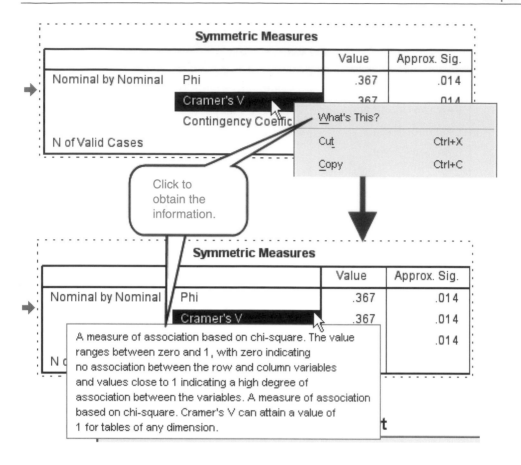

Figure 12. Getting help with unfamiliar terms in the output

11.5.7   Some cautions and caveats

As with any other statistical technique, the making of an approximate chi-square test implies that the requirements of the underlying statistical model have been met.   One requirement is that there must be sufficient data. The frequencies in the cells of the contingency table must also meet certain requirements.

Low expected frequencies

A word of warning about the misuse of chi-square should be given here. In the first place, it is important to bear in mind that the 'chi-square' statistic is only *approximately* distributed as a true chi-square variable. The greater the expected frequencies, the better the approximation, hence the rule about minimum expected frequencies.   When the expected frequencies fall below the recommended levels, the approximation can be poor and the *p*-value of the approximate chi-square statistic can be misleading.   The default output of a chi-square test gives the **asymptotic *p*-value**, that is, the *p*-value for a true chi-square statistic.   The asymptotic *p*-value, however, can be wide of the mark with small samples. SPSS, however, can provide **exact *p*-values**, which should be requested when the data are scarce.

Returning to our current example, suppose that the study had involved only 19 patients. The contingency table (Output 10) shows the same pattern as before: there is a clear predominance of the antibody in the Critical tissue group.

Tissue Type * Presence of antibody Crosstabulation

Count

		Presence of antibody		Total
		No	Yes	
Tissue Type	Type A	4	2	6
	Type B	3	0	3
	Type C	1	0	1
	Critical	2	7	9
Total		10	9	19

Output 10. A contingency table of a small set of nominal data

Were you to proceed to use the Pearson chi-square statistic to test the null hypothesis of independence, you would find that the *p*-value of chi-square was greater than 0.05 and be forced to accept the null hypothesis. With the table displaying the 'aymptotic' *p*-value, however, would come a warning that there are too many cells with low expected frequencies. The correct procedure here is to request an exact test.

When completing the Crosstabs dialog, click the **Exact ...** button at the side of the dialog box, enter the **Exact Tests** dialog box, and activate the **Exact** radio button (Figure 13).

The results of both the approximate (Asymptotic) chi-square test and the exact test are shown in Output 11. The exact tests do not agree with the asymptotic tests: on the exact tests, the result is significant beyond the 0.05 level. This is the result we should accept. We have evidence for a greater presence of the antibody in the Critical group.

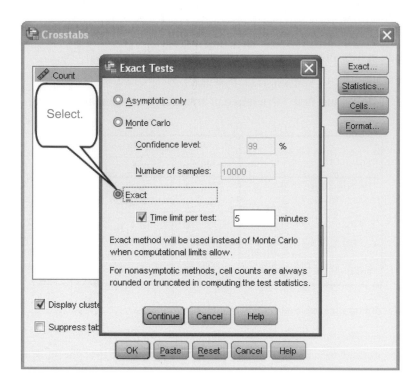

Figure 13. Choosing an exact test

Chi-Square Tests

	Value	df	Asymp. Sig. (2-sided)	Exact Sig. (2-sided)
Pearson Chi-Square	7.412[a]	3	.060	.035
Likelihood Ratio	9.114	3	.028	.035
Fisher's Exact Test	6.795			.035
Linear-by-Linear Association	3.803[b]	1	.051	.065
N of Valid Cases	19			

a. 8 cells (100.0%) have expected count less than 5. The minimum expected count is .47.
b. The standardized statistic is 1.950.

Output 11. Results of the exact tests

Non-independent observations: correlated nominal data

The use of the chi-square test requires that each individual studied contributes to the count in one cell only of the contingency table. In other words, the observations must be independent. Suppose that a researcher is interested in the effects of hearing a debate upon people's response to a contentious political issue. One hundred people are asked whether they support the motion before and after hearing the debate. One might be tempted simply to count the proportions of the participants in favour of the motion before and after hearing the debate and proceed with a chi-square test for a possible association between the variables of Stage of Monitoring (Before/After) and Response (Yes/No). To analyse the data in this way, however, would be to violate the requirement that each person must contribute to the tally in only one cell of the two-way frequency table. There would be twice as many responses as there were participants! Since the same people are giving their Yes/No response on different occasions, an experiment of this kind will yield **correlated nominal data**. We shall see that correct approach here is to follow a different data-gathering strategy and make a test of **goodness-of-fit**, rather than a test for association.

The way to proceed is to identify the individuals as they give their responses to the motion before and after hearing the debate. It can then be seen whether a person's views have changed or not. Suppose the participants' responses are as shown in Table 8.

Table 8. Number of people supporting a political motion

Before	After	Frequency
Yes	Yes	27
	No	13
No	Yes	38
	No	22

The **McNemar test** uses only the data on those participants who *changed* their views. We can see from Table 8 that a total of 51 participants changed their minds after hearing the debate; but while only 13 participants changed their minds against the motion, 38 changed their minds in favour of the motion. If the null hypothesis is true and listening to the debate had no effect, we could expect as many participants to change their responses in the negative direction as in the positive direction. Under the null hypothesis, if a participant's responses can be assumed to be independent of those of the other participants, we have a series of 51 **Bernoulli trials** like tosses of a coin (see Chapter 6). We could test the null hypothesis by running a **binomial test**, setting the expected proportion at 0.5, as described in Chapter 6. The McNemar test uses an approximate chi-square test of goodness-of-fit to test the same null hypothesis.

To run the McNemar test on SPSS Statistics 19, prepare the data file by defining two nominal variables named Before and After and a scale variable named Frequency. When defining the nominal variables, label the values 1 and 2 as Yes and No, respectively. The **Measure** levels must be set at **nominal**. *This is essential.* When the data have been entered, Data View should appear as in Figure 14.

Before	After	Frequency
Yes	Yes	27
Yes	No	13
No	Yes	38
No	No	22

Figure 14. The appearance of Data View before running the McNemar test

At this point, SPSS must be instructed to weight the rows by their frequencies of occurrence. Choose **Data➜Weight Cases...** and, in the **Weight Cases** dialog box, transfer the variable label Frequency into the **Frequency Variable** box.

• To run the **McNemar** test, choose **Analyze➜Nonparametric Tests➜Related Samples...** to open the **Nonparametric Tests:Two or More Related Samples** dialog box.

• Click the Fields tab and move the variables Before and After to the Test Fields box (Figure 15).

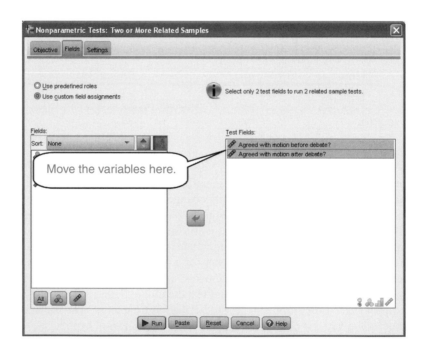

Figure 15. Completing the Fields dialog

- Click the Settings tab and complete the Settings dialog as shown in Figure 16.

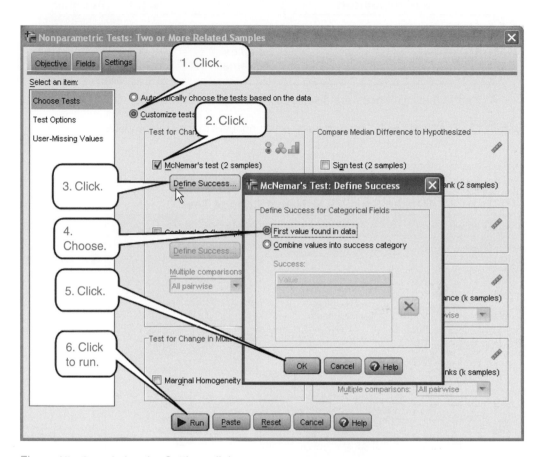

Figure 16. Completing the Settings dialog

In the Output Viewer, the Hypothesis Test Summary appears (Output 12). Double-clicking on the table will show the **Model Viewer**, the auxiliary pane of which is shown in Output 13.

The results of the test are shown in Output 12. The very low p-value (0.001) is strong evidence against the null hypothesis. We have evidence that listening to the debate tended to change more people's views in the direction of the motion rather than against it.

Hypothesis Test Summary

	Null Hypothesis	Test	Sig.	Decision
1	The distributions of different values across Agreed with motion before debate? and Agreed with motion after debate? are equally likely.	Related-Samples McNemar Test	.001	Reject the null hypothesis.

Asymptotic significances are displayed. The significance level is .05.

Output 12. The Hypothesis Test Summary, which appears in the Output Viewer

Related-Samples McNemar Change Test

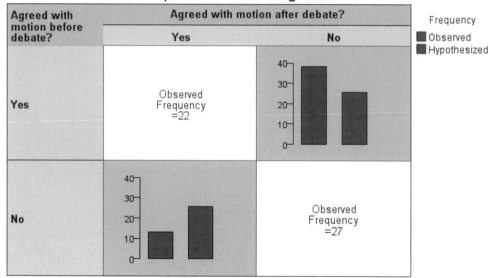

Total N	100
Test Statistic	11.294
Degrees of Freedom	1
Asymptotic Sig. (2-sided test)	.001

Output 13. The auxiliary pane of the Model Viewer, showing the results of the McNemar Change test

Since the McNemar test (like the binomial test) is a test of goodness-of-fit, we can use Cohen's measure g (which we described in Chapter 6) as a measure of effect size, where g is the difference between P, the proportion of outcomes in the target category and p is the probability of the outcome under the null hypothesis:

$$g = |P - p| \quad \text{- - - (15)}$$

Cohen's Effect size index

In Table 9, we reproduce our interpretation of the guidelines suggested by Cohen (1988).

Table 9. Guidelines (from Cohen, 1988) for interpreting the effect size index g

Value of g	Size of effect
$.05 \leq g < .15$	Small
$.15 \leq g < .25$	Medium
$g \geq .25$	Large

A value less than .05 is trivial.

A value between .05 and .15 is a Small effect.

A value between .15 and .25 is a Medium effect.

A value of at least .25 is a Large effect.

Output 13 shows that of the 51 participants who changed their responses, 38 changed in a positive direction, that is, the proportion who changed in a positive direction was $38/51 = 0.75$. The proportion expected under the null hypothesis was 0.5. Substituting in formula (15), we have

$$g = |P - p| = 0.75 - 0.5 = 0.25$$

which, according to Table 9 is a Large effect.

11.5.8   Other problems with traditional chi-square analyses

There are several other potential problems with the making of chi-square tests that the user should be aware of. A lucid account of the rationale and assumptions of the chi-square test is given by Howell (2007) and would be an excellent starting-point for further reading on this topic.

11.6   DO DOCTORS AGREE? COHEN'S KAPPA

Suppose that two psychiatrists assign each of 50 patients to one of a set of five diagnostic categories, A, B, C, D and E. Their assignments are shown in Table 10.

Table 10. Assignments of patients to categories A to E by two doctors

Doctor1	Doctor2	Count	Doctor1	Doctor2	Count
A	A	4	C	D	1
A	B	1	C	E	1
A	C	1	D	A	1
A	D	1	D	B	1
A	E	1	D	C	2
B	A	1	D	D	8
B	B	4	D	E	2
B	C	0	E	A	1
B	D	4	E	B	0
B	E	2	E	C	1
C	A	2	E	D	3
C	B	0	E	E	2
C	C	6			

When these assignments are cast into the form of a contingency table, the data appear as in Output 14. The marked diagonal cells in Output 14 contain the numbers of patients who were assigned to the same diagnostic category by the two doctors. Intuitively, it might seem reasonable to divide the sum of the judgements on the marked diagonal by the total number of judgements and argue that the percentage of agreement is 24/50 = 48%. As with the analysis of any contingency table, however, we must take into consideration the different numbers of patients with different kinds of problem, as indicated by the varying row and column frequencies. Such discrepancies may merely reflect a tendency to make more use of some diagnostic categories than others, rather than truly reliable diagnosis. Accordingly, we need to obtain the **expected frequencies (E)** for the cells along the marked diagonal, given the values of the marginal row and column totals. We obtain the value of E for each cell by multiplying the marginal totals in the row and column and dividing by the total frequency (50). For example, four patients were assigned to diagnostic category B by both doctors. Since the row and column totals for the assignments by the first and second doctor are 6 and 11, respectively, $E = 66/50 = 1.32$.

Second Doctor * First Doctor Crosstabulation

			First Doctor					Total
			A	B	C	D	E	
Second	A	O	4	1	2	1	1	9
Doctor		E	1.4	2.0	1.8	2.5	1.3	9.0
	B	O	1	4	0	1	0	6
		E	1.0	1.3	1.2	1.7	.8	6.0
	C	O	1	0	6	2	1	10
		E	1.6	2.2	2.0	2.8	1.4	10.0
	D	O	1	4	1	8	3	17
		E	2.7	3.7	3.4	4.8	2.4	17.0
	E	O	1	2	1	2	2	8
		E	1.3	1.8	1.6	2.2	1.1	8.0
Total		O	8	11	10	14	7	50
		E	8.0	11.0	10.0	14.0	7.0	50.0

Output 14 . Contingency table showing the diagnoses of 50 patients by two doctors.(The observed frequencies are given in the rows labelled O; the expected frequencies are given in the rows labelled E.)

Cohen (1960) suggested the statistic **kappa (κ)** as a measure of agreement between the doctors. Kappa is defined as

$$\kappa = \frac{\sum\limits_{\text{diagonal}} O - \sum\limits_{\text{diagonal}} E}{N - \sum\limits_{\text{diagonal}} E} \quad \text{- - - (16)} \quad \textbf{Kappa coefficient}$$

where O and E are, respectively, the observed and expected frequencies *for the diagonal cells only* in Output 14 and N is the *total* number of patients. (For the *entire* contingency table, the totals for O and E would be equal.) Substituting in the formula, we have

$$\sum\limits_{\text{diagonal}} O = 4 + 4 + 6 + 8 + 2 = 24$$

$$\sum\limits_{\text{diagonal}} E = 1.44 + 1.32 + 2.00 + 4.76 + 1.12 = 10.64$$

$$\kappa = \frac{24 - 10.64}{50 - 10.64} = 0.34$$

The value 0.34 is even lower than the 48% agreement we arrived at using the intuitive measure.

Cohen's kappa statistic is available in SPSS. The data for the following example are in the file *Ch11 Cohen's kappa.sav* at http://www.psypress.com/spss-made-simple.

- In **Variable View**, set up the variables *Doctor1* and *Doctor2* as nominal variables and *Count* as a scale variable. For the nominal variables Doctor1 and Doctor2, assign to the values 1, 2, ..., 5 the labels A, B, ...,E respectively. Enter all the data for each combination of doctors (Table 10).

- Choose **Data➔Weight Cases...** to weight the cases by Frequency.

- Choose **Analyze➔Descriptive Statistics➔Crosstabs...** to open the **Crosstabs** dialog box.

- Highlight and transfer the grouping variable names to the **Row(s)** and **Column(s)** boxes respectively

- Click the **Statistics...** button and select the **Kappa** check box. Click **Continue** to return to the **Crosstabs** dialog box and then click **OK**.

First Doctor * Second Doctor Crosstabulation

Count

		Second Doctor					Total
		A	B	C	D	E	
First Doctor	A	4	1	1	1	1	8
	B	1	4	0	4	2	11
	C	2	0	6	1	1	10
	D	1	1	2	8	2	14
	E	1	0	1	3	2	7
Total		9	6	10	17	8	50

Symmetric Measures

		Value	Asymp. Std. Error[a]	Approx. T[b]	Approx. Sig.
Measure of Agreement	Kappa	.339	.088	4.760	.0000019
N of Valid Cases		50			

a. Not assuming the null hypothesis.
b. Using the asymptotic standard error assuming the null hypothesis.

Output 15. The kappa statistics

The crosstabulation and the value and *p*-value of kappa are given in Output 15.

The value of kappa is given as 0.339, in agreement with the value 0.34, as calculated previously. The output also contains a test of the significance of kappa which is of little importance, because a value such as 0.34, while significant beyond the 0.01 level, is much too low for a reliability: a minimum value of at least 0.75 would be expected with a reliable diagnostic system. This example well illustrates the difference between statistical and substantial significance.

The result should be reported as follows:

> "Cohen's kappa statistic was used as a measure of diagnostic agreement between the two doctors: $\kappa = .34$; $p < .01$".

11.7   PARTIAL CORRELATION

In experimental (as opposed to correlational) research, provided there are adequate controls, the independent variable (IV) can be shown to have a causal effect upon the dependent variable (DV). In correlational research, however, in which variables are measured as they occur in participants, it can be difficult or impossible to demonstrate unequivocally that one variable in any sense "causes" another. In some situations, in fact, even when two variables are substantially correlated, *neither* variable causes the other: both are at least partly determined by a third variable. In such circumstances, although the correlation between the two variables may be both statistically significant and substantial, it is a 'spurious' correlation, in the sense that it suggests the presence of a direct causal link between the two variables when actually there is none.

Suppose that, as a continuation of the research described at the beginning of this chapter, further data were gathered with fresh participants, not only on Actual violence and Exposure to screened violence, but also their parents' attitudes towards aggression, violence and their preparedness to use violence in certain situations. Let us call this new variable Parental Aggression.

Once again, as in the earlier study, Actual violence and Exposure to screened violence turned out to be highly positively correlated: $r(27) = 0.707$; $p < 0.01$.

The hypothesis that motivated the original study was that Exposure to screened violence increases Actual violence. This hypothesis can be represented diagrammatically as a simple **causal model**:

Model 1

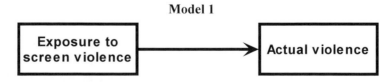

The high correlation between Exposure and Actual obtained in both studies is certainly consistent with this model. The existence of a positive correlation, however, is equally compatible with the view that the amount of screen violence watched is a reflection of the strength of the child's own violent tendencies:

Model 2

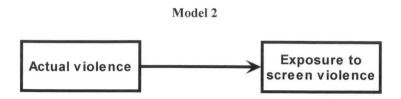

Here then, we have two contradictory models, each able to live quite happily with the high correlations yielded by the two studies.

There is, however, still another possibility.   In the second study, the correlations of the Parental variable with Actual violence and Exposure to violence were even higher than the correlation between Actual and Exposure: the correlation between Parental aggression and Actual violence was 0.801 and the correlation between Parental aggression and Exposure was 0.845.   Such a pattern of correlations is consistent with – indeed suggestive of – a third hypothesis, namely, that the Parental variable has a strong causal influence on both Exposure to and Actual violence, as shown in Model 3:

Model 3

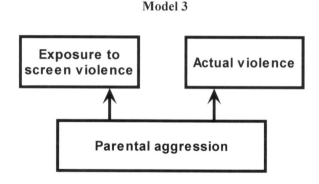

If Model 3 is correct, the high correlation observed between Exposure to and Actual violence in our two studies has been driven almost entirely by the variable of Parental aggression.

We have not exhausted the possibilities for models of causation here.   The point is that it is often impossible to determine unequivocally which model is the correct interpretation of a correlation coefficient, unless additional, collateral data are available or theoretical considerations compel the acceptance of one particular model and rejection of the others.

Had we no additional evidence beyond a high correlation between Exposure and Actual, we should have to accept that the findings were compatible with any of the three models of causation that we have described, and perhaps with others that we have not described.   The high correlations of both variables with Parental aggression, however, show the original correlation between Exposure and Actual in a different light, as we shall see in the next section.

A **partial correlation** is what remains of the correlation between two variables when their correlations with a third variable have been taken into consideration. If r_{AC} and r_{BC} are, respectively, the correlations of variables A and B with a third variable C, the partial correlation between *A* and *B* with *C* 'partialled out' (for which we shall use the subscript notation $r_{AB.C}$) is given by the following formula:

$$r_{AB.C} = \frac{r_{AB} - r_{AC}r_{BC}}{\sqrt{\left(1 - r_{AC}^2\right)\left(1 - r_{BC}^2\right)}} \quad \text{- - - (19) \textbf{Partial correlation}}$$

If the two variables correlate substantially with the third variable, the partial correlation between them may be much smaller than the original correlation; indeed, an initially high correlation may be reduced to insignificance. In that case, it may be reasonable to interpret the original correlation as having been driven by the third variable, as in the third causal model shown above.

The data for the following demonstration are available in *Ch11 Violence & Parents.sav* at http://www.psypress.com/spss-made-simple.

Proceed as follows:

- Select **Analyze➔Correlate➔Partial…** to enter the **Partial Correlations** dialog box.

- Complete the dialog box as shown in Figure 17.

- By clicking the **Options** button and checking the **Zero-order correlations** box in the **Options** dialog, you can obtain the original Pearson correlation between Exposure to and Actual violence for comparison.

The upper part of the edited output (Output 16) gives the Pearson correlations among the three variables. The lower part of the table gives the partial correlation between Actual Violence and Exposure to Screen Violence, after the potential confounding variable of Parental Aggression has been controlled or **partialled out**. The original value of 0.707 has been reduced to 0.095: in other words, little remains of the original correlation when the correlations of Exposure to Screen Violence and Actual Violence with the Parental Aggression variable have been taken into consideration. It would appear that the original correlation was driven largely by Parental Aggression.

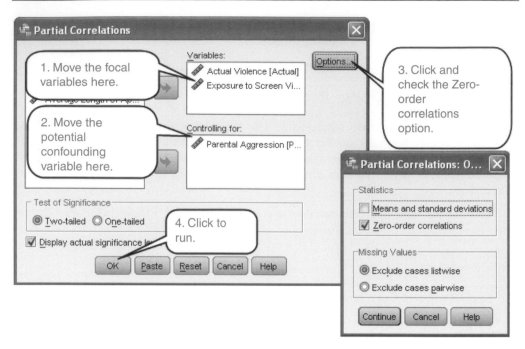

Figure 17. The **Partial Correlations** dialog box

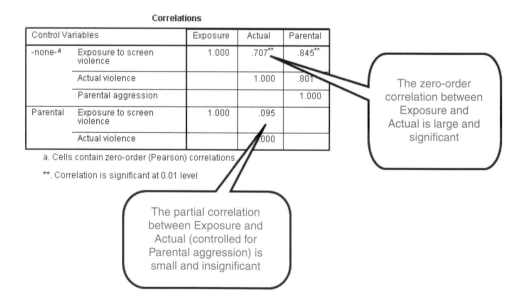

Output 16. Edited table of correlations showing the original (zero-order) correlations and the partial correlation. (The original table also gave the *p*-value of the partial correlation, which appears in the report below.)

Report this result as follows:

> "The partial correlation between Actual violence and Exposure with Parental Aggression partialled out is insignificant: $r_{partial}$ (27) = .095; p = .644."

11.8   A FINAL WORD

In this chapter, we switched out attention from statistics that were designed to compare means (or other averages such as the median) to those designed to measure association. In particular, we discussed two of the most used (and misused) of all statistics, namely, the Pearson correlation and the chi-square statistic. A correlation should never be taken at its face value without first examining the scatterplot; and the user of the approximate chi-square test for association should make sure that the contingency table conforms to the requirements of minimum expected frequencies and independence of responses.

Recommended reading

Howell (2007) has excellent chapters on correlation (Chapter 9) and on the analysis of contingency tables (Chapter 6).

Howell, D. C. (2007). *Statistical methods for psychology (6th ed.)*. Belmont, CA: Thomson/Wadsworth.

Exercises

Exercise 17 *The Pearson correlation*, Exercise 18 *Other measures of association* and Exercise 19 *The analysis of nominal data* are available in www.psypress.com/spss-made-simple . Click on Exercises.

CHAPTER 12

Regression

12.1   INTRODUCTION

The associative coin has two sides. On the one hand, a single number, a correlation coefficient, can be calculated which expresses the *strength* of the association between two variables. On the other, however, there is a set of techniques, known as **regression**, which utilise the presence of an association between two variables to predict the values of one variable (the **dependent**, **target** or **criterion** variable) from those of another (the **independent variable**, or **regressor**). In **simple** regression, there is just one IV or regressor; in **multiple regression**, there are two or more IVs.

Prediction of an individual's score on one variable from their scores on other variables has obvious practical value. Another, equally important, aspect of regression, however, is the determination of the extent to which the variance of the dependent variable can be accounted for by the variance of one or more independent variables. It is on this second, explanatory, aspect of regression that we shall concentrate in this chapter.

In **simple** regression, there is just one IV.   In **multiple regression**, there are two or more IVs. In certain circumstances, provided the data meet certain requirements, the addition of more IVs can result in more accurate prediction of the DV.   For many researchers, however, the purpose of multiple regression is to test **models of causation**.   The more accurately we can predict one variable from others, the more we can say that we have accounted for variance in the target variable in terms of variance in the predictors.   On the other hand, if there are two, three or perhaps several more IVs in the regression, it can be difficult to establish the precise role of each IV in the regression and its relative importance in accounting for variance in the DV.   In this chapter, we shall also be touching upon some of the problems of interpreting the output of a multiple regression.

12.1.1   Simple, two-variable regression

Returning to the study of the association between Actual violence and Exposure to screened violence (Chapter 11), we shall begin with the same elliptical scatterplot that served as our point of departure in the previous chapter. (The cautions and caveats about the use and abuse of the Pearson correlation all apply, with equal force, to regression as well. In particular, the scatterplot must either be elliptical in shape, indicating a basically linear relationship between the DV and the IV, or circular, indicating that they are independent.)

Figure 1 shows the **regression line** drawn through the points in the scatterplot. The equation of this line is

$$\text{Actual}' = 2.09 + 0.74 \text{ Exposure}$$

If we represent the IV and DV by the algebraic symbols X and Y respectively, we can write:

$$Y' = 2.09 + 0.74X$$

where Y' is the point on the line above X. (It is important to distinguish carefully between the observed value Y and Y', which is the corresponding point on the line for the same value of the independent variable X.)

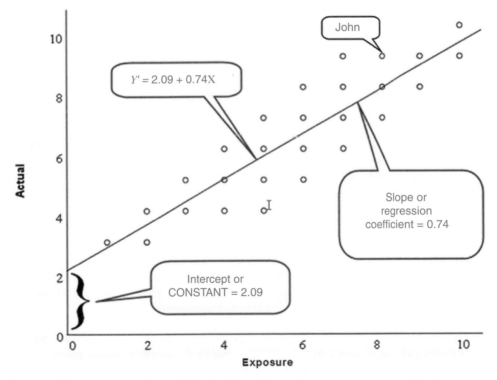

Figure 1. The regression line of Actual violence upon Exposure to screen violence

The general form of this **linear regression equation** is

$$Y' = b_0 + b_1 X \; \text{- - -} \; (1)$$

The linear regression equation

where b_0 is the **intercept** of the line and b_1 is its **slope**. The intercept is the distance from the origin to the point at which the line cuts the y-axis. At this point, $X = 0$: that is, $Y' = b_0$ (equation 1). In SPSS output, the intercept b_0 is referred as the **constant**.

The slope of the regression line b_1 is known as the **regression coefficient**. The regression coefficient measures the estimated average change in the dependent variable Y that results from increasing the value of X, (the regressor or IV), by one unit. In our example, $b_1 = 0.74$, so an increase of one unit in Exposure results in an estimated average increase of 0.74 units in the Actual violence score.

Suppose that we had no access to the regression statistics at all and were to be told only that the mean score on Actual violence is 6.37 and that John has an Exposure score of 8. Without further information, our best guess of John's Actual score would be the mean Actual score M_Y, that is, 6.37. We should be obliged to make this guess whatever the value of John's Exposure score. We could do much better, of course, if we knew the equation of the regression line and were to take as our guess of John's Actual score the point on the regression line above $X = 8$. From the regression equation calculated from our data, we see that John's predicted Actual score (the point on the regression line above Exposure = 8) is

$$Y' = 2.09 + 0.74 \times 8 = 8.0$$

This estimate is much closer than the value of M_Y (6.37) to John's real score Y on Actual violence, which was 9 (Figure 1).

12.1.2   Residuals

Although we can predict the participant's real score on Actual violence more accurately when we use the regression line, we shall still make errors.

The error or **residual** (e) is the participant's real score on Actual violence minus the prediction from regression:

$$e = Y - Y' \; \text{- - -} \; (2) \; \textbf{The residual score}$$

In John's case, since $Y = 9$ and $Y' = 8$, $e = 9 - 8 = 1$. Since we are predicting a person's score on the vertical scale of the graph, the residual is measured in the units of the vertical scale (Figure 2).

In regression, the study of the residuals is of great importance, because they form the basis for various measures of the accuracy of the estimates and of the extent to which the regression model   gives a good account of the data in question. (See Tabachnick & Fidell, 2007 for advice on **regression diagnostics**, which are based largely upon residuals and their transformations.)

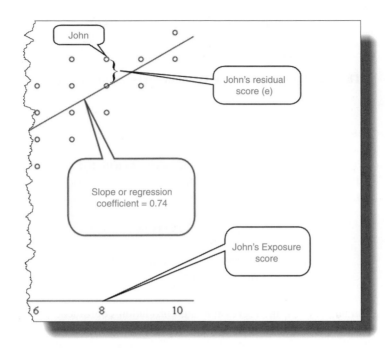

Figure 2. A residual score

12.1.3 The least squares criterion for 'the best-fitting line'

The regression line shown in Figure 1 is the line that 'fits' the data best according to what is known as the **least squares criterion**, whereby the values of b_0 and b_1 must be such that the sum of squares of the residuals $\Sigma\ e^2 = SS_{\text{residual}}$ is a minimum. There is a unique mathematical solution to this problem. The values of b_0 and b_1 that meet the criterion are given by the following formulae:

$$b_1 = \frac{SP}{SS_X}$$

--- (3) **Slope and intercept of the regression line**

$$b_0 = M_Y - b_1 M_X$$

In formula (3), SS and SP are, respectively, the **sum of squares** and **sum of cross-products**, as in the formula for the Pearson correlation (Chapter 11):

$$SS_X = \sum \left(X - M_X\right)^2; \quad SS_Y = \sum \left(X - M_Y\right)^2; \quad SP = \sum \left(X - M_X\right)\left(X - M_Y\right)$$

The (easily memorised) *SS/SP* formula for the Pearson correlation is reproduced below:

$$r = \frac{\sum (X - M_X)(Y - M_Y)}{\sqrt{\sum (X - M_X)^2 \sum (Y - M_Y)^2}} = \frac{SP}{\sqrt{SS_X SS_Y}}$$

The SS/SP formula for the Pearson correlation   - - - (4)

12.1.4   Regression and correlation

It is clear from formulae (3) and (4) that the regression coefficient and the Pearson correlation are closely related. The regression coefficient b_1 is directly proportional to the correlation coefficient r_{XY} thus:

$$b_1 = r_{XY} \frac{s_Y}{s_X} \; \text{- - - (5)}$$

Relation between the regression coefficient
and the Pearson correlation

It is clear from formula (5) that the regression and correlation coefficients must always have the same sign. In Figure 3 are two scatterplots showing positive and negative associations of the same strength. The regression and correlation coefficients have the same sign in each plot.

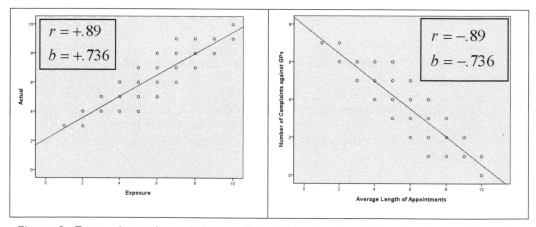

Figure 3. Regression and correlation coefficients for pairs of variables showing positive and negative association

Figure 4 shows the scatterplot of two uncorrelated variables, namely, two random samples of a million values from a normal population with a mean of 100 and a standard deviation of 25. (With such a huge sample, we are virtually looking at a population, rather than merely a sample, and our estimates of its parameters will be virtually free of error.) As expected, the scatterplot is circular, which is characteristic of dissociated variables. Notice that, in this case, the regression line is horizontal: its slope is zero, as indicated by the value of the regression coefficient.

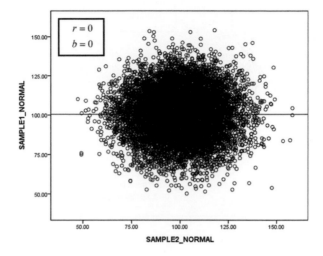

Figure 4. Scatterplot and regression line for uncorrelated variables

12.1.5   The coefficient of determination revisited

In Chapter 11, it was observed that the **coefficient of determination (CD)** can be represented diagrammatically as the proportion of overlap between two circles, the total area of each circle representing 100% of the variance of either variable (Figure 5). In this section, we shall review the coefficient of determination in terms of regression rather than correlation.

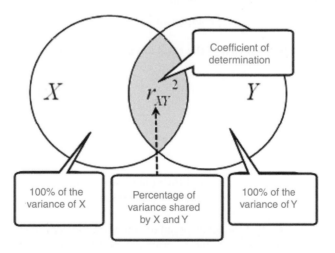

Figure 5. Diagrammatic representation of the coefficient of determination (CD)

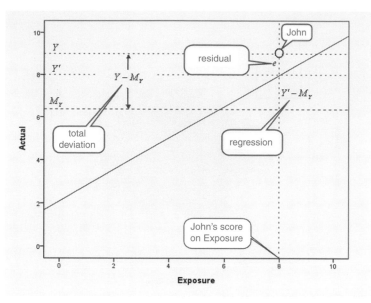

Figure 6. Breakdown of a score on the dependent variable

It can be seen from Figure 6 that the total deviation score on the dependent variable Y can be broken down (or **partitioned**) as follows:

$$Y - M_Y \quad = \quad (Y' - M_Y) \quad + \quad (Y - Y')$$

$$\begin{bmatrix} \text{total} \\ \text{deviation} \end{bmatrix} \qquad \begin{bmatrix} \text{regression} \\ \text{component} \end{bmatrix} \qquad \begin{bmatrix} \text{residual} \\ \text{component } (e) \end{bmatrix} \text{ --- (6)}$$

Breakdown of the total deviation score on Y

It can be shown that if the squares of these deviation scores are summed over all the participants in the study, the sum of squares for the dependent variable Y can be broken down into regression and residual components according to the following equation:

$$SS_Y = SS_{\text{regression}} + SS_{\text{residual}} \quad \text{--- (7)}$$

Partition of the sum of squares
of the DV in regression

In words, formula (7) states that the total spread of scores on the dependent variable is the sum of a regression component and a residual or error component. The cross-product terms have disappeared because deviations about the mean sum to zero.

It is clear from formulae (6) and (7) that if the points in the scatterplot were all to lie along a straight line, the residual sum of squares would be zero and the regression sum of squares would be equal to SS_Y. If, on the other hand, the scatterplot were to show complete independence or dissociation, then the regression sum of squares would be zero and SS_Y would consist entirely of error variance. The **coefficient of determination (CD)** expresses the regression sum of squares as a proportion of SS_Y and is given by the square of the Pearson correlation:

$$CD = r^2 = \frac{SS_{\text{regression}}}{SS_Y} \quad \text{--- (8)}$$

The coefficient of determination

The Pearson correlation between the Actual and Exposure scores is 0.89. The value of the coefficient of determination is therefore $0.89^2 = 0.80$. So 80% of the variance of Actual scores is accounted for by regression of Actual violence upon Exposure to screened violence.

In the coefficient of determination, we have a useful measure of effect size applicable to regression. In Table 1, we reproduce part of a table from Chapter 11, which offers a rough guide to the classification of effect size in regression.

Table 1. Guidelines (from Cohen, 1988) for classifying association strength, as measured by a correlation coefficient and the coefficient of determination

Absolute value of r	r squared	Size of effect
$0.1 \leq |r| < 0.30$	$0.01 \leq r^2 < 0.09$	Small
$0.30 \leq |r| < 0.50$	$0.09 \leq r^2 < 0.25$	Medium
$|r| \geq 0.50$	$r^2 \geq 0.25$	Large

12.1.6   Shrinkage with resampling: cross-validation

So far, all the statistics we have described refer to a single sample of scores. The purpose of running a regression, however, is ultimately to generalise beyond the data to the bivariate population or joint distribution of Actual violence and Exposure, which can be visualised as a scatterplot with an infinite number of points. The coefficient of determination as calculated from the square of the Pearson correlation will tend to overstate the predictive power of regression in the population, with the consequence that predictive power will be lost if the regression equation is re-applied to a fresh set of data on the same variables. This loss in predictive power with re-sampling is known as **shrinkage**.

In the procedure known as **cross-validation**, the regression statistics from the analysis of one data set are applied to another on exactly the same variables. To achieve comparability, a large data set is sometimes divided in two, the first regression being run on one half-set and the cross-validation on the other. Shrinkage will be very evident from such an operation, particularly if the samples are small. It will inevitably be found that the predictions from the first regression will correlate less strongly with the DV when applied to the data in the second set.

Often, however, our data will be less plentiful than we would have wished and we must content ourselves with adjusting the regression estimates to anticipate shrinkage should more data on the same variables become available at some future point. This is done by using the degrees of freedom of the regression statistics of a single sample to adjust the value of r^2 downwards to remove its positive bias. This is the reason for the 'adjustment' referred to in the SPSS output for various regression-related routines; in fact, **adjusted R^2** is referred to by some authors as '**shrunken R^2**'.

12.1.7 Beta coefficients

The **beta weight** β_1 is the slope of the regression line when the DV and IV have both been transformed to the **standardised variables** z_Y and z_X, respectively, where

$$z_Y = \frac{Y - M_Y}{s_Y} \text{ and } z_X = \frac{X - M_X}{s_X} \quad \text{- - - (9)}$$

Standardised variables

It follows immediately from the formula for the intercept in the regression equation (formula 3) that, since the mean and standard deviation of a set of standardised scores are 0 and 1, respectively, the intercept in the regression equation of z_Y upon z_X is zero and the regression equation of z_Y upon z_X is

$$z_Y' = \beta_1 z_x \quad \text{- - - (10)}$$

Standardised form of the
simple regression equation

In words, transforming the IV and DV to standard scores results in the regression line passing through the origin and having a slope equal to the Pearson correlation (Figure 7).

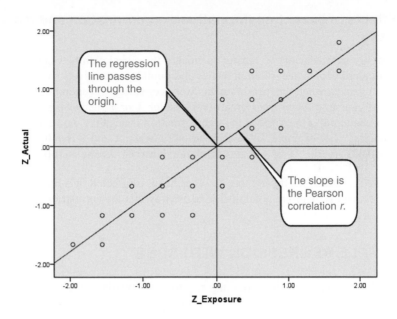

Figure 7.   Regression with standard (Z) scores.

The slope β_1 of the standardised form of the regression equation is the average change in the dependent variable Y, measured in standard deviation units, produced by an increase of one standard deviation in the IV or regressor X. The beta-weight therefore has the advantage of providing a unit-free measure of the slope of the regression line.

We have seen (formula 5) that the slope of the regression line is directly proportional to the Pearson correlation, the constant being the ratio of the standard deviations of Y and X. Since the standard deviations of a set of standard scores is unity, the slope of the standardised regression line is simply the Pearson correlation r and we can write:

$$z'_Y = \beta_1 z_X = r z_X \;\text{---}\; (11)$$

**Identity of beta with r in the
standardised simple regression equation**

We should note that formula (11) holds only in the case where there is a single IV or regressor.

12.1.8   Effects of linear transformations on correlation and regression coefficients

It would be highly unsatisfactory if, having calculated the correlation between the heights and weights of a hundred people, measured in inches and pounds, respectively, we were to find that the correlation changed when the measurements were converted to centimetres and kilograms! It would not, of course: a *linear* transformation of either X or Y leaves the *absolute* value of the correlation unaltered; if the slope of the transformation is negative, however, the sign of the correlation changes. For example, if the correlation between X and Y is $+ 0.6$, the correlation between X and $100Y$ is still $+ 0.6$; but the correlation between X and $- 100Y$ is $- 0.6$.

The value of the regression coefficient, on the other hand, is affected by a linear transformation of either variable, and is therefore not unit-free in the way that the correlation is.

12.2   SIMPLE REGRESSION WITH SPSS

Always get to know your data before running any formal statistical tests. We have, however, already examined the scatterplot of the data on children's violence in Chapter 11 and seen that the cloud of points is elliptical in shape, indicating that the two variables are in a basically linear relationship and that the joint distribution is bivariate normal, as required for correlation and regression.

12.2.1   Drawing scatterplots with regression lines

The data are available in the file *Violence & Parents.sav* at www.psypress.com/spss-made-simple. We shall begin by obtaining the scatterplot and drawing the regression line through the points. Formal tests of the estimates of the regression parameters will then be made by running SPSS's **Linear Regression** procedure.

Drawing the regression line through the points

Proceed as follows:

- Open the file *Ch12 Violence & Parents.sav* . Alternatively, simply enter the data (the entire set of which is shown in Chapter 11) into the Data Editor in the usual way.

- Use the **Chart Builder** to draw a scatterplot of Actual against Exposure.

- Double-click the plot to enter the **Chart Editor** and double-click the vertical axis to view the **Scale** tab in **Properties** (Figure 8). Uncheck **Minimum** and enter 0 as the Minimum point on the vertical axis. Click **Apply** to show the zero point on the vertical scale of the scatterplot and close the **Properties** dialog.

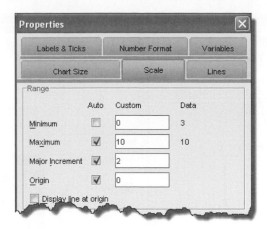

Figure 8.   Including the zero point on the vertical axis

- To add a regression line, stay in the **Chart Editor** and click the icon marked by the white cursor in Figure 9 labelled **Add Fit Line at Total**.

At this point, we should note that the safe use of regression makes certain assumptions about the data. In the first place, perhaps, the relationship between the IV and the DV should be **linear**. The appearance of the scatterplot, especially with the regression line drawn in, will be strongly indicative of whether that assumption is true.

Another important assumption is that the residuals should be uncorrelated. Statistics in the regression output such as estimates of standard errors, confidence intervals and p-values all assume independence of the residuals. This assumption is typically violated in **time series** (e.g the FTSE), the analysis of which we do not consider in this book. A **serial correlation** or **autocorrelation** is the correlation of a variable with itself when measured repeatedly over time. An autocorrelation may well be a function of separation in time, as measured by **lag**. The presence of autocorrelations violates one of the central assumptions in ordinary least squares regression and special methods have been developed for the purpose of analysing time series data.

The residuals should have constant variance over the range of the IV. This property is known as **homoscedasticity**. Heteroscedasticity can indicate nonlinearity of the association between the DV and the IV.

The distribution of errors should be **normal** at all levels of the IV.

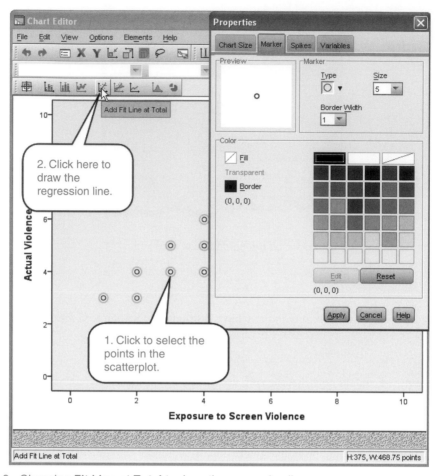

Figure 9. Choosing **Fit Line at Total** to draw the regression line

- Clicking on **Fit Line at Total** will access the **Properties** dialog box again and the **Fit Line** tab, in which the **Linear** radio button is checked as the default setting. Close the **Properties** dialog box and exit from the **Chart Editor** to see the regression line (Output 1).

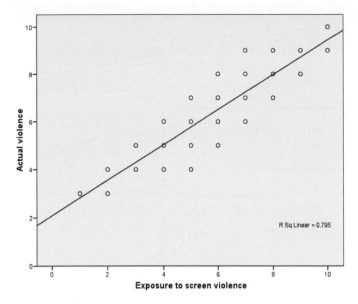

Output 1. The regression line

In Output 1, the vertical axis has been displaced slightly to the left, with the result that the intercept appears to be nearer the origin than the correct value of 2.09 (the intercept or regression constant). To rectify this, double-click the figure to enter the **Chart Editor** again and click the icon labelled **Add a reference line to the X axis** (Figure 10).

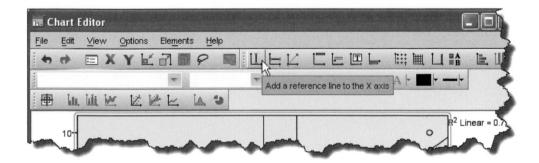

Figure 10. Adding a vertical reference line to the X axis

Clicking this icon will access the **Reference Line** tab in the **Properties** dialog box (Figure 11). Set the **Position** to zero and click the **Apply** button at the foot of the dialog box. The graph will now appear as in Output 2. The regression line intercepts the vertical reference line 2.09 units above zero on the vertical axis.

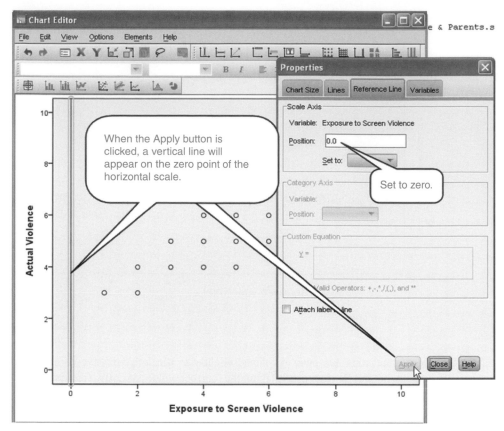

Figure 11. The **Properties** dialog box for drawing a vertical reference line on the X axis

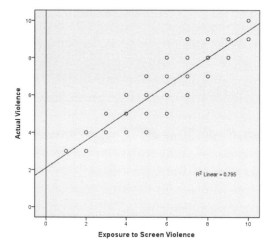

Output 2. Scatterplot with regression line and vertical reference line above the zero point on the X axis

Running the regression

Proceed as follows:

- Choose **Analyze➔Regression ➔Linear...** to open the **Linear Regression** dialog box (the completed dialog is shown in Figure 12).

- Transfer the variable names as shown in Figure 12, taking care to select the appropriate variable names for the dependent variable (target) and the independent variable (regressor): Actual is the DV; Exposure is the IV.

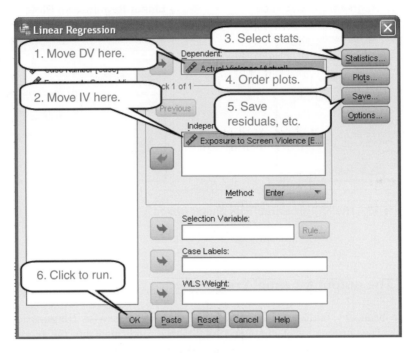

Figure 12. Completing the Linear Regression dialog

- Request additional descriptive statistics and a residuals analysis by clicking the **Statistics...** button to open the **Linear Regression: Statistics** dialog box (Figure 13a) and activating the **Descriptives** checkbox. Analysis of the residuals gives a measure of how good the predictions are and whether there are any cases that are so discrepant as to be considered outliers and perhaps dropped from the analysis. Click the **Casewise diagnostics** checkbox to include a listing of any exceptionally large residuals in the output. Click **Continue** to return to the **Linear Regression** dialog box.

- Since systematic associations between the predicted values and the residuals can indicate violations of the assumption of linearity, we also recommend that a plot of the standardised residuals (*ZRESID) against the standardised predicted values (*ZPRED) should be requested. Click **Plots...** to open the **Linear Regression: Plots** dialog box

(Figure 13b) and transfer *ZRESID to the **Y:** box and *ZPRED to the **X:** box. Check the boxes for a histogram and a **normal probability plot** as well. Click **Continue** to return to the **Linear Regression** dialog box.

* Back in the **Linear Regression** dialog, predicted values and residuals can be saved to **Data View** by clicking the **Save…** button. Click **OK** to run the regression.

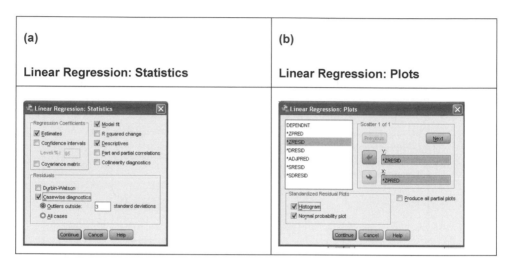

(a)	(b)
Linear Regression: Statistics	**Linear Regression: Plots**

Figure 13. The Statistics and Plots dialog boxes

12.2.2 The output for simple regression

Had there been any outliers in the data set, a table of **Casewise Diagnostics** would have appeared. The information it contained might have indicated that the regression analysis should be terminated and re-run after the outliers had been removed from the data set. There is no such table in the present output, because the data contain no outliers.

The output begins with a table of **Descriptive Statistics** (not shown), including the means and standard deviations of the scores on Actual Violence and Exposure to Violence, followed by a **Correlations** table (not shown) giving the correlation between the two variables as 0.892.

The next two items, a table headed **Variables Entered/Removed** and **Model Summary** (Output 3), may not seem to make much sense until it is realised that in **multiple regression**, where there are two or more IVs, a major issue is the question of which IVs to include in the final **model** for the data. The output for simple regression contains items that appear in any SPSS regression output, however many IVs there may be. For the present example, the Variables Entered/Removed table is of limited interest, because with a single IV, only one model is possible.

The **Model Summary**, however, tells us that the regression model is a significant improvement upon intercept-only prediction. Notice also the columns headed **R**, **R Square** and **Adjusted R Square**. The statistic R, which is known as the **multiple correlation coefficient**, is the correlation between the DV and the predictions of the DV from regression, that is, the corresponding points on the regression line. This statistic can be calculated in *any* regression, however many IVs there may be and therefore appears in *all* regression outputs, incuding the output from the simple regression procedure.

> **The multiple correlation coefficient R**

The multiple correlation cannot have a negative value: unlike the Pearson correlation, which ranges in value from − 1 to +1, R can vary only within the range from 0 to +1, inclusive. This is because even if the original correlation had been negative, the slope of the regression line would also have been negative, so that the correlation between Y and the estimates of Y from regression would still have been positive. When, as in the present example, there is only one regressor, R is therefore the *absolute value* of the Pearson correlation between the DV or criterion and the IV or regressor. Had the correlation between Actual and Exposure been negative (−0.892), the value of R would still have been 0.892 .

Variables Entered/Removed[b]

Model	Variables Entered	Variables Removed	Method
1	Exposure to Screen Violence	.	Enter

a. All requested variables entered.
b. Dependent Variable: Actual Violence

Model Summary[b]

Model	R	R Square	Adjusted R Square	Std. Error of the Estimate
1	.892[a]	.795	.787	.933

a. Predictors: (Constant), Exposure to Screen Violence
b. Dependent Variable: Actual Violence

Output 3. The Variables Entered/Removed and Model Summary tables.

Notice that in the **Model Summary**, **R Square** is 0.795 and **Adjusted R Square** is 0.787 . The first value is simply the **coefficient of determination (CD)**, that is, the square of the Pearson correlation (0.892). The second value has been calculated by using the degrees of freedom to reduce the estimate to allow for **shrinkage** with resampling. It is better, therefore, to report the value of Adjusted R Square, rather than R Square. The **effect size**, as estimated by **adjusted R Square** is, then, 0.787 (79%). This, following Cohen's classification, is a still a 'large' effect.

The next item in the output is the **ANOVA** table (Output 4). The ANOVA tests for a linear relationship between the variables. The F statistic is the ratio of the mean square for regression to the residual mean square. In this example, the value of F in the ANOVA table is significant beyond the 0.01 level. We have already seen that the elliptical shape of the scatterplot indicates that there is indeed a linear relationship between Exposure and Actual.

Further support for the assumption of linearity is provided by items in the output which we shall consider presently.

ANOVA[b]

Model		Sum of Squares	df	Mean Square	F	Sig.
1	Regression	84.517	1	84.517	97.017	.000[a]
	Residual	21.779	25	.871		
	Total	106.296	26			

a. Predictors: (Constant), Exposure to Screen Violence
b. Dependent Variable: Actual Violence

Output 4. The ANOVA summary table

Output 5 is the table of **Coefficients**. This contains the kernel of the regression analysis, namely, the regression equation itself.

Coefficients[a]

Model		Unstandardized Coefficients		Standardized Coefficients	t	Sig.
		B	Std. Error	Beta		
1	(Constant)	2.091	.470		4.449	.000
	Exposure to Screen Violence	.736	.075	.892	9.850	.000

a. Dependent Variable: Actual Violence

Output 5. The Coefficients table

The values of the **regression coefficient** and **constant** are given in column **B** of the table, from which it is clear that the regression equation is:

$$\text{Actual}' = 2.091 + 0.736 \text{ Exposure}$$

Two further features of Output 5 are worthy of note. In the column headed **Standardized Coefficients: Beta**, there is no entry in the row labelled **Constant**. This is because, as we have seen, the intercept of the regression equation disappears when the scores are standardised. In the same column, the regression coefficient (**beta**) is given as 0.892, which (in the case of regression with one IV) is the value of the Pearson correlation r: when the variables are standardised, the slope of the regression line is the Pearson correlation.

Output 6 is a table of the **Residuals Statistics**. The row labelled **Predicted Value** summarises the unstandardised predicted values. The row labelled **Residual** summarises the raw residuals. The row labelled **Std. Predicted Value** (identified as *ZPRED in the **Plots** dialog box in Figure 13) summarises the standardised predicted values (i.e. Predicted Value transformed to a scale with Mean = 0 and SD = 1). The row labelled **Std. Residual** (identified as *ZRESID in the **Plots** dialog box) summarises the standardised residuals (with Mean = 0 and SD = 1).

Residuals Statistics^a

	Minimum	Maximum	Mean	Std. Deviation	N
Predicted Value	2.83	9.45	6.37	1.803	27
Residual	-1.771	1.757	.000	.915	27
Std. Predicted Value	-1.965	1.708	.000	1.000	27
Std. Residual	-1.897	1.883	.000	.981	27

a. Dependent Variable: Actual Violence

Output 6. Table of statistics relating to the residuals

Output 7 is a histogram of the **Standardised Residuals**. As required by the regression model, the distribution is indeed symmetrical and bell-shaped (ie., normal).

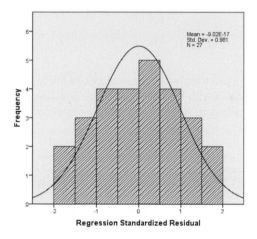

Output 7. Histogram of the standardised residuals

The scatterplot of the standardised residuals (*ZRESID) against the standardised predicted values (*ZPRED) is shown in Output 8. The plot shows an essentially shapeless pattern, thereby confirming that the assumptions of linearity and homogeneity of variance are tenable. A crescent-shape or a 'funnel' would have indicated that a linear regression model was not a convincing interpretation of the data.

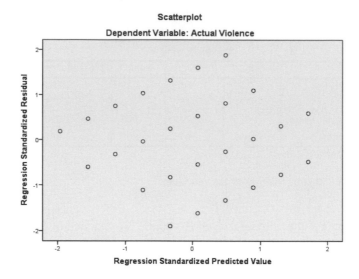

Output 8. Scatterplot of Standardized Residuals against Standardized Predicted Value

The final item (Output 9) is a **cumulative normal probability plot (P-P)**, which compares sample cumulative probabilities with the corresponding cumulative probabilities of the normal distribution. If the match is good, the points should lie approximately along a straight line. Clearly, they do in this case.

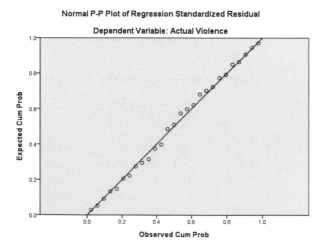

Output 9. Cumulative normal probability plot of Regression Standardized Residual. (Expected cumulative probabilities are plotted against observed cumulative probabilities.)

12.3   MULTIPLE REGRESSION

In this section, we turn to **multiple regression**, the construction of an equation predicting the values of a DV from those of two or more IVs.   The addition of further IVs can improve the predictive power of the regression model.   Usually, however, the purpose of a multiple regression is to develop an appropriate **causal model** of a target variable or DV; indeed; the results of a regression can be difficult or impossible to interpret in the absence of a substantive model of causality.

We shall now consider a situation in which we have a data set containing, in addition to the variables of Actual and Exposure, a third variable of Parental Aggression.   Figure 13 is a fragment of Data View showing some values of this Parental variable.

Case	Exposure	Actual	Parental	VAR
1	1	3	2	
2	2	3	4	
3	1	5	3	
4	3	3	3	
5	4	4	5	
6	5	4	5	
7	3	5	4	
8	4	5	5	
9	3	7	4	
10	6	5	5	
11	4	6	5	
12		6		

Figure 14.   Part of Data View showing the scores of some parents on Parental Aggression

12.3.1   The multiple regression equation

As in simple regression, the objective is to construct a linear equation predicting values of Actual as accurately as possible, so that the sum of squares of the residuals is minimised.   This time, however, the regression equation will have two IVs: Exposure and Parental.   We shall see presently that the best-fitting equation (according to the least squares criterion) is:

$$\text{Actual}' = 2.115 + 0.082\ \text{Exposure} + 0.652\ \text{Parental}\ \text{- - -} (12)$$

Multiple regression equation of Actual upon Exposure and Parental

When the second IV is added to the regression equation, the accuracy of prediction increases. Recall that the **multiple correlation R** is the correlation between the observed values of the DV and the corresponding predictions from the regression equation. (We also saw that R is defined even in the case of simple regression with one IV.) The **coefficient of determination (CD)**, that is, the proportion of the variance of the DV

> **The multiple correlation coefficient R**

accounted for by the regression is R^2. (In simple regression, $R^2 = r^2$: that is, the proportion of variance accounted for is the square of the Pearson correlation between the DV and the IV.) When Actual is regressed upon Exposure, the value of the coefficient of determination (R^2) is 0.50 (50%); but when the Parental variable is added to the regression equation, the value of R^2 increases to 0.645 (65%). (See Figure 15.)

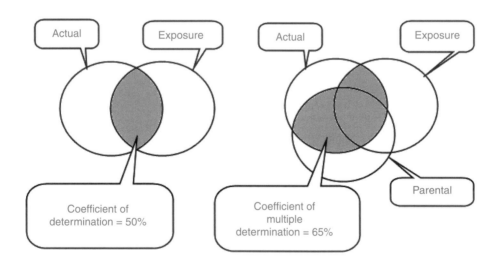

Figure 15. The coefficient of multiple determination

The coefficients of the variables of Exposure and Parental in formula (17) are known as **partial regression coefficients**. A partial regression coefficient is the average change in the DV resulting from an increase of one unit in the IV when *all the other IVs in the regression are held constant*. Thus, we see from formula (17) that, if the Parental variable is held constant, an increase of one unit in Exposure increases Actual violence by a small fraction of a unit; whereas when the Exposure variable is held constant, an increase of one unit in the Parental variable increases Actual violence by 0.652 units.

In the general case, the values of one variable (the dependent variable, target or criterion, Y) are estimated from those of p independent variables or regressors X_1, X_2, ..., X_p . This is achieved by the construction of a **multiple linear regression equation** of the general form:

$$Y' = b_0 + b_1 X_1 + b_2 X_2 + ... + b_p X_p \text{ --- (13)}$$

Multiple linear regression equation

where the parameters b_1, b_2, ..., b_p are the **partial regression coefficients** and the intercept b_0 is the **regression constant**. This equation is known as the **multiple linear regression equation** of Y upon $X_1, X_2, ..., X_p$.

12.3.2 Partial and semipartial (part) correlations

In Chapter 11, we discussed the **partial correlation coefficient**. Correlation does not imply causation: an obtained correlation can often be explained by more than one **causal model**. A correlation between Exposure and Actual, for example, may indeed reflect a direct causal effect of Exposure upon a child's actual violence; but it can be explained by several different models, just three of which are as follows:

1. Exposure causes Actual.

2. Actual causes Exposure

3. Both Actual and Exposure are caused by a third variable, in this case, Parental Aggression.

Reviewing the partial correlation in the light of what we have been considering in this chapter, suppose that we were to run two regressions: Actual upon Parental; Exposure upon Parental. We should now have two sets of residuals from these regressions: Actual (with Parental removed) and Exposure (with Parental removed). The partial correlation is the correlation between these two sets of residuals. In Chapter 11, we found that the partial correlation between those components of Actual and Exposure that are independent of Parental was small (0.095) and insignificant, suggesting that the original high correlation between Actual and Exposure was driven largely by causation of both variables by the Parental variable.

The results of the multiple regression are entirely consistent with the partial correlation. The regression equation shows that when the Parental IV is included in the equation, the influence of Exposure is seen to be negligible.

With the support of a coherent causal model (and credible rival models), multiple regression can, to an even greater extent than the partial correlation, help to resolve complex issues of causation. In multiple regression, a key statistic is the **semipartial** (or **part**) **correlation**, which is the correlation between the DV and one of the IVs in the regression, the values of the other IVs being held constant. Partial and part correlations are referred to as **first-order** correlations, in contradistinction to **zero-order** correlations, which are the correlations between variables from which no other variables have been partialled out.

The semipartial correlation between the DV and one of the IVs is the correlation between the DV and the residuals of the IV when the IV has been regressed upon the other IVs in the regression. The square of the semipartial correlation is the proportion of the DV that is accounted for by variance in the IV with all the other IVs held constant. Figure 16 shows the squared semipartial correlation between Actual and Exposure with Parental held constant (light grey area) and between Actual and Parental with Exposure held constant (dark grey area). It is clear that the partial correlation of Actual with Parental is larger than that of Actual with Exposure.

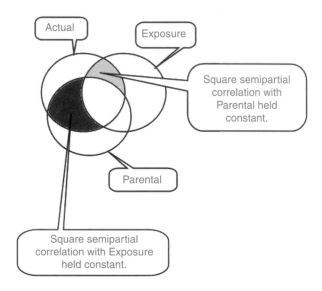

Figure 16. Squared semipartial correlations of Actual with Exposure and Parental

The semipartial correlation is closely related to the partial regression coefficient: in fact, a test of the significance of the partial regression coefficient is at the same time a test of the significance of the semipartial correlation.

It can be seen from Figure 15 that the semipartial correlation between the DV and either IV is less than the correlation would have been if either IV had been the only regressor. If we think of the DV sharing variance among the IVs, the squared semipartial correlation puts the IV 'at the end of the queue', in the sense that it allocates to the IV the shared DV variance that is left after the other IVs have received their portions.

While we can usually expect a partial or semipartial correlation to be smaller than the corresponding zero-order correlation, this is not always the case. A **suppressor** variable is an IV which, while been virtually uncorrelated with the DV, correlates strongly with another IV which does correlate (modestly) with the DV. As a result, the denominator of the zero-order correlation of the DV with the second IV contains a factor of variance that is shared between the two IVs, but not between the DV and the second IV. When this variance is removed by calculating the part or partial correlation (which in this situation will have almost identical values), the correlation increases. Suppose that two IVs are strongly correlated (r = 0.6), that the DV correlates 0 with the first IV (the suppressor) and 0.2 with the second. The value of the part (and partial) correlation is:

$$\frac{0.2-0}{\sqrt{1-0^2}\sqrt{1-0.6^2}} = 0.25$$

In this situation, the part (and partial) correlation is larger than the zero-order correlation. This is because variance shared between the two IVs (but not with the DV) has now been removed and in this sense, the correlation between the DV and the second IV has been 'decontaminated' of the influence of the suppressor.

The best situation for a successful multiple regression is to have IVs that correlate reasonably strongly with the DV but not with one another. It may take some years of research to develop variables that are representative of certain characteristics, so that inclusion of several measures of, say, educational level (some good, some bad) does not occur and the presence of suppressors in the data set is less likely.

From Figure 16, we can also see that the squared semipartial correlation is the increase in R^2 that results from adding that particular independent variable to the regression equation. For this reason, the squared semipartial correlation is referred to by some authors as ΔR^2 (**delta R^2**). This expression appears in the regression output of several statistical computing packages. (SPSS Statistics, however, uses the term **R squared change** instead of **delta R^2** .)

In the unlikely event of complete dissocation among the IVs, the squared semipartial correlations with the DV would simply be the squares of the Pearson correlations of the DV with the IVs, which could be represented as non-overlapping portions of the variance of the DV (Figure 17).

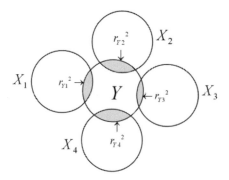

Figure 17. Regression with uncorrelated independent variables

12.3.3 Measuring the importance of an IV in multiple regression

Were the situation to be as pictured in Figure 16, variance in the DV (Y) could be unequivocally attributed to each of the IVs, and we could take the simple Pearson correlation as a serviceable measure of the importance of each regression. In practice, correlations among the IVs necessitate a shift of emphasis to the semipartial correlations.

The sharing of variance among the independent variables in multiple regression makes it impossible to assign variance in Y unequivocally to any one independent variable. There is, therefore, a large literature on the question of which of the variables in a multiple regression should be regarded as the 'most important' in explaining the variance of the dependent variable. The paper and textbook by Darlington (1968, 1990) still provide a lucid discussion of the problems with the various measures of 'importance' that have been proposed. Cohen, Cohen, West & Aiken (2003) have a comprehensive treatment of all aspects of multiple regression.

We have already seen that the unstandardised regression coefficient is often unsuitable as a measure of "importance", because its value is dependent upon the units of measurement. The standardised regression coefficient β is in this sense an improvement, because it permits comparison between variables originally measured in different units. It might be thought that the simple Pearson correlation between an independent variable and the criterion would be an appropriate measure of the importance of an IV in accounting for variance in the DV; but there are situations in which the largest squared semipartial correlation ΔR^2 is not obtained with the variable showing the highest Pearson correlation with the criterion.

No matter which measure of 'importance' we adopt, there remains the possibility that the addition of another IV to the regression equation could change the order of merit of the DVs. In the absence of a clear model of causation (backed up with additional collateral evidence), a regression equation is often impossible to interpret unequivocally.

12.3.4 Strategies in multiple regression

In **simultaneous** multiple regression, all the IVs are entered into the equation at once. This is an appropriate strategy when the purpose of the research is to investigate a situation in which the variables are predetermined. A north American university, for example, might test each student on certain aptitude tests at matriculation and award each student a grade point average (GPA) at the end of their first year. A simultaneous multiple regression of GPA upon the aptitude tests might afford useful information about the importance of the aptitude tests.

Suppose, however, that a research team has developed a compelling model of the causal relationships among the variables they have been studying. Some variables (such as Parental Aggression) in our example, might be seen as causally prior to others (Exposure of children to screened violence). Rather than allowing each variable to take its place at the end of the queue as in simultaneous regression, we might wish to force some variables (or groups of variables) into the equation first and thus attribute part of the variance of the DV to them before we add other DVs to the regression equation. Such a theory-driven approach to regression is known as **hierarchical multiple regression**.

There is another approach to multiple regression, known as **stepwise regression**, in which variables are added successively to the regression equation on purely statistical grounds. In the **forward** approach, they are added successively if they meet the criteria; in the **backward** approach, they are removed successively. Stepwise regression, however, has many critics, who argue that multiple regression should always be theory-driven and that a purely statistical model is insufficient without a substantive causal model also. The technique may be best applied in relatively new research areas, where the most representative and best IVs have yet to be identified and where there is, as yet, no coherent body of theory to guide the researcher.

12.4   MULTIPLE REGRESSION WITH SPSS

One potential problem with multiple regression is that if we have measured several variables, some of which are highly correlated, the multiple regression package the researcher is using may not work at all. (In the extreme case, where one variable is an exact function of others in the set, the matrix of correlations is **singular**, that is, its determinant is zero.) This is known as the problem of **multicollinearity**. A key measure here is the **tolerance** of a regressor, that is, one minus the square of the multiple correlation between the regressor and estimates of its values from its regression upon all the other regressors. If the tolerance is too low, the multiple regression will fail to run. In practice, a researcher will include an IV because, since it is known to be representative of a category of IVs, it should not correlate too highly with IVs representing other categories. Good correlational research requires such background knowledge.

Before running a regression, it is good practice to **centre** the variables, that is transform them to deviation scores by subtracting their means. The process of centring (or **centering**) leaves the correlations among the variable unchanged; but the regression algorithm is less likely to crash when there are high correlations among some of the variables.

12.4.1   Running a simultaneous multiple regression with SPSS

Proceed as follows:

- Complete the **Linear Regression** dialog box, as outlined in Figure 18.

- Select the other optional items as in Figure 19, then click **OK**.

In Figure 19, the statistic labelled **R squared change** is the squared semipartial correlation **delta R squared** ΔR^2, which we discussed earlier. This statistic, as we shall see, is most at home in **heirarchical multiple regression**, where we shall want to attribute variance in the DV to each of the groups of DVs that are successively added to the regression equation. We shall also want to look at the **Part** (semipartial) **and partial correlations**. As usual, we shall want **Descriptives**. We shall also want measures of **Model fit**. A very important choice is **Casewise diagnostics**: With a small data set like this especially, the presence of outliers can exert undue leverage upon the values of the statistics in the output.

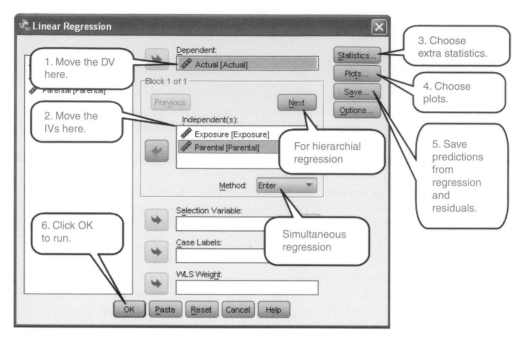

Figure 18.   Completing the **Linear Regression** dialog box for multiple regression

In the Plots dialog (Figure 20), several useful choices can be made. We show the choice of a plot of ZRESID against ZPRED, that is, the standardised residuals against the predictions from regression; but additional choices can be made by clicking the Next button, which will clear the first entry from view and allow another plot to be specified.   Check the boxes labelled **Histogram** and **Normal probability plot** as well. Such graphics are very useful in **regression diagnostics**.

Figure 21 shows some useful choices of variables that might be saved in Data View.   You might want to confirm, for example, that the value of the multiple correlation R is indeed identical with the absolute value of the Pearson correlation between the IV and the predictions from regression. Measures such as **Cook distances** identify data points that are exerting undue leverage on the estimates of the regression statistics.

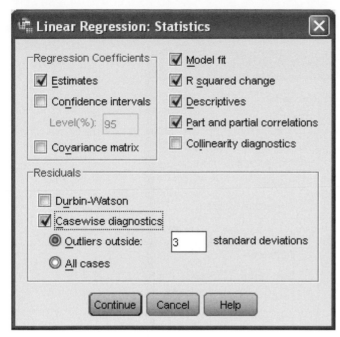

Figure 19. Choosing some extra statistics

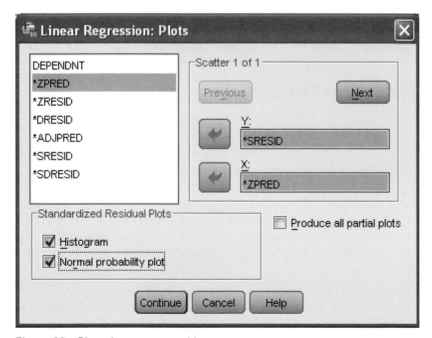

Figure 20. Choosing some graphics

Figure 21. Choosing some variables to save in Data View

12.4.2   The output from simultaneous multiple regression

We shall omit the first three tables, **Descriptive Statistics**, **Correlations** and **Variables Entered/Removed**. The values given in the first two tables, however, should match exactly those obtained in a preliminary survey of the data with such routines as **Descriptives** and **Correlate**. We know that both IVs will be entered together, since we have requested a simultaneous multiple regression.

Output 10 is a transposed version of the **Model Summary**. Notice that the value of R (0.803) is only very slightly higher than the correlation between the DV and the Parental variable. The value of **R Square Change** is 0.645 (65%). The tiny p-value given for **Sig. F Change** shows that the regression is a significant improvement upon intercept-only prediction of the DV. The value of **R Square Change** (0.645) is a 'large' effect, according to Cohen's classification.

Model Summary[b]

	Model
	1
R	.803[a]
R Square	.645
Adjusted R Square	.615
Std. Error of the Estimate	1.196
Change Statistics R Square Change	.645
F Change	21.793
df1	2
df2	24
Sig. F Change	.000

a. Predictors: (Constant), Parental, Exposure
b. Dependent Variable: Actual

Output 10. The Model Summary

The ANOVA table (not shown) shows that the regression is significant – a fact which is also evident from the **Model Summary**. Note, however, that the degrees of freedom of the regression sum of squares is 2, because, in addition to the intercept, there are now two regression coefficients in the regression model.

Output 11 is a transposed version of the table of **Coefficients**. From the values in the first row, we can see immediately that the multiple regression equation of Actual upon Exposure and Parental is:

$$\text{Actual}' = 2.115 + 0.082 \text{ Exposure} + 0.652 \text{ Parental}$$

Once again, we see that of the two IVs, only Parental makes a significant contribution to the regression, a fact backed up by the small values of the partial and semipartial correlations. In this example, where the Exposure and Parental variables were measured on the same scale, a direct comparison of the unstandardised regression coefficients is meaningful. In real research, however, that is unlikely to be the case.   It is usually safer to compare the beta-weights which, in this case, have similar values to the unstandardised regression coefficients. From the beta-weights, we learn that a change of one unit in the Parental and Exposure variables, result in increases in the DV of 0.711 SD and 0.106 SD, respectively.

Coefficients^a

		Model		
		1		
		(Constant)	Exposure	Parental
Unstandardized Coefficients	B	2.115	.082	.652
	Std. Error	.712	.175	.208
Standardized Coefficients	Beta		.106	.711
t		2.970	.467	3.131
Sig.		.007	.644	.005
Correlations	Zero-order		.707	.801
	Partial		.095	.539
	Part		.057	.381

a. Dependent Variable: Actual

Output 11. The Coefficients table

The table of **Residuals Statistics** (not shown) would have been of central interest, had a table of **Casewise diagnostics** appeared revealing the presence of outliers.   Since no casewise diagnostics have appeared in the output, the residuals statistics are unlikely to be of interest. Residuals are the basis of **regression diagnostics**, a set of procedures for identifying rogue scores that can distort the values of multiple regression statistics.   The raw residuals e are themselves valuable measures of **distance**.   But distances exert more **leverage** on the regression statistics if they are far from the mean of the IV concerned than if they are near the centre. Leverage is captured by the statistic known as h_i, where h stands for 'hat'. (The hat is used to denote an estimate in the mathematical development of the statistic.)   To have influence, however, a score must have both distance and leverage.   The statistic known as **Cook's D** is a respected measure of both distance and leverage. (See Howell, 2007, pages 515-520, for a helpful introduction to regression diagnostics.   Cohen et al., 2003, have a full treatment.)

Output 12 (edited) is a histogram of the **Standardized Residuals**.   These should have the standard normal distribution with Mean $= 0$ and SD $= 1$.   The appearance of the histogram is consistent with this requirement.

Output 13 is the requested normal probability plot. The points all lie close to a straight line, which is the required pattern, confirming the impression given by the histogram that the residuals are normally distributed.

Output 14 is a scatterplot of the **Studentized Residuals** against the **Standardized Predicted Values**.   No trend is evident in this shapeless cloud of points, indicating that the linear regression model is appropriate for these data.

Finally, turning now to the saved variables, you will see that they now appear in Data View. You might wish to confirm, for example that the correlation between the scores on Actual and the Unstandardized predicted values is 0.803, the value of the multiple correlation coefficient *R*. The correlation of the DV with the standardized predicted values is also 0.803, since the value of the Pearson correlation is unaltered by linear transformation of either variable involved.

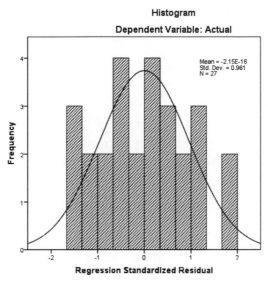

Output 12. Histogram of the Standardized Residuals

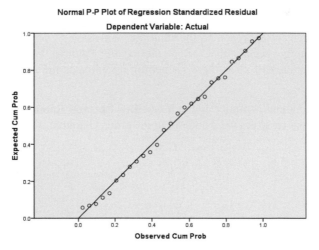

Output 13. Normal probability plot

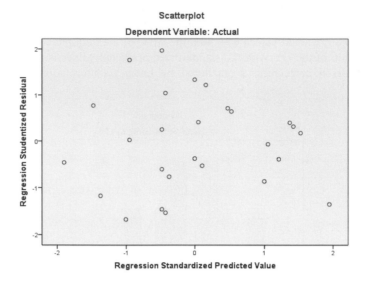

Output 14.   Scatterplot of the Regression Studentized Residuals against the Regression Standardized Predicted Values

12.4.3   An hierarchical multiple regression

Since, according to the researchers' causal model, the correlation between Actual and Exposure is driven by the variable of Parental Aggression, we have a sound theoretical basis for taking the hierarchical approach to the multiple regression.   We can omit most of the procedural details, noting simply that, after entering the Parental Variable as the first IV, clicking the **Next** button will clear the slot, permitting entry of the second IV of Exposure (Figure 22).

The first item in the output to notice is the **Variables Entered/Removed** table (Output 15), which confirms that the variables were entered in the order: Parental, Exposure.

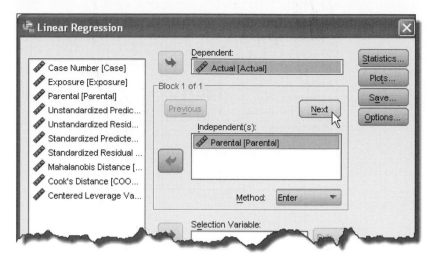

Figure 22. Entering the first variable in an hierarchical regression. Clicking Next will clear the way for the next group of IVs

Variables Entered/Removed[b]

Model	Variables Entered	Variables Removed	Method
1	Parental[a]	.	Enter

a. All requested variables entered.
b. Dependent Variable: Actual

Output 15. The Variables Entered/Removed table, showing that the Parental variable was entered as the first IV in the multiple regression

The **Model Summary** is shown in Output 16.   The values of **R** and **R Square** are slightly lower than for the simultaneous regression; but this is because the addition of the Exposure variable makes no significant contribution to the variance accounted for by the simpler regression model.

Model Summary[b]

		Model
		1
R		.801[a]
R Square		.642
Adjusted R Square		.627
Std. Error of the Estimate		1.177
Change Statistics	R Square Change	.642
	F Change	44.767
	df1	1
	df2	25
	Sig. F Change	.000

a. Predictors: (Constant), Parental
b. Dependent Variable: Actual

Model Summary[b]

		Model
		1
R		.803[a]
R Square		.645
Adjusted R Square		.615
Std. Error of the Estimate		1.196
Change Statistics	R Square Change	.645
	F Change	21.793
	df1	2
	df2	24
	Sig. F Change	.000

a. Predictors: (Constant), Parental, Exposure
b. Dependent Variable: Actual

Output 16. The Model Summary for the hierarchical regression.

Output 17 is the ANOVA summary table for the hierarchical regression. (The summary table for the simultaneous regression is shown below for comparison.) Notice that the Regression degrees of freedom is given as 1 (rather than 2, as in the simultaneous regression). This is because the final model has only one IV. In the hierarchical ANOVA table, the degrees of freedom of the residual is given as 25, rather than 24, as in the corresponding table for the simultaneous multiple regression.

Output 18 is the Coefficients table, with the corresponding table from the simultaneous regression below it for comparison. The hierarchical final model has dropped the Exposure IV from the regression model. As a result, the part and partial correlations both have the value 0.801, which is simply the Pearson correlation between Parental and Actual.

ANOVA[b]

Model		Sum of Squares	df	Mean Square	F	Sig.
1	Regression	62.027	1	62.027	44.767	.000[a]
	Residual	34.639	25	1.386		
	Total	96.667	26			

a. Predictors: (Constant), Parental
b. Dependent Variable: Actual

ANOVA[b]

Model		Sum of Squares	df	Mean Square	F	Sig.
1	Regression	62.340	2	31.170	21.793	.000[a]
	Residual	34.327	24	1.430		
	Total	96.667	26			

a. Predictors: (Constant), Parental, Exposure
b. Dependent Variable: Actual

Output 17. The ANOVA summary table for the hierarchical regression.

Coefficients[a]

		Model	
		1	
		(Constant)	Parental
Unstandardized Coefficients	B	2.064	.735
	Std. Error	.693	.110
Standardized Coefficients	Beta		.801
t		2.980	6.691
Sig.		.006	.000
Correlations	Zero-order		.801
	Partial		.801
	Part		.801

a. Dependent Variable: Actual

Coefficients[a]

		Model		
		1		
		(Constant)	Exposure	Parental
Unstandardized Coefficients	B	2.115	.082	.652
	Std. Error	.712	.175	.208
Standardized Coefficients	Beta		.106	.711
t		2.970	.467	3.131
Sig.		.007	.644	.005
Correlations	Zero-order		.707	.801
	Partial		.095	.539
	Part		.057	.381

a. Dependent Variable: Actual

Output 18. The ANOVA summary table for the hierarchical regression. (The corresponding table for simultaneous regression is given below for comparison.)

12.5   RUNNING THE ANOVA AS A MULTIPLE REGRESSION

The similarities between the ANOVA tables in regression output and those in the output of the the ANOVA procedures are by no means coincidental; in fact, as we shall see in this section, the ANOVA itself can be run as a multiple regression.

The link between the ANOVA and regression, on the other hand, may seem far from self-evident. In the one-way ANOVA, for example, there is no continuous IV: we have a set of qualitatively different categories among which there is no inherent order. The results of the one-way ANOVA, in fact, are unaffected by the order in which the scores of the various groups are entered in the Score column in Data View. In this section, however, we shall show that the one-way ANOVA can be viewed as the multiple regression of the scores (the DV) upon a set of coding variables specifying group membership and the resulting regression statistics are exactly equivalent to the usual ANOVA F test and to tests of differences among the treatment means.

12.5.1   The two-group case

We shall begin by returning to the caffeine experiment, in which the performance of a group of participants who had ingested caffeine was compared with that of a placebo group.

Case	Score	Group	X	var
28	15	Placebo	0	
29	12	Placebo	0	
30	7	Placebo	0	
31	14	Caffeine	1	
32	14	Caffeine	1	
33	10	Caffeine	1	
34	10	Caffeine	1	
35	8	Caffeine	1	

Figure 23. A fragment from Data View showing some of the data from the caffeine experiment and values of a dummy variable carrying group membership.

Figure 23 shows a fragment of Data View, to which has been added, in addition to Score and the grouping variable, an additional variable X. We have used the code number 0 for the Placebo group and 1 for the Caffeine group. A variable consisting of the values 0 and 1 is known as a **dummy variable**; and the use of dummy variables to indicate group membership is known as **dummy coding**.

So far, we haven't said anything about the grouping variable. Up to this point, it hasn't mattered which code numbers you assign to the two groups, so long as they are different. For this exercise, it does matter. When assigning values to the Placebo and Caffeine groups, assign the larger value to the group you want to be treated as the comparison: e.g. 2 = Placebo; 1 = Caffeine, not vice versa. In its ANOVA procedures, SPSS will always treat the group with the largest code value as the comparison group.

Running the ANOVA

First, we shall run the one-way ANOVA, for which the new variable X will not be required. To bring out the identity of the ANOVA with regression, however, we shall need to run the ANOVA from the **General Linear Model (GLM)** menu, rather than use the **One-Way ANOVA** procedure. Proceed as follows:

- Choose **Analyze➔General Linear Model➔Univariate...** to open the **Univariate** dialog box. Transfer Score to the **Dependent List** slot and Group to the **Fixed Factor(s)** box on the right.

- Click the **Options** button and, in the **Univariate: options** dialog, transfer Group to the **Display Means for** box on the right and check **Descriptive statistics** and **Parameter estimates** in the boxes in the **Display** panel underneath.

- Click **Continue** to return to the **Univariate** dialog. Click the **Save** button and, in the **Univariate: Save** dialog, check **Unstandardized** in the **Predicted Values** panel at top left. Click **Continue** to return to the **Univariate** dialog.

- Click **OK** to run the ANOVA.

The **Tests of Between Subjects Effects** table is shown in Output 19. The table is considerably more elaborate than the corresponding table in the output from the **One-Way** procedure in the **Compare Means** menu; but you will find that if you run the One-Way procedure on the same data, the results will appear as in the lower table in Output 19, which is an edited version of the full **Tests of Between-Subjects Effects** table.

Notice, in the full table of **Tests of Between-Subjects Effects**, the row labelled **Intercept** and, underneath the table itself, the statistic **R squared = 0.078**. These are clearly regression statistics: in fact, the ANOVA has actually been run as a regression, rather than in the manner described in Chapter 7.

Tests of Between-Subjects Effects

Dependent Variable:Number of Hits

Source	Type III Sum of Squares	df	Mean Square	F	Sig.
Corrected Model	84.899ᵃ	1	84.899	4.913	.031
Intercept	7598.615	1	7598.615	439.743	.000
Group	84.899	1	84.899	4.913	.031
Error	1002.222	58	17.280		
Total	8685.736	60			
Corrected Total	1087.121	59			

a. R Squared = .078 (Adjusted R Squared = .062)

Tests of Between-Subjects Effects

Dependent Variable:Number of Hits

Source	Sum of Squares	df	Mean Square	F	Sig.
Group	84.899	1	84.899	4.913	.031
Error	1002.222	58	17.280		
Total	1087.121	59			

Output 19. Some of the GLM output from the one-way ANOVA. The lower table is an edited version of the upper table.

Output 20 shows the **Parameter Estimates** and the **Descriptive Statistics**. In the table of parameter estimates, notice that the intercept of the regression equation is 10.064, which is the mean score of the Placebo group. The value of the slope of the regression equation (2.379) is the difference between the Caffeine and Placebo means.

Parameter Estimates

Dependent Variable:Number of Hits

Parameter	B	Std. Error	t	Sig.	95% Confidence Interval	
					Lower Bound	Upper Bound
Intercept	10.064	.759	13.261	.000	8.545	11.583
[Group=1]	2.379	1.073	2.217	.031	.231	4.528
[Group=2]	0ᵃ	.	.	.	.	.

a. This parameter is set to zero because it is redundant.

Descriptive Statistics

Dependent Variable:Number of Hits

Treatment Group	Mean	Std. Deviation	N
Caffeine	12.443	3.719	30
Placebo	10.064	4.553	30
Total	11.25	4.293	60

Output 20.   Tables of Parameter Estimates and Descriptive Statistics

Running the regression

Now we are going to run a simple regression of the scores from the caffeine experiment upon the dummy variable X, which also carries group membership.   Proceed as follows:

- Choose **Analyze➔Regression ➔Linear...** to open the **Linear Regression** dialog box. Transfer Score to the **Dependent Variable** slot and the dummy variable X to the **Independent Variable(s)** box.

- Click the **Statistics** button and, in the **Linear Regression: Statistics** subdialog, check **Descriptives, Estimates, Model fit** and **R squared change** (Figure 24).

- Back in the **Linear Regression** dialog, click the **Save** button and, in the **Linear Regression: Save** dialog, check **Unstandardized** (Predicted Values). Click **Continue** to return to the **Linear Regression** Dialog.

- Click **OK** to run the regression.   The Coefficients and ANOVA tables are shown in Output 21.

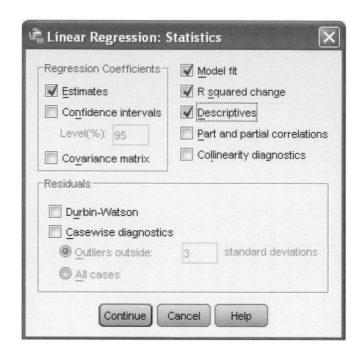

Figure 24. Choosing some relevant statistics from the **Linear Regression: Statistics** dialog box

Coefficients[a]

Model		Unstandardized Coefficients		Standardized Coefficients	t	Sig.
		B	Std. Error	Beta		
1	(Constant)	10.064	.759		13.261	.000
	Treatment Group	2.379	1.073	.279	2.217	.031

a. Dependent Variable: Number of Hits

ANOVA[b]

Model		Sum of Squares	df	Mean Square	F	Sig.
1	Regression	84.899	1	84.899	4.913	.031[a]
	Residual	1002.222	58	17.280		
	Total	1087.121	59			

a. Predictors: (Constant), Treatment Group
b. Dependent Variable: Number of Hits

Output 21. The regression output from the **Linear Regression** procedure

In Output 21, the values of the statistics in the ANOVA table (the sums of squares, the mean squares, the degrees of freedom and F) are identical with those given in the output from the **GLM Univariate** procedure shown in Output 19. Notice also that the value of the intercept in the regression output is the value of the Placebo mean given in the Descriptives table. Finally, the slope of the regression line given in the Coefficients table is the difference between the Caffeine and Placebo means given in the Descriptives table in Output 20.

Recall that the regression methods we have been discussing in this chapter minimise the sum of the squares of the residuals. It is easy to show that the sum of the squared deviations of scores about their mean is a minimum: that is, the sum of squared deviations about the mean is less than the sum of squares about any other value. Since there are only two groups, therefore, the regression line must pass through the group means (Figure 25).

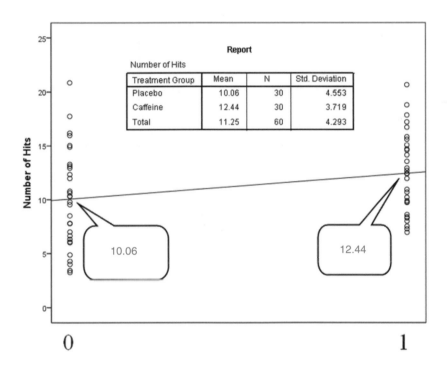

Figure 24. The regression line

For the Placebo group, the dummy variable has the value 0. Recalling that the regression equation is

$$Y' = b_0 + bX$$

and knowing that the predicted value of Y for $X = 0$ is the Placebo mean, it is clear that the intercept b_0 is the Placebo mean. Similarly, substituting the value 1 for X in the regression equation and knowing that the predicted value for $X = 1$ is the Caffeine mean and that the intercept is the Placebo mean, we can see that the slope b of the regression line is simply the difference between the Caffeine and Placebo means.

We can see, therefore, that the test of the null hypothesis that the slope of the regression line is zero is also the test that, in the population, the Placebo and Caffeine means are equal. The regression and the ANOVA are doing equivalent things.

Finally, Output 22 shows the **Model Summary** for the regression. Notice that **R square** is given as 0.078, which is exactly the value given in the **GLM Univariate** output shown in Output 19. The statistic **F Change** (4.913) is exactly the value of the ANOVA *F* ratio given in Output 19.

Model Summary

		Model
		1
R		.279[a]
R Square		.078
Adjusted R Square		.062
Std. Error of the Estimate		4.157
Change Statistics	R Square Change	.078
	F Change	4.913
	df1	1
	df2	58
	Sig. F Change	.031

a. Predictors: (Constant), X

Output 22. The Model Summary

12.5.2   The k-group case

The parallel with regression can easily be extended to the one-factor experiment with three or more treatment groups. We shall illustrate this with the data we used for the one-way ANOVA in Chapter 7. Once again, we can use dummy variables to specify group membership, as shown in Table 2. The data are to be found in the file *One-way ANOVA with dummy coding.sav* at http://www.psypress.com/spss-made-simple.

The use of four dummy variables ensures that each of the five groups is identified by a different sequence of four binary numbers. In general, if there are *k* groups, we shall need ($k - 1$) dummy variables to code group membership. We can regard each of the dummy variables *X* as referring to one of the four active treatment conditions; but no dummy variable need be defined for the Placebo group.

Table 2. Coding group membership with dummy variables

	X1	X2	X3	X4
Placebo	0	0	0	0
Drug A	1	0	0	0
Drug B	0	1	0	0
Drug C	0	0	1	0
Drug D	0	0	0	1

As before, we shall run the GLM version of the one-way ANOVA, then compare the output with that of the regression of the scores upon the four dummy variables. As with the Caffeine data set, make sure that when you are assigning values to the categories making up the grouping variable, assign the highest value to the Placebo group; otherwise, the ANOVA and regression parameters won't agree.

Running the ANOVA

- Choose **Analyze→General Linear Model→Univariate...** to open the **Univariate** dialog box and proceed exactly as described in Section 12.5.1.

In Output 23 is the table of **Tests of Between-Subjects Effects**, which clearly summarises the results of a regression.

In Output 24, are the **Descriptive Statistics** and **Parameter Estimates**. As in the two-group ANOVA with the caffeine data, the value of the Intercept is the mean score of the Placebo group. It can also be confirmed from the means in the Descriptive Statistics table, that each of the four regression coefficients is the difference between the mean score of participants in one of the experimental groups and the Placebo mean.

Tests of Between-Subjects Effects

Dependent Variable:Score

Source	Type III Sum of Squares	df	Mean Square	F	Sig.
Corrected Model	351.520[a]	4	87.880	9.085	.000
Intercept	6116.180	1	6116.180	632.272	.000
Group	351.520	4	87.880	9.085	.000
Error	435.300	45	9.673		
Total	6903.000	50			
Corrected Total	786.820	49			

a. R Squared = .447 (Adjusted R Squared = .398)

Output 23. Results of the one-way ANOVA in the GLM Univariate output

Descriptive Statistics

Dependent Variable:Score

Drug Condition	Mean	Std. Deviation	N
Drug A	7.90	2.132	10
Drug B	12.00	2.494	10
Drug C	14.40	4.502	10
Drug D	13.00	3.742	10
Placebo	8.00	1.826	10
Total	11.06	4.007	50

Parameter Estimates

Dependent Variable:Score

Parameter	B	Std. Error	t	Sig.	95% Confidence Interval	
					Lower Bound	Upper Bound
Intercept	8.000	.984	8.134	.000	6.019	9.981
[Group=1]	-.100	1.391	-.072	.943	-2.901	2.701
[Group=2]	4.000	1.391	2.876	.006	1.199	6.801
[Group=3]	6.400	1.391	4.601	.000	3.599	9.201
[Group=4]	5.000	1.391	3.595	.001	2.199	7.801
[Group=5]	0[a]	.	.	.	.	.

a. This parameter is set to zero because it is redundant.

Output 24. Descriptive Statistics and Parameter Estimates from the GLM Univariate version of the one-way ANOVA

Running the regression

Figure 26 shows a section of Data View with the four dummy variables in place. Proceed as follows:

- Choose **Analyze➜Regression ➜Linear…** to open the **Linear Regression** dialog box. Transfer Score to the **Dependent** slot and the dummy variables X1, X2, X3 and X4 to the **Independent(s)** box.

- Make exactly the same choices as those described in Section 12.5.1 and run the regression.

	Group	Score	X1	X2	X3	X4	var
7	Placebo	7	0	0	0	0	
8	Placebo	6	0	0	0	0	
9	Placebo	8	0	0	0	0	
10	Placebo	8	0	0	0	0	
11	Drug A	8	1	0	0	0	
12	Drug A	10	1	0	0	0	
13	Drug A	7	1	0	0	0	
14	Drug A	7	1	0	0	0	
15	Drug A	7	1	0	0	0	
16	Drug A	12	1	0	0	0	
17	Drug A	7	1	0	0	0	
18			1				

Figure 26. A section of Data View showing group membership coded by four dummy variables

Output 25 shows the **ANOVA** and **Coefficients** tables in the Linear Regression output. (The Descriptives table from the GLM Univariate output is reproduced below them for reference.) Once again, as in the two-group example, the values given in the ANOVA table in the regression output are identical with those given in the **GLM Univariate Tests of Between-Subjects Effects** summary table. Moreover, the value of the regression constant is that of the Placebo mean and those of the four regression coefficients are the differences between each group mean and the Placebo mean.

ANOVA[b]

Model		Sum of Squares	df	Mean Square	F	Sig.
1	Regression	351.520	4	87.880	9.085	.000[a]
	Residual	435.300	45	9.673		
	Total	786.820	49			

a. Predictors: (Constant), X4, X3, X2, X1
b. Dependent Variable: Score

Coefficients[a]

Model		Unstandardized Coefficients		Standardized Coefficients	t	Sig.
		B	Std. Error	Beta		
1	(Constant)	8.000	.984		8.134	.000
	X1	-.100	1.391	-.010	-.072	.943
	X2	4.000	1.391	.403	2.876	.006
	X3	6.400	1.391	.645	4.601	.000
	X4	5.000	1.391	.504	3.595	.001

a. Dependent Variable: Score

Descriptive Statistics

Dependent Variable:Score

Drug Condition	Mean	Std. Deviation	N
Drug A	7.90	2.132	10
Drug B	12.00	2.494	10
Drug C	14.40	4.502	10
Drug D	13.00	3.742	10
Placebo	8.00	1.826	10
Total	11.06	4.007	50

Output 25. The ANOVA and Coefficients tables in the output from Linear Regression

The **Model Summary** is shown in Output 26. You can easily confirm that if the given value of R^2 (0.44676) is multiplied by the total sum of squares, we obtain the sum of squares for the treatment factor:

$$R^2 (SS_{total}) = 0.44676(786.820)$$
$$= 351.52$$
$$= SS_{between}$$

The statistic R^2 is the **coefficient of determination (CD)**, that is, the proportion of the variance of the DV accounted for by regression on the IV. (Its value was also given in Output 23.) When we multiply the CD by the total sum of squares, we have the ANOVA between groups sum of squares.

Model Summary[b]

		Model
		1
R		.668[a]
R Square		.446760
Adjusted R Square		.398
Std. Error of the Estimate		3.110
Change Statistics	R Square Change	.447
	F Change	9.085
	df1	4
	df2	45
	Sig. F Change	.000

a. Predictors: (Constant), X4, X3, X2, X1
b. Dependent Variable: Score

Output 26. The Model Summary

Inspection of Data View will show that the regression procedure has placed, as the predicted value for each score, the mean of the group to which it belongs.

Note that, with the dummy coding of group membership that we have used in this example, each dummy variable carries one of a set of simple contrasts. The **Coefficients** table in the regression output reports the results of tests of the four simple contrasts. Were you to run the one-way ANOVA in the usual way and request simple contrasts (using the Placebo group as the reference group), you would obtain exactly the same results.

Eta squared revisited

In Chapter 7, we discussed the measure of effect size known as **eta squared (η^2)** , where η, the **correlation ratio**, is the proportion of the variance of the scores that is attributable to differences among the group means. We saw in Chapter 7 that the positive square root of this measure, **eta**, is the correlation between the scores the participants achieved in the experiment and their group means. In this chapter, we have seen that the **multiple correlation R** is the Pearson correlation between the observed scores Y and the corresponding predicted values from regression Y'. Eta is thus a multiple correlation coefficient; and Eta squared is the square of the multiple correlation between the scores and their predicted values from multiple regression upon coding variables carrying information about group membership.

Since the value of eta, like those of the statistics from the one-way ANOVA itself, is unaffected by the ordering of the scores from the different groups, it is applicable to a situation in which there is no continuous independent variable. Eta can thus be regarded as a **function-free correlation** expressing the total regression (linear and curvilinear) of the scores upon the numbers that have been assigned to the treatment groups.

12.5.3   Other systems of coding: contrast coding and effects coding

Dummy coding is not the only system we could have used to run the one-way ANOVA as a regression. Two other systems are **contrast coding** and **effects coding**. In contrast coding, the values in each column sum to zero. We could, for example, have used a set of four Helmert contrasts to code membership of the five groups in the drug experiment. In that case, since Helmert contrasts make an **orthogonal contrast set**, the contrasts would also be independent or **orthogonal**, so that the unique contribution of each contrast to the variance of the scores could be estimated. With orthogonal contrast coding, the semipartial or part correlations of the coding variables with the scores (the DV) are equal to the zero-order correlations.

Effects coding resembles dummy coding; but the group that would have received a sequence of zeros receives instead repetitions of the value –1. We saw that in regression with dummy coding, the intercept is the mean of the group we wish to use as a comparison and that the regression coefficients are the differences between the comparison (Placebo) mean and the means for the active conditions in the experiment. In effects coding, the intercept is the grand mean and the regression coefficients are deviations of the group means from the grand mean. Of the three systems, effects coding has some advantages over the other systems when running factorial experiments as multiple regressions (see below).

It does not matter which system of coding we use (dummy variables, contrast coding, or effect coding): provided there are exactly one fewer coding IVs than there are groups, the regression equation will always predict the group mean.

The **general linear model** is an interpretation of a score as being made up of three types of component: (1) the **grand mean**; (2) **effects**, which are deviations of various kinds; (3) a random **error** component. Effects coding parallels this interpretation of a score, so that the parameter estimates in the regression equation cast direct light upon the types of effects that have emerged from the research. Effects coding is particularly useful in the investigation of interactions in factorial experiments.

12.5.4   The factorial ANOVA as a regression

The factorial ANOVA can also be run as a multiple regression. To illustrate the procedure, we shall take as an example the two-factor factorial experiment from Chapter 8. The dependent variable was Driving Performance and the factors were Drug (Placebo, A and B) and Alertness (Fresh, Tired). The data are available in the file *Ch12 Factorial Contrast Coding.sav* at http://www.psypress.com/spss-made-simple.

To code group membership of the regression, we shall use **contrast coding**, rather than dummy coding (though dummy coding works perfectly well – as does effects coding). In particular, we shall use Helmert contrasts to carry the main effects and interaction sources. Since Helmert contrasts have the property of independence or **orthogonality**, the regression will enable us to ascertain the portion of the total sum of squares that is accounted for by each contrast and each source of variance in the two-way ANOVA. Contrast coding of group membership is shown in Table 3.

Table 3. Contrast coding for the Drug experiment

Alertness	Drug	Alert_Coding	Drug1	Drug2	Interaction1	Interaction2
Fresh	Placebo	1	2	0	2	0
Fresh	Drug A	1	-1	1	-1	1
Fresh	Drug B	1	-1	-1	-1	-1
Tired	Placebo	-1	2	0	-2	0
Tired	Drug A	-1	-1	1	1	-1
Tired	Drug B	-1	-1	-1	1	1

You can see that the Drug factor (which has three levels) has been coded with two Helmert contrasts: 1. the Placebo mean with the mean of the two drug means; 2. the contrast between the two drug means. The two interaction variables Interaction1 and Interaction2 are the products of the entries for Alert_Coding with the corresponding entries for Drug1 and Drug2, respectively. Notice that the coefficients in the columns sum to zero and that the sum of the products of corresponding entries in any two columns is also zero. The five sets of contrasts are thus orthogonal, which is very important for the demonstration that follows.

Figure 27 shows a fragment of Data View with the contrasts in place.   When entering the values of the coding variables, it is only too easy to make an error. To check that all is well, choose   **Analyze➔Correlate ➔Bivariate…** , transfer all five coding variables to the Variable box and run the correlations. All the correlations must be zero, as shown in Output 27.

Alertness	Drug	DrivingPerf	Alert_Coding	Drug1	Drug2	Interaction1	Interaction2	var
Fresh	Placebo	24	1	2	0	2	0	
Fresh	Placebo	25	1	2	0	2	0	
Fresh	Placebo	13	1	2	0	2	0	
Fresh	Placebo	22	1	2	0	2	0	
Fresh	Placebo	16	1	2	0	2	0	
Fresh	Placebo	23	1	2	0	2	0	
Fresh	Placebo	18	1	2	0	2	0	
Fresh	Placebo	19	1	2	0	2	0	
Fresh	Placebo	24	1	2	0	2	0	
Fresh	Placebo	26	1	2	0	2	0	
Fresh	Drug A	14	1	-1	1	-1	1	
Fresh	Drug A	18	1	-1	1	-1	1	
Fresh	Drug A	15	1	-1	1	-1	1	
Fresh	Drug A	18	1	-1	1	-1	1	
Fresh	Drug A	14	1	-1	1	-1	1	
Fresh	Drug A	11	1	-1	1	-1	1	
Fresh	Drug A	16	1	-1	1	-1	1	
Fresh	Drug A	11	1	-1	1	-1	1	
Fresh	Drug A	8	1	-1	1	-1	1	

Figure 27.   A fragment of Data View showing the use of contrast coding to specify group membership and to carry the main effect and interaction sources of variance

Correlations

		Alert_Coding	Drug1	Drug2	Interaction1	Interaction2
Alert_Coding	Pearson Correlation	1	.000	.000	.000	.000
	Sig. (2-tailed)		1.000	1.000	1.000	1.000
	N	60	60	60	60	60
Drug1	Pearson Correlation	.000	1	.000	.000	.000
	Sig. (2-tailed)	1.000		1.000	1.000	1.000
	N	60	60	60	60	60
Drug2	Pearson Correlation	.000	.000	1	.000	.000
	Sig. (2-tailed)	1.000	1.000		1.000	1.000
	N	60	60	60	60	60
Interaction1	Pearson Correlation	.000	.000	.000	1	.000
	Sig. (2-tailed)	1.000	1.000	1.000		1.000
	N	60	60	60	60	60
Interaction2	Pearson Correlation	.000	.000	.000	.000	1
	Sig. (2-tailed)	1.000	1.000	1.000	1.000	
	N	60	60	60	60	60

Output 27.   The correlation between every pair of coding variables must be zero

To ensure that each effect is tested against the same error term, we must run a simultaneous multiple regression. Proceed as follows:

- Choose **Analyze➜Regression ➜Linear…** to open the **Linear Regression** dialog box. Transfer Score to the **Dependent** slot and the coding variables Alert_Coding, Drug1, Drug2, Interaction1 and Interaction2 to the **Independent(s)** box. Leave the **Method** setting at **Enter**.

- Click the **Statistics** button and check **Estimates, Descriptives, Model fit, R squared change** and **Part and partial Correlations**. Click **Continue** to return to the main **Regression** dialog.

- Back in the main dialog, click the **Save** button and check **Unstandardized** (Predicted Values).

- Click **OK** to run the regression.

The ANOVA table from the regression output is shown in Output 28. The summary table from the GLM ANOVA procedure is shown below for comparison. The two outputs are entirely compatible. The regression sum of squares is the sum of the sums of squares for the main effect and interaction sources in the two-way ANOVA. The Residual sum of squares and degrees of freedom are equal to the Error sum of squares and degrees of freedom in the ANOVA table. The total sums of squares are the same in both tables. The total sums of squares in the two tables have equal values.

Inspection of Data View will show that the regression procedure has saved, as the predicted values, the group means. This will always be so, irrespective of the system of coding used, provided that the number of coding variables is the sum of the degrees of freedom of all the effect sources – which it is in this case.

The Coefficients table is shown in Output 29. At first this may not appear very similar to the ANOVA summary table from the GLM output. Once again, however, the two tables are exactly equivalent. Each contrast sum of squares has one degree of freedom. To generate the GLM ANOVA sums of squares, therefore, we need only square the value of t and multiply it by the error mean square in the regression ANOVA. For example, the sum of squares for the Alertness factor is $3.491^2 \times 21.711 = 264.60$, which is the entry for the SS in the GLM ANOVA summary table. In a similar way, the sum of squares for the interaction is found to be $21.711(3.9967^2 + 3.5291^2) = 617.20$, which is the value given in the GLM ANOVA summary table.

Notice that in Output 29, the values of the part (semipartial) and zero-order (Pearson) correlations are equal. This is because of the system of orthogonal coding that we used to carry group membership. When IVs are correlated, the semipartial correlation is smaller than the correlation between an IV and the DV; but in this example, the orthogonal coding has created a set of uncorrelated IVs.

ANOVA[b]

Model		Sum of Squares	df	Mean Square	F	Sig.
1	Regression	1032.333	5	206.467	9.510	.000[a]
	Residual	1172.400	54	21.711		
	Total	2204.733	59			

a. Predictors: (Constant), Interaction2, Interaction1, Drug2, Drug1, Alert_Coding
b. Dependent Variable: Driving Performance

The regression Residual SS and the ANOVA Error SS have the same value and *df*.

The Regression SS is equal to the sum of the SS's of the ANOVA main effects and interaction sources.

Tests of Between-Subjects Effects

Dependent Variable: Driving Performance

Source	Type III Sum of Squares	df	Mean Square	F	Sig.
Alertness	264.600	1	264.600	12.187	.001
Drug	150.533	2	75.267	3.467	.038
Alertness * Drug	617.200	2	308.600	14.214	.000
Error	1172.400	54	21.711		
Total	2204.733	59			

Output 28. Equivalence of the regression and GLM outputs

Coefficients[a]

Model		Unstandardized Coefficients		Standardized Coefficients	t	Sig.	Correlations		
		B	Std. Error	Beta			Zero-order	Partial	Part
1	(Constant)	16.767	.602		27.873	.000			
	Alert_Coding	2.100	.602	.346	3.491033	.001	.346	.429	.346
	Drug1	-.633	.425	-.148	-1.488956	.142	-.148	-.199	-.148
	Drug2	-1.600	.737	-.216	-2.171746	.034	-.216	-.283	-.216
	Interaction1	1.700	.425	.397	3.996672	.000	.397	.478	.397
	Interaction2	-2.600	.737	-.350	-3.529087	.001	-.350	-.433	-.350

a. Dependent Variable: Driving Performance

Output 29. The Coefficients table

12.6   MULTILEVEL REGRESSION MODELS

Underlying all the methods described so far in this chapter has been a very important assumption, namely, that the observations are independent. Suppose, however, that we are interested in the factors that lead to school success and that we have data on the exam results of a large number of children, together with their scores on a reading test, as well as information about their school's gender admission policy and other variables.

If we are interested in the effect of the children's reading levels on their exam success at school, it might seem natural to regress their school exam scores on their reading scores in the manner described earlier in this chapter. We could easily enter the data into SPSS and apply the methods of least squares regression to estimate the regression coefficient and test it for significance. The difficulty with this approach is that the assumption of independence of observations is manifestly false: it is well known that schools vary considerably in the stringency of their selection processes, their policy with regard to the issue of segregation of boys and girls and so on. For a variety of reasons, therefore, observations from one school are likely to be more similar to one another than they are to observations from another school.

Data of this kind are not a simple random sample from a pool of possible observations, as required by ordinary least squares regression models: on the contrary, they are clustered in an hierarchical fashion: students are nested within schools; schools are nested within districts and so on. Just as the data of children within a particular school will be more similar than the data of children from different schools, there will be characteristics of a district that tend to make data from that district more similar than data from another district. Research in many areas of study (e.g. education and health psychology) typically yield data that are hierarchically clustered in this way.

If the hierarchical dependencies in such a data set are ignored, the consequences can be serious. Ordinary least squares (OLS) regression will produce underestimates of the standard errors of the test statistics and the researcher may be led to conclude that there is strong evidence for non-existent effects. Rasbash et al. (2004) provide some striking examples of the consequences of inappropriate use of OLS regression with clustered data and the different conclusions the researcher would come to using multilevel modelling.

There is now available some excellent software for multilevel or hierarchical modelling, including the SPSS MIXED procedure. Jon Rasbash and his associates (Rasbash et al., 2004) have developed MLwiN, a dedicated package which provides excellent graphical feedback and an interactive learning environment for the user, backed up by an excellent manual and other documentation.

For a readable introduction to multilevel modelling, we recommend Chapter 19 in Andy Field's (2009) book *Discovering Statistics Using SPSS (3rd ed.)*, which discusses the use of SPSS Statistics for multilevel modelling.

12.7   A FINAL WORD

Multiple regression is a highly complex topic and a full treatment is beyond the scope of this book. The following is a small selection from the wide choice of excellent books available.

Recommended reading

Many years ago Jacob Cohen wrote a book on multiple regression which, perhaps more than any other, has made this difficult topic accessible to those other than professional statisticians. The book has continued to be updated and the latest edition has kept fully abreast with recent developments. It is strongly recommended to anyone wishing to make progress in multiple regression.

Cohen, J., Cohen, P., West, S. G., & Aiken, L. S. (2003). *Applied multiple regression/correlation analysis for the behavioral sciences (3rd ed.)*. Mahwah, NJ: Lawrence Erlbaum Associates.

There is a very readable chapter on multiple regression in:

Dugard, P., Todman, J., & Staines, H. (2010). *Approaching multivariate analysis: a practical introduction (2nd ed.)*. London & New York: Routledge.

A more comprehensive, in-depth treatment of multiple regression will be found in:

Tabachnick, B. G., & Fidell, L. S. (2007). *Using multivariate statistics (5th ed.)* Boston: Allyn & Bacon (Pearson International Edition).

The article and book by Darlington are still well worth reading:

Darlington, R. B. (1968). Multiple regression in psychological research and practice. *Psychological Bulletin, 69*, 161 – 182.

Darlington, R. B. (1990). *Regression and linear models*. New York: McGraw-Hill.

Multilevel modelling

The topic of multilevel modelling is introduced in Tabachnick & Fidell (2007), Chapter 15. The manual by Jon Rasbash and his associates would be an excellent follow-up:

Rasbash, J., Steele, F., Browne, W., & Prosser, B. (2004). *A User's Guide to MLwiN Version 2.0*. London: Centre for Multilevel Modelling, University of London.

Exercises

Exercise 20 *Simple, two-variable regression* and Exercise 21 *Multiple regression* are available in www.psypress.com/spss-made-simple and click on Exercises.

The analysis of covariance (ANCOVA)

13.1   INTRODUCTION

In an experiment on the effects upon skilled performance of four supposedly performance-enhancing drugs (A, B, C and D), five groups of participants were tested: (1) a Placebo group; (2) a group who had ingested Drug A; (3) a group who had ingested Drug B; (4) a group who had ingested Drug C; (5) a group who had ingested Drug D.   Output 1 is the **Report** table from the output of the **Means** procedure.

As expected, the performance levels of some of the drug groups, particularly Drug B and Drug C, were somewhat higher than that of the Placebo group.   Output 2, however, which is the summary table of the one-way ANOVA of the data, does not confirm that any of the differences in the Report table is robust to replication of the study: the p-value is 0.065.

Report

Score

Drug Condition	Mean	Std. Deviation
Placebo	22.80	4.881
Drug A	23.81	5.606
Drug B	28.46	4.254
Drug C	26.22	5.143
Drug D	25.93	1.564
Total	25.45	4.772

Output 1.   The report table from the Means procedure

ANOVA

Score

	Sum of Squares	df	Mean Square	F	Sig.
Between Groups	195.479	4	48.870	2.390	.065
Within Groups	920.262	45	20.450		
Total	1115.741	49			

Output 2.   The ANOVA summary table from the One-Way ANOVA procedure

After the experiment had been run, further data on the same participants became available to the research team.   Unknown to the researchers at the time of the experiment, all the participants had previously taken a set of skills tests closely resembling the one used in the experiment.   On that earlier occasion, each participant had received an Aptitude score summarising his or her aptitude for tasks of this kind.   The Aptitude data, it should be emphasised, were unknown to the researchers at the time of the experiment and *played no part in the assignment of the participants to the experimental conditions*: they were added later to the SPSS data file.

The participants' scores in the experiment are likely to have depended partly on their aptitude for such skilled activities, irrespective of the condition under which they were tested.   In this context, a variable such as Aptitude is what is known as a **covariate**.   A covariate is a variable which, although it may have had an influence on the dependent variable in the experiment, is uncorrelated with the treatment factor.   Since the participants were assigned randomly to the three treatment conditions, there should, in this case, be no correlation between Drug Condition and Aptitude.

The **analysis of covariance (ANCOVA)** is a regression technique which corrects for the influence of one or more covariates upon the dependent variable, so that the ANOVA can be run on a set of data that are uncontaminated by the covariate.   In the one-way ANOVA, the between groups variance is compared with the within groups variance.   The purpose of the ANCOVA is to reduce the within groups variance by removing the component associated with the covariate.   After the covariate has been removed, or **partialled out**, the ANOVA is run on the residual scores, with reduction of the degrees of freedom of the error term.   Should the covariate correlate substantially with the DV, the new within groups variance estimate will be smaller than the original value and the *F* test will benefit from an increase in power.

The rationale of the ANCOVA is pictured in Figure 1.   In the upper part of the figure, is a situation in which the factor (IV) in the experiment accounts for some of the variance of the DV. (The proportion of variance accounted for is represented as the shaded area of overlap between the two circles on the left).   The error variance, the proportion of the DV unaccounted for by the treatment factor, is the shaded area on the right.   In the lower part of the figure, is shown the presence of a covariate that correlates with the DV, but not with the treatment factor.   (The circles representing the Factor and the Covariate do not overlap.) When the component of variance shared between the covariate and the DV is removed, the error term for the ANOVA is reduced (as represented by the shaded area on the right), with the result that the power of the ANOVA *F* test is increased.

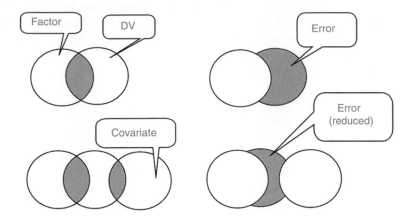

Figure 1. Rationale of the analysis of covariance

The model underlying the analysis of covariance makes two important assumptions. Firstly, it is assumed that the treatment factor is uncorrelated with the covariate. Secondly, it is assumed that, if the dependent variable is regressed upon the covariate within each of the experimental groups, the regression slopes are homogeneous. Both assumptions are very important.

In Figure 1, as we said, the circles representing the treatment factor and the covariate do not overlap: the treatment factor must not be correlated with the covariate. In Figure 2, is shown a situation in which the treatment factor correlates substantially with the covariate, as indicated by the large area of overlap between the Factor and Covariate circles. This could have arisen because participants' scores on the covariate played a role in determining the groups to which they were assigned.

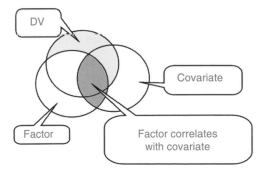

Figure 2. Confounding of the dependent variable with the covariate

Here, the results of the ANCOVA would be impossible to interpret unequivocally. Were we to proceed with the ANCOVA, whatever effects the treatment factor might have had could disappear completely, leaving open the question of which variable, treatment or covariate, was responsible for the differences among the treatment means. In this situation, the covariate and the treatment factor are seriously confounded.

13.2   THE ANCOVA WITH SPSS

In view of the cautions and caveats in the previous section, we shall begin by finding the correlation between the DV and the covariate. A substantial correlation would indicate that the analysis of covariance could result in a more powerful F test. We shall also compare the group means on the covariate. They should have similar values across the groups. We shall also examine the within groups regression lines.

13.2.1 Preliminary analysis

The data are available in the file *Placebo & Four Drugs plus Covariate.sav*, on our website at http://www.psypress.com/spss-made-simple. To find the correlation between the DV (Score) and the covariate (Aptitude), proceed as follows:

- Choose **Analyze➔Correlation➔Bivariate…** to open the **Bivariate correlations** dialog (not shown).

- Complete the dialog in the usual way and click **OK** to run the procedure.

The output shows that there is a substantial correlation between the covariate and the DV: $r = 0.440$.

Turning now to the question of whether the treatment factor and the covariate are correlated, Output 3 is the **Report** table in the output of the **Means** procedure. The table shows clearly that, on the covariate (Aptitude), the means in all five groups have similar values; moreover, the one-way ANOVA shows a value of F near to unity, with a high p-value ($p = 0.497$). It would appear, then, that our data meet the requirement that the covariate should be uncorrelated with the treatment factor.

Report

Aptitude

Drug Condition	Mean	Std. Deviation
Placebo	17.82	4.036
Drug A	19.06	3.118
Drug B	18.49	3.095
Drug C	16.61	3.206
Drug D	18.55	2.541
Total	18.10	3.216

ANOVA

Aptitude

	Sum of Squares	df	Mean Square	F	Sig.
Between Groups	35.897	4	8.974	.858	.497
Within Groups	470.866	45	10.464		
Total	506.762	49			

Output 3. The Report table from the output of the Means procedure

13.2.2 The five within groups regression lines

We shall turn now to the question of whether the data meet the requirement of homogeneity of regression slopes within groups. Proceed as follows:

- Use the **Chart Builder** to draw the scatterplots of the DV against the covariate for the five treatments groups as described in Chapter 4.

- Double-click on any of the scatterplots to enter the **Chart Editor**.

- Click on the icon **Add Fit Line at Total** (Figure 3) to fit the five regression lines (Output 4).

- Close the **Properties** box (which appears with the regression lines), and exit from the **Chart Editor**. (Before leaving the Chart Editor, you may want to remove the caption by clicking it once to get a yellow border and then clicking **Delete**.)

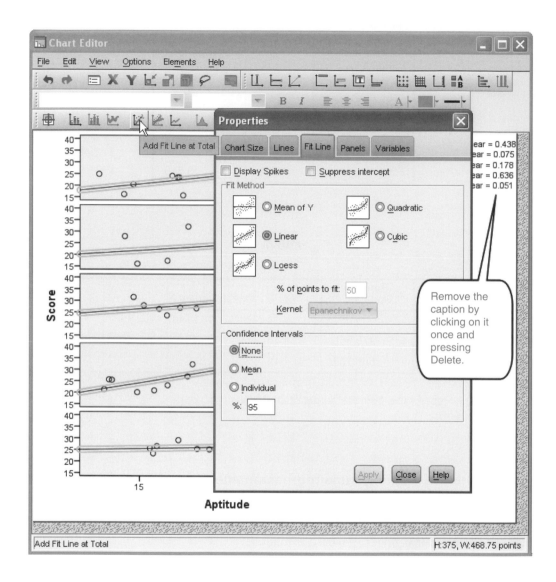

Figure 3. Obtaining the five regression lines

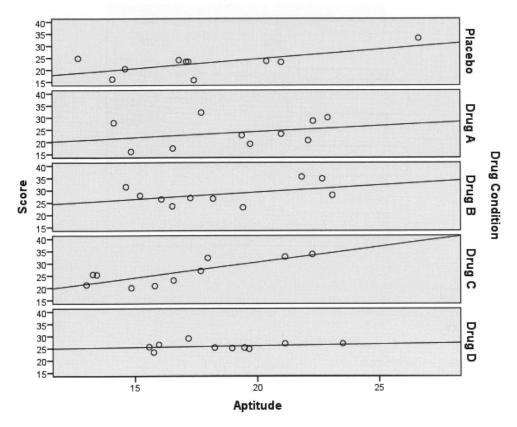

Ouput 4. The five regression lines

The five regression lines all have positive slopes. A mixture of positive and negative slopes would have been cause for serious concern. There are, however, differences among the slopes of the lines: the steepest is within the Drug C group; the flattest is for the Drug D group.

13.2.3 The ANCOVA

- Choose **Analyze➔General Linear Model➔Univariate…** to open the **Univariate** dialog box. Complete the dialog as shown in Figure 4.

The ANCOVA summary table is shown in Output 5, with the original ANOVA table below it for comparison. Clearly, there is now strong evidence against the null hypothesis of equality of the five treatment means: the p-value is given as 0.013.

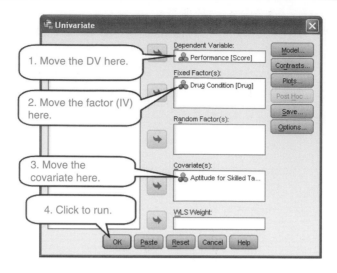

Figure 4. Completing the ANCOVA dialog

Tests of Between-Subjects Effects

Dependent Variable:Score

Source	Type III Sum of Squares	df	Mean Square	F	Sig.
Corrected Model	436.268[a]	5	87.254	5.650	.000
Intercept	218.174	1	218.174	14.128	.000
Aptitude	240.789	1	240.789	15.593	.000
Group	220.095	4	55.024	3.563	.013
Error	679.473	44	15.443		
Total	33489.466	50			
Corrected Total	1115.741	49			

a. R Squared = .391 (Adjusted R Squared = .322)

ANOVA

Score

	Sum of Squares	df	Mean Square	F	Sig.
Between Groups	195.479	4	48.870	2.390	.065
Within Groups	920.262	45	20.450		
Total	1115.741	49			

Output 5. The ANCOVA summary table. (The uncorrected ANOVA summary table from the One-Way ANOVA procedure is shown below for comparison.)

From Output 5, it can also be seen that, the error mean square is now 15.443, whereas it was 20.450 in the ANOVA. The ANCOVA, in reducing the noisiness of the data, has resulted in a more powerful F test, despite the loss of a degree of freedom from the error term.

13.2.4 Further analysis

So far, we have described only the basic ANCOVA analysis. The **Univariate** dialog offers several additional choices, some of which can help to clarify the results of the ANCOVA.

Descriptives

- Choose **Analyze➔General Linear Model➔Univariate...** to open the **Univariate** dialog box. Set up the basic analysis by transferring the variable names in the usual way.

- Click the **Options** button to open the **Univariate: Options** dialog box. Complete the dialog as shown in Figure 5. Click **Continue** to return to the **Univariate** dialog.

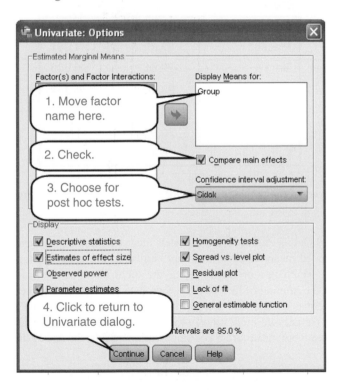

Figure 5. Ordering descriptives and unplanned or post hoc pairwise comparisons

Estimates

Dependent Variable:Score

Drug Condition	Mean	Std. Error	95% Confidence Interval	
			Lower Bound	Upper Bound
Placebo	23.009[a]	1.244	20.503	25.516
Drug A	23.130[a]	1.255	20.602	25.659
Drug B	28.180[a]	1.245	25.672	30.689
Drug C	27.289[a]	1.272	24.726	29.853
Drug D	25.618[a]	1.245	23.109	28.128

a. Covariates appearing in the model are evaluated at the following values: Aptitude = 18.10.

Report

Score

Drug Condition	Mean	Std. Deviation
Placebo	22.80	4.881
Drug A	23.81	5.606
Drug B	28.46	4.254
Drug C	26.22	5.143
Drug D	25.93	1.564
Total	25.45	4.772

Ouput 6. Descriptives of the adjusted scores for the five groups. (The Report table is shown underneath for comparison.)

The upper table in Output 6 shows the adjusted means and standard deviations for the five groups. The amended means have values very similar to those in the **Report** table from the **Means** procedure, which is reproduced under the table of adjusted means for comparison. This is reassuring: the running of the ANCOVA on data sets that do not meet the requirements of factor-covariate dissociation and homogeneity of regression slopes can result in the means being pulled apart (or pressed more closely together) quite disturbingly. Dramatic changes in the values of the treatment means are a contraindication against the use of the ANCOVA.

Pairwise Comparisons

Dependent Variable:Score

(I) Drug Condition	(J) Drug Condition	Mean Difference (I-J)	Std. Error	Sig.[a]	95% Confidence Interval for Difference[a]	
					Lower Bound	Upper Bound
Placebo	Drug A	-.121	1.772	1.000	-5.343	5.101
	Drug B	-5.171	1.762	.052	-10.363	.021
	Drug C	-4.280	1.771	.182	-9.499	.939
	Drug D	-2.609	1.762	.793	-7.803	2.585
Drug A	Placebo	.121	1.772	1.000	-5.101	5.343
	Drug B	-5.050	1.760	.061	-10.238	.138
	Drug C	-4.159	1.813	.236	-9.501	1.183
	Drug D	-2.488	1.760	.834	-7.674	2.699
Drug B	Placebo	5.171	1.762	.052	-.021	10.363
	Drug A	5.050	1.760	.061	-.138	10.238
	Drug C	.891	1.790	1.000	-4.385	6.167
	Drug D	2.562	1.757	.808	-2.617	7.741
Drug C	Placebo	4.280	1.771	.182	-.939	9.499
	Drug A	4.159	1.813	.236	-1.183	9.501
	Drug B	-.891	1.790	1.000	-6.167	4.385
	Drug D	1.671	1.792	.988	-3.610	6.953
Drug D	Placebo	2.609	1.762	.793	-2.585	7.803
	Drug A	2.488	1.760	.834	-2.699	7.674
	Drug B	-2.562	1.757	.808	-7.741	2.617
	Drug C	-1.671	1.792	.988	-6.953	3.610

Based on estimated marginal means

a. Adjustment for multiple comparisons: Sidak.

Ouput 7. Results of the conservative multiple pairwise comparisons

The results of the post hoc multiple pairwise comparisons (Sidak method) are shown in Output 7. We should not be surprised to find that, despite the significant result of the ANCOVA F test, none of the comparisons shows significance: the Sidak adjustment, though less conservative than the Bonferroni method, still results in a very conservative test. The differences among the five treatment means are small. Output 8 shows the **means plot**, which can be ordered from the **Univariate** dialog by clicking the **Plots** button and completing the **Univariate: Profile Plots** dialog as shown in Figure 6.

The default means plot, since it has a microscopic scale on the vertical axis, presents a greatly exaggerated picture of the differences among the means (Output 8a). Double-click on the graph to enter the **Graph Editor** and reset the scale to show zero. The true picture, with the zero now showing on the vertical scale, is shown in Output 8b. The differences among the means are clearly small.

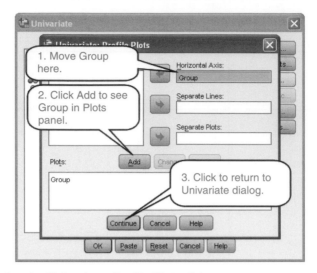

Figure 6. Completing the **Univariate: Profile Plots** dialog

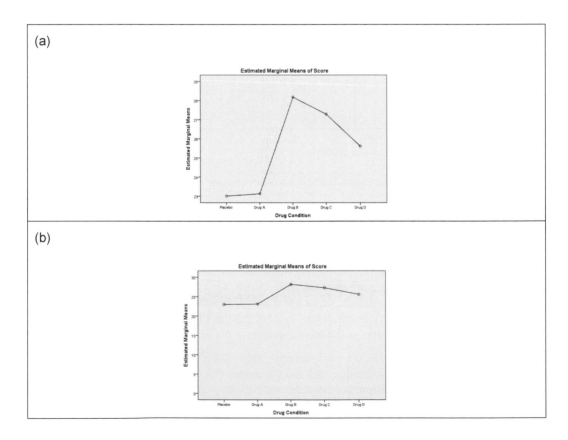

Output 8. The default and edited means plots

Helmert contrasts

The researchers had expected that at least one of the four drugs would enhance performance; on the other hand, they had no expectations about which drug would be the most effective. The GLM version of the one-way ANOVA and ANCOVA does not allow us to specify particular contrasts as we could in the One-Way ANOVA dialog. Instead, we are offered a choice from among several sets of contrasts. If we order a set of Helmert contrasts, the first contrast will be a comparison of the first treatment mean (the mean for the Placebo group) with the average of the remaining means, that is, the mean of the means for Drugs A, B, C and D. This is a contrast the researchers could reasonably have planned to make before the data were gathered.

- Click the **Contrasts** button and complete the **Univariate: Contrasts** dialog, as shown in Figure 7. You must click the **Change** button to register the type of contrast you have chosen from the drop-down menu. Notice that, in the **Factors** box, the word Helmert now appears in brackets after the name of the treatment factor. Check that this has happened before clicking **Continue** to return to the **Univariate** dialog.

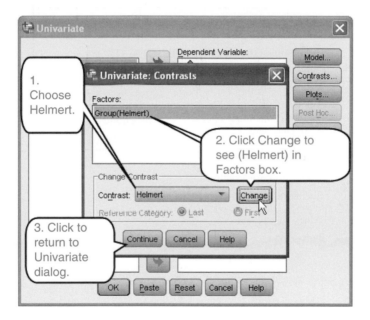

Figure 7. Ordering Helmert contrasts

The results of the tests of Helmert contrasts are shown in Output 9. The first contrast is significant beyond the 0.05 level, a result consistent with the result of the ANCOVA *F* test, which would lead us to expect at least one difference among the means in the array. The second contrast (between the Drug A mean and the other drug means combined) also shows significance; but since this wasn't predicted, we should perhaps view that result with caution.

Custom Hypothesis Tests

Contrast Results (K Matrix)

Drug Condition Helmert Contrast		Depende...
		Score
Level 1 vs. Later	Contrast Estimate	-3.045
	Hypothesized Value	0
	Difference (Estimate - Hypothesized)	-3.045
	Std. Error	1.391
	Sig.	.034
	95% Confidence Interval for Difference Lower Bound	-5.848
	Upper Bound	-.242
Level 2 vs. Later	Contrast Estimate	-3.899
	Hypothesized Value	0
	Difference (Estimate - Hypothesized)	-3.899
	Std. Error	1.451
	Sig.	.010
	95% Confidence Interval for Difference Lower Bound	-6.823
	Upper Bound	-.975
Level 3 vs. Later	Contrast Estimate	1.727
	Hypothesized Value	0
	Difference (Estimate - Hypothesized)	1.727
	Std. Error	1.531

Output 9. Results of the first two Helmert contrasts

13.3   THE ANCOVA AS AN HIERARCHICAL MULTIPLE REGRESSION

In the procedure known as   **hierarchical multiple regression** (Chapter 12),   some variables are forced into the regression equation at an earlier stage than they would be in **simultaneous multiple regression**, in which each variable, as it were, 'goes to the end of the queue'.   In the hierarchical approach, that is, IVs entered earlier get a bigger slice of the cake, in that they are allowed to account for more of the variance of the DV. When there are compelling theoretical reasons for entering a variable earlier, rather than later, the hierarchical approach can be used to test specific causal models and is preferable to simultaneous multiple regression, which puts all the IVs on an equal footing. Hierarchical multiple regression is, arguably, also preferable to a **stepwise** method which, lacking a substantive rationale, would inevitably leave the user wondering what would have happened if other variables had been included in the regression.

The analysis of covariance is essentially an hierarchical multiple regression, in which the first variable entered is the covariate, so that the residual variance of the DV is shared out among the other IVs. The subsequent IVs are coding variables carrying information about group membership. As we saw in Chapter 12, we shall need one fewer coding variables than the number of conditions or groups making up the treatment factor.

13.3.1   Setting up the regression

We shall use **contrast coding** (Helmert contrasts) to identify the groups, as shown in Table 1. The first contrast compares the first (Placebo) mean with an aggregate of the means of the two drug conditions; the second compares the means of the two drug conditions.

Table 1.   Coding group membership with Helmert contrast coding

	X1	X2	X3	X4
Placebo	− 4	0	0	0
Drug A	1	− 3	0	0
Drug B	1	1	− 2	0
Drug C	1	1	1	− 1
Drug D	1	1	1	1

Output 10 is an R-matrix, that is, an array or **matrix** of correlations in which each row (or column) displays the correlations between one variable and the others in the set. The ones in the cells of the **principal diagonal** running from top left to bottom right are the correlations of the tests with themselves. With Helmert contrast coding, the correlation in all off-diagonal cells should be zero.

Correlations

		X1	X2	X3	X4
X1	Pearson Correlation	1	.000	.000	.000
	Sig. (2-tailed)		1.000	1.000	1.000
	N	50	50	50	50
X2	Pearson Correlation	.000	1	.000	.000
	Sig. (2-tailed)	1.000		1.000	1.000
	N	50	50	50	50
X3	Pearson Correlation	.000	.000	1	.000
	Sig. (2-tailed)	1.000	1.000		1.000
	N	50	50	50	50
X4	Pearson Correlation	.000	.000	.000	1
	Sig. (2-tailed)	1.000	1.000	1.000	
	N	50	50	50	50

Output 10. R-matrix of correlations among the contrast coding variables. (The correlations in all the off-diagonal cells are zero.)

13.3.2   Running the regression

- Choose   **Analyze➔Regression➔Linear…**   to open the **Linear Regression** dialog box Complete the dialog as shown in Figure 8.   Note carefully that the covariate is moved to the **Independent(s)** box first and the **Next** button is pressed *immediately*, before further IVs are moved to the box. Pressing **Next** will clear the Independent(s) box of all variable names. This ensures that the covariate will be partialled out before the other IVs (X1, X2, X3 and X4) are entered (together) into the regression equation. Keep the **Method** set at **Enter** throughout, which will ensure that the correct error term is used for the analysis.

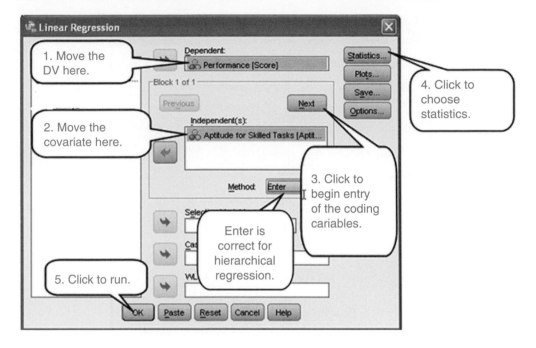

Figure 8. Completing the regression dialog

- After move number 4 (clicking on the **Statistics** button), complete the **Linear Regression: Statistics** dialog as shown in Figure 9.

- Click **OK** to run the hierarchical multiple regression.

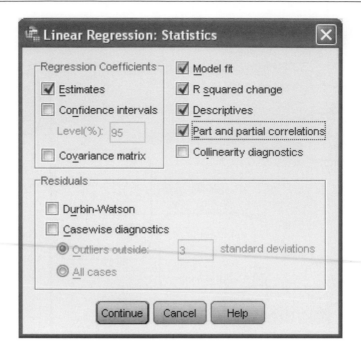

Figure 9. Choosing some statistics

13.3.3 Interpreting the output

The first two items in the output (not shown) are a table of descriptive statistics and the correlations among the variables, including the two contrast coding variables. The third item (Output 11) is a table headed **Variables Entered/Removed**.

Variables Entered/Removed[b]

Model	Variables Entered	Variables Removed	Method
1	Aptitude[a]	.	Enter
2	X1, X3, X2, X4	.	Enter

a. All requested variables entered.
b. Dependent Variable: Score

Output 11. The sequence in which variables were added to the regression equation

Output 11 confirms that the regression proceeded hierarchically, with Aptitude having been entered first, followed by the contrast coding variables representing the treatment factor.

ANOVA[c]

Model		Sum of Squares	df	Mean Square	F	Sig.
1	Regression	216.173	1	216.173	11.535	.001[a]
	Residual	899.568	48	18.741		
	Total	1115.741	49			
2	Regression	436.268	5	87.254	5.650	.000[b]
	Residual	679.473	44	15.443		
	Total	1115.741	49			

a. Predictors: (Constant), Aptitude
b. Predictors: (Constant), Aptitude, X1, X3, X2, X4
c. Dependent Variable: Score

Tests of Between-Subjects Effects

Dependent Variable:Score

Source	Type III Sum of Squares	df	Mean Square	F	Sig.
Corrected Model	436.268[a]	5	87.254	5.650	.000
Intercept	218.174	1	218.174	14.128	.000
Aptitude	240.789	1	240.789	15.593	.000
Group	220.095	4	55.024	3.563	.013
Error	679.473	44	15.443		
Total	33489.466	50			
Corrected Total	1115.741	49			

a. R Squared = .391 (Adjusted R Squared = .322)

Output 12. The ANOVA table from the Linear Regression output

Output 12 (upper table) is the ANOVA summary table from the linear regression. Comparing the values in the table with those in the Tests of Between-Subjects Effects from the Univariate output (reproduced underneath the regression ANOVA table), we see that the Residual source in the regression output has the same value (15.443) as the Error in the Tests of Between-Subjects Effects table from the Univariate output.

The ANCOVA produced a value of F with a p-value of 0.013. Output 13 is the Model Summary for the hierarchical multiple regression. The table shows clearly that, after the covariate has been partialled out, the four contrast coding variables add significantly to the predictive power of the model ($p = 0.013$). This is the p-value given in the ANCOVA summary table. The values of **R** and **R Square** have increased substantially as a result of the removal of the covariate from the regression.

Model Summary[c]

	Model 1	Model 2
R	.440[a]	.625[b]
R Square	.194	.391
Adjusted R Square	.177	.322
Std. Error of the Estimate	4.329	3.930
Change Statistics R Square Change	.194	.197
F Change	11.535	3.563
df1	1	4
df2	48	44
Sig. F Change	.001	.013

a. Predictors: (Constant), Aptitude
b. Predictors: (Constant), Aptitude, X1, X3, X2, X4
c. Dependent Variable: Score

Output 13. The Model Summary. (The Pivot procedure was used to transpose the original table.)

Output 14 is a table showing the regression coefficients.   The p-values given in the Sig. column are exactly the same as those given in the Helmert contrasts output of the Univariate ANCOVA.

Coefficients[a]

Model		Unstandardized Coefficients B	Unstandardized Coefficients Std. Error	Standardized Coefficients Beta	t	Sig.	Correlations Zero-order	Correlations Partial	Correlations Part
1	(Constant)	13.621	3.535		3.853	.000			
	Aptitude	.653	.192	.440	3.396	.001	.440	.440	.440
2	(Constant)	12.499	3.325		3.759	.000			
	Aptitude	.715	.181	.482	3.949	.000	.440	.512	.465
	X1	.609	.278	.258	2.189	.034	.280	.313	.258
	X2	.975	.363	.320	2.688	.010	.250	.376	.316
	X3	-.576	.510	-.133	-1.128	.265	-.184	-.168	-.133
	X4	-.836	.896	-.112	-.932	.356	-.019	-.139	-.110

a. Dependent Variable: Score

Output 14. The regression coefficients

13.4   A FACTORIAL ANALYSIS OF COVARIANCE

For our next example, we shall turn to a two-factor completely randomised factorial experiment of design similar to the one we described and analysed in Chapter 8. (This, however, is a fresh set of data.) As in Chapter 8, the DV was performance in a driving simulator and the factors were Alertness (Fresh, Tired) and Drug Treatment (Placebo, Drug A, Drug B). We shall suppose that, in a manner reminiscent of the one-factor experiment of the previous section, further data have become available to the researchers since the experiment was carried out: the incomes of the parents of the participants tested in the driving simulation experiment. The researchers consider that differences in parental income among the participants might have added to the noisiness of the data and that the analysis would be improved by running an ANCOVA. Once again, we should emphasise that the data on parental income played no part in the assignment of the participants to the experimental conditions at the time of the experiment.

The data are available at http://www.psypress.com/spss-made-simple. The file name is *Factorial ANCOVA.sav*.

The ANOVA and the ANCOVA

The main motivation for the research was the possibility that while one (or both) of the drugs should enhance performance in tired participants, its effects upon well-rested participants had been called into question, raising the possibility of an interaction between the factors of Alertness and Drug Treatment. As usual, we shall run the ANOVA first. Proceed as follows:

- Choose **Analyze➜General Linear Model➜Univariate…** to open the **Univariate** dialog box and opt for the usual extras, such as profile plots and descriptives. The procedure is exactly as in the one-factor experiment, except that when completing the **Univariate** dialog, the two factor names, Alertness and Drug Treatment, are transferred to the **Fixed Factor(s)** box.

The results of the ANOVA are shown in Output 15. They are disappointing: the expected interaction has failed to appear. An examination of the profile plots (Output 16) suggests a tendency towards an interaction; but the formal statistical ANOVA F test does not confirm this.

Tests of Between-Subjects Effects

Dependent Variable:Driving Performance

Source	Type III Sum of Squares	df	Mean Square	F	Sig.
Corrected Model	397.750[a]	5	79.550	1.978	.097
Intercept	90559.350	1	90559.350	2251.579	.000
Alertness	212.817	1	212.817	5.291	.025
Drug	12.900	2	6.450	.160	.852
Alertness * Drug	172.033	2	86.017	2.139	.128
Error	2171.900	54	40.220		
Total	93129.000	60			
Corrected Total	2569.650	59			

a. R Squared = .155 (Adjusted R Squared = .077)

Output 15. The ANOVA summary table from the Univariate output

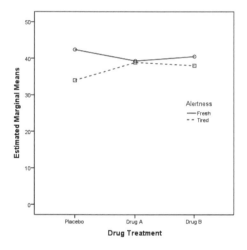

Output 16. The profile plots

- Choose **Analyze➔Correlate➔Bivariate…** to open the **Bivariate Correlations** dialog box, transfer Parents' Income and Driving Performance to the **Variables** box and click **OK** to run the correlation.

The correlation is 0.757, which suggests that, provided there are no contraindications, the ANCOVA should be very effective in reducing the noisiness of the data.

- Choose **Analyze→Compare Means→Means ...** to open the **Means** dialog box, transfer Parents' Income to the **Dependent List** box and Drug Treatment and Alertness to the **Independent List** box. Click Options, check **Anova table and eta**, click **Continue** to return to the **Means** dialog and click **OK** to calculate the mean Parents' Income across levels of the Drug and Alertness factor.

In the **Report** tables for the Alertness and Drug factors (not shown), there are some differences among the group means. In neither case, however, does the one-way ANOVA show significance. The way is clear for the analysis of covariance.

- Choose **Analyze→General Linear Model→Univariate...** to open the **Univariate** dialog box. After transferring the two factor names, Alertness and Drug Treatment to the **Fixed Factor(s)** box, transfer the covariate, Parents' Income, to the Covariate(s) box. Opt for **Profile plots** and **Descriptives** as well (in **Options**), before running the ANCOVA.

The results of the ANCOVA are shown in Output 17. As we should expect from the high correlation between the DV and the covariate, the error term has been reduced very considerably from 40.220 to 17.093. As a result, the test for the interaction term now shows significance: $p = 0.048$. There is now evidence that the Drug factor interacts with Alertness. The profile plots and the Descriptives, however, indicate that the differences among the means are relatively small, so that conservative data-snooping is unlikely to confirm pairwise differences.

Tests of Between-Subjects Effects

Dependent Variable:Driving Performance

Source	Type III Sum of Squares	df	Mean Square	F	Sig.
Corrected Model	1663.746[a]	6	277.291	16.223	.000
Intercept	82.205	1	82.205	4.809	.033
Income	1265.996	1	1265.996	74.067	.000
Alertness	24.694	1	24.694	1.445	.235
Drug	53.102	2	26.551	1.553	.221
Alertness * Drug	110.299	2	55.150	3.227	.048
Error	905.904	53	17.093		
Total	93129.000	60			
Corrected Total	2569.650	59			

a. R Squared = .647 (Adjusted R Squared = .608)

Output 17. The ANCOVA summary table

In Chapter 12, we described how to run a factorial ANOVA as a multiple regression of the DV against coding variables carrying group membership. In Table 2, is reproduced the system of Helmert contrast coding that we used to illustrate the running of the factorial ANOVA as a regression in Chapter 12.

Table 2. A Helmert contrast coding scheme for the Drug experiment

Alertness	Drug	Alert_Coding	Drug1	Drug2	Interaction1	Interaction2
Fresh	Placebo	1	2	0	2	0
Fresh	Drug A	1	-1	1	-1	1
Fresh	Drug B	1	-1	-1	-1	-1
Tired	Placebo	-1	2	0	-2	0
Tired	Drug A	-1	-1	1	1	-1
Tired	Drug B	-1	-1	-1	1	1

In Table 2, the Contrasts carrying the interaction were obtained by multiplying the values of the contrast carrying the Alertness factor by the corresponding values of the contrasts Drug1 and Drug2. As a result, variables Interaction1 and Interaction2 are tests of simple main effects of the Drug factor at the Fresh and Tired levels of the Alertness factor.

Output 18 is the **Coefficients** table from the output of an hierarchical multiple regression of Driving Performance upon Parents' Income (which was partialled out first) and the five contrast coding variables. It is clear from the table that the only significant source (apart from the covariate, Parents' Income) is the final contrast coding variable Interaction2. This a test of the simple main effects of the Drug factor at the Fresh and Tired levels of Alertness.

Coefficients[a]

Model		Unstandardized Coefficients		Standardized Coefficients	t	Sig.
		B	Std. Error	Beta		
1	(Constant)	10.710	3.237		3.309	.002
	Parents' Income	.608	.069	.757	8.827	.000
2	(Constant)	7.958	3.629		2.193	.033
	Parents' Income	.668	.078	.831	8.606	.000
	Alert_Coding	.664	.552	.101	1.202	.235
	Drug1	.521	.390	.113	1.336	.187
	Drug2	.794	.661	.099	1.201	.235
	Interaction1	.215	.393	.046	.546	.587
	Interaction2	1.695	.703	.211	2.412	.019

a. Dependent Variable: Driving Performance

Output 18. The Coefficients table from the output of the hierarchical linear regression of Driving Performance upon Parents' Income and five contrast coding variables carrying the main effects and interaction sources.

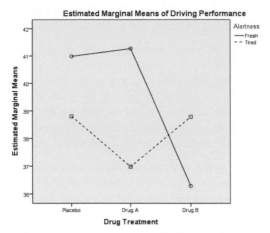

Output 19. Profile plots of Alertness against Drug after removal of the covariate

Output 19 show the profile plots of the mean performance of the Fresh and Tired participants over the three drug conditions. It is quite clear, both from the graph and the result of the test of the contrast in Interaction2, that the significant interaction has been driven almost entirely by a reversal of the simple difference between Drug A and Drug B in Fresh and Tired participants.

Since the research was driven by the question answered by the contrast in Interaction2, this can be regarded as a planned contrast and, arguably, no adjustment to the *p*-value need be made. This example illustrates the ability of the regression approach to pinpoint effects more precisely than is possible with the Univariate procedure for ANCOVA.

13.5   A FINAL WORD

The analysis of covariance is a modication of the analysis of variance and, as such, is most at home in the context of experimental as opposed to correlational research. The technique was designed to utilise additional information about participants to, in a sense, 'clean up' the dependent variable in an experiment and thus reduce the error term in the analysis of variance. The technique requires the presence of a variable known as a **covariate** which, although correlated with the dependent variable, is uncorrelated with the treatment factor or independent variable. The dependent variable is regressed upon the covariate and the analysis of variance is run on the residuals from the regression. Despite the loss of degrees of freedom from the error term arising from the regression, the *F* test is likely to gain power from the reduction in error or data noise.

The analysis of covariance cannot be used to negate the effects of a confounding variable in a piece of research of dubious design. The safe use of the technique carries the important requirement that the covariate must be uncorrelated with the treatment factor. If there is such a correlation, the effect of the analysis of covariance may be a marked change in the values of the treatment means on the residual dependent variable. Such a change, however, leaves open the question of the causal priorities of the treatment factor and the covariate.

If there are adequate numbers of participants and random assignment to the treatment conditions or groups, there should be dissociation between the covariate and the treatment factor. In particular, knowledge of participants' scores on the covariate should play no part in the assignment of participants to conditions or groups. In some applied research situations, however, the principle of random assignment can be difficult to implement. It is easy to imagine situations in which a whole group of participants might become available as a result of their performance on a task other than the dependent variable in the experiment.

A second important assumption in the analysis of covariance is that the slopes of the lines of the regression of the dependent variable upon the covariate should be homogeneous. As with the assumption of dissociation between the treatment factor and the covariate, violation of the assumption of homogeneity of regression within groups can result in marked changes in the treatment means which are confounded with the results of the treatment factor.

This chapter was intended only as an introduction. There are many additional aspects of this topic that lie beyond the scope of this elementary book. The analysis of covariance is much more versatile than we have indicated so far: for example, the technique can be applied to the analysis of the results of factorial experiments with repeated measures on one or more of the factors. The ANCOVA can also be extended to include two or more covariates, so that the dependent variable is estimated by multiple regression of the DV upon the covariates and the ANOVA performed on the residuals. With such additional complexity, of course, come additional potential pitfalls. The ANCOVA is a technique which should be used with great caution.

Recommended reading

As a first port of call, we suggest the informal (but informative) introduction by

Dugard, P., Todman, J., & Staines, H. (2010). *Approaching multivariate analysis: A practical introduction (2nd ed.).* London & New York: Routledge. Chapter 5.

You might follow their highly readable chapter with a more advanced and very much more extensive treatment in

Tabachnick, B. G., & Fidell, L. S. (2007). *Using multivariate statistics (5th ed.).* Boston: Allyn & Bacon (Pearson International Edition). Chapter 6.

The analysis of multiway frequency tables

14.1   INTRODUCTION

The construction of a contingency table is the first step in the investigation of a possible association between categorical variables in a set of nominal data.   In Chapter 11, we described the use of approximate chi-square statistics to test for the presence of an association between two categorical variables: 1. Tissue Type; 2. Presence of an Antibody.

In this chapter, we shall consider the investigation of associations among the variables in multivariate nominal data sets with three or more attributes.   The traditional Pearson chi-square test was designed for use with two-way frequency tables.   The situation often arises, however, in which the researcher has nominal data on three or more attributes and wants to test for associations among the attributes. For many years, the standard approach to this problem was to combine or 'collapse' the frequencies across the categories of some of the variables, thus creating a two-way table, upon which the usual chi-square test could then be made.   This is a dangerous practice.   Todman & Dugard (2007), for example, show how an apparent association between sex and mathematical ability (seemingly revealed by collapsing across a third variable and testing in the usual way) actually arises from the association of both gender and mathematical aptitude with a third variable, namely, the relative lengths of the index and third fingers.   (Later in this chapter, we shall see that there are circumstances in which multiway frequency tables can safely be collapsed across the categories of some variables, but this move must be justified by preliminary analysis.)   It is also possible to generalise the traditional chi-square test to multi-way tables without collapsing across any of the attributes. Such an approach, however, as we shall see, rarely answers the researcher's specific questions.

Recent years have seen great advances in the analysis of multiway contingency tables, and these new methods, collectively known as **loglinear analysis**, are now available in computing packages such as SPSS. Loglinear analysis allows the user to do much more than merely reject the hypothesis of independence of all the variables in the classification, which (when there are three or more attributes) is very unlikely to be true anyway.   The great advantage of loglinear analysis is that it makes possible the formulation of a model of the data that shows the unique contribution of each attribute and of its interactions with the other attributes.

14.2 SOME BASICS OF LOGLINEAR MODELLING

There is little or no advantage in using loglinear analysis to analyse a two-way contingency table: the Pearson and likelihood ratio chi-square tests which we described in Chapter 11 (together with follow-up measures of strength of association) are sufficient for this purpose. In the simple context of the two-way table, however, the essential features of loglinear modelling emerge very clearly; moreover, the comparison with the traditional chi-square analysis of the same data is also instructive. In this section, therefore, we shall apply loglinear analysis to the same data that we analysed in Chapter 11, namely, the incidence of an antibody in four different tissue groups. The data are reproduced in Table 1 below.

Table 1. Contingency table with a pattern of observed frequencies suggesting an association between Tissue Type and Presence of an antibody

Tissue type	Presence		Total
	Yes	No	Total
A	8	14	22
B	7	11	18
C	7	5	12
Critical	21	6	27
Total	43	36	79

14.2.1 Loglinear models and ANOVA models

The full loglinear model of a two-way contingency table is very similar in appearance to the fixed-effects model for the two-factor, between subjects ANOVA. In this subsection, we shall review the ANOVA model before discussing the loglinear model.

Review of the two-way ANOVA model

In the ANOVA model, each score X is expressed as the sum of several components:

1. The **grand mean** μ;

2. A **main effect** of factor A which, in the population, is the deviation of a marginal group mean on the A classification from the grand mean;

3. A **main effect** of factor B, which is the deviation of a marginal mean on the B classification from the grand mean;

4. The **interaction** AB, which is what remains of the deviation of a cell mean from the grand mean when the two main effects have been subtracted;

5. A random **error** component.

The **two-way ANOVA model** states that:

$$X = \begin{bmatrix} \text{grand} \\ \text{mean} \end{bmatrix} + \begin{bmatrix} \text{main effect} \\ \text{of factor A} \end{bmatrix} + \begin{bmatrix} \text{main effect} \\ \text{of factor B} \end{bmatrix} + \begin{bmatrix} \text{AB} \\ \text{interaction} \end{bmatrix} + \begin{bmatrix} \text{random} \\ \text{error} \end{bmatrix} \;\text{- - - (1)}$$

The two-way ANOVA model

A main effect of factor A is estimated with $M_j - M$, the deviation of the mean on the A classification from the grand mean. A main effect of factor B is estimated with $M_k - M$, the deviation of the mean on the B classification from the grand mean. The interaction component AB is what is left of the deviation of the cell mean from the grand mean when the main effects have been removed: $M_{jk} - M_j - M_k + M$.

With the exception of the grand mean, the components of the fixed effects ANOVA model are deviation scores, which have the property that they sum to zero at any level of either factor.

A loglinear model of a two-way contingency table

The full loglinear model for the cell frequencies in a two-way contingency table is similar in form to the ANOVA model:

$$\ln E = \text{constant} + \begin{bmatrix} \text{main effect} \\ \text{of A} \end{bmatrix} + \begin{bmatrix} \text{main effect} \\ \text{of B} \end{bmatrix} + \begin{bmatrix} \text{interaction} \\ \text{AB} \end{bmatrix} \;\text{- - - (2)}$$

A loglinear model

In formula 2, $\ln E$ is the natural logarithm of the cell frequency.

Notice that, rather than modelling an individual score X as in the two-way ANOVA, we are modelling an **aggregate** (the cell frequency) in the contingency table. There is thus no separate random error term in the loglinear model. Rather than modelling the cell frequency itself, we are modelling the natural logarithm of the cell frequency. As we said in Chapter 11, the values of the expected frequencies are derived from *products* of the marginal frequencies in the contingency table. Formula 2 is linear in form because the log of a product is the *sum* of the logs of the factors involved. In fact, there is a multiplicative equivalent of the model in formula 2, in which the expected frequencies themselves (rather than their logs) are modelled as a *product* of main effect and interaction terms. This multiplicative model can be obtained from (2) by taking the antilogs of both sides of the equation.

These differences aside, there are important similarities between the ANOVA and loglinear models. The 'constant' in the loglinear model is the equivalent of the grand mean in the ANOVA model: it is the mean of the logs of the cell frequencies. The main effects are the deviations of the logs of the marginal frequencies from the grand mean of the logs. An interaction effect (there is one for each cell in the table) is what remains of the deviation of the log of the cell mean from the grand mean when the main effects have been removed. As in the two-way ANOVA model, the main effects sum to zero over all the levels of either factor; and the interaction effects sum to zero at any level of either factor.

Although the ANOVA is predicated upon a score model, the ANOVA is not an exercise in modelling as such: the various components of the model (main effects and interactions) are tested for significance and the results are interpreted accordingly. Throughout the testing process, however, the same model remains intact with all its original components, regardless of the outcomes of the tests.

In contrast, loglinear analysis is a process of **model-building**, the aim of the exercise being to find the model which, while having as few components as possible, accounts for the cell frequencies adequately. In the tissue type example, for instance, the hypothesis that the two attributes are independent implies that the cell frequencies can be modelled adequately by omitting the interaction term and retaining only the main effect components of the model.

14.2.2   Model-building and the hierarchical principle

Having identified some important parallels between the loglinear and ANOVA models, we must now consider a very important difference. In the ANOVA, we are dealing with the means of samples of scores. The values of means are independent of the numbers of observations from which they are calculated. In ANOVA, therefore, the values of the various effects are unaffected by the sizes of the samples. In loglinear analysis, however, we are modelling cell frequencies as a function of other frequencies. As a consequence, the values of the marginal frequencies do affect estimates of the main effects and the interaction.

Because of these interdependencies, loglinear modelling should generally follow what is known as the **hierarchical principle**: that is, if an interaction term is included in the model, the main effects of all the factors involved in the interaction must also be included; and if the interaction involves three or more factors, the model must include all the lower-order interactions involving those factors. For example, if the model includes the three-way interaction term ABC, it must also include the main effects A, B and C, plus the two-way interactions AB, AC and BC. In most (though not all) SPSS loglinear procedures, only the interaction term of highest order need be specified: the procedure will automatically **generate** the lower-order effects. Hence a model which includes the effects A, B, C, D, BC, BD, CD and BCD is said to be of **generating class** A, BCD: the term BCD implies the presence in the model of the main effects of B, C and D, and also of the two-way interactions BC, BD and CD.

Saturated models

A loglinear model that contains all possible effect terms is known as a **saturated model**. A saturated model will always predict the observed cell frequencies exactly. In our current example, since the interaction has been defined as the residual difference between the (logs of the) cell frequencies and the grand mean when the main effects have been removed, the sum of the main effects plus the interaction is the (log of the) cell frequency.

Each effect term in a loglinear model has an associated number of degrees of freedom and parameters that must be estimated. In our 4×2 contingency table, the Group variable has $(4 - 1) = 3$ degrees of freedom, the Presence variable has $(2 - 1) = 1$ degree of freedom and the

Group × Presence interaction has $(4 - 1)(2 - 1) = 3$ degrees of freedom. That makes 7 degrees of freedom in total, making 7 parameters that would be estimated with the saturated model. If we add the grand mean, we have as many parameters as there are cells in the contingency table, leaving no room for any deviation from the observed cell frequencies.

Unsaturated models

The purpose of a loglinear analysis is often to see whether the cell frequencies can be adequately approximated by a model that contains *fewer* than the full set of possible treatment effects, subject to the hierarchical constraint. A model that contains fewer than the total number of possible terms is known as an **unsaturated model**.

When there is no association between two variables, the expected frequencies can be accounted for adequately in terms of the marginal frequencies in the table and the model will contain no interaction terms. This model is known as the **total independence** or **main-effects-only** model:

$$\ln E = \text{constant} + \begin{bmatrix} \text{main effect} \\ \text{of A} \end{bmatrix} + \begin{bmatrix} \text{main effect} \\ \text{of B} \end{bmatrix} \text{ - - - (3)}$$

Loglinear main-effects model

Note the absence of the interaction term from this unsaturated model.

The role of the chi-square test in loglinear model-building

When we make a traditional chi-square test for an association in a contingency table, the null hypothesis states that the attributes are independent. On that assumption, expected frequencies are calculated from the marginal frequencies in the table and the chi-square test statistic expresses the extent to which the observed cell frequencies O deviate from the corresponding expected frequencies E. The greater the deviations $(O - E)$ tend to be, the greater the value of chi-square and the stronger the evidence against the null hypothesis of independence. In Chapter 11, we described two versions of the chi-square statistic: the Pearson version and the likelihood ratio version. The likelihood ratio chi-square plays the more important role in loglinear analysis.

In Chapter 11, we observed that the traditional chi-square test is used for two purposes. When we have data on a single variable, we can use the chi-square statistic to measure the extent to which our data are approximated by a theoretical distribution and test the null hypothesis that the data have been sampled from this theoretical population. This is a **goodness-of-fit** test. Where we have data on two attributes in the form of a contingency table, we can use chi-square to test for an **association** between the two attributes. In a test of goodness-of-fit, a *small* value of chi-square indicates a *good* fit. In a test for association, a *large* value of chi-square indicates the presence of an association.

In loglinear modelling, the (likelihood ratio) chi-square statistic is used as a measure of goodness-of-fit of the model to the data. A small value for chi-square indicates a good fit; a large value indicates a poor fit. There are several approaches to loglinear modelling. In the **backward hierarchical** approach, we begin with the saturated model, which we know in advance will predict the cell frequencies exactly. Next, we remove the most complex interaction term from the model. The expected frequencies and LR chi-square are now recalculated on the basis of the simpler model. The effect of this simplification of the model will be to increase the value of chi-square from zero, because there are now fewer parameters in the model than there are cells in the table and the degrees of freedom of the chi-square statistic will increase from zero to the degrees of freedom of the effect that has been removed. This increment in chi-square can be tested to see whether the removal of the interaction significantly worsens the goodness-of-fit of the model to the data. If the goodness-of-fit is not significantly worse, that is, the value of chi-square has not been significantly increased, we remove the term from the model. We continue the process of removing terms, recalculating the expected frequencies and re-testing the **residuals** with chi-square. The process ends when the removal of a term from the model results in a significant increase in chi-square, indicating that the term should be retained in the model. (If the term is an interaction, we must also, in accordance with the hierarchical principle, retain any lower order interactions and the main effects of all the factors involved.)

In the context of loglinear modelling, the likehihood ratio chi-square measure of goodness-of-fit is often known as G^2 (or as the **Goodman statistic**, in honour of Goodman's pioneering work in this area). A great advantage of the Goodman statistic over the traditional Pearson chi-square is that it has the **additive property**: that is, its total value can be apportioned among the different terms being tested, enabling us to see whether the removal of any term from the model makes a significant difference to the model's goodness-of-fit. By 'total value' here, we mean the value of chi-square that we should obtain if we tried to fit the data with a model containing only a constant and no effect terms at all.

The significance of any particular interaction effect is tested with G^2_{effect}, where

$$G^2_{\text{effect}} = G^2_{\text{effect present}} - G^2_{\text{effect absent}} \quad \text{- - - (4)}$$

Testing the increase in chi-square resulting
from the removal of a term from the model

This increase in G^2 is distributed approximately on chi-square with degrees of freedom equal to that of the effect itself.

14.2.3   The main-effects-only loglinear model and the traditional chi-square test for association

The **main-effects-only** model is the equivalent, in loglinear analysis, of the null hypothesis of no association between two variables, which is the hypothesis tested by the traditional chi-square test. In the loglinear analysis of a two-way contingency table, the value of the Goodman statistic will be exactly that of the likelihood ratio chi-square that we described in Chapter 11:

$$\chi^2 = 2 \sum_{\text{all cells}} O \ln\left(\frac{O}{E}\right) \text{ --- (5)}$$

Likelihood ratio chi-square

If r and c are the numbers of rows and columns, respectively, the likelihood ratio chi-square is distributed approximately as chi-square on $(r-1)(c-1)$ degrees of freedom. For the data in Table 1, the value of the likelihood ratio chi-square is

$$\chi^2(3) = 2 \sum_{\text{all cells}} O\left[\ln\left(\frac{O}{E}\right)\right]$$

$$= 2\left[6 \ln\left(\frac{6}{12.3}\right) + 21 \ln\left(\frac{21}{14.7}\right) + \ldots + 14 \ln\left(\frac{14}{10.0}\right) + 8 \ln\left(\frac{8}{12.0}\right)\right]$$

$$= 11.09$$

We shall see that this is exactly the value of G^2 when the interaction term has been removed from the loglinear model and the main effects model is tested for goodness-of-fit.

Note carefully that when we apply the main-effects-only model to the data and run a test of significance, we are not testing the *main effects* for significance: we are testing the increase in the value of chi-square resulting from the *removal* of the interaction term from the model. We are, in fact, testing the *interaction term* for significance.

14.2.4   Analysis of the residuals

As in regression analysis, it is good practice to assess the goodness-of-fit of a loglinear model by examining the distribution of the **residuals** (the differences between the observed and expected frequencies). There are different kinds of residuals, designed for different purposes. The **raw** residuals are obtained by subtracting the expected frequencies generated by the model from the observed frequencies. Other residuals, such as **Adjusted residuals** and **deviance residuals**, have been rescaled, so that they have a mean of zero and a standard deviation of 1. They are more useful than raw residuals for identifying outliers and cells where the estimates of the expected frequencies are particularly poor.

Quantile-quantile Q-Q plots

A special kind of graph, which will be included in the SPSS output if requested, displays the distribution of the residuals. A **quantile-quantile Q-Q plot** is a plot of the quantiles of the standardised scores of the obtained distribution against the values of the standard normal distribution that have the same quantile values. (Quantiles are points taken at regular intervals from the cumulative distribution function of a random variable – the **100-quantiles** are called **percentiles**.) The same range of values of the standard normal variable Z is stepped out on both axes. If the points tend to lie (approximately) along the straight line running diagonally from bottom left to top right, the obtained distribution is normal; non-normal distributions have points that deviate systematically from the line in an obviously non-linear fashion.

Detrended Q-Q plots

In a **detrended Q-Q plot**, the deviations of the scores from the line in the Q-Q plot (i.e. their deviations from expectation) are plotted against their standard scores. If the distribution is normal, all values will lie reasonably close to the horizontal baseline through zero on the vertical axis. The points in the detrended plot should show no obvious pattern: should, for instance, those points on the left tend to lie above the horizontal baseline and those to the right below (or vice versa), non-normality of distribution is indicated.

14.3   MODELLING A TWO-WAY CONTINGENCY TABLE

We shall now run a loglinear analysis of the Tissue Type × Presence contingency table in Table 1. Since we have already explored this table thoroughly in Chapter 11, we can dispense with the preliminaries here and proceed with the loglinear analysis itself.

Follow the usual procedure to enter the data into the **Data Editor**, which will appear as in Figure 1. (To view the value labels rather than the numerical values themselves, check **Value Labels** in the **View** menu or click the label icon at the tops of either of the **Data Editor** windows.)

	Group	Presence	Count
1	Type A	No	14
2	Type A	Yes	8
3	Type B	No	11
4	Type B	Yes	7
5	Type C	No	5
6	Type C	Yes	7
7	Critical	No	6
8	Critical	Yes	21

Figure 1. **Data View** showing the two grouping variables and the counts of presence or absence of the antibody

14.3.1   SPSS procedures for loglinear analysis

Figure 2 shows the menu for loglinear analysis. Any of the three choices on the Loglinear menu will fit a loglinear model to the data. **Model Selection**, however, accesses the HILOGLINEAR program; whereas the **General** and **Logit** choices access the GENLOG program. Here we shall concentrate on the Model Selection choice.

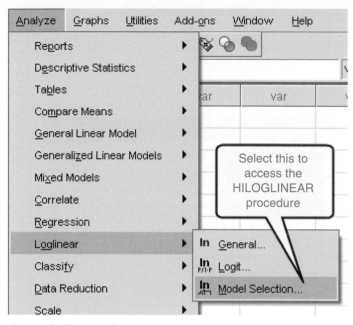

Figure 2. The **Loglinear** menu

Procedure

There are important differences between the HILOGLINEAR and GENLOG programs. (GENLOG is accessed by choosing General from the Loglinear menu.) All three choices from the **Loglinear** menu will produce parameter estimates and tests for significance. **Model Selection**, however, will run a backward elimination analysis and report direct tests of significance of the various components of the model. In our view, this is the easiest way of testing the components of the loglinear model. Tests of the significance of model components can also be made in GENLOG; but in order to make such tests, the user must take extra steps. We shall therefore take the **Model Selection** approach first.

- Select **Data➔Weight Cases…** to open the **Weight Cases** dialog box and transfer the variable Count to the **Frequency Variable** box. Click **OK**. (This move is not necessary for a loglinear analysis; however, loglinear analysis should be run in conjunction with the Crosstabs procedure, which does require that the cases be weighted according to frequency.)

- Select Analyze➔Loglinear➔Model Selection… to enter the Model Selection Loglinear Analysis dialog box (Figure 3).

- Transfer the variable names Group and Presence to the **Factor(s)** panel on the right. Each factor name in the **Factor(s)** box will be followed by the expression (? ?), which is a request for the minimum and maximum values of the code numbers that have been selected for the categories.

- Follow the steps described in Figure 3 to specify the minimum and maximum values of each factor.

- Click **OK** to run the procedure.

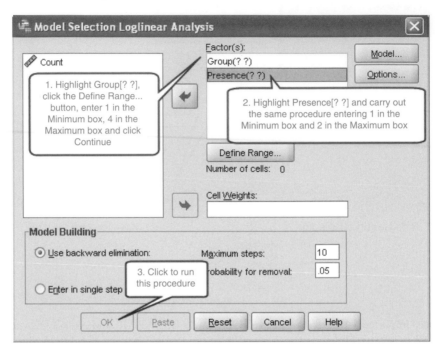

Figure 3.   Defining the range of factor values in the **Model Selection Loglinear Analysis** dialog box.

The output

An early item in the output (not shown here) is a table headed **Convergence Information**. In this table, check that the generating class is given as Group*Presence, which means that SPSS has applied a saturated model to the data.

The next item (Output 1) is a table of **Cell Counts and Residuals**. From this table, it is immediately apparent that the saturated model is a perfect fit: all the residuals are zero. For technical reasons, however, the frequency in every cell in the table has been incremented by 0.5. Later in the **Backward Elimination Statistics** section of the output, however, another table, also with the caption **Cell Counts and Residuals**, appears with the observed frequencies as they were in the original data set.

Cell Counts and Residuals

Tissue Type	Presence	Observed Count[a]	Observed %	Expected Count	Expected %	Residuals	Std. Residuals
Type A	No	14.500	18.4%	14.500	18.4%	.000	.000
	Yes	8.500	10.8%	8.500	10.8%	.000	.000
Type B	No	11.500	14.6%	11.500	14.6%	.000	.000
	Yes	7.500	9.5%	7.500	9.5%	.000	.000
Type C	No	5.500	7.0%	5.500	7.0%	.000	.000
	Yes	7.500	9.5%	7.500	9.5%	.000	.000
Critical	No	6.500	8.2%	6.500	8.2%	.000	.000
	Yes	21.500	27.2%	21.500	27.2%	.000	.000

a. For saturated models, .500 has been added to all observed cells.

Output 1. Table of **Cell Counts and Residuals**, showing that the saturated model predicts the cell frequencies perfectly

The table headed **Goodness-of-fit Tests** (Output 2) shows that the chi-square statistic has no degrees of freedom and hence a value of zero: this is entirely consistent with information in the table of cell counts and residuals.

Goodness-of-Fit Tests

	Chi-Square	df	Sig.
Likelihood Ratio	.000	0	.
Pearson	.000	0	.

Output 2. The **Goodness-of-Fit Tests**. The saturated model leaves chi-square with no degrees of freedom

Note carefully that the test reported in Output 2 is not a test of the significance of any of the components of the model: the chi-square statistic measures any residual difference that might remain (in this case there is none) between the predictions of the model and the actual cell frequencies.

The tests of significance for individual components of the model are reported in the table of **Backward Elimination Statistics**, which is shown in Output 3. In this table, it can be seen that when the interaction term is removed from the model, the value of the **LR chi-square** (i.e. G^2) increases from zero to 11.093 on 3 degrees of freedom. Since this value is significant beyond the 0.05 level, the interaction term must be retained in the model. Note that the value 11.093 is *exactly the value we obtained when we applied the likelihood ratio chi-square formula to the same contingency table.*

Backward Elimination Statistics

When the interaction term is removed from the model, the value of chi-square increases to 11.093

A saturated model leaves chi-square with 0 degrees of freedom

Step Summary

Step[a]		Effects	Chi-Square[c]	df	Sig.	Number of Iterations
0	Generating Class[b]	Group*Presence	.000	0	.	
	Deleted Effect 1	Group*Presence	11.093	3	.011	2
1	Generating Class[b]	Group*Presence	.000	0	.	

a. At each step, the effect with the largest significance level for the Likelihood Ratio Change is deleted, provided the significance level is larger than .050

b. Statistics are displayed for the best model at each step after step 0

c. For 'Deleted Effect', this is the change in the Chi-Square after the effect is deleted from the model

Output 3. Table (edited and annotated) of backward elimination statistics

The process of backward elimination ceases after the first step because, by the hierarchical principle, the retention of an interaction necessitates also the retention of its component factors, Group and Presence.

Output 4 is part of a table with the caption **K-Way and Higher Order Effects**. (In the original table, the Pearson chi-square values were also given. They present a very similar picture to the LR chi-square statistics.) Here the term **Order** refers to the number of factors involved in the effect concerned: a first-order effect (K=1) is a main effect; a second-order effect (K = 2) is a two-way interaction, and so on.

$df_{Group} + df_{Presence}$

K-Way and Higher-Order Effects

	K	df	Likelihood Ratio Chi-Square	Likelihood Ratio Sig.	Pearson Chi-Square	Pearson Sig.	Number of Iterations
K-way and Higher Order Effects[a]	1	7	18.048	.012	20.342	.005	0
	2	3	11.093	.011	10.655	.014	2
K-way Effects[b]	1	4	6.955	.138	9.686	.046	0
	2	3	11.093	.011	10.655	.014	0

a. Tests that k-way and higher order effects are zero.
b. Tests that k-way effects are zero.

$df_{Group} + df_{Presence} + df_{Group*Presence}$

Output 4. Table showing the chi-square values associated with effects at different levels. The upper part of the table gives the chi-square value associated with effects at a level as high as or higher than a specified level; the lower part gives the total chi-square associated with the effects at each level alone

In the upper part of Output 4, the chi-square value opposite each level of effect is the chi-square attributable to all effects at that level, *plus* those associated with any (and every) higher-order effect. The chi-square value for K = 1 (18.048) is the total chi-square value of the two main effects, plus the chi-square value for the two-way interaction. Since there are no effects of order higher than K = 2, the chi-square for K = 2 is, in this example, the chi-square associated with the interaction alone, namely, 11.093.

The meaning of the terms in Output 4 may be clearer upon consideration of the values in the degrees of freedom column. In the upper part of the table, the entries are the total degrees of freedom of all effects at each level, *plus* the degrees of freedom of the effects at all higher levels. Thus at level K = 1, we have the main effect of Group ($df = 3$), plus the main effect of Presence ($df = 1$), *plus* the degrees of freedom of the interaction (3), making seven degrees of freedom in all. At level K = 2, there is only one effect, namely, the interaction ($df = 3$).

In the lower half of the table, the df value for K = 1 is now 4 (not 7), because here we are being given the total degrees of freedom of the effects at one level only. The total degrees of freedom for the two main effects is 4 (1 for Presence plus 3 for Group), which is the value opposite K = 1.

The topmost entry for the LR chi-square (or G^2) is 18.048. This is the total value of chi-square: it is the increment in G^2 that would result from applying a model that contained no effects at all, that is, one containing the constant only. You will see that when we add the two values in the lower part of the table (those associated with the main effects and the interaction), we obtain 18.048, which is exactly the value of the total G^2 in the upper part of the table. (This is also approximately true of the corresponding Pearson chi-square values.)

Notice also that the value of G^2 given for the interaction alone (11.093) is what remains of the total G^2 when the portion attributable to the main effects only (6.955) has been subtracted.

Finally, we note from the entry for K = 1 in the lower part of Output 4 that the tests for main effects do not show significance. The only significant component in the model, therefore, is the interaction.

14.3.2 Fitting an unsaturated model

A saturated model, which contains all possible effect terms, must (as explained earlier) always predict the cell frequencies exactly, as in the present example.

We have just seen, however, that in order to account adequately for the pattern of frequencies in Table 1, we must include the interaction term in the model; otherwise, the value of chi-square increases significantly. We know, therefore, that an unsaturated model containing only main effect terms will fit the data poorly. It is, however, instructive to apply an (albeit ill-fitting) main-effects-only model to the data of our current example, so that we can obtain some of the graphs from SPSS's regression diagnostics. The goodness-of-fit of a model is readily apparent from the appearance of such diagnostic graphs. We shall begin at the point where we have completed the dialog shown in Figure 3. In that exercise, we were then able to proceed with the backward elimination analysis simply by clicking **OK**.

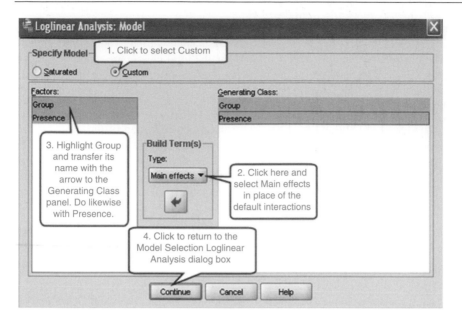

Figure 4. The completed **Loglinear Analysis: Model** dialog, showing that a main-effects-only model has been specified

- This time, click the **Model** button in the top right-hand corner of the dialog box, to obtain the **Loglinear Analysis: Model** dialog box (Figure 4). Follow the steps shown in Figure 4 to specify a main-effects-only model. In the central pillar in the dialog box is the **Build Term(s)** caption, with the **Type** button underneath. The default setting is **Interactions**. Change this setting to **Main effects** and return to **Model Selection Loglinear Analysis**.

- In the **Model Selection Loglinear Analysis** dialog box, click the **Options** button to open the **Loglinear Analysis: Options** dialog box (Figure 5). Select a **Residuals** plot and click **Continue** to return to **Model Selection Loglinear Analysis**.

- Finally click **OK** to run the procedure.

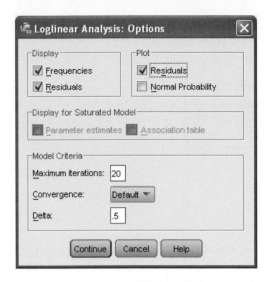

Figure 5. The completed **Loglinear Analysis: Options** dialog

Output for an unsaturated model

The first table in the output (not shown here) is **Convergence Information**. Check that the generating class is given as Group, Presence, not Group*Presence, which was the generating class given when we were fitting a saturated model.

Output 5 shows the plots of observed counts and residuals for our current data set. The fit is now far from perfect: the expected and observed frequencies no longer match and there are non-zero entries in the **Residuals** and **Standardised Residuals** columns.

Cell Counts and Residuals							
Tissue Type	Presence	Observed		Expected		Residuals	Std. Residuals
		Count	%	Count	%		
Type A	No	14.000	17.7%	10.025	12.7%	3.975	1.255
	Yes	8.000	10.1%	11.975	15.2%	-3.975	-1.149
Type B	No	11.000	13.9%	8.203	10.4%	2.797	.977
	Yes	7.000	8.9%	9.797	12.4%	-2.797	-.894
Type C	No	5.000	6.3%	5.468	6.9%	-.468	-.200
	Yes	7.000	8.9%	6.532	8.3%	.468	.183
Critical	No	6.000	7.6%	12.304	15.6%	-6.304	-1.797
	Yes	21.000	26.6%	14.696	18.6%	6.304	1.644

Output 5. **Cell Counts and Residuals** table when the main-effects-only model is applied

Output 6 summarises the **Goodness-of-fit Tests**. The significant increase in G^2 shows that the main-effects-only (independence) model is not a good fit for these data.

Goodness-of-Fit Tests

	Chi-Square	df	Sig.
Likelihood Ratio	11.093	3	.011
Pearson	10.655	3	.014

Output 6. Summary of the **Goodness-of-Fit Tests**

The values of the **Likelihood Ratio** and **Pearson Chi-Square** in Output 6 are exactly the same as those we obtained by the backward elimination analysis in the previous section. They are also the values we obtain when we make the traditional chi-square test of association between Presence and Group. The significance test for the goodness-of-fit of a main-effects-only loglinear model is the exact equivalent of the traditional chi-square test for association, in which the null hypothesis is that the two variables are independent.

It may be worth repeating our earlier point that the test reported in Output 6 is a test of the component *omitted* from the model, not of those remaining in the model. The test of G^2 when the main-effects-only model is applied is a test of the *interaction* component of the full model.

The residual plots

If a loglinear model is a good fit and the observed cell counts are plotted against the expected counts from the loglinear model, the points on the graph should lie close to a straight line. Another characteristic of a good fit is that both the adjusted and deviance residuals should have approximately normal distributions. Thirdly, a plot of either kind of residual against the expected values should result in an amorphous cloud of points, and there should be no outstandingly large values.

Output 7 shows what the residual plots would look like if the main-effects-only model were a good fit for the data, as it would be with a data set showing no association between Group and Presence. Only the cells either above or below the diagonal of blank cells are relevant: the cells on the other side simply reproduce the same plots with the axes reversed. The data from which Output 7 was obtained are available in the file *Ch14 Tissue Type (Main Effects Only).sav* on our website at http://www.psypress.com/spss-made-simple.

Hiloglinear Model

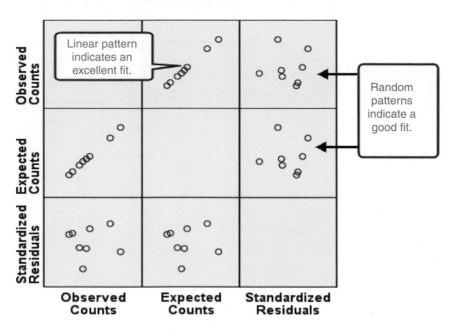

Cases weighted by Count

Output 7. Plots of **Observed Counts, Expected Counts** and **Standardized Residuals** when a model fits the data well

The strongly linear pattern in the plot of observed counts against expected counts indicates an excellent fit, as do the shapeless plots of observed counts against standardised residuals.

Output 8 shows the plots of counts and residuals for the data in our current example (the data in Table 1). The plots clearly do not meet the criteria for a good fit: the plot of observed counts against expected counts is far from linear; and the plots of the observed and expected counts against the standardised residuals show patterns that are far from random.

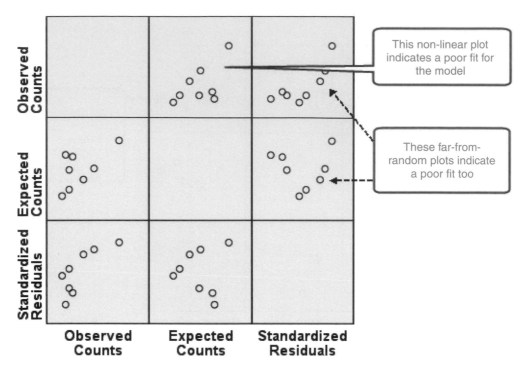

Output 8. Plots of **Observed Counts, Expected Counts** and **Standardized Residuals** for the data in Table 1 showing that the main-effects model fits the data poorly

14.3.3   Summary

The purpose of the foregoing sections has been to introduce the fundamentals of loglinear modelling in the simplest possible context and to familiarise the reader with the general procedure and the main features of the output. As we said in Section 14.1, if you actually have a two-way contingency table you want to analyse, you should use one of the chi-square tests described in Chapter 11: there would be no advantage in running a loglinear analysis (although that would produce the same result). In the next section, however, the essential features we have discussed in this section will be put to good use in the analysis of a three-way frequency table, where the loglinear analysis has great advantages over the traditional chi-square approach. Faced with a more complex table, loglinear modelling can not only confirm the existence of associations among the data, but also pinpoint the precise nature of those associations.

14.4   MODELLING A THREE-WAY FREQUENCY TABLE

We shall illustrate the loglinear modelling of a three-way frequency table with some data from an imaginary experiment on gender and helpfulness. Suppose that male and female interviewers asked 50 male and 50 female participants whether, in a hypothetical situation, they would offer to help someone in difficulties. The factors of sex of interviewer and sex of participant were varied orthogonally, so that each of 50 male and 50 female interviewers interviewed 25 male and 25 female participants.

The purpose of the investigation was not to compare the helpfulness of the sexes, but to test the opposite-sex dyadic hypothesis, which holds that, in certain pre-specified circumstances, we are more likely to help someone of the opposite sex than someone of our own.

14.4.1   Exploring the data

The data are shown in Table 2. They are available in the file *Helping (Three-way Interaction Only).sav*, available at http://www.psypress.com/spss-made-simple. We suggest, however, that it would be a valuable exercise to enter the data by following the instructions below.

Table 2. Three-way contingency table showing the results of the gender and helpfulness experiment

Sex of Interviewer	Sex of Participant	Would you help?		
		Yes	No	Total
Male	Male	4	21	25
	Female	16	9	25
Female	Male	11	14	25
	Female	11	14	25
	Total	42	58	100

The measures known as the **odds** and the **odds ratio (OR)** were introduced in Chapter 11. There, we used them to explore the pattern of the frequencies in a two-way contingency table. These measures can also be used to explore more complex frequency tables, provided at least two of the factors are dichotomies.

What is the effect of the sex of the interviewer on whether male participants will help or not? When the interviewer is male (first row of entries in the table), the odds in favour of males helping are 4/21 = 0.190. When the interviewer is female (third row of data in the table), the odds in favour of males helping are 11/14 = 0.786. Male participants, then, are more likely to help when the interviewer is female. The OR is 0.786/0.190 = 4.13: that is, male participants are four times as likely to help when the interviewer is a female.

When we turn to the female participants, we find that, when we compare their helpfulness with male and female interviewers, the odds ratio is 2.26. Again, the participants are more likely to help someone of the opposite sex than one of their own. A superficial exploration of the data, therefore, seems to confirm the opposite-sex dyadic hypothesis.

Suppose for a moment that instead of recording whether someone was prepared to help or not, we had taken some continuous measure of helpfulness on an independent scale with units. We should then have had an experiment of between subjects, two-factor design and could consider running an ANOVA on the data. The opposite-sex dyadic hypothesis implies what, in the context of ANOVA, would be a two-way interaction between Sex of Participant and Sex of Interviewer. In the present context of loglinear modelling, however, the same hypothesis implies a *three-way* interaction between the factors of Sex of Participant, Sex of Interviewer and whether Help was given. Here, the Help × Sex of Participant interaction has replaced the continuous measure of helpfulness. In Chapter 9, we saw that a three-way interaction is said to occur when the interaction between two of the variables is not homogeneous across the levels of the third factor. In the present example, the opposite-sex dyadic hypothesis implies that the interaction between Gender and Help will be different with male and female interviewers: with male interviewers, females will be more helpful than they would be with female interviewers; with female interviewers, the reverse pattern should be obtained.

14.4.2   Loglinear analysis of the data on gender and helpfulness

An important consideration before embarking upon a loglinear analysis of a multiway frequency table is whether the data are sufficiently numerous to meet the requirements of loglinear modelling. According to Tabachnick and Fidell (2007; p862), there should be at least five times as many cases as there are cells in the multiway table. Those authors also recommend that, in every possible two-way contingency table, all expected frequencies must be greater than 1 and no more than 20% should be less than 5. Since, in our data set, there are 100 cases and 8 cells in the multiway table, the first criterion is satisfied. We can test the data on the second criterion by using **Crosstabs** to create three two-way tables (Interviewer × Help, Participant × Help and Participant × Interviewer) and calculate the expected frequencies for each table.

Procedure

Proceed as follows:

- In **Variable View**, create three grouping variables: *Participant (Sex of Participant), Interviewer (Sex of Interviewer), Help (Would you help?)* and a fourth variable, *Count*, for the frequencies. Use the **Values** column to assign values to the code numbers, such as, for the *Help* variable, 1 = Yes, 2 = No. The complete SPSS data set is shown in Figure 6.

- We now need to weight the cases with the frequencies in Count. (This step would not be required if the data consisted of records of individual cases.) Choose **Data➔Weight Cases…** to open the **Weight Cases** dialog box and transfer the variable Count to the **Frequency Variable** box. Click **OK**.

	Interviewer	Participant	Help	Count
1	Male	Male	Yes	4
2	Male	Male	No	21
3	Female	Male	Yes	11
4	Female	Male	No	14
5	Male	Female	Yes	16
6	Male	Female	No	9
7	Female	Female	Yes	11
8	Female	Female	No	14

Figure 6. **Data View** showing the Gender and Helping data set

- The next stage is to confirm, with **Crosstabs**, that the expected frequencies are sufficiently large. (The procedure is described in Section 11.5.5.) The output tables (which we have omitted) show that no cell has an expected frequency of less than 1 and over 80% of cells have expected frequencies of 5 or more. We have, therefore, sufficient data for a loglinear analysis.

> See Section 11.5.5

- Select **Analyze→Loglinear→Model Selection...** to open the **Model Selection Loglinear Analysis** dialog box (the completed version is shown in Figure 8).

- Follow the steps in Figure 7. You will notice that, since each variable contains two categories, to which we have consistently assigned the values 1 and 2, we need only complete the **Define Range** dialog once; had the variables had different numbers of categories or different values been used from variable to variable, it would have been necessary to enter the ranges separately for each grouping variable.

- The default model is **backward elimination**. Makes sure its radio button is on.

- Click **OK**.

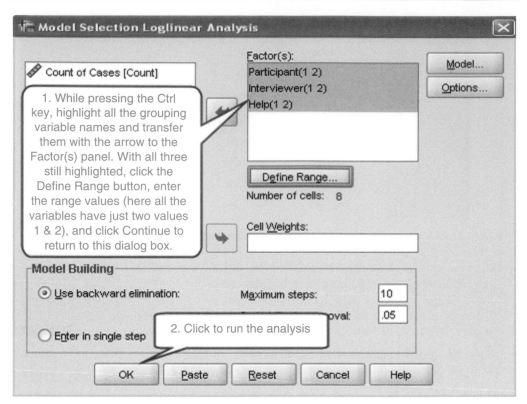

Figure 7. The completed **Model Selection Loglinear Analysis** dialog box for three factors

The output for the loglinear analysis

The first table in the output (Output 9) lists the number of cases and the names of the variables (factors) in the analysis. Check that the information is consistent with the design of the experiment as we have described it: in this example, there should be three factors, each having two levels. In Output 10, the factors, Help, Interviewer and Participant, are listed under the heading 'Categories'.

Data Information

		N
Cases	Valid	8
	Out of Range[a]	0
	Missing	0
	Weighted Valid	100
Categories	Sex of Interviewer	2
	Sex of Participant	2
	Would you help?	2

a. Cases rejected because of out of range factor values.

Output 9. Information about the number of cases and the category names (factors)

The next item (not shown here) is a table listing the observed and expected counts for the combinations of the three factors. At this stage, SPSS is fitting a **saturated model**, with generating class Sex of Interviewer × Sex of Participant × Help. In this section of the output, therefore the observed and expected frequencies have the same values.

The third item in the output, with the caption **K-Way and Higher-Order Effects** (Output 10), lists the results of the statistical tests for the various effects. As explained in Section 14.3.1, the term *Order* denotes the number of factors involved in the effect concerned: a first-order effect (K=1) is a main effect; a second-order effect (K = 2) is a two-way interaction, and so on. In the present example, there is one three-way interaction (K = 3).

In the upper part of Output 10, the chi-square value opposite each level of effect is the chi-square attributable to all effects at that level, *plus* that associated with any (and every) higher-order effect. The chi-square value for K = 1 (15.382) is the *total* of the chi-squared values for the three main effects, the three two-way interactions and the three-way interaction. This is clear from the degrees of freedom: 3 (main effects) + 3 (two-way interactions) + 1 (three-way interaction) = 7, the value given in the degrees of freedom column opposite K = 1 in the upper half of the table. Since there are no effects of order higher than K = 3, the chi-square for K = 3 is the chi-square associated with the three-way interaction alone (6.659), on one degree of freedom.

In the lower half of the table, the value of the degrees of freedom for K = 1 is now 3 (not 7), because now we are being given the degrees of freedom associated with *one* level only. The total degrees of freedom for the three main effects alone is 3, which is the value opposite K = 1 in the lower part of the table. The chi-square value (and degrees of freedom) are the same for K = 3 in both the upper and the lower parts of the table, because in either case, there is just one three-way interaction. From the entries for K = 3 in either half of the table, we see that, as we should expect from the hypothesis, there is indeed a significant three-way interaction (Sex of Interviewer × Sex of Participant × Help) : Chi-Square = 6.659 on one degree of freedom; *p* = .01.

From the lower part of Output 10, which gives the results of tests of the individual components of the model, we also learn that no other effect makes a significant contribution to the total chi-square value, as can be seen from the *p*-values in the rows for K = 1 and K = 2. The loglinear analysis, therefore, has given us something that the traditional chi-square test cannot offer: a direct test for a three-way interaction.

The fourth part of the SPSS output, the **Backward Elimination Statistics** (Output 11) shows that the saturated model containing the three-way interaction is the best one for the data, because removal of the interaction term would result in a significant increase in Chi-square. At Step 1, the saturated model is therefore adopted as the final model.

The loglinear analysis has confirmed the opposite-sex dyadic hypothesis, which implies that the best-fitting loglinear model contains the three-way interaction term.

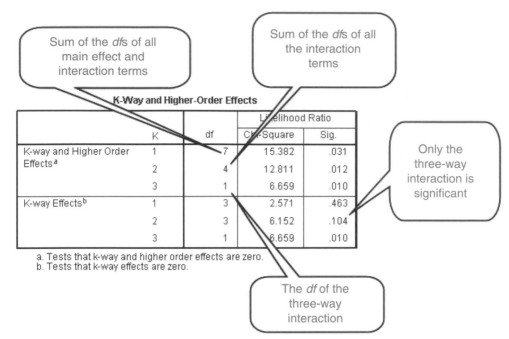

Sum of the *df*s of all main effect and interaction terms

Sum of the *df*s of all the interaction terms

K-Way and Higher-Order Effects

	K	df	Likelihood Ratio Chi-Square	Sig.
K-way and Higher Order Effects[a]	1	7	15.382	.031
	2	4	12.811	.012
	3	1	6.659	.010
K-way Effects[b]	1	3	2.571	.463
	2	3	6.152	.104
	3	1	6.659	.010

a. Tests that k-way and higher order effects are zero.
b. Tests that k-way effects are zero.

Only the three-way interaction is significant

The *df* of the three-way interaction

Output 10. Part of the **Tests of Effects** table. The subscripts P, I and H represent Participant, Interviewer and Help respectively

Backward Elimination Statistics

Since deletion of the three-way interaction term results in a significant increase in chi-square, this term must be retained in the final model

Step Summary

Step[a]		Effects	Chi-Square[c]	df	Sig.	Number of Iterations
0	Generating Class[b]	Participant*Interviewer*Help	.000	0	.	
	Deleted Effect 1	Participant*Interviewer*Help	6.659	1	.010	2
1	Generating Class[b]	Participant*Interviewer*Help	.000	0	.	

a. At each step, the effect with the largest significance level for the Likelihood Ratio Change is deleted, provided the significance level is larger than .050
b. Statistics are displayed for the best model at each step after step 0
c. For 'Deleted Effect', this is the change in the Chi-Square after the effect is deleted from the model

Output 11. The final model for the gender and professed helpfulness data

14.4.3   The main-effects-only model and the traditional chi-square test

The formula for the likelihood ratio chi-square statistic (and indeed the Pearson formula also) can readily be adapted for use with multiway contingency tables. We can represent a three-way frequency table as a set of two-way tables, one at each level of the third attribute, where r and c are the number of rows and columns in each table and each table is said to be at a different **layer** of the third attribute, which has l layers. Let R, C and L be the marginal totals associated with a particular combination of the categories of the three attributes. By extension of the reasoning for the two-way contingency table, the expected cell frequency E under the null hypothesis of total independence among the three attributes is given by

$$E = \frac{R}{N} \times \frac{C}{N} \times \frac{L}{N} \times N = \frac{RCL}{N^2} \ \text{- - - (6)}$$

Expected cell frequency for total independence model

For the three-way frequency table, the likelihood ratio chi-square statistic is

$$\chi^2 = 2 \sum_{\text{all cells}} O \ln\left(\frac{O}{E}\right) \ \text{- - - (7)}$$

The LR Chi-square

This statistic is distributed approximately as chi square on $(r-1)(c-1)(l-1)$ degrees of freedom.

Table 3 shows the observed frequencies O, together with the expected frequencies E for each of the eight cells in the frequency table of the results of the helping experiment. Also given are the marginal total frequencies for the three variables: Sex of Participant; Sex of Interviewer; Help.

For example, we can use (6) to calculate the expected frequency of the first cell in Table 3(a) (Male Interviewer, Male Participant, Help Given) using the values of the marginal totals in Table 3(b) :.$(50 \times 50 \times 42)/100^2 = 10.5$. The expected frequencies for the other cells are found in a similar way. Applying the likelihood ratio chi-square formula, we have

$$\chi^2 = 2 \sum_{\text{all cells}} O \ln\left(\frac{O}{E}\right)$$

$$= 2\left[4 \times \ln\left(\frac{4}{10.5}\right) + 21 \times \ln\left(\frac{21}{14.5}\right) + \dots + 14 \times \ln\left(\frac{14}{14.5}\right) \right]$$

$$= 12.81$$

This value is significant beyond the 0.05 level: (

Table 3. Observed and expected frequencies for the data in Table 2. (In (a), the expected frequencies are shown in brackets.)

(a) Table of observed and expected frequencies

Sex of Interviewer	Sex of Participant	Was Help Given? Yes	Was Help Given? No
Male	Male	4 (10.5)	21 (14.5)
	Female	16 (10.5)	9 (14.5)
Female	Male	11 (10.5)	14 (14.5)
	Female	11 (10.5)	14 (14.5)

(b) Marginal row and column frequencies

Sex of Interviewer		Sex of Participant		Was Help Given?	
Male	Female	Male	Female	Yes	No
50	50	50	50	42	58

Goodness-of-Fit Tests

	Chi-Square	df	Sig.
Likelihood Ratio	12.811	4	.012
Pearson	11.987	4	.017

Output 12. The result of the goodness-of-fit test of the main-effects-only model

Output 12 shows the result of the goodness-of-fit test of the main-effects-only model. The value of chi-square is exactly the same as the one we have just calculated from the extension of the usual likelihood ratio formula.

The test of the main-effects-only model is the exact equivalent, in loglinear analysis, of the traditional chi-square test for an association. The problem with the traditional chi-square test is that it can merely reject the total independence (main-effects-only) model. This is fine if there are only two attributes: since in that situation only one association is possible, the interpretation of a significant result is unequivocal. With multiway frequency tables, however, a significant result tells us only that there are at least some dependencies among the variables: it cannot tell us which of several possible effects is responsible for the pattern of frequencies in the frequency table. Could these cell frequencies have arisen from one or more of the possible two-way interactions? Does the three-way interaction account for a significant portion of the chi-square value? Only modern methods such as loglinear analysis can provide the answers to such questions.

14.4.4   Collapsing a multi-way table: the requirement of conditional independence

We might reasonably ask another question of our data: are female participants more inclined to help than male participants? The traditional approach to this question was to create a two-way table by 'collapsing' across the levels of the Interviewer variable. By adding the data for the male interviewers to that of the female interviewers, we can produce a two-way table in which only the variables of Sex of Participant and Help remain. We have already said, however, that there are dangers in 'collapsing' a table in this way. In Output 13, the variable Sex of Interviewer has disappeared and, in both the table and the clustered bar chart, we see a pattern of cell frequencies suggesting that there may be a tendency for female participants to be more helpful. Moreover, this impression is seemingly confirmed by formal statistical testing: **Fisher's Exact** two-tailed probability = 0.03. On the other hand, we have previously seen that the loglinear analysis does not confirm *any* of the two-way interactions: the only statistically robust effect to emerge from the loglinear analysis is a three-way interaction.

Helpfulness in male and female participants: p = .025

Count

| | | Would you help? | | |
		Yes	No	Total
Sex of Participant	Male	15	35	50
	Female	27	23	50
Total		42	58	100

Output 13. Collapsed table, showing levels of helpfulness in male and female participants

Our variables are Help, Participant and Interviewer. In collapsing the three-way table across the Interviewer variable to obtain a two-way Help × Participant table, we have ignored the fact (confirmed by the three-way interaction that emerged from the loglinear analysis) that the Interviewer variable is correlated with the interaction between the other two variables and therefore confounds the simple comparison of males and females on helpfulness.

An important concept in loglinear modelling is that of **conditional independence**. Two variables A and B are said to be conditionally independent at one level of a third variable C if, at that level of C, they show no association. Only if A & B are conditionally independent at *every* level of C, is it permissible to collapse the frequency table across C to investigate the association between A and B with a traditional chi-square test. In our example, A, B and C are Help, Participant and Interviewer, respectively. If we follow the Select Cases procedure and test for an association between Help and Participant in the male inverviewers, we find a striking tendency for the females to be more helpful: $\chi^2(1) = 12.647$; $p < 0.01$. If, however, we make a similar test with the female interviewers, we find no such tendency: $\chi^2(1) = 0$; $p = 1$.) Clearly the requirement of conditional independence of A and B (Help and Participant) at all levels of C (male and female interviewers) has not been met and it is unsafe to collapse the three-way table by combining the data for the male and female interviewers.

A stronger case can be made for collapsing the data across the Participant variable and studying the association between Interviewer and Help. It will be found that if tests for association between Interviewer and Help are made on the data from the male and female participants separately, the chi-square test fails to show significance in either case. When the three-way table is collapsed across Participants (i.e. the data for male and female participants are combined so that we have a two-way Interviewer × Help table), the chi-square test fails to provide evidence for an association. This result is consistent with that of the loglinear analysis.

14.4.5   An alternative data set for the gender and helpfulness experiment

The presence of a three-way interaction, together with the absence of any other significant effects, made the interpretation of the output of the gender and helping experiment very simple. Often, however, several steps will be needed to locate the significant effects. Let us suppose that the data from the gender and helping experiment had been as in Table 4. The data are in the file *Helping (ComplexResult).sav*, which is available on our website at http://www.psypress.com/spss-made-simple.

Table 4. Three-way contingency table showing a more complex outcome of the gender and helping experiment

Sex of Interviewer	Sex of Participant	Would you help?		Total
		Yes	No	
Male	Male	4	10	14
	Female	10	20	30
Female	Male	47	10	57
	Female	58	17	75
	Total	119	57	176

Notice that in Table 4, the row marginal totals show some variation: there were differences both in the numbers of male and female interviewers and in the numbers of male and female participants.

In the table of **Convergence Information** (Output 14), we learn that the generating class is Interviewer*Help, Participant. Remembering the hierarchical principle by which the retention of an interaction term in the model requires the retention of all lower order effect involving the factors in the interaction, we write the final model as follows:

$$\ln(E) = \text{constant} + \begin{bmatrix} \text{main effect} \\ \text{of} \\ \text{Interviewer} \end{bmatrix} + \begin{bmatrix} \text{main effect} \\ \text{of} \\ \text{Help} \end{bmatrix} + \begin{bmatrix} \text{Interviewer} \times \text{Help} \\ \text{interaction} \end{bmatrix} + \begin{bmatrix} \text{main effect} \\ \text{of} \\ \text{Participant} \end{bmatrix} \text{-- (8)}$$

Final loglinear model

This unsaturated model fits the data quite well: the table of **Cell Counts and Residuals** (not shown) shows no residual value larger than 0.713. The **Goodness-of-Fit Tests** (Output 15) show that G^2 is small and insignificant, confirming the appearance of the table of observed and expected frequencies.

Convergence Information[a]

Generating Class	Interviewer*Help, Participant
Number of Iterations	.000
Max. Difference between Observed and Fitted Marginals	.000
Convergence Criterion	.250

a. Statistics for the final model after Backward Elimination.

Output 14 The Convergence Information table in the Backward Elimination Statistics section of the output

Goodness-of-Fit Tests

	Chi-Square	df	Sig.
Likelihood Ratio	2.435	3	.487
Pearson	2.393	3	.495

Output 15. **Goodness-of-Fit Tests** for the unsaturated model

Output 16 shows the table of **K-Way and Higher-Order Effects**. The total **Likelihood Ratio Chi-Square** (G^2) is 110.282; but, unlike the equivalent table from the analysis of the previous data set, most of this value is accounted for by main effects and two-way interactions. There is no evidence for a three-way interaction in these data and therefore no support for the opposite-sex dyadic hypothesis.

K-Way and Higher-Order Effects

	K	df	Likelihood Ratio		Pearson		Number of Iterations
			Chi-Square	Sig.	Chi-Square	Sig.	
K-way and Higher Order Effects[a]	1	7	110.282	.000	123.000	.000	0
	2	4	35.310	.000	37.077	.000	2
	3	1	.431	.512	.425	.514	4
K-way Effects[b]	1	3	74.972	.000	85.923	.000	0
	2	3	34.879	.000	36.651	.000	0
	3	1	.431	.512	.425	.514	0

a. Tests that k-way and higher order effects are zero.

b. Tests that k-way effects are zero.

Output 17. The K-Way and Higher-Order Effects table

Output 17 shows the **Backward Elimination Statistics**. At Step 0, a saturated model is applied first, after which the three-way interaction is tested by fitting a model with the three-way component absent. Since there is no significant increase in G^2, the three-way interaction term is dropped from the model.

At Step 1, each of the three two-way interactions is tested by removing it from the model. Only for the Interviewer × Help interaction is the increase in G^2 significant. At Step 2, therefore, the other two two-way interactions are removed from the model. At Step 3, it is found that if either Interviewer × Help or Participant is removed from the model, G^2 is significantly increased. At Step 4, therefore, both terms are retained and the final model is of generating class Interviewer × Help, Participant.

While the loglinear analysis of this second data set does not confirm the opposite-sex dyadic hypothesis, it should serve as an illustration of how this technique can pinpoint the key associations among the variables in a multiway frequency table.

The significant main effect of the Participant factor arises simply because there were more male participants in the study. While that fact is of no scientific interest, the Participant factor must be retained in the model to achieve an adequate goodness-of-fit to the cell frequencies.

From inspection alone, it is much more difficult to discern any clear-cut pattern in the data of Table 4 than in Table 3. The import of the loglinear analysis is that the only robust effects are an Interviewer × Help interaction and a main effect of Sex of Participant. Since the interaction has received confirmation from the loglinear analysis, there is justification for assuming conditional independence and creating a two-way table by collapsing across the factor of Sex of Participant.

The cross-tabulation of the Interviewer × Help interaction is shown in Output 18. There is an obvious tendency for the participants to be helpful when the interviewer is female:

$$LR\,\chi^2 = 32.875;\ p < 0.01.\ \ OR = 8.33.$$

This odds ratio $(105/27)/(14/30) = 8.33$ is very large indeed.

Backward Elimination Statistics

Step Summary

Abbreviations for Participant, Interviewer and Help, respectively

Step[a]			Effects	Chi-Square[c]	df	Sig.	Number of Iterations
0	Generating Class[b]		P*I*H	.000	0	.	
	Deleted Effect	1	P*I*H	.431	1	.512	4
1	Generating Class[b]		P*I, P*H, I*H	.431	1	.512	
	Deleted Effect	1	P*I	1.029	1	.310	2
		2	P*H	.198	1	.656	2
		3	I*H	32.098	1	.000	2
2	Generating Class[b]		P*I, I*H	.629	2	.730	
	Deleted Effect	1	P*I	1.806	1	.179	2
		2	I*H	32.875	1	.000	2
3	Generating Class[b]		I*H, P	2.435	3	.487	
	Deleted Effect	1	I*H	32.875	1	.000	2
		2	P	6.610	1	.010	2
4	Generating Class[b]		I*H, P	2.435	3	.487	

a. At each step, the effect with the largest significance level for the Likelihood Ratio Change is deleted, provided the Significance level is larger than .050.

b. Statistics are displayed for the best model at each step after Step 0.

c. For 'Deleted Effect', this is the change in the Chi-square after the effect is deleted from the model.

Output 17. The Backward Elimination Statistics table

Sex of Interviewer * Was help given? Crosstabulation					
Count					
			Was help given?		
			Yes	No	Total
Sex of Interviewer	**Female**		105	27	132
	Male		14	30	44
	Total		119	57	176

Output 18. Crosstabulation showing that participants were more likely to help a female interviewer

14.4.6 Reporting the results of a loglinear analysis

Reports of loglinear analyses in the literature have yet to follow a standard format. For example, once a model has been fitted, it would be possible to write out the equation of the loglinear model and report the estimates of each of the terms in the equation. Many journal editors, however, would take the view that such a mathematical presentation is unnecessary and would serve only to obscure the findings of the research.

One of the many excellent features of the book by Tabachnick & Fidell (2007) is their inclusion of sample write-ups of the results of the multivariate procedures they describe, including a report of a loglinear analysis on pages 906-908. In their report they (quite rightly, in our view) do not include any formal equations. They do, however, include the following:

1. Details of the data that were used in the analysis, including information about the incidence of cells with low expected frequencies and the presence of outliers. It is essential to establish that there are no contraindications against the use of loglinear analysis. Make sure that you have sufficient data.

2. The maximum likelihood chi square and p-value for the final model.

3. A table showing the results of the significance tests of the various effects on an individual basis. The entries in the table are chi-square tests of partial association, each on one degree of freedom.

4. A larger table showing the parameter estimates and the ratios of the estimates to their standard errors. This table, however, is very extensive, so the researcher submitting an article might omit it from the first draft (or include it as an appendix): the table can always be included in the body of the text in a revision of the article should the editor insist upon this.

14.5   A FINAL WORD

In this chapter, we have described how loglinear analysis can be used to analyse data in the form of multiway contingency tables. This powerful technique makes it possible to tease out and confirm associations among the attributes in a multivariate nominal data set much more effectively and safely than if the researcher were to adapt the traditional Pearsonian analysis and collapse the multiway table across factors in the classification.

Recommended reading

Howell (2007) has a lucid introductory chapter on the theory of loglinear analysis. Tabachnick & Fidell (2007) have an extensive chapter on loglinear analysis with various computing packages, including SPSS. Todman and Dugard (2007) and Dugard, Todman & Staines (2010) take a more informal, hands-on approach.

Dugard, P., Todman, J., & Staines, H. (2010). *Approaching multivariate analysis: A practical introduction (2nd ed.)*. London & New York: Routledge.

Howell, D. C. (2007). *Statistical methods for psychology (6th ed.)*. Belmont, CA: Thomson/Wadsworth.

Tabachnick, B. G., & Fidell, L. S. (2007). *Using multivariate statistics (5th ed.)*. Boston: Allyn & Bacon (Pearson International Edition).

Todman, J., & Dugard, P. (2007). *Approaching multivariate analysis: An introduction for psychology.* Hove: Psychology Press.

Exercise

Exercise 22 *Loglinear analysis* is available in www.psypress.com/spss-made-simple and click on Exercises.

CHAPTER 15

Predicting category membership: Logistic regression

15.1   INTRODUCTION

In Chapter 12, it was shown how the methods of regression could be used to predict scores on one **dependent** or **criterion** variable from knowledge of scores on one or more independent variables or **regressors**. In the situations we discussed, both the dependent variable and the independent variables were always scale or continuous data. There are circumstances, however, in which one might wish to predict, not scores on a quantitative dependent variable, but category membership: that is, the DV is qualitative, rather than quantitative.

Suppose that a premorbid blood condition (indicated by the presence of a protein) has been discovered, which is suspected to arise in middle age partly because of smoking and drinking. A hundred people are tested for the presence of the condition and a record made of their smoking and alcohol consumption. Can people's levels of smoking and drinking be used to predict whether they have the blood condition?

Here, although the independent variables (smoking and alcohol consumption) are continuous variables, the dependent variable is qualitative, consisting merely of the categories Yes (condition present) and No (condition absent). Could we assign arbitrary code numbers to the categories (dummy coding: 0 = No; 1= Yes) and carry out an OLS (Ordinary Least Squares) regression in the usual way? Well, yes, we could; but there are many problems with that approach, and it is not recommended.

Two techniques have been specially designed to predict category membership:

1.   **Discriminant analysis**.
2.   **Logistic regression**.

The topic of discriminant analysis (DA) was touched upon in Chapter 10, in the context of multivariate analysis of variance (MANOVA). The MANOVA can be viewed as an extension of the ANOVA to situations in which there are two or more measures, or DVs. In the process of the MANOVA, a linear function of the DVs known as a **discriminant function** is determined, the group means on which are spread as widely as possible. The group means, or **centroids** of the discriminant function calculated from the data are used to test the null hypothesis of equality, in the population, of the group means. In discriminant analysis (DA), the same discriminant function is calculated, but here the purpose is to predict group membership from the discriminant function.

Mathematically, the one-way MANOVA and discriminant analysis are equivalent and the outputs from the two techniques contain a common core of key statistics. The difference is one of perspective: what are, for the MANOVA, the dependent variables are, for discriminant analysis, the independent variables. SPSS offers both the MANOVA and DA. The output from both procedures contains many of the same statistics. In the DA output, however, there are additional measures of the success with which the DA has predicted group membership. Discriminant analysis, although more at home in the context of correlational (rather than experimental) research, can also be used as an effective follow-up to the MANOVA.

As with the MANOVA, the safe use of discriminant analysis requires that the data meet certain criteria. The distribution of the data should be **multivariate normal**: for any fixed set of values for $p - 1$ variables, the remaining variable should be normally distributed. As in the MANOVA, there is also the assumption of **homogeneity of variance-covariance matrices**. Failure to meet this requirement is most serious when the sample sizes are unequal.

While it is assumed that the independent variables will usually be quantitative, it is possible, as in multiple regression, to include the occasional qualitative independent variable, such as gender or marital status. In general, however, discriminant analysis does not 'like' categorical IVs, the presence of which can inflate the error rates.

15.1.1   Logistic regression

Logistic regression is a technique which, like discriminant analysis, was designed to predict category membership. Logistic regression, however, carries fewer assumptions than does discriminant analysis: neither multivariate normality nor homogeneity of variance-covariance matrices is assumed. Logistic regression, moreoever, can cope with categorical IVs; in fact, *all* the predictors can be categorical. In recent years, therefore, logistic regression has overtaken discriminant analysis as the preferred technique for prediction of category membership.

15.1.2   Binary and multinomial logistic regression

In this chapter, we shall consider two kinds of logistic regression:

1. **Binary logistic regression**, which is applicable to the situation where the target or dependent variable comprises two qualitative categories.

2. **Multinomial logistic regression**, which is applicable when the DV comprises three or more qualitative categories.

15.2 BINARY LOGISTIC REGRESSION

The method we shall describe in this section is applicable to situations in which the dependent variable consists of two categories only.

Returning to the example of the premorbid blood condition mentioned at the start of this Chapter, suppose that of the hundred people studied, forty-four people have the condition and fifty-six do not. We shall assign code numbers to the two categories: to those who have the condition, we assign 1; and to those who do not, we assign 0. In this section, we shall outline the use of logistic regression to predict category membership.

On the basis of the foregoing information about the patients, a prediction of category membership can be made without running any regression at all. Since the probability that a person selected at random will have the condition is 44/100 = 0.44 (44%) and the probability that they will not have the condition is 56/100 = 0.56 (56%), our best a priori prediction of category membership for any particular person selected at random is to assign them to the 'condition absent' category. If we do that, we shall be right in 100% of the cases in which the condition was absent, but wrong in the 44% of cases in which the condition was present, giving us a net success rate of 56% over the hundred assignments. This prediction, which does not require any regression model, is the equivalent, in logistic regression, of 'intercept-only' prediction in multiple regression, in which we assign the mean value of the dependent variable, irrespective of the values of the regressors. The purpose of logistic regression is to improve upon this baseline success rate by exploiting any association between the dependent and independent variables to predict category membership (the dependent variable) with the greatest possible accuracy.

In logistic regression, it is assumed that, although the condition can only be present or absent, variables such as number of cigarettes smoked and amount of alcohol consumed increase the probability of developing the condition **continuously** throughout the range of either variable. For reasons which will become clear, however, the probability of having the condition cannot be expected to be a linear function of the IVs: it is likely to rise at first with increasing rapidity as scores on the independent variable increase from zero and decelerate at a later stage, so that the probability graph is rather like a flattened S (see Figure 1).

This curve is known as the **logistic regression function**. On the basis of the number of cigarettes that a person smokes, the logistic regression function assigns a probability of belonging to the condition-present category. As in multiple regression with a continuous DV, further IVs, such as alcohol intake, can be added in the hope of improving predictive accuracy and deepening scientific understanding of the nature of the condition.

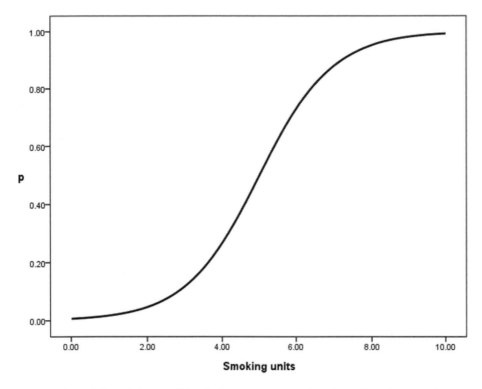

Figure 1. Probability of the condition being present as a function of level of smoking

Probability estimates from the logistic regression function can be used to assign individuals to either of the two categories of the dependent variable. This is achieved by fixing a criterion probability (most commonly 0.5) and, should the probability estimate for a participant exceed the criterion, that person is assigned to the 'condition present' category. A value less than 0.05 will result in assignment to the 'condition absent' category (see Figure 2).

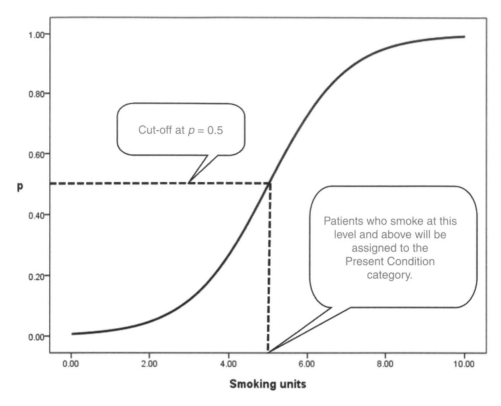

Figure 2. Decision rule for assigning a participant to a category using the logistic regression function

15.2.1   How logistic regression works

In the context of an **experiment of chance**, such as tossing a coin, or rolling a die, the **odds** in favour of an event is the number of ways in which the event could occur divided by the number of ways in which it could fail to occur. If a die is rolled, the odds in favour of a six are 1/5 and the odds in favour of an even number are 3/3 = 1. If we know that among 100 patients, 44 have the blood condition and a patient is selected at random, the odds in favour of the patient selected having the antibody are 44/56 = 11/14.

The odds and the probability

Another measure of likelihood applicable in the same situation is the **probability**.   The probability of an event is the number of ways in which the event could occur divided by the total number of possible outcomes. If a die is rolled, the probability of a six is 1/6 and the probability of an even number is 3/6 = ½ . The two measures of likelihood, the odds and the probability, are closely related as follows:

$$p = \frac{\text{odds}}{1 + \text{odds}} \quad \text{- - - (1)}$$

**Relation between the probability
and the odds**

If we substitute the odds in favour of a six (1/5) into (1), we have p = (1/5)/(6/5) = 1/6. If we substitute the odds in favour of the blood condition (11/14) into (1), we have *p* = (11/14)/(25/14) = 11/25.

The logit (log odds)

As a measure of likelihood, the odds has the disadvantage of **asymmetry of range**. If we start at fifty-fifty (i.e. odds = 1) and regard events with odds in favour greater than 1 as 'likely' and those with odds in favour less than 1 as 'unlikely', there is, in principle, no limit to how great the odds in favour of a 'likely' event could be; whereas those of an 'unlikely' event – however unlikely that event might be short of being an impossibility – can only have a vanishingly small fractional value.

The **logit** is the **natural logarithm** (log to the base *e*) of the odds:

$$\text{logit} = \ln(\text{odds}) = \log_e(\text{odds}) \quad \text{- - - (2)}$$

The logit or log odds

When the logit of an event is zero, the odds themselves are 50/50, because the number whose log is 0 is 1: $10^0 = e^0 = 1$. We have seen that the odds in favour of the blood condition are 11/14. The logit, therefore, is ln(11/14) $^-$ – 0.24, where the negative sign indicates that the odds are against the occurrence of the condition. Had the number of patients with the condition been 56 instead of 44, the odds would have been 14/11 rather than 11/14, and the logit would have been ln(14/11) = + 0.24, which is the same distance from zero, but in the opposite direction. In contrast with the odds, the logit has **symmetry of range**.

The logarithm of a number is the power to which the base must be raised to equal the number itself. The **antilogarithm** function reverses the logarithm function: it raises the base to the power required to give the number itself which, by definition, is the logarithm:

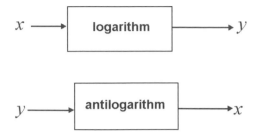

So the base raised to the power of the log of a number (i.e. the **antilogarithm** of the logarithm) is the number itself.

$$\text{If } \; y = \log_{10} x$$

$$\text{antilog } y = 10^y = x$$

In the system of natural logarithms,

$$\text{If } \; y = \ln x \; = \; \log_e x$$

$$\text{antilog } y = e^y = x$$

where e^y is the EXPONENTIAL FUNCTION

and is written as $\exp(y)$.

We can, therefore, write the odds as the antilog of the logit:

$$\text{odds} = \exp\left(\text{logit}\right) = e^{\text{logit}} \quad \text{- - - (3)}$$

The odds expressed as an antilogarithm

The logistic regression function

From the formula expressing the probability in terms of the odds, we can express the probability as a function of the logit thus:

$$p = \frac{\text{odds}}{1+\text{odds}}$$

$$= \frac{\exp(\text{logit})}{1+\exp(\text{logit})}$$

$$= \frac{e^{\text{logit}}}{1+e^{\text{logit}}}$$

We have arrived at the **logistic regression function**:

$$p = \frac{e^{\text{logit}}}{1+e^{\text{logit}}} \quad \text{--- (4)}$$

The logistic regression function

Recall that in **multiple regression**, the dependent variable Y is predicted from p independent variables $X_1, X_2, \ldots, X_p$ by means of the linear regression equation

$$Y' = b_0 + b_1 X_1 + b_2 X_2 + \ldots + b_p X_p \text{ --- (5)}$$

Multiple linear regression equation

where b_0 is the regression constant and b_1, b_2, …,b_p are the regression coefficients.

In logistic regression, it is clear from formula (4) that p is a nonlinear function of the logit (Figure 1). It is assumed, however, that the logit is a linear function of the independent variables:

$$\text{logit} = b_0 + b_1 X_1 + b_2 X_2 + \ldots + b_p X_p$$

constant

partial
regression
coefficients

**The logit equation as a linear function
of the independent variables** - - - (6)

A typical graph of the logit function is shown in Figure 3.

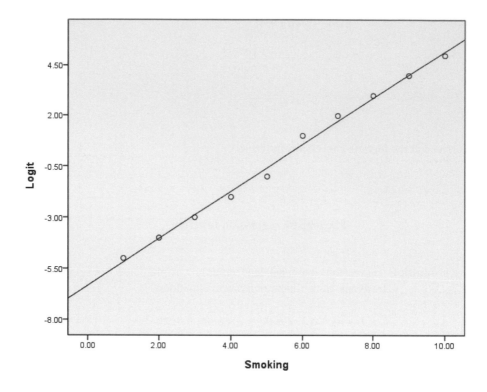

Figure 3.   A typical logit function

On the assumption that the logit function is linear, we can estimate the probability p of the antibody with $\hat{p}$, where

$$\hat{p} = \frac{e^{\text{logit}}}{1+e^{\text{logit}}} = \frac{e^{b_0 + b_1 X_1 + b_2 X_2 + \ldots + b_p X_p}}{1 + e^{b_0 + b_1 X_1 + b_2 X_2 + \ldots + b_p X_p}} \quad \text{--- (7)}$$

The logistic regression equation

Estimating the regression parameters

In logistic regression, as in ordinary multiple regression, the values of the parameters b_0, b_1, ..., b_p in the logit formula (6) are chosen so that the logistic regression equation predicts the independent variable (in this case category membership) as accurately as possible.

We should note that, in contradistinction to ordinary least squares (OLS) regression, there is no mathematical solution to the problem of determining the values of the parameter estimates in the logit equation. Instead, a highly computing-intensive algorithm is used to arrive at the estimates by a series of repetitions or **iterations**. If all goes well, the estimates of the parameters from successive iterations approximate ever more closely to, or **converge** upon, stable values for the parameter estimates. It is essential, however, when running logistic regression, that the user checks the **iteration history** to make sure that convergence really has been achieved; otherwise the output may contain bizarre and self-contradictory information!

Centring the independent variables

As with OLS regression, it is often a good idea to **centre** continuous IVs by subtracting the mean from each score. While this transformation does not affect the correlations among the variables, it can sometimes enable the logistic regression algorithm to converge upon stable estimates that it could not produce from the raw data. Centring the variables is particularly important if the researcher is testing a model containing interaction terms.

The meaning of a logistic regression coefficient

A logistic regression coefficient b is the increase in the logit produced by an increase of one unit in the independent variable. In logistic regression, the IVs are often referred to as **covariates**. If one unit is added to the IV (covariate), the logit becomes:

$$\text{logit} + b$$

The new odds are therefore:

$$\begin{aligned}
\text{antilog}\left(\text{logit} + b\right) &= \exp\left(\text{logit} + b\right) \\
&= \exp\left(\text{logit}\right) \times \exp\left(b\right) \\
&= \text{odds} \times e^b
\end{aligned}$$

In words, the effect of adding a unit to the IV *multiplies* the original odds by exp(b). Suppose, for example, that we were to find that, for the IV Smoking, the value of the partial regression coefficient b is 1.1. This means that if Smoking increases by a unit, the log odds in favour of having the condition (the logit) increase by 1.1 units. But in the scale of odds, rather than logit units, the original odds are *multiplied* by exp(1.1) = 3: that is, an increase of one unit in Smoking *multiplies* the odds in favour of having the condition by 3.

15.2.2   A binary logistic regression with quantitative independent variables

For our first example, we return to the data set on the premorbid blood condition, smoking and drinking.   Figure 4 shows the data on the first eight cases only - the complete data set is available in the file *Ch15 Blood, Smoke, Alcohol.sav* at www.psypress.com/spss-made-simple. We shall assume that at the point when the data were being transcribed, convenient units for smoking and alcohol had been decided upon: one smoking unit might have been ten cigarettes; one drinking unit might have been the equivalent of a large glass of wine or a half-pint of beer.

	Blood	Smoking	Alcohol	va
1	Yes	7	18	
2	Yes	6	15	
3	Yes	1	10	
4	Yes	7	16	
5	Yes	5	11	
6	Yes	2	18	
7	No	0	0	
8	Yes	6	12	

Figure 4.   A fragment of Data View, showing the first few cases in a set of data on the presence or absence of a premorbid blood condition and levels of smoking and alcohol consumption

Exploring the data

As usual, we recommend that you explore the data first before embarking upon any formal analysis.   For example, an examination of the correlations among the three variables (Output 1) shows that Presence of the blood condition correlates substantially with the Smoking variable ($r = + 0.586$). and with Alcohol intake ($r = + 0.267$).   The independent variables of Alcohol intake and Smoking level are also correlated ($r = + 0.443$).

Correlations

		Blood Condition	Number Smoked	Alcohol consumption
Blood Condition	Pearson Correlation	1.000	.586**	.267**
	Sig. (2-tailed)		.000	.007
	N	100.000	100	100
Number Smoked	Pearson Correlation	.586**	1.000	.443**
	Sig. (2-tailed)	.000		.000
	N	100	100.000	100
Alcohol consumption	Pearson Correlation	.267**	.443**	1.000
	Sig. (2-tailed)	.007	.000	
	N	100	100	100.000

**. Correlation is significant at the 0.01 level (2-tailed).

Output 1. **Correlations** among category membership (presence or absence of the premorbid blood condition), amount of smoking and level of alcohol consumption

Centring the independent variables

You will find from running **Descriptives** that the means for the smoking and alcohol variables are 1.38 and 3.87, respectively, with standard deviations 2.461 and 4.907. To centre the smoking and alcohol scores, use **Compute** to subtract their means from the raw values of their respective variables. The new smoking and alcohol means will now be zero. You may wish to confirm that the standard deviations are still 2.461 and 4.907, respectively, and that the correlations among the three variables are still exactly as they are in Output 1.

Running binary logistic regression

In its **Logistic Regression** dialog box, SPSS uses the term **covariate** to denote continuous independent variables. In this example, both IVs are continuous, so they are both covariates.

- Choose **Analyze➔Regression➔Binary Logistic …** to open the **Logistic Regression** dialog box (Figure 5).

- Follow the steps in Figure 5. Leave the **Method** setting at **Enter**, which includes both IVs in the regression simultaneously.

- Click **Options…** to obtain the **Options** dialog box (Figure 5). Select **Hosmer-Lemeshow goodness-of-fit** and **Iteration history**. (The iteration history is essential.) Click **Continue** to return to the **Logistic Regression** dialog box.

- Click **OK** to run the logistic regression.

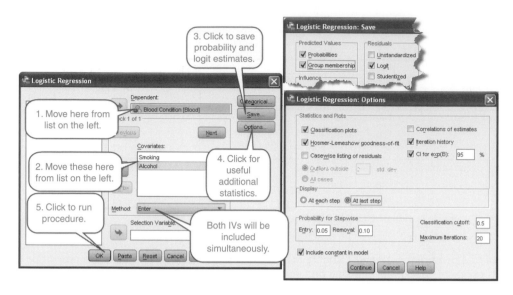

Figure 5 The **Logistic Regression** dialog box, together with the **Save** and **Options** subdialog boxes

We have seen that the logistic regression procedure maximises its predictions of category membership by a highly computer-intensive process which generates successive approximations called **iterations**. If all goes well, the estimates should converge upon (i.e. become progressively closer to) stable values, which are taken to be the best estimates. By choosing the item **Iteration history** in the **Options**, you can check that the successive iterations really have converged. (It may sometimes be necessary to increase the number specified in the **Maximum Iterations** slot to, say, 100 to achieve convergence.)

The analysis of a data set with many variables may take some time to complete. If some of the IVs are highly inter-correlated, the logistic regression algorithm may fail to converge upon stable estimates (the **multicollinearity** problem, which can occur with any regression method). The solution is to exclude one or more of the redundant variables from the analysis.

Output for binary logistic regression

The output for logistic regression is extensive (see Output 2), even if no options are selected. Notice that the output, after the preliminaries, essentially consists of two Blocks. The first, **Block 0: Beginning Block**, gives the statistics of the baseline, intercept-only or guessing approach to prediction of category membership. The second, **Block 1: Method = Enter**, gives the statistics of prediction from the regression model with both IVs present in the regression equation.

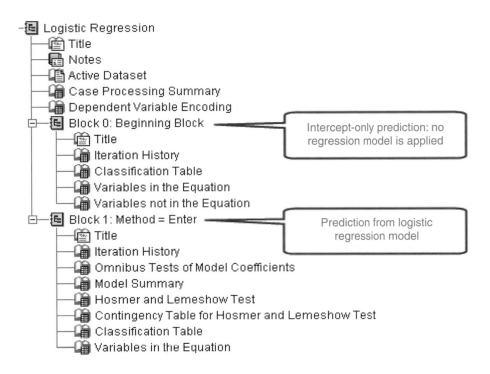

Output 2. The left-hand pane of **SPSS Statistics Viewer** showing the details of the output

In logistic regression, pivotal use is made of a statistic termed the **likelihood ratio**, which, in the output for logistic regression, is written as − **2 Log likelihood**. This statistic behaves as chi-square: it has a large value when a model fits poorly, and a small value when the model fits well. The log likelihood statistic is analogous to the residual sum of squares in OLS (ordinary least squares) regression: the larger its value, the more the variance that remains to be accounted for. A small, statistically insignificant value indicates that the regression model fits the data well.

The first two tables in the output (not shown here) are a **Case Processing Summary** table specifying how many cases were selected and a **Dependent Variable Encoding** table tabulating the numerical values and value labels of the dependent variable (presence or absence of the blood condition). Examine both tables to make sure that the logistic regression procedure has processed all the data and that the value labels have been correctly assigned to the numerical values of the categorical dependent variable.

Next, there is a block of tables under the heading **Block 0: Beginning Block** in which the logistic regression procedure applies a model containing neither of the independent variables (i.e. the 'intercept only' model). Block 0 begins with the **Iteration History** (Output 3).

Iteration History[a,b,c]

Iteration		-2 Log likelihood	Coefficients Constant
Step 0	1	137.186	-.240
	2	137.186	-.241
	3	137.186	-.241

a. Constant is included in the model.
b. Initial -2 Log Likelihood: 137.186
c. Estimation terminated at iteration number 3 because parameter estimates changed by less than .001.

Output 3. **Iteration History** for Step 0 (the intercept-only model)

The convergence to stable values for the likelihood ratio and the estimate of the regression constant was almost instantaneous: the values in the second and third rows agree to three places of decimals.

In the introduction, we saw that, in the absence of any information about regression, the best bet of a person's category membership is the more frequently occurring category (i.e. condition absent). This 'guessing stage' is called **Step 0** by SPSS. Included in this block is the Step 0 **Classification Table** (see Output 4). There are no surprises here: we have already seen that the success rate without any regression is 56%.

Classification Table[a,b]

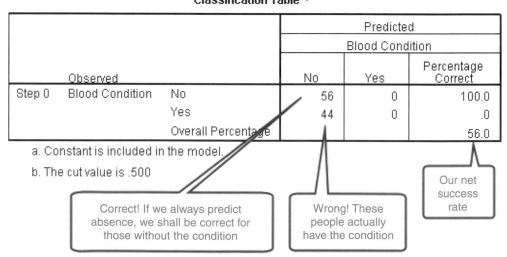

Output 4. The 'no regression' or 'intercept only' **Classification Table**

Two other tables in Block 0 (not shown here) are **Variables in the Equation** and the **Variables not in the equation**. The first table gives the statistics of the intercept, which are not generally of interest. The second table tells us that neither of the independent variables is in the regression equation.

The next block of tables of output is headed **Block 1: Method = Enter**. The first item in the block is the **Iteration History** (Output 5).

Iteration History[a,b,c,d]

Iteration		-2 Log likelihood	Coefficients		
			Constant	Smoking	Alcohol
Step 1	1	98.522	-.906	.472	.004
	2	88.269	-1.030	.875	-.029
	3	80.474	-1.202	1.530	-.061
	4	78.107	-1.355	2.108	-.078
	5	77.999	-1.392	2.256	-.079
	6	77.999	-1.394	2.264	-.078
	7	77.999	-1.394	2.264	-.078

a. Method: Enter
b. Constant is included in the model.
c. Initial -2 Log Likelihood: 137.186
d. Estimation terminated at iteration number 7 because parameter estimates changed by less than .001.

Output 5. The **Iteration History** for Step 1, the simultaneous regression of presence of the blood condition upon smoking and alcohol intake

In the last three rows of entries in the iteration history table, the entries agree to three places of decimals, indicating that convergence to stable estimates has been achieved.

The next three items, **Omnibus Tests of Model Coefficients**, **Model Summary** and **Hosmer-Lemeshow test**, are shown in Output 6. The first table shows that the regression model improves significantly upon chance in predicting category membership: the p-values are very small. In the **Model Summary** table, the **Nagelkerke R Square** statistic imitates the coefficient of determination R^2 in multiple regression: it can be interpreted as the proportion of variance of the dependent variable that is accounted for by the regression model. The other statistic in the table, **Cox & Snell R Square**, compares the log likelihood for the model with the log likelihood for the baseline, intercept-only model. The Nagelkerke R Square, unlike the Cox & Snell R Square, can take values over the full range from 0 to 1. The size of R Square (60% after Step 2) indicates that the model contributes powerfully to the prediction of the presence or absence of the blood condition.

In the Hosmer-Lemeshow table, the p-value is high, which indicates that all the systematic variance has been accounted for by the model: the rest is error.

Omnibus Tests of Model Coefficients

		Chi-square	df	Sig.
Step 1	Step	59.187	2	.000
	Block	59.187	2	.000
	Model	59.187	2	.000

Model Summary

Step	-2 Log likelihood	Cox & Snell R Square	Nagelkerke R Square
1	77.999[a]	.447	.599

a. Estimation terminated at iteration number 7 because parameter estimates changed by less than .001.

Hosmer and Lemeshow Test

Step	Chi-square	df	Sig.
1	6.155	7	.522

Output 6. Some output statistics indicating that regression accounts significantly for presence of the antibody

Output 7 shows the **Contingency Table for the Hosmer and Lemeshow Test**. The first column categorises, in order of increasing magnitude, the probabilities assigned by the regression model into divisions known as **deciles** (deciles divide the distribution into ten parts): the lowest probabilities are in deciles 1 and 2; the highest are in deciles 8 and 9. The table shows the association between assigned probability and presence or absence of the blood condition. Notice that, in general, there is close agreement between the **Expected** frequencies (the assignments by the regression model and category assignment on the basis of the cut-off point of 0.05 for probability) and the **Observed** or actual frequencies of patients in those categories. In particular, notice that in deciles 1 and 2 (the first two rows of entries), both Observed and Expected frequencies are very low; whereas in deciles 8 and 9 (the last two rows of entries), both the Observed and Expected frequencies are considerably higher – and in complete agreement.

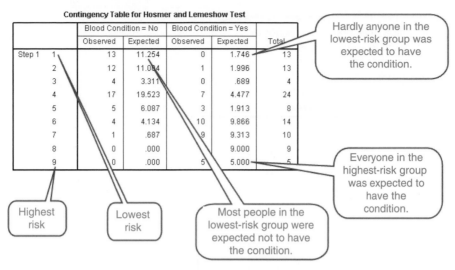

Output 7. Contingency table showing the association between the size of the probability assigned by the regression model and presence or absence of the blood condition

Output 8 is the Classification Table showing the proportion of correct assignments when the regression model has been applied to the data. The new success rate of 85% is a spectacular improvement upon the baseline, intercept-only rate of 56%.

Classification Table[a]

			Predicted		
			Blood Condition		
Observed			No	Yes	Percentage Correct
Step 1	Blood Condition	No	51	5	91.1
		Yes	10	34	77.3
		Overall Percentage			85.0

a. The cut value is .500

Output 8. The **Classification Table** with the regression model applied

Output 9 (actually the transpose of the original output table) tabulates the variables that are included in the regression equation. Since we chose the **Enter** method, both DVs will be entered in the equation, even if one does not make a significant contribution when added to the other. It can be seen from the p-values that Alcohol, although correlating substantially with the incidence of the antibody, does not make a significant contribution when the Smoking variable is also present in the equation. For Smoking, the 95% confidence interval on Exp(B) does not include 1; whereas it does for Alcohol. (The value 1 is the antilog of zero, the ex hypothesi value of the coefficient in the logit equation.)

> The antilog of B, that is, the factor by which an increase of one unit in Smoking multiplies the odds in favour of the presence of the condition

Variables in the Equation

		Step 1[a]		
		Smoking	Alcohol	Constant
B		2.264	-.078	-1.394
S.E.		.513	.085	.373
Wald		19.490	.846	13.979
df		1	1	1
Sig.		.000	.358	.000
Exp(B)		9.623	.925	.248
95% C.I.for EXP(B)	Lower	3.522	.783	
	Upper	26.294	1.092	

a. Variable(s) entered on step 1: Smoking, Alcohol.

Output 9. The table (transposed) of **Variables in the Equation**

In Output 9, the entries in the row headed Exp(B), are the factors by which the raw odds in favour of the occurrence of the blood condition are *multiplied* by increasing the independent variable by one unit. The term Exp(B) is e^B, the **exponential function** of B. It is the antilog of the regression coefficient. For example, the value of B for Smoking is given as 2.264. This means that an increase in smoking level of one unit produces, on average, an increase of 2.264 units in the logit (i.e. the natural log of the odds) in favour of having the blood condition. But an increase of 2.264 units in the logarithm corresponds to *multiplication* of the raw odds by $\text{Exp}(2.264) = e^{2.264} = 9.623$. In words, an increase of one unit in Smoking, multiplies the likelihood of having the blood condition by ten, approximately.

It is clear from Output 9 that Smoking makes both a significant and a substantial contribution to the regression: $p < 0.01$; Exp(B) = 9.623. Alcohol, on the other hand, makes neither a significant ($p = 0.358$) nor a substantial [Exp(B) = 0.925] contribution. That suggests that, in our regression exercise, we might dispense with the services of the Alcohol variable altogether.

The **Wald statistic** for Smoking has a much higher value for Smoking than for Alcohol. The Wald statistic tests a regression coefficient for significance. As with OLS regression, the null hypothesis is that, in the population, the value of B is 0. The Wald statistic is defined as follows:

$$\text{Wald} = \left(\frac{b}{s_b}\right)^2 \quad \text{---} (8)$$

The Wald statistic

The Wald statistic is distributed approximately as chi-square on one degree of freedom.

Output 10 shows the logit equation, in which the values of the constant and the two regression coefficients have been obtained from Output 9 (shown in edited form in Output 10).

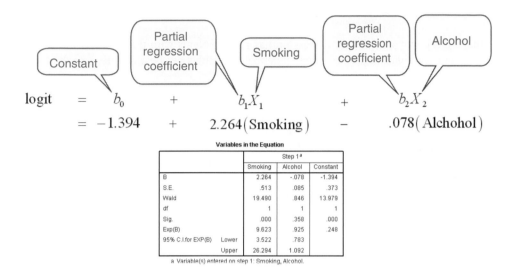

Variables in the Equation

		Step 1 ª		
		Smoking	Alcohol	Constant
B		2.264	-.078	-1.394
S.E.		.513	.085	.373
Wald		19.490	.846	13.979
df		1	1	1
Sig.		.000	.358	.000
Exp(B)		9.623	.925	.248
95% C.I.for EXP(B)	Lower	3.522	.783	
	Upper	26.294	1.092	

a Variable(s) entered on step 1: Smoking, Alcohol.

Output 10.   The logit equation

Since we have the logit equation, we are now in a position to write the logistic regression equation:

$$p' = \frac{e^{\text{logit}}}{1 + e^{\text{logit}}}$$

$$= \frac{e^{-1.394+2.264(\text{Smoking})-0.078(\text{Alcohol})}}{1 + e^{-1.394+2.264(\text{Smoking})-0.078(\text{Alcohol})}}$$

The logistic regression equation - - - (9)

We have been describing the output resulting from **simultaneous** logistic regression, that is, regression with both the IVs having been entered into the regression equation in a single step. Returning to the **Logistic Regression** dialog box, the drop-down menu for **Method** gives us several other possible approaches. If we select, say, **Backward LR** (i.e. Backward Likelihood Ratio), we shall find that the regression will eliminate the Alcohol variable from the regression and still achieve a hit rate of 85% of accurate classifications. (As a matter of fact, you will obtain the same result if you select any of the other methods.) We suggest that, as an analytic strategy, it is often helpful to begin with simultaneous regression, the output of which is easier to understand, and then proceed to the sequential methods in order to clarify the results of the simultaneous regression.

15.2.3   Binary logistic regression with categorical independent variables

Neither binary nor multinomial regression has any problems with the inclusion of categorical independent variables: in fact, *all* the independent variables can be qualitative, as the following example will illustrate.

In Chapter 14, we described an experiment on gender and professed helpfulness, in which participants were asked by a male or female interviewer whether they would be prepared to help in a certain situation. The research hypothesis was the opposite-sex dyadic hypothesis, which holds that one is more inclined to help someone of the opposite sex than someone of one's own sex. The results are reproduced in Output 11.

Incidence of helping by male and female participants with male and female interviewers

Count

Sex of Interviewer			Would you help?		Total
			Yes	No	
Male	Sex of Participant	Male	4	21	25
		Female	16	9	25
	Total		20	30	50
Female	Sex of Participant	Male	11	14	25
		Female	11	14	25
	Total		22	28	50

Output 11.   Contingency table of the results of the gender and helping experiment

Here the implicit dependent variable was Help, a categorical, dichotomous variable with two values: 1 = Yes; 2 = No. The independent variables were Sex of Interviewer and Sex of Participant. As we saw in Chapter 14, however, the loglinear analysis does not frame the problem in regression terms. Loglinear analysis models the expected cell frequencies in the multiway contingency table. In terms of loglinear analysis, confirmation of the opposite-sex dyadic hypothesis would take the form of a *three-way* interaction among the factors: in participants of either sex, there would be a higher helping rate (itself a two-way interaction between Help (Yes/No) and Sex of Participant) when the sex of the interviewer was opposite to that of the participant.

The data on helping are also suitable for analysis with logistic regression: there is a categorical dependent variable Help; and there are two categorical IVs, Sex of Participant and Sex of Interviewer. In the present regression context, however, confirmation of the opposite-sex dyadic hypothesis would take the form of a two-way interaction between Sex of Participant and Sex of Interviewer.

The running of logistic regression with these data involves two new moves: 1. the addition of an interaction term to the model; 2. the specification of the IVs as **categorical**, as opposed to continuous. The data are available in the file *Ch14 Helping(3WayInteractionOnly).sav* at www.psypress.com/spss-made-simple. With this file in the **Data Editor**, proceed as follows:

- Having first weighted the cases by the Count variable, Choose
  Analyze➔Regression➔Binary Logistic ... to open the **Logistic Regression** dialog box
  (Figure 6).

- Transfer the name of the DV to the **Dependent** slot and the names of the two IVs to the
  Covariates panel.

- Add the interaction term by selecting both IVs. (Highlight the first IV, press and hold Ctrl
  and click the second IV.) The **interaction button** marked **>a*b>** will become active.
  Click the interaction button to transfer the interaction term Interviewer*Participant to the
  Covariates panel.

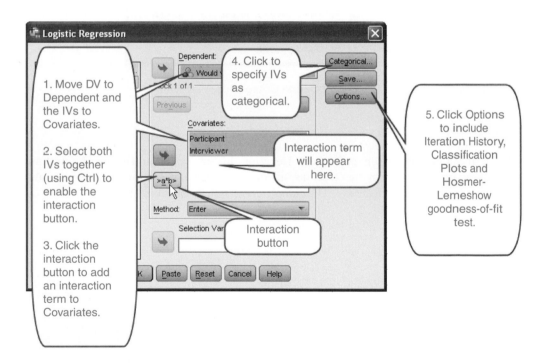

Figure 6. The **Logistic Regression** dialog box. The IVs are registered as categorical by clicking the **Categorical** button and completing the **Define Categorical Variables** dialog box (see Figure 7)

- Click the **Categorical...** button to obtain the **Define Categorical Variables** dialog box (Figure 7). Transfer the names Participant and Interviewer to the **Categorical Covariates:** box. The default type of **Contrast** is **Indicator**, which registers the presence or absence of the target category. Click **Continue** to return to the **Logistic Regression** dialog box, where you will now see the variable names marked with **(Cat).**

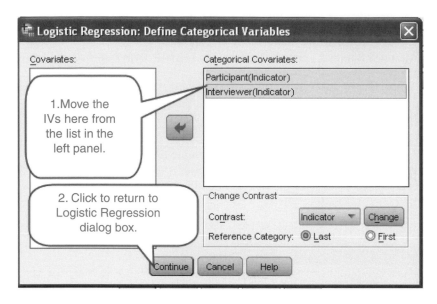

Figure 7. The completed dialog box for **Define Categorical Variables**

- Click the **Options** button and select **Iteration history** and the **Hosmer-Lemeshow goodness-of-fit test** from the **Options** dialog box. Click **Continue** to return to the **Logistic Regression** dialog box. The completed version is shown in Figure 8.

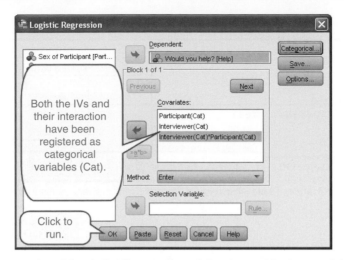

Figure 8. The completed **Logistic Regression** dialog box, with the two IVs registered as categorical

- Click **OK** to run the regression.

The output

As usual, following the preliminaries, the output is presented under the headings Step 0 (intercept-only prediction) and Step 1 (prediction from the regression model). As always, we check the iteration history for convergence to stable estimates. Output 12 shows the classification table at Step 0. The baseline success rate is 58%.

Classification Table[a,b]

			Predicted		
			Would you help?		
Observed			Yes	No	Percentage Correct
Step 0	Would you help?	Yes	0	42	.0
		No	0	58	100.0
	Overall Percentage				58.0

a. Constant is included in the model.

b. The cut value is .500

Baseline, 'intercept-only' success rate

Output 12. The baseline classification success rate with 'intercept-only' prediction

Classification Table[a]

			Predicted		
			Would you help?		
	Observed		Yes	No	Percentage Correct
Step 1	Would you help? Yes		16	26	38.1
		No	9	49	84.5
		Overall Percentage			65.0

a. The cut value is .500

Success rate when regression model is applied

Output 13. **Classification Table** showing an increase in the success rate when the regression model is applied

Output 13 shows the classification success rate when the regression model is applied. The classification success rate from regression is 65%, which is an improvement upon the baseline, intercept-only success rate of 58%.

Output 14 shows the final table of **Variables in the Equation**.

Variables in the Equation

		B	S.E.	Wald	df	Sig.	Exp(B)
Step 1	Interviewer(1)	-.817	.580	1.985	1	.159	.442
	Participant(1)	.000	.570	.000	1	1.000	1.000
	Interviewer(1) by Participant(1)	2.234	.892	6.268	1	.012	9.333
	Constant	.241	.403	.358	1	.549	1.273

Output 14. Final table of **Variables in the Equation**

It can be seen from Output 14 that the only significant term in the regression is the **Interviewer × Participant** interaction. Notice that the value of Exp(B), the multiplier of the raw odds, is much greater (9.333) than it is for the other terms in the regression equation. This result is the equivalent, in logistic regression, of the significant three-way interaction that we obtained when we used loglinear analysis to model the cell frequencies of the same contingency table. The outcome of the logistic regression is in complete agreement with that of the loglinear analysis of the same data.

15.3   MULTINOMIAL LOGISTIC REGRESSION

Binary logistic regression can be used to predict a dichotomous dependent variable only. If the DV has more than two categories, we must use **multinomial logistic regression**. In multinomial logistic regression, as in binary logistic regression, the independent variables can be either categorical or continuous (scale). In multinomial logistic regression, however, categorical IVs are termed **factors**.

To illustrate the use of multinomial logistic regression, we shall return to the prediction of a pre-morbid blood condition from level of smoking. Let us suppose that the patients fall into three categories: (1) Condition absent; (1) Protein A is present; (2) Proteins A and B are both present. (We shall assume that, while protein A can be present without protein B, the converse is not true; however, both proteins can be present in the same person.)

The motivation for the study was a strong suspicion that level of smoking helps to determine the presence or absence of certain proteins in the blood. Reports of incidence, however, have been inconsistent, a fact that the researchers attribute to a tendency in men to develop the premorbid condition as a consequence of high levels of smoking; whereas in females that might not be the case. The main purpose of the research is to investigate the possibility of this interaction between Gender and Smoking.

We need to give some thought to the naming of the categories making up the dependent variable. We shall assign the values as follows: 0 = None; 1 = A; 2 = Both. Suppose, for a moment, that we were about to run a MANOVA and that these three categories were the levels of a single treatment factor and Smoking and Gender were the DVs. We want to decide upon a common **reference category** for two simple comparisons. The obvious 'control' group would be None and the groups 'A' and 'Both' could be compared with this control group. Our two comparisons, therefore are: A versus None; Both versus None. Returning to logistic regression, where Smoking and Gender are the IVs and Blood Condition is the DV, we can think of multinomial regression as two simultaneous binary logistic regressions in which the dichotomies are the two comparisons we have just described.

15.3.1   Accessing the data set

The full data set is available in the file *Ch15 Trinomial Interaction.sav* at www.psypress.com/spss-made-simple. A fragment of **Data View** (with value labels displayed) is shown in Figure 9.

Case	blood	smoking	Gender	var	var
44	None	2	Female		
45	None	2	Female		
46	None	3	Male		
47	None	3	Male		
48	A	3	Female		
49	A	3	Female		
50	Both	3	Female		
51	A	3	Female		
52	A	3	Female		
53	None	4	Male		
54	None	4	Female		
55	Both	4	Female		
56	None	4	Female		
57	Both	5	Male		
58	A	5	Female		
59	None	5	Female		

Figure 9. Part of Data View showing the three outcome categories

15.3.2   Running multinomial logistic regression

To run the multinomial logistic regression procedure, proceed as follows:

- Choose **Analyze➜Regression➜Multinomial Logistic…** to open the **Multinomial Logistic Regression** dialog box (Figure 10).

The completion of the **Multinomial Logistic Regression** dialog differs from the Binary dialog in two important ways.   Firstly, there is no interaction button in the main dialog box. Interactions terms are added to the model by clicking the **Model** button and completing the **Model** subdialog appropriately (see below).   Secondly, in the **Multinomial** dialog, Categorical IVs are known as **factors** and are moved to the box labelled **Factors** in the main dialog box. There is no need to click a special **Category** button.

- Move Blood condition (the DV) to the **Dependent** slot. Initially, the entry in the Dependent slot will read Blood(Second), because, as the default, SPSS selects the last category as the reference category. Since we have chosen the first category, None, as our reference category, we need to change the **Reference Category** to First.

- Click **Reference Category** and complete the dialog as shown in Figure 11. Click **Continue** to return to the **Multinomial Logistic Regression** dialog, where you will find that the enty in the **Dependent** slot is now Blood(First).

- Transfer Number Smoked to the **Covariate(s)** box and Gender to the **Factor(s)** box.

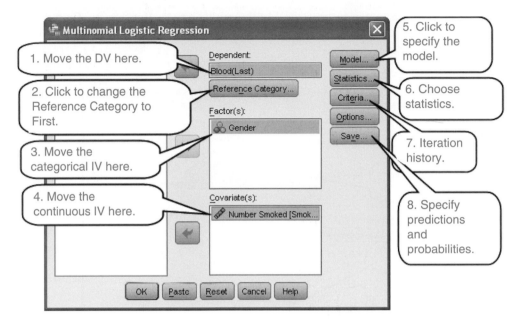

Figure 10. The Multinomial Logistic Regression dialog box

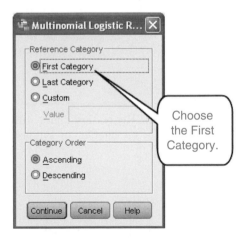

Figure 11. The **Reference Category** dialog box

- Click **Model...** to open the **Model** dialog box (Figure 12). Follow the steps shown and click **Continue** to return to the main dialog box. Note that, although we are not really interested in main effects, they must be included in the model by transferring them to the upper box in the **Model** dialog.

- Click the **Critera** button to open the **Multinomial Logistic Regression: Convergence Criteria** dialog box (Figure 13). Check the box labelled **Print iteration history**. This is very important.

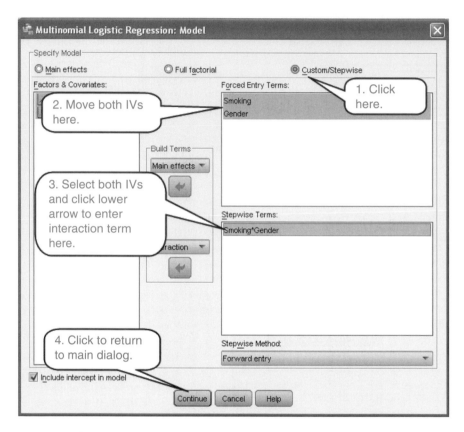

Figure 12. Specifying the model

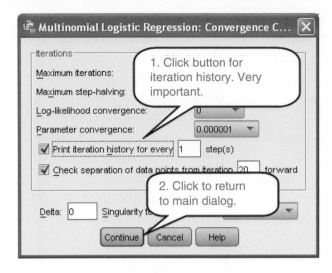

Figure 13. The **Convergence Critera** dialog box with the **Print interation history** button checked

- Click **Statistics** to open the **Multinomial Logistic Regression: Statistics** dialog box (Figure 14). Check the boxes as shown in the figure. Click **Continue to** return to the **Multinomial Logistic Regression dialog box.**

- In the main dialog box, click **Save** and choose the items marked in Figure 15.

- **Click OK to run the** multinomial logistic regression.

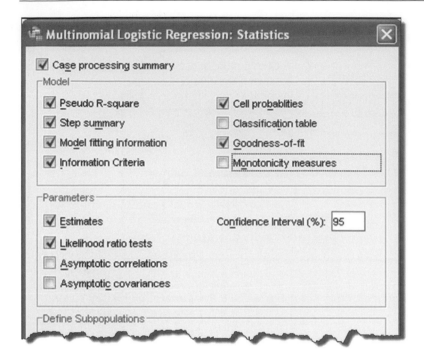

Figure 14. Statistics options for multinomial logistic regression

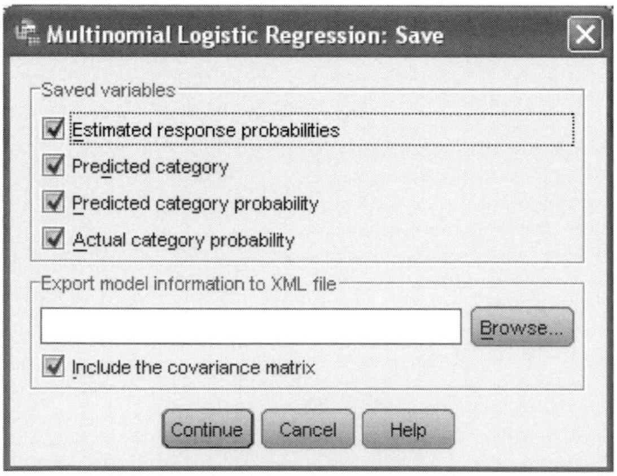

Figure 15. The Multinomial Logistic regression: Save dialog box

Output for multinomial logistic regression

One of the first items to appear is a warning (not shown here) that 43.3% of the cells have zero frequencies. Since such a warning always appears in the output of this procedure, there is no cause for alarm. The warning is issued because the procedure is treating the values of the continuous IV as if they were categories of a contingency table and expecting to find every possible combination of each of these 'categories' with those of the other IV and the DV.

The next item is a **Case Processing Summary** (not shown here), which should show that 100% of the cases were processed.

The output consists of several tables. First there is a **Case Summary Table** (not shown here) listing the categories of the Blood Condition and Gender variables and the number in each Category.

The next item is a **Step Summary** table (Output 15) showing the order of entry of terms into the model. We notice immediately that the addition of Gender*Smoking interaction makes a significant contribution to the model's goodness-of-fit: it reduces a chi-square of 96.006 to one of 63.287.

Step Summary

Model	Action	Effect(s)	Model Fitting Criteria			Effect Selection Tests		
			AIC	BIC	-2 Log Likelihood	Chi-Square[a]	df	Sig.
0	Entered	Intercept, Smoking, Gender	108.006	123.637	96.006	.		
1	Entered	Gender * Smoking	79.287	100.128	63.287	32.719	2	.000

Stepwise Method: Forward Entry

a. The chi-square for entry is based on the likelihood ratio test.

Output 15. The **Step Summary** table showing which IVs were entered in the model

The iteration history is shown in Output 16. It is clear from inspection of this table that the algorithm was able to converge upon stable estimates of all the parameters. Here, at least, is one sign that all is well with the analysis.

Iteration History

Iteration	-2 Log Likelihood	Blood Condition							
		A				Both			
		Intercept	Smoking	[Gender=1]	[Gender=1] * Smoking	Intercept	Smoking	[Gender=1]	[Gender=1] * Smoking
0	114.456	-.794930	.000000	.000000	.000000	-1.824549	.000000	.000000	.000000
1	74.405	.045911	-.060603	-2.892486	.628459	-2.289247	.117667	-.990160	.361432
2	67.713	-.073771	-.046688	-4.389625	.915780	-2.437581	.131235	-1.210883	.474760
3	64.995	-.073383	-.046737	-6.147486	1.204642	-2.439427	.131404	-1.366832	.537757
4	63.765	-.073383	-.046737	-8.169227	1.513122	-2.439428	.131404	-1.486420	.578852
5	63.339	-.073383	-.046737	-10.142460	1.805040	-2.439428	.131404	-1.573450	.605607
6	63.287	-.073383	-.046737	-11.118615	1.947260	-2.439428	.131404	-1.605601	.614698
7	63.287	-.073383	-.046737	-11.244612	1.965466	-2.439428	.131404	-1.608571	.615488
8	63.287	-.073383	-.046737	-11.246238	1.965701	-2.439428	.131404	-1.608601	.615495
9	63.287[a]	-.073383	-.046737	-11.246238	1.965701	-2.439428	.131404	-1.608601	.615495

Redundant parameters are not displayed. Their values are always zero in all iterations.

a. The parameter estimates converge. Last absolute change in -2 Log Likelihood is .000, and last maximum absolute change in parameters is 2.64194E-007.

Output 16. The Iteration History, showing clear convergence of all the parameter estimates

The next three tables, **Model Fitting Information**, **Goodness-of-Fit** and **Pseudo R-Square**, are shown in Output 17. The two measures of goodness-of-fit, Pearson and Deviance, agree in being statistically insignificant; and a difference between their values is usual. The chi-square value in the uppermost table is not a measure of goodness-of-fit: it is the increase in chi-square resulting from removal of the effect terms from the final model.

Of the three **Pseudo R-Square** measures, the Nagelkerke measure is regarded as the most successful in imitating the coefficient of multiple determination in ordinary least squares (OLS) multiple regression. Its value, 0.483, is of 'medium' size in Cohen's classification.

The table of **Likelihood Ratio Tests** is shown in Output 18. It is clear from the table that the interaction term Gender*Smoking makes a statistically significant contribution to the goodness-of-fit of the model. The principal scientific hypothesis that motivated the study has been confirmed.

Model Fitting Information

Model	Model Fitting Criteria			Likelihood Ratio Tests		
	AIC	BIC	-2 Log Likelihood	Chi-Square	df	Sig.
Intercept Only	118.456	123.667	114.456			
Final	79.287	100.128	63.287	51.170	6	.000

Goodness-of-Fit

	Chi-Square	df	Sig.
Pearson	29.076	32	.615
Deviance	35.565	32	.304

Pseudo R-Square

Cox and Snell	.401
Nagelkerke	.483
McFadden	.290

Output 17. Model information, goodness-of-fit and effect size

Likelihood Ratio Tests

Effect	Model Fitting Criteria			Likelihood Ratio Tests		
	AIC of Reduced Model	BIC of Reduced Model	-2 Log Likelihood of Reduced Model	Chi-Square	df	Sig.
Intercept	79.287	100.128	63.287[a]	.000	0	.
Smoking	79.287	100.128	63.287[a]	.000	0	.
Gender	103.657	119.288	91.657	28.370	2	.000
Gender * Smoking	108.006	123.637	96.006	32.719	2	.000

The chi-square statistic is the difference in -2 log-likelihoods between the final model and a reduced model. The reduced model is formed by omitting an effect from the final model. The null hypothesis is that all parameters of that effect are 0.

a. This reduced model is equivalent to the final model because omitting the effect does not increase the degrees of freedom.

Output 18. Likelihood Ratio Tests confirming the effect of the interaction term

Parameter Estimates

Blood Condition[a]		B	Std. Error	Wald	df	Sig.	Exp(B)	95% Confidence Interval for Exp (B)	
								Lower Bound	Upper Bound
A	Intercept	-.073	.565	.017	1	.897			
	Smoking	-.047	.093	.251	1	.617	.954	.795	1.146
	[Gender=1]	-11.246	5.084	4.893	1	.027	1.306E-5	6.140E-10	.278
	[Gender=2]	0[b]	.	.	0	.	.	.	.
	[Gender=1] * Smoking	1.966	.769	6.539	1	.011	7.140	1.583	32.213
	[Gender=2] * Smoking	0[b]	.	.	0	.	.	.	.
Both	Intercept	-2.439	1.202	4.115	1	.042			
	Smoking	.131	.170	.595	1	.440	1.140	.817	1.592
	[Gender=1]	-1.609	1.640	.962	1	.327	.200	.008	4.986
	[Gender=2]	0[b]	.	.	0	.	.	.	.
	[Gender=1] * Smoking	.615	.310	3.935	1	.047	1.851	1.007	3.400
	[Gender=2] * Smoking	0[b]	.	.	0	.	.	.	.

a. The reference category is: None.
b. This parameter is set to zero because it is redundant.

Output 19. Table of **Parameter Esimates**, showing that, in the males, Gender is associated with the presence of protein A and with the presence of Both proteins

Output 19 is the table of **Parameter Estimates**. The table is divided into an upper part (A present) and a lower part (Both present). Each part of the table can be thought of as the results of a binary logistic regression of a Present/Absent dichotomy against the IVs of Smoking and Gender. In (A), the term [Gender = 1]*Smoking is not an interaction: it is the equivalent of a simple main effect of Smoking upon category membership at one level (Male) of the Gender variable. We have seen that the antilog Exp(B) is a useful comparative measure of effect size. Here, Exp(B) = 7.140, which means that in Males, an increase of one unit in Smoking multiplies the odds in favour of having protein A by seven.

The lower part of the table presents a similar picture – though the effects are not so marked. Once again, there is the equivalent of a simple main effect of Smoking in the Males. The antilog Exp(B) is 1.851, a value which, although considerably smaller than the corresponding value in the upper table, means that an increase of one unit in Smoking doubles the odds of having Both proteins. Here, once again, we have confirmation of the hypothesis of a link between Smoking and the presence of a protein in the male patients.

Notice that there is no parameter estimate for the effect of Smoking in the female patients. While the significance of the Gender*Smoking interaction implies that the effects of Smoking differ in males and females, we must take a closer look at the interaction to see what is going on. First, we shall find the correlation between Smoking and the presence of protein A in the males only.

- Choose **Data→Select Cases→If condition is satisfied** to open the **Select Cases: If** dialog box (Figure 16). Complete the dialog as shown in the figure.

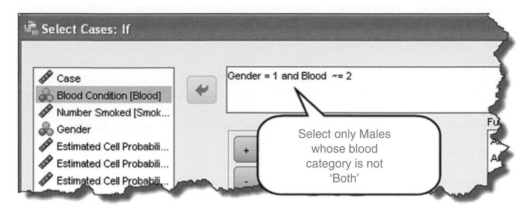

Figure 16. Selecting the males only and excluding the category 'Both'

- Choose **Analyze➔Correlate➔** and obtain the Pearson correlation, which is 0.887 .

- Choose **Data➔Select Cases➔If condition is satisfied** and, in the **Select Cases: If** dialog, enter 'Gender = 2 and Blood ~=2'. Obtain the Pearson correlation, – 0.074, which is negligible.

- Make similar selections of Gender while excluding the Blood value 1 and find the correlations. (In the **Select Cases: If** dialog, Enter 'Gender = 1 and Blood ~=1', find the correlation, then enter 'Gender = 2 and Blood ~=1' and find the correlation.) You will find that, once again, the correlations are substantial in the males, but negligible in the females.

It is clear from the examination of the Parameter Estimates table that the hypothesis of an interaction between Smoking and Gender in the males is strongly confirmed by the analysis. A descriptive follow-up analysis with the female data indicates that, in the females, there is no evidence of an association between Smoking and the presence of either premorbid category.

15.4   A FINAL WORD

In this chapter, we have described some regression methods that have been specially designed for data sets in which the DV is a set of categories, rather than a continuous variable. Logistic regression makes fewer assumptions than does discriminant analysis, which can also be applied to data of this kind. We began with binary logistic regression, which is appropriate when the dependent variable consists of two categories and ended with multinomial logistic regression, which is appropriate when the DV consists of three or more categories.

The user of logistic regression does not, thereby, evade all the potential problems that are attendant upon any regression exercise. Multicollinearity can be an issue. As with ordinary least squares (OLS) multiple regression, there is inevitably doubt about which of several correlated independent variables makes the greatest contribution to the variance of the dependent variable. There exists no automated solution to this problem. It is incumbent upon the user to supply, in addition to a statistical model, a compelling causal model.

Finally, we should note that, because logistic regression uses maximum likelihood estimation, sample size is even more of an issue than it is in ordinary least squares (OLS) regression. The ratio of sample size to the number of parameters should be carefully monitored. As a rule of thumb, it has been suggested that the number of cases in the smallest group should be at least ten times the number of predictors (Hosmer & Lemeshow, 2000). An insufficiency of data results in loss of power and difficulty in interpreting statistically insignificant results.

Recommended reading

Dugard, Todman & Staines (2010) have a lively and helpful chapter on logistic regression, which would be a good starting point. Tabachnick & Fidell (2007) go into the technicalities in more detail.

Dugard, P., Todman, J., & Staines, H. (2010). *Approaching multivariate analysis: A practical introduction (2ⁿᵈ ed.).* London & New York: Routledge.

Tabachnick, B. G., & Fidell, L. S. (2007). *Using multivariate statistics (5ᵗʰ ed.)* Boston: Allyn & Bacon (Pearson International Edition).

Exercise

Exercise 23 *Predicting category membership: Binary logistic regression* is available at www.psypress.com/spss-made-simple. Click on Exercises.

CHAPTER 16

The search for latent variables: factor analysis

16.1   INTRODUCTION

Suppose that some schoolchildren are tested on a battery of variables, including an assortment of school subjects and a test of orientation and spatial skills we shall refer to as mapwork. The correlations of performance on each test with every other test in the battery can be arranged in a rectangular array known as a **correlation matrix**, or **R-matrix** (Table 1).

Table 1. A correlation matrix (from SPSS output).

Correlation Matrix

		French	German	Latin	Music	Maths	Mapwork
Correlation	French	1.000	.836	.742	.032	.083	.312
	German	.836	1.000	.715	-.081	.008	.118
	Latin	.742	.715	1.000	.022	.222	.131
	Music	.032	-.081	.022	1.000	.713	.783
	Maths	.083	.008	.222	.713	1.000	.735
	Mapwork	.312	.118	.131	.783	.735	1.000

In its basic form, a correlation matrix is **square**, that is, there are as many rows as there are columns. The diagonal of cells running from top left to bottom right is known as the **principal diagonal** of the matrix. The values in the off-diagonal cells are repeated above and below the principal diagonal: e.g., the correlation of French with German is the same as that of German with French. Each row (or column) of the R-matrix contains all the correlations involving one particular test in the battery. Since the variables are labelled in the same order in the rows and columns of the R-matrix, each of the cells along the principal diagonal contains the correlation of one of the variables with itself (i.e. 1). The R-matrix is the starting point for a variety of multivariate statistical procedures, but in this chapter we shall consider just one technique: **factor analysis.**

Factor analysis is a set of techniques designed to enable the researcher to classify data on several variables with reference to a smaller number of supposed underlying dimensions or **factors**. Is it possible, for example, to account for the patterns shown by the correlations in Table 1 in terms of fewer factors than there were tests in the battery?

Since the entries below the principal diagonal of the R-matrix in Table 1 are identical with those above it, we shall concentrate on the upper half of the table only. In Figure 1, we see that there are two groups of subjects with high correlations among the members of each group: 1. German, French and Latin; 2. Music, Maths and Mapwork.

Correlation Matrix

		French	German	Latin	Music	Maths	Mapwork
Correlation	French	1.000	.836	.742	.032	.083	.312
	German	.836	1.000	.715	-.081	.008	.118
	Latin	.742	.715	1.000	.022	.222	.131
	Music	.032	-.081	.022	1.000	.713	.783
	Maths	.083	.008	.222	.713	1.000	.735
	Mapwork	.312	.118	.131	.783	.735	1.000

Group 1: French, German and Latin show high intercorrelations, but each shows low correlations with the subjects in Group 2

Group 2: Maths, Mapwork and Music show high intercorrelations, but each shows low correlations with the subjects in Group 1

Figure 1. Exploring the R-matrix

While the members of each group correlate strongly with the other group members, they show much lower correlations with the members of the other group. For example, German (Group 1) correlates 0.008 with Maths and 0.118 with Mapwork. And Maths (Group 2) correlates 0.083 with French and 0.222 with Latin.

It is tempting to surmise that the clustering among the tests in the R-matrix arises because, although the tests in each group are measuring the same underlying ability (or very similar abilities), the two groups are tapping different abilities. The tests in Group 1 might be tapping general linguistic ability; whereas those in Group 2 might be tapping nonverbal, visuo-spatial ability.

It would appear, therefore, that the 15 correlations among the six tests in the R-matrix can be accounted for in terms of just *two* underlying, independent dimensions. In general, the purpose of an exploratory factor analysis is to determine the minimum number of dimensions necessary to account for an R-matrix.

The **factors** produced by factor analysis are mathematical entities, which can be thought of as classificatory axes for plotting the tests as points on a graph. The greater the value of a test's co-ordinate, or **loading**, on a factor/axis, the more important that factor is in accounting for the variance of scores on that test. Theoretically, a loading can vary throughout the range from – 1 to +1, inclusive. In practice, however, errors in measurement restrict this theoretical range considerably.

The term **factor** has also an equivalent algebraic interpretation as a linear function of the observed scores that people achieve on the tests in a battery. If a battery contains six tests (as in the present example), and each person tested were also to be assigned a seventh score consisting of the sum of the six test scores, that seventh (summative) score would be a **factor score**, and it would make sense to speak of correlations between the factor scores and the real test scores. Factor scores, in fact, can be used as representative variables for input into subsequent analyses.

We have seen that the loading of a test on a factor is, geometrically speaking, the co-ordinate of the test point on the factor axis. But that axis also represents a 'factor' in the second, algebraic sense, and (in the technique we shall be considering in this chapter) the loading is the correlation between the original test scores and those on the factor. Ultimately, however, a factor (originally a mathematical entity) is assumed to represent an underlying or latent variable, in terms of which the correlations in the R-matix can be accounted for or explained and with reference to which the tests in the battery can be classified.

In **exploratory factor analysis**, the aim is to determine the number and nature of the factors necessary to account adequately for the correlations in the R-matrix. The researcher will hope that the correlations among the observed variables can be accounted for in terms of comparatively few factors. In **confirmatory factor analysis**, on the other hand, the researcher hypothesises that there should be a predetermined number of factors, on which the tests in the battery should show specified patterns of loadings. Such a model can then be put to the test by gathering data and testing the favoured model against other models of the same data, positing different number of factors and other specifications. Recent years have seen dramatic developments in what is known as **structural equation modelling (SEM)**, of which confirmatory factor analysis is one aspect. (See, for example, Tabachnick & Fidell, 2007, Chapter 14.)

At present, SPSS itself offers exploratory factor analysis only. Under the aegis of SPSS, however, there is also AMOS, a structural equation modelling (SEM) package, which (if installed) can be accessed through the **Analyze** menu. We shall not consider AMOS in this book.

16.1.1   Stages in an exploratory factor analysis

An exploratory factor analysis usually takes place in three stages:

1. A **correlation matrix** is generated for all possible pairings of the variables (i.e. the tests).

2. From the correlation matrix, **factors** are **extracted.** The most common method of extraction is called **principal factors** or **principal components**. (Technically, there is a difference between factors and components, but this need not concern us at the moment.)

3. The factors (axes) are **rotated** to facilitate the interpretation of the results of the factor analysis.

16.1.2   The extraction of factors

The factors (or axes) in a factor analysis are **extracted** one at a time, leaving after each extraction a set of **residual** scores that do not correlate with the extracted factor. The process is repeated with the residuals until it is possible, from the loadings of the tests on the factors so far extracted, to generate good approximations to the correlations in the original R-matrix. One of the main purposes of exploratory factor analysis is to ascertain the number of factors necessary to achieve an adequate reconstruction of the R-matrix.

16.1.3   The rationale of rotation

We can think of the tests in the battery and the origin of the classificatory axes or factors as stationary points and rotate the axes around the origin of this graph to produce a new pattern of loadings known as a **rotated factor matrix**. We can do this because, although rotation will cause the values of all the loadings to change, the new set of loadings, *whatever the new position of the axes*, can still be used to produce exactly the same estimates of the correlations in the R-matrix. In this sense, the position of the axes is arbitrary: the factor matrix (or **F-matrix**) only tells us *how many* axes are necessary to classify the data adequately: it does not thereby establish that the initial position of the axes (the **unrotated F matrix**) is the best position. (There is, in fact, no unique position for the axes that is 'best' in every possible respect.)

The factors or axes are rotated in order to make the results of the factor analysis easier to interpret. In general, it is easier to endow mathematical factors with substantive meaning if the tests in the R-matrix have substantial loadings on comparatively few factors, as opposed to having small loadings on many factors. The position of the axes (or rotated factor matrix) that best achieves this economy is said to have the property of **simple structure**. That term, however, which was coined many years ago by Thurstone, is open to different interpretations and there exists no method of achieving, in a single rotation, all the properties that Thurstone described. Modern computing packages such as SPSS offer a selection of rotation methods, each based upon a different (but reasonable) interpretation of simple structure.

16.1.4   Some issues in factor analysis

As we have described it so far, the outcome of a factor analysis will have seemed entirely objective and automatic. While the researcher will almost certainly have expectations about how many factors are likely to emerge, the process of factor extraction proceeds automatically until a criterion for termination is reached. The results of a factor analysis, however, are notoriously dependent upon the manner in which the participants and the test materials have been sampled by the researcher and the type of factor analysis the researcher is using.

When children are selected from the full main stream ability range, the pattern of correlations shown in Figure 1 is extremely unlikely. Years of research with primary school children have shown the predominance of a factor on which *every* test has substantial loadings. This is known as the **general factor (g)**. Study after study has confirmed the pattern known as the **positive manifold**, that is, substantial correlations among all the tests in the battery. Figure 1 shows an unusual predominance of **group factors**, that is, factors on which only *some* of the tests in the battery have substantial loadings. Such a **group factor profile** is characteristic of children selected for their high academic ability.

Even when the same battery of tests has been used in different projects, the precise number of factors extracted and the pattern of the loadings have been found to vary from study to study. The goal of **factor invariance** has, in detail, proved to be somewhat elusive.

The pattern shown by the loadings in the final rotated factor matrix depends upon the method of rotation used. The most commonly used method of rotation is **varimax**, which maintains independence among the mathematical factors. Geometrically, this means that during rotation, the axes or factors remain **orthogonal** (i.e. they are kept at right angles). **Orthogonal factors** are uncorrelated factors. There are other methods of rotation, however, which allow the axes to be non-orthogonal or **oblique**, so that they represent correlated or **oblique factors**. There has been much argument about which method of rotation is best, and the preferred method tends to reflect the theoretical views of the user. In view of the multiplicity of considerations that can influence the outcome of a factor analysis, it has often been argued that traditional factor analytic methods are ill-suited to the testing of specific hypotheses and are appropriate only in the early, exploratory stages of research. **Confirmatory factor analysis**, however, in contrast with **exploratory factor analysis**, allows the formulation of hypotheses that are sufficiently specific to be put to the empirical test.

16.1.5   Some key technical terms

An understanding of the SPSS output requires at least an intuitive grasp of the meaning of several technical terms.

- Provided the factors remain uncorrelated or orthogonal during rotation, the **loading** of a test on a factor is the correlation between the test and the factor.

- The **communality** of a test is the total proportion of its variance that is accounted for by the extracted factors. The communality is the **squared multiple correlation R^2** between the test and the factors emerging from the factor analysis. If the factors are orthogonal or independent (as they will be in the example we shall consider), the communality is given by the sum of the squares of the loadings of the test on the extracted factors. The communality of a test is a measure of its **reliability**.

- The **eigenvalue** (or **latent root**) of a factor is a measure of the total variance (taken across all the tests) accounted for by the factor. If the total variance of each test is unity, the eigenvalue of the first factor extracted has a theoretical maximum equal to the number of tests in the battery. (In practice, of course, this cannot be achieved with variables having an element of measurement error.) The eigenvalue can be converted to a measure of the proportion of the total variance by dividing by the total number of tests in the battery. Before the rotation phase, the first factor extracted always has the largest eigenvalue, the second the next largest, and so on. The process of extraction continues until the factors extracted account for negligible proportions of the total variance.

- If the eigenvalues of successive factors are plotted against the ordinal numbers of the factors, the curve eventually flattens out and its appearance thereafter has been likened to the rubble or scree on a mountainside. The eigenvalue plot is therefore known as a **scree**

plot (see Output 6). There is general agreement that this 'factorial litter' begins when the eigenvalues fall below one.

* The process of **rotation** changes the eigenvalues of the factors that have been extracted, so that the common factor variance accounted for by the extraction is more evenly distributed among the rotated factors. The communalities, on the other hand, are unchanged by rotation, because their values depend only upon the number of factors and the correlations among the tests.

16.1.6   Preliminaries

Before you proceed with a factor analysis, it is advisable to inspect the R-matrix first. Since the purpose of factor analysis is to account for correlations among the tests, the exercise is pointless if no substantial correlations exist. By convention, all variables should show at least one correlation of the order of 0.3 before it is worth proceeding with a full factor analysis. Should any variables show no substantial correlation with any of the others, they should be removed from the R-matrix. It is also advisable to check that the correlation matrix does not possess the highly undesirable property of **multicollinearity**, that is, the presence of very high correlations arising from the inclusion of very similar tests in the battery. Should the R-matrix show multicollinearity, some of the variables must be omitted from the analysis; otherwise the factor analysis will not run.

The process of preparing the data for a factor analysis includes checking them for transcription errors, the presence of extreme scores and outliers and missing values. Some writers insist that at least 300 cases are required for a factor analysis; others, however, accept fewer cases. Should the data be less plentiful than one would wish, however, extreme scores and outliers can distort the correlations in the R-matrix.

Missing data present problems for any kind of analysis. One approach is to exclude cases from the analysis; another is to substitute the mean score for the variable concerned. **Listwise** exclusion of cases removes from the analysis any case that does not have values on all the variables in the set. This is a strict criterion: should even a single score be missing, all the data from the case concerned are excluded. **Pairwise** exclusion removes only those cases that do not have both scores for any one pair of variables, so that data from a case may be included in the calculation of some correlations, but not for others. This is clearly a less stringent criterion than listwise exclusion.

A potential problem with pairwise exclusion is that the correlations in the R-matrix may be based upon data from different samples of participants. The result may be what is known as an **ill-conditioned** matrix, that is, one that does not yield stable solutions to mathematical operations essential to factor analysis and other multivariate methods.

The **Kaiser-Meyer-Olkin (KMO)** statistic tests for **sampling adequacy**, that is, absence of multicollinearity among the variables. It is generally recommended that its value should be at least 0.6.

A preliminary inspection of the R-matrix in order to check for the presence of correlations among the variables should be supported by some statistical analysis. **Bartlett's test** of sphericity, which is included in the SPSS output, is rather too sensitive to be very useful and typically shows significance with large data sets. SPSS ouput, however, also includes tests for the significance of the correlations in the R-matrix, which is more helpful.

The claim that a subset of the tests in a battery really do measure a particular underlying factor can be supported by additional statistics, such as **Cronbach's alpha**, which are obtained from a separate reliability analysis.

16.2 AN EXPLORATORY FACTOR ANALYSIS

Table 2 contains the raw data from which the correlations in Table 1 were calculated. These data will be found in the file *Ch16 School marks.sav*, which is available on our website at http://www.psypress.com/spss-made-simple.

Table 2. Marks of 10 children in six examinations

Case	French	German	Latin	Music	Maths	Mapwork
1	56	66	53	47	50	48
2	46	48	43	53	69	55
3	56	51	43	40	49	45
4	29	42	39	53	56	48
5	71	67	84	66	67	60
6	56	47	58	59	67	74
7	62	69	48	59	58	66
8	46	42	38	46	38	42
9	66	73	85	34	49	42
10	36	42	48	53	59	48

Once these raw data have been entered into SPSS, we can run a factor analysis by choosing from menus and completing dialogs. Should we, however, wish to input a correlation matrix such as that shown in Table 1, we should have to use SPSS syntax. We shall describe how that is done in a later section.

16.2.1 Entering the data for a factor analysis

Enter the data using the procedures described in Section 2.3. In **Variable View**, name the six variables for the factor analysis. It's good practice to include an extra variable for the case number. Ensure that there are no decimals by changing the value in the **Decimals** column to 0. Click the **Data View** tab at the foot of **Variable View** and enter the data in **Data View**.

16.2.2　Running a factor analysis with SPSS

To run the factor analysis, proceed as follows:

- Choose **Analyze➜Dimension Reduction➜Factor...** (Figure 2) to open the **Factor Analysis** dialog box (Figure 3).

- Transfer all the variable names except Case Number to the **Variables** box.

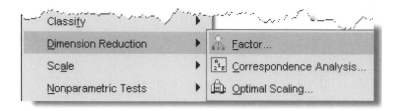

Figure 2. Finding the **Factor Analysis** dialog box in the **Analyze** menu

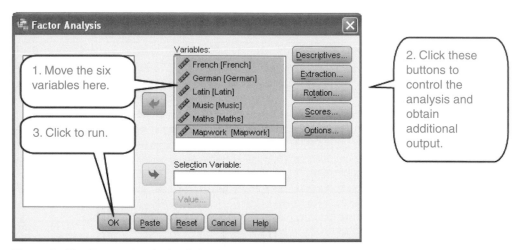

Figure 3. The **Factor Analysis** dialog box

Before running the analysis, you should select some options to control the analysis and add some useful extra items to the output.

- Click **Descriptives...** to open the **Descriptives** dialog box (Figure 4). Click the following check boxes: **Univariate descriptives**, to tabulate descriptive statistics; **Initial solution**, to display the original communalities, eigenvalues and the percentage of variance explained; **Coefficients**, to tabulate the R-matrix; **Reproduced**, to obtain an approximation of the R-matrix from the loadings of the factors extracted by the analysis; **Significance levels**, to identify the significant correlations in the R-matrix; **KMO and Bartlett's test of sphericity** for tests of sampling adequacy and complete independence. The **Reproduced** option will also obtain communalities and the residual differences between the observed and reproduced correlations.

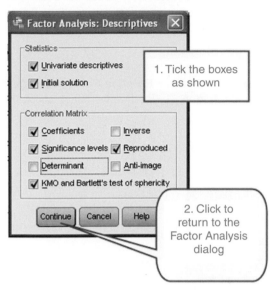

Figure 4. The **Descriptives** dialog box with appropriate selections

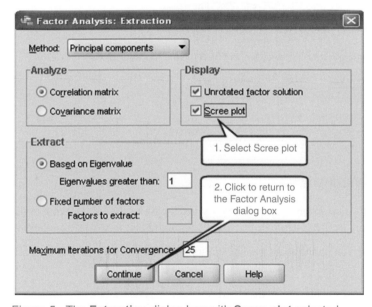

Figure 5. The **Extraction** dialog box with **Scree plot** selected

- Click **Continue** to return to the **Factor Analysis** dialog box.

- Click **Extraction…** to open the **Extraction** dialog box (Figure 5). Click the **Scree plot** check box. The scree plot is a useful display showing the relative importance of the factors extracted.

- Click **Continue** to return to the **Factor Analysis** dialog box.

- To obtain the rotated F-matrix, click **Rotation…** to obtain the **Rotation** dialog box (Figure 6). In the **Method** box, click the **Varimax** radio button. In the Display panel, check the boxes labelled **Rotated solution** and **Loading plots**.

- Click **Continue** and then **OK** to run the factor analysis procedure.

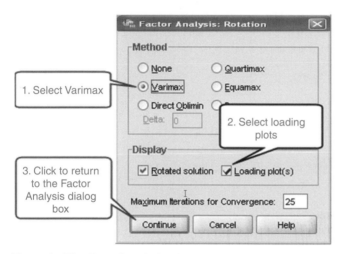

Figure 6. The **Rotation** dialog box with **Varimax** selected

16.2.3   Output for factor analysis

The output of the factor analysis is extensive, as shown by the length of the list of items in the **SPSS Statistics Viewer**. Any desired item can be viewed immediately, however, by clicking on its name in the list.

Descriptive statistics

Output 1 shows the specially requested descriptive statistics for the variables.

Descriptive Statistics

	Mean	Std. Deviation	Analysis N
French	52.00	13.167	10
German	55.00	12.561	10
Latin	54.00	17.233	10
Music	51.04	9.524	10
Maths	56.18	9.854	10
Mapwork	52.74	10.854	10

Output 1. Descriptive statistics of the variables in the test battery

The correlation matrix (R-matrix)

The correlation matrix (edited by adding additional shading) is shown in the upper part of Output 2. This is exactly the same R-matrix that we discussed in Section 15.1. (The shaded groups in Output 2 look larger than the ringed groups in Figure 1; but note the duplication of correlations with the inclusion of elements on both sides of the principal diagonal.)

Correlation Matrix

		French	German	Latin	Music	Maths	Mapwork
Correlation	French	1.000	.836	.742	.032	.083	.312
	German	.836	1.000	.715	-.081	.008	.118
	Latin	.742	.715	1.000	.022	.222	.131
	Music	.032	-.081	.022	1.000	.713	.783
	Maths	.083	.008	.222	.713	1.000	.735
	Mapwork	.312	.118	.131	.783	.735	1.000
Sig. (1-tailed)	French		.001	.007	.465	.410	.190
	German	.001		.010	.411	.491	.373
	Latin	.007	.010		.476	.269	.359
	Music	.465	.411	.476		.010	.004
	Maths	.410	.491	.269	.010		.008
	Mapwork	.190	.373	.359	.004	.008	

Output 2. The correlation matrix (**R-matrix**) with additional shading (see text) and the *p*-values of the correlations

In the lower part of Output 2 are the *p*-values of the correlations in the upper part. The *p*-values corresponding to the correlations in the shaded areas in the upper table, which are shown in similarly shaded and correspondingly placed rectangles in the lower table, are all very small, indicating that the correlations are statistically robust.

We saw in Section 16.1 that we should be able to account for the pattern of correlations in terms of two independent dimensions of ability. The important question now is whether this view is confirmed by the results of the formal factor analysis. Are two factors sufficient to account for the correlations among the tests? Are the results of the factor analysis consistent with the simple interpretation we have arrived at through inspection of the R-matrix?

The KMO statistic and Bartlett's test

It can be seen from Output 3 that the value of the KMO statistic is 0.606, which is within the acceptable range. (The value of the KMO should be at least 0.5.) There is unlikely to be a problem with multicollinearity. In view of the large (and statistically significant) correlations in the R matrix, it would be very surprising if Bartlett's test were not significant, even with such a small data set as the present one.

KMO and Bartlett's Test

Kaiser-Meyer-Olkin Measure of Sampling Adequacy.		.606
Bartlett's Test of Sphericity	Approx. Chi-Square	28.455
	df	15
	Sig.	.019

Output 3. A measure of sampling adequacy and Bartlett's test

Communalities

Output 4 is a table of communalities assigned to the variables by the factor analysis. The communality of a test is, as we have seen, the proportion of the variance of the test that has been accounted for by the factors extracted. For example, we see that 89% of the variance of the scores on French is accounted for by the factoring.

Communalities

	Initial	Extraction
French	1.000	.888
German	1.000	.870
Latin	1.000	.783
Music	1.000	.852
Maths	1.000	.801
Mapwork	1.000	.862

Extraction Method: Principal Component Analysis.

Output 4. Table of the communalities of the six variables

The next table (Output 5) displays information about the factors (SPSS calls them 'components') that have been extracted. Technically, a 'component' is not identical with a 'factor'. In principal components analysis (as opposed to factor analysis), the analysis produces as many components as there are tests in the battery. You can see that this is so in Output 5, where 6 components are listed. A principal components analysis accounts for *all* the variance of the test scores, including error variance. In contradistinction, a factor analysis accounts only for that portion of the variance that is **common factor variance**, that is, variance that is shared among the tests in the battery. The common factor variance is the *reliable* part of the total variance.

Proportion of variance accounted for by each factor (SPSS calls factors 'components')

Proportion of variance accounted for by each factor *before* rotation

Proportion of variance accounted for by each factor *after* rotation. (Note that the total variance accounted for by the two factors is the same as for the unrotated model)

Total Variance Explained

Comp-onent	Initial Eigenvalues			Extraction Sums of Squared Loadings			Rotation Sums of Squared Loadings		
	Total	% of Variance	Cumul-ative %	Total	% of Variance	Cumul-ative %	Total	% of Variance	Cumul-ative %
1	2.81	46.82	46.82	2.81	46.82	46.82	2.56	42.60	42.60
2	2.25	37.45	84.27	2.25	37.45	84.27	2.50	41.67	84.27
3	.44	7.35	91.62						
4	.23	3.85	95.47						
5	.19	3.19	98.66						
6	.08	1.34	100.00						

Extraction Method: Principal Component Analysis.

Output 5. Edited table of statistics relating to the two components extracted

A principal components analysis begins with the R-matrix and proceeds until the entries in R can be produced exactly. This includes all the values in R, including the unit entries along the principal diagonal, each of which represents 100% of the variance of the test in the row or column of R. Exact reproduction of the unit entries will require as many components as there are tests. In a true factor analysis, an initial estimate of the communality of each test is made and that value is substituted for the initial unit value in the cell of the principal diagonal of R. The amended R-matrix (known as the **reduced R-matrix**) is sometimes denoted by R*. A factor analysis attempts to reproduce this reduced R-matrix, rather than the original R-matrix, which has ones along the principal diagonal. We can see the results of a true factor analysis in the last six columns on the right of Output 5, each of which contains only two entries.

Earlier, we saw that the **eigenvalue** of a factor is a measure of the total test variance that is accounted for by that factor alone. The eigenvalue is an aggregate of the proportions of the variances of the individual tests that are accounted for by the factor and is the sum of the squares of the loadings of the tests on the factor. Since each loading is the correlation between a test and the factor, the square of the loading gives the proportion of test variance that is accounted for by regression of the test scores upon the factor scores. The squared loading is the **coefficient of determination**. Since the maximum value of each component of the eigenvalue is 1, the theoretical total value of an eigenvalue is the number of tests in the battery. If, therefore, we divide the eigenvalue by the number of tests and multiply by 100, we shall have the percentage of the total test variance that is accounted for by each factor.

In Output 5, the first block of three columns, labelled **Initial Eigenvalues**, contains the eigenvalues and the contributions they make to the total variance. The eigenvalues determine which factors (components) remain in the analysis: following Kaiser's criterion, factors with an eigenvalue of less than 1 (i.e. factors 3-6) are excluded. From the eigenvalues, the proportions of the total test variance accounted for by the factors are readily obtained. For example, the eigenvalue of the first factor is 2.81. Since the total test variance that could possibly be accounted for by a factor is 6 (the total number of tests), the proportion of the total test variance accounted for by the first factor is 2.81 ÷ 6 = 46.82%, the figure given in the **% of Variance** column. In this analysis, the two factors that meet the Kaiser criterion account for over 84% of the variance (see the column labelled **Cumulative %**).

The second block of three columns (**Extraction Sums of Squared Loadings**) repeats the output of the first block, but only for the two factors that have met Kaiser's criterion.

The third block (**Rotation Sums of Squared Loadings**) tabulates the output for the rotated factor solution. Notice that the proportions of variance explained by the two factors are more similar in the rotated solution than they are in the unrotated solution, in which the first factor accounts for a much greater percentage of the variance. Notice also that the accumulated proportion of variance from the two components/factors is the same for the unrotated and rotated solutions.

Scree plot

Output 6 (edited) shows the **scree plot**, which was specially requested in the **Factor Analysis: Extraction** dialog box. The eigenvalues are plotted against the ordinal numbers of the factors extracted. The amount of variance accounted for (the eigenvalue) by successive components plunges sharply as the first factors are extracted.

The point of interest is where the curve begins to flatten out. It can be seen that the 'scree' begins to appear between the second and third factors. Notice also that Component 3 has an eigenvalue of less than 1, so that only the first two components have been retained as common factors.

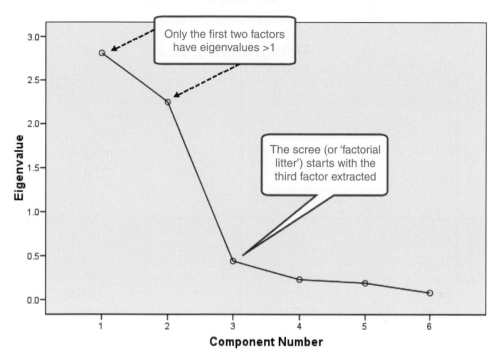

Output 6 (annotated). The scree plot

The component matrix (unrotated factor matrix)

Output 7 shows the component (factor) matrix containing the loadings of the six tests on the two factors extracted.

Component Matrix^a

	Component	
	1	2
French	.764	-.551
German	.661	-.659
Latin	.714	-.523
Music	.566	.729
Maths	.647	.618
Mapwork	.735	.568

Extraction Method: Principal Component Analysis.

a. 2 components extracted.

Output 7. The unrotated component matrix

Since the components or factors can be thought of as graphical axes, each test can be plotted as a point on the graph with its loadings on the factors as coordinates. When this is done, the graph appears as in Output 8.

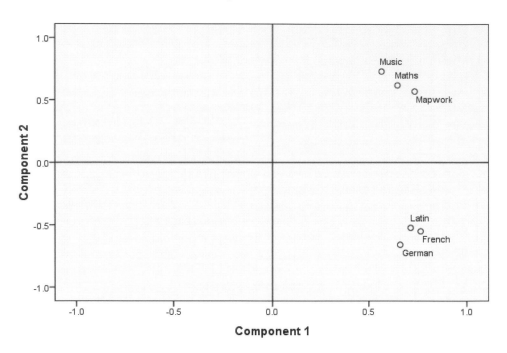

Component Plot

Output 8. Plot of the unrotated factor matrix, in which each of the six tests in the battery appears as a point in space with its loadings on the axes (factors) as coordinates

Note that the plot of the unrotated factor matrix shown in Output 8 will not appear in the output if a rotation has been requested. This graph can be obtained in a second run of the factor analysis procedure by clicking the **Rotation** button in the **Factor Analysis** dialog box and, in the **Factor Analysis: Rotation** dialog box**,** changing the choice of rotation from **Varimax** to **None** and checking the square labelled **Loading plots**.

It can be seen that, in agreement with the impression given by the correlation matrix, the factor analysis has extracted two factors. On the other hand, it is not easy to interpret the unrotated factor matrix. Both groups of tests show substantial loadings on both factors, which is not in accord with the obvious psychological interpretation of the pattern of correlations in the original R-matrix, which seemed to arise from two independent abilities, each required for one of the two clusters of highly correlated tests.

Another awkward feature of the unrotated factor matrix is that, whereas the mathematical group of tests loads positively on both factors, the verbal group is negatively loaded on the second factor. In other words, the higher one's score on the language subjects, the lower one's score on the first factor/component, whatever that factor may be. A factor such as factor 1, upon which one group of tests loads negatively and the other loads positively, is known as a **bipolar factor**. Bipolar factors are very difficult to interpret without collateral evidence or a sound theoretical rationale.

The Reproduced correlation matrix and residuals

Reproduced Correlations

		French	German	Latin	Music	Maths	Mapwork
Reproduced Correlation	French	.888[a]	.868	.834	.031	.154	.249
	German	.868	.870[a]	.816	-.107	.020	.111
	Latin	.834	.816	.783[a]	.022	.139	.228
	Music	.031	-.107	.022	.852[a]	.817	.830
	Maths	.154	.020	.139	.817	.801[a]	.826
	Mapwork	.249	.111	.228	.83?	.826	.862[a]
Residual[b]	French		-.032	-.092	.002	-.071	.063
	German	-.032		-.101	.025	-.012	.007
	Latin	-.092	-.101		-.001	.083	-.096
	Music	.002	.025	-.001			-.046
	Maths	-.071	-.012	.083			-.091
	Mapwork	.063	.007	-.096			

The diagonal entries are the communalities

The residual correlations are small

The reproduced correlations are close to the values in the R-matrix

Extraction Method: Principal Component Analysis.

a. Reproduced communalities

b. Residuals are computed between observed and reproduced correlations. There are 8 (53.0%) nonredundant residuals with absolute values greater than 0.05.

Output 9 The reproduced correlation matrix and residuals

Output 9 shows the **reproduced correlation matrix** of coefficients, computed from the extracted factors (components), together with the **residuals**, which are the differences between the values in the R-matrix and the corresponding values in the reproduced matrix. The residuals are small, indicating that the two factors extracted give a good account of the correlations in the R-matrix.

Each reproduced correlation between two tests is the sum of the products of their loadings on the factors emerging from the analysis. For example, the sum of the products of the loadings of French and German on the two factors extracted is, from the loadings in the unrotated F-matrix in Output 7, $[(0.764 \times 0.661) + (-0.551 \times -0.659)] = 0.868$, which is the value given for the reproduced correlation between French and German in Output 9. The diagonal values labelled **a** are the communalities listed in Output 4. Each communality is the sum of the squares of the loadings of a test on the two factors extracted. Confirm that the sum of the squares of the entries in the first row of Output 7 is 0.888, the value given as the communality for French in Output 9. Notice that all the communalities are very large – at least 78%.

The **residuals** are the differences between the actual and reproduced correlations. For example, the actual correlation between French and German is 0.836 (Output 2) and the reproduced correlation is 0.868, so the difference is –0.032, which is the residual shown in the lower half of Output 9. Footnote *b* gives the number and proportion of residuals (i.e. the differences) that are greater than 0.05. There are eight such residuals (53%); but none is greater than 0.10.

The rotated factor (component) matrix

Output 10 shows the rotated factor (component) matrix, which should be compared with the unrotated matrix in Output 7.

Rotated Component Matrix [a]

	Component	
	1	2
French	.936	.105
German	.932	-.045
Latin	.880	.092
Music	-.070	.920
Maths	.065	.892
Mapwork	.163	.914

Extraction Method: Principal Component Analysis.
Rotation Method: Varimax with Kaiser Normalization.

[a]. Rotation converged in 3 iterations.

Output 10. The rotated component matrix

Now we have a pattern that is much easier to interpret: there are two groups of tests; and the tests in each group are loaded upon (i.e., they correlate substantially with) one factor only. The purpose of rotation is not to change the number of components extracted, but to try to arrive at a new position for the axes (components) that is easier to interpret in substantive terms. In the previous Section, we showed that the sum of the products of the loadings of any two tests on the factors extracted gives the 'reproduced' value of the correlation between the two tests in R. You will find that you will arrive at exactly the same value for the reproduced correlation if you take the sum of the products of the loadings of the tests on the rotated factors given in Output 10. This will be so whatever the position of the axes.

Output 11 is a graph of the rotated F-matrix, in which each of the six tests is plotted as a point in space with its new loadings on the rotated axes as coordinates. It can be seen from the graph in Output 11 that the rotated component/factor matrix is much easier to interpret than the unrotated matrix in Output 7. The three language tests now have high loadings on one factor only (Component 1); whereas Mapwork, Mathematics and Music have high loadings on the other factor only (Component 2). Since the rotation was orthogonal, that is, the axes were kept at right angles, the two factors are uncorrelated. This is quite consistent with what we concluded from our inspection of the original R-matrix, namely, that the correlations among the six tests in our battery could be accounted for in terms of two independent psychological dimensions of ability and that each group of tests measured a separate dimension of ability.

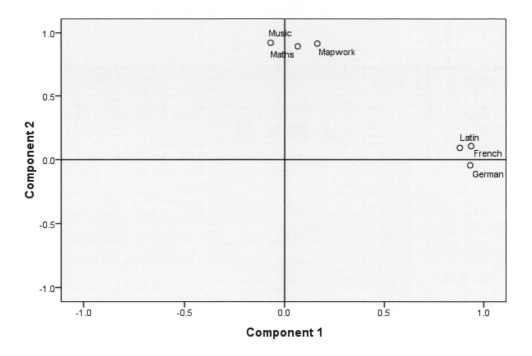

Output 11. Graph of the rotated R-matrix

Tests with high loadings on one factor only are said to be **indicators** of the factor concerned. Clearly, Output 11 shows that Music, Maths and Mapwork are indicators of Factor 1; whereas Latin, French and German are indicators of Factor 2.

16.3   USING SPSS SYNTAX TO RUN AN EXPLORATORY FACTOR ANALYSIS

Initially, the easiest way to run a factor analysis on SPSS is by using the Windows graphical interface with its dialog boxes. When the user is more familiar with the procedure, however, the syntax approach has much to recommend it. If you have several factor analyses to run, for example, it is much quicker to edit the syntax file and run the procedure from the syntax window, rather than complete the dialogs with every new data set.

16.3.1   Procedure with the raw data as input

With the scores from Table 1 in **Data View**, access the **Factor Analysis** dialog box in the usual way. Make the selections as before, remembering to select the buttons at the bottom of the dialog box to specify the rotation, order a scree test, request a correlation matrix and so on. Now click **Paste**. When this is done, the **syntax window**, will appear, with the commands that have just been specified by your choices from the dialog boxes written in the editor pane (see Figure 7).

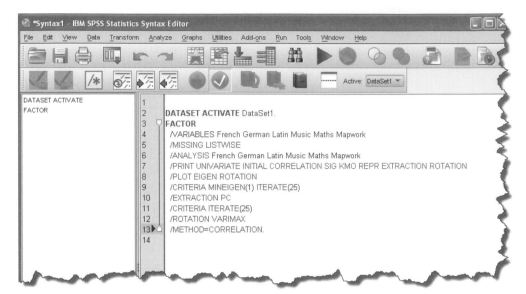

Figure 7. The syntax window after clicking **Paste** in the completed **Factor** dialog box

To run the factor analyis, you can select the entire command (by left-clicking and dragging the cursor from its initial position at the beginning of the top line) and clicking the run button in the toolbar above the window. You can also run the procedure by choosing Run➔All from the drop-down menu at the top of the syntax window.

It is easy to see that with another data set, consisting of scores on a different battery of tests, it would be easy to edit the **FACTOR** command by changing the variable names and other specifications to match the active data set in **Data View**. Inevitably, the experienced user of syntax will have built up a library of written commands, because it is quicker to carry out the analysis by editing the display in the **SPSS Statistics Syntax Editor** than to complete all the dialog and subdialog boxes again.

16.3.2 Procedure with a correlation matrix as input

The Windows graphical interface with its dialog boxes is a comparatively recent development. SPSS (like several other major statistical packages) was originally designed to be run with syntax exclusively. The translation of all the SPSS procedures to dialog boxes is as yet incomplete: there are some procedures that cannot yet be accessed through the graphical interface. We have seen, for example, that in order to test for simple effects following a significant interaction from the two-factor ANOVA, the user must run a syntax command: simple effects are not an option in the dialogs.

So far, we have concentrated on running the factor analysis procedure from the raw data, that is, participants' scores on the various tests. There are occasions when we might wish to run a factor analysis with the R-matrix, not the raw data, as our starting-point. It is not possible to do this using the SPSS graphical interface, but it can easily be done using syntax.

Running a factor analysis from a correlation matrix

The procedure has two stages, each of which requires a separate syntax command:

1. the entry of the correlation matrix into **Data View**;
2. the running of the factor analysis.

We have already noted that the R-matrix (shown again in the upper part of Figure 8) is square and symmetric: the correlations below the principal diagonal of cells extending from top left to bottom right are duplicates of the values above the principal diagonal. In such cases, a **lower triangular matrix** (Figure 9, lower part), which contains only the values along the principal diagonal and below, contains all the correlations in the full square matrix.

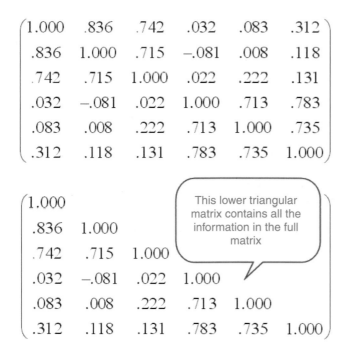

Figure 8. R-matrix (upper) and lower triangular matrix (lower)

When we come to enter the correlations in the R-matrix into the SPSS syntax editor, we shall enter the matrix in lower diagonal form. There are other modes of entry, but they require more complicated syntax.

Entry of the correlation matrix into Data View

- Choose **File➜New➜Syntax** to open the **SPSS Statistics Syntax Editor** window.

- Type in the words MATRIX DATA, as shown in Figure 9.

- On the same row, type VARIABLES=ROWTYPE_ exactly as we have it here. (The lower case can be used.) There must be no spaces at all between the two words, only the hyphen. Create the final underline by pressing and holding down the shift key and pressing the hyphen key.

- Click on the **Variables** icon and paste the names of the six tests into the row, finishing with a full stop.

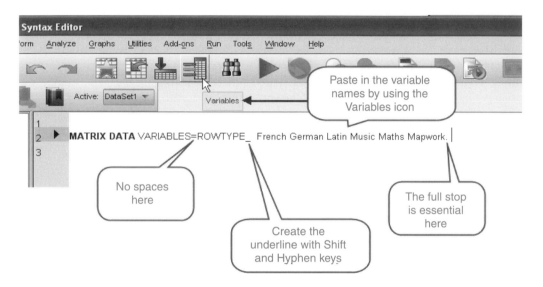

Figure 9. The MATRIX DATA command

This first command, MATRIX DATA, prepares SPSS to receive a matrix with dimensions equal to the number of variables in the list. As with all commands, there is a full stop at the end.

In the expression VARIABLES=ROWTYPE_ , ROWTYPE_ is a special string variable which prepares the syntax editor for rows of data, each row beginning with another keyword indicating the type of data in that row. If the first word is CORR, the row contains correlations, which is what we shall be entering. If the first word is N, the data in the row will be the sample sizes of each of the variables listed in the MATRIX DATA command. Had means and standard deviations been available (which is not the case in this example), they could be given in rows beginning with MEAN and STDEV, respectively. The data, however, must be contained within the envelope of the BEGIN DATA – END DATA command structure.

The next step is to write the BEGIN DATA command and enter the correlation matrix in lower triangular form, beginning each line of values with the keyword CORR. The lower triangular form of the R-matrix is not obligatory; but other forms, such as the upper triangular, would require a special format command. Note that BEGIN DATA is a command in itself and ends with a full stop.

The complete syntax for entering the R-matrix into the SPSS Data Editor is shown in Figure 10. We have entered the sample sizes underneath the correlations; but they could also have been entered above the correlations, just underneath the BEGIN DATA command. We should note that the information about samples sizes is not required for the basic factor analysis; but it is needed for some of the additional statistics.

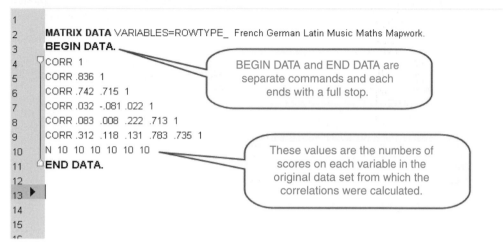

```
1
2    MATRIX DATA VARIABLES=ROWTYPE_ French German Latin Music Maths Mapwork.
3    BEGIN DATA.
4    CORR 1
5    CORR .836 1
6    CORR .742 .715 1
7    CORR .032 -.081 .022 1
8    CORR .083 .008 .222 .713 1
9    CORR .312 .118 .131 .783 .735 1
10   N 10 10 10 10 10 10
11   END DATA.
12
13
14
15
```

BEGIN DATA and END DATA are separate commands and each ends with a full stop.

These values are the numbers of scores on each variable in the original data set from which the correlations were calculated.

Figure 10. The commands for entering the R-matrix into the SPSS data editor

To run the MATRIX DATA command, proceed as follows:

- Click **Run** in the toolbar above the syntax window and select **All**.

- The matrix will appear in **Data View**, not in the **SPSS Statistics Viewer** (Figure 11).

ROWTYPE_	VARNAME_	French	German	Latin	Music	Maths	Mapwork
N		10.000	10.000	10.000	10.000	10.000	10.000
CORR	French	1.000	.836	.742	.032	.083	.312
CORR	German	.836	1.000	.715	-.081	.008	.118
CORR	Latin	.742	.715	1.000	.022	.222	.131
CORR	Music	.032	-.081	.022	1.000	.713	.783
CORR	Maths	.083	.008	.222	.713	1.000	.735
CORR	Mapwork	.312	.118	.131	.783	.735	1.000

Figure 11. The data set that appears in Data View after the **MATRIX DATA** command has been run

Syntax of the FACTOR command

Return to the syntax window and type the **FACTOR** command below the previous syntax, as shown in Figure 12.

- Notice that the identification of the matrix in the /**MATRIX** =**IN** subcommand is given as (**CORR=***). This informs SPSS that the input will be a correlation matrix (and not, say, a factor matrix), and that it is in the current data file (represented by *), which can be seen in the **Data View** window. The /**PRINT** options are those selected in the **Descriptives** dialog box and the /**PLOT** option is that selected in the **Extraction** dialog box. It is not necessary to enter /**ROTATION VARIMAX**, because that is the default rotation method. *Again note the full stop at the end of the command: this terminator is absolutely essential.*

```
1    ▽ FACTOR
2    │  /MATRIX =IN (CORR=*)
3    │  /PRINT INITIAL EXTRACTION ROTATION CORRELATION REPR
4    │  /PLOT EIGEN
5    ▶◿ /ROTATION VARIMAX.
```

Figure 12. The **FACTOR** command for running a factor analysis from a correlation matrix in **Data View**

- Run the **FACTOR** command by clicking **Run** in the toolbar at the top of the syntax window and selecting **All**. The output for the factor analysis will be more or less identical with that previously described in Section 16.2.3, depending upon which statistics were specified in the /PRINT subcommand.

16.3.3   Progressing with SPSS syntax

As we said earlier, we believe that the best way of learning SPSS syntax is by pasting the minimal basic commands into the **syntax window** from the appropriate dialog boxes in the usual way, and observing how the syntax becomes more elaborate when extra options are chosen from the subdialog boxes.

You can obtain more information about a command by selecting it and clicking on the Syntax Help icon at the top of the syntax window (Figure 13).

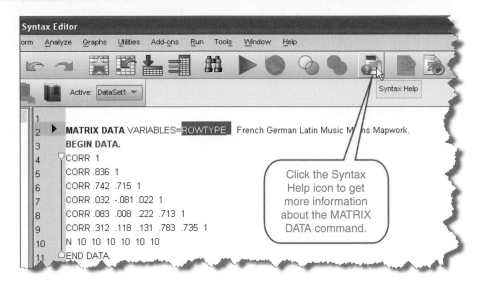

Figure 13. Getting help with syntax

Figure 14 shows **the Online Help** window.

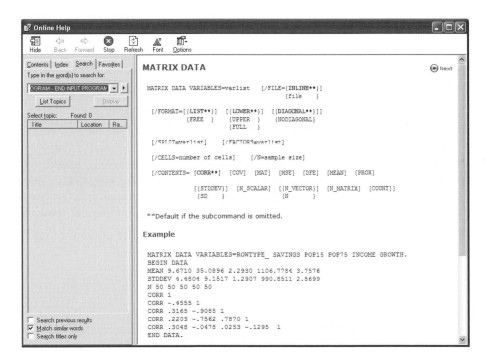

Figure 14. The **Online Help** window

The Online Help window is initially rather daunting. The user, however, will find the examples very helpful. In the **syntax map** at the top, square brackets indicate optional subcommands and (within the square brackets) the curly brackets {} indicate alternatives.

16.4   A FINAL WORD

In this chapter, we have described techniques designed to classify measured variables with reference to relatively few hypothetical reference variables or factors, which are taken to represent underlying substantive (medical, social or psychological) characteristics. In exploratory factor analysis (the topic of this chapter), the aim is to ascertain the minimum number of factors needed to generate reasonably close approximations to the correlations in the original R-matrix. Another important aspect of exploratory analysis is rotation, whereby the factors, viewed as mathematical axes with respect to which each variable can be plotted as a point in space, are rotated in order to achieve the 'simple structure' needed to interpret the factors.

Recommended reading

If you are unfamiliar with factor analysis, we suggest you read the lucid texts by Kim and Mueller (1978a, 1978b), before proceeding to more difficult books, such as Tabachnick and Fidell (2007). Tabachnick and Fidell also have a chapter on structural equation modelling, a development of multiple regression which incorporates confirmatory factory analysis.

The great advantage of confirmatory factor analyis is that it enables the researcher to compare and evaluate different factor models to determine which gives the most convincing account of the correlations in the R-matrix.

A strong feature of the books by Kim and Mueller is that they present factor analysis as an aspect of the analysis of covariance structures, which makes these texts an admirable preparation for more advanced treatments.

Dugard, Todman & Staines (2010) describe, with commendable clarity, how to develop a full structural equation model (of which confirmatory factor analyis is an aspect) and have some interesting examples. Their treatment of such highly technical material must be one of the most accessible in the literature. They achieve this by avoiding formal mathematical expressions wherever possible. On the other hand, they emphasise the importance of checking that the assumptions underlying the statistical model really are met by the data in hand.

Dugard, P., Todman, J., & Staines, H. (2010). *Approaching multivariate analysis: a practical introduction (2nd ed.)* London & New York: Routledge.

Kim, J., & Mueller, C. W. (1978a). *Factor analysis: statistical methods and practical issues.* Newbury Park, CA: Sage.

Kim, J., & Mueller, C. W. (1978b). *Introduction to factor analysis: what it is and how to do it.* Newbury Park, CA: Sage.

Tabachnick, B. G., & Fidell, L. S. (2007). *Using multivariate statistics (5th ed.).* Boston: Allyn & Bacon (Pearson International Edition).

Exercise

Exercise 24 *Factor analysis* is available in www.psypress.com/spss-made-simple. Click on Exercises.

APPENDIX

The use of looping structures in Syntax

Syntax has many uses other than simply running stock statistical routines. By using Syntax, you can perform complex transformations on your data; in fact, you can create completely new data sets. A **loop** is a command which returns control to the point just before a transformation was first run so that the transformation can be repeated as often as desired, either on the same (or next) case or on new variables. By using loops, it is possible to sample from specified distributions and so run simulations to investigate sampling distributions.

A **looped structure** is an assembly of commands which implements a looping operation. In this section, we shall describe four common looped structures: 1. LOOP – END LOOP; 2. INPUT PROGRAM – END INPUT PROGRAM; 3. DO IF – END IF; and 4. DO REPEAT – END REPEAT.

For the following exercise open the caffeine data once again. The data are in the file *Ch2 Caffeine experiment(60).sav*, at http://www.psypress.com/spss-made-simple.

The LOOP – END LOOP structure

We shall first illustrate the use of a looping structure to perform a simple arithmetical operation: we shall create, in the caffeine data set, a new variable named Sum, which contains, in every row, the sum of the first hundred counting numbers: $1 + 2 + 3 + ... + 98 + 99 + 100$. As a check on what the computer is about to do, we recall that the sum of the first n counting numbers is $n(n + 1)/2$, so the sum of the counting numbers from 1 to 100 is $100(101)/2 = 5050$. We are going to command the computer to arrive at this value in a different way, by creating a new variable Sum with value zero, looping back and adding 1 to this value, looping back and adding 2, and so on. At the end of the looping operation, therefore, the variable named Sum should contain the value 5050 in every row of Data View.

The syntax of the LOOP – END LOOP structure is shown in Figure 1a. The command COMPUTE Sum = 0, will create a new variable Sum, with zero in every row. The default position of Sum will be to the right of the variables already in the data set; but you can place the new variable anywhere you want by inserting a new variable in the desired position among those already in Variable View.

The looping structure itself begins with the LOOP command. The looping operation repeatedly returns control to the beginning of the COMPUTE command, so that progressively higher counting numbers are added to the initial value of zero. The variable #i is termed a **scratch indexing variable**, that is, #i is a temporary variable used in counting operations. With each loop, the variable #i is assigned the next number in the count from 1 to 100; but after the looping function is complete, it is removed (or **scratched**) from the data set.

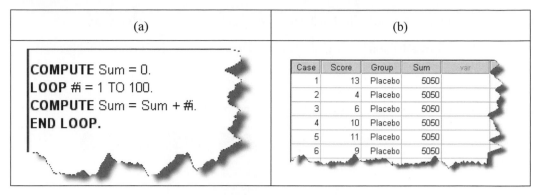

(a)	(b)

```
COMPUTE Sum = 0.
LOOP #i = 1 TO 100.
COMPUTE Sum = Sum + #i.
END LOOP.
```

Case	Score	Group	Sum	var
1	13	Placebo	5050	
2	4	Placebo	5050	
3	6	Placebo	5050	
4	10	Placebo	5050	
5	11	Placebo	5050	
6	9	Placebo	5050	

Figure 1. The LOOP – END LOOP structure

The LOOP command must always be followed by an END LOOP command.

Proceed as follows:

- In Variable View, highlight the fourth row by clicking on the blue cell labelled 4, choose **Edit➔Insert Variable** and type *Sum* in the **Name** column of the new variable. You may want to confirm that, in Data View, the new variable Sum now appears at the head of the fourth column; but every row contains the system-missing value (.).

- Since the cases are whole numbers, set **Decimals** to zero.

- In the Syntax Editor, type the commands shown in Figure 1a.

- Run the commands by highlighting them (so that they appear in inverse video) and clicking the **Run Selection** icon (at right). Confirm that, in Data View, the system-missing values (.) have now been replaced by the value 5050, as in Figure 1b.

Inserting CASE NUMBERS into an existing data set

We can also use the LOOP – END LOOP structure to insert case numbers into an existing data set. The caffeine data set already contains a variable Case. For the following exercise, therefore, open the dataset *Ch2 Heights and weights(ungrouped, no case numbers).sav* at http://www.psypress.com/spss-made-simple.

- In Variable View, highlight the first variable, MENS_HEIGHTS, choose **Edit➔Insert Variable** and type *Case* in the Name column of the new variable, which will appear *above* the highlighted row. (We want the new variable Case to appear in Data View as the first variable on the left.)

- Since the cases are whole numbers, set **Decimals** to zero.

- Choose **File➔New➔Syntax** to open the **Syntax Editor**.

- In the editor pane, type the Syntax shown in Figure 2a.

- Highlight the commands, which will then appear in inverse video (Figure 2b).

- Click the **Run Selection** button (labelled in the upper right part of Figure 2b) to place 1000 case numbers in Data View.

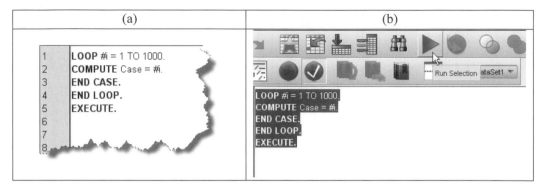

Figure 2. Syntax for inserting case numbers into a data set

The END CASE command causes control to progress to the next case, so that the next counting number can be assigned to that case; otherwise the loop will continue to operate on the first case. The END LOOP command terminates the loop. The looped structure will not run without a final additional command, such as EXECUTE or LIST.

Inspection of the navigation pane (Figure 3a) shows the hierarchical structure of the syntax: the indentation of the COMPUTE and END CASE indicates that they are nested within the LOOP – END LOOP structure. Indentation can also be used when writing Syntax, as in Figure 3b.

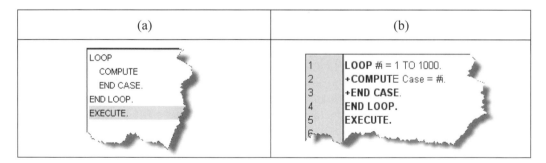

Figure 3. The hierarchical structure of the Syntax for inserting case numbers

Inserting case numbers into an empty Data Editor

Syntax can also be used to paste case numbers into an empty Data Editor. There is, however, an important difference between adding case numbers to a data set that is already in the Data

Editor and entering them when the Editor is empty: SPSS does not yet 'know' the size of the data set. In addition to the LOOP – END LOOP structure, we shall need an additional END FILE command to inform the Data Editor that the fullest extent of the new data set has now been reached. Moreover, we shall need to carry both the LOOP – END LOOP structure and the END FILE command in the envelope of another looping structure, namely, INPUT PROGRAM – END INPUT PROGRAM, which is used for entering fresh data into an empty Data Editor, rather than operating on an existing data set.

- Open *any* data file in SPSS – the caffeine data will serve the purpose. There must be an active file in the Data Editor before Syntax will run; but, since the case numbers will be entered into a new data set, the size of the active data set doesn't matter. (The active data set need contain only a single data point!)

- Choose **File➜New➜Syntax** to open the **Syntax Editor**.

- Write the Syntax shown in Figure 4a. The display in the navigation pane of the Syntax Editor window (Figure 4b) makes it clear, from the indentations, that the INPUT PROGRAM – END INPUT PROGRAM structure carries nested within it both the LOOP – END LOOP structure and the END FILE command.

- Highlight the Syntax and Click the **Run Select** button. The case numbers will now appear (with two places of decimals displayed) in Data View.

- In **Variable View**, set **Decimals** to zero to see whole numbers only in **Data View**.

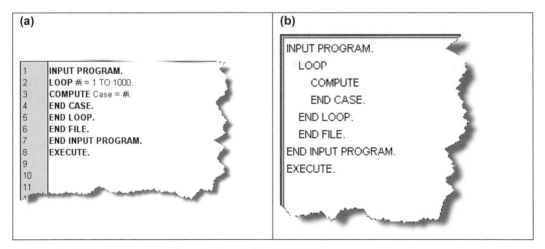

Figure 4. Entering case numbers before data with Syntax

Sampling with Syntax

Random samples can be drawn from specified populations (distributions) by using the Compute command. This command is found in the Transform menu; but here we shall show how it can be used in Syntax to draw samples. When we are entering the samples into an empty Data Editor, the size of the sample is controlled by the scratch indicator variable #i in the LOOP – END LOOP structure.

In the following exercise, we shall take a sample of 1000 values from a normal distribution with mean 1 and SD 0.5 and a sample of the same size from a skewed distribution: F on 4 and 45 degrees of freedom. We shall then graph the distributions of the two samples. (We have set the parameters of the normal distribution at small values such as 1 and 0.5 so that we can view the two distributions together in the same figure.)

- Enter 2000 case numbers into a new, initially empty data file with the following syntax (Figure 5):

```
INPUT PROGRAM.
LOOP #i = 1 TO 2000.
COMPUTE Case = #i.
END Case.
END LOOP.
END FILE.
END INPUT PROGRAM.
EXECUTE.
```

Figure 5. Entering 2000 case numbers into a new, empty data file

- In Variable View, name two new variables: 1. Group (with 1 = Normal; 2 = F); 2. Distribution. Set Decimals to zero for all three variables. Set the Measure level at **Nominal** for Group. Variable View will now appear as in Figure 6. In Data View, the system-missing value (.) will appear in the Group and Distribution columns.

Name	Type	Width	Decimals	Label	Values	Missing	Columns	Align	Measure	Role
Case	Numeric	9	0		None	None	11	≡ Right	✦ Scale	↘ Input
Group	Numeric	9	0		{1, Normal}...	None	9	≡ Right	♣ Nominal	↘ Input
Distribution	Numeric	9	0		None	None	9	≡ Right	✦ Scale	↘ Input

Figure 6. Variable View after naming two new variables

- Enter values of Group into Data View with the syntax shown in Figure 7. This looping structure is known as DO IF – END IF.

```
DO IF (Case LE 1000).
COMPUTE Group = 1.
ELSE IF (Case LE 2000).
COMPUTE Group = 2.
END IF.
EXECUTE.
```

Figure 7. Entering values into a grouping variable with DO IF – END IF

- Sample from the specified normal and F distributions with the syntax shown in Figure 8.

```
DO IF (Case LE 1000).
COMPUTE Distribution = RV.NORMAL(1, 0.5).
ELSE IF (Case LE 2000).
COMPUTE Distribution = RV.F(4, 45).
END IF.
EXECUTE.
```

Figure 8. Sampling from specified normal and F distributions

- Draw histograms of the two distributions with the syntax shown in Figure 9.

```
GRAPH
  /HISTOGRAM=Distribution
  /PANEL ROWVAR=Group ROWOP=CROSS.
```

Figure 9. Graphing the distributions

The appearance of the distributions is shown in Output 1. As we should expect, the distribution of the scores in the NORMAL group is symmetrical and bell-shaped; whereas the distribution of the F group shows marked positive skewness.

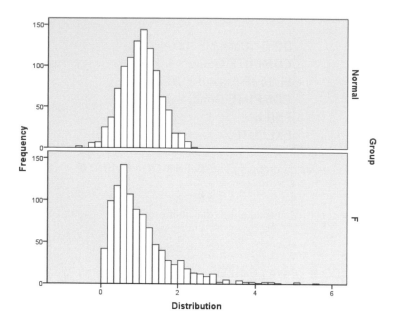

Output 1. Comparison of normal and F distributions

Sampling distributions

The (probability) distribution of a statistic such as the mean or the standard deviation is known as its **sampling distribution**. With small samples from a skewed population, such as an *F* distribution, the sampling distribution will be also be skewed – though not to the same extent as the parent population. If all sampling distributions are graphed on the same scale, the shape of a distribution will depend partly upon the size of the sample: the sampling distribution becomes taller and narrower as the sample size increases. It also becomes more symmetrical and normal in shape, in accordance with the **central limit theorem**.   Roughly speaking, the central limit theorem states that the sampling distribution of the mean of samples drawn from *any* continuous distribution, whatever its shape, can be made to approximate the normal distribution to any degree of closeness by taking a sufficiently large sample. In this section, we shall study the distribution of the means of samples from a skewed population. To do so, we shall need a new looped structure: DO REPEAT – END REPEAT. Hitherto, the structures we have used have operated on cases; DO REPEAT – END REPEAT creates (and operates upon) variables.

In the following exercise, we shall enter 1000 cases into a new data set and divide them into two groups of 500 cases. We shall pair each of the first 500 cases with a single value drawn from the F distribution on 4 and 45 degrees of freedom. We shall pair each of the second 500 cases with the mean of a sample of size 20 drawn from the same F distribution. (We shall use the DO REPEAT – END REPEAT structure to do this.) Finally, we shall draw histograms of the parent and sampling distributions on the same scale for comparison.

- Open any SPSS data file (the caffeine data will do).

- Open the Syntax Editor and write the Syntax shown in Figure 10.

- Highlight the Syntax so that it appears in inverse video and click the **Run Select** icon to run the commands.

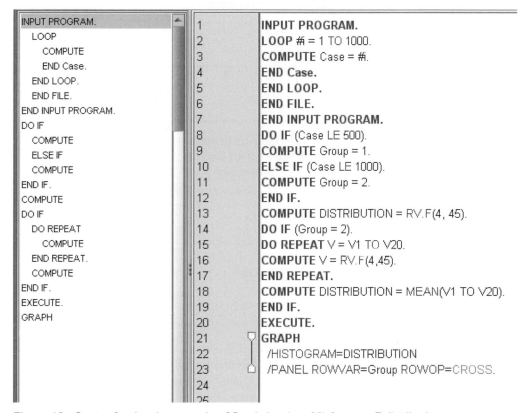

Figure 10. Syntax for drawing sample of fixed size (n = 20) from an F distribution

The rationale of the Syntax in Figure 10 is made more explicit in the display in the navigator pane on the left. Note the DO REPEAT – END REPEAT looped structure starting on line 15. This creates twenty new variables, which will contain the values in the samples from the F distribution. The COMPUTE command on line 18 creates a new variable DISTRIBUTION, which is the mean of the twenty values in V1 to V20.

When the Syntax shown in Figure 10 is run, the variables V1 to V20 and DISTRIBUTION will appear in Data View. The final GRAPH command will plot the parent distribution and the sampling distribution to the same scale (Output 2).

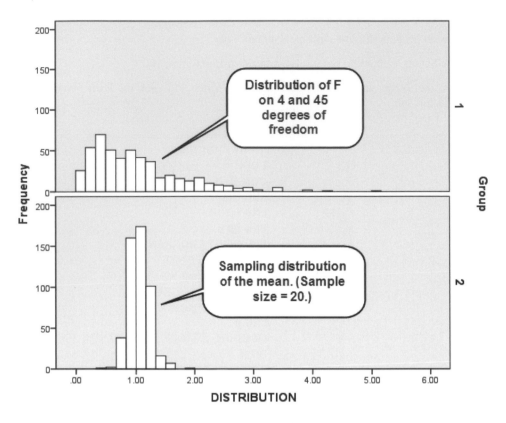

Output 2. The sampling distribution of means drawn from an *F* distribution

The striking feature of the sampling distribution of the mean is that, in accordance with the central limit theorem, it is considerably more symmetrical than the *F* distribution from which the samples were drawn.   By taking sufficiently large samples, we can make the sampling distribution approximate the normal distribution to any required degree of closeness.

In this section, we have examined four different looping structures: LOOP – END LOOP; DO IF – ELSE IF, INPUT PROGRAM – END INPUT PROGRAM and DO REPEAT – END REPEAT.   These structures enable the user to sample repeatedly from specified theoretical distributions.

Glossary

Adjusted R squared   A measure of effect size in **Regression** and **Analysis of Variance (ANOVA)**. The adjustment corrects for positive bias.

Alternative hypothesis (H_1)   In **hypothesis-testing**, the proposition that the **null hypothesis** is false.

Analysis of covariance (ANCOVA)   In the context of **analysis of variance (ANOVA)**, an ancillary technique which corrects for the association between the dependent variable and one or more additional variables known as **covariates**. A covariate is a potential nuisance variable, which may inflate the error term of the F-ratio and result in an incorrect decision about the null hypothesis.

Analysis of variance (ANOVA)   A set of **univariate** statistical techniques for comparing means from experiments with three or more treatment conditions or groups. In the one-way ANOVA, the total variance is divided into treatment and error components, which are compared by means of an **F ratio**.

Behrens-Fisher problem   A problem with making an independent samples t test when the population variances are heterogeneous. Underlying the t test for independent samples is the assumption of homogeneity of variance. If that assumption is true, the t statistic is distributed as t on $n_1 + n_2 - 2$ degrees of freedom. With heterogeneity of variance, particularly when the sample sizes are unequal, the ordinary t statistic, in which there is a pooled estimate of the supposedly constant population variance, does not have this distribution. In such cases, the sample variances are no longer pooled for the calculation of the test statistic. The Behrens-Fisher T statistic is used instead and the df are adjusted downwards by means of the Welch-Satterthwaite formula or an equivalent.

Between groups   See **Between subjects designs**.

Between subjects designs   Comparative experimental designs yielding independent samples of data, in which each participant is tested under only one condition and there is no basis for pairing the scores from one group with those in another. The term **between groups** is also used to describe this kind of design. (cf. **Repeated measures** and **Within subjects**.)

Between subjects factors   Factors to the levels of which different samples of subjects or participants are assigned. (cf. **Within subjects factors**.)

Bivariate normality   Two variables are said to have a bivariate normal distribution if, given a value of one variable, the distribution of the other variable at that value is normal. More technically, the conditional distributions are normal. The correct application of the **Pearson correlation** assumes bivariate normality, which is indicated by an elliptical (or, where there is dissociation or independence, circular) scatterplot. (cf. **Multivariate Normality**.)

Bonferroni correction   A procedure, based on the Bonferroni inequality in probability theory, for controlling the **familywise** (or **experimentwise**) **Type I error rate**. A more stringent criterion for significance can be set by dividing the ordinary (per comparison) significance level by the number of planned comparisons or (with unplanned or **post hoc** comparisons) by the number of pairwise comparisons possible from an array of means of specified size. An equivalent procedure is to multiply the *p*-value by the same factor.

Centring In **multiple regression**, the computing algorithm may not produce a solution when the correlations among the independent variables or regressors are high. (The extreme case is multicollinearity.) The risk of failure is greater if interaction terms or powers are included in the regression model. The program is more likely to run if the raw scores on a variable are first transformed into deviations by subtracting the mean, an operation known as centring.

Chi-square distribution The sum of the squares of *n* independent squared standard normal variables has a chi-square distribution on *n* degrees of freedom. A chi-square variable has a continuous distribution. The familiar chi-square statistic used in the analysis of nominal data is only an approximation to a true chi-square variable, and the approximation becomes poor when expected cell frequencies are low. The (controversial) **correction for continuity** (**Yates' correction**) is an attempt to improve the approximation.

Coefficient of determination (CD) In simple regression, the proportion of the variance of the target, criterion or dependent variable that is accounted for by regression upon another variable (the regressor or independent variable). Its value is given by the square of the Pearson correlation. In multiple regression, the coefficient of determination is the square of the multiple correlation coefficient.

Cohen's *d*   A measure of effect size, defined as the difference between the two treatment means divided by the standard deviation.

Cohen's kappa A measure of agreement between raters who are assigning cases to the same set of mutually exclusive categories, as when following a diagnostic system.

Communality In **factor analysis**, the total proportion of the variance of scores on a variable that is accounted for by the common factors extracted in the analysis.

Comparison See **Contrast**.

Confidence interval An interval constructed around the value of a statistic such as the mean which would 'cover' or include the population value in a specified proportion of samples. A confidence interval is an **interval estimate**, in contradistinction to a **point estimate** such as the value of the mean or SD.

Confirmatory factor analysis A set of techniques designed to account for an R-matrix in terms of a model in which the number of factors and other aspects of the model are pre-specified. Confirmatory factor analysis is an aspect of **structural equation modelling**.

Contingency table A table classifying individuals with respect to two or more sets of categories (see **Qualitative variables**). The entries in the cells of a contingency table are the frequencies of individuals with various combinations of attributes. For example, if patients are classified with respect to tissue type and presence or absence of an antibody, the contingency table would show the numbers of patients with and without the antibody in each tissue category. A contingency table is the starting point for various statistical analyses. For example, with a two-way contingency table, an approximate chi-square test can be used to test for an association between the two attributes. Complex multi-attribute contingency tables can be analysed with **loglinear analysis**.

Continuous variable   A quantitative variable that can have an infinite number of values within a specified interval.   Height and weight are examples.   SPSS uses the term **scale** to denote variables at the continuous level of measurement.

Contrast   The comparison between two of an array of k treatment means (or combinations of means) can be written as a **linear contrast**, which is a weighted sum of the treatment means, such that the coefficients (weights) add up to zero.   (See **Orthogonal contrasts**.)

Correction for continuity   When a discrete variable is used as an approximation to a continuous one or vice versa (as when using the normal distribution as an approximation to a binomial distribution or an approximate chi-square statistic with frequency data), the value 0.5 is first subtracted from the difference between the observed and expected values before the test statistic is calculated.

Correlation   A measure of a supposed linear relationship between two continuous variables X and Y.   The value of a correlation can vary only within the range from -1 to $+1$, inclusive.

Correlation ratio   See **eta**.

Correlational research   A research strategy whereby variables are measured as they occur in the individuals studied.   Correlational research contrasts with **experimental** research, in which the supposedly causal variable is manipulated by the experimenter, independently of the characteristics of the participants.

Covariance   A measure of a supposed linear association between two variables.   The covariance is the sum of the cross-products of the deviations of pairs of scores on the two variables from their respective means divided by the number of pairs of scores minus one.   If the scores on both variables are standardised, the covariance is identical with the **Pearson correlation**.

Covariate[1]   In the context of the **analysis of variance (ANOVA)**, a variable that may be correlated with the measure or dependent variable and therefore must be taken into consideration in the analysis.

Covariate[2]   In some SPSS procedures, such as **logistic regression** and canonical correlation, a covariate is a continuous independent variable.

Cross-validation   A procedure for attempting to generalise the results of a multiple regression. One approach is to divide the original data set into two sub-samples, fit a regression model to the first sub-sample and then assess the predictive value of the model when applied to the second sub-sample.   Applying a regression model to a fresh sample will show a weakening of predictive power known as **shrinkage**.   Shrinkage will be minimal with very large samples: Howell (2007, p506) reviews various recommendations, including the stipulation that in multiple regression we should have at least 40 or 50 more participants than there are predictors in the regression equation.   The guiding principle is that, with multiple regression (as with many other techniques), the more data one has, the better.

Cumulative probability   The probability of a value of a random variable or variate less than or equal to a specified value.   Cumulative probabilities are given by **distribution functions**.

Degrees of freedom   A term borrowed from physical science, in which the degrees of freedom of a system is the number of constraints needed to determine its state completely at any point.

In statistics, the degrees of freedom *df* are given by the number of independent observations minus the number of parameters estimated.

Deleted residual In **regression diagnostics**, it is often important to determine the influence of one particular case upon the regression statistics. Two regressions are run: the first with the entire data set; the second with the case omitted. The difference in magnitude between the raw residual (with all the data present) and the deleted residual (with the case removed) is a measure of the influence of the target case upon the regression statistics.

Dependent (or outcome) variable In the context of a true experiment, the variable (such as performance) that is measured during the course of the investigation, as opposed to the variable that is manipulated by the experimenter (the **independent variable** or IV). The purpose of an experiment is to determine whether the IV has a causal effect upon the DV.

Discriminant analysis (DA) A **multivariate** statistical technique which is mathematically equivalent to the one-way **multivariate analysis of variance (MANOVA)**. In DA, the objective is to predict group membership from two or more measured variables, which are therefore regarded as independent (rather than dependent variables, as in the MANOVA). Linear **discriminant functions** of the independent variables, which are constructed so that they maximise inter-group differences, are used to predict group membership.

Discriminant function See **Discriminant analysis**.

Distribution Any table, display or formula that pairs each of the values of a variable with a frequency or a probability. With continuous variables, the **distribution function** gives the cumulative probability of specific values; the **density function** gives the **probability density** of a particular value, that is, the derivative of the distribution function at that point. (Note that with a continuous variable, the probability of any particular value is zero.)

Distribution function See **Distribution**.

Dummy variables Variables consisting of the values 0 and 1. In several contexts, dummy variables are used to code group membership.

Eigenvalue or **latent root** In **factor analysis**, a measure of the variance accounted for by a factor extracted by the analysis. If the eigenvalue is divided by the total number of variables or tests in the R-matrix, the measure becomes the proportion of the total variance that is accounted for by the treatment factor.

Eta The **correlation ratio**, a measure of effect size in the **analysis of variance (ANOVA)**. In the **one-way ANOVA**, eta is the correlation between the scores and their group means. **Eta squared** or R^2 is a measure of the proportion of the total variance that is accounted for by differences among the treatment means. In the one-way ANOVA, eta squared is the ratio of the between groups sum of squares to the total sum of squares. As an estimator, eta squared is positively biased. Statistics such as **adjusted R squared** and **omega squared** correct the bias.

Event A category of outcome in an **experiment of chance**.

Event space In an **experiment of chance**, the subset of the sample space containing those elementary outcomes that qualify as instances of a defined event.

Experiment A research technique in which the independent variable (IV) is manipulated to ascertain its effects upon the dependent variable (DV). Such direct manipulation is the hallmark of a true comparative experiment, as opposed to a **correlational** study or a **quasi-experiment**.

Experimentwise Type I error rate   See **Familywise Type I error rate**.

Experiment of chance In probability theory, a procedure with an uncertain outcome, such as tossing a coin or rolling a die. The entire set of possible **elementary outcomes** (an elementary outcome is one of the simplest possible ways in which the experiment can turn out) is termed the **sample space**. An **event space** is a subset of the sample space.

Exploratory factor analysis A set of techniques designed to account for an **R-matrix** in terms of the minimum number of classificatory axes or dimensions, the latter being known as **factors**. (See **Confirmatory factor analysis**.)

Factorial experiments   Experiment with two or more treatment factors.

F distribution   The distribution of the ratio of two chi-square variables, each of which has been divided by its degrees of freedom. An F distribution has two parameters, namely, df_1 and df_2, the degrees of freedom of the chi-square variables. The mean of the distribution is $df_1/(df_2 - 2)$, provided that $df_2 > 2$. It can be shown that the ratio of two independent estimates of the variance of a normal population is distributed as $F(df_1, df_2)$. The F test in **analysis of variance (ANOVA)** is an application of this result.

F ratio   See **F distribution**.

Factor[1]   In **Analysis of Variance (ANOVA)**, a set of related categories, treatments or conditions. A factor is thus a qualitative or categorical **independent variable**.

Factor[2]   See **Factor analysis**.

Factor analysis (FA)   A set of techniques enabling the researcher to account for the correlations among a battery of tests in terms of a relatively small number of classificatory axes or **factors**, which are assumed to represent theoretical dimensions, **latent variables** or hypothetical constructs. Since a factor is also a function of the observed variables, individuals receive, in addition to scores on the tests in the battery, a **factor score** locating them on the dimension concerned. (See **R-matrix**.)

Factor score An individual's aggregate score on a combination of the scores on the tests in a battery.

Factorial experiments   Experiments in which there are two or more independent variables or factors. If each level of one factor is found in combination with every level of another factor, the two factors are said to **cross** and the factors are independent or **orthogonal**. In nested or hierarchical factorial designs, on the other hand, the levels of some factors are distributed among the levels of other factors, so that not every combination of conditions can be found in the experimental design.

Familywise Type I error rate   This term, which we owe to Tukey, has largely replaced the older term **experimentwise**. Following the analysis of variance of data from an experiment with three or more conditions, the researcher will often wish to make planned or unplanned comparisons among the means for specified groups or conditions. If the null hypothesis is true, the probability of at least one comparison showing significance is known as the familywise Type I error rate. The familywise Type I error rate may be considerably higher than the significance level set for any one comparison (the Type I error rate per comparison) and increases with the size of the array of treatment means. With large sets of comparisons, the familywise error rate greatly exceeds the per comparison significance level, which is usually set at 0.05: for example, if we have a set of 5 treatment means and make all 10 possible pairwise comparisons, the probability that at least one comparison will show significance (the familywise error rate) is approximately $1 - 0.95^{10} = 0.40$. (This is an approximation, because the comparisons are not independent.)   Conservative tests such as the **Bonferroni**, the **Sidak** and **Tukey** methods are designed to control the experimentwise Type I error rate.

The problem with basing the familywise Type I error rate on the entire experiment is that the criteria for the significance of comparisons can become extremely stringent. (For this reason, some recommend setting the familywise Type I error rate at 0.10, rather than 0.05.) There may be grounds for defining the reference set of means as those making up only part of the experiment and thus working with a smaller comparison 'family'. Such a redefinition of the 'family' must first be justified by, for example, demonstrating the presence of **simple effects**.

Greenhouse-Geisser correction   In **within subjects** or **repeated measures** experiments, the data may not have the property of **sphericity**, or **homogeneity of covariance**. If so, the ordinary F test may be positively biased, that is, it may give too many significant results when the null hypothesis is true. The correction adjusts the numerator and denominator degrees of freedom of the F ratio downwards by multiplying them by a constant (epsilon), which takes its maximum value of 1 when there is homogeneity of covariance. Another corrective procedure is the Huynh-Feldt method, which is less conservative than the Greenhouse-Geisser correction. SPSS offers a choice of several different corrections.

Grouping variable   In SPSS, a qualitative variable consisting of a set of arbitrary code numbers indicating group membership. In **Variable View**, the numbers, or **values**, should always be assigned meaningful **value labels**.

Homogeneity of covariance (sphericity)   A property of the **variance-covariance matrix**, which is calculated from the data obtained from an experiment with a repeated measures factor.

Hypothesis   A supposition about the state of nature. In statistics, a hypothesis is a statement about a population or distribution, such as the value of a parameter or the shape of the distribution. (See **Null hypothesis**; **Alternative hypothesis**; **Hypothesis testing**.)

Hypothesis testing   In statistical inference, a procedure for testing the null hypothesis (H_0) against the alternative hypothesis (H_1).   On the basis of the null hypothesis, the range of possible values of the **test statistic** (e.g., z, t, F, χ^2) is divided into an acceptance region and a **critical region**. The critical region contains values of the test statistic that are unlikely under H_0: that is, under H_0, there is a low probability α that the value of the test statistic will fall within the critical region. The value of α is known as the **significance level** and is conventionally set at 0.05, 0.01 (or sometimes 0.001), depending on the research area. Should the value of the test statistic fall within the critical region, the statistic is said to be **significant** beyond the pre-specified alpha-level. Such a significant result is regarded as evidence against the null hypothesis and therefore, by implication, as evidence for the **alternative hypothesis**. The location of the critical region depends upon the alternative hypothesis. In a t test, for example, if H_1 is the two-sided assertion that the population mean is not that specified by H_0 (i.e. μ_0), the critical region is located symmetrically in both tails of the distribution, that is, above the $(1 - \alpha/2)^{th}$ percentile and below the $\alpha/2^{th}$ percentile. If, on the other hand, H_1 states that the mean is greater than μ_0, that is, H_1 is a **one-sided** alternative, the critical region is located entirely in the upper tail of the t distribution, above the $(1 - \alpha)^{th}$ percentile. This is known as a one-tailed test.

Independent samples Two samples are said to be independent if the values in each have been drawn at random from their respective populations and there is no basis for pairing the data they contain.

Independent variable In a true experiment, a variable manipulated by the experimenter, to determine whether it has a causal effect upon the dependent variable. In correlational research, the term is used to denote a predictor variable or regressor, a variable that is being investigated as possibly having a causal effect upon a target, criterion or dependent variable. In that context, although the regressor is often referred to as the 'independent variable' or IV, it is not manipulated by an experimenter, but is measured as a characteristic of the participant during the course of the investigation. The investigator attempts to neutralise the influence of possible confounding variables by statistical, rather than experimental means. Where natural groups are being compared, the researcher attempts to balance potential confounds across groups by following an appropriate sampling strategy.

Interaction In analysis of variance (ANOVA), two factors are said to interact when the simple effects of one factor are not the same at all levels of the other.

Interval data Data yielded by measurement on a scale whose units are equally spaced on the property concerned. There has been much debate about whether data in the form of ratings (and other psychological measures) have the interval property. Those who argue that ratings do not have the interval property tend to eschew the use of parametric tests and favour nonparametric or distribution-free tests. Others, however, take the view that this issue is irrelevant to the choice of a statistical test.

Interval estimate (See Confidence Interval.)

Latent variable A variable supposedly underlying associations among the variables in a multivariate data set. In several multivariate methods, such as factor analysis and structural equation modelling (of which confirmatory factor analysis is an application), linear functions are constructed which serve as reference variables, factors or axes with reference to which the observed variables can be classified. Such linear functions are taken to represent latent variables.

Level In Analysis of Variance, one of the conditions or categories that make up an independent variable or factor[1]. Since, in the general case, a factor is a set of qualitatively different categories rather than a continuous independent variable, the term 'level' does not, in this context, carry its usual comparative meaning: one blood group, for example, cannot be regarded as 'higher' or 'lower' than another.

Levene's test Tests for homogeneity of variance, a requirement for the independent samples t test and the analysis of variance (ANOVA). A significant result on Levene's test indicates that the homogeneity assumption is untenable, a contraindication against the use of the traditional t test or the one-way ANOVA, the error terms of which incorporate a pooled estimate of the supposedly uniform population variance.

Leverage The values of some statistics can be unduly influenced by atypical cases or outliers. In regression, for example, measures are available for measuring the influence or leverage that outliers exert upon the parameter estimates in the **regression model**. The further from the mean an outlier is, the greater the leverage it exerts.

Linear Of the nature of a straight line. The straight line function is the simplest in the family of **linear equations**. The analogues of the straight line when there are two or more IVs are, respectively, the **plane** (two IVs) and the **hyperplane** (three or more IVs). (See **Regression**.)

Loading In **factor analysis,** the loading of a test on a factor (assuming that the factors are independent or **orthogonal**) is the correlation between scores on the test and the scores of the participants on that particular factor (i.e., their **factor scores**). The loading is thus a measure of the extent to which performance on the test can be accounted for in terms of the factor concerned. The square of the loading is the proportion of the common factor variance of the test that is accounted for by that particular factor.

Logistic regression A method of regression applicable when the dependent variable is a set of categories. The independent variables may be either continuous or categorical.

Loglinear analysis A set of techniques for modelling the expected frequencies of observations in the cells of a multi-way **contingency table**. The expected raw cell frequencies can be estimated by multiplicative functions of the relevant marginal frequencies, in which the factors are estimates of main effects and interactions. Since, however, the logarithm of a product is the sum of the logarithms of its factors, the (natural) **logarithm** of the expected cell frequency is modelled by a **linear function** of the various effect terms, which are estimated from the logarithms of the marginal frequencies.

Main effect In **factorial analysis of variance (ANOVA)**, a factor is said to have a **main effect** if, in the population, the means on the dependent variable do not have the same value at all levels of the factor (ignoring any other factors in the design).

Mann-Whitney test The nonparametric equivalent of an independent samples t test. In the Mann-Whitney test, the null hypothesis is that the two populations have identical distributions. **Wilcoxon's rank-sum test**, another nonparametric test, is the exact equivalent of the Mann-Whitney test.

MANOVA See **Multivariate analysis of variance**.

Model An interpretation of data, usually in the form of an equation or a **path diagram**, in which an observed score is presented as the sum of systematic and error components. The use of any formal statistical test requires that the assumptions of a specific model are applicable to the data.

Multiple correlation coefficient R In **regression**, the Pearson correlation between the target or criterion variable and the estimates of its values from the regression equation. The value of R, however, unlike the Pearson correlation, cannot be negative, because the slope of the regression line, plane or hyperplane is always consistent with the orientation of the cloud of points in the scatterplot.

Multiple responses The compiler of a questionnaire may be interested in the mode of transport used by the respondents to get to their work. A single question in the form of a checklist inviting respondents to tick those modes of transport they use is likely to receive two, three or more responses, which would create problems for entry of the data into SPSS. Another approach, however, is to have a Yes/No question for each item in the list and record the response to each question as a separate **dummy variable**. SPSS has a Multiple Response procedure which computes and displays the frequencies with which different modes of transport are used by the respondents.

Multivariate analysis of variance (MANOVA) A generalisation of the analysis of variance (ANOVA) from the **univariate** to the **multivariate** situation, where there are two or more dependent variables.

Multivariate data A data set containing observations on three or more variables.

Multivariate normality A set of k variables is said to have a multivariate normal distribution if, given any set of values of $k - 1$ of them, the remaining variable is normally distributed. More technically, not only is the distribution of each variable considered separately (its **marginal distribution**) normal, but also the **conditional distributions** are normal. Techniques such as **Multivariate analysis of variance (MANOVA)** and **Discriminant Analysis (DA)** assume multivariate normality.

Multivariate statistics Statistical techniques for analysing data sets with two or more dependent variables. Examples are **Multivariate analysis of variance (MANOVA)**, **Factor analysis (FA)** and **Principal components analysis (PCA)**. (See **Univariate statistics**.)

Nagelkerke's R^2 In **logistic regression**, a statistic which mimics the **coefficient of determination** (R^2) in ordinary least squares (OLS) regression. Nagelkerke's statistic was designed to overcome the inability of another measure, **Cox and Snell's R^2**, to achieve its maximum value.

Nominal data Numerical data consisting of records of category membership. Nominal data result from observations of qualitative variables.

Non-parametric or distribution-free test A test, such as the **Mann-Whitney** test or the **Friedman** test, which does not make specific assumptions about the population distribution such as normality or homogeneity of variance. Such tests, however, do carry the assumption that the distributions are identical in all conditions or groups.

Normal (or Gaussian) distribution The famous 'bell curve', upon which much of classical statistical theory is based. A normal distribution has two parameters, the mean and the variance. Some naturally occurring variables, such as height and weight, have an approximately normal distribution. Since a linear function of two normal variables has itself a normal distribution, the mean of a sample of fixed size n drawn from a normal distribution is itself normally distributed, even if $n = 2$. Moreover, according to the **Central Limit Theorem**, the mean of a sample of fixed size n from a non-normal distribution has a distribution which can be made to approximate a normal distribution to any degree of closeness provided the sample is sufficiently large. It is this theorem that gives the normal distribution its central position in classical statistical theory.

Null hypothesis In statistical hypothesis-testing, the null hypothesis (H_0) is the supposition of 'no effect': there is *no* difference between the means; there is *no* association between two variables; the sample we have selected has *not* been drawn from a population with a mean different from that of the standardisation sample, and so on. The null hypothesis, therefore, is usually the negation of the **scientific** hypothesis. The null hypothesis cannot be proved. This truth reflects the logical asymmetry of truth and falsification. In classical, **Fisherian** hypothesis-testing, should a statistical test fail to show significance, the null hypothesis is not regarded as 'proved', but is 'retained' or 'accepted'. In Neyman-Pearson hypothesis testing on the other hand, the emphasis shifts to the alternative hypothesis (H_1), the supposition that the null hypothesis is false.

Odds   In an experiment of chance, the odds in favour of an event is the number of ways in which the event can occur, divided by the number or ways in which it can fail to occur. (cf. **Probability**.)

Omega squared   A measure of effect size in **analysis of variance (ANOVA)** which corrects for the positive bias of **eta squared**.

One-tailed versus two-tailed tests   In hypothesis testing, a **critical region** of values for the test statistic is set up such that, under the **null hypothesis**, the probability of a value in the region is equal to a small value known as the **significance level** (usually 0.05). In a **two-tailed test**, the critical region is distributed equally between the tails of the sampling distribution of the test statistic. Some argue, however, that the location of the critical region should depend upon the scientific or alternative hypothesis. There are situations in which it makes sense to look for a difference in one direction only: e.g. since brain injury is unlikely to improve test performance, the critical region for a suspiciously low performance on a diagnostic test should, arguably, be located entirely in the lower tail of the t distribution. Since the null and alternative hypotheses are **complementary** (i.e. they exhaust the possibilities), the null hypothesis is the asymmetrical proposition that the population mean is 'equal to or greater than', rather than 'equal to' a specified value. An unexpected result in the 'wrong' direction, therefore, cannot be declared to be significant.

Ordinal data   Data containing only information about order or sequencing. Examples of ordinal data are sets of ranks and lengths of sequences of dichotomous outcomes over a set of trials. There is some doubt about whether data in the form of ranks are ordinal data.

Ordinary least squares (OLS) regression   A set of techniques designed to predict value of a continuous target, **criterion** or **dependent** variable from values of one, two or more continuous predictors, **regressors** or **independent variables (IVs)**. The regression line, plane or hyperplane is positioned (by assigning values to its parameters) so as to minimise the sum of the squares of the residuals $Y - Y'$, , where Y and Y' are the target variable and the estimate from the regression equation, respectively. This is known as the **least-squares criterion**.

Orthogonal contrasts   Two contrasts are said to be orthogonal (independent) if the products of their corresponding coefficients sum to zero. In the one-way ANOVA of data from an experiment with k treatment groups, a set of $k - 1$ orthogonal contrasts can be constructed, each member of which accounts for a portion of the between groups sum of squares, so that the total of the sums of squares of the contrasts is the between groups sum of squares itself.

Orthogonal rotation   In **factor analysis**, the classificatory axes (factors) can be rotated around the origin in relation to the test points in order to produce a pattern of loadings that is easier to interpret than the original pattern. If the axes are kept at right angles during rotation, the process is known as **orthogonal rotation**. Axes at right angles represent uncorrelated factors. In **oblique rotation**, however, the axes are not maintained at right angles: that is, the axes represent correlated factors.

Outcome variable See **Dependent variable**.

Parameters Characteristics of the population, as opposed to the corresponding properties of the sample, which are known as **statistics**. Conventionally, Greek letters (μ, σ) are used to denote parameters; whereas Roman letters (M, s) denote the corresponding statistics.

Part correlation See **Semipartial correlation**.

Partial correlation What remains of the correlation between two variables when a third variable has been neutralised or **partialled out**. A partial correlation is a correlation between the residuals of two variables that have been regressed upon a third variable.

Path analysis A development of multiple regression, the purpose of which is to utilise the associations among a set of variables to help to determine, with the assistance of a special graphical representation known as a **path diagram**, the most convincing causal model for the data. In path analysis, regression coefficients are termed **path coefficients**.

Path coefficient See **Path analysis**.

Path diagram   A graphical representation of a causal model, which makes explicit the supposed causal relationships among variables.

Pearson correlation A measure of the strength of a supposed linear (straight line) association between two quantitative variables, each measured on a continuous scale with units, which is so constructed that it can take values only within the range from -1 to $+1$, inclusive. (See **Coefficient of determination**.) The supposition of linearity must always be checked by examining the scatterplot.

Percentile The score or value below which a specified proportion of the distribution lies: the 95th percentile is the score below which 95% of the distribution lies; the 5th percentile is the value below which 5% of the distribution lies. The median (or middle score) is the 50th percentile.

Point-biserial correlation ($r_{pt\text{-}bis}$) The Pearson correlation between a dichotomous qualitative variable (such as gender) and a continuous or scale variable. The sign of the point-biserial correlation is of no importance, because it reflects only the ordinal relation between the arbitrary code numbers used to denote the two categories. If the t test between the group means on the scale variable is significant, then so will be the point-biserial correlation, because the two statistics are related according to:

$$r^2_{pt-bis} = \frac{t^2}{t^2 + df}$$

where $df = n_1 + n_2 - 2$.

Point estimate The value of a statistic such as the mean or SD as an estimate of the corresponding population parameter (cf. **Interval estimate**.)

Polynomial A sum of terms, each of which is a product of a constant and a power of the same variable thus

$$y = a_0 + a_1 x + a_2 x^2 + \ldots + a_n x^n$$

The highest power n is the **degree** or **order** of the polynomial.

Post hoc comparisons Unplanned comparisons of the sort one inevitably makes at the data-snooping stage of a statistical analysis, after the data have been gathered. Planned or *a priori* comparisons are decided upon before the data are gathered. Since the family of possible post hoc comparisons is usually considerably larger than a set of planned comparisons, the **familywise** (or **per family) type I error rate** associated with post hoc comparisons may also be much higher than the nominal per comparison error rate. In either case, the per family error rate can be controlled by the **Bonferroni correction**, whereby the *p*-value for each comparison is multiplied by the number of comparisons in the family. (The **Sidak** correction results in a slightly less conservative test.)

Power The probability, assuming that the null hypothesis is false, that when a statistical test is made, the null hypothesis will be rejected. The power *P* of a statistical test is related to the **Type II error rate** (β) according to the equation: $P = 1 - \beta$. Power is affected by several factors, including the significance or alpha-level, the minimum effect size that the researcher considers worth reporting, the number of participants in the experiment, the design of the experiment (especially whether it is between subjects or within subjects) and the reliability of the measurement.

Principal components (PC) A set of techniques enabling the researcher to account for the correlations among a battery of tests in terms of classificatory dimensions or components. In contrast with **factor analysis (FA)**, principal components is designed to account for 100% of the variance of each of the tests in the battery, rather than the variance it shares with the other tests.

Probability A measure of likelihood so constructed that it can have values only within the range from 0 (for an impossible event) to 1 (a certainty). Probabilities arise in the context of **experiments of chance**, in which an event is viewed as a subset of the entire set of possible elementary outcomes. The results of an experiment can be viewed as an experiment of chance: the researcher's observations are a supposedly random sample from a reference set or **population** of possible observations. On that basis, we can assign probabilities to ranges of values within which the sample mean (or other statistic) might fall, assuming that the **null hypothesis** is true.

Probability density function (frequency function) A continuous random variable *X* assigns an infinite number of possible values within any specified interval in its range. The probability of any particular value of *X*, therefore, is zero. A probability density function, however, assigns a **probability density** to values of *X*. A probability density can be regarded informally as the probability of a value in the neighbourhood of a specified value. More technically, a probability density is the rate of change (i.e., the derivative) of the cumulative probability at that point.

***p*-value** In hypothesis-testing, the probability, under the null hypothesis, of a value of the test statistic at least as unlikely as the one actually obtained from the data. Should the *p*-value be less than the pre-set **significance level** (a small probability, conventionally 0.05, but sometimes set at 0.01), the result is said to be **significant**. (In its output for statistical tests, SPSS Statistics uses the term **Sig.** for the *p*-value.) If the alternative hypothesis is one-sided, the *p*-value must refer to values of the test statistic in *one tail only* of the distribution: extreme values in the opposite direction must result in acceptance of H_0.

Qualitative variables   Characteristics or properties, such as nationality, gender and blood group, which can be possessed only in kind (not in degree) and comprise sets of categories, rather than numerical values.

Quantitative variables   Characteristics or properties, such as height, weight or intelligence, that are possessed in degree, so that one individual can have more or less of the property than another. A quantitative variable consists of a set of values. The term continuous variable is often used for variables of this kind.

Quasi-experiment   A hybrid of a true comparative experiment and correlational research, in which sampling strategy is used in an attempt to create control groups for the purposes of comparison.   In studies of the effects of smoking upon health and longevity, for example, sampling strategies are used in the attempt to equalise possible confounding variables such as education level and lifestyle. The quasi-experiment, however, has the same fundamental weakness as correlational research, namely, that the supposedly causal variable (e.g. smoking) is observed in the participants studied, rather than being manipulated by an experimenter, with the result that other characteristics of the participants are varying at the same time. As a consequence, however much the researcher attempts to make the samples comparable, it can never be claimed that all possible confounds have been controlled.

Random variable (or variate)   In probability theory, a rule for assigning numerical values to outcomes in the sample space arising from an experiment of chance: e.g. 'Let X be the number of spots on the upper face when a die is rolled'; 'When a coin is tossed, Let Y be 1 for a head and 0 for a tail'.

Regression   The prediction of a dependent, target, outcome or criterion variable from other variables known as independent variables or regressors.   The prediction is made by constructing a regression equation, the subject of which is the estimate of the dependent variable from the independent variables.

Reliability   The extent to which a measuring instrument produces consistent results, in the sense that participants achieve scores at similar percentile levels with different testers or from occasion to occasion of testing. The various approaches to the determination of reliability include test-retest, parallel (or equivalent) forms and split-half. (See Validity.)

Repeated measures (or within subjects) design   Experimental designs in which observations are made on the same participants on two or more occasions. The repeated measures design is a special case of the randomised blocks design, a block being a set of observations that are linked in some way, as when fertilizer is applied to plants in the same flowerbed.   Such experiments yield sets of observations that can be paired or matched across samples: these four observations are John's scores; those four are Mary's.   Repeated measures designs yield correlated data, as do experiments with different groups of participants who are matched in some way. (Compare Between subjects design.)

R-matrix   A square array, or matrix, displaying the correlations of each of the tests in a battery with every other test. An *R*-matrix can be the starting point for factor analysis, which is a set of techniques for accounting for the correlations among the tests in terms of relatively few underlying variables or factors.

Rotation   In factor analysis, the factors can be regarded as classificatory axes with respect to which the tests in the battery can be plotted as points. When the axes are orthogonal (at right angles to one another), the co-ordinates of each test point are the correlations between the test and the factors emerging from the analysis. Such a correlation is known as the loading of a test on the factor concerned. Should the axes be rotated around the origin in relation to the test points, all the loadings will change. The sum of the products of the loadings of any two tests on all the axes, however, will remain constant, thus producing the same estimate of the observed correlation between the two tests, irrespective of the position of the axes. Rotation makes it easier to interpret the results of a factor analysis because, in relation to the original pattern of loadings, each test tends (after rotation) to have higher loadings on fewer factors. (See Orthogonal rotation.)

Sample space   In an experiment of chance, the set of all elementary outcomes, each of which is assumed to be equally likely (thus introducing the element of circularity into the definition of probability).

Scale data   A term in SPSS denoting data in the form of independent measurements on a scale with units. Examples are heights, weights, IQs, scores on questionnaires and ratings. Roughly equivalent terms are continuous data and interval data; although those terms arise in somewhat different contexts.

Scatterplot   A graphical display depicting a bivariate distribution, in which the axes represent the scales on the two variables and the individuals are represented as points with co-ordinates equal to their scores on the variables. An elliptical cloud of points indicates a linear association between the two variables: the narrower the ellipse, the stronger the association. A circular cloud of points indicates independence or dissociation. The Pearson correlation is a measure of a supposedly linear association between two variables; but whenever possible, the supposition of linearity should be checked by inspecting the scatterplot.

Semipartial correlation   In multiple regression, what remains of the correlation between a dependent variable (DV) and one of a set of independent variables (IVs) when the variance shared by the IV with the other IVs has been partialled out of the IV (but not the DV) by regression.

Shrinkage   The tendency for the predictive power of a regression model to weaken with resampling.

Sidak correction   A method of controlling the familywise type I error rate when making multiple comparisons. The Sidak correction is less conservative than the Bonferroni correction and the difference between them increases with the number of comparisons.

Significance level   In hypothesis testing, a small probability, often 0.05, fixed by convention and supposedly striking a balance between the type I and type II error rates.

Significant   A result is said to be statistically significant if it is unlikely to have occurred by chance. Here, 'unlikely' means no greater than a small probability known as the significance level, set by convention at 0.05 (but sometimes 0.01 or less, depending upon the field of study).

Simple effects   In factorial analysis of variance, the effect of one factor at one particular level of another. Simple effects analysis provides a way of analysing significant interactions. A two-way interaction can be explored by testing the simple main effects of one factor at different levels of the other. Heterogeneity of simple effects, as when they act in opposite directions, helps to explain a significant interaction. A significant three-way interaction can be further explored by testing the simple two-way interactions between two of the factors at specific levels of the third. In unplanned (**post hoc**) multiple pairwise comparisons, a significant simple effect is sometimes used as a justification for defining a smaller comparison **family**, rather than one based upon all the cell means involved in the interaction.

Simple main effect See **Simple Effects**.

Standard deviation (SD) The positive square root of the variance, often written as s, where

$$s = +\sqrt{\frac{\sum (X - M)^2}{n-1}}$$

Unlike the variance, the standard deviation measures spread or dispersion in the original units of measurement. The square root operation, however, does not negate the distorting effects of extreme scores or outliers on the value of the standard deviation. Adding a constant k to each score leaves the standard deviation unaltered. If each score is multiplied by a constant k, however, the standard deviation is multiplied by k. (Compare **Variance**.)

Standard normal variable See z.

String variable A variable whose values are strings of characters (e.g. names), rather than numbers. By default, SPSS assumes that variables (including grouping variables) have numerical values. A string variable therefore requires special prespecification.

Structural equation modelling A structural equation model (SEM) is a statistical model of causal relationships among the variables in a set of multivariate data. Such a model takes the dual form of a set of regression equations and a pictorial representation showing the causal relationships among the variables. SEM can be used for **confirmatory factor analysis** (CFA), the culmination of which is a **measurement model**. A **latent variable (LV) model** specifies the regression structure among latent variables. A complete or **full** structural equation model comprises both a measurement model (CFA) and a latent variable model.

Sum of squares (SS) The sum of the squares of the deviations of scores X from their mean M. The sum of squares is the numerator of the variance estimate s^2.

t **distribution** In the one-sample case, the distribution of the statistic t, which is defined as

$$t = \frac{M - \mu}{s/\sqrt{n}}$$

where M is the mean of a sample of size n drawn from a normal population. The distribution of t has one parameter, the **degrees of freedom** df, the value of which is given by $df = n - 1$. A t distribution resembles the standard normal distribution in being bell-shaped and symmetrical, and in having a mean of zero. The t distribution, however, has thicker tails and its variance is $df/(df - 2)$. As n increases, the t distribution approximates the standard normal distribution ever more closely.

Test statistic In **hypothesis testing**, a statistic with a known sampling distribution, such as t, F or chi-square, which can be used to test the **null hypothesis**. If the value of the test statistic is sufficiently improbable under the null hypothesis, the result is said to be statistically **significant** and the null hypothesis is rejected.

Trend analysis In **analysis of variance (ANOVA)**, the independent variable, rather than merely being a set of related treatments, groups or experimental conditions, may be quantitative and continuous, as when different groups of patients ingest different measured quantities of a drug. If so, the question arises as to the nature of the functional relationship between the dependent variable and the independent variable. In **trend analysis**, the treatment sum of squares is divided into **orthogonal** (independent) **components** accounted for by linear, quadratic and more complex **polynomial functions**. Each component of trend can be tested for significance.

Type I error The rejection of the null hypothesis when it is true. The probability of a Type I error is the significance level α, which is also known as the **alpha-level**, or the **alpha-rate**.

Type II error The acceptance of the null hypothesis when it is false. Its probability β is known as the **beta-level** or **beta-rate**. The beta-level is determined by several factors, including the sample size and the significance level. (See **Power**.)

Univariate statistics Analyses in which there is only one dependent variable. Examples are the *t* tests and **analysis of variance (ANOVA)**. (Compare **Multivariate statistics**.)

Unrelated samples See **Independent Samples**.

Validity[1] In psychological testing (psychometrics), a test is said to be valid if it measures what it is supposed to measure. This beguilingly simple definition is open to many interpretations, which is why, in Reber's Dictionary of Psychology (1985), there are more than 25 definitions of validity. In personnel selection, the predictive or criterion validity is the Pearson correlation between scores on a psychological test and a target or criterion variable (job efficiency, academic grade). In order to be valid in this sense, a psychological test must also be reliable. Reliability, however, does not ensure validity. A vocabulary test may be highly reliable; but it may have low validity as a predictor of success on an IT course.

Validity[2] An experiment is said to have **ecological validity** when the dependent variable is a characteristic actually seen in everyday life. Is the result of a scenario study of bystander intervention generalisable to a real situation in which the protagonist is asked for (or should offer) help? This is a question of ecological validity.

Validity[3] An experiment is said to be **internally valid** if the independent variable has been shown unequivocally to have had a causal effect upon the dependent variable. The internal validity of an experiment is threatened by such influences as placebo effects, extraneous variables, demand characteristics and experimenter effects.

Validity[4] In psychometrics, a test is said to be have high **internal validity** if its component items correlate positively with the aggregate total score on the test.

Variable A property or characteristic consisting of a set of values or categories. (See **Qualitative variables**, **Quantitative variables**.)

Variance A measure of the extent to which scores are spread (or dispersed) around their mean. The variance estimate s^2 of a set of n scores is the sum of the squares of their deviations from the mean, divided by $n - 1$: that is, $s^2 = SS/(n - 1)$. The denominator of the variance estimate is also known as the **degrees of freedom** (df), and the variance estimate can be expressed as SS/df. The variance is of great theoretical importance but, as a descriptive measure, its value is limited by the fact that it expresses the spread of a set of scores in squares of the original units of measurement. The positive square root of the variance estimate is known as the **standard deviation** s, which expresses spread in the original units of measurement. In the population, the variance is the mean squared deviation of scores from the population mean and the standard deviation is the root mean square. The *df* appears in the denominator of the sample variance to remove negative bias: that is, the expected value of the sample mean squared deviation is less than the value of the population variance. Adding a constant k to each score leaves the variance unaltered. Multiplying by k multiplies the variance by k^2.

Wald-Wolfowitz runs test   There are situations, as when a participant makes a series of choices over a series of trials, in which the investigator is concerned with whether sequences of the same choice indicate a lack of randomness in the participant's strategy. The Wald-Wolfowitz runs test tests for non-randomness.

Welch's *F* test   A variation of the *F* test which is applicable when the assumption of homogeneity of variance has been violated.

Welch-Satterthwaite formula   A formula used to adjust the degrees of freedom for a variant of the *t* statistic in which separate variance estimates are retained.   See **Behrens-Fisher problem**.

Wilks' Lambda (Λ)   In the **multivariate analysis of variance (MANOVA)**, one of several statistics that can be used to test the null hypothesis of equality of the **group centroids**, that is, the group mean values of the discriminant functions calculated during the analysis. Wilks' lambda can be thought of as expressing the error variance as a proportion of the total variance.

Within subjects designs   See **Repeated measures**.

Within subjects factors   Factors with all levels assigned to the same sample of subjects or participants.

Within subjects factorial designs   Designs in which all factors are within subjects.

Yates' correction   A modification of the approximate chi-square formula. See **Correction for continuity**.

z   The **standard normal variable**, with a mean of zero and a standard deviation of 1.   Any normally distributed variable X can be transformed to z by subtracting the mean and dividing by the standard deviation.   A z-score expresses a value in units of standard deviation, not the original units.   A *positive* sign for z indicates that the value is so-many standard deviations *above* the mean; a *negative* sign indicates that the value is so-many standard deviations *below* the mean.   Standardising a variable does NOT normalise its distribution: if the raw scores have a skewed distribution, so will the standardised scores.

References

Agresti, A. (1990). *Categorical data analysis*. New York: Wiley.

American Psychological Association. (2001). *Publication manual of the American Psychological Association (5th ed.)*. Washington, DC: American Psychological Association.

Anscombe, F. J. (1973). Graphs in statistical analysis. *American Statistician, 27*, 17–21.

Brown, M.B., & Forsythe, A.B. (1974). The ANOVA and multiple comparisons for data with heterogeneous variances. *Biometrics, 30*, 719–724.

Cohen, J. (1960). A coefficient of agreement for nominal scales. *Educational and Psychological Measurement, 10*, 37–46.

Cohen, J. (1962). The statistical power of abnormal-social psychological research: A review. *Journal of Abnormal and Social Psychology, 65*, 145–153.

Cohen, J. (1988). *Statistical power analysis for the behavioral sciences (2nd ed.)*. Hillsdale, NJ: Lawrence Erlbaum Associates.

Cohen, J., Cohen, P., West, S. G., & Aiken, L. S. (2003). *Applied multiple regression/correlation analysis for the behavioral sciences (3rd ed.)*. Mahwah, NJ: Lawrence Erlbaum Associates.

Darlington, R. B. (1968). Multiple regression in psychological research and practice. *Psychological Bulletin, 69*, 161–182.

Darlington, R. B. (1990). *Regression and linear models*. New York: McGraw-Hill.

Dodd, D. H., & Schultz, R. F. (1973). Computational procedures for estimating magnitude of effect for some analysis of variance designs. *Psychological Bulletin, 79*, 391–395.

Dugard, P., Todman, J., & Staines, H. (2010). *Approaching multivariate analysis: A practical introduction (2nd ed.)*. London & New York: Routledge.

Erdfelder, E., Faul, F., & Buchner, A. (1996). GPOWER: A general power analysis program. *Behavior Research Methods, Instruments, and Computers, 28*, 1–11.

Faul, F., Erdfelder, E., Lang, A-G., and Buchner, A. (2007). G*Power 3: A flexible statistical power analysis program for the social, behavioral and biomedical sciences. *Behavior Research Methods, 39*, 175–191.

Field, A. (2005). *Discovering statistics using SPSS: And sex and drugs and rock 'n' roll (2nd ed.)*. London: Sage.

Field, A. (2009). *Discovering statistics using SPSS: And sex and drugs and rock 'n' roll (3rd ed.)*. London: Sage.

Field, A., & Hole, G. (2003). *How to design and report experiments*. London: Sage.

Frigge, M., Hoaglin, D. C., & Iglewicz, B. (1989). Some implementations of the boxplot. *American Statistician, 43*, 50–54.

Hosmer, D. W., & Lemeshow, S. (2000). *Applied logistic regression (2nd ed.)* New York: Wiley.

Howell, D. C. (2007). *Statistical methods for psychology (6th ed.)*. Belmont, CA: Thomson/Wadsworth.

Keppel, G., & Wickens, T. D. (2004). *Design and analysis: A researcher's handbook (4th ed.)*. Upper Saddle River, NJ: Pearson Prentice Hall.

Kim, J., & Mueller, C. W. (1978a). *Factor analysis: Statistical methods and practical issues.* Newbury Park, CA: Sage.

Kim, J., & Mueller, C. W. (1978b). *Introduction to factor analysis: What it is and how to do it.* Newbury Park, CA: Sage.

King, B. M., & Minium, E. M. (2003). *Statistical reasoning in psychology and education (4th ed.)* Hoboken, NJ: John Wiley & Sons, Inc.

McGill, R, Tukey, J. W., & Larsen, W. A. (1978). Variations of box plots. *The American Statistician*, 32, 12–16.

Nelson, D. (2004). *The Penguin dictionary of statistics*. London: Penguin Books.

Rasbash, J., Steele, F., Browne, W., & Prosser, B. (2004). *A user's guide to MLwiN (Version 2.0)*. London: Centre for Multivel Modelling, Institute of Education, University of London.

Reber, A. S. (1985). *The Penguin dictionary of psychology*. Harmondsworth, Middlesex, England: Penguin Books.

Tabachnick, B. G., & Fidell, L. S. (2007). *Using multivariate statistics (5th ed.)*. Boston: Allyn & Bacon (Pearson International Edition).

Todman, J., & Dugard, P. (2007). *Approaching multivariate analysis: An introduction for psychology.* London: Psychology Press.

Tukey, J. W. (1977). *Exploratory data analysis*. Reading, Mass. : Addison-Wesley series in behavioral science.

Welch, B.L. (1951). On the comparison of several mean values: An alternative approach. *Biometrika, 38*, 330–336.

Winer, B. J., Brown, D. R., & Michels, K. M. (1991). *Statistical principles in experimental design (3rd ed.)*. New York: McGraw-Hill.

Index